W9-CBU-727

Fodor's

BRAZIL

5th Edition

Where to Stay and Eat
for All Budgets

Must-See Sights
and Local Secrets

Ratings You Can Trust

Fodor's Travel Publications   New York, Toronto, London, Sydney, Auckland
www.fodors.com

FODOR'S BRAZIL
Editor[s]: Margaret Kelly

Editorial Production: Tom Holton
Editorial Contributors: Lucy Bryson, Ana Cristina, Daniel Corry, Rhan Flatin, Doug Grey, Katya Hodge, Anna Katsnelson, Shannon Kelly, Carolina Berard Kreusch, Fabio Kreusch, Stephen Silva, Mark Sullivan, Simon Tarmo, Alastair Thompson, Carlos Tornquist
Maps & Illustrations: David Lindroth, Mark Strand, *cartographers*; Bob Blake, Rebecca Baer, and William Wu, *map editors*
Design: Fabrizio LaRocca, *creative director*; Guido Caroti, Siobhan O'Hare, *art directors*; Tina Malaney, Chie Ushio, Ann McBride, *designers*; Melanie Marin, *senior picture editor*; Moon Sun Kim, *cover designer*
Cover Photo: (Copacabana, Rio de Janeiro): Hugh Sitton/zefa/Corbis
Production/Manufacturing: Angela L. McLean

5th Edition

ISBN 978-1-4000-1966-3

ISSN 0163-0628

SPECIAL SALES
This book is available at special discounts for bulk purchases for sales promotions or premiums. Special editions, including personalized covers, excerpts of existing books, and corporate imprints, can be created in large quantities for special needs. For more information, write to Special Markets/Premium Sales, 1745 Broadway, MD 6-2, New York, New York 10019, or e-mail specialmarkets@randomhouse.com.

AN IMPORTANT TIP & AN INVITATION
Although all prices, opening times, and other details in this book are based on information supplied to us at press time, changes occur all the time in the travel world, and Fodor's cannot accept responsibility for facts that become outdated or for inadvertent errors or omissions. So **always confirm information when it matters**, especially if you're making a detour to visit a specific place. Your experiences—positive and negative— matter to us. If we have missed or misstated something, **please write to us.** We follow up on all suggestions. Contact the Brazil editor at editors@fodors.com or c/o Fodor's at 1745 Broadway, New York, NY 10019.

PRINTED IN THE UNITED STATES OF AMERICA
10 9 8 7 6 5 4 3 2 1

Be a Fodor's Correspondent

Your opinion matters. It matters to us. It matters to your fellow Fodor's travelers, too. And we'd like to hear it. In fact, we need to hear it.

When you share your experiences and opinions, you become an active member of the Fodor's community. That means we'll not only use your feedback to make our books better, but we'll publish your names and comments whenever possible. Throughout our guides, look for "Word of Mouth," excerpts of your unvarnished feedback.

Here's how you can help improve Fodor's for all of us.

Tell us when we're right. We rely on local writers to give you an insider's perspective. But our writers and staff editors—who are the best in the business—depend on you. Your positive feedback is a vote to renew our recommendations for the next edition.

Tell us when we're wrong. We're proud that we update most of our guides every year. But we're not perfect. Things change. Hotels cut services. Museums change hours. Charming cafés lose charm. If our writer didn't quite capture the essence of a place, tell us how you'd do it differently. If any of our descriptions are inaccurate or inadequate, we'll incorporate your changes in the next edition and will correct factual errors at fodors.com immediately.

Tell us what to include. You probably have had fantastic travel experiences that aren't yet in Fodor's. Why not share them with a community of like-minded travelers? Maybe you chanced upon a beach or bistro or B&B that you don't want to keep to yourself. Tell us why we should include it. And share your discoveries and experiences with everyone directly at fodors.com. Your input may lead us to add a new listing or highlight a place we cover with a "Highly Recommended" star or with our highest rating, "Fodor's Choice."

Give us your opinion instantly at our feedback center at www.fodors.com/feedback. You may also e-mail editors@fodors.com with the subject line "Brazil Editor." Or send your nominations, comments, and complaints by mail to Brazil Editor, Fodor's, 1745 Broadway, New York, NY 10019.

You and travelers like you are the heart of the Fodor's community. Make our community richer by sharing your experiences. Be a Fodor's correspondent.

Boa viagem!

Tim Jarrell, Publisher

CONTENTS

CONTENTS

ABOUT THIS BOOK

OUR RATINGS

Sometimes you find terrific travel experiences and sometimes they just find you. But usually the burden is on you to select the right combination of experiences. That's where our ratings come in.

As travelers we've all discovered a place so wonderful that its worthiness is obvious. And sometimes that place is so experiential that superlatives don't do it justice: you just have to be there to know. These sights, properties, and experiences get our highest rating, **Fodor's Choice**, indicated by orange stars throughout this book.

Black stars highlight sights and properties we deem **Highly Recommended**, places that our writers, editors, and readers praise again and again for consistency and excellence.

By default, there's another category: any place we include in this book is by definition worth your time, unless we say otherwise. And we will.

Disagree with any of our choices? Care to nominate a place or suggest that we rate one more highly? Visit our feedback center at www.fodors.com/feedback.

BUDGET WELL

Hotel and restaurant price categories from ¢ to $$$$ are defined in the opening pages of each chapter. For attractions, we always give standard adult admission fees; reductions are usually available for children, students, and senior citizens. Want to pay with plastic? **AE, D, DC, MC,** and **V** following restaurant and hotel listings indicate if American Express, Discover, Diners Club, MasterCard, and Visa are accepted.

RESTAURANTS

Unless we state otherwise, restaurants are open for lunch and dinner daily. We mention dress only when there's a specific requirement and reservations only when they're essential or not accepted—it's always best to book ahead.

HOTELS

Hotels have private bath, phone, TV, and air-conditioning and operate on the European Plan (aka EP, meaning without meals), unless we specify that they use the Continental Plan (CP, with a Continental breakfast), Breakfast Plan (BP, with a full breakfast), or Modified American Plan (MAP, with breakfast and dinner) or are all-inclusive (AI, including all meals and most activi-

ties). We always list facilities but not whether you'll be charged an extra fee to use them, so when pricing accommodations, find out what's included.

Many Listings	
★	Fodor's Choice
★	Highly recommended
⊠	Physical address
↔	Directions
⌂	Mailing address
☎	Telephone
🖷	Fax
⊕	On the Web
✎	E-mail
☞	Admission fee
◷	Open/closed times
Ⓜ	Metro stations
▭	Credit cards

Hotels & Restaurants	
▥	Hotel
↵	Number of rooms
⚲	Facilities
†◎†	Meal plans
✕	Restaurant
⚑	Reservations
↘	Smoking
🍸	BYOB
✕▥	Hotel with restaurant that warrants a visit

Outdoors	
🏌	Golf
⛺	Camping

Other	
☺	Family-friendly
⇨	See also
⊠	Branch address
☞	Take note

WHAT'S WHERE

RIO DE JANEIRO 	On the map, the city of Rio de Janeiro dangles from the south-central edge of the state by the same name. The city cascades down and between dramatic mountains and out to beaches that ribbon the metropolitan area. A national park since 1961 and the first one within an urban area, the Tijuca Forest, near Barra da Tijuca Beach, has more than 900 species of plants. The open-armed Christ the Redeemer statue atop Corcovado, often seen in postcards, lies within this park. On the west side of the city is White Rock (Pedra Branca) State Park, four times bigger than Tijuca park, with 30,888 acres of the original Mata Atlântica rain forest. When visiting Rio, make sure you take safety precautions 24 hours a day. Try to walk around accompanied and, in parks, do not stay by yourself. Bring cameras, because the landscape is wonderful, but take good care of them.
SIDE TRIPS FROM RIO 	Rio de Janeiro State bulges from Brazil's southeast coast, just at the point where the country starts to narrow. Although the state is best known for its eponymous city, with famous beaches like Copacabana and Ipanema, inland you'll find several historical towns such as Petrópolis in refreshingly cool (relatively speaking) and lush mountainous settings; and along the coasts are quieter beach and water-sports destinations like Angra dos Reis, Ilha Grande, and Búzios; and the colonial town of Paraty.
SÃO PAULO	The capital of São Paulo State, this huge city is on a plateau 46 mi from the coast. Strolling along Avenida Paulista, once a country road, now lined with skyscrapers, you can almost hear the urgent buzz of business. Indeed, if you are looking for peace and tranquillity, the city of São Paulo is not the place for you. The city breathes business, rush, pollution, and traffic. And many of its inhabitants enjoy the fast pace. To compensate for the stress, São Paulo has seemingly countless distractions in the form of restaurants, cinema, theater, galleries, museums, and much, much more.
SIDE TRIPS FROM SÃO PAULO 	South and west of Rio de Janeiro State is the industrial coastal state of São Paulo. Beautiful beaches, the large ocean port of Santos, ecological sanctuaries—including some patches of the Mata Atlântica (Atlantic Forest)—all run along its shores. Like the state of Rio de Janeiro, São Paulo's heartland includes mountainous regions covered with charming historical and resort towns like Águas de São Pedro, with its

hot springs; handicraft center Embu; and 16th-century Santana de Parnaíba. Ilhabela is São Paulo's destination of choice for beach bums and water-sports fanatics.

THE SOUTH

The three southernmost states—Paraná, just below São Paulo, Santa Catarina, and Rio Grande do Sul—run along the coast and stretch inland to the borders of Uruguay, Argentina, and Paraguay. Together they compose the narrowest section of Brazil's territory, covering 220,000 square mi, an area about the size of France. Curitiba, the capital of Paraná, is on a plateau 50 mi from the sea. Santa Catarina's capital, Florianópolis, literally straddles the Atlantic, its coastal mainland portion connected by a bridge to its offshore island portion. Rio Grande do Sul's capital, Porto Alegre, is halfway between São Paulo and Buenos Aires (about a 1½-hour flight from either city). Far to the west is the mighty Foz de Iguaçu (Iguaçu Falls).

If you visit the south in June or July (Brazil's winter), bring jackets and coats, as temperatures can drop as low as in Europe or the U.S. (about 32° F). Snow is rare, but not completely unheard-of in Santa Catarina and Rio Grande do Sul. Bring umbrellas, especially for Curitiba. If people in the south don't seem as friendly as those from Rio or Bahia, don't be offended. People tend to be more reserved, but are open to making friends or giving a helping hand when asked.

MINAS GERAIS

Roughly the size of Spain, the inland state of Minas Gerais is northwest of Rio de Janeiro and São Paulo. Near the center of the state is the capital, Belo Horizonte. Just southeast of Belo is the Serra do Espinhaço, where most of the state's gold towns lie a short drive from one another. Diamantina, land of diamonds, is north of Belo Horizonte, and Mariana, founded in 1696, is to the southwest. The state's southern region is dominated by spas, such as those in Poços de Caldas and Caxambú. Ouro Preto, known for its baroque architecture, is embedded 3,500 feet high in mountains that rise well above 6,200 feet in the Serra do Espinhaço. Tiradentes, with its waterfalls and breathtaking views of the São José Sierra, is 130 mi southwest of Belo Horizonte.

WHAT'S WHERE

BRASÍLIA & THE WEST 	Built in five years and inaugurated in 1960, Brasília became a global model of urbanism and modern architecture. The nation's capital lies in the geographical center of the country in a vast, flat region dominated by the *cerrado,* or Brazilian savanna. The cerrado extends west through the sparsely populated "frontier" states of Goiás, Tocantins, Mato Grosso, and Mato Grosso do Sul. The massive Pantanal—an untamable mosaic of swamp and forest teeming with wildlife, including vultures in all hues of the rainbow—is the dominant feature of the far west both in geography and in tourist appeal. Despite its beauty, Brasília has one major drawback: it is not a "pedestrian-friendly" city. Be prepared to either take taxis often or rent a car. Between June and September, it doesn't rain at all and you must drink a lot of water. It is a good time of the year for swimming or sports on the lake (Lago Paranoá).
SALVADOR & BAHIA 	On a huge bay, the city of Salvador, the capital of Bahia State, is divided between valley and hill. The enormous Lacerda Elevator connects the two parts, the Cidade Baixa (Lower City) and the Cidade Alta (Upper City). In the nearby waters of All Saints' Bay, with island settlements dating from colonial times (Frades and Itaparica), all is full of life and history. Salvador has plenty to do and see, from beaches to craftsmanship. The city's cuisine is quite unique within Brazil, thanks to its African influence. Eating at a restaurant with local specialties is an experience that should not be missed. To the west of Salvador in the state's heartland is Lençóis, a village lying in the splendor of the Chapada Diamantina, a plateau covered with rare flowers and orchids. In the state's southern region are some of Brazil's most beautiful beaches, near Porto Seguro.
RECIFE, NATAL & FORTALEZA 	On Brazil's most curvaceous bit of coast, nearly 600 mi north of Salvador, are two colonial cities, Olinda and Recife, with beaches lapped by warm waters and caressed by cooling breezes. The capital of Pernambuco State, Recife is affectionately called the Venice of Brazil because it is bathed by the sea and crisscrossed by rivers and bridges dating from the 1640s. Recife can be seen from the hills of Olinda 3½ mi away. About 130 mi to the north is Natal, the capital city of Rio Grande do Norte, where the sun shines an average of 300 days a year. Appropriately dubbed the "Cidade do Sol" (City of the Sun), Natal is geographically the closest Brazilian city to Europe and Africa. The state's coastline of dunes, beaches,

and fishing villages unfolds 50 mi to the south and 180 mi to the north. In the southern part of the state are some of Brazil's most spectacular beaches: Ponta Negra, Pirangi, and Búzios. In Fortaleza, capital of Ceará, 340 mi north of Natal, you can revel in miles of urban beaches with warm ocean waters and cool breezes. Thirty miles east of Fortaleza is Iguapé, where dunes are so high and smooth you can ski down their slopes. These cities are very touristy, even among Brazilians. Many people from São Paulo vacation here.

THE AMAZON

Through the centuries many have tried in vain to conquer Brazil's vast northwest, a mythical land of a thousand rivers dominated by one giant, the Amazon River. Flowing for more than 4,000 mi, this gargantuan waterway is so wide in places you can't see the shore from a riverboat's deck. It is banked by a rain forest that houses the greatest variety of life on earth. Manaus, the capital city of Amazonas State, is a free-trade zone with electronic gadgets buzzing around magnificent 19th-century buildings, and lies almost exactly at the longitudinal center of the continent. Santarém is a bit less than 500 mi downriver and halfway between Manaus and the Atlantic. Before reaching the ocean, the river splits in two, leading northeast to Macapá and east to Belém. In the 200 mi between the river's opposite banks lies the Ilha do Marajó, the world's largest river island, roughly the size of the U.S. state of Indiana.

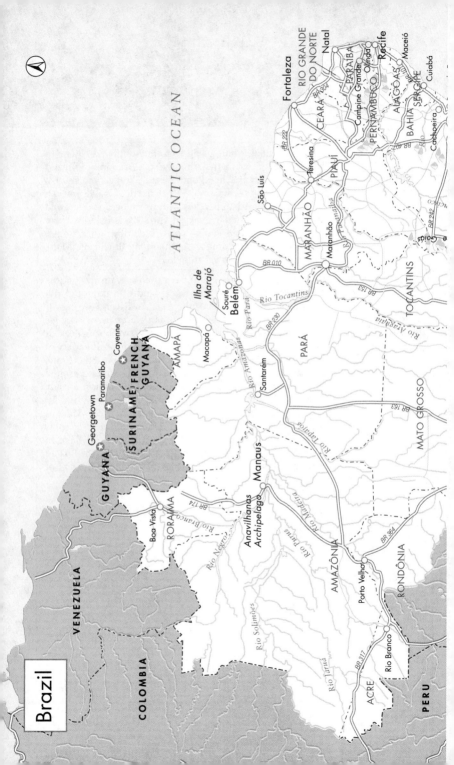

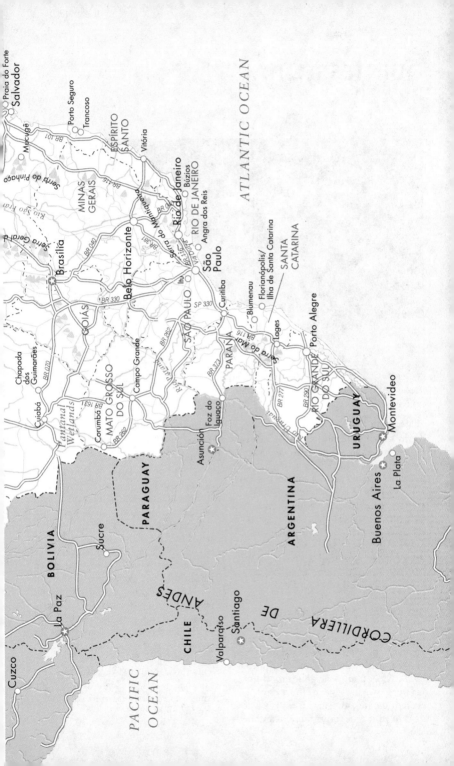

QUINTESSENTIAL BRAZIL

Historic Places

Many of Brazil's cultural distinctions can be explained by its past. To understand modern Brazil, it is essential that one know something about Portugal's colonization of the country and Brazil's slave trade with Africa. Salvador is undoubtedly one of the best places to learn about the Africans' influence on Brazilian way of life, because it was the major port during the slave trade. Ouro Preto, a UNESCO World Heritage Site in Minas Gerais State, and other Gold Towns are important for their historic and distinctive Brazilian baroque architecture. Rio de Janeiro was the seat of power for the Portuguese and then the Brazilian monarchy from the 16th to the 19th centuries, and the seat of Brazil's government until 1960. Rio's Centro neighborhood holds well-preserved vestiges of those days. The current capital, Brasília, is worth a few days of your time for its modern architec-

ture and its importance in Brazil's modern political history.

Carnival

In the heat of the South American summer (February or March, depending on the date of Easter), the country explodes in gaiety. Brazil comes alive, from such cities as Rio de Janeiro, Salvador, and Recife—where hundreds of thousands dance in formal parades as well as spontaneous street parties fueled by *trio elétricos,* which are flatbed trucks that carry bands from neighborhood to neighborhood—to the small towns of Pará or Goiás. Carnival season involves not only the days right before Lent (Friday through Ash Wednesday), but also months of rehearsal beforehand. And the sparks of passion flow over into other events throughout the year: religious festivals, ball games, weekend dances. Some of the best Carnivals are in Rio de Janeiro, Salvador, and Olinda.

A good place to start learning about Brazil and Brazilians is with the country's so-called "national passions"—music, soccer, and Carnaval. Brazil's past can also help you understand its present, and some cultural activities will undoubtedly enrich your trip.

Music

You will inevitably be exposed to Brazilian music while you are here, whether on your taxi driver's radio or in live-music bars in every town. Go to Rio for live bossa nova and samba, northeastern cities for *axé* and *pagode,* Brasília for rock, and the southeast for pop. Bossa nova, which is sort of the equivalent of classic rock in Brazil, is seeing somewhat of a comeback among younger generations, thanks to Maria Rita, daughter of bossa-nova icon Elis Regina, and a handful of other singers. Samba is undoubtedly the most popular music *du jour.* If you want to get a handle on Brazilian music, you'll have to do your homework: there are as many varieties of samba as there are of rock music; add to that the many variations of axé, bossa nova, *forró, frevo, lundu, maxixe,* and *tropicalismo,* and you'll be thoroughly overwhelmed . . . and exhilarated.

Soccer

Fûtebol (soccer) is called *o jogo bonito* (the beautiful game) in Brazil, and is considered an art form. Matches can be a blast: expect to see fans at their passionate best and sometimes at their worst. To avoid getting caught in a skirmish among fans, buy the best reserved seats (despite the cost) and ask about which matches are calmer. For example, in Rio, avoid matches between Flamengo and Fluminense—the "Fla-Flu" rivalry is notoriously heated. Simply watching matches on TV with Brazilians can be more fun than you ever had in your life. And when Brazil wins the World Cup . . . well, to say the celebrations are unique is an understatement. Top soccer players in Brazil are treated like deities. Pelé retired in the 1980s and is still revered as a national hero. The biggest stars today are Ronaldo, or "O Fenômeno" ("The Phenomenon"); Ronaldinho Gaúcho; and Robinho.

WHEN TO GO

Prices in beach resorts are invariably higher during the Brazilian summer season (December–February) and in July (school-break month). If you're looking for a bargain, stick to May–June and August–October. Rio and beach resorts along the coast, especially in the northeast, suffer from oppressive heat November through April, but in Rio the temperature can drop to uncomfortable levels for swimming June through August. If you want sun and hot weather and want to enjoy beaches and cities in the south, come in the high season, as temperatures can be very low from May to December.

Climate

Seasons below the equator are the reverse of the north—summer in Brazil runs from December to March and winter from June to September. The rainy season in Brazil occurs during the summer months. Showers can be torrential but usually last no more than an hour or two. The Amazon and the Pantanal have the most pronounced rainy seasons, running roughly from November to May and marked by heavy, twice-daily downpours.

Rio de Janeiro is on the tropic of Capricorn, and its climate is just that—tropical. Summers are hot and humid. The same pattern holds true for the entire Brazilian coastline north of Rio, although temperatures are slightly higher year-round in Salvador and the northeastern coastal cities. In the Amazon, where the equator crosses the country, temperatures in the high 80s to the 90s (30s C) are common all year. In the south, São Paulo, and parts of Minas Gerais, winter temperatures can fall to the low 40s (5° C–8° C). In the southern states of Santa Catarina and Rio Grande do Sul, snowfalls occur in winter, although they're seldom more than dustings.

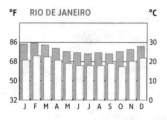

°F   RIO DE JANEIRO   °C

°F   SALVADOR   °C

IF YOU LIKE

Beaches

Brazil has thousands of gorgeous beaches, so you're bound to find a little slice of heaven wherever you are. In the northeast you find sweeping, isolated expanses of dunes; warm aquamarine waters; and constant breezes. Rio's famous beaches are vibrant, social, and beautiful. The south has glorious sands and cooler climes. A short list doesn't do them justice, but these are some of our favorite beach destinations:

 Rio de Janeiro. Barra da Tijuca, Prainha, and Grumari are the most naturally beautiful beaches in the city of Rio. Copacabana and Ipanema are the best beach "scenes." Out of the city, Búzios has some of the country's most gorgeous beaches.

■ **Ceará.** Canoa Quebrada, near Fortaleza, and Jericoacoara are our two favorite northeastern beaches for sheer beauty and relaxation.

■ **Paraná.** Ilha do Mel is known as the Paradise of the South Atlantic, and is one of the best ecotourism destinations in Brazil.

■ **Santa Catarina.** It's difficult to choose one beach to recommend on Ilha de Santa Catarina and Florianópolis. Garopaba, Praia dos Ingleses, and Praia Mole are the most famous, and Jurerê Internacional is the favorite among the well-to-do.

■ **São Paulo.** Ilhabela is a paradise of more than 25 beaches.

■ **Bahia.** Praia do Forte has plenty of leisure activities, 12 km (7 mi) of beaches, and is the number-one place to see sea turtles in Brazil.

Nature

This is one of the best places on earth for nature-lovers. There are so many things to see that you will need to prioritize your itinerary. The Amazon and the Pantanal, Brazil's two ecological wonderlands, are givens, but some lesser-known gems are waiting to be discovered by tourists, like Curitiba, known as the "ecological city" because of its many parks and green areas. Our favorite nature destinations follow.

■ **Pantanal Wetlands.** This vast floodplain is the best place to see wildlife outside sub-Saharan Africa. Its savannas, forests, and swamps are home to more than 600 bird species as well as anacondas, jaguars, monkeys, and other creatures.

■ **The Amazon Rain Forest.** A visit to the world-famous Amazon is one of those "life-list" experiences. Its scope and natural wealth are truly awe-inspiring.

■ **Parque Nacional da Chapada Diamantina, west of Salvador.** One of Brazil's most spectacular parks, Chapada Diamantina was a former diamond mining center. Today it is a center for hard and soft adventure.

■ **Parque Nacional do Iguaçu.** This amazing preserve has one of the world's most fantastic waterfalls.

■ **Parque da Pedreira, Curitiba.** Impressive landscaping and unique structures have given an abandoned quarry new life.

■ **Projeto Tamar, Praia do Forte.** Each year, September through March, more than 400,000 baby turtles are hatched along this beach northeast of Salvador.

IF YOU LIKE

Partying

Brazilians are famous for their Carnival, the biggest party of the year, but any time of year is occasion for revelry in Brazil. Even small towns have multitudes of festivals that may start out with a mass but end with dancing in the streets. Nearly every town has live-music venues playing samba, axé, forró, and MPB (Brazilian pop music) year-round—most with dancing. Brazilians—men and women alike—seem to have been born shaking their groove thing. If you can't dance the samba, don't worry, a lot of Brazilians can't either—they just know how to fake it.

■ **Rio de Janeiro.** Music and dance clubs stay open all night long here, especially in Lapa. This is one of the top places in Brazil to hear great samba and jazz. Carnival is the biggest party of the year, but New Year's Eve in Rio is also a fabulous celebration.

■ **Salvador.** The center of axé (Brazilian pop) music in Brazil and of Afro-Brazilian culture, Salvador has an easygoing party scene, bit its Carnival is considered Brazil's biggest and craziest party, where you can dance in the streets for eight days straight.

■ **Belo Horizonte.** With more bars per capita than any other city in Brazil, it's obvious that BH knows how to party. The music scene is quite lively here—especially for MPB.

■ **São Paulo.** If you crave elite clubs and rubbing elbows with Brazilian stars and millionaires, and sipping martinis at rooftop skyscraper bars, head to São Paulo, Brazil's poshest place to party.

Food & Drink

Trying cuisines unique to Brazil can be a highlight of your trip. Each region has its own specialties: exotic fish dishes in the Amazon; African spiced casseroles in Bahia; and the seasoned bean paste *tutu* in Minas Gerais. Much was inherited from the Portuguese, including the popular fish stews, *caldeiradas,* and beef stews, *cozidos,* boiled with vegetables.

■ **feijoada.** The national dish, feijoada, is a thick stew with a base of black beans, combined with sausage, bacon, pork loin, and other meats that originated in Bahia. Traditional versions may include pig's feet, ears, and other "choice" meats that some say add the best flavor. Feijoada is usually accompanied by *farofa* (toasted manioc flour), rice, and collard greens.

■ **churrasco.** Served at *churrascarias,* churrasco is meat, poultry, or fish roasted on spits over an open fire. In a *rodízio*-style churrascaria, you get all the meat and side dishes you can eat, prix-fixe. Rodízio means "going around," which explains the waiters who constantly circle the restaurant, only resting their skewers to slice another piece of meat onto your plate.

■ **caipirinha.** The national drink is *caipirinha,* crushed lime, ice, sugar, and *cachaça,* a liquor distilled from sugarcane.

■ **guaraná.** Be sure to try this carbonated soft drink made with the Amazonian fruit of the same name. It has a unique but subtle flavor.

■ **cafezinhos.** These thimble-size cups of coffee with tons of sugar keep Brazilians going between meals.

Rio de Janeiro

WORD OF MOUTH

"I love the city, the people, the food and the beaches. There are also some great museums that are often overlooked. My impression is that more adventurous travelers really enjoy Rio. If time permits there are great side trips also."

—hotnphoenix

Updated by
Stephen Silva

WELCOME TO THE CIDADE MARAVILHOSA, or the Marvelous City, as Rio is known in Brazil. Synonymous with the girl from Ipanema, the dramatic view from Christ the Redeemer atop Corcovado Mountain, and famous Carnival celebrations, Rio is also a city of stunning architecture, abundant museums, and marvelous food. Rio is also home to 23 beaches, an almost continuous 73-km (45-mi) ribbon of sand.

As you leave the airport and head to Ipanema or Copacabana, you'll drive for about a half hour on a highway from where you'll begin to get a sense of the city's dramatic contrast between beautiful landscape and devastating poverty. In this teeming metropolis the very rich and the very poor live in uneasy proximity. But by the time you reach breezy, sunny Avenida Atlântica—flanked on one side by white beach and azure sea and on the other by condominiums and hotels—your heart will leap with expectation as you begin to recognize the postcard-famous sights. Now you're truly in Rio, where the 10 million *cariocas* (residents of the city of Rio) dwell and live life to its fullest.

Enthusiasm is boundless and contagious in Rio. Prepare to have your senses engaged and your inhibitions untied. Rio seduces with a host of images: the joyous bustle of vendors at Sunday's Feira Hippie (Hippie Fair); the tipsy babble at sidewalk cafés as patrons sip their last glass of icy beer under the stars; the blanket of lights beneath Pão de Açúcar; the bikers, joggers, strollers, and power walkers who parade along the beach each morning. Borrow the carioca spirit for your stay; you may find yourself reluctant to give it back.

ORIENTATION & PLANNING

ORIENTATION

Cariocas divide their city into four main sections: the suburban Zona Norte (North Zone), the chic Zona Sul (South Zone), the sprawling Zona Oeste (West Zone), and the urban Centro.

Most tourist activity is in beach- and hotel-laden Zona Sul, the heartbeat of Rio, where you'll find a mix of residential areas, office buildings, shops, restaurants, bars, and beaches. It's the most affluent part of the city, with beautiful condos housing Rio's middle and upper class. It's also the most culturally diverse part of the city, home to dozens of theaters and music halls.

Centro is filled with the remnants of the old Portuguese colony, including some impressive neoclassical architecture housing churches, museums, and art galleries. The Zona Norte is primarily a residential area, but the international airport and the soccer stadium are here. Zona Oeste is the "up and coming" part of Rio, occupied by the nouveaux riches and replete with malls, superstores, and untouched beaches.

TOP REASONS TO GO

■ Rio's 70 km of **beaches** are stunning, so unpack your Speedo or thong bikini and join the masses.

■ Head to the streets or the Sambódromo for **Carnival**, Rio's biggest party.

■ Samba, bossa nova, funk, and pagode are just a few of the uniquely Brazilian styles of **music** to be enjoyed in Rio's myriad clubs and venues offering live music.

■ Brace yourself for exquisite **dining** in Rio's diverse repertoire of restaurants; meat lovers and vegetarians alike are welcome.

■ You'll quickly notice that Rio is nestled between beach and mountain; there are endless possibilities to enjoy the breathtaking **landscapes**.

CENTRO

Architectural gems left behind from the days of Portuguese colonialism share space with modern high-rises in Rio's financial district. Ornately decorated churches, museums, and palaces are just some of the highlights. The neighborhood is a virtual ghost town from Saturday afternoon until Monday morning, when the workweek begins. Have a look in one of Centro's many used book stores for good buys on Brazilian literature, *literatura de cordel,* and foreign books, too.

SANTA TERESA & LAPA

Adjacent to Centro, the historic neighborhood of Lapa has some of the best music halls and dance clubs in the city. If you're looking to explore Rio's nightlife, you'll become intimately familiar with Lapa. One of the first residential neighborhoods in Rio, Santa Teresa is worth a visit to explore its narrow, cobblestone streets lined with beautiful, Portuguese-style homes. Take a ride on the Bonde de Santa Teresa, Rio's last trolley. It also has some traditional Brazilian restaurants, excellent local craft stores, and art galleries.

FLAMENGO & BOTAFOGO

Home to some of the cheapest accommodations, least-popular beaches, but plenty of restaurants, including the exquisite beachside Porcão. Beaches in both neighborhoods are populated each morning by walkers, runners, and joggers. The stunning, palm-lined Rua Paissandu in Flamengo is clearly visible from any high point in Rio.

URCA

If you continue along the bay east from Botafogo you arrive at the tiny, mainly residential neighborhood of Urca, where you can ascend the Pão de Açúcar (Sugar Loaf). Adventurers will love the Sugar Loaf's first hill, which is climbable, and everyone will enjoy the view from inside the glass-lined *bonde,* the tram that ascends this oddly shaped landmark. It's quite windy up top, so hold on to your hats.

COPACABANA

Copacabana beach is the main attraction in the city's most tourist-packed neighborhood. It's the perfect place to stroll, people-watch, buy souvenirs at the open-air night market, soak up the sun, or gaze in awe at the giant old apartment buildings and hotels (including the Copacabana Palace) that line the Avenida Atlântica.

IPANEMA

Famous for being the place where the "Girl from Ipanema" was spied and then written into lyrical history by Tom Jobim and Vinicius de Moraes back in the '60s, this posh neighborhood today is a collection of tree-lined streets harboring upscale condos, fabulous restaurants, and trendy shopping. The beach is beautiful and attracts not only travelers but cariocas from all over the city.

WHAT'S A CARIOCA?

The term *carioca* was an indigenous word meaning "white man's house" and was used in the city's early history to describe the Portuguese colonizers. Today the word is used more broadly, to identify residents of the city of Rio. But the word defines much more than birthplace, race, or residence: it represents an ethos of pride, a sensuality, and a passion for life. Poor or rich, cariocas share a common identity and a distinct local accent, considered by foreigners and Brazilians alike to be the most beautiful within the Portuguese language.

LEBLON

Extending west from Ipanema, this affluent, intimate community borrows some of its neighbor's trendy charms, but is slightly funkier. The narrow streets are flush with small restaurants and bars. Sadly, the beach here is not great for swimming since the water is often polluted, though it's a popular spot for families.

SÃO CONRADO & BARRA DA TIJUCA

West of Leblon, these low-key neighborhoods have long stretches of unspoiled beach. Residential condos and malls crowd the streets in these wealthy parts. It's best to take a cab straight to the beaches, which are quieter than Copacabana and Ipanema and are especially recommended for kids. Hang gliders and paragliders land just behind São Conrado Beach. Stop by Barra Shopping, a huge mall in Barra da Tijuca, for a glimpse of a scaled-down Statue of Liberty in the New York wing and a flick in the state-of-the-art cinema.

THE LUSH INLAND

You can find Jardim Botânico, Gávea, Lagoa, Cosme Velho, and Tijuca to be much more residential than Ipanema and Copacabana, but it's definitely worth it to visit these neighborhoods, especially if you enjoy long walks or nature. Don't miss Rio's Botanical Garden in Jardim Botânico, the ascension to the Christ statue in Cosme Velho, Gávea's planetarium, Tijuca's samba school, or a refreshing lap around the massive lagoon in Lagoa.

PLANNING

WHEN TO GO

Rio is a year-round destination, but Carnival (usually in February) is the best time to soak up the city's energy. Arrive a few days before the celebrations begin, or stay a few days after they end in order to enjoy the museums and other sights that close for the four days of revelry. Last-minute Louies need not apply: you'll have to book your hotel and flight at least one year in advance for Carnival.

The hottest months in Rio tend to be January through March, when temperatures often soar above 100 degrees. The city generally sees the most rain during December, when it might rain for days at a time. To tour the city at a quieter time with gentler temperatures and at lower prices, come in the off-season, from May to October (Brazil's winter). The temperature in the winter tends to be in the upper 70s during the day and rarely falls below 50 degrees at night.

SAFETY & PRECAUTIONS

IN THE CITY Despite Rio's reputation, crime is no more likely than in any large city, and many cariocas feel that the city's safety is unfairly portrayed by the media. Most crimes involving visitors occur in crowded public areas: beaches, busy sidewalks, intersections, and city buses. Pickpockets, usually children, work in groups. One will distract you while another grabs a wallet, bag, or camera. Be particularly wary of children who thrust themselves in front of you and ask for money or offer to shine your shoes. Another member of the gang may strike from behind, grabbing your valuables and disappearing into the crowd. Another tactic is for criminals to approach your car at intersections. Always keep doors locked and windows partially closed. Leave valuables in your hotel safe, don't wear expensive jewelry or watches, and keep cameras strapped to your wrist.

ON THE BEACH Don't shun the beaches because of reports of crime, but *do* take precautions. Leave jewelry, passports, and large sums of cash at your hotel; don't wander alone and at night; and be alert when groups of friendly youths engage you in conversation (sometimes they're trying to distract you while one of their cohorts snatches your belongings). A big danger is actually the sun. From 10 AM to 3 PM the rays are merciless, making heavy-duty sunscreen, hats, cover-ups, and plenty of liquids essential; you can also rent a beach umbrella from vendors on the beach or your hotel. Ambulant vendors stroll the beaches with beverages, food, and trinkets. Unlike in other beach destinations you may have experienced, these guys are no-nonsense salespeople, and quickly move on if you shake your head no. Most beachgoers take advantage of their services. Beach vendors aren't supposed to charge more than R$5.50 for a bottle of beer or other alcoholic beverage, R$3 for a coconut water. Lifeguard stations, including bathrooms and showers, are found every kilometer.

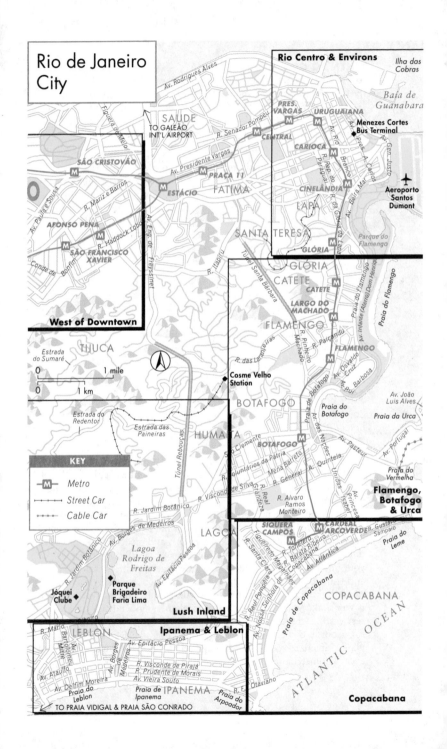

GETTING AROUND

The metro extends from the Zona Norte to Copacabana, with shuttles to Ipanema, Leblon, Gávea, São Conrado, and even Barra da Tijuca. Within Ipanema and Copacabana, it's quite easy to get around on foot, but some attractions are a bit far apart, so a taxi might be the way to go. After dark you should always take a taxi if you're venturing into unexplored territory, and it's easy to hail taxis on every main street. Public buses are cheap and cover every inch of the city, but are difficult to figure out if you don't speak Portuguese. Avoid the bus at night. Vans are a form of informal public transportation that are much more frequent, quicker than buses, 100% safe, and only R$2 per ride; if you're staying in Copacabana or Ipanema, vans are a good and inexpensive option because they ride along the beaches, and you'll be able to easily recognize where you should get out.

> ### THE COPS
>
> Once known as the murder capital of the world, Rio is now much less dangerous than a decade ago. Simple changes such as installing lights on the beaches have greatly improved safety in certain parts of the city. An increased police presence has also helped. In Rio there are three types of police: the gray-uniformed Military Police, the beige-uniformed Municipal Guard, and the black-uniformed special forces called the BOPE (pronounced "boppy"). For a glimpse at Rio's SWAT team, the BOPE, check out the film *Tropa de Elite* (2007).

ABOUT THE RESTAURANTS & CUISINE

With more than 900 restaurants, Rio's dining choices are broad, from low-key Middle Eastern cafés to elegant contemporary eateries with award-winning kitchens and first-class service. The succulent offerings in the *churrascarias* (restaurants specializing in grilled meats) can be mesmerizing for meat lovers—especially the places that serve *rodízio* style (grilled meat on skewers is continuously brought to your table—until you can eat no more). Hotel restaurants often serve the national dish, *feijoada* (a hearty stew of black beans and pork), on Saturday—sometimes Friday, too. Wash it down with a *chopp* (the local draft beer; pronounced "shop") or a caipirinha (Brazilian rum, lime, and sugar).

WHAT IT COSTS IN REAIS					
	¢	$	$$	$$$	$$$$
AT DINNER	under R$15	R$15–R$30	R$30–R$45	R$45–R$60	over R$60

Prices are per person for a main course at dinner or for a prix-fixe meal.

ABOUT THE HOTELS

Most hotels are in Copacabana and Ipanema. Copacabana hotels are close to the action (and the metro), but the neighborhood is noisier than Ipanema (which is itself noisier than São Conrado and Barra da Tijuca). ⚠ Note that "motels" aren't aimed at tourists. They attract couples looking for privacy and usually rent by the hour.

Expect to pay a premium for a room with a view. Many hotels include breakfast in the rate, but the quality varies from a full buffet to a hard roll with butter. If you're traveling during peak periods (December–March), make reservations as far in advance as possible.

	WHAT IT COSTS IN REAIS				
	¢	$	$$	$$$	$$$$
FOR 2 PEOPLE	under R$125	R$125–R$250	R$250–R$375	R$375–R$500	over R$500

Prices are for a standard double room in high season, excluding tax.

EXPLORING: THE BEACHES

Rio's circuit of *praias* (beaches) begins with Flamengo, on Guanabara Bay, but the best strands are farther south. Beaches are the city's pulse points: exercise centers, gathering places, lovers' lanes. Although cariocas wander into the water to cool off, most spend their time sunning and socializing, not swimming. Copacabana and Ipanema are nerve centers. Beaches west of Barra da Tijuca are increasingly isolated and undeveloped.

For beaches not accessible by metro, consider taking a taxi. City buses and chartered minivans drop you off along the shore, but they can be confusing if you don't speak Portuguese. Most beaches have parking lots—look for attendants in green-and-yellow vests. Turismo Clássico (⇨ *By Car in Rio de Janeiro Essentials*) can arrange for drivers and guides.

THE ZONA SUL

Praia do Flamengo. Flamengo residents know that this beach is much busier 5 AM–7 AM than during the sunny hours of the afternoon. That's because Praia do Flamengo is a great place to go for a walk, jog, run, or stroll, but not such a great place for a dip in the (usually brown) water. A major attraction here is Porcão Rio's, a not-to-be-missed churrascaria. ⊠ *Rua Praia do Flamengo, Flamengo, 22210-030.*

Praia do Botafogo. Though it's very much a strand, Praia do Botafogo doesn't attract swimmers and sunbathers. Considered to be the most polluted beach, the water is really only suitable for mooring your boat. But don't let that stop you from taking a jog along the sidewalk if you're staying nearby. Early risers will see a stunning sunrise from this shore. ⊠ *Av. das Nações Unidas, Botafogo, 22250-040.*

Praia Vermelha. Closed to civilians until 1938, Praia Vermelha is still the home of the military base installed in the 18th century. These days, this small beach is mostly frequented by local residents. ⊠ *Praça General Tibúrcio, Urca, 22290-270.*

Praia do Leme. A natural extension of Copacabana Beach to the northeast, toward the Pão de Açúcar, is Leme Beach. A rock formation juts into the water here, forming a quiet cove that's less crowded than the rest of the beach. Along a sidewalk, at the side of the mountain overlooking Leme, anglers stand elbow to elbow with their lines dangling into the sea. ⊠*Av. Princesa Isabel to Morro do Leme, Leme, 22010-000.*

Fodor's Choice **Praia de Copacabana.** Maddening traffic, noise, packed apartment blocks, and a world-famous beach—this is Copacabana, or Manhattan with bikinis. Walk along the neighborhood's classic crescent to dive headfirst into Rio's beach culture, a cradle-to-grave lifestyle that begins with toddlers accompanying their parents to the water and ends with silver-haired seniors walking hand in hand along the sidewalk. Copacabana hums with activity: you're likely to see athletic men playing volleyball using only their feet and heads, not their hands—a sport Brazilians have dubbed *futevôlei.* As you can tell by all the goal nets, soccer is also popular, and Copacabana frequently hosts the annual world beach soccer championships. You can swim here, although pollution levels and a strong undertow can sometimes be discouraging. Pollution levels change daily and are well publicized; someone at your hotel should be able to get you the information.

Copacabana's privileged live on beachfront Avenida Atlântica, famed for its wide mosaic sidewalks designed by Burle Marx, and for its grand hotels—including the Copacabana Palace Hotel—and cafés with sidewalk seating. On Sunday two of the avenue's lanes are closed to traffic and are taken over by joggers, rollerbladers, cyclists, and pedestrians. ⊠*Av. Princesa Isabel to Rua Francisco Otaviano, Copacabana, 22070-000.*

NEW YEAR'S EVE IN RIO

Rio's New Year's celebration, or *Réveillon* as it's known in Brazil, is a whirling dervish of a party in which an estimated 2 million people truck over to Copacabana for drinks, dancing, and the much anticipated fireworks show in Guanabara Bay. A word of warning: stay away from the stage. The area immediately surrounding the temporary stage on the beach gets packed with people, and you run the risk of getting pick pocketed Plan your hotel stay well in advance and be prepared to pay more—prices are at least double (hostels charge quadruple) and rooms fill quickly.

NEED A BREAK? Stop in for a drink at one of Avenida Atlântica's few air-conditioned cafés. The windows of Manoel & Juaquim (⊠*Av. Atlântica 1936, Copacabana, 22021-001 ☎021/2236–6768*) face the sands, so you can settle in with a cold draft beer or a light meal (the garlic potatoes are unbeatable) while watching carioca life unfold.

Praia do Diabo. Praia do Diabo is a barely noticeable stretch of sand tucked away between Arpoador and a natural rock wall that extends to Copacabana's fort. The dangerous waves, which can smash an unskilled

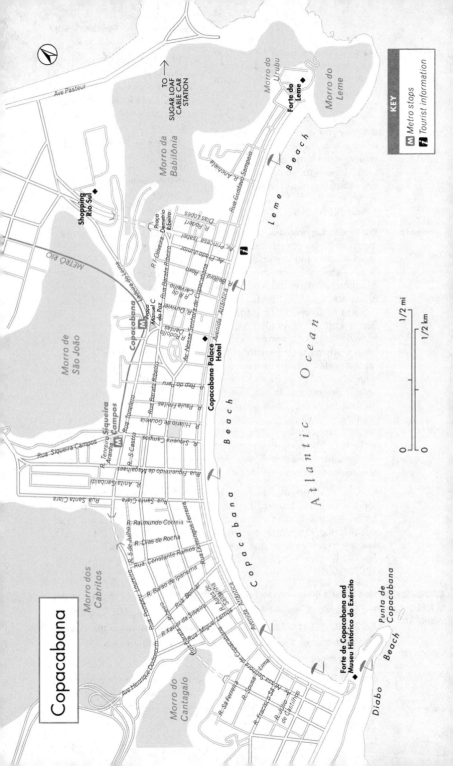

Copacabana

KEY

M Metro stops

🛈 Tourist information

TO
SUGAR LOAF
CABLE CAR
STATION

Ave Pasteur

Morro do Urubu

Morro do Leme

Forte do Leme

Morro da Babilônia

Leme Beach

Morro de São João

Shopping Rio Sul

Rua Gustavo Sampaio

R. Roderi Dias Lopes

Praça Demétrio Ribeiro

R. F. Oliveira

Rua Barata Ribeiro

Av. Princesa Isabel

Av. Prado Junior

R. Bedford Roxo

Av. Nossa Senhora de Copacabana

R. S. de Carvalho

Praça Manuel C. da Paz

METRO RIO

Copacabana

R. Rodolfo Dantas

Av. Nossa Senhora de Copacabana

Copacabana Palace Hotel

R. Dep. do Peru

Rua Barata Ribeiro

Rua Tonelero

R. Paula Freitas

R. Hilário de Gouveia

Praça Siqueira Campos

Siqueira Campos

R. Tenente Atanília

R. S. Castilho

Rua Figueiredo de Magalhães

R. Siqueira Campos

Rua Anita Garibaldi

Rua Santa Clara

Rua Santa Clara

Rua Siqueira Campos

R. Raimundo Correia

R. Dias de Rocha

Rua Constante Ramos

R. 5 de Julho

Rua Pompeu Loureiro

R. Barão de Ipanema

Rua Bolívar

R. Xavier da Silveira

R. Anita de Sousa

R. Julia de Castilhos

Av. Nossa Senhora de Copacabana

Avenida Atlântica

Morro dos Cabritos

Morro do Cantagalo

Ave Henrique Dodsworth

R. Sá Ferreira

R. Souza Lima

R. Francisco Sá

R. Julio de Castilhos

Av. Atlântica

R. Domingos Ferreira

R. Miguel Lemos

Avenida Atlântica

Forte de Copacabana and Museu Histórico do Exército

Atlantic Ocean

Copacabana Beach

Punta de Copacabana

Diabo Beach

0 ——— 1/2 mi

0 ——— 1/2 km

surfer on the nearby rocks, leave no mystery as to why this beach is called the Devil's Beach in Portuguese. Take advantage of the exercise bars, but stay out of the water. ⊠*Between Arpoador rock and Copacabana Fort, Copacabana, 22080-040.*

Praia do Arpoador. This beach, at the east end of Ipanema, has great waves for surfing. Nonsurfers tend to avoid the water for fear of getting hit by boards. But it's popular for sunbathing. ⊠*Rua Joaquim Nabuco to Rua Francisco Otaviano, Arpoador, 22080-040.*

> ### SUBMARINE WATCHING
>
> The Arpoador is essentially a natural rock formation jutting out into the sea where Ipanema begins. Once a popular spot for youths to "watch for submarines" in the evening (aka get some privacy away from home), Arpoador offers a perfect vantage point from which to capture all of Ipanema beach and the most beautiful sunset in Rio.

Fodor's Choice ★ **Praia de Ipanema.** As you stroll along this beach you catch a cross section of the city's residents, each favoring a particular stretch. One area is dominated by families (near Posto [Post] 10), another is favored by the gay community (near Posto 8). Throughout the day you'll see groups playing beach volleyball and soccer, and if you're lucky you'll even get to see Brazilian Olympic volleyball champions practicing on the beach. There are kiosks all along the boardwalk, where you can get anything from the typical coconut water to fried shrimp and turnovers. ⊠*Rua Joaquim Nabuco to Av. Epitácio Pessoa, Ipanema, 22420-000.*

Praia do Leblon. At the far end of Ipanema you'll find Praia do Leblon. As you stroll along the beautifully tiled sidewalk, take note of the sprawling Vidigal favela, which is perched precariously on the hillside overlooking the area. This stretch of beach is usually occupied by families, and it tends to be a quieter spot as far as beach sports are concerned. Continue up the road a bit to one of Leblon's *mirantes,* boardwalklike areas that offer a great view of the entire beach from Leblon to Arpoador. ⊠*Av. Visconde de Albuquerque to Av. Borges de Medeiros, Leblon, 22420-000.*

Praia do Vidigal. Praia Vidigal is a small stretch of sand next to the Sheraton hotel. Calm and clean, it used to be frequented only by dwellers of the favela Vidigal before the Sheraton was built. ⊠*Av. Niemeyer at Sheraton, Vidigal, 22450-221.*

Praia de São Conrado. Undoubtedly the safest beach in Rio, Praia de São Conrado is empty during the week and packed on weekends and holidays. This is the playground of the residents of Rocinha, the world's largest shantytown. It's worth it to stay until sunset; the pumpkin sun makes a beautiful show over Pedra da Gávea. ⊠*São Conrado, 22610-095.*

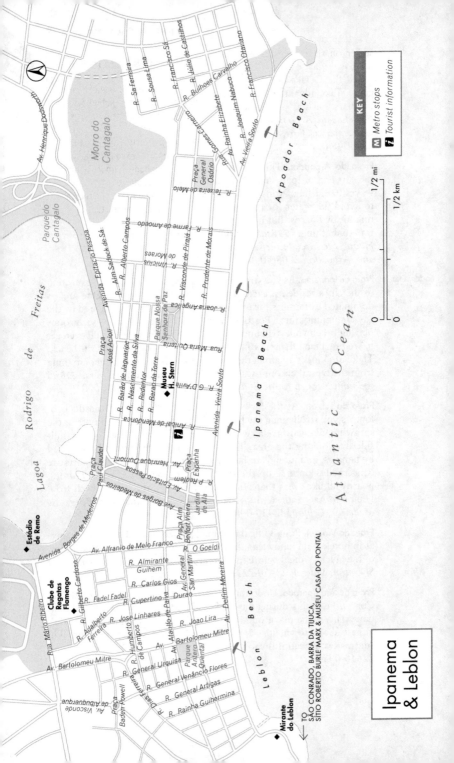

Ipanema & Leblon

KEY

M Metro stops

i Tourist information

Atlantic Ocean

Morro do Cantagalo

Parque do Cantagalo

Lagoa Rodrigo de Freitas

Parque Nossa Senhora da Paz

♦ Estádio de Remo

Clube de Regatos Flamengo

♦ Museu H. Stern

♦ Mirante do Leblon

Ipanema Beach

Arpoador Beach

Leblon Beach

Av. Henrique Dodsworth

R. Sá Ferreira

R. Sousa Lima

R. Francisco Sá

R. Bulhões Carvalho

R. Julia de Castilhos

R. Francisco Otaviana

R. Rainha Elizabete

Av. Joaquim Nabuco

Av. Vieira Souto

R. Teixeira de Melo

Praça General Osório

R. Farme de Amoedo

R. Alberto Campos

R. Aln Sadock de Sá

Avenida Epitacio Pessoa

Praça José Acioli

R. Barão de Jaguaripe

R. Nascimento da Silva

R. Redentor

R. Barata Ribeiro

R. Vinicius de Moraes

R. Visconde de Pirajá

R. Prudente de Morais

R. Joana Angélica

Rua Maria Quiteria

R. G. D'Avila

Avenida Vieira Souto

R. Anibal de Mendonça

Av. Henrique Dumont

Praça Espanha

Praça Paul Claudel

Ave. Borges de Medeiros

Avenida Borges de Medeiros

Praça Alm Belfort Vieira

Jardim de Alá

R. P. Redfern

Av. Epitácio Pessoa

Av. Alfranio de Melo Franco

R. O Goeldi

R. Almirante Guihem

R. Carlos Gios

R. Cupertino Durao

Av. General San Martin

Av. Delfim Moreira

R. Gilberto Cardoso

R. Fadel Fadel

R. Adalberto Ferreira

R. Jose Linhares

R. Joao Lira

Rua Mário Ribeiro

Av. Bartolomeu Mitre

R. Humberto de Campos

R. Ataulfo de Paiva

Av. Bartolomeu Mitre

Parque Antero Quental

Av. Visconde de Albuquerque

Praça Baden Powell

D. Ferreira

R. General Urquisa

R. General Venâncio Flores

R. General Artigas

R. Rainha Guilhermina

TO
SÃO CONRADO, BARRA DA TIJUCA,
SÍTIO ROBERTO BURLE MARX & MUSEU CASA DO PONTAL

0   1/2 mi

0   1/2 km

BEYOND THE ZONA SUL

Praia da Barra. Some cariocas consider the beach at Barra da Tijuca to be Rio's best, and the 18-km-long (11-mi-long) sweep of sand and jostling waves certainly is dramatic. Pollution isn't generally a problem, and in many places neither are crowds. Barra's water is cooler and its breezes more refreshing than those at other beaches. The waves can be strong in spots; this attracts surfers, windsurfers, and jet skiers, so you should swim with caution. The beach is set slightly below a sidewalk, where cafés and restaurants beckon. Condos have also sprung up here, and the city's largest shopping centers and supermarkets have made inland Barra their home. ⊠ *Av. Sernambetiba in Barra, Barra da Tijuca, 22630-010.*

LIGHTS ON THE MOUNTAINSIDE: VIDIGAL

When you go to Ipanema beach, look west, down past Leblon, towards the favela of Vidigal. It is a constant reminder of Brazil's problem of poverty. Just because it's poor though doesn't mean that Vidigal is without vibrance. Its beautiful tiled entrance on the Avenida Niemeyer between Leblon and São Conrado was designed in 2001 when the favela was elevated to "favela-bairro" status (favela-neighborhood). Inside you'll see small parks, signs advertising parties, and a government-funded daycare center.

Recreio dos Bandeirantes. At the far end of Sernambetiba, Barra's beachfront avenue (the name of the street was recently changed to Avenida Lúcio Costa, but most people still know it as Sernambetiba) is **Recreio dos Bandeirantes,** a 1-km (½-mi) stretch of sand anchored by a huge rock, which creates a small protected cove. Its quiet seclusion makes it popular with families. The calm, pollution-free water, with no waves or currents, is good for bathing, but don't try to swim around the rock—it's bigger than it looks. ⊠ *Av. Sernambetiba, Recreio dos Bandeirantes, 22620-905.*

Prainha. The length of two football fields, Prainha is a vest-pocket beach favored by surfers, who take charge of it on weekends. The swimming is good, but watch out for surfboards. On weekdays, especially in the off-season, the beach is almost empty; on weekends, particularly in peak season, the road to and from Prainha and nearby Grumari is so crowded it almost becomes a parking lot. ⊠ *35 km (22 mi) west of Ipanema on coast road; accessible only by car from Av. Lúcio Costa (Av. Sernambetiba), Grumari, 23020-805.*

Praia de Grumari. About five minutes beyond Prainha, off Estrada de Guaratiba, is Grumari, a beach that seems a preview of paradise. What it lacks in amenities—it has only a couple of groupings of thatch-roof huts selling drinks and snacks—it makes up for in natural beauty: the glorious red sands of its quiet cove are backed by low, lush hills. Weekends are extremely crowded. Take a lunch break at Restaurante Point de Grumari (⇨ *Where to Eat, below*), which serves excellent fish dishes. If you've ventured this far, you might as well take a slight detour to the **Museu Casa do Pontal,** Brazil's largest folk-art museum, and the **Sítio Roberto Burle Marx** for an in-depth look at one of Brazil's greatest artists. ⊠*Estrada de Guaratiba, Grumari, 23020-250.*

Farther West. If you continue walking west from Recreio, you'll notice that this part of Rio is largely untouched; in fact, you'll see just three things: the mountains on your right, the road ahead, and the beach to your left. There are numerous trails (maintained by city workers) that lead to the hidden beaches west of Recreio. You'll see Rio's nude beach, Praia do Abricó, among the many short stretches of sand that continue west.

EXPLORING: THE SIGHTS

CENTRO & ENVIRONS

Rio's settlement dates back to 1555, and much of the city's rich history is captured in traditional churches, government buildings, and villas, which are tucked in and around Centro. You can use the metro to get downtown, but wear comfortable shoes and be ready to walk multiple blocks as you explore this city's historic center. If you're not up for a long walk, consider taking an organized bus tour.

What locals generally refer to as Centro is a sprawling collection of several districts that contain the city's oldest neighborhoods, churches, and most enchanting cafés. Rio's beaches, broad boulevards, and modern architecture may be impressive; but its colonial structures, old narrow streets, and alleyways in leafy inland neighborhoods are no less so. The metro stations that serve Centro are Cinelândia, Carioca, Uruguaiana, Presidente Vargas, Central, and Praça Onze.

Numbers in the text correspond to numbers in the margin and on the Rio Centro and Environs map.

MAIN ATTRACTIONS

⓭ Biblioteca Nacional. Corinthian columns adorn the neoclassical National Library (built between 1905 and 1908), the first such establishment in Latin America. Its original archives were brought to Brazil by King João VI in 1808. Today it contains roughly 13 million books, including two 15th-century printed Bibles, and manuscript New Testaments from the 11th and 12th centuries; first-edition Mozart scores as well as scores by Carlos Gomes (who adapted the José de Alencar novel about Brazil's Indians, *O Guarani,* into an opera of the same name); books that belonged to Empress Teresa Christina; and many other manuscripts, prints, and drawings. Tours are available in English. ⊠*Av. Rio Branco 219, Centro, 20040-008* ☎*021/2220–9484* ⊕*www.bn.br* ☜*Tours R$2* ◔*By guided tour only, weekdays at 11 and 3* Ⓜ*Cinelândia.*

⓮ Catedral de São Sebastião do Rio de Janeiro *(Catedral Metropolitana).* The exterior of this circa-1960 metropolitan cathedral, which looks like a concrete beehive, can be off-putting. The daring modern design stands in sharp contrast to the baroque style of other churches. But

CLOSE UP

What's Your Beach Style?

Praia do Flamengo. Power-walkers, volleyballers, and yoga enthusiasts come to Flamengo Beach to work up a sweat. It isn't a tourist destination, and you rarely see people swimming (pollution can be a problem) or sunbathing.

Praia do Botafogo. The view of the bay and the Sugar Loaf from this beach is breathtaking, but it isn't a popular beach with tourists or even locals, due to pollution in the bay waters.

Praia do Vermelha. This tiny beach neighboring the Pão de Açúcar has beautiful scenery but polluted waters. It's generally populated only by cariocas who live nearby.

Praia do Leme. A continuation of Copacabana Beach, Leme has a similar feel. Lined with kiosks and volleyball nets, it's popular with locals and tourists.

Praia do Diabo. Between Ipanema and Copacabana, this small strip attracts surfers. The view is beautiful, and if you're at Ipanema, it's worth the walk to Praia do Diabo.

Praia de Copacabana. The city's grande dame, Copacabana is a 3-km (2-mi) stretch packed to the gills on sunny days with sunbathers, vendors, and athletes. Kiosks along its busy promenade have snacks and drinks. Cafés and high-rise hotels line the waterfront avenue.

Praia de Ipanema. Always-crowded Ipanema is smaller than Copacabana, but equally famous. It's a perfect place to sunbathe and people-watch. At the east end is the dramatic rock formation Pedra do Arpoador; visible to the west, past Leblon, is the Morro Dois Irmaos (Two Brothers Mountain) and the hillside Vidigal favela.

Praia do Leblon. Ipanema Beach extends west to meet Leblon Beach, which has the same feel. It's very popular for exercising on the sand or boardwalk. Water pollution is a problem.

Praia do Vidigal. Sheltered by rock formations, Vidigal doesn't attract many other travelers other than those staying in the nearby hotels, because access is difficult.

Praia de São Conrado. Hang gliders land here after leaping from a nearby peak. The proximity to the Rocinha favela keeps many people away. Tourists are rare.

Praia Barra da Tijuca. Rio's longest beach (18 km/11 mi) has clean and cool waters. Its far end, called Recreio dos Bandeirantes, was a fishing village until the late 1960s. The neighborhood of Barra da Tijuca feels like a suburb, and the beach reflects that. It attracts families with young children and older folks out for a stroll.

Prainha. Just beyond Barra da Tijuca, Prainha has rough seas that make it popular with surfers. It's nearly empty on weekdays.

Praia de Grumari. The copper sands of this lovely beach are packed on weekends. It has little infrastructure but clean sand and water, and is backed by green hills.

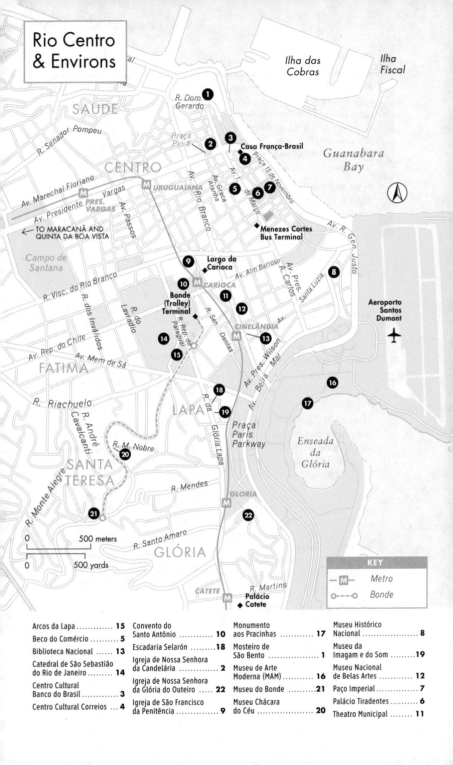

Rio Centro & Environs

R. Dom Gerardo

SAÚDE

R. Senador Pompeu

Praça Pio-X

CENTRO

1

2

3

4 Casa França-Brasil

Av. Marechal Floriano

URUGUAIANA

Av. Presidente Vargas

PRES. VARGAS

Vargas

← TO MARACANÃ AND
QUINTA DA BOA VISTA

Av. Rio Branco

Av. Passos

Av. Graça Aranha

Av. 1 de Março

Praça 15 de Novembro

5

6 **7**

Menezes Cortes
Bus Terminal

*Guanabara
Bay*

*Ilha das
Cobras*

*Ilha
Fiscal*

Campo de
Santana

R. Visc. do Rio Branco

R. dos Inválidos

R. do Lavrado

9 Largo da
Carioca

10 CARIOCA

Bonde
(Trolley)
Terminal

11

12

Av. Alm Barroso

Av. Pres. Carlos

Santa Luzia

8

Av. R. Gen. Justo

**Aeroporto
Santos
Dumont** ✈

FÁTIMA

Av. Rep. do Chile

Av. Mem de Sá

14

R. Sen. Dantas

CINELÂNDIA

13

R. Rep. do Paraguai

15

Av. Pres. Wilson

Av. Beira Mar

LAPA

R. Riachuelo

R. André Cavalcanti

R. da Glória Lapa

18

19

Praça
Paris
Parkway

16

17

*Enseada
da
Glória*

SANTA
TERESA

R. Monte Alegre

R. M. Nobre

20

R. Mendes

R. Santo Amaro

21

GLÓRIA

22

GLÓRIA

0 ——— 500 meters

0 ——— 500 yards

CATETE

R. Martins

**Palácio
Catete** ◆

KEY

—Ⓜ— *Metro*

o—•—•—o *Bonde*

don't judge until you've stepped inside. Outstanding stained-glass windows transform the interior—which is 80 meters (263 feet) high and 96 meters (315 feet) in diameter—into a warm yet serious place of worship that accommodates up to 20,000 people. An 8½-ton granite rock lends considerable weight to the concept of an altar. ⊠ *Av. República do Chile 245, Centro, 20031-919* ☎ *021/2240–2869* 💲 *Free* ⊘ *Daily 7:30–5:30* Ⓜ *Carioca or Cinelândia.*

❸ **Centro Cultural Banco do Brasil.** What was once the headquarters of Brazil's oldest bank is now an enormous cultural space in downtown Rio. With plenty of room for cinema, expositions, music, educational programs, and theater, the options are endless. 2008 marks Banco do Brasil's bicentennial and the arrival of the Portuguese royal family in Rio, fleeing from Napoléon's invading army. Explore the many floors of this impressive edifice or take a nap on the first floor's unusual sound bed. ⊠ *66 Rua Primeiro de Março, Centro, 20010-000* ☎ *021/3808–2020* 💲 *Free* ⊘ *Tues.–Sun. 10–9* Ⓜ *Carioca.*

❿ **Convento do Santo Antônio.** The Convent of St. Anthony was completed in 1780, but some parts date from 1615, making it one of Rio's oldest structures. Its baroque interior contains priceless colonial art—including wood carvings and wall paintings. The sacristy is covered with azulejos (Portuguese tiles). Note that the church has no bell tower: its bells hang from a double arch on the monastery ceiling. An exterior mausoleum contains the tombs of the offspring of Dom Pedro I and Dom Pedro II. At this writing the convent is undergoing renovations, and most parts are roped off. ⊠ *Largo da Carioca 5, Centro, 20050-020* ☎ *021/2262–0129* 💲 *Free* ⊘ *By appointment only, call ahead to set up a visit* Ⓜ *Carioca.*

❾ **Igreja de São Francisco da Penitência.** The church was completed in 1737, nearly four decades after it was started. Today it's famed for its wooden sculptures and rich gold-leaf interior. The nave contains a painting of St. Francis, the patron of the church—reportedly the first painting in Brazil done in perspective. Part of the Convento do Santo Antônio, this church is partially roped off due to renovations, though its beauty still shines through. ⊠ *Largo da Carioca 5, Centro, 20050-020* ☎ *021/2262–0197* 💲 *R$2* ⊘ *Wed.–Fri. 11–4* Ⓜ *Carioca.*

⓱ **Monumento aos Pracinhas.** The Monument to the Brazilian Dead of World War II (the nation sided with the Allies during the conflict) is actually a museum and monument combined. It houses military uniforms, medals, stamps, and documents belonging to soldiers. Two soaring columns flank the tomb of an unknown soldier. The first Sunday of each month Brazil's armed forces perform a colorful changing of the guard. ⊠ *Parque Brigadeiro Eduardo Gomes, Flamengo, 20011-000* ☎ *021/ 2240–1283* 💲 *Free* ⊘ *Tues.–Sun. 10–4* Ⓜ *Cinelândia.*

❶ **Mosteiro de São Bento.** Just a glimpse of this church's main altar can fill you with awe. Layer upon layer of curvaceous wood carvings coated in gold create a sense of movement. Spiral columns whirl upward to capitals topped by cherubs so chubby and angels so purposeful they seem almost animated. Although the Benedictines arrived in 1586, they didn't begin work on this church and monastery until 1617. It was completed in 1641, but such artisans as Mestre Valentim (who designed the silver chandeliers) continued to add details almost through to the 19th century. Every Sunday at 10, mass is accompanied by Gregorian chants. ⊠ *Rua Dom Gerardo 68, Centro, 20090-906* ☏ *021/2206–8100* 🎫 *Free* ⊙ *Weekdays 7–noon and 2–6.*

⑯ Museu de Arte Moderna (MAM). In a striking concrete-and-glass building, the Modern Art Museum has a collection of some 1,700 works by artists from Brazil and elsewhere. It also hosts significant special exhibitions and has a movie theater that plays art films. ⊠ *Av. Infante Dom Henrique 85, Centro, 20021-140* ☏ *021/2240–4944* ⊕ *www.mamrio. org.br* ⊙ *Tues.–Fri. noon–6, weekends and holidays noon–7* 🎫 *R$5* Ⓜ *Cinelândia.*

⑧ Museu Histórico Nacional. The building that houses the National History Museum dates from 1762, though some sections—such as the battlements—were erected as early as 1603. It seems appropriate that this colonial structure should exhibit relics that document Brazil's history. Among its treasures are rare papers, Latin American coins, carriages, cannons, and religious art. ⊠ *Praça Marechal Ancora, Centro, 20021-200* ☏ *021/2550–9224 or 021/2220–2328* ⊕ *www.museuhistorico nacional.com.br* 🎫 *Tues.–Sat. R$6, Sun. free* ⊙ *Tues.–Fri. 10–5:30, weekends and holidays 2–6* Ⓜ *Carioca or Cinelândia.*

⑫ Museu Nacional de Belas Artes. Works by Brazil's leading 19th- and 20th-
★ century artists fill the space at the National Museum of Fine Arts. The most notable canvases are those by the country's best-known modernist, Cândido Portinari, but be on the lookout for such gems as Leandro Joaquim's heartwarming 18th-century painting of Rio (a window to a time when fishermen still cast nets in the waters below the landmark Igreja de Nossa Senhora da Glória do Outeiro). After wandering the picture galleries, tour the extensive collections of folk and African art. At this writing the museum is in its final stage of a six-phase overhaul of the building. ⊠ *Av. Rio Branco 199, Centro, 20040-008* ☏ *021/2240–0068* ⊕ *www.iphan.gov.br* 🎫 *R$4, free Sun. and during construction* ⊙ *Tues.–Fri. 10–6* Ⓜ *Carioca or Cinelândia.*

⑪ Theatro Municipal. If you visit one place in Centro, make it this theater, modeled after the Paris Opera House and opened in 1909. Carrara marble, stunning mosaics, glittering chandeliers, bronze and onyx statues, gilded mirrors, German stained-glass windows, brazilwood inlay floors, and murals by Brazilian artists Eliseu Visconti and Rodolfo Amoedo make the Municipal Theater opulent indeed. The main entrance and first two galleries are particularly ornate. As you climb to the upper floors, the decor becomes simpler, a reflection of a time when different classes entered through different doors and sat in separate sections—but also due in part to the exhaustion of funds toward the end of the project. The theater seats 2,357—with outstanding sight lines—for its dance performances and classical music concerts. English-speaking guides are available. ⊠ *Praça Floriano 210, Centro, 20031-050* ☏ *021/2299–1667* ⊕ *www.theatromunicipal.rj.gov.br* 🎫 *Tours*

R$4 ☉ Guided tours available by request weekdays 1–4 Ⓜ *Cinelândia or Carioca.*

IF YOU HAVE TIME

❺ **Beco do Comércio.** A network of narrow streets and alleys centers on this pedestrian thoroughfare, also called the Travessa do Comércio. The area is flanked by restored 18th-century homes, now converted to offices. The best known is the Edifício Teles de Menezes. Once a functional aqueduct and the source of water for downtown Rio, the **Arco do Teles,** links this area with Praça 15 de Novembro. A great place to grab a bite to eat, the Beco do Comércio offers dining options from low-end quilo-style restaurants to some higher end restaurants and cafés. ✉*Praça 15 de Novembro 34, Centro, 20010-080* Ⓜ*Uruguaiana.*

❹ **Centro Cultural Correios.** The Post Office Cultural Center always hosts a few surprisingly good (and free) art exhibits just around the corner from the more impressive Bank of Brazil Cultural Center. The beautiful interior and old-fashioned elevator are photograph-worthy in and of themselves. ✉*Rua Visconde de Itaboraí 20, Centro, 20010-976* ☏*021/2253–1580* ✍*Free* ☉*Tues.–Sun. noon–7* Ⓜ*Carioca. .*

❷ **Igreja de Nossa Senhora da Candelária.** The classic symmetry of Candelária's white dome and bell towers casts an unexpected air of sanity over the chaos of downtown traffic. The church was built on the site of a chapel founded in 1610 by Antônio de Palma after he survived a shipwreck; paintings in the present dome tell his tale. Construction on the present church began in 1775, and although it was formally dedicated by the emperor in 1811, work on the dome wasn't completed until 1877. The sculpted bronze doors were exhibited at the 1889 world's fair in Paris. ✉*Praça Pio X, Centro, 20091-040* ☏*021/2233–2324* ✍*Free* ☉*Weekdays 7:30–4, Sat. 8–noon, Sun. 9–1* Ⓜ*Uruguaiana.*

❼ **Paço Imperial.** This two-story colonial building with thick stone walls and an ornate entrance was built in 1743, and for the next 60 years was the headquarters for Brazil's captains (viceroys), appointed by the Portuguese court in Lisbon. When King João VI arrived, he made it his royal palace. After Brazil's declaration of independence, emperors Dom Pedro I and II called the palace home. When the monarchy was overthrown, the building became Rio's central post office. Restoration work in the 1980s transformed it into a cultural center and concert hall. The building houses a restaurant, a coffee shop, a stationery-and-CD shop, and a movie theater. The square on which the palace sits, Praça 15 de Novembro, known in colonial days as Largo do Paço, has witnessed some of Brazil's most significant historic moments: it's where two emperors were crowned, slavery was abolished, and Emperor Pedro II was deposed. The square's modern name is a reference to the date of the declaration of the Republic of Brazil: November 15, 1889. ✉*Praça 15 de Novembro 48, Centro, 20010-010* ☏*021/2533–4407* ⊕*www.pacoimperial.com.br* ✍*Free* ☉*Weekdays 1–5.*

❻ **Palácio Tiradentes.** The Tiradentes Palace runs a permanent exhibit on its own history: it was once the seat of Brazilian parliament before Brasília was built in the late 1950s. Getúlio Vargas, Brazil's President for almost 20 years and by far the biggest force in Brazilian 20th-century politics, used the Palace as a nucleus for propaganda diffusion in the 1940s. Tours are given in Portuguese, English, and Spanish. ⊠*Rua Primeiro de Março, Centro* ☎*021/2588-1411* ⊠*Free* ⊘*Mon.–Sat. 10–5, Sun. noon–5.*

NEED A BREAK?

Elegance joins good but simple food at Café do Odeon BR (⊠*Praça Floriano 7, Centro, 20031-050* ☎*021/2240-2573*), close to the Theatro Municipal. Appetizers and sandwiches can revitalize after walking downtown. The Odeon BR is one of Rio's most traditional movie theaters and was renovated in 2000. The café's veranda has a view to Praça Cinelândia. To taste a little of the carioca life, try the bar Carlitos (⊠*Rua Álvaro Alvim 36, Loja E, Centro, 20031-010* ☎*021/2262-6567*), on a street parallel to Theatro Municipal. Don't expect a fashionable place, but a spot where the *chopp* (draft beer) is good and *batidas* (sweet alcoholic drinks mixed in a blender) come in many flavors—from tropical fruits to gingerbread.

CATETE, GLÓRIA & LAPA

These three neighborhoods surround the city center. Catete formerly housed the national government and still has beautiful buildings (such as the Palácio do Catete) that are worth visiting. Gloria is famous for its beautiful churches. Lapa also has beautiful architecture that can be explored on foot during the day, but at night it's best to get around in taxis. Lapa is also home to some of the best music halls in the city, and attracts music lovers every night of the week.

Numbers in the margin correspond to numbers on the Rio Centro and Environs map.

MAIN ATTRACTIONS

㉒ **Igreja de Nossa Senhora da Glória do Outeiro.** Perched atop a hill, this baroque church is visible from many spots in the city, making it a landmark that's truly cherished by the cariocas. Its location was a strategic point in the city's early days. Estácio da Sá took this hill from the French in the 1560s and then went on to expand the first settlement and found a city for the Portuguese. The church, which wasn't built until 1739, is notable for its octagonal floor plan, large dome, ornamental stonework, and vivid tile work. The church has a small museum inside with baroque art. Tours are given by appointment only. ⊠*Praça Nossa Senhora da Glória 135, Glória, 22211-110* ☎*021/2557–4600* ⊕*www.outeirodagloria.com.br* ⊠*Church free, museum R$2* ⊘ *Weekdays 9–noon and 1–5, weekends 9–noon. Museum closed Mon.* Ⓜ*Glória.*

⑱ **Escadaria Selarón.** After traveling the world and living in more than 50 countries, Chilean painter Selarón began working in 1990 on the iconic tile staircase that is now one of the highlights of Lapa. With tiles from around the world, Selarón's staircase is the product of years of dedication, artistic vision, and many donations of tiles from places far and near. At night the staircase is filled with people seeking to escape the noise and action that define Lapa. In the daytime Selarón can be found at the staircase, forever at work on his masterpiece. He's happy to talk to interested travelers, patient to pose for photos, and grateful for donations (of tiles) to his work. ⊠ *Escadaria Selarón 24, Lapa, 20241-120* ⊕ *www.selaron.net. .*

IF YOU HAVE TIME

⑲ **Museu da Imagem e do Som.** The first audiovisual museum in Brazil, the Museum of Image and Sound (MIS) was founded to acquire, preserve, and exhibit important collections tied to Rio's cultural history. The museum houses collections of images and sound in a range of mediums, including engravings, drawings, caricatures, musical instruments, photographs, books, discs, recordings, and even antique gramafones, microfones, and musical instruments. The collections highlight the works of many of Rio's lesser-known names of the past, such as the Batista sisters of Brazil's Golden Age of Radio, and Elizeth Cardoso, considered to be one of the greatest female singers of Brazilian popular music. ⊠ *Rua Visconde de Maranguape 15, Lapa, 20021-390* ☎ *021/2224–8461* ⊠ *Free* ⊙ *Weekdays 11–5.*

SANTA TERESA

With its cobblestone streets and bohemian atmosphere, Santa Teresa is a delightfully eccentric neighborhood. Gabled Victorian mansions sit beside alpine-style chalets as well as more prosaic dwellings—many hanging at unbelievable angles from the flower-encrusted hills. Cafés, galleries, and antiques shops have nudged their way into nooks and crannies between the colorful homes, many of which house artists and their studios.

Numbers in the text correspond to numbers on the Rio Centro and Environs map.

MAIN ATTRACTIONS

⑮ **Arcos da Lapa.** Formerly the Aqueduto da Carioca (Carioca Aqueduct), this structure with 42 massive stone arches was built between 1744 and 1750 to carry water from the Carioca River in the hillside neighborhood of Santa Teresa to Centro. In 1896 the city transportation company converted the then-abandoned aqueduct into a viaduct, laying trolley tracks along it. Since then Rio's distinctive trolley cars (called "*bondes*" because they were financed by foreign bonds) have carried people between Santa Teresa and Centro. ⚠ **Guard your belongings particularly closely when you ride the open-sided bondes.** ⊠ *Estação Carioca, Rua Professor Lélio Gama, Centro, 20021-180* ☎ *021/2240–5709 or 021/2240–5709* ⊠ *R$1* ⊙ *Bondes leave every 20 min 6 AM–10 PM* Ⓜ *Carioca or Cinelândia.*

⑳ **Museu Chácara do Céu.** The collection of mostly modern works at the
★ Museum of the Small Farm of the Sky was left—along with the hilltop house that contains it—by one of Rio's greatest arts patrons, Raymundo de Castro Maya. Included are originals by 20th-century masters Picasso, Braque, Dalí, Degas, Matisse, Modigliani, and Monet. The

Brazilian holdings include priceless 17th- and 18th-century maps and works by leading modernists. From the grounds you have great views of the aqueduct, Centro, and the bay. ⊠*Rua Murtinho Nobre 93, Santa Teresa, 20241-050* ☎*021/2507–1932* ⊕*www.museuscastro maya.com.br/chacara* ⊠*R$2, free on Wed.* ☺*Daily noon–5 except Tues.*.

IF YOU HAVE TIME

㉑ **Museu do Bonde.** If you're waiting around for the *bonde* (tram) close to Largo do Guimarães, have a peek inside this small, memorabilia-packed homage to Rio's trolleys. ⊠*Rua Carlos Brand 14, Santa Teresa, 20240-290* ☎*021/2242–2354* ⊠*Free* ☺*Mon–Fri 9–4:30.*

NEED A BREAK? Santa Teresa attracts artists, musicians, and intellectuals to its eclectic slopes. One of their popular hangouts is Bar do Arnaudo (⊠*Rua Almirante Alexandrino 316-B, Santa Teresa, 20241-260* ☎*021/2252–7246*), which is always full.

FLAMENGO & BOTAFOGO

These largely residential neighborhoods connect the southern beach districts and Centro via a series of highways that intersect here. It's very easy to reach these neighborhoods by metro. Apartment buildings dominate, but Rio Sul—one of the city's most popular shopping centers—is here, as are some of the city's best museums and public spaces.

The eponymous beach at Flamengo no longer draws swimmers (its gentle waters look appealing but are polluted; the people you see are sunning, not swimming). A marina sits on a bay at one end of the beach, which is connected via a busy boulevard to the smaller beach (also polluted), at Botafogo. The city's yacht club is here, and when Rio was Brazil's capital, it was also the site of the city's glittering embassy row. The embassies were long ago transferred to Brasília, but the mansions that housed them remain. Among Botafogo's more interesting mansion- and tree-lined streets are Mariana, Sorocaba, Matriz, and Visconde e Silva.

Numbers in the text correspond to numbers on the Flamengo, Botafogo & Urca map.

MAIN ATTRACTIONS

❸ **Museu das Telecomunicações.** Housed in the Oi Futuro, this high-tech museum is a multimedia adventure. The Telecommunications Museum was purposely designed so that each visitor has a unique experience, with no prescribed order to how the museum is viewed. After being oriented in the use of the MP3 headsets, a light- and mirror-filled airlock-like room awaits. The myriad monitors, blinking lights, and artifacts that lie ahead may seem a bit overwhelming at first, but the start of your journey begins with a click of your MP3 player. Even if you don't speak Portuguese, the English guide will explain the various exhibits, and the sights in this tiny exhibit space will mesmerize you. One word

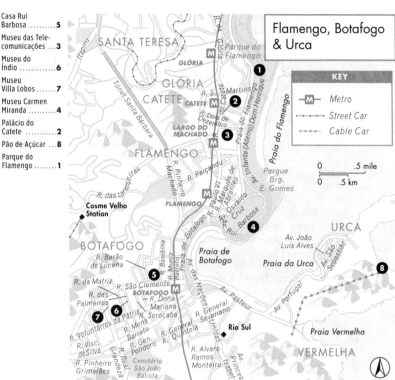

Flamengo, Botafogo & Urca

of caution: be careful not to get trapped in the antique phone booth. The other floors of the Oi Futuro building house other cultural spaces devoted to theater performances, film screenings, and art exhibits. There's also a small library and a café. ⊠ *Rua Dois de Dezembro 63, Flamengo, 22220-040* ☎ *021/3131–3050* 🖾 *Free* ☉ *Tues.–Sun. 11–8* Ⓜ *Largo do Machado or Catete.*

❻ Museu do Índio. Just a few blocks away from the Botafogo metro station is Rio de Janeiro's Indian Museum, an homage to Brazil's many Amazonian tribes. The first floor is free, but the second floor, which houses the main exhibition, is not. Head to the gift shop to browse the native handicrafts and buy your tickets before going up the stairs of the museum. ⊠ *Rua das Palmeiras 55, Botafogo, 22270-070* ☎ *021/2286—8899,* ⊕ *www.museudoindio.org.br* 🖾 *R$3* ☉ *Tues.–Fri. 9–5:30, weekends 1–5* Ⓜ *Botafogo.*

❹ Museu Carmen Miranda. This tribute to the Brazilian bombshell is in a circular building that resembles a concrete spaceship (its door even opens upward rather than out). On display are some of the elaborate costumes and incredibly high platform shoes worn by the actress, who was viewed as a national icon by some and as a traitor to true Brazilian culture by others. Hollywood photos of Miranda, who was only 46 when she died of a heart attack in 1955, show her in her trademark turban and jewelry. Also here are her records and movie posters and such memorabilia as the silver hand mirror she was clutching when she died. Guided tours are given by appointment, but guides do not speak English. ⊠ *Atêrro do Flamengo park, Av. Rui Barbosa s/n, across from Av. Rui Barbosa 560, Flamengo, 22250-020* ☏ *021/2299–5586* ⊕ *www.sec.rj.gov.br* ☏ *Free* ⊗ *Tues.–Fri. 11–5, weekends and holidays 1–5* Ⓜ *Flamengo.*

② **Palácio do Catete.** Once the villa of a German baron, the elegant, 19th-century granite-and-marble palace became the presidential residence after the 1889 coup overthrew the monarchy and established the Republic of Brazil. Eighteen presidents lived here. Gaze at the palace's gleaming parquet floors and intricate bas-relief ceilings as you wander through its **Museu da República** (Museum of the Republic). The permanent exhibits include a shroud-draped view of the bedroom where President Getúlio Vargas committed suicide in 1954 after the military threatened to overthrow his government. Presidential memorabilia, furniture, and paintings that date from the proclamation of the republic to the end of Brazil's military regime in 1985 are also displayed. A small contemporary art gallery, a movie theater, a restaurant, and a theater operate within the museum. ⊠ *Rua do Catete 153, Catete, 22220-000* ☏ *021/2558–6350* ☏ *Tues. and Thurs.–Sat., R$6. Wed. and Sun., free* ⊗ *Tues., Thurs., and Fri. noon–5, Wed. 2–5, weekends 2–6* Ⓜ *Catete.*

FodorsChoice ★

IF YOU HAVE TIME

⑦ **Museu Villa Lobos** A short walk from the Museu do Índio is a small museum dedicated to Brazil's best-knowm classical composer, Heitor Villa Lobos. Inside this former two-story house, you'll find a collection of Villa Lobos's handwritten compositions, conducting batons, and a small viewing room. At this writing the Museu Villa Lobos is undergoing renovations, and sections were closed to the public. ⊠ *Rua Sorocaba 200, Botafogo, 22271-110* ☏ *021/2266–1024* ⊕ *www.museuvillalobos.org.br* ☏ *Free* ⊗ *Weekdays 10–5:30* Ⓜ *Botafogo.*

⑤ **Casa Rui Barbosa.** Slightly inland from the Atêrro is a museum in what was once the house of 19th-century Brazilian statesman and scholar Rui Barbosa (a liberal from Bahia State who drafted one of Brazil's early constitutions). The pink mansion dates from 1849 and contains memorabilia of Barbosa's life, including his 1913 car and an extensive library that's often consulted by scholars from around the world. ⊠ *Rua São Clemente 134, Botafogo, 22260–000* ☏ *021/3289–4600* ⊕ *www.casaruibarbosa.gov.br* ☏ *R$2, free on Sun.* ⊗ *Tues.–Fri. 9–5:30, weekends and holidays 2–6* Ⓜ *Botafogo.*

NEED A BREAK? Flamengo has some of Rio's better small restaurants. For authentic Brazilian fare, the bohemian community heads to Lamas (⊠ *Rua Marquês de Abrantes 18, 22230-060* ☏ *021/2556–0799*), which is a quick taxi ride from the Carmen Miranda Museum.

① **Parque do Flamengo.** Flanking the Baía de Guanabara from the Glória neighborhood to Flamengo is this waterfront park. It gets its name from its location atop an *atêrro* (landfill), and was designed by landscape architect Roberto Burle Marx. Paths used for jogging, walking, and biking wind through it. There are also playgrounds and public tennis and basketball courts. On weekends the freeway beside the park is closed to traffic, and the entire area becomes one enormous public space. ⊠*Inland of beach, from Glória to Botafogo, 22210-030* 🚳*Free* 🕙*Daily 24 hrs* Ⓜ*Glória or Flamengo.*

URCA

Tiny sheltered Urca faces Botafogo. The quiet neighborhood with single-family homes and tree-lined streets is separated by the Pão de Açúcar from a small underwhelming patch of yellow sand called Praia Vermelha. This beach is, in turn, blocked by the Urubu and Leme mountains from the 1-km (½-mi) Leme Beach at the start of the Zona Sul. Besides having one of the city's most famous attractions, the Pão de Açúcar, Urca has our favorite branch of the world-famous churrascaria Porcão *(⇨ Where to Eat).*

❽ **Pão de Açúcar** *(Sugar Loaf).* This soaring 1,300-meter (approximately
★ 4,290-foot) granite block at the mouth of Baía de Guanabara was originally called *pau-nh-acugua* (high, pointed peak) by the indigenous Tupi people. To the Portuguese the phrase seemed similar to *pão de açúcar;* the rock's shape reminded them of the conical loaves in which refined sugar was sold. Italian-made bubble cars holding 75 passengers each move up the mountain in two stages. The first stop is at Morro da Urca, a smaller, 212-meter (705-foot) mountain; the second is at the summit of Pão de Açúcar itself. The trip to each level takes three minutes. In high season long lines form for the cable car; the rest of the year the wait is seldom more than 30 minutes. ■TIP➡ **Consider visiting the Pão de Açúcar first as the view can be somewhat anticlimactic after climbing the considerably higher Corcovado.** ⊠*Av. Pasteur 520, Praia Vermelha, Urca, 22290-902* ☎*021/2546–8400* ⊕*www.bondinho.com.br* 🚳*R$35 adults, R$17.50 children under 13, free for children under 6* 🕙*Daily 8 AM–9 PM.*

ZONA SUL

Copacabana is Rio's most famous tourist neighborhood thanks to its fabulous beach and grande-dame hotels like the Copacabana Palace. The main thoroughfare is Avenida Nossa Senhora de Copacabana, two blocks inland from the beach. The commercial street is filled with shops, restaurants, and sidewalks crowded with colorful characters. Despite having some of the best hotels in Rio, Copacabana's heyday is over, and the neighborhood is quite a bit grittier than Ipanema or Leblon. It's no secret to thieves that tourists congregate here, so keep your eyes peeled for shady types when walking around after dark.

Ipanema, Leblon, and the blocks surrounding Lagoa Rodrigo de Freitas are part of Rio's money belt. For an up-close look at the posh apartment buildings, stroll down beachfront Avenida Vieira Souto and its extension, Avenida Delfim Moreira, or drive around the lagoon on Ave-

Gay Rio

Gay Rio rocks almost every night with a whole menu of entertainment options. During the day, dedicated areas of the beach in Copacabana (Posto 6) and Ipanema (in front of Rua Farme de Amoedo) are gay and lesbian havens. After dark, the nightlife is welcoming and inclusive. Kick off the evening at **Galeria Café** or the **Copa**, and as it nudges 1 AM, head toward **Le Boy,** the more intimate **La Girl,** or the impressive new club **The Week.** **La Cueva** is one of Copacabana's longest-running gay venues, and most of the livelier underground clubs

(see **Dama De Ferro, Fosfobox,** and **Bunker**) run GLS (Gay/Lesbian/Sympathizer) nights during the week. The best online source for information is at ⊕ *www.guiagaybrasil.com.br,* or pick up monthly leaflets from most of these venues and tourist offices. The sporadic circuit party B.I.T.C.H (Barbies In Total Control) ⊕ *www.bitch.com.br* has been one of the biggest events in the gay calendar since the '80s. The excellent ⊕ *www.xdemente.com* has details of regular bimonthly parties in venues around the city.

nida Epitácio Pessoa. The tree-lined streets between Ipanema Beach and the lagoon are as peaceful as they are attractive. The boutiques along Rua Garcia D'Ávila make window-shopping a sophisticated endeavor. Other chic areas near the beach include Praça Nossa Senhora da Paz, which is lined with wonderful restaurants and bars; Rua Vinicius de Moraes; and Rua Farme de Amoedo.

Forte de Copacabana and Museu Histórico do Exército. Copacabana Fort was built in 1914 as part of Rio's first line of defense. Still visible are many of the fort's original features, such as the thick brick fortification and old Krupp cannons. In the '60s and '70s, during Brazil's military dictatorship, political prisoners were kept here. Today it houses a history museum and a lovely little café with views of the beach and excellent coffee, pastries, and desserts. ⊠*Praça Coronel Eugênio Franco 1, Copacabana, 22070-020* ☎*021/2287–3781* ⊕*www.fortedecopa cabana.com* ☜*R\$2 to enter and another \$2 for exhibition* ۞*Tues.– Sun. 10–4.*

Museu H. Stern. The world headquarters of H. Stern has a small museum where you can see rare gems. A self-guided audio tour explains the entire process of cutting, polishing, and setting stones. Afterward, you get a personal consultation with a salesperson and a gift box with five small stones. The museum can arrange transport back to your hotel. ⊠*Rua Visconde de Pirajá] 490, Ipanema, 22410-002* ☎*021/2106– 0000* ☜*Free* ۞*Tours by appointment only.*

SÃO CONRADO & BARRA DA TIJUCA

West of the Zona Sul lie the highly residential (and considerably affluent) neighborhoods of São Conrado and Barra da Tijuca. If you're accustomed to the shop-lined and restaurant-filled streets of Copacabana and Ipanema, you're in for a shock if you head to these neighborhoods, dominated mainly by towering, modern apartment buildings. São Conrado's main attractions are the nearby favelas of Rocinha and Vila Canoas and the chic Fashion Mall. Its quiet beach serves as a landing site for hang gliders and paragliders. Barra has more to offer to the shopper, with plenty of malls and high-end restaurants for the middle-upper class that dwells there.

MAIN ATTRACTIONS

Fodor'sChoice
★

Sítio Roberto Burle Marx *(Roberto Burle Marx Farm).* Beyond Grumari, the road winds through mangrove swamps and tropical forest. It's an apt setting for the plantation-turned-museum where Brazil's famous landscape designer Roberto Burle Marx is memorialized. Marx, the mind behind Rio's swirling mosaic beachfront walkways and the Atêrro do Flamengo, was said to have "painted with plants," and was the first designer to use Brazilian flora in his projects. More than 3,500 species—including some discovered by and named for Marx as well as many on the endangered list—flourish at this 100-acre estate. He grouped his plants not only according to their soil and light needs but also according to their shape and texture. Marx also liked to mix the modern with the traditional—a recurring theme throughout the property. The results are both whimsical and elegant. In 1985 he bequeathed the farm to the Brazilian government, though he remained here until his death in 1994. His house is now a cultural center full of his belongings, including collections of folk art. The grounds also contain his large ultramodern studio (he was a painter, too) and a small, restored colonial chapel dedicated to St. Anthony. ⊠*Estrada Roberto Burle Marx 2019, Pedra da Guaratiba, 23020-240* ☎*021/2410–1412* ⊡*R$5* ⊙*Tues.–Sun. by appointment only; tours at 9:30* AM *and 1:30* PM.

Museu Casa do Pontal. If you're heading toward Prainha or beyond to Grumari, consider taking a detour to Brazil's largest folk-art museum. One room houses a wonderful mechanical sculpture that represents all of the *escolas de samba* (samba schools) that march in the Carnival parades. Another mechanical "scene" depicts a circus in action. This private collection is owned by a French expatriate, Jacques Van de Beuque, who has been collecting Brazilian treasures—including religious pieces—since he arrived in the country in 1946. ⊠*Estrada do Pontal 3295, Grumari, 22785-560* ☎*021/2490–3278* ⊕*www.museu casadopontal.com.br* ⊡*R$10* ⊙*Tues.–Sun. 9:30–5.*

IF YOU HAVE TIME

São Conrado. Blocked by the imposing Dois Irmãos Mountain, Avenida Niemeyer snakes along rugged cliffs that offer spectacular sea views on the left. The road returns to sea level again in São Conrado, a natural amphitheater surrounded by forested mountains and the ocean. Development of what is now a mostly residential area began in the late '60s with an eye on Rio's high society. A short stretch along its beach includes the condominiums of a former president, the ex-wife of another former president, an ex-governor of Rio de Janeiro State, and a one-time Central Bank president. The far end of São Conrado is marked by the towering Pedra da Gávea, a huge flattop granite boulder. Next to it is Pedra Bonita, the mountain from which gliders depart.

(Although this beach was the city's most popular a few years ago, contaminated water has discouraged swimmers.)

Ironically, the neighborhood is surrounded by favelas (shantytowns). Much of the high ground has been taken over by Rio's largest favela, Rocinha, where an estimated 200,000 people live. This precarious city within a city seems poised to slide down the hill. It and others like it are the result of Rio's chronic housing problem coupled with the refusal by many of the city's poor to live in distant working-class neighborhoods. Though the favelas seem dangerous for the uninitiated, they have their own internal order, and their tremendous expansion has even upper-class cariocas referring to them not as slums but as neighborhoods. The favelas enjoy prime vistas, and most are constructed of brick. It's generally not advisable to enter a favela unless you're with an organized tour that has assured you of its safety, especially if you don't speak Portuguese. ⊠ *Just west of Leblon, 22610-095.*

THE LUSH INLAND

In the western portion of the city north of Leblon, trees and hills dominate the landscape in the neighborhoods of Jardim Botânico, Lagoa, Cosme Velho, and Tijuca. In addition to their parks and gardens, these primarily residential neighborhoods have marvelous museums, seductive architecture, and tantalizing restaurants. The architecture is a mix of modern condominiums and colonial houses. They tend to be quieter neighborhoods during the day because they're not on the beachfront, but also have some of the hippest nightclubs in Rio. You can't say you've seen Rio until you've taken in the view from Corcovado and then strolled through its forested areas or beside its inland Lagoa (Lagoon) Rodrigo de Freitas—hanging out just like a true carioca.

Public transportation doesn't conveniently reach the sights here; take a taxi or a tour.

Numbers in the margin correspond to numbers on the Lush Inland map.

MAIN ATTRACTIONS

❸ Corcovado. There's an eternal argument about which view is better, from Pão de Açúcar (Sugar Loaf) or from here. In our opinion, it's best to visit Sugar Loaf *before* you visit Corcovado, or you will remember Sugar Loaf only as an anticlimax. Corcovado has two advantages: at 690 meters (2,300 feet), it's nearly twice as high and offers an excellent view of Pão de Açúcar itself. The sheer 300-meter (1,000-foot) granite face of Corcovado (the name means "hunchback" and refers to the mountain's shape) has always been a difficult undertaking for climbers.

Fodor'sChoice
★

It wasn't until 1921, the centennial of Brazil's independence from Portugal, that someone had the idea of placing a statue atop Corcovado. A team of French artisans headed by sculptor Paul Landowski was assigned the task of erecting a statue of Christ with his arms apart as if embracing the city. (Nowadays, mischievous cariocas say Christ is get-

Favelas

A BIT OF HISTORY

Named after the flowers that grow on the hills of Rio, the first favela began as a squatter town for homeless soldiers at the end of the 19th century, and later, freed slaves illegally made their homes on these undeveloped government lands. The favelas flourished and expanded in the 1940s as the population in Brazil shifted from a rural-based to an urban-based one. In the 1970s, during the military dictatorship, the government moved favela dwellers into public housing projects.

RIO'S LARGEST FAVELA

Rocinha is Rio's largest and most developed favela. Between 150,000 and 300,000 people reside in this well-developed community (there are three banks, a nightclub, and a plethora of shops and small markets). Brace yourself for a variety of smells, both good and bad: you'll find savory-smelling, grilled churrasquinho (meat skewers) sold in the street and any number of delicous aromas drifting out of nearby restaurants. On the flip side, residents dump their trash on the side of the road (in designated areas) and in some places, raw sewage flows in open canals.

EXPLORING

The main thoroughfare, the Estrada da Gávea, begins in São Conrado and ends on the other side of Rocinha, in Gávea. Anyone can take a stroll up this street, and visitors are likely to hear English being spoken. If you're feeling intrepid and want to explore Rocinha on foot without a guide, be aware of the following: Rocinha has been controlled by the drug faction Amigos dos Amigos (ADA) since 2006. The gang is heavily armed with handguns, automatic weapons, and gre-

nades. They use these arms to protect the drug trade, which is a thriving, though illegal, business. It's clear who the gang members are, and drugs are sold in plain sight. The drug dealers don't hustle, they don't call out visitors or people on tours, and they will assume that foreigners are either on a tour or working for one of the many NGOs stationed inside Rocinha. Do not take pictures of the police or of armed men inside the favela. Favelas are not safe when the police are invading; firecrackers and a police blockade are the most obvious signs of an invasion. Normally, there are a few patrol cars stationed at Rocinha's entrance, and a police cruiser tends to circle the block in front of Rocinha, stopping individuals to check for drugs.

If you're interested in exploing Rocinha or other favelas, but don't want to go it alone, we recommend the following tour operators.

Favela Tour, led by Marcelo Armstrong (⊕ *www.favelatour.com.br* ☎ *021/3322–2727 or 021/9989–0074* ✉ *R$65/person min 2 people*), takes tours twice daily through Rocinha and Vila Canoas. Marcelo has an impeccable reputation and offers tours in English, Spanish, Portuguese, French, Italian, and German.

Be a Local (⊕ *www.bealocal.com* ☎ *021/9643–0366* ✉ *R$65*) offers walking tours of Rocinha with various stops inside the community. They accept donations of clothes, food, and medicine. They also offer a favela funk party tour on Sunday (R$50) that includes entrance and admission to a VIP area.

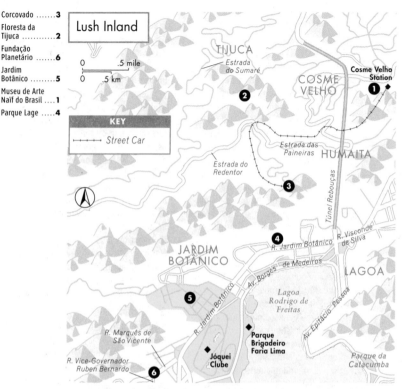

Lush Inland

0   .5 mile

0   .5 km

KEY

⊢——⊣ *Street Car*

ting ready to clap for his favorite escola de samba.) It took 10 years, but on October 12, 1931, the *Cristo Redentor* (Christ the Redeemer) was inaugurated by then president Getúlio Vargas, Brazil's FDR. The sleek, modern figure rises more than 30 meters (100 feet) from a 6-meter (20-foot) pedestal and weighs 700 tons. In the evening a powerful lighting system transforms it into a dramatic icon.

There are four ways to reach the top: by cogwheel train (R$36), by taxi (R$10 per person), car (R$13 per person), or on foot (R$5 per person, free on Catholic holidays). The fee to enter on foot was instituted in December 2007 and is a highly controversial matter, with both the Catholic Church and Rio governor César Maia against the fee. The train, built in 1885, provides delightful views of Ipanema and Leblon from an absurd angle of ascent, as well as a close look at thick vegetation and butterflies. (You may wonder what those oblong medicine balls hanging from the trees are, the ones that look like spiked watermelons tied to ropes—they're *jaca*, or jackfruit.) Trains leave the **Cosme Velho station** (✉ *Rua Cosme Velho 513, Cosme Velho, 22241-090* ☎ *021/2558–1329* ⊕ *www.corcovado.com.br*) for the steep, 5-km (3-mi), 17-minute ascent. Trains run from 9 AM to 6 PM and depart every 30 minutes. Late-afternoon trains are the most popular; on weekends be prepared for a long wait. To get to the summit, you can climb up 220 steep, zigzagging steps (which was the only option available prior to 2003), or take an escalator or a panoramic elevator. If you choose the stairs, you pass little cafés and shops selling film and souvenirs along the way. Save your money for Copacabana's night market; you'll pay at least double atop Corcovado. Once at the top, all of Rio stretches out before you.

Visit Corcovado on a clear day; clouds often obscure the Christ statue and the view of the city. Go as early in the morning as possible, before people start pouring out of the tour buses, and before the haze sets in. ⊠ *Estrada da Redentor, Cosme Velho, 20531-540* ⊕ *www.corcovado. org.br* ⊞ *R$36* ⊙ *Daily 9–6.*

❻ Fundação Planetário. Rio's planetarium is a great escape if your vacation gets rained on or if you simply have a passion for astronomy. The ajoining interactive Museu do Universo, beefed up in recent years, illustrates the history of space discovery and travel in a futuristic exhibition space. The Planetarium has two projection domes: a 23-meter diameter Carl Zeiss Universarium VIII as well as a 12.5-meter diameter Galileu Galilei Spacemaster. The larger dome, projecting around 9,000 stars, is among the most modern in Latin America. The planetarium frequently updates its programming, which consists of a mixture of fictitious adventures in space (recommended for kids) and nonfiction shows about the constrellations and our Solar System. If your aim is stargazing without the voice-over and music, the Praça dos Telescópios is open for sky observation from Tuesday to Friday, between 7:30 PM and 9:30 PM. ⊠ *Rua Vice-Governador Ruben Bernardo 100, Gávea* ☎ *021/2274-0046* ⊞ *Museum: R$6; museum and planetarium session: R$12; weekends: half price* ⊙ *Tues.–Fri. 3–7:30, weekends 3–7 with shows at 4, 5:30, and 7, with frequent changes of dates and times, so call ahead.*

❺ Jardim Botânico. The 340-acre Botanical Garden contains more than 5,000 species of tropical and subtropical plants and trees, including 900 varieties of palms (some more than a century old) and more than 140 species of birds. The temperature is usually a good 12°C (22°F) cooler in the shady garden that was created in 1808 by Portuguese king João VI during his exile in Brazil. In 1842 the garden gained its most impressive adornment, the Avenue of the Royal Palms, a 720-meter (800-yard) double row of 134 soaring royal palms. Elsewhere in the gardens the Casa dos Pilões, an old gunpowder factory, has been restored and displays objects that pertained to both the nobility and their slaves. Also on the grounds are a library, a small café, and a gift shop that sells souvenirs with ecological themes. ⊠ *Rua Jardim Botânico 1008, Jardim Botânico, 22470-180* ☎ *021/3874–1808 or 021/3874–1214* ⊕ *www.jbrj.gov.br* ⊞ *R$4* ⊙ *Daily 8–5. Guided tours in English, Spanish, and Portuguese available by appointment weekdays 9–4.*

❹ Parque Lage. This lush green space, down the road from Jardim Botânico was aquired by Antônio Martins Lage Junior, whose grandson, Henrique Lage, fell head-over-heels in love with the Italian singer Gabriela

Bezanzoni. He had a magnificent palace constructed for her in 1922. The space was later turned into a public park in 1960. It's a good place to relax and explore the grounds—there are aquariums and a few caves with some impressive stalactites and stalagmites. The Escola de Artes Visuais do Parque Lage and a café are housed in the impressive converted mansion. If you want to tackle Corcovado on foot to make your pilgrimage to see Christ the Redeemer, start in Parque Lage; trails are clearly marked, though you shouldn't go alone your first time. ⊠*Rua Jardim Botânico 414, Jardim Botânico, 22461-000* ☎*021/2538-1091* ⊕*www.eavparquelage.org.br* ⊡*Free* ⊙*Daily 7–6.*

IF YOU HAVE TIME

❶ **Museu de Arte Naïf do Brasil.** More than 8,000 art naïf works by Brazil's best (as well as works by other self-taught painters from around the world) grace the walls of this colonial mansion that was once the studio of painter Eliseu Visconti. The pieces, in what is reputedly the world's largest and most complete collection of primitive paintings, date from the 15th century through contemporary times. Don't miss the colorful, colossal 7×4–meter (22×13–foot) canvas that depicts the city of Rio; it reportedly took five years to complete. This museum sprang from a collection started decades ago by a jewelry designer who later created a foundation to oversee the art. ⊠*Rua Cosme Velho 561, Cosme Velho, 22241-090* ☎*021/2205–8612 or 021/2205–8547* ⊕*www.museunaif. com.br* ⊡*R$8* ⊙*Tues.–Fri. 10–6, weekends and holidays noon–6.*

❷ **Floresta da Tijuca** *(Quagmire Forest).* Surrounding Corcovado is the dense, tropical Tijuca Forest. Once part of a Brazilian nobleman's estate, it's studded with exotic trees and thick jungle vines and has a delightful waterfall, the Cascatinha de Taunay. About 180 meters (200 yards) beyond the waterfall is the small pink-and-purple Capela Mayrink (Mayrink Chapel), with painted panels by the 20th-century Brazilian artist Cândido Portinari.

From several points along this national park's 96 km (60 mi) of narrow winding roads the views are breathtaking. Some of the most spectacular are from Dona Marta, on the way up Corcovado; the Emperor's Table, supposedly where Brazil's last emperor, Pedro II, took his court for picnics; and, farther down the road, the Chinese View, the area where Portuguese king João VI allegedly settled the first Chinese immigrants to Brazil, who came in the early 19th century to develop tea plantations. A great way to see the forest is by jeep; you can arrange tours through a number of agencies, such as **Trilhas do Rio Ecoturismo & Aventura** (☎*021/2425–8441 or 021/2424–5455* ⊕*www.trilhasdorio. com.br*), a highly professional tour company with fun programs and well-trained guides. Request an English-speaking guide when you book. **Jeep Tour** (☎*21/2589–0883* ⊕*www.jeeptour.com.br*) is another option. ⊠*Entrance at Praça Afonso Viseu 561, Tijuca, 20531-580* ☎*021/2492–2253* ⊡*Free* ⊙*Daily 8–5.*

West of
Downtown

0   1/2 mile
0   1/2 km

R. São Luiz Gonzaga
R. Sinimbu
Av. do Exército
R. Fonseca Teles
R. Eclydes da Cunha
Av. Rotary Internacional
R. Dez
Área Verde
Av. Bartolomeu Gusmão
R. Gen. Herculano Gomes
R. Francisco Eugênio
MARACANÃ   Av. Osvaldo Aranha   R. M. Machado   SÃO CRISTOVÃO
São Francisco   R. Prof. Eurico Rabelo   R. Teixeira Soares
R. Sen. Furtado
R. Ibituruna
R. Gen. Canabarro
R. Moraes E. Silva
R. Mariz e Barros
Av. Prof. Manoel de Abreu   Xavier
R. Santa Luiza   R. Prof. Gabizo
R. Jacegual
R. Maracanã   AFONSO PENA
Av. Den.   R. H. Beltrão
Av. Paula e Sousa   R. Haddock Lobo
SAENS PEÑA   Av. Soares Filho   SÃO FRANCISCO XAVIER
Av. Maracanã

Mons. Manuel Gomes
Figuera de Melo

WEST OF DOWNTOWN

Neighborhoods west of downtown are mainly residential. Some are middle-class and some are poor. Unless you're a local, it's hard to know which areas are safe and which are not, so you should avoid wandering around. (Though wandering around Quinta da Boa Vista is fine.) You can easily get to Maracanã and Quinta da Boa Vista by metro, but avoid coming here after dark.

Numbers in the margin correspond to numbers on the West of Downtown map.

MAIN ATTRACTIONS

1 Maracanã. From the Igreja de Nossa Senhora da Candelária, walk 3½ blocks to the Uruguaiana station and take the metro to the world's largest soccer stadium. Officially called Estádio Mário Filho after a famous journalist, it's best known as Maracanã, which is the name of the surrounding neighborhood and a nearby river. The 178,000-seat stadium (with standing room for another 42,000) was built in record time to host the 1950 World Cup. Brazil lost its chance at the cup by losing a match 2–1 to Uruguay—a game that's still analyzed a half-century later. Soccer star Pelé made his 1,000th goal here in 1969. The smaller 17,000-seat arena in the same complex has hosted Madonna, Paul

McCartney, and Pope John Paul II. Guided stadium tours are available. ⊠*Rua Professor Eurico Rabelo, Gate 16, 20550-013* ☎*021/2568–9962 or 021/2569–4916* ☜*Tours R$3* ☉*Tours daily 9–5, except on match days* Ⓜ*Maracanã.*

IF YOU HAVE TIME

❷ **Quinta da Boa Vista.** West of downtown, on the landscaped grounds of a former royal estate, are pools and marble statues, as well as the **Museu Nacional** and the **Jardim Zoológico.** Housed in what was once the imperial palace (built in 1803), the museum has exhibits on Brazil's past and on its flora, fauna, and minerals—including the biggest meteorite (5 tons) found in the southern hemisphere. At the zoo you can see animals from Brazil's wilds in re-created natural habitats. Glimpse bats and sloths at the Nocturnal House. ⊠*Av. Paulo e Silva and Av. Bartolomeu de Gusmão, São Cristóvão, 20940-000* ☎*021/2568–8262 for museum, 021/2569–2024 for zoo* ☜*Museum R$3; zoo R$5 weekends, R$4 Tues.–Fri.* ☉*Museum Tues.–Sun. 10–4; zoo Tues.–Sun. 9–4:30* Ⓜ*São Cristóvão.*

WHERE TO EAT

CENTRO

BRAZILIAN

Updated by Lucy Bryson

¢–$

✗**Amarelinho.** The best spot for city-center people-watching, this vast pavement *boteco* (bar) sits directly in front of the Biblioteco Nacional, and to the side of the imposing Theatro Nacional. A city-center institution since 1921, the bar attracts hordes of lunchtime and afterwork diners, competing for the tables and chairs that sit directly on the flagstones of the busy Praça do Floriano. Waitstaff in bright yellow waistcoats and bow ties flit among the tables delivering simple Brazilian dishes such as the mixed grill (R$20) served with rice and fries. Pizzas are also popular here, as is the ice-cold draft beer. Given the prime location, prices are surprisingly reasonable. Don't confuse Amerelinho with the adjoining bar, Vermelhino. Both have yellow roof canopies and yellow plastic chairs, but Amerelinho serves superior food. ⊠*Praça Floriano 55 B, Cinelândia, Centro, 20031-050* ☎*2122408434* ⊕*www.amarelinhodacinelandia.com.br* ☐*AE, DC, MC, V* ☉*Closed Sun.* Ⓜ*Cinelândia.*

CAFÉS

¢

Fodor'sChoice

★

✗**Confeitaria Colombo.** At the turn of the 20th century this belle epoque structure was Rio's preeminent café, the site of elaborate balls, afternoon teas for upper-class *senhoras,* and a center of political intrigue and gossip. Enormous jacaranda-framed mirrors from Belgium, stained glass from France, and tiles from Portugal add to the art nouveau decor. Today locals come here to nibble on above-average *salgados* (savory snacks) and melt-in-the-mouth sweet treats. The waffles here are a local legend. Savory pastries are stuffed with shrimp and chicken, and vegetarian nosh includes spinach and ricotta quiche and heart-of-palm pie. You can wash it all down with a creamy coffee, a European lager or, on a hot day, a fruity cocktail (served virgin or laced with alcohol). Perhaps the best way to absorb the opulence is to do as Rio's high society did a century ago: with *chá da tarde*, or afternoon tea (R$50 buys a lavish spread for two). ⊠ *Rua Gonçalves Dias 32, Centro, 20050-030* ☎ *021/2232-2300* ⊕ *www.confeitariacolombo.com. br* ▤ *AE, DC, MC, V* ⊗ *Closed Sun. No dinner* Ⓜ *Carioca.*

ECLECTIC

¢–$$ ✗ **Bistrô do Paço.** Housed inside the cool, whitewashed Emporio do Paço Cultural Center, this is a good option for a light lunch. The vegetarian-friendly menu includes a lunchtime salad buffet that incorporates fresh, healthy options, such as carrot salad with oranges, potatoes, and apples. There are various quiches, good sandwiches (we recommend the Bella Italia—eggplant, sundried tomato, and buffalo mozzerella on Italian bread). Carnivores might want to try the beef carpaccio with Gruyère cheese. For sightseeing purposes, the bistro is well placed; close to the Palacio Tirandentes and inside Cultural Center itself. ⊠ *Praça Quinze 48, Centro, 20010-010* ☎ *021/2262-3613* ▤ *AE, DC, MC, V* ⊗ *Weekdays 7:30; weekends 7* Ⓜ *Uruguaiana.*

GERMAN

$ ✗ **Bar Luiz.** This informal restaurant and bar specializes in tasty German dishes. Established in 1887, it has held its current location since 1927. House specialties include white bratwurst with potato salad dressed in a delicious homemade mayonnaise (R$25). Bypass the less-than-impressive wine list in favor of the draft *chopp* (beer), which comes in light and dark varieties, both served *estupidamente gelado* (stupidly cold). The wooden tables, tiled floor, and wall-mounted photographs of old Rio combine to create a pleasingly rustic ambience. ⊠ *Rua da Carioca 39, Centro, 20050-008* ☎ *021/2262-6900* ⊕ *www.barluiz. com.br* ▤ *AE, DC, MC, V* ⊗ *Closed Sun.* Ⓜ *Carioca.*

SEAFOOD

$–$$$ ✗ **Rio Minho.** Enjoy a slice of history along with your afternoon snack. This downtown restaurant has been serving up seafood to hungry cariocas since 1884. The simple blue-and-white facade of this pretty colonial building harks back to that time, as do the costumes of the attentive waiters who show you to your seats. For a real taste of culinary history, order the Sopa Leáo Veloso—this fortifying Brazilian soup was created in honor of the Brazilian ambassador. It's an adaptation of the French seafood broth bouillabaisse marselhesa, and combines every type of seafood imaginable, along with onion, garlic, and herbs. It's

---

CHICKEN OF THE SEA

Between Rua da Acre and Rua Mayrink Veiga in Centro, you'll find a street filled with plastic tables and chairs and known locally as Beco das Sardinhas, or sardine alley. Five informal restaurants here serve up the much-loved battered and fried sardines that have been nicknamed *Frango Maritimo* (chicken of the sea). The best time to come is 5 PM on a Friday, when you can grab a good table and watch as the street begins to fill with people and, as the beer flows, slip into party mode.

Where to Eat in Rio de Janeiro

now a staple on menus across Rio de Janeiro State, but Minho still serves up the best version. ⊠*Rua do Ouvidor 10, Centro, 20010-150* ☎*21/2509–2338* ⊟*AE, DC, MC, V* ☾*No dinner* Ⓜ*Uruguaina.*

$–$$ ✕**Alba Mar.** Opened in 1933, Alba Mar is not hard to spot—it's housed in a distinctive circular green building facing Guanabara Bay. While the building's 360-degree views are a draw in themselves, the real reason people come is for the outstanding seafood. The chef works magic with the daily specials, and

> **DINING TIPS**
>
> Most restaurants serve a *couvert* (a little something to nibble), usually bread, olives, or another type of munchie. The couvert is not free. If you don't want to pay for it, just hand it to your waiter. Also, restaurants will include a 10% service charge, only half of which is distributed among the restaurant staff. Feel free to leave some bills on the table for your server.

the haddock soufflé is fluffy, creamy culinary nirvana. If you're just looking to nibble, check out the classic codfish balls, sit back, and take in the spectacular view across the bay. ⊠*Praça Marechal Âncora 186, Centro, 20021-200* ☎*021/2240–8428* ⊕*www.albamar.com.br* ⊟*AE, DC, MC, V* ☾*No Dinner* Ⓜ*Carioca.*

COPACABANA & LEME

BRAZILIAN

$$$$ ✕**Marius Carnes.** This well-regarded churrascaria overlooks Leme beach and serves more than a dozen types of sizzling meats rodízio style. The meat here is from organic farms, and there's also an extremely tempting seafood buffet and salad bar. The elaborate decor incorporates items recovered from 19th-century *fazendas* (coffee farms), but don't let that distract you from the task of eating as much as you possibly can. For those who prefer the flavors of the sea to the flavors of the farm, Marius Crustacoes sits right next door and offers the same rodizio-style service, but this time with seafood, and a slightly higher price tag (R$125). ⊠*Av. Atlântica 290A, Leme, 2010-000* ☎*021/2104–9000* ⊕*www.marius.com.br* ⊟*AE, DC, MC, V.*

$$$–$$$$ ✕**Siri Mole & Cia.** For seafood served Bahian style (from the northeast), this is the place. The restaurant takes its name from a soft-shell crab native to Brazil, and the signature dish here is the moqueca—a Bahian stew combining dendê oil and coconut milk with seafood. (Beware, this dish is delicious but very high in saturated fat. It can have disastrous effects on the digestion if you're not used to it.) You can take your pick from squid, lobster, fish, or, of course, siri mole crab. There's also a branch in Centro, or, to sample Siri Mole's northeastern cuisine in a less formal environment, you can visit the offshoot beach kiosk, right on the sands at Copacabana. ⊠*Rua Francisco Otaviano 50, Copacabana, 22080-040* ☎*021/2267–0894* ⊕*www.sirimole.com.br* Ⓜ*Siqueira Campos, then shuttle bus to Praça General Osório, get off at last stop in Copacabana* ⊟*AE, DC, MC, V.*

$–$$ ✕**Boteco Belmonte.** A block back from the beach, the Copacabana branch of this seven-strong Rio chain is a great place for a relaxed meal and a drink after a hard day's sunbathing. On the menu are good pizzas, meat and fish dishes, and an extensive line of finger foods. For a light lunch we recommend three or four empadas with different fillings—they're delicous little pies with a light, buttery pastry. Wash it all down with Chopp Escura (dark draft beer). Queues snake out into the street on weekend evenings, but you'll have plenty of elbow room on weekday afternoons. ✉ *Rua Domingos Ferreira 242, Copcabana* ⊕ *www.botecobe lmonte.com.br* ⊟ *AE, DC, MC, V* Ⓜ *Cantagalo.*

FRENCH

$$$$ ✕ **Le Pré-Catalan.** Considered the best French cuisine in Rio, this is the *carioca* version of the charming Parisian restaurant of the same name in the Bois du Boulogne. This highly reputed establishment has several prix-fixe menus, ranging in price from R$158 for three courses, to R$215 for R$10. The degustation menu is R$185. À la carte includes delicious dishes like lamb chops with fondant potato, rosemary, and ratatouille. ✉ *Sofitel Rio Palace, Av. Atlântica 4240, Level E, Copacabana, 22070-002* ☏ *021/2525–1160* ✍ *Reservations essential* ⊟ *AE, DC, MC, V* ☾ *No lunch* Ⓜ *No metro.*

ITALIAN

$$$–$$$$ ✕ **Cipriani.** This restaurant is housed in the plush environs of Copaca-
★ bana Palace and overlooking the hotel's enormous pool. Start with a Cipriani, champagne with fresh peach juice (really a Bellini), and then take your pick from an extensive North Italian menu that includes appetizers like sea-bass salad with fava beans and burrata cheese, and excellent mains such as wild-rice risotto with asparagus and squid. The freshly made pasta dishes are prepared with great care, and the meat and fish entrées are appropriate to their lavish surroundings. Service, as one would expect, is excellent. The degustation menu is R$191, or R$342 with wine. ✉ *Copacabana Palace Hotel, Av. Atlântica 1702, Copacabana, 22021-001* ☏ *021/2545–8747* ⊕ *www.copa cabanapalace.com.br* ✍ *Reservations essential* ⊟ *AE, DC, MC, V* Ⓜ *Cardeal Arcoverde.*

$$$–$$$$ ✕ **D'Amici.** The diverse menu at D'Amici offers specialties from various
★ regions of Italy. Diners can take their pick from Sicilian and Milanese pasta and fish dishes, among others. To keep hunger at bay while the main course is prepared, the mixed Italian antipasti includes Parma ham and grana padano cheese (R$34 for four). This place has the largest wine list in Rio, with 300 labels, ranging from R$26 to R$10,000—for the Romanée Conti—and also serves 30 types of wine by the glass

---

BEST OF THE BEACH

As recently as 2006, the best that hungry Copacabana beachgoers could expect to find was a plate of fish or fries from one of the many traditional beach kiosks. That's all changed now with the introduction of handsome glass booths offering sophisticated meals to be enjoyed in your bathing suit right on the beach. There's Bahian seafood at Siri Mole and Cia, Chinese at China in Copa and, at Champanheria Copacabana, you can wash a salmon dish down with a bottle of Veuve Clicquot Brut.

(R$9–R$26). The restaurant is consistently a hit in Rio for its food and atmosphere. ⊠ *Rua Antônio Vieira 18, Leme, 22010-100* ☎ *021/2541-4477* ▤ *AE, DC, MC, V* ⌖ *Reservations essential.*

SEAFOOD

$–$$$$ ✕ **Shirley.** Homemade Spanish seafood casseroles and soups are the main draw at this rustic Leme restaurant tucked onto a shady street. The restaurant is small and the decor simple, but the ambience is relaxed and the food is terrific. The waitstaff, clad in white suits, add to the old-time atmosphere. Try the *zarzuela,* a seafood soup, or *cazuela,* a fish fillet with white-wine sauce. ⊠ *Rua Gustavo Sampaio 610, loja A, Leme, 22010-010* ☎ *021/2275–1398* ⌖ *Reservations not accepted* ▤ *No credit cards.*

$–$$ ✕ **Azul Marinho.** You'll catch superb sunsets from the beachside tables at this quiet little spot in Arpoador, which serves high-quality seafood and pasta dishes. The restaurant occupies the ground floor of the Arpoador Inn hotel, and boasts a giant panoramic window looking out onto a barely trafficked street across from Arpoador beach. *Moqueca* is the specialty, made with shrimp, cod, lobster, crab, or octopus—or a mix of them all. Service is excellent and the seafood is fresh, but our favorite reason to go to Azul Marinho is to sit at its outdoor tables next to the sands, enjoying early-evening appetizers, drinks, and the sunset. ⊠ *Av. Francisco Bhering s/n, Arpoador, 22080-050* ☎ *021/3813–4228* ⊕ *www.cozinhatipica.com.br* ▤ *AE, DC, MC, V.*

> ### SAVING THE BEST FOR LAST
>
> Pacing yourself is key to making the most of a meal at one of Rio's many all-you-can-eat churrascarias. Many of the best cuts aren't brought to the table until later in the evening, so don't be tempted to fill up too early. Many places operate a card scheme with a green side for go and a red card for no. Make the most of this by flipping the card over onto red when you feel like a break. Flip it back again when your appetite has returned.

FLAMENGO & BOTAFOGO

BRAZILIAN

$$$$ ✕ **Porcão Rio's.** The ultimate in Brazilian churrascaria experiences, Por-
Fodor's Choice   cão has bow-tied waiters who flit between linen-draped tables, wield-
★   ing giant skewers, and slicing your portions of sizzling barbecued beef, pork, and chicken until you can eat no more. The buffet is huge, with salads, sushi, and, on Saturday, more than 15 types of feijoada. (Hats off if you can do churrasco *and* feijoada in one sitting!) Porcão is a chain, with four restaurants in Rio—including the one in Ipanema *(*⇨*below)*—and another in the suburb of Niterói, but the nearly floor-to-ceiling windows with a view over Guanabara Bay to the Sugar Loaf make the Flamengo branch our top choice. ⊠ *Av. Infante Dom Henrique, Parque do Flamengo, 20021-140* ☎ *021/2554–8535* ▤ *AE, DC, MC, V.*

$$–$$$$ ✕ **Yorubá.** Exotic and delicious dishes are served at this restaurant, one of the few places that go beyond traditional African–Brazilian cuisine.

Try the Afro menu, a selection of contemporary West African dishes. Service can be slow, but you're well rewarded for the wait. The *piripiri* (a spicy rice with ginger, coconut milk, and shrimp) is worth the price of R$80 for two. ✉*Rua Arnaldo Quintela 94, Botafogo, 22280-070* ☎*021/2541–9387* ⊟*AE, V* Ⓜ*Botafogo* ☼*Closed Mon. and Tues.*

ECLECTIC

$$–$$$$ ✗**Alho & Óleo.** Homemade pasta is the hallmark of this fashionable restaurant and bar. There are many meat and fish options, including salmon with honey and mustard, and the sage-and-ricotta tortellini is always mouth watering. Finish with a pear dessert cooked in white wine with vanilla ice cream and chocolate or guava topping. The restaurant also serves a good set lunch on weekdays (R$21–R$26). ✉*Rua Buarque de Macedo 13, Flamengo, 22220-060* ☎*021/2225–3418* ⊕*www.alhoeoleo.com.br* ⊟*AE, DC, MC, V* Ⓜ*Catete.*

$$–$$$ ✗**Miam Miam** Don't expect to get anywhere near this hip Botafogo eatery without reservations. The restaurant is in a tiny white colonial building, and furnished entirely with pieces from the 1950s, '60s and '70s. The French–Brazilian owners have created a relaxed, casual dining space delivering hearty portions of tasty comfort food—the wild-mushroom risotto is a treat for vegetarians, and the fish and meat dishes are good. Leave room for dessert; the shared platter of miniature puddings is a specialty of the house and creamily delicious. The relaxed vibe and kitsch decor ensures Miam Miam's popularity with Rio's bohemian crowd. Even the waitstaff is casually dressed. ✉*Rua General Góes Monteiro 34, Botafogo, 22290-080* ☎*021/2244–0125* ⊕*www.miammiam.com.br* ⌂*Reservations essential* ⊟*AE, DC, MC, V* ☼*Closed Mon. and Tues. No lunch.*

FRENCH

$$$$ ✗**Carême.** This acclaimed bistro offers inventive and high-quality French cuisine that makes good use of fresh, largely organic, ingredients. The à la carte menu offers something different each day, or you can opt for the *menu decouverté*—a selection of entrées, main courses, and desserts served in miniature portions. The head chef, Flávia Quaresma, has become something of a televison celebrity in Brazil. ✉*Rua Visconde de Caravelas 113, Botafogo, 22271-030* ☎*021/2537–2274* ⌂*Reservations essential* ☼*Closed Sun. and Mon. No lunch* ⊟*AE, DC, MC, V* Ⓜ*Botafogo.*

A NEW KIND OF DOGGY BAG

If you like the look of the furniture and artwork at Miam Miam, you can actually buy it. All the furnishings here are for sale—they're sourced by local antiques and artisan products store Holly Gully, and the restaurant's owners like to keep things fresh by continually changing and replacing the kitsch fixtures and fittings. There's even a cut-price sale every couple of months—check with staff for dates.

ITALIAN

$-$$ ✕**Pizza Park.** This enormous pizzeria is part of the hip Cobal Humaitá complex, which houses about a dozen bars and restaurants, whose mostly outdoor tables and chairs abut one another to create a lively scene that extends late into the night. There's a smaller branch in Leblon, but we prefer this spot—it's a great place to hang out with friends, and the waitstaff will let you linger over your pizza and beer for as long as you like. More than 30 varieties of pizza are on the menu. ⊠ *Rua Voluntários da Pátria 446, Botafogo* ☎ *021/2537–5383 or 021/2537–2602* ⊕ *www.pizza-park.com.br* ▭ *AE, DC, MC, V.*

> ### PIZZA RIO STYLE
>
> Cariocas love pizza, and they've certainly added some touches of their own to the established formula. As well as sharing the pan-Brazilian penchant for pizza bases covered in chocolate, Rio residents are also known to indulge in unusual topping combinations such as cheese with pepperoni, banana, and cinnamon. In one last break with tradition, many cariocas eschew the idea of tomato sauce *beneath* the cheese, in favor of squirting ketchup on the surface.

IPANEMA & LEBLON

BRAZILIAN

$$$$ ✕**Porcão.** A convenient location makes this branch of Rio's famous
★ churrascaria the most popular one with travelers, but we prefer the Flamengo branch (⇨*above*) for its fabulous view. You'll get the same excellent service and quality of food here, but in a smaller space with no view. ⊠ *Rua Barão da Torre 218, Ipanema, 22411000* ☎ *021/2522–0999* ⊕ *www.porcao.com.br* ▭ *AE, DC, MC, V* Ⓜ *Sigueiro Campos, then shuttle bus to Praça General Osório.*

$$$–$$$$ ✕**Esplanada Grill.** This churrascaria serves high-quality meat like T-bone steak or *picanha*, a tasty Brazilian cut of beef marbled with some fat. All the grilled dishes come with fried palm hearts, seasoned rice, and a choice of fried, baked, or sauteed potatoes. An average meal is R$90. ⊠ *Rua Barão da Torre 600, Ipanema, 22411-002* ☎ *021/2512–2970* ▭ *AE, DC, MC, V* Ⓜ *Sigueira Campos, then shuttle bus to Praça General Osório.*

$-$$$ ✕**Barril 1800** The perfect place for a relaxed bite while admiring the view over Ipanema beach, Barril 1800 attracts hordes of swimwear-clad locals and travelers. Although service is formal, the atmosphere is anything but. The seafood dishes are good choices during the week, and on Saturday you can sample the rodizio de feijoada (R$28 for one person, R$47 for two). Also, the draft beer here is very well kept. ⊠ *Av V Souto 104, Ipanema, 22420-000* ☎ *21/ 2523–0085* ▭ *AE, DC, MC, V.*

$$ ✕**Casa da Feijoada.** Many restaurants serve Brazil's savory national dish
★ on Saturday, but here the huge pots of the stew simmer every day. You can choose which of the nine types of meat you want in your stew, but if it's your first time, waiters will bring you a "safe" version with sausage, beef, and pork—sans feet and ears. The feijoada comes with the

traditional side dishes of rice, collard greens, *farofa* (toasted and seasoned manioc flour), *aipim* (fried yuca), *torresminho* (pork rinds), and orange slices (to lower your cholesterol!). The set meal price includes an appetizer portion of black-bean soup and sausage, a choice of dessert, and a lime or passion-fruit *batida* (creamy cachaça cocktail). Not feeling like the feijoada? The menu also features options such as baked chicken, shrimp in coconut milk, grilled trout, and filet mignon. Desserts include *quindim* (a yolk-and-sugar pudding with coconut crust) and Romeo and Juliet (guava compote with fresh cheese). The caipirinhas are made not only with lime but also with tangerine, passion fruit, pineapple, strawberry, or kiwi. Be careful—they're strong. ⊠*Rua Prudente de Morais 10, Ipanema, 22420-040* ☎*021/2247–2776* ⊕*www.cozinhatipica.com.br* ⊟*AE, DC, MC, V* Ⓜ*Sigueira Campos, then shuttle bus to Praça General Osório.*

¢–$$ ✕**Jobi.** Not to be missed, Jobi is a Leblon institution—and since it's open daily from 9 AM to 4 AM, you should be able to squeeze it in. It's the sort of place you can go to in your bikini straight from the beach. Basic sandwiches and salads are on the menu, but the reason to go is the fabulous seafood. Order a full meal or just try various appetizers. The *bolinho de bacalhau* (mini cod cakes) may be the best in town. ⊠*Rua Ataulfo de Paiva 1166, Leblon, 22440-035* ☎*021/2274–0547* ⊟*AE.*

¢–$ ✕**Colher de Pau.** The name means wooden spoon, and there are plenty of them mounted on the walls of this simple eatery two blocks from Ipanema Beach. This chilled-out place is a great place for a bite during or after a day in the sun. It's open from breakfast through dinner, and serves good sandwiches and salads plus healthy grilled fish or steak, and great desserts. ⊠*Rua Farme de Amoedo 39, Ipanema, 22420-020* ☎*021/2523–3018* ⊟*AE, DC, MC, V.*

¢–$ ✕**New Natural.** One of many restaurants in Rio where you pay per kilo, this one stands out for its use of natural and organic products. The food is mainly vegetarian, with lots of soy-based dishes, but there are a couple of fish and chicken options. They also serve delicious fruit juices. On hot days seek out the somewhat hidden upstairs dining room, which is air-conditioned. Attached to the restaurant is Emporia Natural—a health-food shop offering delicious oven-baked pastries to take-out. The palmito with catupiry cheese option comes recommended. ⊠*Rua Barão da Torre, Ipanema* ☎*021/2247–1335* ⊟*AE, DC, MC, V.*

CAFÉS

¢–$$ ✕**Garcia & Rodrigues.** Cariocas breakfast at this cozy combination café, ★ delicatessen, liquor shop, and trendy restaurant. At lunchtime choose from a selection of sandwiches, such as marinated salmon, pastrami, or buffalo-milk cheese. Dinner, based on French cuisine, is served until 12:30 AM Monday–Thursday and until 1 AM Friday and Saturday. Menu choices are broad and it's updated regularly to make the most of seasonal ingredients. On Sunday nights the café is open until midnight, but à la carte meals are not served. ⊠*Av. Ataulfo de Paiva 1251, Leblon, 22440-034* ☎*021/2512–8188* ⊕*www.garciaerodrigues.com. br* ⊟*AE, DC, MC, V.*

¢–$$ ✕**Gula Gula.** Salads at upscale café chain Gula Gula are anything but boring. Beyond classics like Caesar and chicken pesto, fresh local fruits and veggies are mixed into salads like smoked salmon with cream cheese and herb sauce, or organic palm-heart salad with tomatoes, watercress, and raisins. Grilled fish or steak, baked potatoes, and soups are good nonsalad options. There are 11 Gula Gula restaurants across the city, and another across the bay in Niterói, but the Ipanema branch is the best because of its excellent location a couple of blocks back from the beach. ⊠*Rua Henrique Dumont 57, Ipanema, 22410-050* ☏*021/2259–3084* ⊕*www.gulagula.com.br* ⊟*AE, DC, MC, V.*

ECLECTIC

¢–$ ✕**Doce Delícia.** Make your own dish by choosing from 5 to 15 of the 42 combinations of vegetables, side dishes, hot dishes, and fruit. Quiche, salmon, grilled tenderloin, chicken, and cold pasta are some of the choices. Dressings range from the light and yogurt-based to innovative creations combining mustard and lemon. There are plenty of vegetarian options. The slick decor and fresh ingredients make this a popular post-beach choice for fashionable cariocas. Annexed to the restaurant is Doce Deli—a delicatessan-bakery where you can pick up sweet and savory tarts and pies to enjoy at home. ⊠*Rua Aníbal de Mendonça 55, Ipanema, 22410-050* ☏*021/2259–0239* ⊕*www.docedelicia.com. br* ⊟*AE, MC, V.*

¢–$ ✕**Fazendola.** The name means "small farm," and this restaurant is reminiscent of a Brazilian farm with its wooden furniture and dim lighting. Homemade dishes prepared with fresh ingredients are sold by the kilo. The other option is to try their delicious pizza, which you can order either à la carte or rodizio-style (all you can eat). ⊠*Rua Jangadeiros 14B, Ipanema, 22420-010* ☏*021/2247–9600* ⊟*AE, DC, MC, V* Ⓜ*Siqueira Campos, then shuttle bus to Praça General Osório.*

INDIAN

$–$$ ✕**Natraj.** One block from Leblon's beachfront, this traditional Indian restaurant has a tasting menu for two, with eight portions of different dishes, a good option for a reasonable price. It can be ordered in vegetarian or nonvegetarian versions. Other suggestions are the many *pulau* (rice) and *dhal* (lentil, or pea) dishes, which may come with vegetables, coconut, fresh white cheese, or *panir,* and spices, or masala. You can also order à la carte. Good options for starters, the *samosas* are fine pastries with chicken, beef, mixed-vegetable, or potato-and-pea fillings. ⊠*Av. General San Martin 1219, Leblon, 22441-015* ☏*021/2239–4745* ⊟*DC, MC, V.*

ITALIAN

$$–$$$$ ✕**Gero.** This chic, beautifully appointed restaurant serves wonderful pastas and risottos along with excellent fish and meat dishes. Vegetarian options are plentiful, and the tiramisu is the perfect blend of creamy, espresso-laced mascarpone. The restaurant is owned by the Fasano chain, and the high-ceiling, wooden-floor building exhibits the clean, contemporary design that is the hallmark of the Italian chain. ⊠*Rua Anibal de Mendonca 157, Ipanema, 22410-050* ☏*21/2239–8158* ⌕*Reservations essential* ⊟*AE, DC, MC, V.*

1

$–$$$$ ✗**Margutta.** A block from Ipanema Beach, Margutta has a reputation for outstanding Mediterranean-style seafood, such as broiled fish in tomato sauce and fresh herbs or lobster cooked in aluminum foil with butter and saffron rice. Veggie options include homemade rigatoni with dried wild mushrooms and olive oil flavored with white truffles. ⊠*Av. Henrique Dumont 62, Ipanema, 22410-060* ☎*021/2511–0878* ☰*AE, DC, MC, V* ⊘*No lunch weekdays.*

$–$$ ✗**Capricciosa.** There are lots of pizza places in Rio, but the Ipanema branch of this upmarket chain emerges at the top of the list. Delicious thin-crust pizzas are served with every topping imaginable, from the standard margheritta to fancy prosciuttos and interesting spices. Capricciosa has recently opened branches in Jardim Botanico, Barra da Tijuca, and Copacabana, but the original venue stands out for its perfect location and tall glass windows that are perfect for people-watching. ⊠*Rua Vinicius de Moraes 134, Ipanema, 22420-021* ☎*021/2523–3394* ⊕*www.capricciosa.com.br* ☰*AE, DC, MC* ⊘*No lunch.*

JAPANESE

$$–$$$$ ✗**Madame Butterfly.** At this sophisticated Japanese restaurant, start with crisp pancakes filled with duck and shiitake mushrooms and served with a cream sauce, or the tataki mix with tuna and salmon, covered with seaweed strips. Main dishes include grilled salmon with honey and miso, and the best sukiyaki in Rio. If you simply can't choose, opt for the all-you-can eat rodizio (R$34 until 5 PM on weekdays, R$44 at other times). ⊠*Rua Barão da Torre 472, Ipanema, 22411-002* ☎*021/2267–4347* ⊕*www.madamebutterfly.com.br* ☰*AE, V.*

MEXICAN

$–$$ ✗**Guapo Loco.** Bustling crowds feast on tamales, enchiladas, and other Mexican delicacies until the last customer leaves. Tequila has garnered quite a following in Rio, making Guapo Loco one of the most well-liked Mexican places thanks to its good margaritas. ⊠*Rua Rainha Guilhermina 48, Leblon, 22441-014* ☎*021/2294–2915* ☰*MC, V* ⊘*No lunch weekdays.*

PORTUGUESE

$$$–$$$$ ✗**Antiquarius.** This much-loved establishment is famous for its flawless rendering of Portuguese classics. A recommended dish is the lobster with rice, lime, and fried greens. The *cataplana*, a seafood stew with rice, is also marvelous, and the *perna de cordeiro* (leg of lamb) is the most-requested dish on the menu. The wine list impresses even Portuguese gourmands. ⊠*Rua Aristides Espínola 19, Leblon, 22440-050* ☎*021/2294–1049* ⊕*www.antiquarius.com.br* ⊛*Reservations essential* ☰*DC, MC.*

FodorsChoice
★

SEAFOOD

$$$–$$$$ ✗**Satyricon.** Some of the best seafood in town is served at this eclectic Italian seafood restaurant, which has impressed the likes of Madonna and Sting. The fish baked in a thick layer of rock salt is a specialty, and the sushi and sashimi are well loved. ⊠*Rua Barão da Torre 192, Ipanema, 22411-000,* ☎*021/2521–0627* ⊕*www.satyricon.com.br* ☰*DC, MC,*

FodorsChoice
★

V Ⓜ*Siqueira Campos, then shuttle bus to Praça General Osório.*

VEGETARIAN

$-$$ ✗ **Vegetariano Social Clube.** Vegan restaurants are rare in Rio, and this is by far the most sophisticated. The small, friendly eatery has carefully prepared dishes free of any animal products that go much beyond brown rice or burdock. The Saturday feijoada, prepared with smoked tofu, tempeh, kale, and farofa, is a real treat. ✉*Rua Conde de Bernadotte 26, Loja L, Leblon, 22430-200* ☎*021/2294–5200* ⊕*www. vegetarianosocialclube.com.br* ▭*DC, MC, V.*

¢–$$ ✗ **Celeiro.** One of Rio's few organic eateries, Celeiro is a combination restaurant, café, and health-food store, and is popular with models (and their admirers). There's a staggering 50 types of salad on the menu, as well as oven-baked pies and pasties, hot dishes, and even low-cal desserts. ✉*Rua Dias Ferreira 199, Leblon, 22431-050* ☎*021/2274–7843* ▭*DC, MC, V* ⊗*Closed Sun. No dinner.*

FOOD ON THE GO

There's a street snack for every taste in Rio—from low-cal treats such as corn on the cob and chilled pineapple slices to less virtuous, but absolutely delicious, barbecued sticks of grilled cheese served with or without herbs. Tasty bags of roasted and salted peanuts and cashews are found everywhere, as are giant hotdogs, served on a stick and covered in manioc flour. Barbecued chicken heart (*coraçao*) is not for the fainthearted, and the grilled shrimp at the beach is best avoided unless you want a side order of food poisoning.

JARDIM BOTÂNICO

FRENCH

$$$$ ✗ **Olympe.** This top-notch venue is run by Claude Troisgros, of the celebrated Michelin-starred Troisgros family of France. The menu's all-Brazilian ingredients are a unique trait of this innovative restaurant that blends native flavors with nouvelle techniques. Every dish—from the crab or lobster flan to chicken, fish, and duck prepared with exotic herbs and sauces—is exceptionally light. The passion-fruit crepe soufflé is highly recommended. ✉*Rua Custódio Serrão 62, Jardim Botânico, 22470-230* ☎*021/2537–8582* ⌕*Reservations essential* ▭*AE, MC, V.*

Fodor's Choice
★

ITALIAN

$$–$$$$ ✗ **Quadrifoglio.** Considered by most locals to be the best Italian restaurant in the city, cozy Quadrifoglio is tucked away on a quiet street. The food and the service are impeccable; the restaurant has been around since 1991 and much of the original waitstaff still works there. Some favorite entrée choices are spinach ravioli and the fabulous salads. Leave room for one of the deservedly famous desserts, such as ice cream with baked figs. ✉*Rua J.J. Seabra 19, Jardim Botânico, 22470-130* ☎*021/2294–1433* ▭*AE, DC, MC, V* ⊗*No dinner Sun., no lunch Sat.*

Fodor's Choice
★

LAGOA

CHINESE

$$$ ✕**Mr Lam.** Mr Lam, head chef of
★ Mr Chow in New York, leads the
kitchen at this glamorous 2006
addition to the Rio dining scene. In
a city where Chinese food has long
been associated with low-budget
dining, this restaurant has burned
the rule book, serving top-qual-
ity Peking cuisine to a discerning
clientele. The downstairs dining
room is spacious and well illuminated by enormous windows, but for
the ultimate experience book a table on the top floor—at night the
roof comes right off to allow dining beneath the stars, and you can
request a spot directly beneath the gaze of the Christo Redentor. À la
carte is an option, but most diners choose from one of the set menus
(R$75–R$125 per person). ✉ *Av. Maria Angélica 21, Lagoa, 22470-
201* ☎*21/2286–6661* ⊕*www.mrlam.com.br* ⚑*Reservations essential*
▤*AE, DC, MC, V* ⊗*No lunch weekdays.*

> ### HOT STUFF
>
> You might think you can handle
> your chilies, but exercise caution
> before piling on the sauce at Bar
> do Arnaudo. It's a fiery north-
> eastern combination of dende
> (palm oil) and super-hot red
> peppers that can take the roof
> off your mouth.

SANTA TERESA

BRAZILIAN

$$–$$$ ✕**Aprazível.** A tropical garden filled with exotic plants, monkeys, and
★ birds is the spectacular setting for this family restaurant serving pan-
Brazilian dishes. The owner and chef, Ana Castilha, hails from Minas
Gerais but was formally trained at the French Culinary Institute in New
York, and there's a distinctly French twist to the traditional Brazilian
dishes on offer. There are some unusual salads, including one featuring
mixed lettuce with mango, whole green peppercorns, Minas cheese,
and sundried tomatoes (R$24). The all-Brazilian wine list is chosen
with great care, and may surprise those who have previously dismissed
national wines. The outdoor tables enjoy excellent views of downtown
and Guanabara Bay during the day, and at night the garden is illumi-
nated by numerous hanging lanterns. If you're lucky you might spot the
pair of toucans that regularly visit the garden. Grass and bamboo roofs
keep diners dry if the weather takes a turn for the worse, and there
are several indoor tables, too, for those who don't fancy alfresco din-
ing. ✉*Rua Aprazível 62, Santa Teresa, 20241-270* ☎*21/2508–9174*
⊕*www.aprazivel.com.br* ▤*AE, DC, MC, V* ⊗*Closed Mon.*

¢–$$ ✕**Bar do Arnaudo.** A neighborhood favorite for 30-plus years, this infor-
★ mal tavern serves excellent Bahian cuisine in more than ample portions.
Sun-dried beef is a popular choice, and vegetarians will love the set
meal of *queijo coalho* (grilled cheese) with brown beans, rice, assorted
vegetables, and seasoned farofa. Reservations are not necessary, but
the restaurant is always packed on weekend evenings. Lunchtimes are
much quieter, and you may be able to bag one of the two tables that
offer views down to Guanabara Bay. Portions are large enough to serve

two or even three. ⊠*Rua Almirante Alexandrino 316-B, Santa Teresa, 20241-260* ☎*021/2252–7246* ▤*MC, V.*

SÃO CONRADO, BARRA DA TIJUCA & BEYOND

BRAZILIAN

$$–$$$ ✕**Barra Grill.** A nice place to stop after a long day at Praia Barra, this informal and popular steak house serves some of the best meat in town. Prices for the rodízio-style meals are slightly higher on weekends than during the week. Reservations are essential on weekends. ⊠*Av. Ministro Ivan Lins 314, Barra da Tijuca, 22620-110* ☎*021/2493–6060* ▤*AE, DC, MC, V.*

ITALIAN

$$–$$$$ ✕**Alfredo.** The pasta here is excellent, especially the fettuccine Alfredo and the spaghetti carbonara. They also serve a delicious lamb dish. The degustation menu (R$89) changes each month to make the most of fresh seasonal ingredients. The restaurant has a view of the hotel pool. ⊠*InterContinental Rio hotel, Av. Prefeito Mendes de Morais 222, São Conrado, 22610-095* ☎*021/3323–2200* ▤*AE, DC, MC, V* ⊗*No lunch.*

SEAFOOD

$$–$$$ ✕**Restaurante Point de Grumari.** From Grumari Beach, Estrada de Guaratiba climbs up through dense forest, emerging atop a hill above the vast Guaratiba flatlands. Here you find this eatery famed for grilling fish to perfection. With its shady setting, glorious vistas, and live music performances (samba, bossa nova, jazz), it's the perfect spot for lunch (it's open daily 11:30–6:30) after a morning on the beach and before an afternoon at the Sítio Roberto Burle Marx or the Museu Casa do Pontal. Alternatively, come here in the early evening to catch the spectacular sunset. ⊠*Estrada do Grumari 710, Grumari, 23020-340* ☎*021/2410–1434* ⊕*www.pointdegrumari.com.br* ▤*AE, DC, MC, V* ⊗*No dinner.*

$–$$$ ✕**476.** At the end of a road with stunning coastal views, 476 is all **Fodor'sChoice** about simplicity, with seven delicious entrées that include *moquecas* ★ (seafood stews), grilled seafood, and curries. It has only 20 tables, some in a lovely garden at the water's edge. The quiet fishing village 13 km (8 mi) west of Barra da Tijuca is a nice respite from the bustling Zona Sul. Tell the taxi driver to take you to "Quatro Sete Meia." ⊠*Rua Barros de Alarcão 476, Pedra da Guaratiba, 23027-010* ☎*021/2417–1716* ⚑*Reservations essential* ▤*AE, MC, V.*

URCA

BRAZILIAN

$ ✕**Bar e Restaurante Urca** This relaxed little spot close to Sugar Loaf mountain has wonderful sea views and is a good place to relax and take in the ambience of this gentile neighborhood. Enjoy a cold *chopp* (beer) and finger food while you contemplate the menu—cold dishes, such as the tomato and palm-heart salad, are good, as are the Portuguese-influenced hot dishes such as fried fish fillet with rice and creamed spinach. The very good Saturday feijoada is R$55 for two, and there's a daily children's set meal at R$17.50. ⊠*Rua Cândido Gaffrée 205, Urca* ☎*21/2295–8744.*

WHERE TO STAY

CENTRO & GLÓRIA

$$$$ 🏨 **Glória.** The grande dame of Rio's hotels, this is the oldest in the city and retains plenty of historic charm. The hotel is in wonderful tropical gardens, and front-facing rooms have a great view over Guanabara Bay and Sugar Loaf. Glória is stuffed full of antique French furniture, and a major renovation in 2005 means that rooms are now crisp and clean. There are three restaurants and two pools—one of which is absolutely enormous. The fitness center is very well equipped and has good views of the bay. Make sure you request a room in the original building as opposed to the new annex, where rooms are pokey and uninspired. The hotel's good convention center and location close to Centro makes it popular among business travelers (and a helicopter landing pad on the roof means Lula is a regular guest), but it's a bit of a trek to Zona Sul beaches. **Pros:** Main building is attractive and has plenty of atmosphere. Great gardens and pools. Good restaurant. **Cons:** Annex rooms not good value, bus or cab ride to Zona Sul, Glória not very safe at night. ⊠*Rua do Russel 632, Glória, 22210-010* ☎*021/2205–7272 or 0800/21–3077* 🖷*021/2555–7282* ⊕*www.hotelgloriario.com.br* ⇌*579 rooms, 21 suites* ♿*In-room: safe, refrigerator, Ethernet (some), Wi-Fi (some). In-hotel: 3 restaurants, room service, bars, pools, gym, spa, concierge, laundry service, parking (fee), no-smoking rooms* ▭*AE, DC, MC, V* ⦿⦚*BP* Ⓜ*Glória.*

Updated by
Lucy Bryson

$$ 🏨 **Guanabara Palace Hotel.** A member of the Windsor chain that was remodeled in 2001, the Guanabara is one of the few solid hotel choices right in Centro. Rooms are reasonably sized and tastefully done in brown and beige. The restaurant serves elaborate buffet meals. The contemporary rooftop pool area, with its stunning views of Guanabara Bay, absolutely gleams thanks to its pristine white tiles, white trellises, and white patio furnishings. **Pros:** Great views from pool, close to downtown attractions and nightlife, good value. **Cons:** Far from beaches, Centro is dangerously deserted on Sunday. ⊠*Av. Presidente Vargas 392, Centro, 20071-000* ☎*021/2195–5000* ⊕*www.windsorhoteis.com/en-us/gu_loca.asp* ⇌*510 rooms, 3 suites* ♿*In-room: safe, refrigerator, Ethernet, Wi-Fi (some). In-hotel: restaurant, room service, bar, pool, gym, laundry service, parking (fee), no-smoking rooms* ▭*AE, DC, MC, V* ⦿⦚*BP* Ⓜ*Uruguaiana.*

COPACABANA & LEME

These neighborhoods can be dangerous at night, so it's wise to get around by taxi after dark.

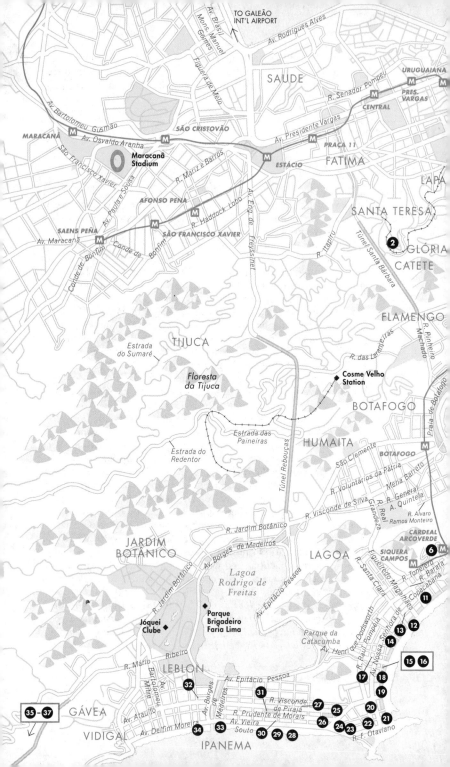

Where to Stay in Rio de Janeiro

$$$$ **Copacabana Palace.** The addition
Fodor'sChoice of a seven-room luxury spa in 2007
★ has brought this iconic hotel up to
date. Built in 1923 for the visiting
king of Belgium and inspired by
Nice's Negresco and Cannes's Carl-
ton, the Copacabana was the first
luxury hotel in South America, and
it's still one of the top hotels on the
continent. Marlene Dietrich, Rob-
ert De Niro, and Princess Di are
among the many famous faces to
have stayed here. The hotel's neo-

> **FLYING DOWN TO RIO**
>
> Copacabana Palace was the set-
> ting for Fred Astaire and Ginger
> Rogers' first on-screen dance,
> in the 1933 film *Flying Down to
> Rio.* However, although the film
> cemented the hotel's glamorous
> repution, the actual scene was
> filmed thousands of miles away, in
> a studio replica.

classical facade is beautifully maintained and remains a glimmering
white. Inside you can find one of the city's largest and most attractive swimming pools. One of Copacabana Palace's two restaurants, the
Cipriani, is rated among the city's best for its northern Italian cuisine,
while the Saturday feijoada, served in the less formal Pergula restaurant by the pool, is legendary. The interior of the hotel is as glittering
white as its facade, and the look is cool, elegant, and luxurious—from
the marble reception desk to the immaculately attired bellboys. Ocean-
view rooms are more expensive than those at the back, whose view
of the Copacabana streets somewhat detracts from the glamorous
atmosphere. A genuine Rio landmark, Copacabana Palace remains the
stomping ground of the rich and fabulous despite a growing preference for Ipanema and Leblon over Copacabana. However, the nightlife here is less sophisticated, and you're likely to find yourself making
nightly cab journeys to Ipanema and Leblon. **Pros:** A historic landmark, front-facing rooms have spectacular views, great on-site restaurant. **Cons:** Dearth of nightlife, dangerous neighborhood at night, "city
view" rooms have poor view of backstreets, dated in-room facilities.
⊠*Av. Atlântica 1702, Copacabana, 22021-001* ☎*021/2548–7070,
0800/21–1533, 800/237–1236 in U.S.* ⊕*www.copacabanapalace.
com.br* ⌨*122 rooms, 111 suites* &*In-room: safe, DVD (some), VCR
(some), Ethernet, Wi-Fi (some). In-hotel: 2 restaurants, room service,
pools, spa, beachfront, public Internet, public Wi-Fi, bars, tennis
court, pool, gym, spa, concierge, laundry service, no-smoking rooms,
some pets allowed* ⊟*AE, DC, MC, V* Ⓜ*Cardeal Arcoverde.*

$$$$ **Marriott Rio de Janeiro.** You could be walking into a Marriott in any
part of the world, which is a comfort for some and a curse for others. Expect spotlessly clean rooms and public areas, an efficient English-speaking staff, and the most modern (and expensive) services and
facilities available. Despite the enormous lobby, rooms here are smaller
than at most Marriott hotels. Some have views of Avenida Atlântica
and Copacabana, others look onto the interior atrium. Business travelers are the Marriott's bread and butter, but thanks to its location—the
front door spits you out onto Copacabana Beach—it attracts quite
a few tourists as well. The sushi bar ($$$) gets rave reviews. **Pros:**
Close to beach, efficient service, modern hotel. **Cons:** Lacks character,
dangerous area at night. ⊠*Av. Atlántica 2600, Copacabana, 22041-*

001 ☎*021/2545–6500* ⊕*hoteis.marriott.com.br* 🛏*229 rooms, 16 suites* ♿*In-room: safe, Ethernet (some), Wi-Fi (some). In-hotel: restaurant, room service, pool, gym, concierge, laundry service, no-smoking rooms, executive floor, public Wi-Fi, laundry service, parking (fee)* ▱*AE, DC, MC, V.*

$$$$ ▦ **Sofitel Rio Palace.** Anchoring one end of Copacabana Beach, this huge hotel was given a top-to-bottom face-lift in 2007 and is once again one of the best on the strip. The building's H shape gives breathtaking views of the sea, the mountains, or both from the balconies of all rooms. The hotel has two pools—one catches the morning sun; the other, afternoon rays. All beds are brand new, and wonderfully comfortable. The look is understated yet luxurious, with decor dominated by neutral creams, whites, and light browns. The wooden paneled elevators and corridors have a classic sophistication, and the executive floors combine modern facilities with antique mirrors, clocks, and chests of drawers. Holiday makers enjoy the beachfront location and the picture-perfect views that take in the entire length of Copacabana beach, while business executives appreciate the top-notch business facilities. The restaurant Le Pré-Catalan is as good as its Parisian original. **Pros:** Handy for Ipanema and Arpoador beaches and nightlife, fantastic views. **Cons:** Very large, could feel impersonal, bar and restaurant expensive. ✉*Av. Atlântica 4240, Copacabana, 22070-002* ☎*021/2525–1232 or 0800/703–7003, 800/7763–4835 in U.S.* ⊕*www.accorhotels.com.br* 🛏*388 rooms, 53 suites* ♿*In-room: safe, Ethernet, Wi-Fi. In-hotel: 2 restaurants, bar, pools, gym, laundry service, concierge, executive floor, parking (fee), no-smoking rooms, some pets allowed, public Internet, public Wi-Fi* ▱*AE, DC, MC, V.*

$$$–$$$$ ▦ **Excelsior.** This hotel, part of the Windsor chain, may have been built in the 1950s, but its look is sleek and contemporary—from the sparkling marble lobby to the guest-room closets paneled in gleaming jacaranda (Brazilian redwood). Service is top-rate. The expansive breakfast buffet is served in the hotel's window-banked restaurant facing the avenue and beach. The equally elaborate lunch and dinner buffets cost roughly R$35. The rooftop bar–pool area offers an escape from the hustle and bustle. Ask for a room with a view over Copacabana Beach. **Pros:** Top-notch service, rooftop pool. **Cons:** Chain hotel so slightly impersonal, busy street that can be dangerous at night. ✉*Av. Atlântica 1800, Copacabana, 22021-001* ☎*021/21955800 or 0800/704–2827, 800/444–885 in U.S.* ⊕*www.windsorhoteis.com.br* 🛏*233 rooms, 12 suites* ♿*In-room: safe, refrigerator, Ethernet (some), Wi-Fi (some). In-hotel: restaurant, room service, bars, pool, gym, concierge, laundry service, public Internet, public Wi-Fi, no-smoking rooms* ▱*AE, DC, MC, V* ⏀*BP* Ⓜ*Cardeal Arcoverde.*

$$$–$$$$ ▦ **Rio Atlântica.** Guests at the Rio Atlântica can enjoy rooftop sunbathing and swimming, or a drink at the bar, which has a great view of Copacabana Beach. Service is good, but many of the cheaper rooms are small and in need of a facelift. Some fixtures, such as carpets, could be cleaner. Excellent restaurants, shopping, and nightlife in Copacabana are all within walking distance. Bathrooms are large and very clean. Standard rooms do not have a view, but oceanfront suites have oversize balconies and guests in these suites are served breakfast at the rooftop bar. **Pros:** Suites are good value, rooftop pool and bar, good beachfront location. **Cons:** Some rooms need revamping, some carpets not particularly clean. Can feel a little crowded. ☒*Av. Atlântica 2964, Copacabana, 22070-000* ☎*021/2548–6332 or 0800/26–6332* ⊕*www.pestana.com* ➪*109 rooms, 105 suites* ⚃*In-room: safe, refrigerator, kitchen (some), Ethernet, Wi-Fi (some). In-hotel: 2 restaurants, room service, bar, pool, gym, spa, concierge, laundry service, public Wi-Fi, parking (no fee), no-smoking rooms* ▭*AE, DC, MC, V* Ⓜ*Cantagalo.*

$$–$$$$ 🖾**Rio Othon Palace.** The flagship of the Brazilian Othon chain, this 30-story hotel is not new, and the ambience is functional rather than luxurious, but it does have a prime view of Copacabana's distinctive black-and-white sidewalk mosaic from the rooftop pool, bar, and sundeck. The executive floor has secretarial support, fax machines, and computer hookups. Executive rooms are modern and smart with a gray-and-white decor, but standard rooms are dated. All suites, junior and executive, have a balcony facing Copacabana and are spacious and well appointed for the price. Although some will love the Copacabana beachfront setting, the hotel is in a spot that is known for red-light activity and can be dangerous at night. ⚠Avoid the area around Help Discoteque, and take taxis after dark. **Pros:** Good beach views from front-facing rooms and pool, handy for beach, reasonable prices. **Cons:** Seedy area, taxis necessary at night, some rooms dated. ☒*Av. Atlântica 3264, Copacabana, 22070-001* ☎*021/2522–1522* ⊕*www.hoteisothon.com.br* ➪*556 rooms, 30 suites* ⚃*In-room: Ethernet (some). In-hotel: 2 restaurants, room service, bars, pool, gym, concierge, laundry service, public Wi-Fi, airport shuttle, parking (no fee), no-smoking rooms* ▭*AE, DC, MC, V.*

$$–$$$ 🖾**Luxor Regente Hotel.** The best of the Luxor hotels in Rio, the Regente was renovated in 2004. Rooms are now spic-and-span and reasonably tasteful—some in bright blue-and-yellow hues, and other in more refined off-whites and browns. The downstairs lounge is modern and vibrant, with leather chairs, red sofas, and glass tables. The restaurant Forno e Fogão has a good Saturday feijoada, though it's not as celebrated as that of the Copacabana Palace. The suites have whirlpool baths. The gym area is small, but the hotel is committed to continually updating its equipment. If you choose a standard room, be sure that it's not one that faces south; those rooms have an unfortunate view of a trash-can-filled alley. Other rooms look out over Avenida Atlântica and Copacabana Beach. **Pros:** Good for families, modern, pool. **Cons:** Some rooms have poor views, breakfast has cold dishes only, Copacabana not the safest area. ☒*Av. Atlântica 3716, Copacabana, 22070-001* ☎*021/2525–2070 or 0800/16–5322* ⊕*www.luxor-hotels.com* ➪*228 rooms, 2 suites* ⚃*In-room: safe, Ethernet (some). In-hotel: restaurant, room service, bars, pool, gym, concierge, laundry service, parking (fee), no-smoking rooms* ▭*AE, DC, MC, V* ⎊*BP.*

$$$$ 🖾**Rio Internacional.** All rooms at this Copacabana landmark hotel have
★ balconies with sea views, a rarity on Avenida Atlântica. The distinctive black- and red-fronted hotel is Swiss-owned, and the tidy and modern

Scandinavian design is one of its best assets. Crisp white decor is a trademark of the hotel, and the rooftop pool with its wood-paneled sun deck is first rate, with excellent views across the bay, and of the Corvovado and the Christ statue. The hotel attracts a well-to-do clientele made up of business travelers and holiday-makers alike; all guests are welcomed with a glass of Champagne. **Pros:** Good design and tasteful decor, excellent service, good views, beachfront. **Cons:** Some rooms are smallish, some mattresses lack support ⊠ *Av. Atlântica 1500, Copacabana, 22021-000* ☎ *021/2543–1555 or 0800/21–1559* ⊕ *www.rio internacional.com.br* ⤶ *117 rooms, 11 suites* ⌂ *In-room: safe, Ethernet. In-hotel: restaurant, room service, bars, pool, gym, beachfront, public Internet, public Wi-Fi, concierge, laundry service, parking (fee), no-smoking rooms* ▤ *AE, DC, MC, V* Ⓜ *Cardeal Arco Verde.*

$–$$$ 🏨 **Leme Othon Palace.** Unexciting but adequate, this hotel has large rooms and a quiet beachfront location. Built in 1964, it was given a top-to-toe revamp in 2006, and now has modern, if subdued, interiors. The lobby and reception area are attractively furnished, with a huge mirror and comfy chairs. The English speaking staff are very helpful. Its location near Leme Beach and many transportation choices is the reason to stay here, and the hotel is popular with business executives. The metro station is six blocks away. **Pros:** Quiet location, safer than many parts of Copacabana, metro access. **Cons:** Far from Ipanema and Leblon nightlife, uninspired interiors ⊠ *Av. Atlântica 656, Leme, 22010-000* ☎ *021/3873–5900* ⊕ *www.hoteis-othon.com.br* ⤶ *163 rooms, 28 suites* ⌂ *In-room: safe, ethernet (some). In-hotel: restaurant, room service, bar, concierge, laundry service, public Internet* ▤ *AE, DC, MC, V* Ⓜ *Cardeal Arco Verde.*

$–$$$ 🏨 **Parthenon Arpoador.** The flexibility of an apartment is combined with the services of a hotel in this luxurious building just steps from Copacabana Beach and a few minutes' walk from Ipanema. All units are apartment-style, each with a bedroom, living room, bathroom, and small kitchen. Though a bit smaller than you might expect, apartments are modern, almost futuristic, with bright-white furniture, and everything is sparkling clean. The building is new and extremely well maintained. Each room has a balcony, but only a few have an ocean view. **Pros:** Great location, reasonably priced. **Cons:** Small rooms, some units have limited views ⊠ *Rua Francisco Otaviano 61, Copacabana, 22070-010* ☎ *021/3222–9600* ✐ *parthenonarpoador@accorhotels. com* ⤶ *48 apartments* ⌂ *In-room: Ethernet. In-hotel: pool, gym, concierge, parking (no fee), no-smoking rooms, restaurant* ▤ *AE, DC, MC, V* ⦿ *EP.*

$$ 🏨 **Miramar Palace.** A mix of old and new, this beachfront hotel has some of the largest rooms in Rio, with some of the best views. Classic accents like the Carrara marble floor of the lobby and the spectacular glass chandeliers that light the restaurant are contrasted with modern amenities like wireless Internet and the contemporary 16th-floor bar with an unobstructed view of the entire sweep of Copacabana. **Pros:** Beachfront location, large rooms, good views. **Cons:** Busy area, must use taxis to Ipanema and Leblon at night. ⊠ *Av. Atlântica 3668, Copacabana, 22070-001* ☎ *021/956-200 or 0800/23–2211* ⊕ *www.*

BEST BAR NONE

Rio's hotel bars range from super chic to shabby. Here's our pick of the best:

■ **Bar D'Hotel, Marina All Suites:** an enduringly fashionable favourite in trendy Leblon, attracting models, footballers, and Brazilian soap stars.

■ **Londra, Fasano Rio:** a 2007 newcomer, but an extremely cool one, full of rock-and-roll attitude and Italian glamour.

■ **Horse's Neck Bar, Sofitel Rio Palace:** the traditional British pub gets an African-influenced makeover at this Copacabana hot spot. Great range of Belgian beers.

■ **Pergula, Copacabana Palace:** strictly speaking, a restaurant, but the location by the hotel's pool makes this a fabulously glamorous spot for a light snack and a cocktail.

windsorhoteis.com ⇆*147 rooms, 9 suites* ♿*In-room: safe, refrigerator, Ethernet, Wi-Fi (some). In-hotel: restaurant, room service, bars, concierge, laundry service, public Internet, public Wi-Fi, parking (no fee), no-smoking rooms* ⊟*AE, DC, MC, V* ⦙⊙⦙*BP.*

$$ 🏨**Windsor Palace Hotel.** Close to the shopping area of Copacabana, the Windsor Palace has standard, cookie-cutter hotel rooms. From the fifth floor up, rooms have balconies, but only those from the 12th floor up have ocean views. Overall, this is a solid mid-range option with decent services. The rooftop pool has a view of Copacabana Beach, and it's two blocks from the Siqueira Campos metro station. **Pros:** Rooftop views, good amenities, close to Metro. **Cons:** Bland rooms, not the best location. ⊠*Rua Domingos Ferreira 6, Copacabana, 22050-010* ☎*021/2545–9000* ⊕*www.windsorhoteis.com* ⇆*73 rooms, 1 suite* ♿*In-room: safe, Ethernet, Wi-Fi (some). In-hotel: restaurant, room service, bar, pool, concierge, laundry service, public Internet, parking (no fee), no-smoking rooms* ⊟*AE, DC, MC, V* ⦙⊙⦙*BP* Ⓜ*Siqueira Campos.*

$–$$ 🏨**Copacabana Rio Hotel.** Brightly decorated in blues, yellows, and reds, the rooms here are nicer than those you find at many more expensive places. A few rooms have wonderful views of Pedra da Gávea (Gávea Rock). Single, double, and triple rooms and suites are all reasonably priced and are good value for the location—one block back from the beach. From the heated rooftop pool you can see Copacabana Beach and Sugar Loaf, and the on-site restaurant serves buffet-style and à la carte meals. You're practically in Ipanema here, which is handy for nightlife, but it's a 10 block walk to the nearest metro station at Canto Galo. **Pros:** Good price, comfortable rooms, handy for Copacabana and Ipanema beaches. **Cons:** No metro, busy and noisy street. ⊠*Av. Nossa Senhora de Copacabana 1256, Copacabana, 22070-010* ☎*021/2267–9900* ⊕*www.copacabanariohotel.com.br* ⇆*90 rooms, 8 suites* ♿*In-room: safe. In-hotel: restaurant, pool, gym, concierge, laundry service, parking (fee)* ⊟*AE, DC, MC, V* ⦙⊙⦙*BP* Ⓜ*Siqueira Campos.*

$–$$ 🏨**Ouro Verde Hotel.** Since the 1950s this hotel has been favored for
★ its efficient, personalized service. Quirky touches such as the huge art deco reception desk, enormous gilt-framed mirrors, and reading room

with antique furnishings give this hotel an air of old-time decadence, while the modern bar, which features DJs and live music several nights a week, brings things up to date for younger guests. The quiet beachfront location, at the Leme end of Copacabana, is excellent, and the prices are low for Avenida Atlântica, although it should be noted that some of the fixtures and fittings are a little past their prime. All front rooms face the beach; those in the back on the 11th and 12th floors have a view of Corcovado. **Pros:** Good location, good price, quirky hotel with lots of character. **Cons:** Far from Ipanema and Leblon, furnishings are a little worn. ⊠ *Av. Atlântica 1456, Copacabana, 22021-000* ☎ *021/2543-4123* ⊕ *www.dayrell.com.br* 🛏 *60 rooms, 2 suites* ♿ *In-room: safe, Wi-Fi (some). In-hotel: restaurant, room service, bar, laundry service, public Internet, public Wi-Fi, no-smoking rooms* ⊟ *AE, DC, MC, V* Ⓜ *Cardeal Arco Verde.*

ALTERNATIVE HOUSING

Rio has accommodations to suit virtually every taste and wallet. There are plenty of self-catering options for those who value their own space over hotel luxury. Agencies specialize in everything from luxury Ipanema penthouses right down to pokey Copacabana digs. Recommended companies include Rioholidays (www.rioholidays.com), which offers 1–4 bedroom apartments and penthouses, and Gringo Management (www.gringomanagent.com), which has offices in Rio and New York, and offers solid but basic cost-friendly options in Copacabana and Ipanema.

$-$$ 🏨 **Royalty Copacabana.** Three blocks from the beach, this hotel is in a relatively quiet, semi-residential area. The back rooms from the third floor up are the quietest and have mountain views; front rooms face the sea. **Pros:** Great view from the pool, fairly quiet location. **Cons:** Basic amenities, not on the beach. ⊠ *Rua Tonelero 154, Copacabana, 22030-000* ☎ *021/2548-5699* ⊕ *www.royaltyhotel.com.br* 🛏 *123 rooms, 13 suites* ♿ *In-room: safe, Ethernet. In-hotel: restaurant, bar, pool, gym, parking (fee), no-smoking rooms* ⊟ *AE, DC, MC, V* ⊙|*BP* Ⓜ *Siqueira Campos.*

$ 🏨 **Hotel Debret.** This former apartment building scores points for keeping its prices moderate despite a beachfront location. The decor honors Brazil's past: the lobby has baroque statues and prints depicting colonial scenes, and the rooms are furnished in dark, heavy wood. The hotel has a loyal following among diplomats and businesspeople, who are more interested in functionality and low prices than elegance. The buffet breakfast with a view of the beach from the 12th-floor restaurant is one of the hotel's best assets. Corner rooms tend to be most spacious, and the hotel's "business room" features a standard room with well-equipped office attached. **Pros:** Beachfront location, good price. **Cons:** Less-than-attractive facade, usual Copacabana safety problems. ⊠ *Av. Atlântica 3564, Copacabana, 22060-040* ☎ *021/2522–0132* 🖨 *021/2521–0899* ⊕ *www.debret.com* 🛏 *94 rooms, 13 suites* ♿ *In-room: safe, Ethernet (some). In-hotel: restaurant, bar, laundry service, public Internet* ⊟ *AE, DC, MC, V* ⊙|*BP* Ⓜ *Cantagalo.*

$ ⛭**Vilamar Copacabana.** A small hotel by Rio's standards, Vilamar has petite rooms. The pool is small, too, but since you're only 200 meters (about 660 feet) from the beach, the size of the pool shouldn't be a problem. Rooms on the lower level get some street noise. **Pros:** Close to beach, pool and gym. **Cons:** Traffic noise, small rooms. ⊠*Rua Bolívar 75, Copacabana, 22061-020* ☎*021/3461–5601* ⊕*www.hotelvilamar-copacabana.com.br* ⮑*56 rooms, 14 suites* ⚒*In-room: safe, refrigerator, Ethernet. In-hotel: restaurant, bar, pool, gym, parking (fee), no-smoking rooms* ▤*AE, DC, MC, V* �ĨOĨ*BP* Ⓜ*Cantagalo.*

¢–$ ⛭**Toledo.** Although it has few amenities, the Toledo goes the extra mile to make the best of what it does have. The staff is friendly, the service is efficient, and the location—on a quiet backstreet of Copacabana, a block from the beach—isn't bad either. Back rooms from the 9th to the 14th floors have sea views and sliding floor-to-ceiling windows. Some rooms are much larger than others, so specify if you have a preference. **Pros:** Reasonably quiet location, decent service, good price. **Cons:** Not on the beach, basic amenities. ⊠*Rua Domingos Ferreira 71, Copacabana, 22050-010* ☎*021/2257–1990* ⊕*www.hoteltoledo. com.br* ⮑*92 rooms* ⚒*In-room: safe. In-hotel: public Internet* ▤*AE, DC, MC, V* ĨOĨ*BP* Ⓜ*Siqueira Campos.*

FLAMENGO

$–$$ ⛭**Novo Mundo.** A short walk from the Catete metro station and five minutes by car from Santos Dumont Airport, this traditional hotel is on Guanabara Bay in Flamengo, near Glória. Convention rooms are popular with the business crowd. Deluxe rooms have a view of the bay and also of the Pão de Açúcar. The traditional restaurant, Flamboyant, has buffet and à la carte service during the week and feijoada every Saturday. **Pros:** Good for business travelers, some rooms have good views. **Cons:** Far from Zona Sul. ⊠*Praia do Flamengo 20, Flamengo, 22210-030* ☎*021/2105–7000 or 0800/25–3355* ⊕*www.hotelnovo mundo-rio.com.br* ⮑*209 rooms, 22 suites* ⚒*In-room: safe, refrigerator, Ethernet (some). In-hotel: restaurant, bar, laundry service, parking (fee), no-smoking rooms* ▤*AE, DC, MC, V* ĨOĨ*BP* Ⓜ*Catete.*

IPANEMA & LEBLON

$$$$ ⛭**Caesar Park.** In the heart of Ipanema, close to high-class shops and gourmet restaurants, this beachfront hotel has established itself among business travelers, celebrities, and heads of state, who appreciate its impeccable service. The hotel has a business center including secretarial services and fax machines. Disappointingly, rooms lack balconies, and although the rooftop pool has excellent views, it's very small. However, the fitness center is superb, and the hotel has an excellent Italian restaurant, Galani, which serves a fabulous Sunday brunch and an impeccable executive lunch. A second restaurant serves feijoada every Saturday. The black-theme lobby is modern, comfortable, and cool, but corridors and rooms are quite plainly furnished and, although the suites are impressive, other rooms feel functional rather than luxurious. **Pros:** Great location, good business facilities, good views. **Cons:** No balco-

nies, small pool, uninspired decor. ⊠ *Av. Vieira Souto 460, Ipanema, 22420-000* ☎ *021/2525–2525 or 0800/21–0789, 877/223–7272 in U.S.* ⊕ *www.caesarpark-rio.com* ⟐ *221 rooms, 24 suites* ⌂ *In-room: safe, Ethernet, Wi-Fi. In-hotel: 2 restaurants, room service, bar, pool, gym, concierge, laundry service, parking (fee), no-smoking rooms* ⊟ *AE, DC, MC, V.*

$$$$ ✕🏠 **Fasano Rio.** Fasano Rio opened to great fanfare in 2007, and with good reason. The Italian-owned Fasano Group is renowned for its stylish, elegant hotels and restaurants, and Fasano Rio has the added glamour of having been crafted by French designer Philippe Starck. The location, in front of Ipanema Beach, could not be better, and the understated facade of the building masks a wealth of quirky style inside. A key theme is the use of Amazonian wood—the reception desk is carved from a huge tree trunk—and modern glass and chrome. Elsewhere, specially commissioned furnishings re-create the style of the 1950s and '60s. You'll find unique touches everywhere, such as the huge pink-and-white candy-stripe armchairs in the middle of each corridor, but the real star of the show is the white-marble plunge pool on the rooftop terrace. With breathtaking views across Ipanema Beach, it's the ultimate in Rio decadance. A poolside bar and restaurant serves wonderful tropical juices, light meals, and cocktails. Egyptian cotton sheets, goosedown pillows, and plasma-screen televisions are further indulgent touches. The hotel's elegant Italian restaurant, Fasano Al Mare, has already picked up awards, and the intimate lounge bar Londra, which blends English punk-rock attitude with Italian glamour, has a waiting list a mile long. ⊠ *Av. Viera Souto 80, Ipanema, 22420 000* ☎ *21 3202 4000* ⊕ *www.fasano.com.br* ⟐ *82 rooms, 10 suites* ⌂ *In room: safe, refrigerator, DVD (some), Ethernet, Wi-Fi. In hotel: 2 restaurants, room service, bar, pool, gym, bicycles, laundry service, public Internet, public Wi-Fi, some pets allowed.*

$$$$ 🏠 **Marina All Suites.** In front of Leblon Beach and surrounded by designer stores and upmarket restaurants, Marina All Suites is a favorite with chic holidaymakers (Gisele Bundchen and Calvin Klein are regulars). The lofty building is home to 37 spacious suites, and those on the upper floor have each been signed by a different designer. As well as slick design, each of the rooms is equipped with a stereo system, and many have ocean views. The service is superb, and the hotel has some wonderfully eccentric touches such as a home cinema (film requests can be made at reception and will be picked up at no charge from the local rental store). There's also a shared "living room" with

CHOOSING A HOTEL

While the beaches and natural beauty of the Zona Sul are the principal draw for most visitors, making your base away from the tourist hot spots can be a rewarding experience. The middle class area of Botafogo enjoys the city's best view of the Christ statue, as well as having some of the hippest nightlife and restaurant options. Santa Teresa and Lapa offer multiple opportunities to party the night away. Accomodation prices outside the main tourist zones are competitive, and some of the city's finest colonial architecture will be right on your doorstep.

lounge and bar, where you can receive friends. At the time of writing, the rooftop pool was being completely overhauled to provide a clearer view of the ocean. The top-floor bar, Bar D'Hotel, is considered one of the best nightlife spots in the area. **Pros:** Good location, well equipped, spacious, excellent service. **Cons:** Leblon Beach is not quite as pretty as Ipanema. ⊠ *Avenida Delfim Moreira 696, Praia do Lebolon, 22441 000* ⊕ *www.hoteismarina.com.br* ⇰ *37 rooms* ⚿ *In room: safe, kitchen (some), refrigerator, DVD (some), Wi-Fi. In hotel: restaurant, room service, bar, pool, gym, bicycles, laundry service, concierge, public Internet, public Wi-Fi, airport shuttle, parking (no fee), no-smoking rooms.*

$$$–$$$$ **Best Western Sol Ipanema.** Another of Rio's crop of tall, slender hotels, this one has a great location between Rua Vinicius de Moraes and Farme de Amoedo, where there are several bars, anchoring the eastern end of Ipanema Beach. While it isn't luxurious, the hotel has comfortable accommodations, and the interiors are crisp, clean, and modern. The lobby is small and functional, but the all-white furnishings are a nice touch. Deluxe front rooms have panoramic beach views, and back rooms from the eighth floor up, which are the same size, have views of the lagoon and Corcovado. **Pros:** Great location, friendly staff, modern. **Cons:** Standard facilities. ⊠ *Av. Vieira Souto 320, Ipanema, 22420-000* ☎ *021/2525–2020* ⊕ *www.solipanema.com.br* ⇰ *90 rooms* ⚿ *In-room: refrigerator, Ethernet. In-hotel: restaurant, room service, bars, pool, laundry service, parking (no fee), no-smoking rooms* ▭ *AE, DC, MC, V* ❍|*BP.*

$$$–$$$$ **Everest Rio Hotel.** With standard service but a great rooftop view—a postcard shot of Corcovado and the lagoon—this hotel is in the heart of Ipanema's shopping and dining district, a block from the beach. Back rooms have sea views, but the hotel lacks any compelling decor and some carpets look a little worn. However, there are good amenities for business travelers. The restaurant 360°, on the top floor close to the swimming pool, has seafood and some specialties from the south of Brazil. There's also a sushi bar on the ground floor. **Pros:** Good roof views, good location, rooftop pool. **Cons:** Uninspired interiors, views slightly hampered by other buildings. Rooms clean but not spotless. ⊠ *Rua Prudente de Morais 1117, Ipanema, 22420-041* ☎ *021/2525–2200 or 0800/24–4485* ⊕ *www.everest.com.br* ⇰ *148 rooms, 8 suites* ⚿ *In-room: safe, Ethernet, Wi-Fi (some). In-hotel: 2 restaurants, room service, bar, pool, concierge, laundry service, parking (fee), no-smoking rooms, public Internet* ▭ *AE, DC, MC, V.*

$$$–$$$$ **Ipanema Plaza.** European standards and solid service are the hallmarks of this hotel. The rooms are large, with white-tile floors and modern facilities, and the decor is tastefully tropical. In the center of Ipanema, very close to the beach, the hotel is on a street that's rife with restaurants and bars. From the rooftop pool it's possible to see not only the ocean, but also the lagoon and the statue of Christ the Redeemer. In 2005 the hotel introduced Ipanema Floor—an executive floor with all the bells and whistles, including rooms and suites with spectacular views over Ipanema Beach, elegant Italian fixtures, and fine linens with impossibly high thread counts. **Pros:** Attractive, comfortable accommodation, good views from pool, attention to detail. **Cons:** Pool often used for private parties during high season, pricey neighborhood. ⊠*Rua Farme de Amoedo 34, Ipanema, 22420-020* ☎*021/3687–2000* ⊕*www.ipanemaplazahotel.com* ⬎*118 rooms, 13 suites* ♿*In-room: safe, Ethernet (some), Wi-Fi. In-hotel: restaurant, room service, pool, gym, concierge, laundry service, executive floor, parking (fee), no-smoking rooms* ⊟*AE, DC, MC, V* ❏|*BP.*

$$$–$$$$ ▦ **Praia Ipanema.** This hotel isn't deluxe, but it has a great location across from the beach and between Ipanema and Leblon. You can see the sea from all its rooms. Choose the higher floors to enjoy the view and avoid the traffic noise. Take in the dramatic beach view from the pool area on the roof of the 15-story building. You can also catch a breeze from your private balcony (every room has one) or enjoy live music at the hotel bar every Friday night. **Pros:** Great views, beach-front location, close to both Ipanema and Leblon shopping and night-life. **Cons:** Some furnishings a little shabby. ⊠*Av. Vieira Souto 706, Ipanema, 22440-000* ☎*021/2540–4949* ⊕*www.praiaipanema.com. br* ⬎*103 rooms* ♿*In-room: safe, Ethernet, Wi-Fi (some). In-hotel: restaurant, room service, bars, pool, gym, concierge, laundry service, parking (no fee)* ⊟*AE, DC, MC, V* ❏|*BP.*

$$ ▦ **Hotel Vermont.** Another good budget option in Ipanema, Hotel Vermont is in a great location on the main shopping strip, a few minutes' walk from the beach. The hotel has been under new management since 2007, and a new restaurant has already been installed. Rooms are small and basic with no views, but the price is good and includes a buffet breakfast of hot and cold food. ⊠*Rua Visconde de Pirajá 254 Ipanema, 22410-000* ☎*21/3202-5500* ⊕*www.hotelvermont.com.br* ⬎*84 rooms* ♿*In room: safe, refrigerator, Wi-Fi (some). In hotel: restaurant, bar, laundry service, public Internet, no-smoking rooms.*

$$ ▦ **Leblon Flat Service.** Simply decorated, small furnished apartments with one or two bedrooms and balconies are offered at this hotel-like tower block apartment complex. Leblon Beach is three blocks away. This is a good option for those who want to save money by cooking at home, and a buffet breakfast is included in the daily rate. **Pros:** Good rate for Leblon area, shopping, restaurants, and nightlife nearby. **Cons:** Building is unattractive. ⊠*Rua Professor Antônio Maria Teixeira 33, Leblon, 22430-050* ☎*021/2529–8332 for information, 021/2239–4598 for reservations* ☎*021/2259–2191* ⬎*120 apartments* ♿*In-room: safe, kitchen. In-hotel: restaurant, bar, pool, gym, laundry facilities* ⊟*AE, DC, MC, V.*

$–$$ ▦ **Arpoador Inn.** This simple pocket-size hotel occupies the stretch of sand known as Arpoador. Surfers ride the waves, and pedestrians rule the roadway—a virtually traffic-free street allows direct beach access. At sunset the view from the landmark rock that juts out into the ocean at the end of the beach is one of Rio's most beautiful. The spectacle is visible from the hotel's back (deluxe) rooms that face Arpoador Beach. Avoid the front rooms, which can be noisy. Built in the '70s, the hotel has since been renovated and has a good seafood restaurant, Azul Marinho, on the ground floor overlooking the beach. The restaurant has tables right next to the sand, and guests can choose to take their buffet breakfast here. Some rooms are much larger than others, so specify if you have a preference. **Pros:** Great sunset, good restaurant, good price. **Cons:** Some rooms a little noisy, can be busy with groups of surfers. ✉*Rua Francisco Otaviano 177, Ipanema, 22080-040* ☎*021/2523–0060* ⊕*www.arpoadorinn.com.br* ☛*50 rooms* ⚑*In-room: safe. In-hotel: restaurant, room service, bar, laundry service, public Internet* ▭*AE, DC, MC, V* ⊙❙*BP.*

$–$$ 🏨 **Ipanema Inn.** If you want to stay in Ipanema and avoid the high prices of beachfront accommodations, this no-frills hotel with great service fits the bill. Rooms are simply furnished and have no view, but the fact that the hotel is just seconds from the beach should sugar the pill. The hotel owners also run Arpoador Inn, so you can expect the same relaxed atmosphere and youthful clientele. Ipanema Inn is attached to a Brasil & Cia shop, which sells brightly colored artisan paintings and figurines, many of which are on display in the hotel's lobby. Close to Praça Nossa Senhora da Paz, it's convenient not only for sun worshippers but also for those seeking to explore Ipanema's varied nightlife. **Pros:** Great location, good value. **Cons:** Basic rooms, no views. ✉*Rua Maria Quitéria 27, Ipanema, 22410-040* ☎*021/2523–6092 or 021/2274–6995* ⊕*www.ipanemainn.com.br* ☛*56 rooms* ⚑*In-room: safe. In-hotel: bar, laundry service, public Internet* ▭*AE, DC, MC, V* ⊙❙*BP.*

$ 🏨 **Ipanema Sweet.** In this smart residential building in the heart of Ipanema, owners rent out their units by the night, week, or month. Two blocks from the beach and steps away from Ipanema's best bars, restaurants, and shops, the location cannot be beat. Rooms are well equipped and tastefully appointed, and the lobby's design (comfy sofas, framed modern art on the walls, and gleaming white walls and floors) deliberately appeals to a young, fashionable clientele. All units have their own bathroom, kitchen, and living room, and some are also equipped with television, DVD player, and Internet connection. If you like the idea of experiencing Rio like a local, this is a good place to start. A grocery store across the street makes preparing meals easy. The building has a small swimming pool and small exercise room. The bus connecting Ipanema to the metro in Copacabana is one block from the building. **Pros:** Good for budget travelers who want to cook for themselves, great location, more space than standard hotel rooms. **Cons:** Not all apartments have safe boxes, maid service is extra. ✉*Rua Visconde de Pirajá 161, Ipanema, 22420-010* ☎*021/2551–0488, 021/82774815 Sonia Maria Cordeiro* ✆*soniacordeiro@globo.com* ▭*No credit cards* ⊙❙*EP.*

SANTA TERESA

$$$–$$$$ 🏨 **Relais Solar.** In a leafy courtyard set back from a quiet street, Relais Solar is the perfect boutique hideaway in bohemian Santa Teresa. The expansive colonial building comprises two 2-room suites, plus a separate bungalow. Next to each suite is a smaller room that can only be rented in conjunction with the main suite. Polished wooden floors in the dining room lead to a wide, winding staircase. Each room is flooded with light when the old-fashioned shutters are flung open to reveal a hammock-strewn veranda. A breakfast of tropical fruit, cheeses, breads, meat, and pastries can be had outdoors beneath the trees or indoors at the vast dining table. When night falls a bartender mixes cocktails beneath the stars, and there are occasional live music performances. **Pros:** Quiet and peaceful, gorgeous indoor and outdoor space, lively eating and drinking scene nearby. **Cons:** A long way from the beach, Santa Teresa can feel isolated from the rest of the city. ⊠*Ladeira do Meirelles 32, Santa Teresa, 20241-340* ☏*21/2221–2117* ⊕*www.solardesanta.com* ⇋*2 suites, 1 bunglow* ⚒*In-room: refrigerator, Wi-Fi. In-hotel: room service, bar, pool, no elevator.*

HAPPY HOSTELLERS

Rio's hostelling options range from vast party hostels with multiple bars and enormous dorm rooms to small boutique hostels with double rooms in pretty colonial buildings. In Ipanema a quiet little street off Barão da Torre houses six friendly little hostels right next door to each other. The gated street, with security at night, has been nicknamed "Hostel Alley" and is just a couple of blocks from the beach. Most of the hostels have double rooms, at prices much lower than the area's hotels. www.hostelworld.com has booking facilities and guest reviews for all Rio hostels.

SÃO CONRADO, BARRA DA TIJUCA & BEYOND

$$$$ 🏨 **InterContinental Rio.** One of the city's few resorts is in São Conrado, on its own slice of beachfront next to the Gávea Golf and Country Club. Attractions include a cocktail lounge, an Italian restaurant (Alfredo), and a buffet with feijoada every Saturday. All rooms have a balcony with ocean view, and all have been recently renovated, with new curtains, carpets, and furnishings. The nearby mall is much less crowded than those with more central locations. The club floor has extra facilities like daily newspapers and a tearoom. One major safety concern is the hotel's proximity to Rocinha, the largest favela in South America. **Pros:** Modern, good facilities, views. **Cons:** Taxis needed to get to Zona Sul and Centro, favela nearby. ⊠*Av. Prefeito Mendes de Morais 222, São Conrado, 22610-090* ☏*021/3323–2200, 800/327–0200 in U.S.* ⊕*www.interconti.com* ⇋*429 rooms, 58 suites, 20 cabanas* ⚒*In-room: safe, Ethernet (some). In-hotel: 2 restaurants, room service, bars, tennis courts, pools, gym, spa, concierge, laundry service, parking (no fee), no-smoking rooms* ▭*AE, DC, MC, V.*

$$$$ 🏨 **Sheraton Rio Hotel & Resort.** Between the upmarket neighborhoods of ♻ São Conrado and Leblon, this is the only hotel in Rio with a "private" beach. (It's open to the public, but so closed off to anything but the hotel that usually only Sheraton guests use it.) The leisure area is possibly the best in Rio, with three pools, two tennis courts, and a children's playground. However, the hotel also sits directly in front of the sprawling favela of Vidigal, which may make some guests uncomfortable. Rooms are tastefully decorated, and all have balconies with sea views, although some are very limited. The lobby was modernized in

2007, and now has a comfortable lounge with Internet access. Floors in the Towers section are reserved for business travelers. Be prepared for numerous taxi rides because of the hotel's isolated location. **Pros:** Great for families, wonderful beach, good amenities. **Cons:** Isolated, close to Vidigal favela. ✉ *Av. Niemeyer 121, Vidigal, 22450-220* ☎ *021/2274– 1122 or 0800/21–0750, 800/325–3589 in U.S.* ⊕ *www.sheraton-rio. com* ↪ *500 rooms, 59 suites* ⚐ *In-room: safe, Ethernet (some), Wi-Fi (some). In-hotel: 3 restaurants, bars, tennis courts, pools, gym, beach-front, concierge, laundry service, public Internet, public Wi-Fi, parking (fee), no-smoking rooms* ☰ *AE, DC, MC, V* ⦿ *BP.*

$$–$$$$ ⛌ **Sheraton Barra Hotel e Suites.** Opened in 2003, this mammoth gleaming-white hotel has balconies in each room that overlook Barra Beach. The decor is futuristic, with white walls, brushed nickel and mahogany accents, skillful lighting, widescreen TVs, and clean lines. Be prepared to rent a car or spend a good deal of money on taxis when staying in this neighborhood, as there's no metro station and unreliable bus service. The hotel is particularly popular with business travelers attending conventions nearby. **Pros:** Barra Beach is quieter than Zona Sul, good facilties. **Cons:** Traffic is bad, can take well over an hour to reach Zona Sul, neighborhood is more like Miami than Rio. ✉ *Av. Lúcio Costa 3150, Barra da Tijuca, 22630-010* ☎ *021/3139–8000* 🖷 *021/3139– 8025* ⊕ *www.sheraton.com/barra* ↪ *264 rooms, 28 suites* ⚐ *In-room: Ethernet. In-hotel: restaurant, room service, bar, pool, gym, spa, concierge, parking (fee)* ☰ *AE, DC, MC, V.*

NIGHTLIFE & THE ARTS

Updated by
Doug Grey

Rio is light years beyond the seedy reputation that it once had. Never before has the city housed such a rich variety of cultural centers and cutting-edge nightlife, and even though the classic rhythms of samba may still dominate the clubs, bars, and street corners, it's now possible to find something to suit every kind of taste almost every night of the week. Venues for theater, opera, ballet, and classical music are plentiful, and smaller, more intimate (and often more intriguing) events happen in most neighborhoods.

More discerning arts enthusiasts should pick up the Portuguese-language *Mapa Cultural* or bilingual *Guia do Rio* published by Riotur, the city's tourist board. The Portuguese-language newspapers *Jornal do Brasil* and *O Globo* publish schedules of events in the entertainment supplements of their Friday editions, which are also to be found online at ⊕ *www.jb.com.br* and ⊕ *www.oglobo.com.br*. Finally, *Veja Rio* is the city's best entertainment guide, published every Saturday and available in all newsstands.

NIGHTLIFE

It's sometimes said that cariocas would rather expend their energies on the beach and that nighttime is strictly for recharging their batteries and de-sanding their *çungas,* but witnessing the masses swarming into

Lapa at 10 PM on a Friday night make this a tricky argument to side with. New nightclubs and bars continue to sprout up with remarkable regularity, and there' are cutting-edge underground rhythms and musical styles that are competing with samba, chorro, and MPB in the locals' hearts.

BARS

A much-loved local pastime is drinking a well-chilled *chopp* (draft beer) and enjoying the lively atmosphere of a genuine Rio *botequim* (bar). Every neighborhood has its share of upmarket options (branches of *Belmonte, Devassa,* and *Conversa Fiada* are dotted around town), but no less enjoyable are the huge number of down-to-earth hole-in-the-wall options, offering ice-cold bottles of *cerveja* (beer) and some interesting regulars.

> ## PLAYING IT SAFE
>
> Safety after dark is of paramount importance in Rio. You should be aware of your surroundings at all times. Always take a taxi after dark, and be sure it has the company name and phone number painted on the outside before you get in. Some drivers are reluctant to go to certain areas of town such as Santa Teresa due to protection rackets; in such situations simply ask to be taken to a taxi rank where they will continue your journey. Pickpockets love Copacabana and Lapa, so keep valuables either at the hotel or at least well hidden.

BOTAFOGO & FLAMENGO

Maldita. It seems that the streets of Botafogo can cope with any number of new bars and this is one of the best. Opened in 2007 and translated curiously as the Cursed, Maldita's tables and chairs line the road either side of the entrance, while the cozy indoors has some great electronic music to offer. ✉ *Rua Voluntarios Da Patria 10, Botafogo, 22011-040* ☎ *21/2527–2456.*

The Cobal. More than just a bar, this collection of bars, restaurants, and shops in the style of an open-air market is always lively and has great views of Cristo Redentor. The largely outdoor Espirito Do Chopp is the best option, weather permitting. ✉ *Rua Voluntarios Da Patria 446, Botafogo, 22270-010* ☎ *21/2266–5599* ⊕ *www.espirito dochopp.com.br.*

Belmonte. If you find yourself in need of refreshment after a stroll through the beautiful Parque Do Flamengo, then your best stop is Belmonte. The original outlet of a now successful chain, it keeps the carioca spirit alive and well with its carefree air, great food and icy chopp. ✉ *Praia Do Flamengo 300, Flamengo, 22210-903* ☎ *(21) 2266 5599.*

COPACABANA

Relatively light on hip new bars, the vibe in Copacabana is more for laid-back time-honored locals. Although the tourist traps that litter Avenida Atlantica are overpriced and underbaked, the kiosks on the beachfront itself were refurbished in 2007 and are nice places to while away the hours.

★ **Bip Bip.** Here the *roda de samba*—where musicians sit and play instruments around a central table (in fact the *only* table in this tiny bar)—is legendary, as is the help-yourself beer policy. The gnarled old owner makes drink notations and keeps the crowd in check ☒*Rua Almirante Gonçalves 50, Copacabana, 22060-040* ☎*021/2267–9696.*

Cervantes. This no-frills Copacabana institution marries great beer with great sandwiches made with fresh beef, pork, and cheese crammed into French bread (with obligatory pineapple slice). Its closed on Monday, but merely to give the staff a chance to recover—the rest of the week they cater to even the most tardy diners. They're known for their lively late night–early morning crowd. ☒*Av. Prado Júnior 335, Copacabana, 22011-040* ☎*021/2275–6147.*

IPANEMA   Though better equipped with clothes shops and restaurants, there are some great bars in Ipanema. General Osorio Square houses two of the city's three genuine pubs, Shenanigans and The Irish Pub, while Rua Vinicius De Moraes has the more upmarket options.

Bar Garota de Ipanema. This is the original Garota (there are branches all over the city), where Tom Jobim and Vinicius de Moraes penned the timeless song "The Girl from Ipanema" back in the '60s. They serve well-priced food and drink that no doubt originally appealed to the two great songsmiths. ☒*Rua Vinicius de Moraes 39, Ipanema, 22411-010* ☎*021/2523–3787.*

★ **Devassa.** Another cross-city chain of bars, Devassa is particularly notable for its own-brand beers, including delicious Pale Ales and Chopp Escuro (dark beer). It also has a great menu of meat-related staples. This branch in particular shines for its plum location a block back from Ipanema Beach. ☒*Rua Prudente de Moraes 416, Ipanema, 22420-041* ☎*21/2522–0627* ⊕*www.devassa.com.br.*

JARDIM   **Lagoa.** The collection of kiosks to the western edge of the city's lagoon
BOTANICO &   simply goes by the name Lagoa. Along with the usual beers and cock-
LAGOA   tails, the food—Italian, Arabian, burgers, and other nontraditional Brazilian—may not be spectacular, but the view of surrounding water and mountains, with Cristo Redentor lighted up in the distance, most certainly is. The kiosks close down around 1 AM. ☒*Parque Brigadeiro Faria Lima, turnoff near BR gas station, 22411-072.*

Caroline Cafe. One of several laid-back bars in the Jardim Botanico area that manages to attract a hip, friendly crowd away from Leblon. Dark-wood finished interior, an open balcony upstairs, and some unusual snacks help create the atmosphere for a good night of straightforward drinking. ☒*Rua J. J. Seabra 10, Jardim Botanico, 22470-130* ☎*21/2540–0705* ⊕*www.carolinecafe.com.br.*

LAPA   As well as the many bars that line the Avenida Mem de Sá (beginning near the Arcos da Lapa), there are literally hundreds of shabby stalls and ice buckets full of booze waiting to be snapped up. Our advice? Grab a drink from one and take a stroll to see which hostelry appeals to you.

Bar Luiz. It's been well over a century since Bar Luiz first opened its doors, and you could be excused for thinking that little has changed since, including the affable waiters. Claiming the best chopp in the city would arouse controversy from a lesser venue, but few here would bother to argue. They draw a mixed and entertaining crowd of young and old with a simple menu and some stunning black-and-white photos adorning the walls. Oh, and excellent beer. ⊠ *Rua Da Carioca 39, Centro, 20050-008* ☎ *21/2262–6900* ⊕ *www.barluiz.com.br.*

> **THE REAL GIRL FROM IPANEMA**
>
> Have you ever wondered if there really *was* a girl from Ipanema? The song was inspired by schoolgirl Heloisa Pinheiro, who caught the fancy of songwriter Antônio Carlos (aka Tom) Jobim and his pal lyricist Vinicius de Moraes as she walked past the two bohemians sitting in their favorite bar. They then penned one of last century's classics. That was in 1962, and today the bar has been renamed **Bar Garota de Ipanema**.

Mangue Seco Cachaçaria. Specializing in some of Brazil's finest institutions—strong and unusual *cachaças* (Brazilian rum), mouthwatering *moquecas* (stews), and, of course, live samba—Mangue Seco's location on the popular Rua do Lavradio makes it a perfect place to start a night out. ⊠ *Rua do Lavradio 23, Centro, 20230-70* ☎ *021/3147–9005* ⊕ *www.manguesecocachacaria.com.br.*

LEBLON   **Academia da Cachaça.** If a top-quality caipirinha is what you're after, then look no further than the specialists at the Academia. Although techniques and quality for this potent local mixture can vary wildly across the city, here they take Brasil's number-one liquor reassuringly seriously. ⊠ *Rua Conde de Bernadotte 26G, Leblon, 22430-200* ☎ *021/2239–1542* ⊕ *www.academiadacachaca.com.br.*

Bar D'Hotel. It's hard to escape the fact that it's just a good hotel bar with a nice view of the sea, but expect to find socialites rubbing shoulders over a more upmarket selection of drinks, cocktails, and food with prices to match. For a more laid-back experience and a balcony overlooking the water, try Bar Da Praia at the sister hotel (the Marina Palace) next door. ⊠ *Marina All Suites, Av. Delfim Moreira 696, Leblon, 22441-000* ☎ *021/2540–4990* ⊕ *www.marinaallsuites.com.br/allsuites.*

Bracarense. A trip to Bracarense after a hard day on the beach is what Rio is all about. Crowds spill onto the streets while parked cars double as chairs and the sandy masses gather at sunset for ice-cold chopp and some of the best pork sandwiches, fish balls, and empadas in the neighborhood. ⊠ *Rua José Linhares 85B, Leblon, 22430-220* ☎ *021/2294–3549.*

Carnival in Rio

By far the biggest event of the year, planning and preparation start months before the four-day Carnival weekend that's marked on every Brazilian's calendar. What began as a pre-Lent celebration has morphed into the massive affair of street parties, masquerades, and samba parades. Elaborate costumes, enormous floats, and intensive planning all unfurl magically behind the scenes as Brazilians from all walks of life save their money for the all-important *desfile* down the Sambódromo. Even though Carnival has set dates based on the lunar calendar that determines when Lent occurs, the *folia* (Carnival festivities) start at least a week before and end at least a week after the samba schools parade. Five-star hotels like the Sheraton and Copacabana Palace have balls that are open to the public, as long as you can afford tickets (which run upward of R$3,000). A cheaper option is partying with the Carnival blocks and Carnival bands, which revel along the streets and beaches of the Zona Sul. If you really want to get close to the action, then you'll need to buy tickets (well in advance) for a seat at the Sambódromo. Most samba schools begin their rehearsals around October; if you're in Rio from October to January, visit one of the samba schools *(see Nightlife)* on a rehearsal day. Whether your scene is hanging out at the bars, partying in the street, parading along the beach, masked balls for the elite, or fun in a stadium, Rio's Carnival is an experience of a lifetime.

★ **Jobi Bar.** Authentically carioca and a smart but down-to-earth must for taking in the local spirit; on weekends it stays open until the last customer leaves. ⌂*Av. Ataulfo de Paiva 1166, Leblon, 22440-035* ☎*021/2274–0547.*

NIGHT CLUBS & LIVE MUSIC

Live music is Rio's raison d'etre, with street corners regularly playing host to impromptu renditions and during Carnival the entire city can feel like one giant playground. The electronic music scene is also very much alive and the underground popularity of Funk (the city's very own X-rated genre not to be confused with James Brown version) is slowly seeping into the mainstream, down from the huge *bailes* or open-air parties held weekly in the city's favelas. In addition to samba and Brazilain pop (MPB), hip-hop, electronica, and rock can be heard in clubs around the city.

BOTAFOGO **Casa Da Matriz.** Undoubtedly one of the more adventurous clubs in Rio both in terms of appearance and music policy. Young crowds flock to this shabbily decorated venue that has the appearance of a house party with its multiroom layout, staircase, and kitchen, and even old school arcade games and a small junk shop. ⌂*Rua Henrique de Novaes 107, Botafogo, 22281-050* ☎*021/2226–6342.*

Cinemathèque. Close to Botafogo Metro Station, Cinemathèque is a new edition to the Matriz empire slowly taking over Botafogo with its inventive bars and clubs. Expect a variety of Brazilian music old and new with live shows upstairs from 10:30 PM, or simply relax in the open air garden downstairs. ⊠*Rua Voluntários da Pátria 53, Botafogo, 2227-000* ☎*021/2286–5731.*

COPACABANA **Fosfobox.** For the more serious dance music enthusiast, Fosfobox, in the heart of Copacabana, plays the best underground dance music as well as rock and pop from Wednesday to Sunday. It's in an industrial-feeling basement and has a newly opened second room, which offers a bit more comfort with its cosy red sofas. ⊠*Rua Siqueira Campos 143, Copacabana, 22031-070* ☎*021/2548–7498* ⊕*www.fosfobox.com.br.*

La Girl. A well-known girls-only gay club that attracts the famous and fabulous females of Rio. ⊠*Rua Raul Pompéia 102, Copacabana, 22080-000* ☎*021/2513–4993* ⊕*www.lagirl.com.br.*

DOWNTOWN CLUBLAND

"Clubland" might be overstating the point, but tucked in a corner of downtown, close by the dingy old port, is Pier Mauà, a renovated waterside venue that hosts seasonal bands and DJs from November through to February. The Week has arrived from São Paulo as one of the city's most stylish gay clubs, Cabaret Kalesa is putting the fun back into Saturday nights with burlesque shows and an eclectic music policy, and for a more traditional slice of choro in a beautiful old building, Trapiche De Gamboa is hard to beat. All can be found on Rua Sacadura Cabral, just off Praça Mauà.

Le Boy. Right next door to La Girl, this is, unsurprisingly, the gay male mecca, playing pop and house music along with outrageous stage shows at the weekends. ⊠*Rua Paul Pompéia 102, Copacabana, 22080-000* ☎*021/2513-4993* ⊕*www.leboy.com.br.*

GAVEA **00 (Zero Zero).** Alongside the Planetarium, 00 is at once a buzzing nightclub, chic sushi restaurant, and open-air bar, all of which combines to give it the air of something special. Music ranges from modern Brazilian samba and house music to drum and bass. ⊠*Av. Padre Leonel Franca 240, Gávea, 22451-000* ☎*021/2540–8041* ⊕*www.00site.com.br.*

IPANEMA **Lounge 69.** A sleek new option in the heart of Ipanema, Lounge 69 with its attractive wooden facade and dashing interior provides a fresh taste of late night glamour in this happening street. ⊠*Rua Farme de Amoedo, Ipanema, 22420-041.*

LARANJEIRAS **Casa Rosa.** This former brothel is now a stunning bright pink mansion in the Laranjeiras hillside. It's loved by locals for its traditional musical repertoire. Sunday afternoon *feijoada* and samba on the terrace is a must for anyone seeking out a true carioca experience. ⊠*Rua Alice 550, Laranjeiras, 22241-020* ☎*021/8877 8804* ⊕*www.casarosa.com.br.*

LAPA **Carioca da Gema.** The original template for Lapa's samba clubs since
★ opening in 2000, Carioca da Gema remains one of the liveliest spots in the area, with local musical talent six nights a week (closed Sunday). By 11 PM it can be hard to find a place to stand, but regulars still find a way to samba, so call ahead and book a table if you are more keen on spectating. ⊠*Rua Mem de Sá 79, Lapa, 20230-150* ☎*021/2221 0043* ⊕*www.barcariocadagema.com.br.*

Circo Voador. A great venue in an excellent location right by the Lapa arches, Circo Voador hosts club nights during the week, but it's the varied live shows that really stand out, with a big stage set under a huge open-sided circular tent and room for up to 1,500 people to dance the night away. ⊠*Rua dos Arcos, Lapa, 20230-060* ☎*021/2533 0354* ⊕*www.circovoador.com.br.*

Estrela da Lapa. Open from 9 PM Tuesday to Saturday, Estrela da Lapa is one of the area's more upmarket nightspots, with a mixture of cutting-edge music and classic samba, and MPB. ⊠*Rua Mem de Sá 69, Lapa, 20230-150* ☎*021/2509–7602* ⊕*www.estreladalapa.com.br.*

> **THE ART OF BEER**
>
> Beer is always a good conversation topic with cariocas: who serves the best; how cold it should be; what's the tastiest salty snack to go with it. It's not uncommon for the barman to whisk your glass away before you're done. They would rather see a full, ice-cold glass on the table than dare to let one go warm. Also, don't be fooled by the "Best Chopp" placards on the walls, there aren't that many prizes each year.

★ **Rio Scenarium.** Rio Scenarium has become an absolute staple for those seeking out live samba in Rio, but despite the hordes of tourists it somehow manages to retain its authenticity and magic. This is due in part to its incredible setting in a former junk shop, still rammed to the rafters with old instruments, bikes, furniture, and puppets, but also the great bands and persevering locals who love to show off their moves and entice novices onto the dancefloor. Arrive early (before 9 PM) to avoid the queues at the weekends or call ahead and book a table. ⊠*Rua do Lavrádio 20, Lapa, 20230-070* ☎*021/3147–9005* ⊕*www.rioscenarium.com.br.*

LEBLON **Melt.** As with many clubs in Rio, don't expect things to get going until near midnight, when this New York–inspired spot starts to fill with a mix of tourists and well-heeled locals. ⊠*Rua Rita Ludolf 47, Leblon, 22440-060* ☎*021/2249 9309* ⊕*www.melt-rio.com.br.*

Plataforma. Very tourist-oriented, but if you're in Rio outside of Carnival season, then the shows at Plataforma give you a taste of the festival's costumes, music, and energy all year round. Capoeira displays complete an enjoyable if expensive look at some great Brazilian traditions. Reservations can be made on the Web site, and there's a restaurant, too. ⊠*Rua Adalberto Ferreira 32, Leblon, 22441-040* ☎*021/2274–4022* ⊕*www.plataforma.com.*

THE ARTS

Theater, classical music (*música erudita*), and opera may be largely the preserve of the affluent upper classes in Rio, but tickets remain reasonably priced by international standards and can be purchased easily from box offices. Although understanding Portuguese can of course prove difficult for some visitors, musicals provide a good opportunity to catch the glitzier side of Rio, and the international language of song and dance is considerably more comprehensible. Since many of the venues are in downtown or more out-of-the-way areas, be sure to get taxis to and from, as the surrounding streets can feel dangerously deserted by night.

Cinema also remains big business in Rio, and the film industry benefited from one of the country's most talked-about films of all time when *Tropa De Elite* (named after the "Elite Troop" police force that patrols the favelas) hit movie theaters in 2007. The annual Rio International Film Festival (⊕ *www.festivaldorio.com.br*) carries a huge buzz every September, when the city's numerous small, private cinemas are awash with avant-garde short films and homegrown acting and directing talent. Multiplexes showing mainstream films can be found in most big malls across the city, and new releases are usually in English with Portuguese subtitles.

Visual-art venues and museums are also very well endowed, with privately funded cultural centers hosting a rich variety of exhibitions, specific details of which are again best sought out in the Friday editions of the Rio press.

CLASSICAL MUSIC

Escola de Música da UFRJ. The music school auditorium, inspired by the Salle Gaveau in Paris, has 1,100 seats, and you can listen to chamber music, symphony orchestras, and opera, all free of charge. ⊠ *Rua do Passeio 98, Lapa, 20241 050* ☎ *021/2240–1391* ⊕ *www.musica. ufrj.br.*

Centro Cultural Municipal Parque Das Ruinas. With a glorious view of Guanabara Bay and downtown Rio, the beautiful Parque Das Ruinas, tucked away in Santa Teresa, was Rio's bohemian epicenter in the first half of the 20th century, and today holds occasional music and art events throughout the summer season. Be sure to check the press for details before going. ⊠ *Rua Murtinho Nobre 169, Santa Teresa, 20241050* ☎ *021/2252 1039.*

Instituto Moreira Salles. Surrounded by beautiful gardens, the institute creates the perfect atmosphere for classical music. Projeto Villa-Lobinhos, whose performances are dedicated to children, is one of their projects. Listen to musicians performing pieces from Bach, Chopin, Debussy, and other classical composers. ⊠ *Rua Marquês de São Vicente 476, Gávea, 22451-040* ☎ *021/3284–7400* ⊕ *www.ims.com.br.*

Sala Cecília Meireles. A popular concert venue for classical music in the city, the Sala hosts regular performances in a mid-sized hall. ⊠ *Largo da Lapa 47, Centro, 20021-170* ☎ *021/2224–4291* ⊕ *www.salaceciliameireles.com.br.*

CONCERT HALLS

Canecão is the traditional venue for the some of the bigger names on the national music scene, and an increasing number of international stars. It seats up to 5,000, but if you can, reserve a table up front. Upcoming events are advertised on a huge billboard outside the main entrance. ✉*Av. Venceslau Brás 215, Botafogo, 22290-140* ☎*021/2543–1241* ⊕*www.canecao.com.br.*

Citibank Hall. This huge venue in Via Parque Shopping in Barra Da Tijuca, Citibank Hall (formerly Claro Hall) has played host to the likes of Red Hot Chili Peppers, Pavaroti, and BB King. Check the Web site for upcoming events. ✉*Av. Ayrton Senna 3000, Barra da Tijuca, 22775-000* ☎*0300 789 6846* ⊕*www.citibankhall.com.br.*

SAMBA-SCHOOL SHOWS
Weekly public rehearsals (*ensaio*) attract crowds of samba enthusiasts and visitors alike to the *escolas de samba* (samba schools) from August through to Carnival (February or March). As the schools frantically ready themselves for the high point of the year, the atmosphere in these packed warehouses is often electric, and with Mangueira and Beija Flor, always sweaty. This may prove one of your liveliest and most chaotic nights on the town. Ticket prices range from R$10 to R$25.

Acadêmicos do Salgueiro. Rehearsals are only on Saturday at 10 PM. ✉*Rua Silva Teles 104, Andaraí, 20541-110* ☎*021/2288–3065* ⊕*www.salgueiro.com.br.*

Beija-Flor. The winning school in 2007, its rehearsals take place on Thursday at 9 PM. ✉*Pracinha Wallace Paes Leme 1025, Nilópolis, 26510-032* ☎*021/2791–2866* ⊕*www.beija-flor.com.br.*

Estação Primeira de Mangueira. One of the most popular schools and always a challenger for the Carnival title, rehearsals are Saturday at 10 PM. ✉*Rua Visconde de Niterói 1072Mangueira, 20943-001* ☎*021/3872–6787* ⊕*www.mangueira.com.br.*

FILM
Estação Ipanema. A charming movie theater in Ipanema with two auditoriums and a coffee shop in a lively area of small restaurants and bookstores, perfect for hanging out before or after the films. Part of the Estação chain of small art-house cinemas that can also be found on the Ipanema beachfront (Estação Laura Alvim), in Flamengo (Estação Paissandu), and in Botafogo (Estação Botafogo). All are well worth a trip on a rainy afternoon. ✉*Av. Visconde de Pirajá 605, Ipanema, 22410-002* ☎*021/2279–4603* ⊕*www.estacaovirtual.com.*

Odeon BR. The last remaining movie theater in historic Cinelândia is one of the most well-preserved and important in the country. The luxurious interior has hosted premieres, exhibits, and events since opening in 1926. ✉*Praça Mahatma Gandhi 2, Cinelândia, 20020-010* ☎*021/2240–1093* ⊕*www.estacaovirtual.com.*

UCI New York City Center. For the first and last word in big, American-style multiplex cinemas you need look no further than this homage to the U.S. in Barra da Tijuca, complete with a fake Statue of Liberty outside. No less than 18 screens can accommodate more than 4,500 cinema goers alongside all the associated amenities you would expect to go with that big blockbuster. ⊠*Av. cas Américas 5000, Barra da Tijuca, 22640-102* ☏*021/2432–4840* ⊕*www.ucicinemas.com.br.*

OPERA

Fodor's Choice
★
Theatro Municipal. Built in 1909, the stunning Municipal Theater at Cinelândia is the city's main performing arts venue, hosting dance, opera (often with international stars as guest artists), symphony concerts, and theater events for most of the year, although the season officially runs from March to December, so don't be surprised to find it closed in January and February and check the press for current events. The theater also has its own ballet company. ⊠*Praça Floriano, Centro, 20020-010* ☏*021/2262–3501 or 021/2299–1717* ⊕*www.theatromunicipal.rj.gov.br.*

THEATER

Fodor's Choice
★
Centro Cultural Banco do Brasil. Formerly the headquarters of the Banco do Brasil, in the late 1980s this opulent six-story domed building with marble floors was transformed into a space for plays, art exhibitions, and music recitals. Today the CCBB is one of the city's most important cultural centers, with a bookstore, three theaters, a video hall, four individual video booths, a movie theater, two auditoriums, a restaurant, a coffee shop, and a tearoom. The guided tours can be invaluable. It's open Tuesday–Sunday 10 AM to 9 PM ⊠*Rua 1° de Março 66, Centro, 20010-000* ☏*021/3808–2020* ⊕*www.bb.com.br/cultura.*

Teatro das Artes. The main theater in the unlikely setting of Gavea shopping mall is one of four in the complex that host some of the city's most popular productions. With one room for children-orientated shows and two smaller, more specialized theaters, there's likely to be something to keep you occupied here, so do check the Web site for information. ⊠*Rua Marques de Sa[t]o Vicente, Gavea, 22459-900* ☏*021/2294–1096* ⊕*www.shoppingdagavea.com.br/teatro.asp.*

Teatro João Caetano. The oldest theater in the city dates to 1813, and with 1,200 seats and a wide variety of inexpensive productions, the program here is worth a look if you don't mind the trip into slightly seedy part of town. ⊠*Praça Tiradentes, Centro, 20060-070* ☏*021/2221–0305.*

Teatro Villa-Lobos. This 463-seat theater has excellent drama productions and occasional dance performances close to Copacabana Beach. ⊠*Av. Princesa Isabel 440, Copacabana, 22011-010* ☏*021/2275–6695 or 021/2541–6799.*

SPORTS & THE OUTDOORS

Updated by
Doug Grey

After the success of the Pan American Games in 2007, Rio has started to think more seriously about staging world sporting events. A serious Olympic bid has been mounted for 2016, and the UEFA (Union of European Football Associations) has confirmed that Brazil will host the 2012 World Cup.

ON THE SIDELINES

HORSE RACING

★ **Jóquei Clube.** This beautiful old stadium manages to conjure a bygone sense of grandeur to even the smallest of race meetings with its impeccably preserved betting hall, 1920s grandstand, and views of the beach in the distance framed by Cristo Redentor and the Dois Irmaos mountain. When the big event of the year, the Grande Premio, comes around every August, expect the crowds to swell as the great and the good seize the opportunity to get dressed up to the nines. Entry is free, too, but you need to dress smart–casual, with no shorts or flip-flops allowed in the main stand. ⊠*Praça Santos Dumont 31, Gávea, 22470-060* ☎*021/3534–9000* ⊕*www.jcb.com.br.*

SOCCER

★ **Estádio Maracanã.** Nothing short of legendary, watching a game of soccer here is a must if the season (mid-January to November) is in swing. Undoubtedly as entertaining as the games are the obsessive supporters, devoted to their team colors but not afraid of trashing their own players, the opposition team, other fans, and of course the referee. Their huge flags and fireworks are always spectacular. Tickets are available in advance and often on the day from the stadium ticket office. The *branco* or white section of the *archibancado* or upper tier is the safest option for the neutral fan. Expect to pay around R$25 for a ticket in that section, and arrive in good time to grab the best seats and soak up the atmosphere. ⊠*Rua Prof. Eurico Rabelo, Maracanã, 20271-150* ☎*021/2568–9962* ⊕*www.suderj.rj.gov.br/visitacao_maracana.asp.*

PARTICIPATORY SPORTS

Rio is an incredibly active city, with people of all ages cycling, jogging, or walking along the beachfront paths, swimming across Ipanema to Leblon, and using municipal tennis courts and football pitches well into the early hours of the morning. Given the natural amenities the city is blessed with, an energetic visitor won't be at a loss for activities.

BOATING & SAILING

Dive Point. Schooner tours around the main beaches of Rio and as far afield as Buzios and Angra are offered here, as well as deep-sea and wreck diving. Be sure to ask if their prices include all the necessary equipment and training (if required). ⊠*Av. Ataulfo da Paiva 1174, basement, Leblon, 22440-035* ☎*021/2239–5105* ⊕*www.divepoint. com.br.*

Saveiro's Tour. Catch one of the daily cruises around Guanabara Bay— views of Sugar Loaf, Botafogo Bay, and the Rio-Niterói Bridge are the highlights. They also hire out speedboats and sailboats by the day. ⊠*Rua Conde de Lages 44, Glória, 20021-140* ☎*021/2225–6064* ⊕*www.saveiros.com.br.*

GOLF

Gávea Golf Club. This is the most upmarket club in town, and has fat greens fees (R$350) to prove it. However, you can get a discount if you're staying at the Copacabana Palace, InterContinental, or Sheraton hotels. It's an impeccable 18-hole course. ⊠*Estrada da Gávea 800, São Conrado, 22610-000* ☎*021/3322–4141* ⊕*www. gaveagolf.com.br.*

Golden Green Golf Club. It may only have six par-3 holes, but given the exclusivity and price of the alternatives this could be your best option in Rio. Clubs can be hired and the greens fees are around R$70. ⊠*Av. Canal de Marapendi 2901, Barra da Tijuca, 22631-050* ☎*021/2434–0429.*

CYCLE RIO

With 132.5 km of bike paths across the city, bikes are a great way to explore Rio. Although hotels can arrange rentals, it's just as easy to find stands along the beachfront avenues or the road ringing the Lagoa (particularly near Parque dos Patins to the western edge). Rates are about R$10 per hour. You're usually asked to show identification and give your hotel name and room number, but deposits are seldom required. (Note that helmets aren't usually available.) A great route runs along the beach from Leblon all the way to Parque do Flamengo.

HANG GLIDING

★ **Just Fly.** For R$200 Just Fly will collect you from your hotel, run you through the basics, and then run you off Pedra Bonita mountain into the sky high above Tijuca Forest. Excellent instructors can also film or photograph the experience for an extra charge. ☎*021/2268–0565 or 021/9985–7540* ⊕*www.justfly.com.br.*

Hilton Fly Rio Hang Gliding Center. DeHilton and his team have years of experience of flying over Tijuca Forest and landing on São Conrado beach. They can arrange pick-up and drop-off from your hotel; price US$125. ⊠*Rua Jose Higino 254, Tijuca, 20520 200* ☎*021/2278–3779 or 021/9964–2607* ⊕*www.hiltonflyrio.com.*

São Conrado Eco-Aventura. This is another reliable and experienced team that can offer you a bird's-eye view of Rio either by hang glider or paraglider. ☎*021/9966–7010* ⊕*www.guia4ventos.com.br.*

HIKING & CLIMBING

Given the changeable weather and the harsh terrain, guides are recommended for all major walks and climbs in Rio. Of particular note within the city itself are the hikes up Corcovado from Parque Lage and the trip through Tijuca Forest to Pico da Tijuca.

Centro Excursionista Brasileiro. You can research and register for all upcoming excursions on Centro Excursionista's Web site. They'll provide guides, maps, and all of the gear that you'll need. They lead treks throughout Rio State and as far as Minas Gerais. ⊠*Av. Almirante Barroso 2, Centro, 20031-000* ☎*021/2252–9844* ⊕*www.ceb.org.br.*

Rio Adventures. A one-stop shop for everything you need to scratch that adventurous itch, but be sure to book well in advance. Their trips run the gauntlet, from hiking and mountain climbing to caving, fishing, and rafting. ☎*021/2705–5747 or 021/8204–7559.*

Rio Hiking. Mother-and-son team Denise and Gabriel Werneck take you to their very favorite spots—hard to find gems that are well off the beaten-path. They also have nightlife tours of some of the best music and dance spots in town. ☎*21/2552–9204 or 21/9721–0594* ⊕*http://www.riohiking.com.br.*

Fodor'sChoice
★
Trilhas do Rio Ecoturismo & Aventura. These ecotourism specialists provide a wealth of options for every age bracket, including more unusual ideas such as horse treks and yoga trails, as well as climbing, mountain biking, and more. ⊠*Rua Francisca Sales 645, Jacarepaguá, 22760-000* ☎*021/2425–8441 or 021/2424–5455* ⊕*www.trilhasdorio.com.br.*

> ### RIO SURF BUS
>
> The Oi Surf Bus goes three times a day from Lago Do Machado to Prainha, which is considered to be the best surfing beach close to the city. The two-hour trip takes in the best surf breaks west of Rio, including all 12 km of Barra, Recreio, and Macumba. There's no snobbery if you don't have a board and you're just going along for the ride. Catch the bus from anywhere along Copacabana, Ipanema, or Leblon beachfront for an easy route to some stunning out-of-town beaches. Check outward and return times at ⊕*www. surfbus.com.br*, because you do not want to be left stranded.

KARTING

Kartodromo Premium. This is the biggest recreational karting track in Rio (1.6 km). They accept group parties, or if you're solo, you can enter in a cup against other members of the public. ⊠*Av Ayrton Senna 3010, Barra da Tijucá, 22775-000* ☎*021/2421–3535 or 021/9995–3535* ⊕*www.kartodromopremium.com.br* ☑*R$45 weekdays, R$49 weekends and holidays* ☉*Daily, 5 PM–midnight.*

SURFING

Surfing remains hugely popular in Rio, but kite surfing is growing rapidly, too, with several schools opening on Barra beachfront and out of town toward Cabo Frio.

Escola de Surf do Arpoador. The most consistent break in the city has its own surf school based on the beach; simply call up or stop by to book an early-morning appointment. ⊠*In front of posto 7, Arpoador beach, Arpoador* ☎*021/9131–2368* ⊕*www.surfboys.com.br.*

Kitepoint Rio. One of several companies based in huts along Avenida do Pepê near Posto 7 that will provide all the equipment and training you need to master the sport of kite surfing. Wind conditions have to be just right though, so patience is a virtue when seeking lessons. ⊠*Ave do Pepê, Kiosk No. 7, Barra* ☎*021/9200–0418.*

TENNIS

Parque do Flamengo. Municipal tennis courts are few and far between in Rio, so the two on Flamengo Beach are popular, but the system is informal and they cannot be booked. Both are in good condition though, so a half-hour wait is likely to be rewarded. ⊠*Parque Do Flamengo, Flamengo.*

SHOPPING

Updated by
Katja Hodge

Rio shopping is most famous for its incomparable beachwear and gemstone jewelry, both of which are exported globally. Brazil is one of the world's largest suppliers of colored gemstones, with deposits of aquamarines, amethysts, diamonds, emeralds, rubellites, topazes, and tourmalines. If you're planning to go to Minas Gerais, do your jewelry shopping there; otherwise stick with shops that have certificates of authenticity and quality. Other good local buys include leather goods (shoes in particular), art, coffee, local music, and summer clothing in natural fibers. With lots of low-quality merchandise around, the trick to successful shopping in Rio is knowing where to find high-quality stuff at reasonable prices.

Ipanema is Rio's most fashionable shopping district. Its many exclusive boutiques are in arcades, with the majority along Rua Visconde de Pirajá. Leblon's shops, scattered among cafés, restaurants, and newspaper kiosks, are found mainly along Rua Ataulfo da Paiva. Copacabana has souvenir shops, bookstores, and branches of some of Rio's better shops along Avenida Nossa Senhora de Copacabana and connecting streets. Walking each of the main shopping streets makes for a great way to explore the different neighborhoods.

CENTERS & MALLS

Although **Barra Shopping** (⊠*Av. das Américas 4666, Barra da Tijuca, 22640-102* ☎*021/4003-4131* ⊕*www.barrashopping.com.br*) is about 30 km (19 mi) from the city center, it's one of South America's largest malls. It has a medical center and a bowling alley as well as more than 600 shops. **Rio Sul** (⊠*Av. Lauro Müller 116, Botafogo, 22290-160* ☎*021/3527–7260* ⊕*www.riosul.com.br*) is one of the city's most popular retail complexes, with four movie screens and a giant food court. Domestic and international fashions are sold at **São Conrado Fashion Mall** (⊠*Estrada da Gávea 899, São Conrado, 22610-000* ☎*021/2111–4444* ⊕*www.scfashionmall.com.br*), Rio's least crowded and most sophisticated mall. It's for those who want to splurge, with shops selling high-end designers like Jean-Paul Gauthier, Blumarine, Prada Sport, Diesel, and Emporio Armani. You will also find a four-screen movie theater and a some very decent restaurants to eat at.

Shopping Leblon (⊠*Av. Afrânio de Melo Franco 290, Leblon, 22430-060* ☎*021/3138-8001* ⊕*www.shoppingleblon.com.br*) is Rio's newest mall. It's easily accessible on foot for those in Ipanema and Leblon, and has a good food court and four movie screens.

Shopping Center Cassino Atlântico (⊠*Av. Nossa Senhora de Copacabana 1417, Copacabana, 22070-012* ☎*021/2523–8709*), adjoining the Rio Palace hotel, is dominated by antiques shops, jewelry stores, art galleries, and souvenir outlets. At **Shopping Center da Gávea** (⊠ *Rua Marquês de São Vicente 52, Gávea, 22451-040* ☎ *021/2294–1096*) with several top art galleries—of which the best are Ana Maria Niemeyer, Borghese, and Toulouse—join a small but select mix of fashionable clothing and leather-goods stores. Four theaters show the best plays in town.

> ### BARGAINING IN RIO
>
> Bargaining in shops is unusual, but you can try your luck and ask if there's a discount for paying in cash, especially if it's a high-priced item. When granted, you can expect a 5% to 10% discount. Market or street-vendor shopping is a different story—bargain to your wallet's content.

DEPARTMENT STORE

Rio's largest chain department store, **Lojas Americanas** (⊠ *Rua do Passeio 42–56, Centro, 20021-290* ☎ *021/2524–0284* ⊕ *www.lojasamericanas.com.br* Ⓜ *Cinelândia* ⊠ *Rua Visconde de Pirajá 526, Ipanema, 22410-002* ☎ *021/2274–0590*) has casual clothing, toys, records, candy, cosmetics, and sporting goods.

MARKETS

In the evening and on weekends along the median of **Avenida Atlântica**, artisans spread out their wares. You can find paintings, carvings, handicrafts, sequined dresses, and hammocks from the northeast. **Babilônia Feira Hype** (⊠ *Jockey Club Brasileiro, Rua Jardim Botânico, Jardim Botânico, 22470-051* ☎ *021/2267–0066* ⊕ *www.babiloniahype.com.br*) takes place every other weekend (although occasionally they skip a weekend or two, call ahead to confirm) from 2 PM to 10 PM. This fair combines fashion, design, art, and gastronomy. It's good not only for shopping but for watching the beautiful people go by. Admission is R$5.

★ The **Feira Hippie** (⊠ *Praça General Osório, Ipanema, 22420-041* ⊕ *www.feirahippie.hpg.ig.com.br*) is a colorful handicrafts street fair held every Sunday 9–7. Shop for high-quality jewelry, hand-painted dresses, paintings, wood carvings, leather bags and sandals, rag dolls, knickknacks, furniture, and samba percussion instruments. The
★ crowded, lively Feira de São Cristovão, better known as the **Feira Nordestina** (*Northeastern Fair* ⊠ *Campo de São Cristóvão, São Cristóvão, 20921-440* ☎ *021/2580–0501 or 021/2580–5335* ⊕ *www.feiradesaocristovao.org.br*) is a social event for Brazilians from the northeast living in Rio. They gather to hear their own distinctive music, eat regional foods, and buy tools and cheap clothing. There's a lot of singing and dancing. If you can't get to that part of the country, come here for a unique day. Although it's best experienced on the weekend, it's open Tuesday–Thursday from 10 AM until 6 PM and from Friday at 10 AM until Sunday at 8 PM (continuously).

Open-air **Feira de Antiquários da Praça 15 de Novembro,** near the Praça 15 de Novembro, has china and silver sets, watches, Asian rugs, and chandeliers (Saturday 10–5, Sunday 9–5); the same fair goes to Praça Santos Dumont, in Jardim Botânico. Vendors at **Feira do Rio Antigo** (*Rio Antique Fair* ✉ *Rua do Lavradio, Centro, 20230-070* ☎ *021/2252–2669*) sell antiques, rare books, records, and all types of objets d'art on every first Saturday afternoon of the month. They move to the Casa Shopping Center in Barra da Tijuca on Sunday. A street fair, **Feirarte** (✉ *Praça do Lido, Copacabana, 22021-020*), similar to the Feira Hippie, takes place weekends 8–6. Cardeal Arcoverde is the closest metro station.

SPECIALTY SHOPS

ART

Contorno (✉ *Gávea Trade Center, Rua Marquês de São Vicente 124, Loja 102, Gávea, 22451-040* ☎ *021/2274–3832*) shows an eclectic selection of Brazilian art. **Gam, Arte e Molduras** (✉ *Rua Garcia D'Ávila 145, Ipanema, 22421-010* ☎ *021/2247–8060*) is good place to find modern and contemporary art and sculptures. They also have a large collection of photographs that can be made to size, and they will ship abroad.

A great way to explore Brazilian art is to make an appointment to visit an artist's atelier. A good choice is **Bia Vasconcellos** (✉ *Ipanema, 22411-001* ☎ *021/9116–3662*). Bia is an artist who works in many different mediums including tapestry, batik, etching, and hand-painted glass pieces. She also designs eyeglasses and jewelry. Check out her trademark puzzle rings.

BEACHWEAR

A bikini shop with many mall locations in addition to the Rio Sul branch, **Bum Bum** (✉ *Rua Visconde de Pirajá 351, Loja B, Ipanema, 22410-003* ☎ *3259–8630* ⊕ *www.bumbum.com.br* ✉ *Shopping Rio Sul, Rua Lauro Müller 116, Loja 401, Botafogo, 22290-160* ☎ *021/2542–9614* ✉ *Barra Shopping, Av. das Américas 4666, Loja 134B, Barra da Tijuca, 22331-004* ☎ *021/2431–8323*) opened in 1979, when the stylist Alcindo Silva Filho, known as Cidinho, decided to create the smallest (and by some accounts, the sexiest) bikinis in town. Two decades later Bum Bum remains a solid beachwear brand.

At **Lenny** (✉ *Fórum Ipanema, Rua Visconde de Pirajá 351, Loja 114, Ipanema, 22410-003* ☎ *021/2523-3796* ⊕ *www.lenny.com.br*) expect sophistication, comfortable sizes, and lots of fashionable beach accessories. Lenny is quite expensive, but the bikinis are particularly creative. If you want a better deal and you don't mind last season's bikinis, check out Lenny Off (✉ *Rua Carlos Góis 234, Loja H, Leblon, 22440-000* ☎ *021/2511–2739*). To find all you need to look great at the beach, visit **Garota de Ipanema Shop** (✉ *Rua Vinicius de Moraes 53, Ipanema, 22411-010* ☎ *021/2521–3168* ⊕ *www.garotadeipanemabrasil.com. br*). It sells great T-shirts and tanks, and has colorful beach bags. For funky T-shirts and great quality swimsuits, go to **Brazilian Soul** (✉ *Rua Prudente de Moraes 1102, Ipanema, 22420-042* ☎ *021/2522–3641*). It's a bit pricey, but the quality is hard to beat.

BEAUTY

O Boticario (✉*Rua Visconde de Pirajá 371, Ipanema,, 22410-003* ☎*021/2287–2944* ⊕*www.oboticario.com.br*) is Brazil's answer to Origins. It carries soaps, lotions, perfumes, shampoos, and cosmetics made from typical local plants and seeds. **Shampoo** (✉*Rua Visconde de Pirajá 581, Ipanema, 22410-003* ☎*021/2259–1699* ⊕*www.shampoo.com.br*) sells local and imported beauty products. Imported products are *very* expensive in Brazil, so if there's something that you need on your trip, stock up beforehand.

The drugstore **Farma Life** (✉*Av. Ataulfo de Paiva 644, Loja A, Leblon, 22440-030* ☎*021/2239–1178* ⊕*www.farmalife.com.br* ✉*Rua Visconde de Pirajá 559 Loja A, Ipanema, 22410-003*

> ### THE BRAZILIAN BIKINI
>
> Urban myth has it that Brazilian model Rose de Primo fashioned the Brazilian string bikini when she hurriedly sewed a bikini for a photo shoot with too little material. Whatever its history, the Tanga (string bikini) provides less than ½ the coverage of conventional bikinis, and makes the itsy bitsy teeny weeny yellow polkadot bikini look rather conservative. If you're looking to buy a Brazilian bikini, but are looking for a little more coverage, some stores have a *modelo exportação*, which is the design intended for export. Not all stores carry this model, but it's worth asking.

☎*021/2274–2017*) has a wide selection of beauty products. If after a day or shopping your feet are moaning, stop by **Spa do Pé** (✉*Av. Nossa Senhora de Copacabana 1052, Loja B, Copacabana, 22060-000* ☎*021/2523–8430* ⊕*www.spadope.com.br* Ⓜ*Siqueira Campos*) for a massage, manicure, or a foot treatment.

BOOKS

All you could need to entertain and guide yourself in Rio is inside **Livraria Letras & Expressõs** (✉*Rua Visconde de Pirajá 276, Ipanema,* ☎*021/2521–6110* ⊕*www.letraseexpressoes.com.br* ✉*Av. Ataulfo de Paiva 1292, Loja C, Leblon,* ☎*021/2511–5085*). Maps and magazines fill the store; the Ipanema location has a cozy coffee shop (with Internet access) on the second floor. **Argumento** (✉*Rua Dias Ferreira 417, Leblon22431-050* ☎*021/2239–5294* ⊕*www.livrariaargumento.com.br* ✉*Rua Barata Ribeiro 502, Loja A, Copacabana, 22051-000* ☎*021/2255—3783*) is an bookstore that carries a large selection of books in English for those who run out of reading material. There's also a CD section and a coffee shop at the back of the store. **Livraria Leonardo da Vinci** (✉*Av. Rio Branco 185, Centro, 20045-900* ☎*021/2533–2237* ⊕*www.leonardodavinci.com.br* Ⓜ*Carioca*), one of Rio's best bookstores for foreign-language titles, has a wide selection of books in English, Spanish, and French.

CACHAÇA

Academia da Cachaça (✉*Rua Conde Bernadote 26, Loja G, Leblon, 22430-200* ☎*021/2239–1542*) is not only *the* place in Rio to try caipirinhas—made with dozens kinds of tropical fruits—but is a temple of cachaça. The small bar with extraordinary appetizers from northeast Brazil sells 50 brands of cachaça by the glass or bottle. At **Garapa Doida**

1

(⊠*Rua Carlos Góis 234, Loja F, Leblon, 22440-040* ☏*021/2274–8186*) learn how to prepare a good caipirinha and to buy everything you need to make it, including glasses, straws, barrels to conserve the alcohol, and cachaça brands from all over the country.

Garrafeira (⊠*Rua Dias Ferreira 259, Loja A, Leblon, 22431-050* ☏*021/2512–3336*) is a charming liquor store that sells cachaça, originating from Minas. Thirty types of cachaça and imported olives, nuts, apricots, salmon, and more are sold at **Lidador** (⊠*Rua da Assembléia 65, Centro, 200-001* ☏*021/2533–4988* Ⓜ*Carioca* ⊠*Rua Barata Ribeiro 505, Copacabana, 22051-000* ☏*021/2549–0091* Ⓜ*Siqueira Campos* ⊠*Rua Vinicius de Morais 120, Ipanema, 22411-010* ☏*2227–0593*).

CLOTHING

Animale (⊠*Rua Joana Angelica 116, Ipanema, 22420-030* ☏*021/2227–3318* ⊕*www.animale.com.br*) sets the trend in women's fashion in Rio. Animale's clothing is original and uniquely Brazilian, ranging from Brazilian blue jeans to elaborate and sensual tops and jackets.

For fashion-forward designs, visit **Alessa** (⊠*Rua Nascimento Silva 399, Ipanema, 22421-020* ☏*021/2287—9939* ⊕*www.alessa.com.br*). Pay special attention to Alessa's fabulously fun underwear line, they make for great presents.

Fun colors and bold patterns make **Farm** (⊠*Rua Visconde de Pirajá 365, Ipanema, 22410-003* ☏*021/3813–3817* ⊕*www.farmrio.com.br* ⊠*Rio Design Leblon Av. Ataulfo de Paiva 270, Loja 313, Leblon, 22440-030* ☏*021/2540–0082*), a popular shop with cariocas. It's a great place to find feminine dresses and cute tops.

Osklen (⊠*Rua Maria Quitéria 85, Ipanema, 22410-040* ☏*021/2227–2911* ⊕*www.osklen.com.br* ⊠*São Conrado Fashion Mall, Estrada da Gávea 899, São Conrado, 22610-001* ☏*021/3322–0317* ⊠*Barra Shopping, Av. das Américas 4666, Barra da Tijuca, 22640-102* ☏*021/3089–1100* ⊕*www.barrashopping.com.br*) is a synonym for sporty casual clothing with a fashionable flair. The clothes—from trousers to coats to tennis shoes—are designed for outdoor use.

Richards (⊠*Rua Maria Quiteria 95, Ipanema, 22410-040* ☏*021/2522–1245* ⊕*www.richards.com.br*) has an English name, but it's actually one of the most traditional clothing stores in Brazil. Originally just for men, Richards now also carries women's clothing. It's the place to go to for good-quality linen clothing.

★ One of Rio's best kept secrets, **Parceria Carioca** (⊠*Forum de Ipanema Rua Visconde de Pirajá 351, Loja 215, Ipanema, 22410-003* ☏*021/2267–3222* ⊕*www.parceriacarioca.com.br* ⊠*Rua Jardim Botânico 728, Jardim Botânico, 22461-000* ☏*021/2259—1437*), carries clothes, beaded jewelry, accessories, shoes, and home decorations all designed and created by local artists from coops and NGOs. A great place to find gift ideas.

COFFEE

Armazém do Café (⊠ *Rua Visconde de Pirajá 547, Ipanema, 22410–003* ☎ *021/3874–2920* ⊠ *Rua Rita Ludolf 87, Loja B, Leblon, 22440-060* ☎ *021/3874–2609*) is a complete coffee shop with several brands of flavorful and high-quality *ouro negro* (black gold), as coffee was once called in the country because of its economic value. The shop also sells coffee machines. The supermarket **Pão de Açúcar** (⊠ *Av. Nossa Senhora Copacabana 493, Copacabana, 22020-002* ☎ *021/2548–5433* Ⓜ *Siqueira Campos*) is a good bet for coffee and is cheaper than buying it at a coffee shop. Open 24 hours, **Zona Sul** (⊠ *Prudente de Morais 49, Ipanema, 22420-041* ☎ *021/2267–0361*) has a wide selection of coffee and other goods at reasonable prices.

HANDICRAFTS

Fodor'sChoice Exhibiting Brazilian craftsmanship at its best, **O Sol** (⊠ *Rua Corcovado*
★   *213, Jardim Botânico* ☎ *021/2294–5149* ⊕ *www.artesanato-sol.com. br*) is a nonprofit, nongovernmental shop promoting and selling the handiwork of artisans from all regions of Brazil. It's one of the best handicraft stores you'll find in Rio and well deserving of a visit. Afterward, head down the street to De Graça, a restaurant with delicious food and a nice ambience. **Pé de Boi** (⊠ *Rua Ipiranga 55, Laranjeiras, 22231-120* ☎ *021/2285–4395* ⊕ *www.pedeboi.com.br*) is a popular art gallery featuring woodwork pieces, ceramics, weaving, and sculptures created by artists from around Brazil, with a special focus on the states of Pernambuco and Minas Gerais. Of good value are the beautiful ceramic bowls and vases. **Chamma da Amazônia** (⊠ *Rio Sul Shopping Center, Rua Lauro Müller 16, 2nd fl. kiosk, Botafogo, 22290-160* ☎ *021/2542–4866* ⊕ *www.chammadaamazonia.com.br*) has jewelry made from seeds from the Amazon and other parts of Brazil. The store also sells beauty products and fragrances made with uniquely Brazilian ingredients.

Many of the handicrafts found at **Feito à Mão** (⊠ *Rua vinícius de Moraes 98, Ipanema, 22411-010* ☎ *021/2247—5752* ⊕ *www.brasilfeitoamao. com.br*) are made with materials offered by the land, such as clay, wood, sand, stones, feathers, gourds. Though a little expensive, you'll find a bright collection of gourd dolls that are worth buying.

La Vereda (⊠ *Rua Almirante Alexandrino 428, Santa Teresa, 20241-260* ☎ *021/2507–0317* Ⓜ *Carioca*) is an art and souvenir store that sells beautiful local crafts, and you'll find items that you probably wouldn't find anywhere else in the city. From the metro station, you take the *bonde* (streetcar) to Santa Teresa, getting off at Largo dos Guimaraes.

JEWELRY

Amsterdam Sauer (⊠ *Rua Visconde de Pirajá 484, Ipanema, 22410-002* ☎ *021/2279–6237, 021/2512–1132 for the museum*), one of Rio's top names in jewelry, has top prices. Jules Roger Sauer, the founder of these stores, is known for his fascination with emeralds. The on-site gemstone museum is open weekdays 10–6 and Saturday 9–2 (tour reservations are a good idea). For beautiful yet affordable jewelry made with semiprecious stones, go to **Chloé Laclau** (⊠ *Rua Garcia d'Ávila*

THE 7 WONDERS OF RIO SHOPPING

■ **A Cowhide Carpet.** The real deal, straight from the hippie fair. (Welcome/bath mat approx. R$85, Carpet approx. R$425)

■ **A Chunky Bangle.** Our favorite is with the famous sidewalk pattern from Francesca Romana Diana. (Approx. R$225)

■ **Havaianas.** MG Bazar sells these so cheaply (R$12 and up) how can you not take home a bag full?

■ **A Gilson Martin Bag.** Whatever style or size you buy will undoubt-

edly be a cool souvenir or gift. (R$12 and up)

■ **Cachaça.** Impress your friends with a caipirinha while showing your vacation pictures. (R$10 and up)

■ **Brazilian Soccer Shirt.** One of the most sought-after gifts. You just can't leave Brazil without one. (Approx. R$35 and up)

■ **A Mini-Cristo.** Made by Sobral, this is a colorful miniversion of one of the world's new 7 wonders. (Approx. R$31).

149, Ipanema, 22421-010 ☎*021/2521–9545).* The necklaces are a particularly good value. **Francesca Romana Diana** (✉*Rua Visconde de Pirajá 547, Ipanema, 22410-900* ☎*021/2274–8511* ⊕*www.francescaromanadiana.com*) has lots of great gold and silver jewelry, and also works with semiprecious stones. Check out the great bangles featuring the famous Copacabana or Ipanema sidewalk pattern.

For chunky, colorful resin jewelry, accessories, and decorative items, visit **Sobral** (✉*Forum Ipanema, Rua Visconde de Pirajá 351, Loja 105, Ipanema22410-003* ☎*021/2267–0009* ⊕*www.rsobral.com.br*)

Hans Stern started his empire in 1945 with an initial investment of about $200. Today his interests include mining and production operations as well as 170 stores in Europe, the Americas, and the Middle East. His award-winning designers create truly distinctive contemporary pieces (the inventory runs to about 300,000 items). At the world headquarters of **H. Stern** (✉*Rua Visconde de Pirajá 490, Ipanema, 22410-002* ☎*021/2274-3447*), you can see exhibits of rare stones and watch craftspeople transform rough stones into sparkling jewels. There's also a museum you can tour that offers a pick-up and drop-off service.The shops downstairs sell more affordable pieces and folkloric items.

SHOES, BAGS & ACCESSORIES

Constança Basto (✉*Av. Afrânio de Melo Franco 290, Loja 311j, Leblon, 22430-060* ☎*021/2511–8801* ⊕*www.constancabasto.com*) has women's shoes made of crocodile and snake leather in original styles. Most pairs cost upward of R$200. **Via Mia** (✉*Rua Anibal de Mendonça 55, Ipanema, 22410-050* ☎*021/2274–9996* ⊕*www.viamia.com.br* ✉*Rio Design Leblon, Av. Ataulfo de Paiva 270, 3rd fl., Leblon, 22440-033* ☎*021/2529–6964*) has a large selection of shoes, bags, and accessories at affordable prices.

Mr. Cat (✉*Botafogo Praia Shopping, Praia de Botafogo 400, Botafogo* ☎*021/2552–5333* ⊕*www.mrcat.com.br* Ⓜ*Botafogo* ✉*Rua Vis-*

conde de Pirajá 414, Ipanema, 22410-003 ☏*021/2227–6521*) carries some of Rio's best handbags and leather shoes for men and women and has stores all over the city. Check the Web site for listings.

Victor Hugo (✉*Rio Sul, Av. Lauro Müller 116, Loja B19, Botafogo, 22290-070* ☏*021/2543–9290*), a Uruguayan who began making handbags when he came to Brazil in the 1970s, has become famous nationally for his quality leather handbags. The bags are similar in quality to more expensive brands like Louis Vuitton, Gucci, and Prada.

Fodor'sChoice
★ Known for its funky bags and accessories, **Gilson Martin's** (✉*Rua Visconde de Pirajá 462, Ipanema, 22410-002* ☏*021/2227–6178* ⊕*www. gilsonmartins.com.br* ✉*Rua Figueredo de Magalhães 304, Copacabana, 22031-010* ☏*021/3816–0552*)is the perfect place to buy fun, colorful Rio-inspired bags at great prices. Gilson Martin is regarded as one of Brazil's most gifted and acclaimed designers, and is quickly gaining international fame.

★ Simply put, **MG Bazar** (✉*Rua Figueiredo Magalhães 414, Copacabana, 22031-030* ☏*021/2548–1664*) is a Havaiana flip-flop-lovers heaven. This one store has all the colors, designs, and sizes you could possibly want.

MUSIC
Modern Sound (✉*Rua Barata Ribeiro 502 D, Copacabana, 22040-000* ☏*021/2548–5005* ⊕*www.modernsound.com.br* Ⓜ*Siqueira Campos*) was a traditional shop that turned into a self-designated megamusic store. Aside from the 50,000 CD titles—which include lots of rarities—the store carries music equipment and accessories and has a charming bistro, where live music, from jazz to bossa nova, is played by the finest carioca musicians. **Musical Carioca** (✉*Rua da Carioca 89, Centro, 20050-060* ☏*021/2524–6029 or 021/2524–6991* ⊕*www. musicalcarioca.com.br*) is a paradise for music lovers, and shares a street with many other music stores. Brazilian percussion instruments are sold here, too.

Fodor'sChoice
★ **Toca do Vinicius** (✉*Rua Vinicius de Moraes 129, Loja C, Ipanema, 22411-010* ☏*021/2247–5227*) bills itself as a "cultural space and bossa nova salon." The shop, though tiny, does indeed seem like a gathering place for bossa nova aficionados from around the world, and if you're one of them, there's a good chance you'll leave the shop with an e-mail address for at least one new pal. Amid the friendly atmosphere, you can find books on music (a few in English), sheet music, and T-shirts as well as CDs. With luck you might catch the one Sunday a month that the store showcases intimate concerts by some of the finest bossa nova musicians around.

SURF & RADICAL SPORTS GEAR
Centauro (✉*Shopping Leblon, Av. Afrânio de Melo Franco 290, Loja 106, Leblon, 22430-060* ☏*021/2512–1246* ⊕*www.centauro.com.br*) is a massive sports store with all possible sporting needs.

Galeria River (✉*Rua Francisco Otaviano 67, Copacabana, 22080-040* ☏*021/2267–1709* Ⓜ*Siqueira Campos*) is an arcade with various stores selling all the clothing and equipment needed for your surfing or sporting vacation. From the metro stop take the shuttle bus toward Praça General Osório, get off at last stop in Copacabana.

RIO DE JANEIRO ESSENTIALS

TRANSPORTATION

BY AIR

Nearly three dozen airlines regularly serve Rio, but most flights (from North America) stop first in São Paulo. Several of the international carriers also offer Rio–São Paulo flights.

AIRPORTS All international flights and most domestic flights arrive and depart from the Aeroporto Internacional Antônio Carlos Jobim, also known as Galeão (GIG). The airport is about 45 minutes northwest of the beach area and most of Rio's hotels. Aeroporto Santos Dumont (SDU), 20 minutes from the beaches and within walking distance of Centro, is served by the Rio–São Paulo air shuttle and a few air-taxi firms.

Airports Aeroporto Internacional Antônio Carlos Jobim (*Galeão, GIG* ☎*021/3398–4526*). **Aeroporto Santos Dumont** (*SDU* ☎*021/3814–7070*).

GROUND Special airport taxis have booths in the arrival areas of both airports. Fares to all parts of Rio are posted at the booths, and you pay in advance (about R$41–R$56). Also trustworthy are the white radio taxis parked in the same areas; these charge an average of 20% less. Three reliable special taxi firms are Transcoopass, Cootramo, and Coopertramo.

Buses run by Empresa Real park curbside outside customs at Galeão and outside the main door at Santos Dumont; for R$5 they make the hour-long trip from Galeão into the city, following the beachfront drives and stopping at all hotels along the way. If your hotel is inland, the driver will let you off at the nearest corner. Buses leave from the airport every half hour from 5:20 AM to 11 PM. Two of the taxi firms have vans at the international airport: Cootramo has a van (with 11 seats) to downtown for R$57 and to Copacabana for R$78. Coopertramo does the same for R$70 and R$80, but the van has a capacity to transport 15.

Contacts Coopertramo (☎*021/2560–2022*). **Cootramo** (☎*021/2560–5442, 021/3976–9944, or 021/3976–9945*). **Empresa Real** (☎*021/2560–7041 or 0800/24–0850*). **Transcoopass** (☎*021/2560–4888*).

BY BUS

ARRIVING & Regular service is available to and from Rio. Long-distance and inter-
DEPARTING national buses leave from the Rodoviária Novo Rio. Any local bus marked RODOVIÁRIA will take you to the station. You can buy tickets at the depot or, for some destinations, from travel agents. Buses also leave from the more conveniently located Menezes Cortes Terminal, near Praça 15 de Novembro. These buses travel to different neigh-

borhoods of Rio (Barra da Tijuca, Santa Cruz, Campo Grande, and Recreio) and to nearby cities Niterói, Petrópolis, and Nova Friburgo, among others.

Contacts **Rodoviária Novo Rio** (⊠ *Av. Francisco Bicalho 1, São Cristóvão* ☎ *021/2291–5151).* **Menezes Cortes Terminal** (⊠ *Rua São José 35, Centro* ☎ *021/2299–1380).*

GETTING AROUND Don't attempt to use the bus unless you know which line to take and you speak enough Portuguese to ask directions (drivers don't speak English). Never take the bus at night. Much has been made of the threat of being robbed on Rio's city buses, and many local residents no longer ride public buses. If you're going to use a public bus, don't wear expensive watches or jewelry, carry a camera or a map in hand, or talk loudly in English. It's also wise to avoid buses during rush hour.

That said, local buses are inexpensive (about R$1–R$2.50) and can take you anywhere you want to go. (Route maps aren't available, but the tourist office has lists of routes to the most popular sights.) You enter buses at the front, where you pay the attendant and pass through a turnstile, then exit at the rear. Have your fare in hand when you board to avoid flashing bills or wallets.

The upscale, privately run, and air-conditioned **Frescão** buses run between the beaches, downtown, and Rio's two airports. These vehicles, which look like highway buses, stop at regular bus stops but also may be flagged down wherever you see them. Minivans run back and forth along beachfront avenues. Fares start at about R$1.40.

BY CAR

ARRIVING & DEPARTING Arriving from São Paulo (429 km/266 mi on BR 116) or Brasília (1,150 km/714 mi on BR 040), you enter Rio via Avenida Brasil, which runs into Centro's beachside drive, the Avenida Infante Dom Henrique. This runs along Rio's Baía de Guanabara and passes through the Copacabana Tunnel to Copacabana Beach. The beachside Avenida Atlântica continues into Ipanema and Leblon along Avenidas Antônio Carlos Jobim (Ipanema) and Delfim Moreira (Leblon). From Galeão take the Airport Expressway (known as the Linha Vermelha, or Red Line) to the beach area. This expressway takes you through two tunnels and into Lagoa. Exit on Avenida Epitácio Pessoa, the winding street encircling the lagoon. To reach Copacabana, exit at Avenida Henrique Dodsworth (known as the Corte do Cantagalo). For Ipanema and Leblon there are several exits, beginning with Rua Maria Quitéria.

GETTING AROUND The carioca style of driving is passionate to the point of abandon: traffic jams are common, the streets aren't well marked, and red lights are often more decorative than functional. Although there are parking areas along the beachfront boulevards, finding a spot can still be a problem. If you do choose to drive, exercise extreme caution, wear seat belts at all times, and keep the doors locked.

There's a gas station on every main street in Rio: for example, on Avenida Atlântica in Copacabana, around the Lagoa Rodrigo de Freitas, and at Avenida Vieira Souto in Ipanema. International companies, such as Shell and Esso, are represented. The gas stations run by Brazilian oil company Petrobras are called BR. Ipiranga is another local option. Half the gas stations are open from 6 AM until 10 PM, and half are open 24 hours and have convenience stores. Gas stations don't have emergency service, so ask when you rent whether your car-rental insurance includes it.

Car rentals can be arranged through hotels or agencies and at this writing cost about R$110–R$250 a day for standard models. Major agencies include Avis, Hertz, and Unidas. Localiza is a local agency. Hertz and Unidas have desks at the international and domestic airports.

Turismo Clássico Travel, one of the country's most reliable travel and transport agencies, can arrange for a driver to get you around within the city, with or without an English-speaking guide (US$30 per hour). Classico's owners, Liliana and Vera, speak English, and each has 20 years of experience in organizing transportation. They also lead sightseeing tours.

Rental Agencies Avis (✉ *Av. Princesa Isabel 350, Copacabana* ☎ *021/2543–8579*). **Hertz** (✉ *Av. Princesa Isabel 334, Copacabana* ☎ *021/2275–7440 or 0800/701–7300* ✉ *Aeroporto Internacional Antônio Carlos Jobim* ☎ *021/3398–4339* ✉ *Aeroporto Santos Dumont* ☎ *021/2262–0612*). **Localiza Rent a Car** (✉ *Av. Princesa Isabel 214, Copacabana* ☎ *021/2275–3340* ✉ *Aeroporto Internacional Antônio Carlos Jobim* ☎ *021/3398–5445* ✉ *Aeroporto Santos Dumont* ☎ *021/2533–2677*). **Unidas** (☎ *021/4001–2222 for main reservations line* ✉ *Aeroporto Santos Dumont, Av. Senador Salgado Filho s/n, Centro* ☎ *021/2240–9181* ✉ *Av. Princesa Isabel 166, Copacabana* ☎ *021/3685–1212* ✉ *Aeroporto Internacional do Galeão, Estrada do Galeão s/n, Ilha do Governador* ☎ *021/3398–2286*).

Transport Agency Turismo Clássico Travel (✉ *Av. Nossa Senhora de Copacabana 1059, Sala 805, Copacabana* ☎ *021/2523–3390*).

BY SUBWAY

Rio's subway system, the metro, is clean, relatively safe, and efficient—a delight to use—but it's not comprehensive and has only two lines. It's a great option to get from Copacabana to Centro, but not to Ipanema or Leblon, since the southernmost metro stop (called Siqueira Campos) is in Copacabana. The metro shuttle can get you to and from Siqueira Campos to Ipanema. Reaching sights distant from metro stations can be a challenge, especially in summer when the infamous carioca traffic fans what is already 90-degree exasperation. Plan your tours accordingly; tourism offices and some metro stations have maps.

Trains run daily 5 AM–midnight Monday–Saturday, and 7 AM–11 PM Sunday and holidays. A single metro ticket at this writing costs R$2.25. Combination metro-bus tickets allow you to take special buses to and from the Siqueira Campos station: one runs to Leblon via Jardim Botânico and Jóckey; the other goes to Leblon by way of Túnel Velho, Copacabana, and Ipanema.

Contact Metrô Rio (☎ *021/3211–6300 information line* ⊕ *www.metrorio.com.br*).

BY TAXI

Taxis are plentiful in Rio, and in most parts of the city you can easily flag one down on the street.

Yellow taxis have meters that start at a set price and have two rates. The "1" rate applies to fares before 8 PM, and the "2" rate applies to fares after 8 PM, on Sunday, on holidays, throughout December, in the neighborhoods of São Conrado and Barra da Tijuca, and when climbing steep hills. Drivers are required to post a chart noting the current fares on the inside of the left rear window.

Radio taxis and several companies that routinely serve hotels (and whose drivers often speak English) are also options. They charge 30% more than other taxis but are reliable and usually air-conditioned. Other cabs working with the hotels also charge more, normally a fixed fee that you should agree on before you leave. Reliable radio-cab companies include Centro de Taxis, Coopacarioca, and Coopatur.

Most carioca cabbies are pleasant, but there are exceptions. Remain alert and trust your instincts. Unless you've negotiated a flat fee with the driver, be sure the meter is turned on. ■ TIP→ **Few cab drivers speak English; it's a good idea to have your destination written down to show the driver, in case there's a communication gap.**

Contacts **Centro de Taxis** (☎ *021/2195–1000*). **Coopacarioca** (☎ *021/2518–1818*). **Coopatur** (☎ *021/2573–1009*).

BY TRAIN

ARRIVING & DEPARTING   Intercity trains leave from the central station that starred in the Oscar-nominated movie of the same name, Estação Dom Pedro II Central do Brasil. Trains, including a daily overnight train to São Paulo, also leave from the Estação Leopoldina Barao de Maria, near Praça 15 de Novembro.

Contact **Estação Dom Pedro II Central do Brasil** (⊠ *Praça Cristiano Otoni on Av. President Vargas, Centro* ☎ *021/2588–9494*).

CONTACTS & RESOURCES

BANKS & EXCHANGE SERVICES

Generally, exchange rates are better in the city than at the airport, and cash gets better rates than traveler's checks. Most Brazilian banks don't exchange money. One that does is Banco do Brasil. The branch at Galeão offers good exchange rates, but it won't provide credit-card advances.

Casas de câmbio (exchange houses) are found all over the city, especially along the beaches and on Avenida Nossa Senhora de Copacabana and Rua Visconde de Pirajá in Ipanema. Many change money without charging a service fee. Sometimes, depending on the amount of money you wish to exchange, exchange houses have a better rate than the banks. American Express is another option.

1

Some hotels, such as the Caesar Park and the Copacabana Palace, offer competitive rates but charge a commission if you're not a guest. On weekends hotels may be your best bet, because few places are open. Or try the Banco 24 Horas automatic teller machines (ATMs) throughout town, which dispense reais.

Contacts **American Express** (✉ *Av. Atlântica 1702 B, Copacabana*). **Banco do Brasil** (✉ *Rua Bartolomeu Mitre 438 A, Leblon* ✉ *Rua Senador Dantas 105, Centro* ✉ *Aeroporto Internacional Antônio Carlos Jobim, 3rd fl.*). **Banco 24 Horas ATM** (✉ *Av. Nossa Senhora de Copacabana 202* ✉ *Av. Nossa Senhora de Copacabana 599* ✉ *Av. Nossa Senhora de Copacabana 1366* ✉ *Rua Visconde de Pirajá 174, Ipanema*). **Casa Universal** (✉ *Av. Nossa Senhora de Copacabana 371 E, Copacabana*).

EMERGENCIES & MEDICAL ASSISTANCE

The Tourism Police station is open 24 hours.

Contacts **Ambulance and Fire** (☎ *193*). **Police** (☎ *190*). **Tourism Police** (✉ *Rua Humberto de Campos 315, Leblon* ☎ *021/3399–7170*).

Medical Clinics **Cardio Plus** (✉ *Rua Visconde de Pirajá 330, Ipanema* ☎ *021/2521–4899*). **Copa D'Or** (✉ *Rua Figueiredo Magalhães 875, Copacabana* ☎ *021/2545–3600*). **Galdino Campos Cardio Copa Medical Clinic** (✉ *Av. Nossa Senhora de Copacabana 492, Copacabana* ☎ *021/2548–9966*). **Medtur** (✉ *Av. Nossa Senhora de Copacabana 647, Copacabana* ☎ *021/2235–3339*).

24-Hour Pharmacies **Drogaria Pacheco** (✉ *Av. Nossa Senhora de Copacabana 534, Copacabana* ☎ *021/2548–1525*). **Farmácia do Leme** (✉ *Av. Prado Júnior 237, Leme* ☎ *021/2275–3847*).

TOUR OPTIONS

CITY TOURS English-speaking guides at Gray Line are superb. In addition to a variety of city tours, the company also offers trips outside town, whether you'd like to go white-water rafting on the Rio Paraíbuna, tour a coffee plantation, or spend time in Petrópolis. Helicopter tours are also an option.

Private Tours take you around old Rio, the favelas, Corcovado, Floresta da Tijuca, Prainha, and Grumari in a jeep. Guides are available who speak English, Hungarian, French, and German. Hang glide or paraglide over Pedra da Gávea and Pedra Bonita under the supervision of São Conrado Eco-Aventura.

Carlos Roquette is a history teacher who runs Cultural Rio, an agency that hosts trips to 8,000 destinations. Most are historic sites. A guided visit costs around US$110 for four hours, depending on the size of the group. Favela Tour offers a fascinating half-day tour of two favelas. For anyone with an interest in Brazil beyond the beaches, such tours are highly recommended. The company's English-speaking guides can also be contracted for other outings.

Rio Hiking takes small groups on nightlife tours to clubs and bars beyond the regular tourist circuit.

Contacts **Cultural Rio** (☎ *021/9911–3829* ⊕ *www.culturalrio.com.br*). **Favela Tour** (☎ *021/3322-2727* ⊕ *www.favelatour.com.br*). **Gray Line** (☎ *021/2512-9919*).

Private Tours (🏢 *021/2232-9710* ⊕ *www.privatetours.com.br*). **Rio Hiking** (🏢 *021/2552-9204 or 021/9721-0594* ⊕ *www.riohiking.com.br*).

ECOLOGY & THE OUTDOORS You can ride around the Floresta da Tijuca and Corcovado or take a tour to Angra dos Reis and Teresópolis in renovated World War II jeeps (1942 Dodge Commanders, Willys F-75s, and others) with the well-organized Ecology and Culture Jeep Tours. Guides speak English, French, German, and Spanish. The company also has a range of ecological tours, including some on horseback.

Trilhas do Rio organizes frequent outdoor trips so you can get to know the Floresta da Tijuca and other ecological treasures in and around Rio. Rio Hiking tours combine city sightseeing with nature hikes to the Floresta da Tijuca and other areas, plus overnight trips to Paraty and Ilha Grande.

Contacts Ecology and Culture Jeep Tours (🏢 *021/2108-5800* ⊕ *www.jeeptour. com.br*). **Rio Hiking** (🏢 *021/2552-9204 or 021/9721-0594* ⊕ *www.riohiking.com. br*). **Trilhas do Rio** (🏢 *021/2425-8441 or 021/2424-5455* ⊕ *www.trilhasdorio. com.br*).

HELICOPTER TOURS Helisight gives a number of helicopter tours whose flights may pass over the *Cristo Redentor,* Copacabana, Ipanema, and/or Maracanã stadium. There are night flights as well; reserve ahead for these daily 9–6.

Contacts Helisight (✉ *Conde de Bernadote 26, Leblon* 🏢 *021/2511-2141, 021/2542-7895, or 021/2259-6995* ⊕ *www.helisight.com.br*).

VISITOR INFORMATION

The Rio de Janeiro city tourism department, Riotur, has an information booth that is open 8–5 daily. There are also city tourism desks at the airports and the Novo Rio bus terminal. The Rio de Janeiro state tourism board, Turisrio, is open weekdays 9–6. You can also try contacting Brazil's national tourism board, Embratur.

Contacts Embratur (✉ *Rua Uruguaiana 174, Centro* 🏢 *021/2509-6292* ⊕ *www. embratur.gov.br*). **Riotur** (✉ *Rua da Assembléia 10, near Praça 15 de Novembro, Centro* 🏢 *021/2217-7575 or 0800/707-1808* ⊕ *www.rio.rj.gov.br/riotur*). **Riotur information booth** (✉ *Av. Princesa Isabel 183, Copacabana* 🏢 *021/2541-7522*). **Turisrio** (✉ *Rua da Ajuda 5, Centro* 🏢 *021/2215-0011* ⊕ *www.turisrio.rj.gov.br*).

Side Trips from Rio

WORD OF MOUTH

"The beaches in Búzios were great. Make sure you absolutely visit Geriba (long and wide and beautiful) and Tarraturaga (calm with beautiful water). All beaches have kiosks or more formal restaurants for food. There are also boat and schooner tours available, scuba, snorkeling and other activities. Rio and Búzios are great combinations. Have fun, bring lots of sunblock."

—tengohambre

ORIENTATION & PLANNING

ORIENTATION

By Alastair
Thompson

The state of Rio de Janeiro is relatively small, yet offers a broad range of distinctly Brazilian attractions, most within three hours of the city. It's worth staying at least two nights in either Búzios or Paraty to unwind after the frenetic pace of Rio. Nature lovers should reserve at least two days for Ilha Grande. While the beaches along the Blue and Green coasts are famous for their beauty, the interior offers mountainous terrain and fabulous hiking.

THE BLUE COAST

The Blue Coast starts just across Guanabara Bay in Niterói, whose ancient forts stand in stark contrast to its ultramodern Museu de Arte Contemporânea. Farther east is Cabo Frio, one of the country's oldest settlements. Nearby Búzios, with its 23 beaches, temperate climate, and vibrant nightlife, is a popular destination for people from around the world.

NORTH OF RIO DE JANEIRO

Northeast of Rio de Janeiro lies Petrópolis, whose opulent imperial palace was once the summer home of the emperor. A twisting road through the mountains takes you to Teresópolis, named after Empress Teresa Christina. Nestled between these two towns is Parque Nacional da Serra dos Órgãos, famous for its strange rock formations.

THE GREEN COAST

West of Rio de Janeiro, Angra dos Reis is the jumping-off point for 365 islands that pepper a picturesque bay. The largest, Ilha Grande, is a short ferry ride from Angra dos Reis and is still somewhat unspoiled. Paraty, a UNESCO world heritage site, is a well-preserved imperial town. Its 18th-century Portuguese architecture and secluded beaches make it the highlight of the region.

PLANNING

WHEN TO GO

The towns along the Blue and Green coasts are packed solid between Christmas and Carnival, so reservations should be made well in advance. The populations of party towns like Paraty and Búzios can more than double as young people arrive from nearby Rio de Janeiro and São Paulo on the weekend.

The weather along the coast is fairly predictable: summers are hot. During low season, from March to October, the weather is mild and the beaches are practically deserted. To top it off, prices can be half of what they are in high season. In the interior, Petrópolis, Teresópolis, and Novo Friburgo offer a refreshing change from the oppressive heat of the coast. Prices are reasonable even during high season.

TOP REASONS TO GO

■ Hanging out with the young and beautiful on the beach at Búzios in the morning, then enjoying the sunset on Orla Bardot.

■ Sailing a schooner to a desert island for some scuba diving, then watching the dolphins play in your wake on the way home.

■ Getting lost in time at the Imperial Museum in mountainous Petrópolis.

■ Taking an early-morning hike through the Atlantic rain forests of Ilha Grande.

■ Washing down the fresh shrimp with caipirinhas at the kiosks on the beach in Cabo Frio.

ABOUT THE RESTAURANTS & CUISINE

The food here is nothing if not eclectic. Coastal towns serve a large selection of fresh seafood, and most have a local specialty that's worth trying. Beachfront restaurants, especially the ubiquitous *baracas* (kiosks), can be a pleasant surprise. Paraty and Búzios have an excellent range of international restaurants. During high season they fill up beginning at 10 PM and may not close until after sunrise. Restaurants in Petrópolis, Teresópolis, and Novo Friburgo serve European cuisine and *comida mineira,* the hearty fare from Minas Gerais. Dinner starts at seven and restaurants generally close around midnight.

■TIP→ To be on the safe side, don't buy seafood from venders strolling along the beach. Be especially careful about the oysters in Búzios and Cabo Frio, which may not be as fresh as the vendor claims.

WHAT IT COSTS IN REAIS				
	¢	$	$$	$$$	$$$$
AT DINNER	under R$15	R$15–R$30	R$30–R$45	R$45–R$60	over R$60

Prices are per person for a main course at dinner or for a prix-fixe meal.

ABOUT THE HOTELS

There are plenty of hotels for all budgets and all tastes, from oceanfront pousadas lining the beaches along the Blue and Green coasts that offer simple rooms with barely more than a bed and a ceiling fan to boutique hotels with luxurious amenities. Many even have nice touches like on-site spas. Paraty and Petrópolis have some gorgeous 18th-century inns, some of which can be a bit drafty.

■TIP→ The staff at the region's smaller hotels speak very little English, so bring along a phrase book. It also helps to arrange as much as your trip as possible while you're still in Rio de Janeiro.

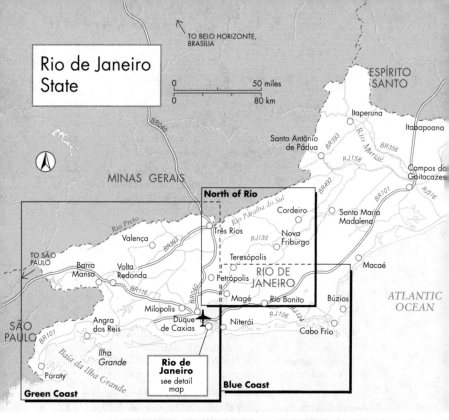

	WHAT IT COSTS IN REAIS				
	¢	$	$$	$$$	$$$$
FOR 2 PEOPLE	under R$125	R$125–R$250	R$250–R$375	R$375–R$500	over R$500

Prices are for a standard double room in high season, excluding tax.

GETTING AROUND

While most resort towns boast an airport of some kind, the state of Rio is small enough that few people fly to destinations within the state. The roads along the Blue and Green coasts and to the resort towns in the mountains tend to be well maintained, so most Brazilians travel by car or bus.

Driving within the city of Rio can be a daunting experience even for the most hardened of city motorists, but once out of the city it's fairly easy to get around. The roads, especially to the major tourist destinations, are well signposted. To get to Ilha Grande you'll need to leave your car in Angra dos Reis and catch a two-hour passenger ferry to the island.

■ TIP➜ Car rental in resort towns can be extortionate, so rent in Rio if you plan to rent a car.

A Bit of History

The history of the state of Rio de Janeiro is as colorful as it is bloody. The first Portuguese trading post was established in 1502 in Cabo Frio to facilitate the export of Pau-Brasil (Brazil Wood). This led to confrontations with Tamoios Indians and their French allies.

The discovery of gold in the state of Minas Gerais in 1696 and the construction of the "Caminho de Ouro" (Path of Gold) from the mines to Paraty bought prosperity. In its wake came pirates and corsairs who used the islands and bays of Angra dos Reis as cover while they plundered the ships bound for Rio de Janeiro.

The mines gave out in the late 1700s, but the relatively new crop called coffee, introduced to the state around 1770, brought another boom. In the mid-19th century the state produced more than 70% of Brazil's coffee. Sadly, vast tracks of Atlantic rain forest were destroyed to make room for the crop across the interior of the state.

In 1808, threatened by Napoléon, King Dom Joáo VI of Portugal moved his court to Rio. He returned to Portugal in 1821 and left his son, Dom Pedro I, behind as prince regent. The following year Dom Pedro I was called back to Portugal, but refused to leave. Instead, he declared Brazil an independent state and himself its emperor. In 1847, his son, Dom Pedro II, inaugurated Petrópolis as the summer capital of Brazil.

Buses are cheap, comfortable, and efficient, but the terminal in Rio can be intimidating, and be sure to travel light. If you feel like splurging, join the rich and famous and charter a helicopter from Rio to Búzios. TEAM offers fixed-wing charters to Búzios, but you need enough people to fill up the flight, and, with wait times and transfers, it's almost quicker by car.

⚠ Avoid leaving the city on a Friday afternoon, when residents flee the city en mass and the traffic is horrific.

THE BLUE COAST

Also known as the Costa do Sol, this stretch of coastline is where you'll find the resort towns of Cabo Frio, Arrial do Cabo, and Búzios. The most popular of the three is Búzios, reminiscent of the French Riviera gone tropical. On its 8-km (5-mi) peninsula are 23 different beaches. Cabo Frio is a family resort famous for its bikini shops and blue water. Arrial do Cabo, sticking out into the Atlantic Ocean, still retains the rustic charms of a fishing village. The wind blows year-round, and sports such as windsurfing, kite surfing, and sailing are common.

■TIP→Currency exchange rates outside of the city of Rio can be exorbitant. Use credit cards where you can because the rates, even with the charges, will be better than those at hotels and exchange buros.

NITERÓI

14 km (9 mi) east of Rio.

Cariocas joke that the best thing about Niterói is the view—on a clear day you can see Rio de Janeiro with the Corcovado and Sugarloaf across the bay. But Niterói has the last laugh, as the city is ranked as having the highest quality of life in the state.

Catch a ferry from Rio's Praça 15 de Novembro and cross the bay in 20 minutes. From the Praça Araribóia or at the Terminal Hidroviário de Charitas, walk along the esplanade to the Forte de Gragoatá and then walk to Museu de Arte Contemporânea where the view is far more impressive than the art. Icaraí beach is a smaller, less touristy version of Copacabana. If you have time, enjoy a beer on the beach and watch the sunset over Rio and the Corcovado. Don't plan to spend more than one afternoon in Niterói. Instead head up the Blue Coast to Búzios or Cabo Frio.

> **KNOCK ON WOOD**
>
> The name of the country is said to have come from the Portuguese word *braza*, meaning ember, after the deep red hue of the trees along the coast of Cabo Frio. Pau-Brasil, which had been previously used to describe a different type of tree found in Asia, soon became synonymous with these unique trees. They became such an important part of the economy of the fledgling country that it became known as Brazil.

TO & FROM

The best way to get to Niterói is by passenger ferry from the Praça 15 de Novembro in Rio de Janeiro. The trip takes about 20 minutes. Barcas S/A boats (R$2) are bigger and slower than the newer Catamaran Jumbo Cat fleet (R$4). Don't travel here by car, unless you have somebody doing the driving. The roads in Niterói are even more confusing than in Rio. To get to Niterói by bus, catch Bus 610 at the Terminal Menezes Cortes.

ESSENTIALS

Airport Niterói is close enough to Rio that it uses both Santos Dumont and Galeão in Rio. Both are about 40 minutes from downtown Niterói. ⚠ **Budget plenty of time, because during rush hour it can sometimes more than two hours to get to either airport.**

Banks & Currency Exchange Banco 24 Horas ATMs (⊠ *Rua Miguel de Frias 180, Icaraí, 24220-003 Niterói*).

Boat Contacts Barcas S/A (⊠ *Praça Araribóia 6-8, 24020-030* ☎ *021/4004–3113* ⊕ *www.barcas-sa.com.br*).

Emergencies & Medical Assistance Hospital Universitário Antônio Pedro (⊠ *Rua Marquês do Paraná 303, Centro, 24033-900* ☎ *021/2620–2828*).

Taxi Rádio Táxi Niterói (☎ *021/2610–0609* ⊕ *www.radiotaxiniteroi.com.br*).

Visitor & Tour Info Niterói Tourism Office (⊠ *Estrada Leopoldo Fróes 773, São Francisco, 24360-005* ☎ *0800/282–7755* ⊕ *www.neltur.com.br*) is open daily 9 to 6.

The Blue Coast

ATLANTIC OCEAN

SAFETY & PRECAUTIONS

Niterói is much safer than Rio de Janeiro, but take the same precautions you would in the city. Keep your valuables out of site and don't stray down any deserted streets or wander by yourself at night.

WHAT TO SEE

Built in 1555, the impressive **Fortaleza de Santa Cruz** was the first fort on Guanabara Bay. The cannons are distributed over two levels, but more impressive are the 17th-century sun clock and Santa Barbara Chapel. It's best to visit in the cool morning hours. It's a 15-minute taxi ride from downtown Niterói (around R$30). ⊠ *Estrada General Eurico Gaspar Dutra, Jurujuba, 24370-375* ☎ *021/2711–0462* ≦ *R$4* ⊙ *Tues.–Sun. 9–5.*

Designed by Oscar Niemeyer, the **Museu de Arte Contemporânea** looks a bit like a spaceship. The modern art collection itself is underwhelming; the exterior is the reason to visit. The museum is five minutes from Praça Araribóia in downtown Niterói. ⊠ *Mirante de Boa Viagem, Boa Viagem, 24210-390* ☎ *021/2620–2400* ⊕ *www.macNiteroi.com. br* ≦ *R$4, free Wed.* ⊙ *Tues.–Thurs. 10–6, Fri.–Sun. 10–7.*

Every Sunday a two-hour-long **tourist ferry** (☎ *021/4004–3113*) departs from Praça Araribóia in Niterói at 9 AM, and then Praça 15 de Novembro in Rio at 10 AM, and circles Guanabara Bay. Along the way it passes the Botafogo Inlet, Niterói beaches, Charitas, Icaraí, and the Rio-Niterói bridge. The trip is R$12.

CABO FRIO

155 km (101 mi) east of Rio.

One of the oldest settlements in Brazil, Cabo Frio was established in the early 1500s as a port from which wood was shipped to Portugal. Today it's best known for its lovely seaside setting. Renowned for fresh seafood, Cabo Frio is a popular weekend getaway for residents of Rio de Janeiro. It's also a favorite destination for watersports enthusiasts. Don't miss the chance to go diving in Arrial do Cabo, which has some of the clearest water in Brazil.

> ### THE LOWDOWN ON FERRIES
>
> **Telebarcas** (☎ *021/4004–3113* ⊕ *www.barcas-sa.com.br*) has information on all ferries within the state of Rio. You can call seven days a week between 6 AM and midnight, or log onto the Web site. The site is easy to navigate, but not every page has an English translation.

Cabo Frio hotels are not as nice as those in nearby Búzios, so you're better off staying in Búzios and taking a day trip to Cabo Frio.

TO & FROM

From Rio de Janeiro, drive across the Rio-Niterói bridge and bear left, following the BR 101. At Rio Bonito take the exit to the Region dos Lagos and follow the signs to Cabo Frio. The trip takes approximately two hours.

Cabo Frio-bound Auto Viação 1001 buses leave the Rodoviária every half hour. The trip takes 2 hours and 40 minutes and costs R$21.60. Probably the easiest way to get to Cabo Frio is to arrange for a shuttle to pick you up from your hotel. Rio's Tourismo Clássico shuttles cost R$70.

ESSENTIALS

Airport Aeroporto Internacional de Cabo Frio (⊠ *Estrada Velha de Arraial do Cabo, 28901-970 Cabo Frio* ☎ *22/2647–9513* ⊕ *www.aeroportocabofrio. com.br*).

Banks & Currency Exchange Banco 24 Horas ATMs (⊠ *Rua Itajuru, 28905-060Cabo Frio*).

Bus Contacts Auto Viação 1001 (☎ *021/4004–5001* ⊕ *www.autoviacao1001. com.br*). **Turismo Clássico** (☎ *21/2523–3390*). **Terminal Rodoviário Cabo Frio** (⊠ *Av. Julia Kubitschek, 28905-000*).

Emergencies & Medical Assistance Hospital Municipal São José Operário (⊠ *Rua Governador Valadares 22, São Cristóvão, 28909-010* ☎ *022/2643-2732*).

Taxi Associação dos Taxistas de Cabo Frio (☎ *22/9967–6951* ⊕ *www.cabofri otaxi.com.br*).

Visitor & Tour Info Cabo Frio Tourism Office (✉ *Av. de Contorno, Praia do Forte, 28906-030 Cabo Frio* ☎ *22/2647–1689* ⊕ *www.cabofrioturismo.rj.gov.br*) is open daily 8–7. **Tridente Dive Center** (✉ *Praça da Bandeira 362, Bairro da Passagem, 28906-320* ☎ *22/2645–1705* ⊕ *www.tridente.tur.br*), open daily 9 to 6, is a full-service dive center that offers trips around the area. Ask for Frederico, who speaks fluent English.

SAFETY & PRECAUTIONS

The biggest problem for travelers is petty theft. Don't leave valuables in your rental car, and keep large amounts of cash in your hotel.

BATHING BEAUTIES

No visit to Cabo Frio is complete without a visit to the bikini shops along Rua das Biquínis. Rumor has it that everything began with a local woman selling her home-made bathing suits on the street. Today more than 70 stores—the largest collection of bikini stores in Latin America, according to the Guinness Book of Records—sell all manner of beach fashion. In summer shops close at around midnight.

WHAT TO SEE

Praia do Forte is popular thanks to its calm, clear waters and long stretch of sand. On weekends it's jammed with colorful beach umbrellas, swimmers, sun lovers, and food kiosks that extend their services to tables at the sand. Be prepared to deal with all kinds of vendors on the sand, some obnoxiously insistent, some selling unique souvenirs.

Some distance away, **Praia Brava and Praia do Foguete** lure surfers to their crashing waves.

Just 10 km (6 mi) south of Cabo Frio is cozy **Arraial do Cabo,** with transparent beaches and the Gruta Azul—a 15-meter-tall cave over the blue sea—and Pontal do Atalaia, an extraordinary viewing point.

WHERE TO STAY

$ 🖼 **Hotel Joalpa.** Three blocks from Praia do Forte, but in front of not-as-crowded Praia das Dunas, Joalpa has rooms that can accommodate five people. **Pros:** Close to the beach, wireless connection. **Cons:** Uninspiring rooms, advance payment required in high season. ✉ *Rua dos Cravos 2, Balneário das Dunas, 28908-280* ☎ *022/2645–4848* ⊕ *www.joalpa.com.br* ⇨ *68 rooms* ⌂ *In-room: refrigerator. In-hotel: restaurant, room service, pool, laundry service, public Wi-Fi* ⊟ *AE, DC, MC, V* ⦿ *BP.*

$ 🖼 **Malibu Palace Hotel.** Probably the most convenient option in Cabo Frio, the Malibu Palace has the advantage of being across the avenue from Praia do Forte and just blocks away from the shops and restaurants of the center. The hotel also provides umbrellas on the beach. **Pros:** Rooms have great views, great breakfast. **Cons:** Can be noisy at night, beach is across the street, showing signs of wear and tear. ✉ *Av. do Contorno 900, at Praia do Forte, 28907-250* ☎ *022/2647–8000* ⊕ *www.malibupalace.com.br* ⇨ *102 rooms, 18 suites* ⌂ *In-room: safe, refrigerator. In-hotel: restaurant, room service, pools, gym, beachfront, laundry service, no-smoking rooms, public Wi-Fi* ⊟ *AE, DC, MC, V* ⦿ *MAP.*

BÚZIOS

24 km (15 mi) northeast of Cabo Frio; 176 km (126 mi) northeast of Rio.

Fodor's Choice
★
Little more than two hours from Rio de Janeiro, Búzios is a string of beautiful beaches on an 8-km-long (5-mi-long) peninsula. It was a fishing village until the 1960s, when Brigitte Bardot holidayed here to escape the paparazzi.

Búzios has something for everyone. Some hotels cater specifically to families and offer plenty of activities and around-the-clock childcare. Many offer spa facilities, and some specialize in weeklong retreats. For outdoor enthusiasts, Búzios offers surfing, windsurfing, kite surfing, diving, hiking, and mountain biking.

> ### BRIGITTE & BÚZIOS
>
> A walk along the Orla Bardot will bring you to the bronze statue of a seated woman looking out over the cobalt-blue waters. This is the statue of Brigitte Bardot, who put the city on the map when she came here on holiday. Bardot, constantly hounded by the press, said Búzios was the one place where she was able to relax. She stayed in Búzios until photographer Denis Albanèse's candid shots allowed the international press to discover her, and, in turn, Búzios.

TO & FROM

From Rio de Janeiro, drive across the Rio-Niterói bridge and bear left, following the BR 101. At Rio Bonito take the exit to the Region dos Lagos. At São Pedro de Aldeia, turn left at the sign for Búzios. The trip takes approximately two hours.

Cabo Frio-bound Auto Viação 1001 buses leave from Rio every half hour. The trip takes 2 hours and 40 minutes and costs R$21.60. Probably the easiest way to get to Cabo Frio is to arrange for a shuttle to pick you up from your hotel.

TEAM has weekend charter flights that depart when there are enough passengers. A round-trip ticket is R$575.

ESSENTIALS

Airline TEAM Transportes Aéreos (☎ *021/3328–1616* ⊕ *www.voeteam.com.br*)

Airport Aeroporto Umberto Modiano (✉ *Av. José Bento Ribeiro Dantas s/n, 28950-000* ☎ *22/2629–1225*).

Banks & Currency Exchange Banco 24 Horas ATMs (✉ *Praça Santos Dumont, Centro, 28950-000*). **Currency Exchange Malizia Tour** (✉ *Avenida José Bento R. Dantes 100, 28950-000* ☎ *022/2623–1226*) operates all the currency exchange offices. The rates aren't so good, so change your cash in Rio.

Bus Contacts Auto Viação 1001 (☎ *021/4004–5001* ⊕ *www.autoviacao1001. com.br*).

Emergencies & Medical Assistance Clínica Búzios (✉ *Estrada J. B. Ribeiro Dantas 3000, Manguinhos, 28950-000* ☎ *22/2623–2465*).

Taxi Búzios Radio Taxi (☎ *22/2623–2509*).

☾ Visitor & Tour Info **Búzios Tourism Office** (✉ *Avenida J.B. Ribeiro Dante s/n, Porceco, 28950-000* ☎ *022/2633-6200* ⊕ *www.buziosonline.com.br*) is open daily 8 to noon. **Tour Shop** (✉ *Orla Bardot 550, Centro, 28950-000* ☎ *22/2623-4733 or 022/2623-0292* ⊕ *www.tourshop.com.br*), the largest tour operator in Búzios, offers different types of tours. It also has a number of activities geared to children.

SAFETY & PRECAUTIONS

A few simple rules: don't eat fresh oysters sold anywhere but in a restaurant, and make sure the drinks you buy from street vendors are made with commercial ice. (The easiest way to check is to look for a circular hole through the middle.)

Avoid visiting Praia da Foca in the late afternoon and evening. Don't go alone during the day, as there have been muggings on the beach.

WHAT TO SEE

Búzios boasts 23 beautiful beaches.

☾ **Praia Azeda** and **Praia Azedinha** both have clear, calm waters and are accessible via a trail from Praia dos Ossos, or by boat. It's one of the few places you may find topless bathing. **Praia da Ferradura,** with its calm water and casual bars, captures the spirit of Búzios. It's a great beach for families with young children. **Praia de Geribá** is a half moon of white sand that is fashionable with a young crowd. The waves make it popular choice for surfers and wind surfers. **Praia João Fernandes** and **Praia João Fernandinho** boast calm seas and crystal waters. Bars on the beach serve fresh seafood.

WHERE TO STAY & EAT

Be sure to book well in advance if you plan to visit Búzios on a weekend between Christmas and Carnival.

$$$$ ✕ **Satyricon.** The Italian fish restaurant famous in Rio has opened up
★ shop here as well. The dishes here are expensive, but always excellent. Go all out and try the grilled mixed seafood plate with cream of Lemon Risotto. Reservations are normally required for parties of four of more on the weekends. ✉ *Av. José Bento Ribeiro Dantas (Orla Bardot) 500, 28950–000* ☎ *022/2623–2691* ▭ *AE, DC, MC, V* ⊗ *No lunch.*

$$$–$$$$ ✕ **Cigalon.** Widely considered the best restaurant in Búzios, Cigalon
★ is an elegant establishment with a veranda overlooking the beach. Though the waiters are bow-tied and the tables covered with crisp linens and lighted by flickering candles, this place still has a casual feel. The food is French-inspired, and includes lamb steak, braised duck breast, and prawns in a lemongrass sauce with almonds. The R$50 bistro menu—including a starter, a main, and a dessert—is a great deal. ✉ *Rua das Pedras 199 Centro28950–000* ☎ *022/2623–6284* ▭ *AE, DC, MC, V.*

$$ ✕ **Buzin.** Behind fashionable Rua das Pedras, Rua Turíbio de Farias is a buffet restaurant featuring many varieties of seafood, steaks, salads, and pizza made to order. The reasonable prices, ample choices, and casual atmosphere make it a great post-beach stop. Try the shrimp fried in oil and garlic or the *picanha* beef, a very tender cut found in

every churrascaria. The house opens at noon and closes when the last person leaves in the evening. ⊠ *Rua Turíbio de Farias 273, 28950-000* ☎ *022/2633–7051* ⊕ *www.buzin.com.br* ⊟ *AE, DC, MC, V.*

$$ ✕ **Capricciosa.** The Búzios branch of this pizzeria has the same high-quality pies as the main branch in Rio. The Margarita Gourmet is a must, with a thin crust topped with tomatoes and buffalo mozzarella. It's on Orla Bardot. ⊠ *Av. José Bento Ribeiro Dantas 500, Praia da Armação, 28950-000* ☎ *022/2623–2691* ⊟ *AE, DC, MC, V.*

$-$$ ✕ **Chez Michou.** This Belgian-owned *crêperie* is the best place for something quick, light, and inexpensive. You can choose from among about 50 savory and sweet fillings. At night the streetside tables buzz with locals and visitors congregating to drink and people-watch. ⊠ *Rua das Pedras 90, 28950-000* ☎ *022/2623–2169* ⊕ *www.chezmichou.com.br* ⊟ *No credit cards.*

$$$$ ⚐ **Casas Brancas.** If you're looking for complete relaxation, and you've
Fodor's Choice got plenty of cash on hand, this is the place to stay in Búzios. The
★ quirky building was constructed on several levels facing the beach, which makes for interestingly shaped rooms. Each is decorated with care, but simple cottage style and Zen-like peace and quiet are the hallmarks here. Get an ocean-view room, and one with a private balcony if you can swing it. The spa is one of the best in town. **Pros:** Great sunset views, on the beach, close to Rua das Pedras. **Cons:** Often booked up in high season, limited wheelchair access. ⊠ *Alto do Humaitá 10, off Orla Bardot, Centro 28950–000* ☎ *022/2623–1458* ⊕ *www.casas brancas.com.br* ⇦ *32 rooms, 3 suites* ⬙ *In-room: safe, refrigerator. In-hotel: restaurant, pool, spa, laundry service, no elevator, public Wi-Fi* ⊟ *AE, DC, MC, V* ❏ *BP.*

$$$$ ⚐ **Hotel le Relais de la Borie.** Imagine a country house with a tropical bent and stairs right down to the beach and you've got La Borie. An inviting warmth pervades the property, especially next to the main fireplace. (Evenings do get chilly here.) The pool area overlooks Geribá Beach. The stylish rooms have tile floors. Be sure to ask for a room facing the beach when you book for spectacular views over the ocean. The excellent restaurant serves lunch by the pool or in the interior courtyard and garden. **Pros:** On the beach, great restaurant, friendly staff. **Cons:** You need a car to get around, a long way from the center. ⊠ *Rua dos Gravatás 1374, Geribá, 28950-000* ☎ *022/2620–8504* ⊕ *www. laborie.com.br* ⇦ *38 rooms, 1 suite* ⬙ *In-room: safe, refrigerator. In-hotel: restaurant, pool, spa, laundry service, public Wi-Fi* ⊟ *AE, DC, MC, V* ❏ *BP.*

$$$-$$$$ ⚐ **Rio Búzios Beach Hotel.** This hotel has a great location a few steps from João Fernandes Beach. Rooms are decorated with wicker furniture, and it has a glass-sided elevator with a view of the beach. At night the hotel has a free shuttle service to downtown. **Pros:** On João Fernandes Beach, intimate setting, fantastic breakfast. **Cons:** 20-minute walk to the center, uninspiring rooms. ⊠ *Rua João Fernandes 2, João Fernandes, 28950-000* ☎ *022/2623–6073* ⊕ *www.riobuzios.com.br* ⇦ *63 rooms* ⬙ *In-room: safe, refrigerator, Wi-Fi. In-hotel: restaurant, room service, bar, pool, gym* ⊟ *AE, DC, MC, V* ❏ *BP.*

2

$$$ ⬚ **Galápagos Inn.** Overlooking the charming Orla Bardot—the continu-
★ ation of Rua das Pedras, where people congregate at night—this hotel
also has a view of the sea and, best of all, a view of the sunset. Rooms
are comfortable, with decoration inspired by the sea. Verandas have
views to João Fernandinho Beach, and there's bar service at the beach.
The hotel is included in Brazil's esteemed Roteiros de Charme club, a
highly exclusive association of the nation's best places to stay. **Pros:** All
rooms have ocean views, close to center. **Cons:** Beach is crowded dur-
ing high season, lots of steps to climb. ⊠*Praia João Fernandinho 3,
28925-000* ☎*022/2620–8800* ⊕*www.galapagos.com.br* ⟿*39 rooms,
5 suites* &*In-room: safe, refrigerator, cable TV. In-hotel: restaurant,
room service, bar, pool, laundry service, exercise room, no-smoking
rooms, public Internet, no elevator* ⊟*AE, DC, MC, V* ¶◎|*BP.*

$$ ⬚ **Ilha Branca Inn.** A stone's throw from João Fernandes Beach, Ilha has
charming and colorful rooms. The hotel has plenty of amenties, such
as a gym and sauna and a pool with panoramic ocean view. Rooms
are individually decorated, with tile floors and wrought-iron furnishings. Try and get one of the oceanfront apartments with a veranda.
Pros: Lovely ocean view, pleasant pool, short walk to center of town.
Cons: Small rooms, unimaginative decor, spotty service. ⊠*Rua João
Fernandes 1, Praia de João Fernandes, 28950-000* ☎*22/2623–2525 or
22/2623–6664* ⊕*www.ilhabranca.com* ⟿*67 rooms* &*In-room: safe,
refrigerator. In-hotel: restaurant, bar, pools, gym, no elevator, public
Internet* ⊟*AE, MC, V* ¶◎|*BP.*

$$ ⬚ **Pousada dos Gravatás.** Its location right on long Praia de Geribá makes
ʘ this pousada the best budget option in Búzios. Both breakfast and lunch
are included in the rates. Suites have verandas and ocean views. Stan-
dard apartments are at the back of the pousada, facing an inside patio.
Rooms aren't big, but they're comfortable, with decor inspired by the
sea. **Pros:** Lunch served on the beach, good value for money, family-
friendly atmosphere. **Cons:** Small rooms, basic restaurant. ⊠*Rua dos
Gravatás 67, Praia de Geribá, 28950-000* ☎*022/2623–1218* ⊕*www.
pousadagravatas.com.br* ⟿*55 rooms, 8 suites* &*In-room: refrigera-
tor. In-hotel: room service, bar, pools, gym, beachfront, public Wi-Fi*
⊟*AE, DC, MC, V* ¶◎|*BP.*

NIGHTLIFE

Anexo (⊠*Av. J. B. Ribeiro Dantes 392, Centro, 28950-000* ☎*22/2623–
6837*) is a low-key alternative to the city's more frenetic clubs. You can
kick back on the veranda as you sip one of the specialty cocktails.

Cervejaria Devassa (⊠*Av. J. B. Ribeiro Dantes 550, Centro, 28950-000*
☎*22/2623–5337* ⊕*www.devassa.com.br*) serves microbrews named
loira (blonde), *ruiva* (redhead), and *negra* (black).

Privilège (⊠*Av. J. B. Ribeiro Dantes 550, Centro, 28950-000*
☎*22/2623–0150*) has space for more than 1,000 people, making it
the city's top night club. Resident DJs play techno Thursday and Sun-
day, while top DJs from around the world fly in to spins on Friday and
Saturday. This is a late-night hangout for the rich and famous, who
head to the exclusive VIP area.

SPORTS & THE OUTDOORS

BIKING   **Nas Trilhas de Búzios** (✉ *Rua canto do Revela 2, Praia de Manguin-hos, 28950-000* ☎ *22/2623–6365 or 22/9234–6707*) offers everything from half-day bike tours around the city to seven-day excursions along deserted beaches and through the mountains.

KITE SURFING   **Búzios Kitesurf School** (✉ *Av. J. B. Ribeiro Dantes 9, Praia Raza, 28950-000* ☎ *22/9956–0668* ⊕ *www.kitenews.com.br*) has a upbeat team of certified instructors.

SURFING   Surf schools set up tents along Geribá Beach, and also rent out boards. Expect to pay R$45 an hour for a private lesson, including board rental, and R$15 to rent a board for an hour. In front of the Hotel le Relais de la Borie, **Marcio's Surf School** (✉ *Praia de Geribá* ☎ *22/9215–3880*) offers personalized classes and a wide range of rental equipment.

NORTH OF RIO

The Swiss heritage of Nova Friburgo is apparent in its architecture and cuisine. Novo Friburgo is surrounded by small districts, like São Pedro da Serra and Lumiar, with waterfalls and pools. Nearby Petrópolis is a charming historical village that was once the summer home of the imperial family. If you enjoy hiking, visit the Parque National da Serra dos Órgãos between Teresópolis and Petrópolis. Temperatures in the mountains are low by Brazilian standards—an average of 55°F (13°C) in winter—and make a welcome change from the stifling heat of the city.

NOVA FRIBURGO

122 km (79 mi) northeast of Petrópolis; 137 km (121 mi) northeast of Rio.

The resort town of Nova Friburgo was settled by Swiss immigrants in the early 1800s, when Brazil was actively encouraging European immigration. Woods, rivers, and waterfalls encircle the city, reminding many newcomers of their native land. Homemade liqueurs, jams, and cheeses pack the town's small markets. Its main export, however, is lingerie. Shops in downtown Friburgo and close to Ponte da Saudade sell high-quality lingerie for reasonable prices.

TO & FROM

By car, take BR 040 and then BR 116 to Teresópolis, and then RJ 130 to Nova Friburgo. The trip takes around 2½ hours. From Rio, Niterói-bound buses frequently continue on to Nova Friburgo. Auto Viação 1001 buses leave every half hour from the Rodoviária in Rio. Trips take around three hours and cost R$19.50.

ESSENTIALS

Banks & Currency Exchange **Banco 24 Horas ATMs** (✉ *Praça Dermerval Barbosa Moreira, 28610-160*).

Bus Contacts **Auto Viação 1001** (☎ *021/4004–5001* ⊕ *www.autoviacao1001. com.br*). **Rodoviária Nova Friburgo Sul** (✉ *Avenida Vereador José Martins da Costa 163, Ponte da Saudade, 4 km (2½ mi) south of town, 28610-160* ☎ *022/2522–0400*).

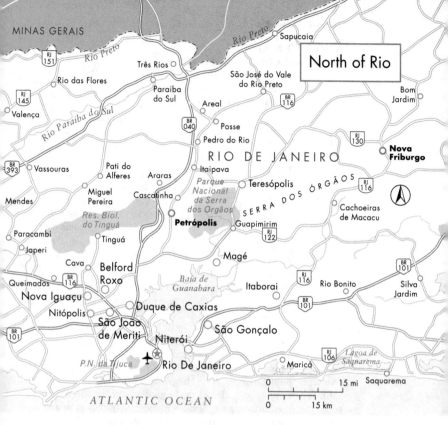

Emergencies & Medical Assistance **Hospital Municipal Raul Sertã** (✉ *Rua General Osório 324, Centro, 28613-001* ☏ *22/2522–9000*).

Taxi **Serra Táxi** (☏ *22/2522–5969* ⊕ *www.serrataxifriburgo.com.br*).

Visitor & Tour Info **Nova Friburgo Tourism Office** (✉ *Praça Dr. Demerval B. Moreira, 28610-390* ☏ *022/2543–6307* ⊕ *www.novafriburgotur.com.br*) is open weekdays 9 to 7 and weekends 9 to noon. **Walk and Bike** (✉ *Estrada Constancia Heringer 260, São Pedro da Aldeia, 28940-000* ☏ *22/2542–3088*) offers mountain biking, horseback riding, white-water rafting, and other activities in the mountains surrounding Novo Friburgo.

SAFETY & PRECAUTIONS

The town itself is relatively safe by Brazilian standards. If you plan to go hiking, always take an experienced guide. The tourist office has plenty to recommend.

WHAT TO SEE

A cable car rises more than 4,750 feet (1,450 meters) to **Morro da Cruz,** where you get a spectacular view of Friburgo. ✉ *Praça Teleférica, 28613-001* ☏ *022/2522–4834* 💳 *R$20* ⏰ *Weekdays 9–noon and 1–5, weekends 9–6.*

WHERE TO STAY

$$$ 🏨 **Hotel Bucsky.** Long walks through the forest are one of the highlights of a stay at this country house. Opened in 1940 by members of a Hungarian family, the inn has a distinctly rustic feel. Rooms, some in knotty pine, aren't large, and the buffet-style restaurant is not luxurious, but it serves tasty European fare. The hotel holds gastronomic festivals that center on German and Hungarian cuisines. **Pros:** Extensive wine cellar, great food, luxurious rooms. **Cons:** Not much to do after dark, rooms sometimes drafty. ⊠ *Estrada Rio-Friburgo, Km 76.5, Ponte da Saudade, 28615-160* ☎ *022/2522–5052* ⊕ *www.hotelbucsky.com.br* 🛏 *70 rooms, 10 suites* ♿ *In-room: refrigerator. In-hotel: room service, tennis court, pool, laundry service, no elevator* ☰ *AE, DC, MC, V* �𝍨 *FAP.*

> **SPICING IT UP IN THE MOUNTAINS**
>
> You wouldn't expect a sleepy mountain town like Nova Friburgo to be known primarily for its lingerie. It began in the late 1980s when job cuts at a local factory meant the town was awash with seamstresses who knew nothing but lingerie. Not to be deterred, the women purchased their old machines and set up their own companies. Novo Friburgo now employs 22,000 people in the lingerie industry.

$$ ★   🏨 **Akaskay.** About 9 km (6 mi) from Nova Friburgo, this hotel is a great place to relax in a natural mountain environment. The rooms have cedarwood walls and electric fireplaces, and the only noise you can hear is from a nearby streamlet. Outdoors, there's a spring-fed swimming pool and a hot tub. The place is surrounded by forest, and Saturday-morning yoga classes in the garden's meditation temple help you relax even further, as do shiatsu massages. Transport to and from nearby restaurants is free. **Pros:** Free yoga lessons, great views. **Cons:** A long way from everything, very little to do after dark. ⊠ *Estrada Norge Hamburgo, access at Km 71 off RJ 116, Mury, 28615-615* ☎ *22/2542–1163* ⊕ *www.akaskay.com* 🛏 *14 rooms, 1 chalet* ♿ *In-room: safe, refrigerator. In-hotel: bar, pool, hot tub* ☰ *AE, DC, MC* �𝍨 *BP.*

PETRÓPOLIS

68 km (42 mi) northeast of Rio.

The highway northeast of Rio de Janeiro rumbles past forests and waterfalls en route to a mountain town so refreshing and picturesque that Dom Pedro II, Brazil's second emperor, moved there with his summer court. From 1889 to 1899 it was also the country's year-round seat of government. Horse-drawn carriages clip-clop between the sights, passing flowering gardens, shady parks, and imposing pink mansions. Be sure to visit the Crystal Palace and the Gothic cathedral, São Pedro de Alcântara. The city is also home to the Encantada—literally "Enchanted"—the peculiar house created by Santos Dumont.

2

TO & FROM

From Rio by car head north along BR 040 to Petrópolis. The picturesque drive—once you leave the city—takes around an hour, depending on the traffic. Única buses leave every 40 minutes—less often on weekends—from Rio's Rodoviária Novo Rio. The 90-minute journey costs R$13. The easiest and safest way to get to Petrópolis is to arrange a shuttle at your hotel in Rio. Both Grayline Tours and Tourism Radical Brazil offer day tours to Petrópolis with English speaking guides. The cost is around R$70.

> ### WALKING IN THE CLOUDS
>
> The Parque Nacional da Serra dos Órgãos, was created in 1939 to protect the region's natural wonders, covers more than 39 square mi of mountainous terrain between Petrópolis and Teresópolis. Overseen by the Brazilian Institute for Environmental Protection, it's one of the best-managed national parks in the country. The Petrópolis to Teresópolis trail—a tough three-day hike with spectacular views—is a must for all hiking enthusiasts.

ESSENTIALS

Banks & Currency Exchange Banco 24 Horas ATMs (⊠ Praça Paulo Carneiro, 25620-140).

Bus Contacts Rodoviária Petrópolis (⊠ Rua Doutor Porciúncula 75, 25610-110 ☎ 024/2237–0101). Única (☎ 021/2263–8792).

Emergencies & Medical Assistance Hospital Municipal Nelson de Sá Earp (⊠ Rua Paulino Afonso 529, Centro, 25680-003 ☎ 024/2237–4062).

Taxi Ponto de Taxi Elite (☎ 0800/282–1412 or 24/2242–4090).

Visitor & Tour Info Petrópolis Tourism Office (⊠ Praça da Liberdade s/n, 25620-000Petrópolis ☎ 24/2246–9300 ⊕ www.petropolis.rj.gov.br) is open Monday to Saturday 9 to 6 and Sunday 9 to 5. **Grayline Tours** (⊠ Av. Niemeyer 121, Rio de Janeiro, 22450-220 ☎ 21/2512–9919 ⊕ www.grayline.com.br) offers guided tours of Petrópolis. **Tourism Radical Rio** (☎ 21/9224–6963 ⊕ www.rioturismoradical. com.br) is a local tour company offering guided tours of Petrópolis and other off-the-beaten-track destinations.

WHAT TO SEE

The **Casa de Santos Dumont** *(Santos Dumont House)* was built in 1918 by one of the world's first aviators. Santos Dumont's inventions fill the house, including a heated shower he invented before most homes had running water. The home doesn't have a kitchen because Dumont ordered his food from a nearby hotel—the first documented restaurant delivery service in Brazil. ⊠ *Rua do Encantado 22, 25685-081* ☎ *024/2247–3158* 💲*R$5* 🕐 *Tues.–Sun. 9:30–5.*

Take a horse-drawn carriage to **Cathedral São Pedro de Alcântara,** the Gothic cathedral containing the tombs of Dom Pedro II; his wife, Dona Teresa Cristina; and their daughter, Princesa Isabel. ⊠ *Rua São Pedro de Alcântara 60, Centro, 25685-300* ☎ *024/2242–4300* 💲*Free* 🕐 *Tues.–Sun. 8–noon and 2–6.*

The **Museu Imperial** is the magnificent 44-room palace that was the summer home of Dom Pedro II, emperor of Brazil, and his family in the 19th century. The colossal structure is filled with polished wooden floors, artwork, and grand chandeliers. You can also see the diamond-encrusted gold crown and scepter of Brazil's last emperor, as well as other royal jewels. ⊠*Rua da Imperatriz 220, Centro, 25610-320* ☎*024/2237–8000* ⊕*www.museu imperial.gov.br* ⊟*R$8* ⊙*Tues.– Sun. 11–6.*

> ### THE "FIRST" MAN TO FLY
>
> On November 12, 1906, Santos Dumont, a dapper young Brazilian adventurer and inventor, launched his airplane, the 14-Bis, into the air above Paris. The pride of Brazil, Dumont found his way into Brazilian history books as the first man to fly—despite the fact that the Wright brothers had been flying since 1903.

The **Palácio de Cristal** *(Crystal Palace)*, a stained-glass and iron building made in France and assembled in Brazil, was a wedding present to Princesa Isabel. During the imperial years it was used as a ballroom: it was here the princess held a celebration dance after she abolished slavery in Brazil in 1888. ⊠*Praça da Confluência, Rua Alfredo Pachá, 25685-210* ☎*024/2247–3721* ⊟*Free* ⊙*Tues.–Sun. 9–6:30.*

WHERE TO STAY & EAT

$–$$ ✕**Trutas do Rocio.** Trout, trout, and more trout is served at this restaurant next to river teeming with—you guessed it—trout. The fish is prepared as appetizers in pâté or in a cassava-dough pastry. Entrées include grilled trout or trout cooked in almond sauce, mustard sauce, or orange sauce. The rustic restaurant seats only 22, so reservations are a must. ⊠*Estrada da Vargem Grande 6333, Rocio, 25725-620* ☎*024/2291–5623* ⊕*www.trutas.com.br* ⌂*Reservations essential.*

$$$ ✕▥**Locanda Della Mimosa.** This cozy pousada is in a valley with trails
★   winding through the colorful bougainvillea trees. The handful of suites are decorated in a classical style with imperial influences. Tea is served in the afternoon and is included in the price of the room. The Italian restaurant, run by the talented Danio Braga, who is always cooking up novelties, is open Thursday through Sunday and includes specialties from different regions of Italy. **Pros:** Spacious rooms, great restaurant, afternoon tea service. **Cons:** Need to book in advance. ⊠*Km 71.5, BR 040, Alameda das Mimosas 30, Vale Florido, 25725-490* ☎*024/2233–5405* ⊕*www.locanda.com.br* ⇌*6 suites* ⌂*In-room: refrigerator, DVD, Wi-Fi. In-hotel: restaurant, room service, bar, pool* ▭*MC* ⏃*BP* ⊙*Hotel closed Mon.–Thurs.*

$$ ✕▥**Pousada de Alcobaça.** Just north of Petrópolis, this is considered by many to be the region's loveliest inn. The grounds have beautiful gardens and a shimmering swimming pool. The kitchen turns out exceptional breakfasts, lunches, and high teas with an emphasis on fresh ingredients. Meals ($–$$$), which include savory pastas, are served in the garden. A pot roast, prepared in a charming farm kitchen, is a must. The hotel grows its own vegetables and herbs. All rooms in the early-20th-century house are cozy and decorated in a rustic style. **Pros:**

Tasty food, great views. **Cons:** Need to book far in advance, it's a 15 minute drive into the city. ✉ *Agostinho Goulão 298, Corrêas, 25730-050* ☎ *024/2221–1240* ➧ *11 rooms* ⊕ *www.pousadadaalcobaca.com.br* ⏷ *In-room: DVD. In-hotel: restaurant, room service, tennis court, pool, laundry service* ☰ *AE, DC, MC, V* ⛻ *BP.*

$ ✕☷ **Pousada Monte Imperial.** A few kilometers from downtown, this European-style inn has a lobby with a fireplace and a comfortable restaurant and bar area. Rooms are cozy and rustic and have views of the historic center of the city. Drinks and meals can be taken in the garden overlooking the city. **Pros:** Close to downtown, great sunset views. **Cons:** Spartan rooms, chilly in the winter. ✉ *Rua José de Alencar 27, Centro, 25610-050* ☎ *024/2237–1664* ⊕ *www.pousadamonteimperial.com.br* ➧ *15 rooms* ⏷ *In-room: refrigerator, Ethernet. In-hotel: restaurant, bar, pool, laundry service, public Internet* ☰ *AE, DC, MC, V* ⛻ *BP.*

THE GREEN COAST

Italy has the charming Costa Azurra, but Brazil has the Costa Verde. The emerald waters in the bay at Angra dos Reis have some of the best diving in the area, with abundant marine life and near year-round visibility. But you don't have to be a diver to enjoy yourself. There are also a variety of boat tours. Getting to beautiful Ilha Grande, the biggest island in the bay, requires an adventurous spirit, as no cars are allowed on the island. Paraty combines historic beauty with unspoiled beaches. During Carnival, normally quiet Paraty holds the Bloco da Lama, a parade where participants smear mud from local Praia do Jabaquara on one another—it's meant to represent the ritual of driving away evil spirits practiced by the prehistoric tribes of the region.

ANGRA DOS REIS

168 km (91 mi) west of Rio.

Angra dos Reis (Bay of Kings) has it all: colonial architecture, beautiful beaches, and clear green waters. Schooners, yachts, sailboats, and fishing skiffs drift among the bay's 365 islands, one for every day of the year. Indeed, Angra dos Reis' popularity lies in its strategic location near the islands. Some are deserted stretches of sand, others patches of Atlantic rain forest surrounded by emerald waters perfect for swimming or snorkeling.

TO & FROM

Angra dos Reis-bound Costa Verde buses leave Rio every hour. The 2½-hour trip costs R$34. Ferries leave the terminal at Angra dos Reis for Ilha Grande every day at 3:30 PM. The 90-minute trip costs R$5.

From Rio by car, get onto the Rio-Santos highway (BR 101) and follow it south for 190 km until you get to Angra dos Reis. Expect the trip to take between two and three hours, depending on traffic.

TEAM airlines offers an irregular service from Rio to Angra dos Reis.

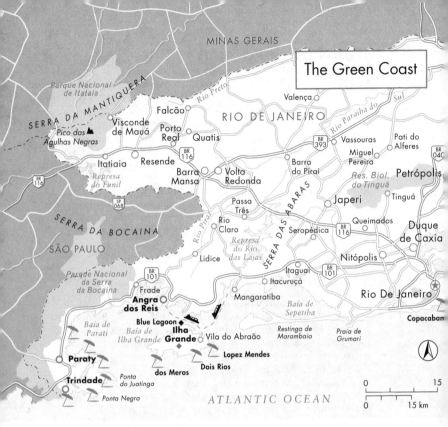

ESSENTIALS

Airline **TEAM Transportes Aéreos** (☎021/3328–1616 ⊕ www.voeteam.com.br)

Airport **Aeroporto Municipal** (✉Rua Pref. João Galindo s/n, Japuíba, 23900-650 ☎24/3365–4073).

Banks & Currency Exchange **Banco 24 Horas ATMs** (✉Rua Júlio Maria 235, 23900-504).

Bus Contacts **Costa Verde** (☎021/2573–1484 ⊕ www.costaverdetransportes. com.br). **Rodoviária Angra dos Reis** (✉Av. Almirante Jair Toscano de Brito 110, 23906-805 ☎024/3365–2041).

Emergencies & Medical Assistance **Santa Casa de Misericórdia** (✉Rua Doutor Coutinho 84, 23900-620 ☎024/3365–5004).

Taxi **Ponto de Táxi** (☎24/3365–1361).

Visitor & Tour Info **Angra dos Reis Tourism Office** (✉Avenida Ayrton Senna 580, 23900-000 ☎24/3367–7789 ⊕ www.angra.rj.gov.br) is open Monday to Sunday 8 to 8. **Mar de Angra** (✉Avenida Júlio Maria 16, 23900-502 ☎24/3365–1097 ⊕ www.mardeangra.com.br) offers guided hikes, boat trips, and diving trips around Angra dos Reis.

SAFETY & PRECAUTIONS

Leaving your car unattended on the street is risky. Park your car in one of the many secure lots, expecially if you plan an overnight trip to Ilha Grande.

WHAT TO SEE

The **Associação dos Barqueiros** (☎024/3365–3165) runs boat tours to the islands. Don't miss the tour to Ilha da Gipóia and its beautiful beaches, like the famous Jurubaíba, which is perfect for snorkeling or diving. ⚠ Some boats have a reputation for playing loud music. Check ahead of time if you prefer a more tranquil environment.

WHERE TO STAY & EAT

$$$$ ✕⊞ **Hotel do Frade & Golf Resort.** Guest-room balconies overlook the
★ sea and the private beach at this modern resort hotel. The many sports options include boat rentals (sailboats, motorboats, catamarans), scuba diving and, of course, golf. It's no surprise that seafood is a standout at the buffet restaurant called Scuna ($$$). Other restaurants, which serve a variety of international cuisines, open in summer. Room rates include both breakfast and an additional meal. **Pros:** Top-notch service, spacious rooms, private beach. **Cons:** Impersonal feel, pricy rates, a long way from the city. ⊠ *Km 123, BR 101, Praia do Frade, 32 km (20 mi) west of Angra do Reis, 23900-000* ☎*024/3369–9500* ⊕*www.hotel dofrade.com.br* ↝*162 rooms* ⌂*In-room: safe, refrigerator, Wi-Fi. In-hotel: 5 restaurants, room service, bar, golf course, tennis courts, pool, laundry service, no-smoking rooms* ⊟*AE, DC, MC, V* ❦*FAP.*

$$$$ ⊞ **Hotel do Bosque.** Inside Parque Perequê, this hotel has boat service to its private beach across the river. The price for the room includes both breakfast and dinner. Apartments look out onto a leafy garden, and suites face the river. There's bar service at the beach. **Pros:** Plenty of activities, private beach, spacious rooms. **Cons:** Out-of-the-way location. ⊠ *Km 533, BR 101, Praia de Mambucaba, 23908-000* ☎*024/3362–3130* ⊕*www.hoteldobosque.com.br* ↝*98 rooms, 4 suites* ⌂*In-room: safe, refrigerator. In-hotel: room service, bar, tennis court, pool, beachfront, laundry service, public Wi-Fi* ⊟*AE, DC, MC, V.*

$$ ⊞ **Portogalo Suíte.** Perched on a hill with a wonderful view of the bay, the exposed-brick buildings at this hotel have a rustic appeal. Rooms have balconies with sea view. Although starkly white and cool, with tile floors, the rooms are clean and right above the beach. A cable car takes guests down the hillside to the beach and the marina. **Pros:** Views of the bay and Ilha Grande. All rooms have verandas with ocean views. **Cons:** A long way from town, basic rooms. ⊠ *Km 71, BR 101, Praia de Itapinhoacanga, 25 km (16 mi) south of town, 23900-000* ☎*024/3361–4343 or 0800/282–4343* ⊕*www.portogalosuite.com.br* ↝*85 rooms* ⌂*In-room: safe, refrigerator, cable TV. In-hotel: room service, bar, tennis courts, sauna, pool, laundry service, public Wi-Fi* ⊟*AE, DC, MC, V.*

ILHA GRANDE

21 km (13 mi) south of Angra dos Reis or Mangaratiba via 90-minute ferry ride.

Ilha Grande, 90 minutes via ferry from Angra dos Reis, is one of the most popular island destinations in Brazil. It boasts 86 idyllic beaches, some of which are sandy ribbons with backdrops of tropical foliage, while others are densely wooded coves with waterfalls tumbling down from the forest.

Ilha Grande once provided refuge for pirates and corsairs, and was the first point of entry for many slaves brought here from Africa. Later it became a leper colony, but for some its use as a political prison during the military dictatorship from 1964 to 1984 was its most insidious incarnation.

Ferries arrive at Vila do Abraão. As there are no cars, it's wise to take only what you can carry. Men waiting at the pier make a living helping tourists carry luggage for about about R$5 per bag.

TO & FROM

Ferries to Ilha Grande are run by Barcas S/A. The ferry for Vila do Abraão on Ilha Grande leaves Angra dos Reis daily at 3:30 PM and returns weekdays at 10 AM and weekends at 11 AM; the price is R$6 during the week and R$12 on weekends.

ESSENTIALS

Banks & Currency Exchange There are no banks or ATMs on the island, and credit cards are not widely accepted. Be sure to bring some extra cash with you.

Emergencies & Medical Assistance **Posto de Saude** (⊠ *Rua Getúlio Vargas, 23968-000*).

Visitor & Tour Info **South America Experience** (☎ *021/2513–4091* ⊕ *www. southamericaexperience.com*) specializes in weeklong adventure trips. **Tourist Information Center** (⊠ *Rua da Praia s/n, 23968-000* ☎ *24/3361–5508*). **Ilha Grande Dive** (⊠ *Rua Buganville, 23968-000* ☎ *24/3361–5512* ⊕ *www.ilhagrande dive.com.br*), the oldest dive operator on the island, offers courses for all levels, including those who have never dived before.

SAFETY & PRECAUTIONS

Avoid taking unlicensed boats. Verify the condition of any boat you plan to board, and check that it has a life preserver for every person aboard.

A DUBIOUS PAST

The Cândido Mendes prison on Ilha Grande was the birthplace of the infamous Comando Vermelho—literally "Red Command"—that controlled most of the criminal activity in Rio de Janeiro in the 1990s. The Comando Vermelho was formed when political prisoners of the Red Phalanx joined forces with convicts from the city. The prison was torn down in 1993.

WHAT TO SEE

Blue Lagoon is popular with day-trippers from the mainland. This natural pool that forms at low tide is home to thousands of small fish that will literally eat out of your hands. Be sure to take a mask and snorkel.

Dois Rios has two rivers that flow out of the forest on either side of this beach, providing a bountiful environment for aquatic life. Just inland are the ruins of the old prison.

★ Locals and visitors alike regard **Lopez Mendes,** a 3 km (2 mi) stretch of white with emerald waters, as one of the most beautiful beaches on Ilha Grande. Organize a boat trip from Vila do Abraão if you don't feel up to the two-hour hike through the forest.

> ### ILHA GRANDE'S SWEET SPOT
>
> They appear late in the afternoon to tempt you with their sweet aromas and delicate flavors. We're talking about Vila do Abraão's sweet carts, of course. They first appeared in 1998, when a resident of the island started producing baked good at his home. His success inspired other dessert makers to sell their sweets on the streets of Abraão. The carts stay out late at night, tempting even the most resolute of travelers.

WHERE TO STAY & EAT

$-$$ ✕**Lua e Mar.** Expect fresh, well-prepared seafood at this longtime favorite. It's a casual establishment, so you can stroll in from the beach still wearing your Havaianas. Try Dona Cidinha's specialty, fish with half-ripe bananas. ⊠*Rua da Praia, Vila do Abraão, 23968-000* ☎*024/3361–5113* ▤*AE, DC, MC, V* ⊘*Closed Wed.*

$-$$ ✕**O Pescador.** Inside the pousada of the same name, this rustic but cozy restaurant mixes local seafood with Italian cooking techniques. The specialties are grilled fish (types of fish vary according to the season), bought from local fishermen. Grilled dourado and grouper are served most of the year. ⊠*Rua da Praia, Vila do Abraão, 23968-000* ☎*024/3361–5114* ▤*AE, MC, V.*

$$ ⊞**Pousada Sankay.** The colorful rooms at Pousada Sankay have names
★ inspired by sea creatures, like Lagosta (lobster) or Golfinho (dolphin). Kayaks, canoes, and other boats are available for rent, as is diving equipment. A boat from the pousada can pick you up at Angra dos Reis. Pros: Plenty of activities, bar extends over the ocean. Cons: You need a boat to get to the Vila do Abraão, small rooms. ⊠*Enseada do Bananal, 23990-000* ☎*024/3365–4065* ⊕*www.pousadasankay.com. br* ⤳*16 rooms* ⌂*In-room: refrigerator. In-hotel: restaurant, bar, pool, gym* ▤*AE, DC, MC, V* ⍟*MAP* ⊘*Closed June.*

$ ⊞**Farol dos Borbas.** Like all the island's lodging options, Farol dos Borbas has simple rooms. Its main advantage is its location near the pier where you disembark from the ferry from Angra dos Reis. The hotel has boat service, with tours around the island. Pros: Walking distance from the pier, close to everything, private schooner. Cons: Can be noisy at night, staff does not speak English. ⊠*Rua da Praia 881, Vila do Abraão, 23960-970* ☎*024/3361–5832* ⊕*www.ilhagrandetur.com.br* ⤳*14 rooms* ⌂*In-room: refrigerator. In-hotel: room service, no elevator* ▤*DC, MC, V* ⍟*BP.*

$ 🔲 **Pousada do Canto.** In a colonial-style house, this pousada faces pretty Praia do Canto. The place has tropical atmosphere, with nice touches like the thatched-roofed bar beside the pretty pool. Some rooms face the ocean and have verandas. **Pros:** On the beach, short walk to the village, pretty pool. **Cons:** Rooms can get chilly in winter, small bathrooms. ⊠*Rua da Praia 121, Vila do Abraão, 23990-000* ☎*19/3455–0986* ⊕*www.ilhagrande.com.br/pages/pousadas/ilhazul/canto.html* ➤*11 rooms* ◇*In-room: refrigerator. In-hotel: pool, beachfront, no elevator* ⊟*AE, DC, MC, V* ⧦*BP.*

A POTENT BREW

One telling has it that cachaça was invented around 1540 by slaves working on the sugarcane plantations. A liquid called *cagaço* was removed from the sugarcane to make it easier to transport. The slaves noticed that after a few days this liquid would ferment into a potent brew. Visit Paraty in August to participate in the Pinga Festival, when cachaça producers from around the country unveil their latest brews.

PARATY

99 km (60 mi) southwest of Angra dos Reis; 261 km (140 mi) southwest of Rio.

This stunning colonial city—also spelled Parati—is one of South America's gems. Giant iron chains hang from posts at the beginning of the mazelike grid of cobblestone streets, closing them to all but pedestrians, horses, and bicycles. Until the 18th century this was an important transit point for gold plucked from the Minas Gerais—a safe harbor protected by a fort. (The cobblestones are the rock ballast brought from Lisbon, then unloaded to make room in the ships for their gold cargoes.) In 1720, however, the colonial powers cut a new trail from the gold mines straight to Rio de Janeiro, bypassing the town and leaving it isolated. It remained that way until contemporary times, when artists, writers, and others "discovered" the community and UNESCO placed it on its list of World Heritage Sites.

Paraty isn't a city peppered with lavish mansions and opulent palaces; rather, it has a simple beauty. By the time the sun breaks over the bay each morning—illuminating the whitewashed, colorfully trimmed buildings—the fishermen have begun spreading out their catch at the outdoor market. The best way to explore is simply to begin walking winding streets banked with centuries-old buildings that hide quaint inns, tiny restaurants, shops, and art galleries.

TO & FROM

From Rio De Janeiro, it's a four-hour drive along the BR 101 to Paraty. Costa Verde buses leave Rio daily every two hours. The journey costs R$42.

ESSENTIALS

Banks & Currency Exchange **Banco 24 Horas ATMs** (⊠*Rua Roberto Silveira, Praça Chafariz, 23970-000*).

2

Banco do Brazil (✉ *Rua Roberto Silveira 192, Praça Chafariz, 23970-000*) has exchange rates that are better than most in town.

Bus Contacts Costa Verde (☏ *21/2573-1484* ⊕ *www.costaverdetransportes.com.br*). **Rodoviária Paraty** (✉ *Rua Jango Pádua, 23970-000* ☏ *024/3371-1177*).

Emergencies & Medical Assistance Santa Casa de Misericórdia (✉ *Av. São Pedro de Alcântara, Pontal, 23970-000* ☏ *024/3371-1623*).

Taxi Tuim Taxi Service (☏ *24/9918-7834* ⊕ *www.eco-paraty.com/taxi*).

MOVE OVER, GATORADE

Coconut water is sold everywhere in Brazil: in supermarkets, in parks, on the beach, in restaurants, and even in bars. But what makes it so popular? The same electrolytic balance found in our blood is also found in coconut water, which makes it ideal for rehydration. It's also much lower in sugar than most sports drinks, and is full of minerals like potassium.

Visitor & Tour Info Paraty Tourism Office (✉ *Av. Roberto da Silveira 1, 23970-000* ☏ *024/3371-1897* ⊕ *www.paraty.com.br*) is open daily 9–9. **Paraty Tours** (✉ *Av. Roberto Silveira 11, 23970-000* ☏ *24/3371-2651* ⊕ *www.paratytours.com.br*) has six-hour jeep tours that go to the Serra da Bocaina National Park, crossing rivers and visiting fantastic waterfalls. **South America Experience** (☏ *021/2513-4091* ⊕ *www.southamericaexperience.com*) offers weeklong adventure trips.

SAFETY & PRECAUTIONS

Although downtown is safe, even late at night, be careful about walking alone in other parts of town.

WHAT TO SEE

Casa da Cultura. The museum in the Casa da Cultura is a good place to get acquainted with the town's history and culture. Downstairs is one of the best gift shops in town, with crafts made by local artisans. ✉ *Rua Dona Geralda 177, at Rua Dr. Samuel Costa, 23970-000* ☏ *24/3371-2325* ⊕ *www.casadaculturaparaty.org.br* ⊠ *Museum R$5* ⊙ *Wed.–Mon. 10–6:30.*

The **Forte Defensor Perpétuo** was built in the early 1700s (and rebuilt in 1822) as a defense against pirates. It's now home to a folk-arts center. ✉ *Morro da Vila Velha, 23970-000* ☏ *No phone* ⊠ *R$1* ⊙ *Wed.–Sun. 9–5.*

The town's slaves built the **Igreja de Nossa Senhora do Rosário** for themselves around 1725, because the other churches in town were reserved for the white population. ✉ *Rua do Comércio, 23970-000* ☏ *024/3371-1467* ⊠ *R$1* ⊙ *Tues.–Sun. 9–5.*

The neoclassical **Igreja de Nossa Senhora dos Remédios** was built in 1787. It holds the small art gallery Pinacoteca Antônio Marino Gouveia, with paintings of modern artists such as Djanira, Di Cavalcanti, and Anita Malfatti. ✉ *Rua da Matriz, 23970-000* ☏ *024/3371-2946* ⊠ *R$1* ⊙ *Tues.–Sun. 9–noon and 2–5.*

The oldest church in Paraty, the simple **Igreja de Santa Rita** was built in 1722 by and for freed slaves. Today it houses a small religious art museum (Museu de Arte Sacra). It's a typical Jesuit church with a tower and three front windows. Religious art objects inside the church are constantly being restored. ⊠ *Rua Santa Rita, 23970-000* ☎ *024/3371–1620* 💲 *R$1* ⊙ *Wed.–Sun. 9–noon and 2–5.*

BEACHES

Sono and **Antigos** are two of the most beautiful beaches in Paraty. They can only be accessed by a trail through the forest. It's an easy hour-long hike, and once here you can catch a ride back by boat.

> **CAMINHO DE OURO**
>
> The Caminho de Ouro, a trail used by the indigenous tribes that once stretched from Paraty to the state of Minas Gerais, was paved with the stones used as ballast for the ships arriving from Europe. The ships then returned to Europe laden with gold from the mines in Minas Gerais.

About 30 km (20 mi) from Paraty, **Trinidade** was once a hippie hangout. Today Trinidade is one of the most happening districts in Paraty, with plenty of activities and even a natural pool that's perfect for children.

WHERE TO STAY & EAT

$$$$ ✗ **Refúgio.** Near the water in a quiet part of town, this seafood restaurant is a great place for a romantic dinner. Café tables out front sit under heat lamps. The codfish cakes are excellent. ⊠ *Praça do Porto, 23970-000* ☎ *024/3371–2447* ⊕ *www.eco-paraty.com/refugio* 🖃 *MC, V.*

$$–$$$$ ✗ **Merlin o Mago.** The German chef and owner, Hado Steinbrecher, was a former photojournalist and food critic who studied in France and traveled through Asia, mainly in Thailand and India. The cuisine here is an interesting mixture of Brazilian, French, and Thai traditions. Entrées include grilled shrimp flambéed in cognac or snook wrapped in a crepe with yogurt and green pepper, topped with caviar. ⊠ *Rua do Comércio 376, 23970-000* ☎ *024/3371–2157* ⊕ *www.paraty.com.br/merlin* 🖃 *DC, MC, V.*

$$–$$$ ✗ **Restaurante do Hiltinho.** This is one of the most elegant restaurants in Paraty. Its specialty is *camarão casadinho*, fried colossal shrimp stuffed with hot *farofa* (cassava flour). Even if you're familiar with jumbo shrimp, you might be astonished at the size of these beauties. Seafood outnumbers other dishes two to one, but the filet mignon is very good. The service borders on perfection, as does the elegant decor, with glass doors opening onto the street. ⊠ *Rua Marechal Deodoro 233, 23970-000* ☎ *024/3371–1432* 🖃 *AE, DC, MC, V.*

$$ 🏠 **Pousada do Sandi.** The town's most upscale lodging is this small inn, which oozes nautical-theme charm. Luxurious by local standards, rooms are tastefully decorated, and some have terraces overlooking the city's cobblestone streets. The lobby, pool area, and restaurant are warm and welcoming. **Pros:** Close to the historic center, large rooms, great breakfasts. **Cons:** Some rooms are noisy, not for people with disabilities. ⊠ *Largo do Rosário 1, 23970-000* ☎ *24/3371–2100* ⊕ *www.pousadadosandi.com.br* 🛏 *25 rooms, 1 suite* � *In-room: safe. In-hotel: restaurant, pool, public Internet* 🖃 *AE, DC, MC, V* ⦿ *BP.*

CONTACTS & RESOURCES

BANKS & CURRENCY EXCHANGE
There are a variety of banks and ATMs in each community, except Ilha Grande, but it's best to get cash before leaving Rio. Some banks accept only cards with Visa/Plus logos and others accept only cards with MasterCard/Cirrus logos. Banco24horas ATMs usually accept all cards, including American Express.

INTERNET
Almost every town has an Internet café, with prices ranging from R$3 to R$6 per hour. On Ilha Grande expect to pay around double that.

VISITOR INFORMATION
The Tourism Information hotline is an English-language information source about the state of Rio de Janeiro and operates from 8 AM to 8 PM.

$$ **Pousada Pardieiro.** The houses that make up this property are decorated in a 19th-century colonial style. Rooms have dark-wood carved beds and antique bureaus. There are no TVs in the rooms, but there's a living room with a home theater. A beautiful patio has birds and orchids. **Pros:** Close to the historic center, great pool and garden. **Cons:** No room TVs, cold floors in winter. ⊠ *Rua do Comércio 74, 23970-000* ☎ *024/3371–1370* ⊕ *www.pousadapardieiro.com.br* ➟ *27 rooms, 2 suites* △ *In-room: no room TV, safe, refrigerator. In-hotel: restaurant, room service, bar, pool, laundry service, public Internet* ⊟ *AE, DC, MC V.*

$$ **Pousada Porto Imperial.** Behind the Igreja da Matriz de Nossa Senhora dos Remédios, this historic hotel has rooms that surround a series of courtyards and a swimming pool. The pousada is decorated with a collection of typical Brazilian artwork—ceramics, tapestries, and colonial furniture—and has a tropical garden filled with bromeliads. **Pros:** In the historic center and close to the beach, beautiful inner garden. **Cons:** Across from a noisy square, simple rooms. ⊠ *Rua Tenente Francisco Antônio s/n, 23970-000* ☎ *024/3371–2323* ⊕ *www.pousadaporto imperial.com.br* ➟ *50 rooms, 3 suites* △ *In-room: safe, refrigerator. In-hotel: room service, bar, pool, laundry service, public Wi-Fi* ⊟ *AE, DC, MC, V.*

$ **Pousada do Príncipe.** The great-grandson of Emperor Pedro II owns this aptly named inn at the edge of the colonial city. The Pousada of the Prince is painted in the yellow and green of the imperial flag, and its quiet, colorful public areas are decorated with photos of the royal family. Rooms are small, decorated in a colonial style, and face either the interior garden or the swimming pool. The restaurant is impressive, too; its chef turns out an exceptional feijoada. **Pros:** Close to the historic center, beautiful buildings. **Cons:** Unimaginative decoration, so-so service. ⊠ *Av. Roberto Silveira 289, Paraty, 23970-000* ☎ *024/3371–2266* ⊕ *www.pousadadoprincipe.com.br* ➟ *34 rooms, 3 suites* △ *In-room: refrigerator. In-hotel: restaurant, room service, tennis courts, pool, laundry service* ⊟ *AE, DC, MC, V.*

Fodor'sChoice

SHOPPING

Paraty is known countrywide for its fine cachaça, including brands like Coqueiro, Corisco, Vamos Nessa, Itatinga, Murycana, Paratiana, and Maré Alta. **Empório da Cachaça** (✉ *Rua Doutor Samuel Costa 22, 23970-000* ☎ *024/3371–6329*) has more than 300 brands of the sugarcane liquor—both local and national brands. **Porto da Pinga** (✉ *Rua da Matriz 12, 23970-000* ☎ *024/9907–4370*) is a good choice for cachaças.

São Paulo

WORD OF MOUTH

"I am female and currently in São Paulo on business. This is my third trip this year. I stay in the Jardins area and feel completely safe there. I even run to and in the Ibirapuera Park on the weekends. Of course, I do follow the recommended precautions. The city is awesome, and the people are very warm. I have not experienced any problems. The city is huge, bigger than I ever could have imagined, so when you hear about crime here, you have to put the size of the city into perspective."

—gromeo

Updated by
Simon Tarmo

SÃO PAULO IS A MEGALOPOLIS of 19 million people, with endless stands of skyscrapers defining the horizon from every angle. The largest city in South America, São Paulo even makes New York City, with its population of about 8 million, seem small in comparison. And this nearly 500-year-old capital of São Paulo State gets bigger every year: it now sprawls across some 8,000 square km (3,089 square mi), of which 1,525 square km (589 square mi) make up the city proper.

The main financial hub in the country, São Paulo is also Brazil's most cosmopolitan city, with top-rate nightlife and restaurants and impressive cultural and arts scenes. Most of the wealthiest people in Brazil live here—and the rest of them drop by at least once a year to shop for clothes, shoes, accessories, luxury items, and anything else that money can buy. *Paulistanos* (São Paulo inhabitants) work hard and spend a lot, and there's no escaping the many shopping and eating temptations.

Despite—or because of—these qualities, many tourists, Brazilian and foreigners, avoid visiting the city. Too noisy, too polluted, too crowded, they say—and they have a point. São Paulo is hardly a beautiful city; it's fast-paced and there's lots to do, but it's also a concrete jungle, with nothing as attractive as Rio's hills and beaches. Yet, even as the smog reddens your eyes, you'll see that there's much to explore here. When you get tired of laid-back beaches, São Paulo is just the right place to go.

ORIENTATION

Situated 70 km (43 mi) inland from the Atlantic Ocean with an average elevation of around 800 meters (2,625 feet), São Paulo has a surprisingly flat and featureless metropolitan area, apart from a few elevated areas, including those around Avenida Paulista and Centro. A major thoroughfare called the "Marginal"—two one-way expressways on either side of a smelly, Pinheiros river—divides the city from both north to south and east to west, with most business and tourist activity occurring in the southeastern quadrant. No matter where you are, though, it's difficult to gain a visual perspective of your relative location, thanks to the legions of buildings in every direction. A good map is a necessity.

CENTRO

This downtown area has the city's most interesting historic architecture and some of its most famous sights; however, many parts are also quite daunting and dirty, so be prepared. Area highlights include the freshly revamped (2006) Praça da Sé, considered the vortex for the São Paulo municipal district. Parque da Luz is just to the north and next to a number of important buildings, including the Estação da Luz, the former headquarters of São Paulo Railway that now houses the Museum of the Portuguese Language.

TOP REASONS TO GO

■ Shop among Brazil's rich and famous in the Jardins or Itaim areas, or visiting one of the city's many fashion malls.

■ Adventurous eating is a sport in São Paulo. There are more than 12,000 restaurants covering some 62 cuisines in São Paulo.

■ Enjoy the music that flows through the streets and can be heard around every corner—dance, sing, or just take in the ambience.

■ Bars of all shapes, styles, and sizes beckon the thirsty traveler—quench your thirst with a cold beer or strong caipirinha.

■ Futebol, or soccer, is truly "the beautiful game" in Brazil, and in São Paulo futebol is played everywhere.

LIBERDADE

Southeast of Centro, Liberdade (meaning "freedom" or "liberty" in Portuguese) is the center of São Paulo's vibrant Japanese, Korean, and Chinese communities, and features a range of Asian-style streetscapes and shopfronts. It's a popular area with travelers, thanks to the many culturally motivated markets and restaurants.

AVENIDA PAULISTA

The imposing Avenida Paulista is home to some of the city's best hotels, biggest financial companies, and most important businesses. Many of São Paulo's cultural institutions center around this impressive, eight-lane-wide thoroughfare. Just 2.8-km (1.7-mi) long, the avenue begins west of Centro and spans several of the city's chicest neighborhoods as it shoots southeast toward the Atlantic.

BIXIGA

Officially called Bela Vista, this is São Paulo's Little Italy. Here are plenty of restaurants, theaters, and nightlife hot spots. Southwest of Centro and right next to Avenida Paulista, Bixiga is an old, working-class neighborhood—the kind of place where everybody knows everybody else's business.

JARDINS

On the southern side of Avenida Paulista sits Jardins, a trendy neighborhood that's ideal for shopping and eating out. The gently sloping, tree-filled area is one of the few parts of São Paulo that's suitable for walking around; it's also one of the safest neighborhoods in the city.

ITAIM BIBI

Moving farther south, Itaim (locals always drop the Bibi part) is similar to Jardins because it also features a plethora of fashionable bars, restaurants, and shops. The suburb is transected by another of the city's most impressive roads, Avenida Brigadeiro Faria Lima, which, along with its many cross-streets, has a ton of expensive and exclusive

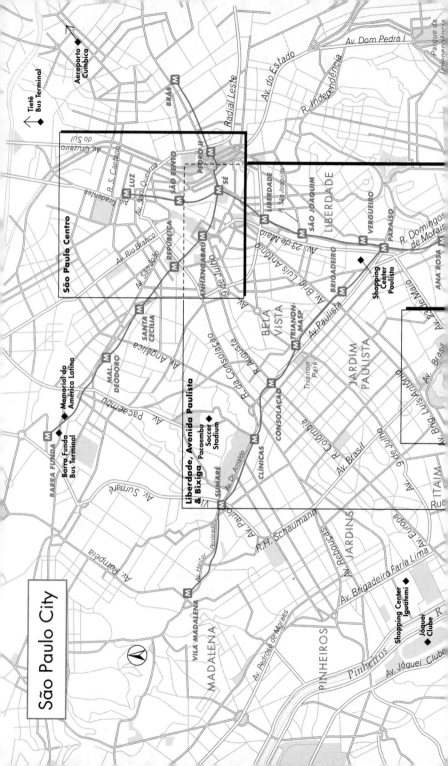

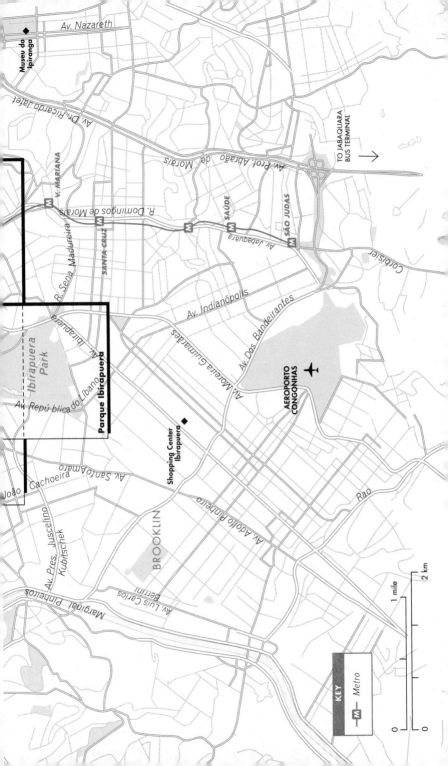

nightlife options. At its western border, Itaim stretches down to the Marginal.

PINHEIROS

Just north of Itaim and west of Jardins sits Pinheiros (pine trees), another nightlife hot spot chockfull of bars, clubs, and late-night restaurants. The area, with some of the city's most expensive low-rise housing, is also traversed by the popular Avenida Brigadeiro Faria Lima and has the Marginal as its western boundary.

VILA MADALENA

One of the hillier parts of São Paulo with impressive views across the city from the uppermost buildings, Vila Madalena is a relatively small suburb just to the north of Pinheiros. It's yet another nightlife mecca with bohemian-style haunts that stay open until dawn. Bars are stacked one on top of the other, making it a great place for a pub crawl, particularly because it's also one of the city's safest after-dark spots.

A VIEW OF THE PAST

Although modern-day São Paulo is a tough place to navigate thanks to the jungle of tall buildings, this certainly wasn't always the case. During the city's first few hundred years, before the the current crop of skyscrapers appeared, there were impressive views from Avenida Paulista, which runs along a natural ridge line, the highest part of the hilly Vila Madalena area.

PLANNING

WHEN TO GO

Cultural events—film and music festivals, and fashion and art exhibits—usually take place between April and December. In South American summer (January–March) the weather is rainy, and floods can disrupt traffic. Be sure to make reservations for beach resorts as far in advance as possible, particularly for weekend stays. In winter (June and July), follow the same rule for visits to Campos do Jordão. Summers are hot—35°C (95°F). In winter temperatures rarely dip below 10°C (50°F).

■TIP→ The air pollution might irritate your eyes, especially in July and August (dirty air is held in the city by thermal inversions), so pack eye drops.

SAFETY

Stay alert and guard your belongings at all times. Avoid wearing expensive sneakers or watches and flashy jewelry, or carrying cameras or laptops—all of which attract attention. Muggers love to target Centro and Liberdade nieghborhoods. Crimes often occur at ATMs throughout the city and at the airports, particularly if you're carrying a laptop.

If you're driving, stay alert during traffic jams and at stop signs, especially at night, and don't deviate from the main streets and beltways. Watch out for motorcycle drivers—there are many who are express couriers, but some are robbers. You should always be wary when there are two people on one bike. It's best to keep your windows up and doors locked.

GETTING AROUND

Navigating São Paulo is not easy, and staying either in the central areas or at least near an inner-city subway station is advisable, especially if you don't plan on renting a car or taking cabs. The subway is quick, easy, inexpensive, and covers much of the city, with stops near the most interesting sites for travelers. Buses can be hard to navigate if you don't speak Portuguese. Driving in São Paulo, particularly in peak hours, can be slow and difficult. For longer stays, obtain a provisional drivers license and a good map—with a little care and a lot of confidence, you can get by. Parking can be perplexing, so it's probably best to use a parking lot (estacionamento), which are numerous and relatively cheap. Cabs rates are reasonable and they're abundant in the popular neighborhoods.

> **THE MOTORBIKE LANE**
>
> Driving along São Paulo's huge Marginal expressway can be memorable for a number of reasons (good and bad). One of the most interesting and downright scary sights is the often endless file of motorbikes that squeeze their own impromtu lane between two of the road's outer lanes. In heavy traffic the "motoboys" virtually fly in between the gridlocked cars, using the few feet of space to make their way. If driving, keep an eye out when changing lanes and try to stick to the opposite side of your lane to avoid collisions.

EXPLORING

CENTRO

Even though the downtown district has its share of petty crime, it's one of the few places with a significant amount of pre-20th-century history. Explore the areas where the city began and see examples of architecture, some of it beautifully restored, from the 19th century. The best way to get here is by metro.

Numbers in the text correspond to numbers in the margin and on the São Paulo Centro map.

MAIN ATTRACTIONS

❺ Catedral da Sé. The imposing 14-tower neo-Gothic church, renovated in 2002, has tours through the crypt that contains the remains of Tibiriçá, a native Brazilian who helped the Portuguese back in 1554. ⊠*Praça da Sé s/n, Centro, 01001-001* ☎*011/3106–2709 or 011/3107–6832 for tour information* ⚞*Tour R$3* ⊙*Mon. and Wed.–Sat. 8–5, Sun. 8:30–6; tour Mon. and Wed.–Sat. 9:30–4:30* Ⓜ*Sé.*

❾ Centro Cultural Banco do Brasil. In a neoclassic 1901 building, this cultural center has become a popular space in town for modern and contemporary art. It has three floors of exhibition rooms, a theater, an auditorium, a movie theater, and a video room. ⊠*Rua Álvares Penteado 112, Centro, 01012-000* ☎*011/3113–3651* ⚞*Free* ⊙*Tues.–Sun. 9–8* Ⓜ*Sé.*

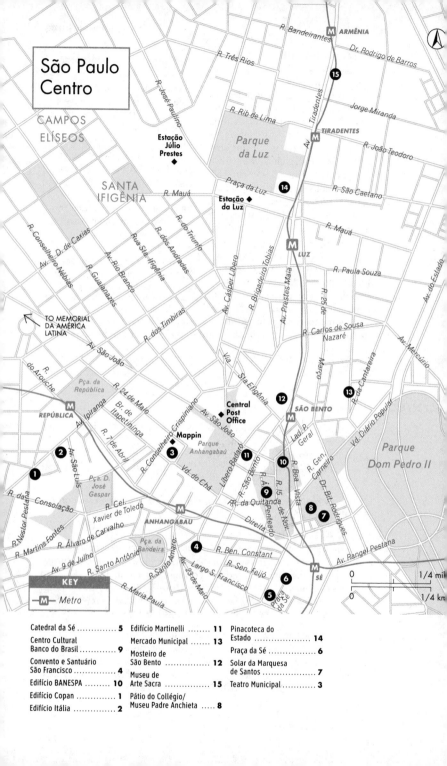

São Paulo Centro

CAMPOS ELÍSEOS

SANTA IFIGÊNIA

Estação Júlio Prestes ◆

Parque da Luz

Praça da Luz

Estação ◆ da Luz

ARMÊNIA

Dr. Rodrigo de Barros

R. Bandeirantes

R. Três Rios

R. José Paulino

R. Rib de Lima

R. Maná

R. Sta. Ifigênia

R. do Triunfo

R. dos Andradas

Av. Rio Branco

R. Guaianazes

R. D. de Caxias

R. Conselheiro Nébias

Av. Conselheiro Nébias

Jorge Miranda

TIRADENTES

R. João Teodoro

R. São Caetano

R. Maná

Av. Tiradentes

LUZ

R. Paula Souza

R. Carlos de Sousa Nazaré

Av. do Estado

Av. Mercúrio

R. Casper Líbero

R. Brigadeiro Tobias

Av. Prestes Maia

R. 25 de Março

R. dos Timbiras

Av. São João

Via Sta. Efigênia

TO MEMORIAL DA AMÉRICA LATINA

R. do Arouche

Pça. da República

R. 24 de Maio

Bt. de Itapetininga

R. 7 de Abril

R. da Consolação

Pça. D. José Gaspar

R. Cel. Xavier de Toledo

ANHANGABAÚ

Pça. da Bandeira

Av. 9 de Julho

R. Santo Antônio

R. Martins Fontes

R. Álvaro de Carvalho

R. Nestor Pestana

REPÚBLICA

Av. Ipiranga

Av. São Luís

R. Conselheiro Crispiniano

Av. São João

Mappin

Parque Anhangabaú

Vd. do Chá

Libero Badaró

Central Post Office

R. Santo Amaro

Largo S. Francisco

R. Ben. Constant

R. Sen. Feijó

R. 23 de Maio

R. Maria Paula

SÃO BENTO

Lad. P. Geral

R. R. São Bento

R. Boa Vista

R. Gen. Carneiro

R. da Cantareira

Vd. Diário Popular

Parque Dom Pedro II

R. da Quitanda

R. 15 de Nov.

Direita

R. Anhaia Penteado

Dr. Blt. Rodrigues

SÉ

Av. Rangel Pestana

Praça da Sé

KEY

Ⓜ — Metro

0   1/4 mil

0   1/4 km

② **Edifício Itália.** To see the astounding view from atop the Itália Building, you'll have to patronize the Terraço Itália restaurant, on the 41st floor. As the restaurant is expensive and not one of the city's best, afternoon tea or a drink is the favored way to get the view. Tea is served 3–5:30, and the bar opens at 6. ⊠ *Av. Ipiranga 344, Centro, 01046-010* ☎ *011/2189-2929 restaurant* ⊕ *www.terracoita lia.com.br* Ⓜ *República.*

STAY ALERT

Pickpocketing can be a problem in Centro, so keep a low profile, don't wear expensive jewelry or watches, and bring only what money you absolutely need. Touring with a guide usually provides some extra security.

3

⑪ ★ **Edifício Martinelli.** Amid São Paulo's modern 1950s-era skyscrapers, the Gothic Martinelli Building is a welcome anomaly. Built in 1929 by Italian immigrant–turned-count Giuseppe Martinelli, it was the city's first skyscraper. The whimsical penthouse is worth checking out. The rooftop has a great view; to go there you need to get permission from the building manager on the ground floor and leave your ID at the front desk. Then take the elevator to the 34th floor and walk up two more flights. ⊠ *Av. São João 35, Centro, 01008-906* ☎ *011/3104-2477* ⊕ *www.prediomartinelli.com.br* ⊡ *Free* ⊙ *8* AM–*6* PM Ⓜ *São Bento.*

⑬ **Fodor's Choice** ★ **Mercado Municipal.** The city's first grocery market, this huge 1928 neo-baroque-style building got a major renovation in 2004 and is now the quintessential hot spot for gourmets and food lovers. The building, nicknamed Mercadão (Big Market) by locals, houses 318 stands that sell just about everything edible, including meat, vegetables, cheese, spices, and fish from all over Brazil. It also has restaurants and traditional snack places—don't miss the salt cod *pastel* at Hocca Bar. ⊠ *Rua da Cantareira 306, Centro, 01024-000* ☎ *011/3228-0673* ⊕ *www. mercadomunicipal.com.br* ⊡ *Free* ⊙ *Mon.–Sat. 5* AM–*6* PM, *Sun. 7–4* Ⓜ *São Bento.*

⑫ ★ **Mosteiro de São Bento.** This unique, Norman–Byzantine church constructed between 1910 and 1922 was designed by German architect Richard Berndl. Its enormous organ has some 6,000 pipes, and its Russian image of the Kasperovo Virgin is covered with 6,000 pearls from the Black Sea. If you go on Sunday, don't miss the 10 AM mass and the monks' Gregorian chants. ⊠ *Largo de São Bento, Centro, 01029-010* ☎ *011/3328-8799* ⊕ *www.mosteiro.org.br* ⊡ *Free* ⊙ *Weekdays 6* AM–*6:30* PM, *weekends 6–noon and 4–6* Ⓜ *São Bento.*

⑮ ★ **Museu de Arte Sacra.** If you can't get to Bahia or Minas Gerais during your stay in Brazil, you can get a taste of the fabulous baroque and rococo art found there at the Museum of Sacred Art. On display is a collection of 4,000 wooden and terra-cotta masks, jewelry, and liturgical objects from all over the country (but primarily Minas Gerais and Bahia), dating from the 17th century to the present. The on-site convent was founded in 1774. ⊠ *Av. Tiradentes 676, Centro, 01101-000* ☎ *011/3326-1373* ⊡ *R$4* ⊙ *Tues.–Fri. 11* AM–*6* PM, *weekends 10* AM–*7* PM Ⓜ *Tiradentes or Luz.*

CLOSE UP
A Bit of History

São Paulo wasn't big and important right from the start. It was founded in 1554 by Jesuit priests who began converting native Indians to Catholicism. The town was built strategically on a plateau, protected from attack and served by many rivers. It remained unimportant to the Portuguese crown until the 1600s, when it became the departure point for the *bandeira* (literally, "flag") expeditions, whose members set out to look for gemstones and gold, to enslave Indians, and, later, to capture escaped African slaves. In the process, these adventurers established roads into vast portions of previously unexplored territory. São Paulo also saw Emperor Dom Pedro I declare independence from Portugal in 1822, by the Rio Ipiranga (Ipiranga River), near the city.

It was only in the late 19th century that São Paulo became a driving force in the country. As the state established itself as one of Brazil's main coffee producers, the city attracted laborers and investors from many countries. Italians, Portuguese, Spanish, Germans, and Japanese put their talents and energies to work. By 1895, 70,000 of the 130,000 residents were immigrants. Their efforts transformed the place from a sleepy mission post into a dynamic financial and cultural

hub, with people of all colors and religions living and working together peacefully.

Avenida Paulista was once the site of many a coffee baron's mansion. Money flowed from these private domains into civic and cultural institutions. The arts began to flourish, and by the 1920s São Paulo was promoting such great artists as Mário and Oswald de Andrade, who introduced modern elements into Brazilian art.

In the 1950s the auto industry began to develop and contributed greatly to São Paulo's contemporary wealth—and problems. Over the next 30 years, people from throughout Brazil, especially the northeast, came seeking jobs, which transformed the city's landscape by increasing slums and poverty. Between the 1950s and today, the city's main revenue moved from industry to banking and commerce.

Today, like many major European or American hubs, São Paulo struggles to meet its citizens' transportation and housing needs, and goods and services are expensive. Like most of its counterparts elsewhere in the world, it hasn't yet found an answer to these problems.

⑭ Pinacoteca do Estado. The building that houses the State Art Gallery was constructed in 1905 and renovated in 1998. The permanent collection has more than 5,000 works of art, including more than 10 Rodin sculptures and several pieces by famous Brazilian artists like Tarsila do Amaral (whose work consists of colorful, somewhat abstract portraits) and Cândido Portinari (whose oil paintings have social and historical themes). The building has a restaurant. ⊠*Praça da Luz 2, Centro, 01120-010* ☎*011/3324–1000* ⊕*www.pinacoteca.org.br* ☒*R$4, Sat. free* ☉*Tues.–Sun. 10–6* Ⓜ*Luz.*

❻ Praça da Sé. Two major metro lines cross under the large, busy Praça da Sé, which marks the city's geographical center and houses its main cathedral (⇨ *Catedral da Sé*, *above*). Here migrants from Brazil's poor northeast often gather to enjoy their music and to sell and buy regional items such as medicinal herbs, while street children hang out trying to avoid the periodic (and controversial) police sweeps to get them off the street. ⊠*Praça da Sé s/n, Centro, 01001-000* Ⓜ*Sé.*

> ### GAROA
>
> One of São Paulo's most famous nicknames is *terra da garoa*, which basically means land of drizzling rain. Although some periods of the year are worse than others, no matter when you visit you'll more than likely get at least a little taste of garoa. An umbrella can be your best friend.

IF YOU HAVE TIME

4 **Convento e Santuário São Francisco.** The baroque building is actually two churches, one run by Catholic clergy and the other by lay brothers. One of the city's best-preserved Portuguese colonial buildings, it was built between 1647 and 1790, and restored in 1997. ⊠*Largo São Francisco 133, Centro, 01005-010* ☎*011/3106–0081* ⊕*www.franciscanos.org.br* ⊠*Free* ⊙*Daily 7:30 AM–8 PM* Ⓜ*Sé or Anhangabaú.*

10 **Edifício BANESPA.** If you can't fit tea or drinks at the top of the Edifício Itália into your Centro tour, get your panoramic view of the city atop the 36-floor BANESPA Building. It was inaugurated in 1947 and modeled after New York's Empire State Building. A radio traffic reporter squints through the smog every morning from here. ⊠*Rua João Brícola 24, Centro, 01014-900* ☎*011/3249–7180* ⊠*Free* ⊙*Weekdays 10–5* Ⓜ*São Bento.*

1 **Edifício Copan.** The architect of this serpentine apartment and office block, Oscar Niemeyer, went on to design much of Brasília, the nation's capital. The building has the clean, white, undulating curves characteristic of his work. The Copan was constructed in 1950, and its 1,160 apartments house about 5,600 people. At night the area is overrun by prostitutes and transvestites. ⊠*Av. Ipiranga 200, Centro, 01066-900* ☎*011/3257–6169* ⊕*www.copansp.com.br* Ⓜ*República.*

OFF THE BEATEN PATH

Memorial da América Latina. A group of buildings designed by Oscar Niemeyer, the Latin American Memorial includes the Pavilhão da Criatividade Popular (Popular Creativity Pavilion), which has a permanent exhibition of handicrafts from all over Latin America. The Salão de Atos Building shows the panel *Tiradentes*, about an independence hero from Minas Gerais, painted by Cândido Portinari in 1949. Regular activities include shows, videos, and films. Ask for an English-speaking guide. ⊠*Av. Auro Soares de Moura Andrade 664, Barra Funda, 01156-001* ☎*011/3823–4600* ⊕*www.memorial.sp.gov.br* ⊠*Free* ⊙*Tues.–Sun. 9–6* Ⓜ*Barra Funda.*

8 **Pateo do Collegio / Museu Padre Anchieta.** São Paulo was founded by the Jesuits José de Anchieta and Manoel da Nóbrega in the College Courtyard in 1554. The church was constructed in 1896 in the same style as the chapel built by the Jesuits. In the small museum you can see some paintings from the colonization period and an exhibition of early sacred art and relics. ⊠ *Praça Pateo do Collegio 2, Centro, 01016-040* ☏ *011/3105–6899* ⊕ *www.pateo collegio.com.br* ⊡ *Museum R$5* ☉ *Museum Tues.–Sun. 9–5; church Mon.–Sat. 8:15–7, Sun. mass at 10 AM* Ⓜ *Sé.*

❼ Solar da Marquesa de Santos. This 18th-century manor house was bought by Marquesa de Santos in 1843, and became famous for housing the emperor's mistress. Now it contains a museum that hosts temporary painting, photo, and sculpture exhibits that usually focus on a São Paulo theme. ⊠ *Rua Roberto Simonsen 136, Centro, 01017-020* ☏ *011/3105–2030* ⊡ *Free* ☉ *Tues.–Sun. 9–5* Ⓜ *Sé.*

❸ Teatro Municipal. Inspired by the Paris Opéra, the Municipal Theater was built between 1903 and 1911 with art nouveau elements. *Hamlet* was the first play presented, and the house went on to host such luminaries as Isadora Duncan in 1916 and Anna Pavlova in 1919. Plays and operas are still staged here; local newspapers have schedules and information on how to get tickets. The fully restored auditorium, resplendent with gold leaf, moss-green velvet, marble, and mirrors, has 1,500 seats and is usually open only to those attending cultural events, although prearranged visits are also available. A dedicated, on-site museum was reopened in 2007. ⊠ *Praça Ramos de Azevedo, Centro, 01037-010* ☏ *011/3223–3022* ⊡ *Tickets from R$10* ☉ *Tours by appointment Tues. and Thurs. at 1 PM* Ⓜ *Anhangabaú.*

NEED A BREAK?

Café Girondino (⊠ *Rua Boa Vista 365, Centro, 01014-010* ☏ *011/3229–4574* ⊕ *www.cafegirondino.com.br* Ⓜ *São Bento*) is crowded with finance types on weekdays, from happy hour until 11 PM. The bar serves good draft beer and sandwiches. Pictures on the wall depict Centro in its early days. **Café do Pateo** (⊠ *Praça Pateo do Collegio 2, Centro, 01016-040* ☏ *011/3106–4303* ⊕ *www.cafedopateo.com.br* Ⓜ *São Bento*) is great for a quick break before or after appreciating the museum. On a large balcony overlooking the east side of town, it serves cold and hot drinks along with typical snacks, such as *pão de queijo* (cheese bread).

LIBERDADE

The red-porticoed entryway to Liberdade (which means "Freedom") is south of Praça da Sé, behind the cathedral. The neighborhood is home to many first-, second-, and third-generation Nippo-Brazilians, as well as to more recent Chinese and Korean immigrants. Clustered around

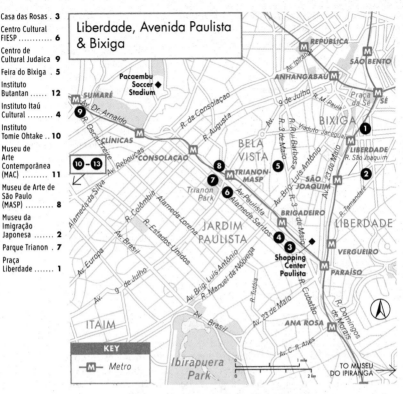

Liberdade, Avenida Paulista & Bixiga

Avenida Liberdade are shops with everything from imported bubble gum to miniature robots and Kabuki face paint.

The best time to visit Liberdade is on Sunday during the street fair at Praça Liberdade, where Asian food, crafts, and souvenirs are sold. The fair will very likely be crowded, so keep your wits about you and do not wander around at night.

Numbers in the text correspond to numbers in the margin and on the Liberdade, Avenida Paulista & Bixiga map.

MAIN ATTRACTIONS

❷ Museu da Imigração Japonesa. The Museum of Japanese Immigration has two floors of exhibits about Nippo-Brazilian culture and farm life, and about Japanese contributions to Brazilian horticulture, along with World War II memorials. Call ahead to arrange for an English-language tour. ⊠*Rua São Joa-*

PAULISTA/PAULISTANO

The Brazilians use nicknames to describe where their citizens come from, and in São Paulo there are two distinct groups. The more commonly used "Paulista" refers to anyone who was born in the state of São Paulo, while "Paulistano" is a special subcategory used only for people from São Paulo city. The tags can be especially useful in conversations about sports, politics, and social hierarchy.

quim 381, Liberdade, 01508-900 ☎011/3209–5465 ⊕www.nihon site.com.br/muse/ ✉R$5 ⊘Tues.– Sun. 1:30–5:30 Ⓜ São Joaquim.

IF YOU HAVE TIME

❶ Praça Liberdade. Every weekend ★ 10–7, this plaza hosts a sprawling Asian food and crafts fair that exhibits São Paulo's eclectic cultural mix. You may see, for example, Afro-Brazilians dressed in colorful kimonos hawking grilled shrimp on a stick. Several religious celebrations are held here, like April's Hanamatsuri, commemorating the

birth of the Buddha. Apart from the fair and special events, another reason to visit this square is to stop by at the nearby Japanese shops and restaurants. ✉Av. da Liberdade and Rua dos Estudantes, Liberdade, 01503-010 Ⓜ Liberdade.

AVENIDA PAULISTA & BIXIGA

Money once poured into and out of the coffee barons' mansions that lined Avenida Paulista, making it, in a sense, the financial hub. And so it is today, though the money is now centered in the major banks. Like the barons before them, many of these financial institutions generously support the arts. Numerous places have changing exhibitions—often free—in the Paulista neighborhood. Nearby Bixiga, São Paulo's Little Italy, is full of restaurants.

MAIN ATTRACTIONS

❸ Casa das Rosas. The House of the Roses, a French-style mansion with gardens inspired by those at Versailles, seems out of place next to the skyscrapers of Paulista. It was built in 1935 by famous *paulistano* architect Ramos de Azevedo for one of his daughters. The building was home to the same family until 1986, when it was made an official municipal landmark. It was later opened as a cultural center, and it's one of the avenue's few remaining early-20th-century buildings. ✉Av. Paulista 37, Paraíso, 01311-902 ☎011/3285–6986 ⊕www.casadas rosas.sp.gov.br ✉Free ⊘Tues.–Sun. 11–9 Ⓜ Brigadeiro.

❻ Centro Cultural FIESP. The cultural center of São Paulo State's Federation of Industry has a theater, a library of art and comic books, and temporary art exhibits. ✉Av. Paulista 1313, Jardim Paulista, 01311-923 ☎011/3146–7405 ✉Free ⊕www.sesisp.org.br/centrocultural/ ⊘Tues.–Sun. 9–7 Ⓜ Trianon.

NEED A BREAK?
A recommended snack is the delicious *bauru*—a sandwich with roast beef, tomato, cucumber, and a mix of melted cheeses—at Ponto Chic (✉*Praça Osvaldo Cruz 26, Paraíso, 04004-070* ☎*011/3289-1480* ⊕ *www.pontochic. com.br* ⊘ *Daily 11 AM–2 AM*), a block east of Instituto Itaú Cultural, across Ave-

nida Paulista. The restaurant claims to have invented the sandwich.

8 **Museu de Arte de São Paulo (MASP).**
Fodor'sChoice One of the city's premier fine-arts
★ collections, with more than 7,000 pieces, is in this striking low-rise, elevated on two massive concrete pillars 256 feet apart. Highlights of the collection are works by Van Gogh, Renoir, Delacroix, Cézanne, Monet, Rembrandt, Picasso, and Degas. Baroque sculptor Aleijadinho, expressionist painter Lasar Segall, and expressionist/surrealist painter Cândido Portinari are three of the many Brazilian artists represented. The huge open area beneath the museum is often used for cultural events and is the site of a charming Sunday antiques fair. ✉ *Av. Paulista 1578, Bela Vista, 01310-200* ☎ *011/3251–5644* ⊕ *www.masp. art.br* 💲 *R$10* ⊗ *Tues.–Sun. 11–6* Ⓜ *Trianon.*

TAKE A WALK

The imposing and almost dead-straight Avenida Paulista a great place to explore on foot. The Museu de Arte de São Paulo (MASP) has one of Brazil's best collections of fine art. Right across the street is Parque Trianon, where locals hang out and eat lunch. Leaving the park, veer right and head for the Centro Cultural FIESP. Here you may be able to catch one of their art shows or perfomances. A few blocks away is the Instituto Itaú Cultural, a great place to see contemporary Brazilian art. Finally, rest your weary feet in Casa das Rosas, a beautiful Versailles-inspired garden.

7 **Parque Trianon.** Originally created in 1892 as a showcase for local vegetation, in 1968 the park was renovated by Roberto Burle Marx, the Brazilian landscaper famed for Rio's mosaic-tile beachfront sidewalks. You can escape the noise of the street and admire the flora and the 300-year-old trees while seated on one of the benches sculpted to look like chairs. ✉ *Rua Peixoto Gomide 949, Jardim Paulista, 01311-400* ☎ *011/3289–2160* 💲 *Free* ⊗ *Daily 6–6* Ⓜ *Trianon.*

IF YOU HAVE TIME

9 **Centro da Cultura Judaica.** A short cab or metro trip northwest of Avenida Paulista, this Torah-shape concrete building is one of the newest architectural hot spots in town. Inaugurated in 2003 to display Jewish history and culture in Brazil, it houses a theater and an art gallery and promotes exhibits, lectures, and book fairs. The café serves local Jewish cuisine. ✉ *Rua Oscar Freire 2500, Pinheiros, 05409-012* ☎ *011/3065–4333* ⊕ *www.culturajudaica.org.br* 💲 *Free* ⊗ *Weekdays 10–9, weekends 2–7* Ⓜ *Sumaré.*

5 **Feira do Bixiga.** Strolling through this flea market is a favorite Sunday activity for paulistanos. Crafts, antiques, and furniture are among the wares. Walk up the São José staircase to see **Rua dos Ingleses,** a typical and well-preserved fin de siecle Bixiga street. ✉ *Praça Dom Orione s/n, Bixiga, 01325-020* 💲 *Free* ⊗ *Sun. 8–5.*

4 **Instituto Itaú Cultural.** Maintained by Itaú, one of Brazil's largest private banks, this cultural institute has art shows as well as lectures, workshops, and films. It also maintains an archive with the photographic history of São Paulo and a library that specializes in works on Brazilian art and culture. ⊠*Av. Paulista 149, Paraíso, 01311-000* ☏*011/2168–1700* ⊕*www.itaucultural.org.br* ▣*Free* ⊙*Tues.–Fri. 10–9, weekends 10–7* Ⓜ*Brigadeiro.*

PARQUE IBIRAPUERA

Ibirapuera is São Paulo's Central Park, though it's slightly less than half the size and is often more crowded on sunny weekends than its NYC counterpart. In the 1950s the land, which originally contained the municipal nurseries, was chosen as the site of a public park to commemorate the city's 400th anniversary. Oscar Niemeyer and Roberto Burle Marx were called in to join the team of professionals assigned to the project. The park was inaugurated in 1954, and some pavilions used for the opening festivities still sit amid its 160 hectares (395 acres). It has jogging and biking paths, a lake, and rolling lawns. You can rent bicycles at a number of places near park entrances for about R$5 an hour.

MAIN ATTRACTIONS

❺ Museu de Arte Moderna (MAM). More than 4,500 paintings, installations, sculptures, and other works from modern and contemporary artists such as Alfredo Volpi and Ligia Clark are part of the Modern Art Museum's permanent collection. Temporary exhibits feature works by new local artists. The giant wall of glass, designed by Brazilian architect Lina Bo Bardi, serves as a window beckoning you to peek inside. ⊠*Av. Pedro Álvares Cabral s/n, Gate 3, Parque Ibirapuera, 04094-000* ☏*011/5085–1300* ⊕*www.mam.org.br* ▣*R$5.50, free Sun.* ⊙*Tues.–Sun. 10–6.*

NEED A BREAK? The Prêt no MAM (⊠*Gate 3, Parque Ibirapuera, 04094-000* ☏*011/5574–1250* ⊕*www.mam.org.br*), inside the Museu de Arte Moderna, has literally hundreds of dishes on offer blending Brazilian, French, and Italian. It's also one of the only places in the park to buy food, apart from hot-dog stands.

❸ Oca. This spacecraft-looking building that hosts art exhibits is pure Oscar Niemeyer. Its temporary traditional- and pop-art exhibits usually break attendance records. When exhibits aren't on, the building is usually not open to the public. Admission varies; check local newspapers for exhibits. ⊠*Gate 3, Parque Ibirapuera, 04094-000* ☏*011/5574–5505, 5579–9912 exhibit information.*

❹ Pavilhão da Bienal. In every even-numbered year this pavilion hosts the Bienal (Biennial) art exhibition, which draws hundreds of artists from more than 60 countries. The first such event was held in 1951 in Parque Trianon and drew artists from 21 countries. It was moved to this Oscar Niemeyer–designed building—with its large open spaces and floors connected by circular slopes—after Ibirapuera Park's 1954 inauguration. Odd-numbered years bring an architecture exhibition. The pavilion also houses a branch of the **Museu de Arte Contemporânea** (MAC ⊠*3rd fl., Parque Ibirapuera, 04094-000* ☏*011/5573–9974 direct line, 011/5574–5922 automated English line* ⊕*www.macvir tual.usp.br* ▣*Free* ⊙*Tues.–Sun. 10–7*). There's much more to see at

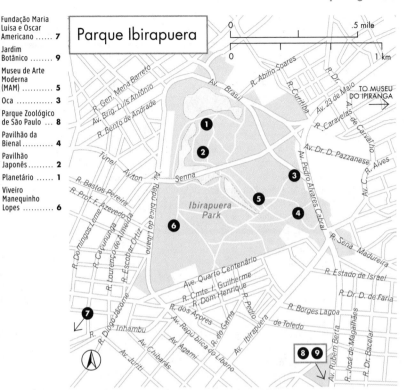

the main branch of the museum, at the University of São Paulo, but this park branch has some temporary exhibits. ✉ *Gate 3, Parque Ibirapuera, 04094-000* ☎ *011/5573–9932 or 011/5574–5922* ⊕ *www. bienalsaopaulo.org.br.*

IF YOU HAVE TIME

② **Pavilhão Japonês.** An exact replica of the Katsura Imperial Palace in Kyoto, Japan, the Japanese Pavilion is also one of the structures built for the park's inauguration. It was designed by University of Tokyo professor Sutemi Horiguti and built in Japan. It took four months to reassemble beside the man-made lake in the Japanese-style garden with a goldfish-filled lake. The main building displays samurai clothes and pottery and sculpture from several dynasties. Rooms upstairs are used for traditional tea ceremonies. ✉ *Gate 10, Parque Ibirapuera, 04094-000* ☎ *011/5573–6453* ✐ *R$3* ◷ *Weds. and weekends 10–noon and 1–5.*

> **LAP OF LUXURY**
>
> Surrounding Parque Ibirapuera are some of the city's most expensive mansions and apartment buildings. Walk around the outskirts of the park and get an eyeful of the rich and famous of São Paulo. Better still, venture into one of the luxurious suburbs and join them for coffee or beer at a trendy *padaria* (part bakery, part bar).

The Hardest Word to Translate

Few words explain the Brazilian character as well as *saudade*. Deriving from the word *solitate* ("loneliness," in Latin), its meaning is close to nostalgia, and defines a feeling of loss of something very dear. When a Brazilian doesn't see a friend for a long time, for example, when they meet again one will say that she felt saudade—a mixture of sadness at not having seen the friend in a long time and a feeling of affection and nostalgia. Considered one of the most difficult words to translate, saudade received a definition from the famous linguist, A.F.G Bell, who wrote that "The famous word *saudade* is a vague and constant desire for something other than the present, a turning towards the past or the future, an indolent dreaming wistfulness." The word appears in the lyrics of famous Brazilian songs like "Chega de Saudade" (No More Saudade), the first bossa nova song and a milestone in Brazilian culture.

❶ **Planetário.** Completely renovated over seven years and reopened in 2006, ☾ the Planetário has 280 seats under its 48-foot-high dome, and features a brand new fiber-optic projection system. ✉ *Gate 2, Av. Pedro Álvares Cabral, Parque Ibirapuera, 04094-000* ☎ *011/5575–5425* 💲*R$5* ☉ *Weekdays 9–6, weekends 10:30 until the final session.*

❻ **Viveiro Manequinho Lopes.** The Manequinho Lopes Nursery is where most plants and trees used by the city are grown. The original was built in the 1920s; the current version was designed by Roberto Burle Marx. Specimens are of such Brazilian trees as *ipê, pau-jacaré,* and *pau-brasil,* the tree for which the country was named (the red dye it produces was greatly valued by the Europeans). ✉ *Gate 7A, Av. República do Líbano, Parque Ibirapuera, 04094-000* ☎ *011/3887–6761* 💲*Free* ☉ *Weekdays 8–6.*

ELSEWHERE IN SÃO PAULO

Several far-flung sights are worth a taxi ride to see. West of Centro is the Universidade de São Paulo (USP), which has two very interesting museums: a branch of the Museu de Arte Contemporânea and the Instituto Butantã, with its collection of creatures that slither and crawl. Head southwest of Centro to the Fundação Maria Luisa e Oscar Americano, a museum with a forest and garden in the residential neighborhood of Morumbi. In the Parque do Estado, southeast of Centro, are the Jardim Botânico and the Parque Zoológico de São Paulo.

MAIN ATTRACTIONS

❼ **Fundação Maria Luisa e Oscar Americano.** A beautiful, quiet private wooded ★ estate is the setting for the Maria Luisa and Oscar Americano Foundation. Paintings, furniture, sacred art, silver, porcelain, engravings, personal possessions of the Brazilian royal family, tapestries, and sculpture are among the 1,500 objects from the Portuguese colonial and imperial periods. There are some modern pieces as well, along with an exclusive tea room and an auditorium that hosts concerts on Sunday. ✉ *Av.*

Morumbi 4077, Morumbi, 05650-000 ☏*011/3742–0077* ⊕*www. fundacaooscaramericano.org.br* ⊡*R$8* ⊙*Tues.–Fri. 11–5, week-ends 10–5.*

⓫ **Museu de Arte Contemporânea** *(MAC).* On the grounds of the country's largest university, Universidade de São Paulo, the main branch of the MAC displays the work of world-renowned European artists Pablo Picasso, Amedeo Modigliani, Wassily Kandinsky, Joan Miró, and Henri Matisse. Also look for the works of well-known Brazilian artists Anita Malfatti, Tarsila do Amaral, Cândido Portinari, and Emiliano Di Cavalcanti. The smaller branch of the

MAC is at the Parque Ibirapuera. ⊠*Rua da Reitoria 160, Cidade Universitária, 05508-900* ☏*011/3091–3039* ⊕*www.mac.usp.br* ⊡*Free* ⊙*Tues.–Fri. 10–6, weekends 10–4.*

Museu do Ipiranga. The oldest and most-visited museum in town, Museu Paulista da Universidade de São Paulo, or Museu do Ipiranga, occupies an 1890 building constructed to honor Brazil's independence from Portugal, declared in the Ipiranga area in 1822 by then-emperor Dom Pedro I. The huge Pedro Américo oil painting depicting this very moment hangs in the main room of this French-inspired eclectic palace, whose famous gardens were patterned after those of Versailles. Dom Pedro's tomb lies under one of the museum's monuments. ⊠*Parque da Independência, Ipiranga, 04218-970* ☏*011/6165–8026* ⊕*www. mp.usp.br* ⊡*R$4* ⊙*Wed.–Sun. 9–4:45.*

❽ **Parque Zoológico de São Paulo.** The 200-acre São Paulo Zoo has more ☪ than 3,000 animals, and many of its 410 species—such as the *mico-* ★ *leão-dourado* (golden lion tamarin monkey)—are endangered. See the monkey houses, built on small islands in the park's lake, and the Casa do Sangue Frio (Cold-Blooded House), with reptilian and amphibious creatures. ⊠*Av. Miguel Stéfano 4241, Água Funda, Parque do Estado, 04301-905* ☏*011/5073–0811* ⊕*www.zoologico.com.br* ⊡*R$12* ⊙*Tues.–Sun. 9–5.*

IF YOU HAVE TIME

⓬ **Instituto Butantan.** In 1888 a Brazilian scientist, with the aid of the state ☪ government, turned a farmhouse into a center for the production of snake serum. Today the Instituto Butantan has more than 70,000 snakes, spiders, scorpions, and lizards in its five museums. It still extracts venom and processes it into serum that's made available to victims of poisonous bites throughout Latin America. ⊠*Av. Vital Bra-*

sil 1500, Butantã, 05503-900 ☎*011/3726–7222* ⊕*www.butantan. gov.br* ✉*R$5* ⊘*Tues.–Sun. 9–4:30.*

❿ **Instituto Tomie Ohtake.** Designed by the architect Ruy Ohtake, this futuristic institute shows modern and contemporary art. It has eight exhibition rooms, a video room, a theater, an auditorium, a bookstore, a café, and a restaurant with a well-reputed Sunday brunch. ✉*Av. Brigadeiro Faria Lima 201, Pinheiros, 05426-010* ☎*011/2245–1900* ⊕*www. institutotomieohtake.org.br* ✉*Free* ⊘*Tues.–Sun. 11–8.*

❾ **Jardim Botânico.** The Botanical Gardens contain about 3,000 plants
Ⓒ belonging to more than 340 native species. The greenhouse has Atlantic rain-forest species, an orchid house, and a collection of aquatic plants. ✉*Av. Miguel Stéfano 3031, Água Funda, Parque do Estado, 04301-012* ☎*011/5073–6300* ⊕*www.ibot.sp.gov.br* ✉*R$3* ⊘*Wed.–Sun. 9–5.*

WHERE TO EAT

ABOUT THE RESTAURANTS & CUISINE

Updated by
Daniel Corry

São Paulo's dynamic social scene centers on dining out, and among the 12,000-plus restaurants, most of the world's cuisines are covered. The most popular options include Portuguese, Japanese, Italian, French, and Lebanese; contemporary fusions are popular and plentiful. The city also offers a massive selection of pizzerias with some world-class offerings. Most places don't require jacket and tie, but Paulistanos tend to dress to European standards, so if you're going to establishments in the $$$ to $$$$ range, looking elegant is key.

On the domestic front the Brazilian *churrascarias* are a carnivores dream, with their all-you-can-eat skewers of barbecued meats and impressive salad buffets. For in-between times, just about every bar will offer a selection of grilled meats, sandwiches, and deep-fried favorites for casual grazing. On Wednesday and Saturday, head to a Brazilan restaurant for *feijoada*—the national dish of black beans and pork. Ask about the other traditional and regional Brazilian dishes as well.

WHAT IT COSTS IN REAIS					
	¢	$	$$	$$$	$$$$
AT DINNER	under R$15	R$15–R$30	R$30–R$45	R$45–R$60	over R$60

Prices are per person for a main course at dinner or for a prix-fixe meal.

BIXIGA

ITALIAN

$$–$$$$ ✕ **Ca' D'Oro.** This is a longtime northern Italian favorite among Brazilian bigwigs, many of whom have their own tables in the old-world-style dining room. Quail, osso buco, and veal-and-raisin ravioli are winners, but the specialty is the Piedmontese *gran bollito misto,* steamed meats and vegetables accompanied by three sauces. ✉*Grande Hotel Ca'*

D'Oro, Rua Augusta 129, Bela Vista, 01305-900 ☎*011/3236–4300* ⊕*www.cadoro.com.br* ⊟*AE, DC, MC, V* Ⓜ*Anhangabaú.*

$$–$$$$ ✕**Roperto.** Wine casks and bottles adorn the walls at this typical Bix-
★ iga cantina, located on a street so charmingly human-scaled you'll hardly believe you're still in São Paulo. You won't be alone if you order the ever-popular fusilli—either *ao sugo* (with tomato sauce) or *ao frutos do mar* (with seafood)—or the traditional baby goat's leg with potatoes and tomatoes. ⊠*Rua 13 de Maio 634, Bixiga, 01327-002* ☎*011/3288–2573* ⊕*www.cantinaroperto.com.br* ⊟*DC, MC, V* Ⓜ*Brigadeiro.*

$–$$ ✕**Montechiaro.** The hardworking folks at this Brazilian-Argentine-owned cantina serve up a massive menu at more than reasonable prices—all of the plates serve two. Lasagna and roasted goat's leg are among the specialties of the house. Tuesday through Friday, they serve a specially priced executive menu, for those on an extra tight budget. Don't leave without picking up one of their cute embroidered bibs. ⊠*Rua Santo Antonio, 844/846, Bixiga, 01314-001* ☎*011/3259–2727* ⊕*www.montechiaro.com.br* ⊟*AE, DC, MC, V* Ⓜ*Brigadeiró.*

$–$$ ✕**Taberna do Julio.** Don't be fooled by the pedestrian, downtrodden exterior: walk through the vestibule and beneath the welcoming brick archway and you just might mistake the interior for an ancient Roman dining chamber. At about R$20, the *rodizio de massas* (all-you-can-eat pasta) is a pretty good deal. If none of the nine varieties offered there tempt you, try the *Espaguete ao vôngole,* which comes chock full of clams. ⊠*Rua Conselheiro Carrão, 392, Bixiga, 01328-000* ☎*011/89–0421* ⊕*www.tabernadojulio.hpg.com.br* ⊟*AE, DC, MC, V* Ⓜ*Brigadeiro.*

PIZZA

$–$$ ✕**Speranza.** One of the most traditional pizzerias in São Paulo, this res-
taurant is famous for its margherita pie. The crunchy *pão de linguiça* (sausage bread) appetizers have a fine reputation as well. Pastas and chicken and beef dishes are also served. ⊠*Rua 13 de Maio 1004, Bela Vista, 04515-001* ☎*011/3288–8502* ⊕*www.pizzaria.com.br* ⊟*DC, MC, V.*

CENTRO

FRENCH

$$–$$$$ ✕**La Casserole.** Facing a little Centro flower market, this romantic, Pari-
sian-style bistro has been around for five decades and has witnessed more than its share of wedding proposals during its years. Surrounded by wood-paneled walls decorated with art that nods at famous French artists, you can dine on such delights as *gigot d'agneau aux soissons* (roast leg of lamb in its own juices, served with white beans) and cherry strudel. ⊠*Largo do Arouche 346, Centro, 01219-019* ☎*011/3331–6283* ⊕*www.lacasserole.com.br* ⊟*AE, DC, MC, V* ⊘*Closed Mon. No lunch Sat.* Ⓜ*República.*

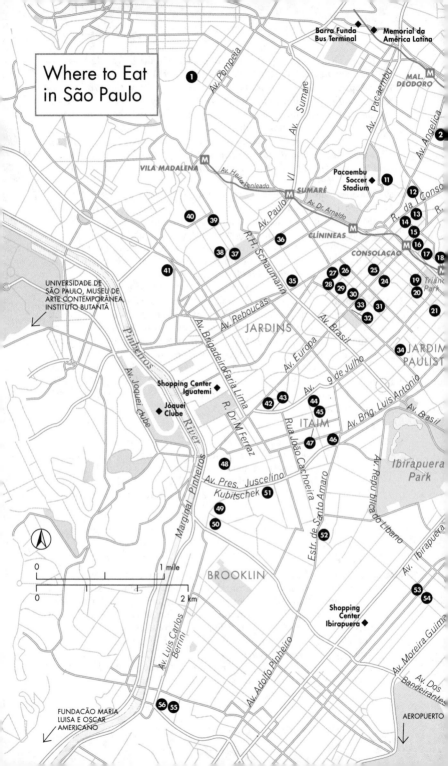

Where to Eat in São Paulo

Barra Funda
Bus Terminal

Memorial da
América Latina

MAL.
DEODORO

Av. Pompeia

Av. Sumaré

Av. Pacaembu

Av. Angelica

1

2

VILA MADALENA

Av. Heitor Penteado

VI.

SUMARÉ

Av. Paulo VI

Av. Dr. Arnaldo

Pacaembu
Soccer
Stadium

11

12

R. da Cons.

R.

40 **39**

R. H. Schaumann

36

CLÍNINEAS

14 **13**

15

CONSOLAÇÃO

M

16

38 **37**

35

41

27 **26**

25

17 **18**

19

Triânc.
Park

UNIVERSIDADE DE
SÃO PAULO, MUSEU DE
ARTE CONTEMPORÂNEA,
INSTITUTO BUTANTÃ

Av. Rebouças

28

29

30

24

20

33

31

21

32

JARDINS

Av. Brasil

34 JARDIM
PAULIST

Pinheiros

Av. Joquei Clube

Av. Brigadeiro Faria Lima

Av. Europa

Av. 9 de Julho

Shopping Center
Iguatemi

Jóquei
Clube

R. Dr. M. Ferraz

Av.

42 **43**

44

45

Av. Brig. Luis Antonio

Av. Brasil

River

ITAIM

47 **46**

Rua João Cacheoira

Av. Repu blica do Libano

Ibirapuera
Park

48

Av. Pres. Juscelino
Kubitschek

51

Marginal Pinheiros

49

50

Estr. de Santo Amaro

52

Av. Ibirapuera

BROOKLIN

1 mile

2 km

0

0

53

54

Shopping
Center
Ibirapuera

Av. Luis Carlos Berrini

Av. Adolfo Pinheiro

Av. Moreira Guima

Av. Dos Bandeirantes

FUNDACÃO MARIA
LUISA E OSCAR
AMERICANO

56 **55**

AEROPUERTO

Tietê
Bus Terminal

KEY

🚇 Metro

JARDIM BOTÂNICO,
JABAQUERO BUS TERMINAL,
PARQUE ZOOLÓGICO
DE SÃO PAULO

3

ITALIAN

$$$–$$$$
Fodor'sChoice
★
X **Famiglia Mancini.** This busy little cantina is well loved for both its cuisine and its location. It's on a singular, unforgettable strip of Rua Avandhandava, where you may find yourself admiring the cobblestones on the street as you wait for a table. An incredible buffet with cheeses, olives, sausages, and much more makes finding a tasty appetizer a cinch. The menu has many terrific pasta options,

> ### CAFEZINHO PLEASE
>
> When you finish the meal, don't forget to ask for a *cafezinho* ("little coffee"). Served at espresso size and strength, it's a great home-grown *digestif*. In this land of coffee, a cafezinho probably won't show up on the bill; a little cup at the end of a sumptuous meal is a standard way of saying thanks.

such as the cannelloni with palm hearts and a four-cheese sauce. All dishes serve two people. ⊠ *Rua Avanhandava 81, Centro, 01306-001* ☏*011/3256–4320* ⊕*www.famigliamancini.com.br* ⊟*AE, DC, MC, V* Ⓜ*Anhangabaú.*

$$–$$$$
X **Gigetto.** A true São Paulo classic, dedicated locals successfully lobbied to have its once slimmed-down menu re-elaborated to include more than 150 delicious options. Try the cappelletti *à romanesca* (with chopped ham, peas, mushrooms, and white cream sauce). Main courses serve two people. ⊠*Rua Avanhandava 63, Centro, 0136-001* ☏*011/3256–9804* ⊟*AE, DC, MC, V* Ⓜ*Anhangabaú.*

CERQUEIRA CÉSAR

BRAZILIAN

$$
X **Bargaço.** The original Bargaço, in Salvador, has long been considered the best Bahian restaurant in that city. If you can't make it to the northeast, be sure to have a meal in the São Paulo branch. Seafood is the calling card. ⊠*Rua Oscar Freire 1189, Cerqueira César, 01426-001* ☏*011/3085–5058* ⊕*www.restaurantebargaco.com.br* ⊟*DC, MC* Ⓜ*Consolação.*

ECLECTIC

$–$$$
X **Spot.** A few blocks west of MASP, this glass-encased diner is futuristic yet quaint. It's a lonely little single story tucked between government skyscrapers. Main dishes like Argentine beef are served up without any sides, so you'll have to order a dish like rice with broccoli to fill the plate. Come early if you want to eat—as the night wears on the extensive drink menu becomes the focus of partying patrons. ⊠*Alameda Rocha Azevedo 72, Cerqueira César, 01410-000* ☏*011/3284–6131 or 011/3283–0946* ⊕*www.restaurantespot.com.br* ⊟*AE, DC, MC, V* Ⓜ*Consolação.*

PIZZA

¢
★
X **Pedaço da Pizza.** This is one of the few places in the city where pizza is served by the slice. Choose from the traditional favorites like pepperoni, or an innovation, like pizza with shimeji mushrooms and kale. It's a good late-night stop, especially on the bar-filled Centro side of Rua Augusta, since it's open until 6 AM on weekends. The place is crowded

with paulistanos once the nearby movie theater lets out. ⊠*Rua Augusta 2931, Jardins, 01413-100* ☎*011/3891–2431* ⊠*Rua Augusta 1463, Cerqueira César* ☎*3285–2117* ▭*No credit cards* Ⓜ*Consolação.*

CONSOLAÇÃO

BRAZILIAN

¢–$$ ✕ **Sujinho–Bisteca d'Ouro.** Occupying corners on both sides of the street, the modest Sujinho honors its roots as an informal bar by serving churrasco without any frills. It's the perfect place for those who simply want to eat a gorgeous piece of meat with a cold bottle of beer. The portions are so large that one dish can usually feed two. A few options on the menu creep into

MEAL TIME
Eating out in São Paulo can be an all-night affair, so most restaurants open late and close even later. The majority will officially throw their doors open around 8 PM but will only get busy after 9 PM, regardless of what day it is. Try a bar that has a good happy hour if you want to eat earlier.

the $$$ price range. ⊠*Rua da Consolação 2078, Cerqueira César, 013002-001* ☎*011/3231–5207* ⊕*www.sujinho.com.br* ▭*No credit cards* Ⓜ*Consolação.*

ECLECTIC

$–$$$ ✕ **Mestiço.** Even the fabulous people have to wait at the bar before getting a table in this large sleek dining room; but for those with a vegetarian in their party, dishes like the California, a tofu and veggie curry, make the wait worth it. The restaurant also makes a point of using free-range chicken and ecologically responsible heart-of-palm throughout the eclectic menu, which also includes Italian, Brazilian, and Bahian dishes. ⊠*Rua Fernando de Albuquerque 277, Consolação, 01309-030* ☎*011/3256–1539 or 011/3256–3165* ⊕*www.mestico.com.br* ▭*AE, DC, MC, V* Ⓜ*Consolação.*

FRENCH

$–$$$ ✕ **La Tartine.** An ideal place for an intimate dinner, this small bistro has a good wine selection and an upstairs bar furnished with mismatched sofas and armchairs. The menu changes daily; a favorite is the classic coq au vin, or you can fill up on entrées such as beef tenderloin or soups and quiches. It's usually crowded with São Paulo's trendy people, and you might have to wait to get a table on weekends. ⊠*Rua Fernando de Albuquerque 267, Consolação, 01309-030* ☎*011/3259–2090* ▭*AE, V* ☉*Closed Sun.* Ⓜ*Consolação.*

HIGIENÓPOLIS

EASTERN EUROPEAN

$ ✕ **Cecília.** Get your gefilte fish, pickled herring, matzo bread, and potato latkes at this small restaurant serving traditional (non-kosher) Jewish cuisine. Pastrami sandwiches are popular, and a special "Jewish feijoada" (with meat, white beans, barley, and potatoes) is served on weekends. A lunch buffet offering most of the house dishes is open from Tuesday to

Friday for 25 reais. The restaurant is family-run, and the owner, Cecilia Judkowitch, is always there. ⊠*Rua Tinhorão 122, Higienópolis, 01241-030* ☎*011/ 3662–5200* ⊟*AE, V* ⊗*Closed Mon.*

ITALIAN

$–$$ ✕**Jardim di Napoli.** The giant neon sign atop this restaurant says it all: classic Italian aesthetics backed up by great traditional food. People keep coming back for the unchanging and unmatchable *polpettone alla parmigiana,* a huge meatball with mozzarella and tomato sauce. There are many other meat dishes, pasta selections, pizzas, and a nice selection of affordable wine. ⊠*Rua Doutor Martinico Prado 463, Higienópolis, 01224-010* ☎*011/3666–3022* ⊟*AE, DC, MC, V.*

PIZZA

$$ ✕**Veridiana** Owner Roberto Loscalzo transformed a 1903 mansion into
Fodor'sChoice   a remarkable dining space; expansive yet intimate, grandiose yet wel-
★   coming. At one end of the room a two-story brick oven presides over diners like a cathedral organ while chefs pull Napoli-style pizzas from its three different mouths. Different place-names lead to different taste combinations: Napoli in Beruit blends goat cheese and zaatar spice, while Napoli in Brasili has sundried meat and Catupiry, the creamy Brazilian cheese. If you don't feel like globetrotting, go for the Do Nonno, topped with juicy whole grilled tomatoes. The recently inaugurated Jardins location is a luxurious update of the original's aesthetic. ⊠*Rua Dona Veridiana 661, Higienópolis, 01238-010* ☎*011/3120–5050* ⊕*www.veridiana.com.br* ⊟*AE, DC, MC V.* ⊠*Rua José Maria Lisboa 493, Jardim Paulista, 01423-000* ☎*011/3559–9151* ⊟*AE, DC, MC V.*

ITAIM BIBI

BRAZILIAN

$$$–$$$$ ✕**Baby Beef Rubaiyat.** The family that owns and runs this restaurant
★   serves meat from their ranch in Mato Grosso do Sul State. Charcoal-grilled fare—baby boar (on request at least two hours in advance), steak, chicken, salmon, and more—is served at the buffet, and a salad bar has all sorts of options. Wednesday and Saturday are feijoada nights, and on Friday the emphasis is on seafood. ⊠*Av. Brigadeiro Faria Lima 2954, Itaim Bibi, 01452-000* ☎*011/3078–9486* ⊟*V* Ⓜ*Paraíso* ⊠*Alameda Santos 86, Paraíso, 01451-901* ☎*011/3141–1188* ⊟*V* Ⓜ*Paraíso.*

CONTINENTAL

$–$$$ ✕**Cantaloup.** That paulistanos take food seriously has not been lost on the folks at Cantaloup. The converted warehouse has two dining areas: oversize photos decorate the walls of the slightly formal room, while a fountain and plants make the second area feel more casual. Try the veal cutlet with blinis of yuca or the stuffed shrimp with clams. Save room for macerated strawberries in port wine sauce or a particularly velvety crème brûlée with ice cream. ⊠*Rua Manoel Guedes 474, Itaim Bibi, 04536-070* ☎*011/3078–9884* ⊕*www.cantaloup.com.br* ⊟*AE, DC, MC, V.*

ECLECTIC

$–$$ ✕ **Bar des Arts.** A great place for lunch or drinks, and a favorite with business people, the Bar des Arts is in a charming arcade with plenty of outdoor seating. Try the artichoke-filled ravioli in sage and tomato butter, or else choose from the ample sushi menu. It's near a lovely flower shop and a wine store. ✉ *Rua Pedro Humberto 9, at Rua Horacio Lafer, Itaim Bibi, 04533-070* ☎ *011/3078–0828* ⊕ *www.bardesarts.com.br* ⊟ *AE, DC, MC, V* ◷ *Closed Mon..*

> **MAMA MIA!**
>
> Since more than half of *paulistanos* claim Italian descendency, the culinary heart of the city might just be boot-shape. Indeed, many claim here, and not New York, to be the pizza capital of the Americas.

FRENCH

$$–$$$$ ✕ **Freddy.** Having recently moved from the location it occupied since 1935, the new Freddy has managed to retain the feel of an upscale Parisian bistro, thanks to a number of small touches as well as some larger ones, like the grand chandeliers hanging from its ceiling. Try the duck with Madeira sauce and apple puree, coq au vin, or the hearty cassoulet with white beans, lamb, duck, and garlic sausage. ✉ *Rua Pedroso Alvarenga 1170, Itaim Bibi, 04531-012* ☎ *011/3167–0977* ⊟ *AE, DC, MC, V* ◷ *No dinner Sun., no lunch Sat..*

$$–$$$$ ✕ **Le Coq Hardy.** Serving haute French cuisine using Brazilian ingredients, this restaurant also features a few Italian dishes, such as porcini mushroom risotto. The sautéed foie gras, braised striped bass, and the roast beef tenderloin, are all highly recommended. Weekday lunch features a prix-fixe menu for 54 reais. ✉ *Rua Jerônimo da Veiga 461, Itaim Bibi, 04536-001* ☎ *011/3079–3344* ⊟ *AE, DC, MC* ◷ *Closed Sun..*

ITALIAN

$$–$$$$ ✕ **La Vecchia Cucina.** Chef Sergio Arno changed the face of the city's Italian restaurants with his *nuova cucina,* exemplified by dishes like frogs' legs risotto and duck ravioli with watercress sauce. Well-to-do patrons dine in the glass-walled garden gazebo or the ocher-color dining room decorated with Italian engravings and fresh flowers. ✉ *Rua Pedroso Alvarenga 1088, Itaim Bibi, 04531-004* ☎ *011/3079–4042* ⊕ *www.lavecchiacucina.com.br* ⊟ *AE, DC, MC, V* ◷ *No dinner Sun..*

JAPANESE

$$–$$$$ ✕ **Nagayama.** Low-key, trustworthy, and well loved, Nagayama consistently serves excellent sushi and sashimi. The chefs like to experiment: the California *uramaki* Philadelphia has rice, cream cheese, grilled salmon, roe, cucumber, and spring onions rolled together. ✉ *Rua Bandeira Paulista 369, Itaim Bibi, 04532-011* ☎ *011/3079–7553* ⊟ *AE, DC, MC* ✉ *Rua da Consolação 3397, Cerqueira César* ☎ *011/3064–0110* ⊟ *AE, DC, MC.*

JARDIM EUROPA

ECLECTIC

$$–$$$$ ✕**La Tambouille.** This Italo-French restaurant with a partially enclosed garden isn't just a place for businesspeople and impresarios to see and be seen; it also has some of the best food in town. Among chef Giancarlo Bolla's recommended dishes are the linguine with fresh mussels and prawn sauce and the filet mignon *rosini* (served with foie gras and saffron risotto). ⊠*Av. Nove de Julho 5925, Jardim Europa, 01406-200* ☎*011/3079–6276* ⊟*AE, DC, MC, V.*

> **PURPLE POWER**
>
> Açai, an antioxidant-rich super fruit, has recently made its way to juice bars around the world. Don't miss your chance to get it close to the source, where it's cheaper and purer than the versions you'll find back home. Always frozen, scoops of it are blended together with syrup of the energy-filled guaraná berry. The most popular way to get it is *na tigela,* in a glass bowl with bananas and granola, though juice stands dedicated to the fruit should serve up a pure milkshake-thick *suco* (juice) as well.

JARDINS

BRAZILIAN

$ ✕**Dona Lucinha.** Mineiro dishes are the specialties at this modest eatery with plain wooden tables. The classic cuisine is served as a buffet only: more than 50 stone pots hold dishes like *feijão tropeiro* (beans with manioc flour). Save room for a dessert of ambrosia. ⊠*Av. Xibarás 399, Moema* ☎*011/5051–2050* ⊟*AE, DC, MC, V* ⊠*Rua Bela Cintra 2325, Jardins, 01415-002* ☎*011/3082–3797* ⊕*www.donalucinha.com.br* ⊟*AE, DC, MC, V* ⊗*Closed Mon..*

¢–$ ✕**Frevo.** Paulistanos of all types and ages flock to this Jardins luncheon-
★ ette on the stylish Rua Oscar Freire for its beirute sandwiches, filled with ham and cheese, tuna, or chicken, and for its draft beer and fruit juices in flavors such as *acerola* (Antilles cherry), passion fruit, and papaya. ⊠*Rua Oscar Freire 603, Jardins, 01426-001* ☎*011/3082–3434* ⊕*frevinho.com.br* ⊟*AE, DC, MC, V.*

ECLECTIC

$ ✕**Ritz.** An animated, gay-friendly crowd chatters at this restaurant with Italian, Brazilian, French, and mixed cuisine, as contemporary pop music plays in the background. Although each day sees a different special and Ritz serves some of the best hamburgers in the city, another popular dish is *bife à milanesa* (a breaded beef cutlet) with creamed spinach and french fries. ⊠*Alameda Franca 1088, Jardins, 01422-001* ☎*011/3088–6808* ⊕*www.ritznet.com.br* ⊟*AE, DC, MC, V* Ⓜ*Consolação.*

FRENCH

$–$$$ ✕**Bistrô Jaú.** Young chef Gilberto César runs the kitchen and the restaurant here. Businesspeople from Avenida Paulista appreciate the fine decor and the lunch menu, which is superb yet inexpensive (compared with the dinner menu). ⊠*Alameda Jaú 1606, Jardins, 01420-002* ☎*011/3085–5573* ⊟*AE, DC, MC, V* Ⓜ*Consolação.*

ITALIAN

$$$–$$$$ ✕**Fasano.** A family-owned north-ern Italian classic subtly ensconced within the elegantly modern lobby of the hotel of the same name, this restaurant is as famous for its superior cuisine as for its exorbi-tant prices. The chef, Salvatore Loi, has added to the menu dishes like seafood ravioli with a white-wine sauce. The luxe decor oozes class—marble, mahogany, and mir-rors, all crowned by a breathtaking skylight—and suggests that proof of one's captainship of industry or other such mastery of the universe must be shown at the door for entrance. ⊠ *Rua Vittorio Fasano 88, Jardins, 01414-020* ☎ *011/3062–4000* ⊕ *www.fasano.com.br* ▭ *AE, DC, MC, V* ☉ *Closed Sun. No lunch.*

> ### A TASTE OF LEBANON
>
> While in São Paulo, be sure to try a *beirute*, a Lebanese sandwich served hot on toasted Syrian bread and filled with roast beef, cheese, lettuce, and tomato. Another quick bite from Lebanon that has established itself in the city is *esfiha*, an open-faced sandwich topped with cheese or spiced meat. Fast-food restaurants serving these snacks are scattered around the city.

$$–$$$$ ✕**Don Pepe Di Napoli.** Good and simple Italian food is what you'll find at this traditional spot. Choose from a great variety of pastas, salads, and meat dishes. A good option is *talharina a Don Pepe,* pasta with meat, broccoli, and garlic. ⊠ *Rua Padre Joao Manoel 1105, Jardins, 01411-001* ☎ *011/3081–4080* ▭ *AE, DC, MC, V.*

LEBANESE

$–$$$$ ✕**Arábia.** For almost 20 years Arábia has served traditional Lebanese
★ cuisine at this beautiful high-ceilinged restaurant. Simple dishes such as hummus and stuffed grape leaves are executed with aplomb. The lamb melts in your mouth. The reasonably priced "executive" lunch includes one cold dish, one meat dish, a drink, and dessert. Don't miss the crepe-like ataife, filled with pistachio nuts or cream, for dessert. ⊠ *Rua Haddock Lobo 1397, Jardins, 01414-003* ☎ *011/3061–2203* ⊕ *www.arabia.com.br* ▭ *AE, DC, MC.*

$ ✕**Almanara.** Part of a chain of Lebanese semi-fast-food outlets, Alma-nara is perfect for a quick lunch of hummus, tabbouleh, grilled chicken, and rice. There's also a full-blown restaurant on the premises that serves Lebanese specialties *rodízio* style, meaning you're served continuously until you can ingest no more. ⊠ *Rua Oscar Freire 523, Jardins, 01426-001* ☎ *011/3085–6916* ▭ *AE, DC, MC, V.*

PIZZA

$$–$$$$ ✕**Pizzaria Camelo.** Though it's neither fancy nor beautiful, Pizzaria Camelo has kept paulistanos enthralled for ages with its wide variety of thin-crust pies. The *chopp* (draft beer) is great, too. Avoid Sunday night unless you're willing to wait an hour for a table. ⊠ *Rua Pamplona 1873, Jardins, 01233-020* ☎ *011/3887–8764* ⊕ *www.pizzariacamelo. com.br* ▭ *DC, MC, V.*

$–$$ ✕**Piola.** Part of a chain started in Italy, this restaurant serves pizzas loaded with toppings like Gorgonzola, Brie, ham, salami, mushrooms, and anchovies. It also has good pasta dishes, like the penne with smoked salmon in a creamy tomato sauce. The young, hip crowd matches the trendy contemporary decor, and there's also a place for kids to play while the grown-ups finish their meal. ⊠*Alameda Lorena 1765, Jardins, 01424-002* ☎*011/3064–6570* ⊕*www.piola.com.br* ▤*AE, DC, MC, V.*

> ### JAPANESE FRUIT
>
> Along with the famous Japanese cuisine, which can be found just about everywhere in São Paulo, Brazil's Japanese immigrants are credited with introducing persimmons, azaleas, tangerines, and kiwis to Brazil.

SEAFOOD

$$$$ ✕**Amadeus.** Since it's not on the ocean, São Paulo isn't known for its seafood, but Amadeus is an exception. Appetizers such as fresh oysters and salmon and endive with mustard, and entrées like shrimp in a cognac sauce make it a challenge to find better fruits of the sea elsewhere in town. It's popular with the business-lunch crowd. ⊠*Rua Haddock Lobo 807, Jardins, 01414-001* ☎*011/3061–2859* ⊕*restauranteamadeus.com.br* ▤*AE, V* ⊘*No dinner weekends* Ⓜ*Consolação.*

VEGETARIAN

¢–$ ✕**Cheiro Verde.** One of the few places in São Paulo where you can eat tasty vegetarian food and not draw funny stares from a staunchly carnivorous public. Cheiro Verde has a simple menu with choices like whole-wheat mushroom pizza and the delicious *gratinado de legumes* (vegetables with Gorgonzola sauce). ⊠*Rua Peixoto Gomide 1413, Jardins, 01409-003* ☎*011/3289–6853* ⊕*www.cheiroverderestaurante. com.br* ▤*AE, DC, MC, V* ⊘*No dinner* Ⓜ*Trianon.*

LIBERDADE

JAPANESE

¢–$$ ✕**Gombe.** At the end of a street packed with sushi restaurants, Gombe is the pick of the pack. The small dining room built of unvarnished wood features low, Japanese-style tables and a barstool-lined grill, where the house specialty, *espetinhos* (juicy chicken and beef skewers), are served hot off the grill until all hours of the night. During more tranquil hours, try the *sashimi teishoku* with generous slices of tuna, salmon, octopus, and squid. The menu is highly interchangeable if you know your way around Japanese cuisine. ⊠*Rua Tomás Gonzaga, 22, Liberdade, 01506-020* ☎*011/3209–8499* Ⓜ*Liberdade* ▤*DC, MC, V* ⊘*Closed Sun.*

MOEMA

PIZZA

$–$$ ✕**Braz.** Its name comes from one of the most traditional Italian neighborhoods in São Paulo, and no one argues that it doesn't have the right.
Fodor's Choice Each of the nearly 20 types of crisp-crusted pizzas is delicious, from the
★ traditional margherita to the house specialty, pizza *braz*, with tomato sauce, zucchini, and mozzarella and Parmesan cheeses. The *chopp*

(draft beer) is also very good. ⊠*Rua Grauna 125, Moema, 04514-000* ☎*011/5561–0905* ⊕*www.casabraz.com.br* ⊟*DC, MC, V.*

MORUMBI

BRAZILIAN

$–$$$ ✕**Esplanada Grill.** The beautiful people hang out in the bar of this highly regarded churrascaria. The thinly sliced *picanha* steak (similar to rump steak) is excellent; it goes well with a house salad (hearts of palm and shredded, fried potatoes), onion rings, and creamed spinach. The restaurant's version of the traditional *pão de queijo* (cheese bread) is widely viewed as one of the best. ⊠*Morumbi Shopping Center, 1st fl., Av. Roque Petroni Jr. 1089, Morumbi, 04707-900* ☎*011/5181–8156* ⊟*AE, DC, MC, V.*

INDIAN

$–$$$$ ✕**Ganesh.** Tucked away from the hub of the shopping center, this unassuming restaurant has a traditional menu that includes curries and tandoori dishes from many regions of India. Indian artwork and tapestries fill the interior. ⊠*Morumbi Shopping Center, Av. Roque Petroni Jr. 1089, Morumbi, 04707-900* ☎*011/5181–4748* ⊟*AE, DC, MC, V.*

> ### WOK THIS WAY
>
> In a street-food scene dominated by forgettable hamburgers and hot dogs, Yakisoba stands out—keep an eye peeled for the spectacle of stir-fried noodles tossed over an open flame in the middle of the crowded sidewalk. Another delicious option, and surprisingly common on public thoroughfares, are homemade *churrascos,* wooden kebabs of beef whose juices send towers of fragrant smoke into the air. A calmer alternative is the corn cart. Rather than on the cob, where kernels are sometimes overcooked, try *pamonha,* steam-cooked sweetened cornmeal wrapped in a husk, or *curau,* sweet creamed corn.

PAN-ASIAN

$–$$$ ✕**House of Siam.** Don't let the shopping-mall atmosphere fool you. This Thai restaurant serves spicy food in a cozy space closed off from the retail outlets. Try the *Ped Yaang* (boneless duck with sweet and sour sauce and Thai spices) or the beef fillet with vegetables and oyster sauce. ⊠ *Morumbi Shopping Center, Av. Roque Petroni Jr. 1089, Morumbi, 04707-900* ☎*011/5181–4748* ⊟*AE, DC, MC, V.*

PINHEIROS

BRAZILIAN

$–$$ ✕**Consulado Mineiro.** During and after the Saturday crafts and antiques
★ fair in Praça Benedito Calixto, it may take an hour to get a table at this homey restaurant. Among the traditional *mineiro* (from Minas Gerais State) dishes are the *mandioca com carne de sol* (cassava with salted meat) appetizer and the *tutu* (pork loin with beans, pasta, cabbage, and rice) entrée. The cachaça menu is extensive, with rare, premium, and homemade brands. Several types of *batidas* (fruit-and-alcohol mixtures) and caipirinhas are served. ⊠*Rua Praça Benedito Calixto 74, Pinhei-*

CLOSE UP

Recipe: Coxinha de Galinha

Brazilians eat *coxinhas* (mock chicken legs) as a snack, but you can also try them as an appetizer.

INGREDIENTS:

3-pound chicken, cut into pieces
3 tablespoons olive oil
3 cloves garlic, minced
1 medium onion, chopped
1 bay leaf
Salt and pepper to taste
1 cup rice flour
2 cups milk
1 cup reserved chicken broth
3 egg yolks, beaten
1 tablespoon butter
1 malagueta pepper (or any red chili pepper), finely chopped
4 cups fine bread crumbs
2 eggs, beaten
Vegetable oil for frying

DIRECTIONS:

Sauté the chicken in olive oil. Add garlic, onion, bay leaf, salt, and pepper to taste. Cover with water and simmer until done. Remove chicken and reserve 1 cup broth. Take the meat off the bones. Reserve 15 thin strips of chicken and finely chop the remainder. Whisk together the flour, milk, and reserved broth until smooth and cook over medium heat until thickened, stirring constantly. Remove from heat and stir in egg yolks, butter, chicken, and malagueta pepper. Adjust the seasonings to taste. Return to heat and stir until quite thick. Completely cool mixture in refrigerator. Take an amount the size of a large egg and shape it around a reserved strip of chicken, forming an oval dough ball. Roll in bread crumbs, dip into beaten eggs, and cover with another layer of bread crumbs. Fry in hot oil until golden brown.

ros, 05414-000 ☎011/3064–3882 ⊕*www.consuladomineiro.com.br* ⊟*AE, DC, MC, V* ⊘*Closed Mon.* ⊠*Rua Cônego Eugenio Leite 504, Pinheiros, 05406-040* ☎011/3898–3241 ⊟*AE, DC, MC, V.*

PIZZA

$–$$ ✕**I Vitelloni.** Running perhaps the most creative pizzeria in town, owner Hamilton Mello Júnior combines disparate ingredients for his specialty pies, while serving up tasty classics as well. In the Pinheiros neighborhood, lively at night, the restaurant sits on a quiet residential street, away from the sidewalk bars an avenue away, so it's prized by locals and well worth searching out. We recommend the authentic rucola pie. There's a stand-up bar outside that's a nice place to finish your drinks before you head off. ⊠*Rua Conde Sílvio Álvares Penteado, 31, Pinheiros, 05428-040* ☎011/3819–0735 ⊕*www.ivitelloni.com. br* ⊟*AE, DC, MC, V.*

JAPANESE

$$$–$$$$ ✕**Jun Sakamoto.** Arguably the best Japanese restaurant in a town famous that's for them, Jun Sakamoto is known for using fish of the highest quality and for employing sushi chefs of the highest caliber and artistry to cut them. This is haute gastronomy at its haughtiest. You're best served if you let the waiters wearing futuristic earpieces guide you through the menu based on what's the freshest fish in the house.

⊠*Rua Lisboa, 55, Pinheiros, 05413-000* ☎*011/3088–6019* 🌐*www.ivitelloni.com.br* ▭*AE, DC, MC, V.*

POMPÉIA

PIZZA

$–$$ ✕**Galpão da Pizza.** Lights that shine from behind bottle bottoms embedded in exposed brick walls is one of the interesting design elements in this restaurant owned by an architect. Service is fast, and the arugula, sundried tomato, and mozzarella pizza is one of the best choices. ⊠*Rua Doutor Augusto de Miranda 1156, Pompéia, 05026-001* ☎*011/3672–4767* 🌐*www.galpaodapizza.com.br* ▭*DC, MC, V.*

3

VILA MADALENA

PIZZA

$$–$$$$ ✕**Allez, Allez!** Chef sensation Luiz Emanuel Cerqueira de Souza riffs on classic French cuisine while still serving up old Provençal favorites. Recommended is the butter-enriched potato puree as a side to the *bacalhau alho e oleo* (baked cod with garlic and oil)—it's delightful. For dessert, try the profiteroles. ⊠*Rua Wisard, 288, Vila Madalena, 05434-000* ☎*011/3032–3325* 🌐*www.allezallez.com.br* ▭*AE, MC, V* ⏲. Ⓜ *Vila Madalena.*

ECLECTIC

$–$$ ✕**Pitanga.** In a comfortable house in Vila Madalena, Pitanga has a diverse buffet every day (R$26 weekdays, R$35 Saturday, R$36 Sunday). Delicious salads, meat dishes, and feijoada are some of the buffet choices. ⊠*Rua Original 162, Vila Madalena, 05435-050* ☎*011/3816–2914* 🌐*www.pitangarestaurante.com.br* ▭*AE, MC, V* ⏲*Closed Mon.* Ⓜ *Vila Madalena.*

PIZZA

$–$$ ★ ✕**Oficina de Pizzas.** Both branches of this restaurant look like something designed by the Spanish architect Gaudí had he spent his later years in the tropics, but the pizzas couldn't be more Italian and straightforward. Try a pie with mozzarella and toasted garlic. ⊠*Rua Purpurina 517, Vila Madalena, 05435-030* ☎*011/3816–3749* ▭*DC, MC, V* ⊠*Rua Inácio Pereira da Rocha 15, Vila Madalena, 05432-010* ☎*011/3813–8389* ▭*DC, MC, V* 🌐*www.oficinadepizzas.com.br.*

VILA OLÍMPIA

FRENCH

$–$$ ✕**Caf é Bistro.** Well known for simple, straightfoward bistro fare with a Brazilian twist like *bacalhau com natas* (salted cod with cream) this place guarantees a solid sit-down meal, even if you happen to be in a hurry. If you're not, stay for the coconut cake with strawberry sauce. ⊠*Avenida Brigadeiro Faria Lima, Vila Olímpia, 05438-133* ☎*011/3045–4040* 🌐*www.cafebistro.net* ▭*AE, DC, MC, V.*

ECLECTIC

$ ✕**Chef du Jour.** Don't fret. There's indeed a permanent chef installed here: Renato Frias, who hails from the state of Pernambuco, though his cuisine straddles French and Italian. Enjoy the vermicelli with mini-meatballs in their spacious, colorfully tiled dining room. ⊠*Alameda Rajá Gabaglia, 133, Vila Olímpia, 04551-090* ☎*011/3845–6843* ▤*AE, DC, MC, V* ☻*No Dinner.*

JAPANESE

$–$$$$ ✕**Nakombi.** Chefs prepare sushi from a *kombi* (Volkswagen van) in the middle of the dining room at this eclectic and fun restaurant where tables are surrounded by a small artificial river teeming with fish. The menu includes a good variety of sushi and non-sushi dishes. Try the salmon fillet with *shimeji* mushrooms. ⊠*Rua Pequetita 170, Vila Olímpia,* ☎*011/3845–9911* ⊕*www.nakombi.com.br* ▤*AE, DC, MC, V.*

WHERE TO STAY

ABOUT THE HOTELS

Updated by
Daniel Corry

São Paulo is all about business, and for the most part so are its hotels. Most of them are near Avenida Paulista, along Marginal Pinheiros, or in the charming Jardins neighborhood, where international businesses are located. But catering to business doesn't mean they've forgotten about pleasure. On the contrary, if you're willing to pay for it, the city can match London or New York for unfettered elegance.

Because of the business influence, rates often drop on weekends. Breakfast is a sumptuous affair and is oftentimes included in the room rate. International conventions and the annual Formula 1 grand prix in September can book hotels completely, so it's wise to make reservations in advance.

WHAT IT COSTS IN REAIS					
	¢	$	$$	$$$	$$$$
FOR 2 PEOPLE	under R$125	R$125–R$250	R$250–R$375	R$375–R$500	over R$500

Prices are for a standard double room in high season, excluding tax.

BELA VISTA

¢ ▨**Pousada dos Franceses.** On rainy days young people lounge on the couches in this classic backpacker's hostel, complete with do-your-own laundry and a cook-for-yourself kitchen. Communal rooms are separated by gender and sleep up to 8 people. There are also 10 private rooms with two to three beds. The bathrooms leave much to be desired—the shower is just a drain in the floor and a curtain drawn across one end of the room. **Pros:** Tips of the Week board indicates cultural happenings, close to Bixiga restaurants, owners speak perfect English. **Cons:** Long, dark walk from Paulista means taking a taxi, spartan rooms. ✉*Rua Dos Franceses 100, Bela Vista, 01329-010* ☎*011/3288–1592* ⊕*www.pousadadosfranceses.com.br* ➪*14 rooms* ৬*In-room: no a/c (some), no phone, no TV. In-hotel: restaurant, laundry facilities, public Internet, public Wi-Fi* ⊟*AE, DC, MC, V* ⊧⊚⊧*BP.*

¢ ⊡ **San Gabriel.** Expect no frills at this budget hotel in a lively neighborhood close to Avenida Paulista. Rooms are small (though there are some larger suites), but have all the basics and are clean. The rates are unbeatable for this part of town, though breakfast is not included in the room rate. **Pros:** Close to malls, bars, and restaurants, in-house convenience store. **Cons:** Surrounding area isn't well lighted, no Internet. ✉*Rua Frei Caneca 1006, Bela Vista, 01307-002* ☎*011/3253–2279* ⊞*011/3253–2279 Ext. 5* ⊕*www.sangabriel.com.br* ➪*75 rooms, 25 suites* ৬*In-room: refrigerator. In-hotel: parking (fee)* ⊟*AE, DC, MC, V* ⊧⊚⊧*EP.*

BROOKLIN & SANTO AMARO

$$$ ⊡ **Hilton São Paulo Morumbi.** George Bush's 2007 stay only cemented this venue's reputation as the brightest star in Brooklin and the new hot spot of the São Paulo business world, one of three skyscrapers forming a Fortune 500 company–loaded office park. The Hilton's glass and marble lobby looks as cool and professional as the staff acts. Apartments feature a large workstation, and suites offer separate living rooms for informal meetings. The rooftop pool and gym, complete with jaw-dropping views of city skyline, are open to all guests, but the five floors below it are pass-key access only. There the executive suites, lounge, and numerous conference rooms serve those who came to close the big deal. **Pros:** Attached by tunnel to a shopping mall, Canvas bar has rotating art exhibit, high-end shopping nearby. **Cons:** Far from anything cultural/historical, need a taxi to get everywhere, terrible rush hour. ✉*Av.das Nações Unidas 12901, Brooklin, 04578-000* ☎*011/6845–0000 or 0800/596–0000* ⊕*www.solmelia.com* ➪*300 suites* ৬*In-room: safe, Ethernet. In-hotel: 2 restaurants, room service, bar, café, pool, gym, laundry facilities, business center, executive floor, airport shuttle, parking (fee)* ⊟*AE, DC, MC, V.*

$$$–$$$$ ⊡ **Transamérica.** Directly across the Pinheiros River from the Centro Empresarial office complex, the home of many U.S. companies, this hotel is a convenient choice for those working in the area. The skylighted lobby—in granite and marble, with Persian carpets, palm trees, leather sofas, and oversize modern paintings—is more impressive than the rooms, with their beige wall-to-wall carpets and floral fabrics, but they're clean, spacious, and quiet. **Pros:** Great location for business travelers, good views. **Cons:** Pinheiros river smells terrible, area paralyzed by traffic at rush hour. ✉*Av. das Nações Unidas 18591, Santo Amaro, 04795-901* ☎*011/5693–4511 or 0800/12–6060* ⊕*www.transamerica.com.br* ➪*389 rooms, 11 suites* ৬*In-room: safe, refrigerator, Ethernet. In-hotel: restaurant, room service, bar, golf course, tennis courts, pool, gym, laundry facilities, parking (fee)* ⊟*AE, DC, MC, V.*

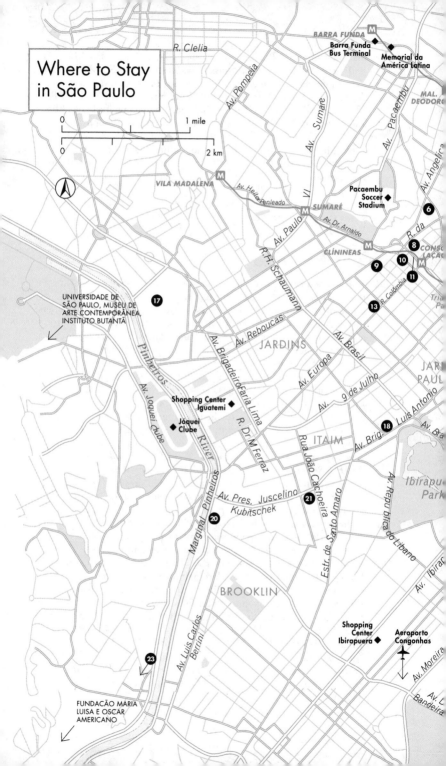

Where to Stay in São Paulo

BARRA FUNDA

Barra Funda Bus Terminal

Memorial da América Latina

R. Clelia

Av. Pompeia

Av. Sumare

Av. Pacaembu

Av. Angelica

MAL. DEODORO

1 mile

2 km

VILA MADALENA

Av. Heitor Penteado

SUMARÉ

Av. Paulo

Av. Dr. Arnaldo

Pacaembu Soccer Stadium

CLININEAS

R. da

6

8 CONSO LAÇÃO

R. H. Schaumann

9 **10**

11

R. Colômbia

Tria Pa

13

UNIVERSIDADE DE SÃO PAULO, MUSEU DE ARTE CONTEMPORÂNEA, INSTITUTO BUTANTÃ

17

Av. Reboucas

JARDINS

Av. Europa

Av. Brasil

JAR PAUL

Pinheiros

Av. Brigadeiro Faria Lima

Av. 9 de Julho

Shopping Center Iguatemi

R. Dr M Ferraz

Av. Joquei Clube

Jóquei Clube

Rua João Cachoeira

ITAIM

Av. Brig. Luís Antonio

18

Av. Bra

Ibirapu Park

Marginal Pinheiros River

Av. Pres. Juscelino Kubitschek

21

Estr. de Santo Amaro

Av. Repu blica do Líbano

20

BROOKLIN

Av. Ibirap

Av. Luis Carlos Berrini

Shopping Center Ibirapuera

Aeroporto Congonhas

23

Av. Moreira

FUNDAÇÃO MARIA LUISA E OSCAR AMERICANO

Av. Bandeira

CENTRO & ENVIRONS

$$ **⊡ Grand Hotel Ca' D'Oro.** A bit like visiting a rich great uncle in Europe, the musty carpet and faded wallpaper of the rooms are more than compensated by the finely worked furniture, gracious staff, and the Continental grandeur of the public spaces. While the cavernous downstairs lobbies are replete with Velázquez replicas, deep leather chairs, and a coffee table made from a giant 1820s English bellows, the panoramic pool is a perfectly preserved window into 1970s splendor: atop the astroturf carpeting sits single-cast plastic pool furniture that would draw crowds at a museum of contemporary design. **Pros:** Classy staff, endless public sitting rooms, unintentional retro charm. **Cons:** Rua Augusta gets a little wild at night. ⊠*Rua Augusta 129, Cerqueira César, 01305-900* ☎*011/3236–4300* ⊕*www.cadoro. com.br* ⌂*240 rooms, 50 suites* ⌂*In-room: safe, Ethernet. In-hotel: restaurant, room service, bars, 2 pools, gym, laundry facilities, public Wi-Fi, parking (fee)* ⊟*AE, DC, MC, V* Ⓜ*Consolação.*

> ### THE FLAT
>
> Need to stay in town for a few months and can't imagine paying hotel rates? Renting or subletting an apartment can be very difficult in São Paulo thanks to laws that require a *fiador,* a city resident who will co-sign the contract. Enter the flat, where you sign monthly contracts at rates much lower than hotels. Flats are located where business is done, Paulista Avenue, Centro, and the South Zone, and they run the gamut between hotel and apartment in terms of amenities. All offer hotel-style maid service, but not all have kitchens.

$ **⊡ Bourbon.** Rich woodwork runs at waist level throughout the halls of this small, classy hotel near Praça da República. It's only one block away from Largo do Arouche, a bar-lined square that's home to a largely gay crowd at night. In each room a wall-length tufted leather cushion serves as headboard, quite comfortable for reading in bed while the city bustles below. The bathrooms are huge cubic rooms flooded with natural light and tiled from floor to ceiling. Since every other tile is emblazoned with the hotel's trademark double B, it can feel like you're showering inside a fancy piece of luggage. **Pros:** Great location for exploring Centro, next door to metro. **Cons:** Small workstations, Plac[cd]a da República should be avoided at night. ⊠*Av. Vieira de Carvalho 99, Centro, 01210-010* ☎*011/3337–2000* 🖷*011/3331–8187* ⌂*127 rooms* ⌂*In rooms: safe, refrigerator, Ethernet. In-hotel: restaurant, bar, parking (fee)* ⊟*AE, DC, MC, V* Ⓜ*República.*

$ **⊡ Novotel Jaraguá.** Built in 1951 to be the headquarters of one of the
★   main newspapers in the city, the building that now houses this hotel is a landmark in downtown São Paulo. The huge mural created by Di Cavalcanti is one of the 1950s attractions. All 415 rooms were renovated in 2004; their decor hovers somewhere between Scandinavian and airport lounge (albeit a well-maintained airport lounge). The furnishings are all blond wood and brushed steel of an indistinguishable contemporary style, which all-in-all makes for pleasant rooms at good prices. **Pros:** Close to many restaurants and sights, 10-minute taxi to Paulista. **Cons:** Area a little spooky at night, since most nearby

businesses are closed. ⊠*Rua Martins Fontes 71, Centro, 01050-000* ☎*011/3120–8000* ⊕*www.novotel.com.br* ⤶*309 rooms, 106 suites* ♿*In-room: Wi-Fi. In-hotel: restaurant, bar, public Wi-Fi, parking (fee)* ▭*AE, MC, V* ⍾*BP.*

¢ ⊡ **Ibis São Paulo Paulista.** This large hotel is one of the best bargains on Paulista. All rooms feature queen-size beds and the decoration is contemporary, with focus on function, not beauty. The staff is bright, helpful, and multilingual. **Pros:** A nonaffiliated airport shuttle bus has a stop next door, close to major thoroughfares. **Cons:** Heavy traffic all day long. ⊠*Av Paulista 2355, Jardins, 01311-300* ☎*011/3523–3000* ⊕*www.accorhotels.com.br* ⤶*236 rooms* ♿*In-hotel: restaurant, room service, laundry facilities, public Wi-Fi, parking (no fee)* ▭*AE, DC, MC, V.*

HIGIENÓPOLIS

$ ⊡ **Meliá Higienópolis.** Tucked imperceptibly among stately apartment buildings in one of the city's oldest and most attractive residential neighborhoods and a 10-minute taxi ride from Centro, this hotel, built in 2000, has bright and spacious rooms with contemporary light-wood furnishings. The 24-story building provides nice views of the city from the top floors. **Pros:** Cool half-indoor, half-outdoor pool, breakfast menu in Braille. **Cons:** Small bathrooms, boring furniture. ⊠*Rua Maranhão 371, Higienópolis, 01240-000* ☎*011/3665–8200 or 0800/703–3399* ⊕*www.solmelia.com* ⤶*213 rooms* ♿*In-room: safe, Ethernet. In-hotel: restaurant, room service, pool, gym, public Internet, parking (fee)* ▭*AE, DC, MC, V* ⍾*BP.*

¢ ⊡ **Ville Hotel.** In the lively Higienópolis neighborhood of apartment buildings, bars, and bookstores abutting Mackenzie University, this hotel has a small lobby with a black-and-pink-granite floor, recessed lighting, and leather sofas. Rooms are plain, with little decoration, but clean. **Pros:** Next door supermarket is open until midnight, Mackenzie Campus is very pretty. **Cons:** Only one person staffs the desk on weekends, heavy rush-hour traffic in the evening. ⊠*Rua Dona Veridiana 643, Higienópolis, 01238-010* ☎*011/3257–5288* ☎*011/3241–1871* ⊕*www.hotelville.com.br* ⤶*54 rooms* ♿*In-room: refrigerator, Wi-Fi. In-hotel: restaurant, parking (fee)* ▭*AE, DC, MC, V.*

ITAIM BIBI

$–$$ ⊡ **Blue Tree Towers Faria Lima.** Techno beats animate the lobby of this chic business hotel halfway between Paulista and Brooklin. Seventy-seven of the apartments can be transformed into offices, their beds folded up and extra tables brought in. Rooms have clean lines and dark-wood furnishings that contrast with the bright-white walls and fabrics. **Pros:** Extremely courteous staff, located on major thoroughfare, close to many multinationals. **Cons:** Need a taxi to get anywhere, heavy rush hour, few restaurants close by. ⊠*Avenida Brigadeiro Faria Lima 3989, Itaim, 04538-133* ☎*011/3896–7544* ☎*011/3896–7545* ⊕*www.bluetree.com.br* ⤶*338 rooms* ♿*In-room: Wi-Fi. In-hotel:*

restaurant, bar, pool, gym, public Wi-Fi, parking (fee) ☐AE, DC, MC, V ❍BP.

JARDINS

$$$$ 🏨**Fasano.** With a decor that hints at 1940s modern, but is undeniably 21st-century chic, Fasano caters to those for whom money is a mere detail. Rooms have Eames chairs, leather headboards, parquet floors, huge windows, and walk-in closets. The restaurant off the lobby with the same name exudes the same deep sense of luxury. **Pros:** Attentive, knowledgeable staff, beautiful top-floor pool. **Cons:** Paying for it all. ⊠*Rua Vittorio Fasano 88, Jardins, 01414-020* 🕾*011/3896-4077* 🖷*011/3896-4156* ⊕*www.fasano.com.br* 🛏*56 rooms, 8 suites* ⚙*In-room: safe, refrigerator, Ethernet. In-hotel: restaurant, room service, bar, pool, gym, spa, concierge, laundry service, airport shuttle, parking (no fee), no-smoking rooms* ☐AE, DC, MC, V ❍EP.

$$$$ ★ 🏨**InterContinental São Paulo.** This exquisite hotel is one of the most attractive of the city's top-tier establishments and consistently gets rave reviews because they pay so much attention to small things—they offer a choice of six different types of pillow. Service is attentive, and both the private and public areas are well appointed. Creams, pastels, and marble come together with seamless sophistication and elegance. **Pros:** Japanese breakfast, Playstation in rooms. **Cons:** Suites aren't much bigger than normal rooms. ⊠*Al. Santos 1123, Jardins, 01419-001* 🕾*011/3179–2600 or 0800/11–8003* 🖷*011/3179–2666* ⊕*www.intercontinental.com* 🛏*189 rooms, 36 suites* ⚙*In room: DVD, Wi-Fi, Ethernet. In-hotel: restaurant, room service, bar, pool, gym, hair salon, parking (fee)* ☐AE, DC, MC, V Ⓜ*Trianon.*

$$$$ Fodor'sChoice ★ 🏨**Unique.** Its hard not see a familiar shape (some say watermelon, some say boat, but neither hits the mark) in the wild but harmonius design of this boutique hotel. Apartments, some with walls that echo the curve of the building's exterior, have plasma TVs with DVD players, mobile phones, king-size beds, and whirlpool baths with remote control, while the pool features a waterslide and submerged hydromassage chairs. The lobby bar and rooftop restaurant are destinations in and of themselves. **Pros:** Steps from Ibirapuera Park and a taxi ride to many top restaurants. **Cons:** Non-stop techno music in public spaces. ⊠*Avenida Brigadeiro Luís Antônio 4700, Jardins, 01402-002* 🕾*011/3055–4710 or 0800/770–8771* 🖷*011/3889–8100* ⊕*www.unique.com.br* 🛏*95 rooms* ⚙*In-room: refrigerator, DVD, Ethernet, Wi-Fi. In-hotel: res-*

taurant, pool, gym, spa, public Wi-Fi, parking (fee) ⊟*AE, DC, MC, V* ⊚|*BP.*

$$–$$$$ 🖭**L'Hotel.** Compared to the top-of-the line chain hotels on Paulista, L'Hotel stands out as truly special experience. Though the famous Parisian hotel of the same name is its declared muse, the luxury here is understated rather than decadent. Rooms are done in soft blue, beige, or rose, the woodwork and cabinets in patina. The French dining room and the English-style piano bar that faces it are twin gems. The top floor pool has a retractable roof, Japanese ofuro baths heated upon request, and every guest gets a complementary brown and gold pair of the famous Havaianas flipflops. **Pros:** Small number of rooms makes for personalized service, L'Occitane bath products. **Cons:** No fitness center. ⊠*Alameda Campinas 266, Jardins, 01404-000* ☎*011/2183–0500* 🖷*011/2183–0505* ⊕*www.lhotel.com.br* ⇌*80 rooms, 7 suites* ♨*In-hotel: 2 restaurants, room service, bar, pool, gym, laundry facilities, parking (fee)* ⊟*AE, DC, MC, V* Ⓜ*Trianon.*

$$–$$$$ 🖭**Maksoud Plaza.** Once the top choice for luxury accommodations in São Paulo, Maksoud must now share the bill with a bevy of high-end hotels. Still, its facilities, comfort, and good location make it one of the best choices in the city. The multilingual staff provides professional service, and the restaurants are excellent, drawing big crowds of businesspeople everyday at lunch and after work. **Pros:** Four different full-service restaurants, huge atrium. **Cons:** Dingy exterior, rush-hour traffic. ⊠*Alameda Campinas 1250, Jardins, 01404-900* ☎*011/3145–8000* 🖷*011/3145–8001* ⊕*www.maksoud.com.br* ⇌*416 rooms, 99 suites* ♨*In-hotel: 4 restaurants, room service, 4 bars, pool, gym, laundry facilities, public Wi-Fi, airport shuttle, parking (fee)* ⊟*AE, DC, MC, V* Ⓜ*Trianon.*

$$–$$$$ 🖭**Renaissance São Paulo.** In case the rooftop helipad doesn't say it all, the striking lines of the red-and-black granite lobby announce one serious business hotel. The fitness center is among the largest in Latin America, complemented by a juice bar/cybercafé. On weekends there's dancing at the Havana cigar bar and even a play at the hotel's own theater. For those staying in suites, there's the executive lounge and an array of ultraluxurious services. However, compared to all the other amenities, the sparsely furnished rooms can be a little underwhelming. **Pros:** You never have to leave hotel, professional staff. **Cons:** Internet isn't free, uninspired decoration. ⊠*Alameda Santos 2233, Jardins, 01419-002* ☎*011/3069–2233, 800/703–1512 in U.S.* ⊕*www.renaissancehotels.com* ⇌*445 rooms, 57 suites, 45 clubrooms* ♨*In-room: refrigerator, safe, DVD, Wi-Fi. In-hotel: 3 restaurants, room service, 2 bars, pool, gym, laundry facilities, parking (fee)* ⊟*AE, DC, MC, V* Ⓜ*Consolação.*

$ 🖭**Pousada Dona Zilah.** Marvelously located in the retail-heavy part of the Jardins district, and easily navigable both to and from, this homey pousada, while not exactly cheap, might be a more affordable alternative if you're seeking to momentarily escape the skyscraper experience. Once you step inside this former private residence, you might easily forget that you're still at the center of a bustling megalopolis. The skylighted café serves breakfast to guests, lunch to those who work at nearby businesses, and a light dinner. Take a peek at the guestbook to see how past guests have raved. ⊠*Alameda Franca 1621, Jardins, 01422-001* ☎*011/3062–1444* 🛏*14 rooms* ⛄*In-hotel: no elevator, restaurant, public Internet* ▭*MC, V* Ⓜ*Consolação.*

PARAÍSO

¢   🛏 **Hotel Formule 1.** With hotels at both ends of Paulista and in Centro, Formule 1 is a great choice if you value location and price over luxury. Like the cockpit of a racecar, rooms have been stripped down to what's necesary for a comfortable stay; a TV, a double bed with a single bunked over it, and an efficent but small bathroom. Perfect for travelers who plan on spending most of their time out and about. The lobby is always full of groups of young people waiting to embark on an excursion. **Pros:** Close to metro, vending machines and pay phones in lobby. **Cons:** Breakfast unspectacular compared to that at other hotels, often fully booked. ⊠*Rua da Consolação, 2303, Consolação, 01301-100* ☎*011/3123–7755* ⊕*www.accorhotels.com.br* 🛏*399 rooms* ⛄*In-hotel: public Internet, parking (fee)* ▭*AE* Ⓜ*Consolação.*

PINHEIROS

$ 🛏 **Golden Tower.** Proximity to important hubs and to Vila Madalena make this a good choice. The hotel was built in 2001, and all rooms have nonallergenic carpet and sheets, as well as anti-noise windows and modern-looking furniture. Rooms are spacious, the location is ideal, and the Mediterranean restaurant is good. Views from the terrace and top floors are privileged. **Pros:** Close to Marginal Pinheiros, quiet neighborhood. **Cons:** Far from Centro. ⊠*Rua Deputado Lacerda Franco 148, Pinheiros, 05418-000* ☎*011/3094–2200 or 0800/10–1525* 🖷*011/3094–2201* ⊕*www.goldentowerhotel.com.br* 🛏*88 rooms, 8 suites* ⛄*In-room: safe, Ethernet (some), Wi-Fi. In-hotel: restaurant, pool, gym, public Internet, parking (fee), no-smoking rooms* ▭*AE, MC, V* ⦿*BP.*

VILA MARIANA

$$–$$$$ 🛏 **Hotel Sofitel São Paulo.** Near the Congonhas Airport and Ibirapuera Park, this modern, luxury hotel is noted for its French style. The restaurant serves French cuisine. Dark-wood furniture fills the rooms, many of which have views of the park. It's refreshing to be able to see trees from your window in São Paulo. **Pros:** Many amenities, convenient helipad for millionaires. **Cons:** Afternoon traffic, far from business centers. ⊠*Rua Sena Madureira 1355, Bloco 1, Vila Mariana, 04021-051* ☎*011/5087–0800* 🖷*011/5575–4544* ⊕*www.accorhotels.com.br* 🛏*219 rooms* ⛄*In-hotel: restaurant, room service, bar, tennis court, pool, gym, laundry facilities, parking (fee)* ▭*AE, DC, MC, V.*

NIGHTLIFE & THE ARTS

NIGHTLIFE

Updated by Simon Tarmo

São Paulo's nightlife options are seemingly endless, and knowing where to go is key. The chic and wealthy head for establishments, most of which serve food, in the Vila Olímpia, Jardins, and Itaim neighborhoods. The Pinheiros and Vila Madalena neighborhoods have a large concentration of Brazilian clubs and bars. Jardins has many gay and lesbian spots, and Pinheiros and Vila Madalena have a large concentration of youthful bars and clubs.

> ### GETTING AROUND AFTER DARK
>
> For safety reasons, we strongly suggest taking cabs at night—its convenient and relatively cheap. Ask your concierge about transportation if finding a cab proves difficult.

São Paulo is a city beset by trends, so clubs and bars come and go at a dizzying pace. Though the places listed here were all thriving spots at this writing, the nightlife scene is always changing, and it's best to check with hotel concierges and paulistanos you meet to confirm that a place is still going strong before heading out on the town.

BARS

Among a massive amount of options, the most sophisticated (and expensive) places are in Jardins, Vila Olímpia, and Itaim; Pinheiros and Vila Madalena are full of trendy places.

CENTRO
Fodor'sChoice ★

First opened in 1949, **Bar Brahma** (⊠ *Av. São João 677, Centro, 01036-000* ☎ *011/3333–3030 reservations* ⊕ *www.barbrahmasp.com* Ⓜ *República*) used to be the meeting place of artists, intellectuals, and politicians. The decor is a time warp to the mid-20th century, with furniture, lamps, and a piano true to the period. This is one of the best places in São Paulo for live music, with a selection of traditional samba and Brazilian pop groups scheduled every week.

FREGUESIA
DO Ó

A stop at off-the-beaten-path **Frangó** (⊠ *Largo da Matriz de Nossa Senhora do Ó 168, Freguesia do Ó, 02925-040* ☎ *011/3932–4818 or 011/3931–2285* ⊕ *www.frangobar.com.br*), northwest of Centro, makes you feel as if you've been transported to a small town. The bar has 150 varieties of beer, including the Brazilian dark beer Xingu. Its rich, molasseslike flavor nicely complements the bar's unforgettable *coxinhas de frango com queijo* (fried balls of chicken with cheese).

ITAIM & VILA
OLÍMPIA

Bar D'A Rua (⊠ *Rua Bandeira Paulista, 327, Itaim, 04532-010* ☎ *011/ 3071–0486* ⊕ *www.bardarua.com.br*) is right in the heart of the Itaim nightlife area and features a popular open deck section. Cold draft beer is served in the traditional tall and thin *tulipa* glasses.

Close to the northern border of Itaim is **Na Mata Café** (⊠ *Rua da Mata, 70, Itaim, 04531-020* ☎ *011/3079–0300* ⊕ *www.namata.com.br*). Considered one of the best live music venues in the city, with shows just about every night of the week and an adjoining restaurant, Na Mata is a great place to catch some upmarket Brazilian entertainment.

Featuring a huge wall lined with more than 500 types of rumlike cachaça, **Bar Do Arnesto** (⊠*Rua Ministro Jesuíno Cardoso, 207, Vila Olímpia, 04544-050* ☎*011/ 3848–9432* ⊕*www.bardoarnesto.com. br*) is a great example of the traditional Brazilian *botequim*. These casual bars generally offer something a little different, and specialize in cold bottled beer, snack foods, and caipirinhas.

JARDINS Crowded from happy hour on, **All Black** (⊠*Rua Oscar Freire 163, Jardins, 01426-001* ☎*011/3088–7990* ⊕*www.allblack.com.br*) is an Irish pub with style—and a great variety of international beer brands. Irish soccer paraphernalia decorates the place, and a New Zealand flag betrays one of the owner's roots. There's usually a live band (with entry fee) later in the night. **Balcão** (⊠*Rua Doutor Melo Alves 150, Jardim Paulista, 01417-010* ☎*011/ 3063–6091* Ⓜ*Consolação*) means "balcony" in Portuguese, and this artsy place has a sprawling one. If you'd like a little food to accompany your drinks and conversation, try one of the famous sandwiches on ciabatta bread.

PARAÍSO **Barnaldo Lucrécia** (⊠*Rua Abílio Soares 207, Paraíso, 04005-000* ☎*011/3885–3425* ⊕*www.barnaldolucrecia.com.br* Ⓜ*Paraíso*) draws crowds with live *música popular brasileira* (MPB, popular Brazilian music). The crowd is intense but jovial.

PERDIZES **Bar do Elias** (⊠*Rua Caraíbas 224, Perdizes, 05020-000* ☎*011/3864– 4722*) changed address in 2007 but remains a hangout for fans of the Palmeiras soccer team, whose stadium is a few blocks away. If you want something to eat, the carpaccio is undoubtedly the best choice on the menu.

PINHEIROS The '60s and '70s bohemian-chic decor at **Astor** (⊠*Rua Delfina 163,*
& VILA *Vila Madalena, 05443-010* ☎*011/3815–1364* ⊕*www.barastor.com.*
MADALENA *br*) sends you back in time. The owner decided to open this place after
★ the success of his other two bars, Pirajá and Original. The quality draft beer and tasty snacks and meals mean this place is always hopping; the menu is full of specialties from classic bars in Brazil. Don't miss *picadinho à astor* (beef stew with rice and black beans, poached eggs, banana, farofa, and beef *pastel*).

Most patrons stop at **Empanadas** (⊠*Rua Wisard 489, Vila Madalena, 05434-080* ☎*011/3032–2116*) for a beer en route to another Vila Madalena bar. It's a good place to "warm up" for an evening out with a quick drink and a bite to eat on the bar's sidewalk tables. Appropriately, the *empanadas* (Argentinian filled pastries) are particularly appealing. When it comes to ending the night, **Filial** (⊠*Rua Fidalga 254, Vila Madalena, 05432-000* ☎*011/3813–9226* ⊕*www.barfilial. com.br*) is considered the best bar in town. Plenty of musicians stop by for an after-hours taste of its draft beer, along with the flavorful snacks (such as *bolinho de arroz,* or rice fritters) and meals (try *galinha afogada,* a stew with incredibly moist chicken and rice).

★ The fashionable patrons at **Grazie a Dio** (⊠*Rua Girassol 67, Vila Madalena, 05433-000* ☎*011/3031–6568* ⊕*www.grazieadio.com.br*) may vary in age, but they always appreciate good music. The best time to go is at happy hour for daily live performances. On Saturday it's jazz, and on Friday, bossa nova. The natural decorations, including trees and constellations, complement the Mediterranean food served in the back. **Pirajá** (⊠*Av. Brigadeiro Faria Lima 64, Pinheiros, 05426-200* ☎*011/3815–6881* ⊕*www.piraja.com.br*), known for its draft beer and sandwiches, attracts a crowd of journalists and designers that work nearby. Pictures of Rio line the walls. The action starts at happy hour, after 6 PM. The *bolinhos de abóbora com carne seca* (pumpkin-and–jerked beef fritters) are very good.

> **HAPPY HOUR**
>
> Unlike in some countries, where the term refers to those few early-evening hours when drinks are cheaper, happy hour (pronounced and written in English) in Brazil simply means the time just after work day, around 6 PM, when you might head to a bar for a drink with friends or colleagues. Despite the lack of discounted cocktails, Paulistanos love to use the term, and many bars are judged purely on their suitability as a happy-hour venue.

MUSIC CLUBS

São Paulo's music clubs might have rock, jazz, or blues artists, but when it comes to Brazilian music, there are many more options. On weekends you find MPB, samba, and *pagode* (similar to samba but with pop-music elements) in clubs throughout the city. At *forró* clubs, couples dance close to the fast beat and romantic lyrics of music that originated in the Northeast.

BIXIGA **Café Piu Piu** (⊠*Rua 13 de Maio 134, Bela Vista, 01327-000* ☎*011/ 3258–8066* ⊕*www.cafepiupiu.com.br*) is best-known for jazz and blues, but it also hosts groups that play rock (between Friday and Sunday), bossa nova, and sometimes even tango. Statues, an antique balcony, and marble tables decorate the place. Doors open at 9 PM Tuesday–Sunday.

ITAIM BIBI Featuring rock, MPB (música popular brasileira) and samba, **6:01** (⊠*Rua Comandatuba, 26, Itaim, 04544-070* ☎*011/3846–3031 and 3845-7396* ⊕*www.seiseum.com.br*) gets packed at night and is known as a great place for flirting, especially on Wednesday and Friday. As the name suggests, the bar opens just after 6 PM Tuesday to Sunday.

JARDINS At **Mr. Blues Jazz Bar** (⊠*Av. São Gabriel 558, Jardim Paulista, 01435-000* ☎*011/3884–5255*), a traditional jazz, blues, rock, and soul venue, the audience drinks beer and whiskey and eats french fries with Parmesan cheese. Doors open at 9 PM Monday–Saturday.

MOEMA With a name right out of New Orleans, it's no wonder that **Bourbon Street** (⊠*Rua dos Chanés 127, Moema, 04087-031* ☎*011/5561–1643 or 011/5095–6100* ⊕*www.bourbonstreet.com.br*) is where the best jazz and blues bands, Brazilian and international, play. Performances are Tuesday–Sunday, after 9:30 PM. On Sunday you can merengue and mambo at the Caribbean dance party.

PINHEIROS   **Canto da Ema** (⊠*Av. Brigadeiro Faria Lima 364, Pinheiros, 05426-200* ☎*011/3813–4708* ⊕*www.cantodaema.com.br*) is considered the best place to dance forró in town. Here you'll find people of different ages and styles coming together on the dance floor. *Xiboquinha* is the official forró drink, made with *cachaça* (a Brazilian sugarcane-based alcohol), lemon, honey, cinnamon, and ginger. Doors open at 10:30 PM Wednesday–Saturday and it's open 7–midnight on Sunday; admission is R$14–R$20.

A *carioca* is a person from Rio de Janeiro, and **Carioca Club** (⊠*Rua Cardeal Arcoverde 2899, Pinheiros, 05407–004* ☎*011/3813–8598* ⊕*www.cariocaclub.com.br*) has the decor of old-style Rio clubs. Its large dance floor attracts an eclectic mix of up to 1,200 college students, couples, and professional dancers who move to *samba, gafieira,* and *pagode* Thursday–Saturday beginning at 10 PM, and Sunday 5–11.

VILA   The tiny round tables at **Piratininga** (⊠*Rua Wizard 149, Vila Madalena,*
MADALENA   *05434-080* ☎*011/3032–9775* ⊕*www.piratiningabar.com.br* Ⓜ*Vila*
★   *Madalena* ⊙*Daily 4 PM*), a small bar-restaurant, are perfect for a quiet rendezvous. The live MPB (música popular brasileira), bossa nova, blues, and jazz music, which starts daily between 7 and 9 PM (R$8 per person cover charge), add to the romance.

VILA OLÍMPIA   People come to **All of Jazz** (⊠*Rua João Cachoeira 1366, Vila Olímpia, 04535-006* ☎*011/3849–1345* ⊕*www.allofjazz.com.br*) to quietly listen to good jazz and bossa nova in an intimate environment. Local musicians jam Monday–Saturday beginning at 7:30 PM. Reserve a table on weekends.

DANCE CLUBS

Most clubs open at 9 PM, but people tend to arrive late (around midnight), and dance until 5 or 6 AM. Still, you should arrive early to be at the front of the lines. Don't worry if the dance floor appears empty at 11 PM; things will start to sizzle an hour or so later. Clubbing can get expensive. Most charge at least R$20 at the door (sometimes women are allowed in for free) and the most popular and upscale places ask as much as R$100 just for entry. If it's a popular club, expect to wait in line for a bit, especially if you're heading out late.

BARRA FUNDA   **Villa Country** (⊠*Av. Francisco Matarazzo 810, Água Branca, 05001-*
AND ÁGUA   *000* ☎*011/3868–5858* ⊕*www.villacountry.com.br* Ⓜ*Barra Funda*)
BRANCA   is *the* place to dance to American country music and *sertanejo,* Brazilian country music. The huge club has a restaurant, bars, shops, game rooms, and a big dance floor. An Old West theme permeates the decor. It's open Thursday–Sunday and entry is R$15–R$25.

Urbano (⊠*Marquês de São Vicente 1767, Barra Funda, 01139-003* ☎*011/3611–3121* ⊕*www.urbanosp.com.br*) closed shop in Pinheiros and relaunched in 2007 in this new location. Now it's only open on Monday and Saturday nights, from 10 PM. The house and funk music is administered by a crew of regular DJs and the venue's cool industrial look attracts big crowds.

CONSOLAÇÃO   Live or recorded indie rock is the musical menu at two-story **Funhouse** (⊠ *Rua Bela Cintra 567, Consolação, 01415-000* ☎ *011/3259–3793* ⊕ *www.funhouse.com.br* Ⓜ *Consolação*), open Wednesday–Saturday. New Brazilian bands play every Saturday, and entry prices are at the low-end of the scale beginning around R$10.

JARDINS   **8 Bar** (⊠ *Rua José Maria Lisboa 82, Jardim Paulista, 01423-000* ☎ *011/3887–3041* ⊕ *www.8bar.com.br*) plays a range of electronic and disco music for dancing or just listening while you're having a drink at the bar. The DJs often interact with the crowd and accept requests in the intimate space.

PINHEIROS   Housed in an unmissable building, **Avenida Club** (⊠ *Av. Pedroso de Morais 1036, Pinheiros, 05420-001* ☎ *011/3814–7383* ⊕ *www.avenidaclub.com.br*) hosts a range of dance events, such as Caribbean or Brazilian dance parties, while Sunday brings contemporary MPB and rock acts. The large wooden dance floor—one of the finest in town—attracts a crowd of twenty- and thirtysomethings.

Every night except Sunday, **Blen Blen Brasil** (⊠ *Rua Inácio Pereira da Rocha 520, Pinheiros, 05432–011* ☎ *011/3815–4999*) has live music ranging from reggae to salsa jazz to Brazilian rock and MPB, beginning at 8 PM. The clientele varies depending on the music—rock generates a younger crowd; salsa jazz an older one. Arrive early and stay at the bar having a drink and snack before going upstairs to dance. Entry from R$25.

VILA MADALENA   At **Dolores Bar** (⊠ *Rua Fradique Coutinho 1007, Vila Madalena, 05416-011* ☎ *011/3031–3604*) DJs spin funk, soul, and hip-hop tunes for a crowd in its twenties and thirties on Friday and Saturday from 10 PM on. Friday nights are the most popular, and people really do fill up the floor only after midnight. Because **A Lanterna** (⊠ *Rua Fidalga 531, Vila Madalena, 05432-070* ☎ *011/3031–0483* ⊕ *www.lanterna.com.br*) is a mixture of restaurant, bar, and nightclub, you can go early for dinner and stay late for dancing. Actors, dancers, and musicians give performances that add to the entertainment. The walls are decorated with local artists' works. It's open Tuesday–Sunday.

VILA OLÍMPIA   **Buena Vista Club** (⊠ *Rua Atílio Innocenti 780, Vila Olímpia, 04538-001*
Fodor'sChoice   ☎ *011/3045–5245* ⊕ *www.buenavistaclub.com.br*) is a good place to
★   take dance classes. On Sunday you can learn to dance *gafieira* and *zouk*. Live music and DJs heat up the dance floor for hours. The club also has good appetizers and drinks and is open Wednesday–Sunday. You might feel like you're on the set of an Austin Powers movie at **Lov.e Club & Lounge** (⊠ *Rua Pequetita 189, Vila Olímpia, 04552-060* ☎ *011/3044–1613* ⊕ *www.loveclub.com.br*). Before 2 AM the music isn't too loud, and you can sit and talk on the '50s-style sofas. After that, the techno and house effects keep people on the small dance floor until sunrise. *Pancadão*, the unique carioca-style funk, can be heard on

some nights, so be sure to check the weekly program. The club is open Tuesday to Saturday from midnight.

GAY & LESBIAN BARS & CLUBS

São Paulo has a large and lively gay scene with a smorgasbord of bars, cafés, and mega nightclubs spread throughout the city. There's a good cluster of watering holes along Avenida Vieira de Carvalho in República, and the Rua Frei Caneca in Consolação (10 minutes from the Consolação metro on Avenida Paulista) is a regular rendezvous point and hangout.

BARRA FUNDA & LAPA In a huge colonial blue house in an old industrial neighborhood, **Blue Space** (⊠ *Rua Brigadeiro Galvão 723, Barra Funda, 01151-000* ☏ *011/3666–1616* ⊕ *www.bluespace.com.br* Ⓜ *Marechal Deodoro*) is one of the largest gay nightclubs in São Paulo. Every Saturday and Sunday, two dance floors and four bars, along with lounge and private rooms, fill with a large crowd interested in the house DJs and go-go-boy and drag shows. Popular **The Week** (⊠ *Rua Guaicurus 324, Lapa, 05033-000* ☏ *011/3872–9966* ⊕ *www.theweek.com.br*) has a whopping 6,000-square-meter area. Two dance floors, three lounge rooms, a deck with a swimming pool, six bars, and several DJs who play house, electro, and techno animate an often shirtless-crowd on Friday and Saturday nights.

BELA VISTA **A Lôca** (⊠ *Rua Frei Caneca 916, Consolação, 01307-002* ☏ *011/3159–8889* ⊕ *www.aloca.com.br* Ⓜ *Consolação*) has a crowded dance floor, a video room, and two bars. A mixed gay, lesbian, and straight crowd often dances until dawn, both to electronic music (Thursday to Saturday) and rock (on Sunday). On Friday and Saturday you can end the night with a light breakfast (yogurt and fruits).

ITAIM BIBI Popular lesbian spot **Clube Z** (⊠ *Rua Tabapuã 1420, Itaim Bibi,* ☏ *011/3071–0030* ⊕ *www.clubz.com.br*), open Friday and Saturday, has Ancient Rome decor, red velvet sofas, and two DJs spinning house and techno.

Vermont Itaim (⊠ *Rua Pedroso Alvarenga 1192, Itaim Bibi04531-004* ☏ *011/3071–1320* ⊕ *www.vermontitaim.com.br*) has a restaurant and bar and offers a variety of live music and dancing. Eight acts divvy up the show times from Wednesday to Saturday; on Sunday a nine-piece all-girl samba band takes the stage. DJs round off the evening's entertainment by spinning late into the night.

THE ARTS

The world's top orchestras, opera and dance companies, and other troupes always include São Paulo in their South American tours. Most free concerts—with performances by either Brazilian or international artists—are presented on Sunday in Parque Ibirapuera. City-sponsored events are usually held in Centro's Vale do Anhangabaú area or in Avenida Paulista.

Listings of events appear in the "Veja São Paulo" insert of the newsweekly *Veja*. The arts sections of the dailies *Folha de São Paulo* and *O Estado de São Paulo* also have listings and reviews. Both papers publish a weekly guide on Friday.

Tickets for many events are available at booths throughout the city and at theater box offices. Many of these venues offer ticket delivery to your hotel for a surcharge. **Ticketmaster** (☎*011/6846–6000* ⊕*www.ticketmaster.com.br*) sells tickets for music concerts and theaters by phone and the Internet, as does **Fun by Phone** (☎*011/5087– 3450* ⊕*www.funbynet.com.br*), which also has theme-park tickets. **Show Tickets at Shopping Center Igua-temi** (⊠*Av. Brigadeiro Faria Lima 1191, 3rd fl., Jardim Paulistano, 01452-002* ☎*011/3031–2098*) sells tickets to the main concerts and performances in town. It's open Monday–Saturday 10 AM–10 PM and Sunday 2–6.

> ### GAY PRIDE PARADE
>
> São Paulo hosts one of the world's biggest and most famous gay parades each year on the Sunday of the Corpus Christi holiday, which generally falls at the end of May or early June. The Gay Pride Parade, which was first held in 1997, runs along Avenida Paulista and attracts more than 2 million people. Organizers of the 2007 event claimed a world record 3.5 million attendees, but city officials have downplayed that number, claiming the Avenue simply cannot hold that many. Whatever the real number, there's no doubt the parade is now one of the biggest events of it's kind in the world.

CLASSICAL MUSIC & OPERA

Many operas and classical performances take place at Teatro Municipal, Teatro Alfa, and Teatro Cultura Artística *(⇨Concert Halls)*.

★ **Espaço Promon** (⊠*Av. Juscelino Kubitschek 1830, Itaim Bibi, 04543– 900* ☎*011/3847–4111*) is a versatile venue with a range of events including chamber music performances. Despite being housed in a magnificent old train station, **Sala São Paulo** (⊠*Praça Júlio Prestes, Centro, 01218-020* ☎*011/3367–9500* ⊕*www.salasaopaulo.art.br* Ⓜ*Luz*) is one of the most modern concert halls for classical music in Latin America. It's also home to the **São Paulo Symphony** (OSESP).

★ Built in neoclassic style in 1917 and entirely renovated in 1998, the **Teatro São Pedro** (⊠*Rua Barra Funda 171, Barra Funda, 01152-000* ☎*011/3667–0499* ⊕*www.teatrosaopedro.sp.gov.br* Ⓜ*Marechal Deodoro*) is the second-oldest theater in São Paulo. It's one of the best places in the city for chamber concerts and operas. There are free morning events Sunday and Wednesday.

DANCE

Dance companies perform at Teatro Alfa, Teatro Cultura Artística, Teatro Municipal, and Via Funchal *(⇨Concert Halls)*.

Ballet da Cidade (⊠*Rua João Passaláqua, 66 Centro, 01326-020* ☎*011/ 3241–3883* ⊕*www.baledacidade.com.br* Ⓜ*Anhangabaú*) is the city's official dance company. It only performs classical acts, mostly in its home theater, the Teatro Municipal. Contemporary pieces are performed by **Ballet Stagium** (⊠ *Rua Augusta 2985, 2nd fl., Cerqueira César, 01413-100* ☎ *011/3085–0151* ⊕ *www.stagium. com.br*). **Cisne Negro** (⊠ *Rua das Tabocas 55, Vila Beatriz, 05445-020* ☎ *011/3813–4966* ⊕ *www.cisnene gro.com.br*) is another esteemed contemporary dance company.

SAMBA

Sometimes it feels like samba is everywhere you look, especially around the nightlife hot spots—be it an impromptu performance by a bar patron or a full-on samba band, there are usually plenty of chances to check out the famous music and dance.

CONCERT HALLS

Credicard Hall (⊠ *Av. das Nações Unidas 17995, Santo Amaro, 04795-100* ☎ *011/6846–6000* ⊕ *www.credicardhall.com.br*) is one of the biggest theaters in São Paulo and can accommodate up to 7,000 people. The venue frequently hosts concerts by famous Brazilian and international artists. Tickets can be bought by phone or Internet using the services of Ticketmaster. Opera, ballet, music, and symphony performances are held at **Teatro Alfa** (⊠ *Rua Bento Branco de Andrade Filho 722, Santo Amaro, 04757-000* ☎ *011/5693–4000* ⊕ *www.teatroalfa. com.br*). It's one of the newest theaters in the country, with all the latest sound and lighting technology—and the biggest foreign stars grace the stage. Tickets can be bought by phone and through Show Tickets, then picked up a half hour before the performance.

Fine acoustics make **Teatro Cultura Artística** (⊠ *Rua Nestor Pestana 196, Cerqueira César, 01303-010* ☎ *011/3258–3616* ⊕ *www.culturaartis tica.com.br* Ⓜ *Anhangabaú*) perfect for classical music performances. It also hosts dance recitals and plays. Avoid walking from the metro stop at night.

Most serious music, ballet, and opera is performed at **Teatro Municipal** (⊠ *Praça Ramos de Azevedo, Centro, 01037-010* ☎ *011/3222–8698 or 011/3223–3022* ⊕ *www.prefeitura.sp.gov.br/theatromunicipal* Ⓜ *Anhangabaú*), a classic theater built in 1911 with an intimate gilt and moss-green-velvet interior. Besides scheduled events, it hosts "guided concerts" (sort of a Classical Music 101) on some Wednesdays, Thursdays, and Fridays at 11 AM. **Teatro da Universidade Católica (TUCA)** (⊠ *Rua Monte Alegre 1024, Perdizes, 05014-001* ☎ *011/3670–8453* ⊕ *www.teatrotuca.com.br*), the Catholic University theater, hosts plays and alternative concerts. **Via Funchal** (⊠ *Rua Funchal 65, Vila Olímpia, 04551-060* ☎ *011/3188–4148 or 011/3897–4456* ⊕ *www.viafunchal. com.br*) is capable of seating more than 3,000 people, and is the site of many large international music, theater, and dance shows.

SAMBA SHOWS

Escolas de samba or samba schools are the heart and soul of many communities. Most people only associate them with the dancing groups that perform during Carnival, but they keep busy all year round. In addition to samba lessons, they organize a range of community services, especially education and health outreach programs. Check them out anytime, but from November to February they're gearing up for Carnival, and often open their rehearsals to the public.

Rosas de Ouro (⊠*Av. Cel. Euclides Machado 1066, Freguesia do Ó, 02713–000* ☎*011/3931-4555* ⊕*www.sociedaderosasdeouro.com.br*) has one of the most popular rehearsals. Up to 3,000 people at a time attend rehearsals at **Mocidade Alegre** (⊠*Av. Casa Verde 3498, Limão, 02520–300* ☎*011/3857-7525* ⊕*www.mocidadealegre.com.br*) just before Carnival.

FILM

Centro Cultural São Paulo (⊠*Rua Vergueiro 1000, Paraíso, 01504–000* ☎*011/ 3383-3402 or 3383–3437* Ⓜ*Vergueiro* ⊕*www.centrocultural. sp.gov.br*) often shows a series of films centered on a theme. Admission is usually free or almost free for some exhibitions. It also has plays, concerts, and art exhibits. **Reserva Cultural** (⊠*Av. Paulista 900, Jardim Paulista, 01310–100* ☎*011/3287-3529* ⊕*www.reservacultural.com. br* Ⓜ*Brigadeiro*) has four movie theaters, a small café, a bar, and a nice deck-style restaurant from which you can see—and be seen by—pedestrians on Paulista Avenue.

Brazilian, European, and other non-blockbuster films are shown at the **Espaço Unibanco** (⊠*Rua Augusta 1475, Consolação, 01307–001* ☎*011/ 3288-6780* Ⓜ*Consolação*). Close by, the **Unibanco ArtePlex** (⊠*Rua Frei Caneca 569, 3rd fl., Consolação, 01307–001* ☎*011/3472-2365* Ⓜ*Consolação* ⊕*www.unibancoarteplex.com.br*) shows Hollywood, European, and independent films.

SPORTS & THE OUTDOORS

Updated by
Simon Tarmo

Maybe it's the environment or maybe the culture, but participating in a range of sporting endeavors is usually not a huge part of a Paulistano's regime. Although many inhabitants will religiously head to a gym or go for a jog a few times a week, there's not a great deal of organized sport in the city. An exception is soccer or "futebol," which you will see in most parks, either on full fields, half-size arenas, or even sandy courts, every weekend and on weeknights.

ON THE SIDELINES

AUTO RACING

Racing fans from all over the world come to São Paulo around September or October for the annual **Formula 1** race, which also attracts massive national attention, especially when a Brazilian driver is in the mix. The race is held at **Autódromo de Interlagos** (⊠*Av. Senador Teotônio Vilela 261, Interlagos, 04801–010* ☎*011/5666-8822* ⊕*www. autodromointerlagos.com*), which also hosts other kinds of races on weekends. For ticket information on the Formule 1 race, contact the

King Ronaldo

Brazilians are so passionate about *futebol* (soccer) that popular wisdom says there are three subjects—soccer, women, and religion—not to be discussed at a bar table among friends, to avoid quarrels. Of these, soccer is surely the most important. The sport, which arrived in Brazil in 1894 with immigrant British railroad workers, is as central to Brazilian culture as samba and the beach.

Soccer is the national passion in no small part thanks to Brazil's world-champion status in 1958, 1962, 1970, 1994, and 2002. The greatest Brazilian soccer players—such as "King" Pelé, as he was known in the 1960s and '70s—are seen as gods, and are treated like royalty. Soccer stars in Brazil are probably more famous than the country's president.

The king of the ball in Brazil today is Ronaldo, who in 1994, at age 17, joined the World Cup team. He didn't play in that game, but went on to score 42 goals in the next two years, in only 13 matches. Shortly afterward he went to play in Europe, but remained an idol in Brazil, where he is known as "The Phenomenon," and is still a hot item in the press, both for his spectacular performances and his tabloid-worthy personal life.

Many lesser stars bring Brazilians to tears and shouts of joy every Sunday afternoon in thrilling games that can be watched live in the fields or on TV. And though soccer reigns supreme in Brazil, you don't have to be royalty to afford a game—even at the world's largest soccer stadium, Maracanã, in Rio, admission is just US$2.

Confederação Brasileira de Automobilismo (⊠ *Rua da Glória 290, 8th fl., Rio de Janeiro, RJ20241-180* ☎ *021/2221–4895* ⊕ *www.cba.org.br*).

HORSE RACING

Thoroughbreds race at the **São Paulo Jockey Club** (⊠ *Rua Lineu de Paula Machado 1263, Cidade Jardim, 05601–000* ☎ *011/2161–8300* ⊕ *www.jockeysp.com.br*), which is open Monday, Wednesday, and Thursday 7:30 PM–11:30 PM, and weekends 2–9. Card-carrying Jockey Club members get the best seats, but you can also go there for its elegant restaurant with a nice view.

SOCCER

Brazilians' reputation for being obsessed with soccer is rightfully earned. Some paulistas, however, prefer to watch soccer on TV at home or in a bar. São Paulo State has several well-funded teams with some of the country's best players. The four main teams—Corinthians, São Paulo, Palmeiras, and Santos—attract fans from other states. The two biggest stadiums are Morumbi and the municipally run Pacaembu. Covered seats offer the best protection, not only from the elements but also from rowdy spectators. Buy tickets at the stadiums or online at ⊕ *www. ingressofacil.com.br*. Regular games usually don't sell out, but finals—where you can buy tickets up to five days in advance—always do.

★ At **Canindé** (⊠ *Rua Comendador Nestor Pereira 33, Canindé, 03034–070* ☎ *011/2125–9400* ⊕ *www.portuguesa.com.br*) the main attraction, besides the game, are *bolinhos de bacalhau* (salt-cod fritters), popular among the Portuguese immigrants. **Morumbi** (⊠ *Praça Roberto Gomes Pedrosa s/n, Morumbi, 05653–070* ☏ *011/3749–8000* ⊕ *www. saopaulofc.net*), the home stadium of São Paulo Futebol Clube, has a capacity of 80,000. The first games of the 1950 World Cup were played at the **Pacaembu** (⊠ *Praça Charles Miller s/n, Pacaembú, 01234–900* ☏ *011/3661–9111* Ⓜ *Clínicas*) stadium, unofficial home of the Corinthians team.

Estádio Palestra Itália (⊠ *Rua Turiassu 1840, Barra Funda, 05005–000* ☏ *011/3873–2111* ⊕ *palmeiras.globo.com* Ⓜ *Barra Funda*), otherwise known as Parque Antártica, has been the home of Palmeiras since 1920 and seats 32,000. The small **Rua Javari** (⊠ *Rua Javari 117, Moóca, 03166–100* ☏ *011/6292–4833* ⊕ *www.juventus.com.br* Ⓜ *Moóca*) stadium is where Juventus plays. It's an ideal place to enjoy the stadium's Italian atmosphere—Moóca is a traditionally Italian neighborhood—and eat a cannoli while cheering for the home team.

VOLLEYBALL

Brazilians love volleyball, both the traditional kind and the beach version. The country has a top-class national competition and hosts regular international matches. Check the **Volleyball Federação Paulista** (⊠ *Rua Abílio Soares, 1370, Paraíso, 04005–005* ☏ *011/3053–9560* ⊕ *www. fpv.com.br*) Web site for details of upcoming matches and venues.

PARTICIPATORY SPORTS

Check the air quality before you practice outdoor sports. During a dry season the air can be bad. Don't take your cues from the paulistas—their lungs are made of steel.

CYCLING & JOGGING

Going for a ride or a run in one of São Paulo's parks can be the best options if you want a little exercise. For cyclists there are usually plenty of rental options (from R$5 per hour) available and special lanes just for riders. **Parque Ibirapuera** (⊠ *Av. Pedro Álvares Cabral s/n, Parque Ibirapuera, 04094-000* ☏ *011/ 5574–5177*) gets busy on the weekends, but is well worth the effort. **Parque Vila Lobos** (⊠ *Av. Professor Fonseca Rodrigues, 1655, Alto de Pinheiros, 05461-010* ☏ *011/3023–0316* ⊙ *Weekdays 7–7*) has fewer trees and history but is big and has plenty of winding pathways wide enough to accommodate everyone. There are bike-rental stands inside the park, as well as a few soccer pitches and a big, concrete square with basketball half-courts, and a few food-and-drink options.

GOLF

Golf is an increasingly popular sport in Brazil, but organizing a round in São Paulo is not easy or inexpensive. The 18-hole **Clube de Campo** (⊠ *Praça Rockford 28, Vila Represa, 04826-410* ☏ *011/5929–3111* ⊕ *www.ccsp.org.br*) can be a good option, but you need to be introduced by a member. It's open Monday, Tuesday, Thursday, and Friday 7–7. **Golf School** (⊠ *Av. Guido Caloi 2160, Santo Amaro, 05802-140*

☎*011/5515–3372*) is a driving range, and for R$50 you get to hit 100 balls.

Golf & Gym (✉*Rua Marquês de São Vicente 1700, Barra Funda, 01139-002* ☎*011/3611–3411* ⊕*www.golfgym.com.br*) has a driving range and a putting green. Fees begin at R$50 for 30 minutes and 70 balls.

SHOPPING

Updated by
Simon Tarmo

Fashionistas from all over the continent flock to São Paulo for the clothes, shoes, and accessories. In fact, shopping is a tourist attraction in its own right. You can get a sampling of what's on offer six days a week: stores are usually open weekdays 9–6:30, Saturday 9–1, and are closed Sunday. Mall hours are generally weekdays and Saturday 10–10; malls open on Sunday around 2 PM.

AREAS

In **Centro** Rua do Arouche is noted for leather goods. The area around Rua João Cachoeira in **Itaim** has evolved from a neighborhood of small clothing factories into a wholesale- and retail-clothing sales district. Several shops on Rua Tabapuã sell small antiques. Also, Rua Dr. Mário Ferraz is stuffed with elegant clothing, gift, and home-decoration stores. In **Jardins,** centering on Rua Oscar Freire, double-parked Mercedes-Benzes and BMWs point the way to the city's fanciest stores, which sell leather items, jewelry, gifts, antiques, and art. Jardins also has many restaurants and beauty salons. Shops that specialize in high-price European antiques are on or around Rua da Consolação. A slew of lower-price antiques stores line Rua Cardeal Arcoverde in **Pinheiros.**

CENTERS & MALLS

D&D Decoração & Design Center (✉*Av. das Nações Unidas 12555, Brooklin, 04578-000* ☎*011/3043–9000* ⊕*www.dedshopping.com.br*) shares a building with the World Trade Center and the Gran Meliá hotel. It's loaded with fancy home-decorating stores, full-scale restaurants, and fast-food spots. **Shopping Ibirapuera** (✉*Av. Ibirapuera 3103, Moema, 04029-200* ☎*011/5095–2300* ⊕*www.ibirapuera.com.br*) has more than 500 stores.

★ One of the newest shopping malls in São Paulo, **Shopping Pátio Higienópolis** (✉*Av. Higienópolis 618, Higienópolis, 01241-000* ☎*011/3823–2300* ⊕*www.patiohigienopolis.com.br*) is a mixture of old and new architecture styles. It has plenty of shops and restaurants, as well as six movie theaters. **Iguatemi São Paulo** (✉*Av. Brigadeiro Faria Lima 2232, Jardim Paulistano, 01489-900* ☎*011/3816–6116* ⊕*www.iguatemis aopaulo.com.br*) is the city's oldest and most sophisticated mall and has the latest in fashion and fast food. Movie theaters often show films in English with Portuguese subtitles. The Gero Café, built in the middle of the main hall, has a fine menu. **Morumbi Shopping** (✉*Av. Roque Petroni Jr. 1089, Morumbi, 04707-000* ☎*011/4003–4132* ⊕*www.*

morumbishopping.com.br), in the city's fastest-growing area, is giving Iguatemi a run for its money. That said, it houses about the same boutiques, record stores, bookstores, and restaurants.

MARKETS

Almost every neighborhood has a weekly outdoor food market, complete with loudmouthed hawkers, exotic scents, and mountains of colorful produce. Nine hundred of them happen every week in São Paulo, so you'll be able to hit at least one; ask around to find out when and where the closest one happens.

> ### EVERYONE'S A MALL RAT
>
> The undefeated champions of the São Paulo shopping scene are the malls; they're constantly growing, evolving, and gaining more shops and attractions. What's more, they're able to offer up the lastest trends in fashion, food, and fun in a safe, clean environment.

On Sunday there are **antiques fairs** near the Museu de Arte de São Paulo (MASP) and (in the afternoon) at the Shopping Center Iguatemi's parking lot. Many stall owners have shops and hand out business cards so you can browse throughout the week at your leisure. An **arts and crafts fair** (⊠*Praça da República, Centro, 01045-000*)—selling jewelry, embroidery, leather goods, toys, clothing, paintings, and musical instruments—takes place Sunday morning. Many booths move over to the nearby Praça da Liberdade in the afternoon, joining vendors selling Japanese-style ceramics, wooden sandals, cooking utensils, food, and bonsai trees. **Flea markets** with secondhand furniture, clothes, and CDs take place on Saturday at the popular Praça Benedito Calixto in Pinheiros (where you can also eat at food stands and listen to music all day long) and on Sunday at the Praça Dom Orione in Bela Vista.

SPECIALTY SHOPS

ANTIQUES

Antiquário Paulo Vasconcelos (⊠*Rua Alameda Gabriel Monteiro da Silva 1935, Jardins, 01441–001* ☎*011/3062–2444*) has folk art and 18th- and 19th-century Brazilian furniture, among other treasures. **Edwin Leonard** (⊠*Rua Oscar Freire 146, Jardins, 01426-000* ☎*011/3088–0294*) is a collective of three dealers that sell Latin American and European antiques.

Head to **Patrimônio** (⊠*Rua Alameda Ministro Rocha Azevedo 1068, Cerqueira César, 01410-002* ☎*011/3064–1750*) for Brazilian antiques at reasonable prices. It also sells some Indian artifacts as well as modern furnishings crafted from iron. **Pedro Corrêa do Lago** (⊠*Rua João Cachoeira 267, Itaim Bibi, 04535-010* ☎*011/3167–0066*) represents Sotheby's. The shop sells and auctions rare and used books, as well as antique maps, prints, and drawings of Brazil. **Renée Behar Antiques** (⊠*Rua Peixoto Gomide 2088, Jardins, 01409-002* ☎*011/3085–3622* ⊕*www.reneebehar.com.br*) has 18th- and 19th-century antiques and temporary exhibitions of antique pieces.

ART

Arte Aplicada (✉*Rua Haddock Lobo 1406, Jardins, 01414-002* ☎*011/3062–5128* ⊕*www.arteaplicada.com.br*) is the place for Brazilian paintings, sculptures, and prints. The staff at **Galeria Fortes Vilaça** (✉*Rua Fradique Coutinho 1500, Vila Madalena, 05416-001* ☎*011/3032–7066* ⊕*www.fortesvilaca.com.br*) has an eye for the works of up-and-coming Brazilian artists.

At **Espaço Cultural Ena Beçak** (✉*Rua Oscar Freire 440, Jardins, 01426-000* ☎*011/3088–7322* ⊕*www.enabecak.com.br*) you can shop for Brazilian prints, sculptures, and paintings and then stop at the café. If *art naif* is your thing, **Galeria Jacques Ardies** (✉*Rua Morgado de Mateus 579, Vila Mariana, 04015-051* ☎*011/5539–7500* ⊕*www.ardies.com* Ⓜ*Paraíso*) is a must. As the name suggests, art naïf is simple, with a primitive and handcrafted look.

At **Galeria Renot** (✉*Alameda Ministro Rocha Azevedo 1327, Jardins, 01410-001* ☎*011/3083–5933* ⊕*www.renot.com.br*) you find oil paintings by such Brazilian artists as Vicente Rego Monteiro, Di Cavalcanti, Cícero Dias, and Anita Malfatti. Many a trend has been set at **Mônica Filgueiras Galeria** (✉*Rua Bela Cintra 1533, Jardins, 01415-001* ☎*011/3082–5292*), which has all types of art, but mostly paintings and sculpture.

BEAUTY

★ **Anna Pegova** (✉*Alameda Lorena 1582, Jardins, 01424-002* ☎*011/3081–2402* ⊕*www.annapegova.com.br*) is a French beauty-product brand famous in Brazil. The shop has hair, skin, face, and body products for men and women. The Jardins store is one of the best. Brazilian brand **O Boticário** (✉*Rua Pamplona 1551, store 20, Jardins, 01405-002* ☎*011/3885–8623* ⊕*www.oboticario.com.br*) was created by dermatologists and pharmacists from Curitiba in the 1970s. Today it's one of the biggest franchising companies in the country, with products for men, women, and children. The company's Fundação O Boticário de Proteção a Natureza (Boticário Foundation for Nature Protection) funds ecological projects throughout Brazil. The shops can be found in most neighborhoods and malls in the city.

BEACHWEAR

Beira Mar Beachwear (✉*Rua José Paulino 592, Bom Retiro, 01120-000* ☎*011/3222–7999* ⊕*www.maiosbeiramar.com.br* Ⓜ*Tiradentes*) was founded in 1948. Since then it has been known for innovative and good-quality products. The Brazilian brand has its own factory and produces a great variety of bikinis and swimming suits. **Track & Field** (✉*Rua Oscar Freire 959, Jardins, 01426-001* ☎*011/3062–4457 or 011/3048–1277* ⊕*www.tf.com.br*) is a very good place to buy beachwear and sports clothing. The store sells bikinis and swimsuits from **Cia. Marítima** (⊕*www.ciamaritima.com.br*), a famous Brazilian beachwear brand. The shops are in almost every mall in São Paulo.

Shopping for Essentials

CLOSE UP

MAPS, BOOKS, NEWSPAPERS

Most Avenida Paulista newsstands sell major U.S. and European papers as well as magazines and paperbacks in English.

Fnac (⊠ *Praça dos Amaguás 34, Pinheiros, 05419-020* ☎ *011/ 3579–2000* ⊕ *www.fnac.com.br*) sells maps and English-language books, magazines, and newspapers.

Livraria Cultura (⊠ *Av. Paulista 2073, Jardins, 01311-940* ☎ *011/3170–4033* ⊕ *www.livcultura. com.br* Ⓜ *Consolação*) has a great selection of maps, and São Paulo's best selection of travel literature.

Livraria Saraiva (⊠ *Shopping Ibirapuera, Av. Ibirapuera 3103, Moema, 04029-200* ☎ *011/5561–7290* ⊠ *Shopping Iguatemi, Av. Brigadeiro Faria Lima 2232, Jardim Paulista, 01451-000* ☎ *011/ 3031–7093* ⊠ *Shopping Morumbi, Av. Roque Petroni Jr. 1089, Morumbi, 04707-000*

☎ *011/5181–7574* ⊕ *www.livrariasar aiva.com.br*) has maps and English-language newspapers and books.

Laselva (⊠ *Shopping Ibirapuera, Av. Ibirapuera 3103, 04029-200* ☎ *011/5561–9561*) usually receives magazines from abroad earlier than other bookstores.

PHARMACEUTICALS

Droga Raia (⊠ *Rua José Maria Lisboa 645, Jardim Paulistano, 01423-001* ☎ *011/3884–8235*).

Drogaria São Paulo (⊠ *Av. Angélica 1465, Higienópolis, 01227-100* ☎ *011/3667–6291*).

Drogasil (⊠ *Av. Brigadeiro Faria Lima 2726, Cidade Jardim, 01451-000* ☎ *011/3812–6276*).

PHOTO EQUIPMENT

Consigo (⊠ *Rua Conselheiro Crispiniano 105, 1st fl., Centro, 01037-001* ☎ *011/3258–4015* ⊕ *www.consigo. com.br* Ⓜ *República*).

CLOTHING

FOR KIDS   Younger family members are the stars at **Petistil** (⊠ *Av. Brigadeiro Faria Lima 2232, Shopping Center Iguatemi, Jardim Paulistano, 01451-000* ☎ *011/3812–5073* ⊕ *www.petistil.com.br*), which sells colorful clothes for infants and children up to 11 years old.

FOR MEN &   Famous Brazilian designer **Alexandre Herchcovitch** (⊠ *Rua Haddock*
WOMEN   *Lobo 1151, Jardins, 01414-003* ☎ *011/3063–2888* ⊕ *www.herchco*
★   *vitch.com.br*) sells prêt-à-porter and tailor-made clothes at his store. At **Cori** (⊠ *Rua Oscar Freire 791, Jardins, 01426-001* ☎ *011/3081– 5223* ⊕ *www.cori.com.br*) everyday outfits with classic lines are the specialty.

Designer-label boutique **Daslu** (⊠ *Avenida Chedid Jafet 131, Itaim Bibi, 04551-065* ☎ *011/3841–4000* ⊕ *www.daslu.com.br*) has built a 17,000-square-meter (183,000-square-foot) megastore of luxurious items: clothes from Chanel, Dior, Pucci, Vuitton, Valentino, Armani, as well as jewelry, purses, objects, shoes, and house decorations. **Ellus** (⊠ *Rua Oscar Freire 990, Jardins, 01426-000* ☎ *011/3061–2900* ⊕ *www.ellus.com.br*) is a good place to buy men's and women's jeans, sportswear, and street wear.

Fórum (✉ *Rua Oscar Freire 916, Jardins, 01426-000* ☎ *011/3085–6269* ⊕ *www.forum.com.br*) has evening attire for young men and women, but it also sells sportswear and shoes. **Richard's** (✉ *Rua Oscar Freire 1129, Jardins, 01426-001* ☎ *011/3082–5399*) is one of Brazil's best lines of sportswear. Collections include outfits suitable for the beach or the mountains. The prices for suits, jackets, jeans, and some women's clothing (silk blouses, for example) at **Vila Romana Factory Store** (✉ *Via Anhanguera, Km 17.5, Osasco, 05112-000* ☎ *011/3604–5293* ✉ *Av. Ibirapuera 3103, Shopping Ibirapuera, Moema, 04029-200* ☎ *011/5535–1808* ⊕ *www.vilaromana.com.br*) are unbeatable. The store is a 40-minute drive from Centro. In-town mall branches are more convenient, but prices are higher. **Zoomp** (✉ *Rua Oscar Freire 995, Jardins, 01426-001* ☎ *011/3064–1556* ⊕ *www.zoomp.com.br*) is famous for its jeans and high-quality street wear. Customers from 13 to 35 mix and match the clothes, creating some unusual combinations.

FOR WOMEN **Ana Capri** (✉ *Alameda dos Arapanés 83, Moema, 04524-000* ☎ *011/5052–4329*) sells plus-size women's underwear, swimsuits, and clothes. **Le Lis Blanc** (✉ *Rua Oscar Freire 809, Jardins, 01426-001* ☎ *011/3083–2549* ⊕ *www.lelisblanc.com.br*) is Brazil's exclusive purveyor of the French brand Vertigo. Look for party dresses in velvet and sheer fabrics. If you have money in your pocket, shop at **Maria Bonita** (✉ *Rua Oscar Freire 705, Jardins, 01426-000* ☎ *011/3082–6649* ⊕ *www.mariabonitaextra.com.br*), which has elegant and fun women's clothes. At Maria Bonita Extra, right next door, the prices are a little lower.

The women's clothing at **Reinaldo Lourenço** (✉ *Rua Bela Cintra 2167, Jardins, 01415-002* ☎ *011/3085–8150* ⊕ *www.reinaldolourenco.com.br*) is sophisticated and of good quality. Young women are intrigued by the unique high-fashion designs of the swimsuits, dresses, shorts, shirts, and pants at **Uma** (✉ *Rua Girassol 273, Vila Madalena, 05433-000* ☎ *011/3813–5559* ⊕ *www.uma.com.br*).

HANDICRAFTS

Art Índia (✉ *Rua Augusta 1371, Loja 117, Cerqueira César, 01305-100* ☎ *011/3283–2102* Ⓜ *Consolação*) is a government-run shop that sells Indian arts and crafts made by tribes throughout Brazil. As its name suggests, **Casa do Amazonas** (✉ *Alameda dos Jurupis 460, Moema, 04088-001* ☎ *011/5051–3098*) has a wide selection of products from the Amazon. Since 1920 **Galeria de Arte Brasileira** (✉ *Alameda Lorena 2163, Jardins, 01424-002* ☎ *011/3062–9452 or 308/5–8769* ⊕ *www.galeriaartebrasileira.com.br*) has specialized in art and handicrafts from

---

BRAZIL'S FASHION

The Brazilian Fashion industry has been in overdrive for the last 10 years and more and more native designers are moving onto the world stage, alongside the country's innumerable beautiful models. Initiated in 1996, São Paulo Fashion Week is now held twice a year (a winter and summer event) and is the best place to check out the latest offerings from the top Brazilian designers and their brands.

all over Brazil. Look for objects made of pau-brasil wood, hammocks, jewelry, T-shirts, *marajoara* pottery (from the Amazon), and lace.

Marcenaria Trancoso (✉ *Rua Harmonia 233, Vila Madalena, 05435-000* ☏ *011/3032–3505* ⊕ *www.marcenariatrancoso.com.br* Ⓜ *Vila Madalena*) sells wooden products that are an elegant mixture of interior design and handicraft. At **Mundareu** (✉ *Rua Mourato Coelho 988, Vila Madalena, 05417-001* ☏ *011/3032–4649* ⊕ *www.mundareu.org. br*), browse through quality products made by different types of artisans from all over Brazil.

JEWELRY

★ An internationally known Brazilian brand for jewelry, **H. Stern** (✉ *Rua Oscar Freire 652, Jardins, 01426-000* ☏ *011/3068–8082* ⊕ *www. hstern.com.br*) has shops in more than 30 countries. This one has designs made especially for the Brazilian stores. Carioca **Antonio Bernardo** (✉ *Rua Bela Cintra 2063, Consolação, 01415-002* ☏ *011/3083–5622* ⊕ *www.antoniobernardo.com.br*) is one of the most famous jewelry designers in Brazil. He can create custom pieces with gold, silver, and other precious stones and metals. The world-famous **Tiffany & Co.** (✉ *Rua Haddock Lobo 1594, Jardins, 01414-002* ☏ *011/3081–8100* ⊕ *www.tiffany.com*) sells exclusive pieces for the very wealthy. Go for the diamonds—you know you want to.

LEATHER GOODS & LUGGAGE

One of the biggest brands for luggage and leather goods in Brazil, **Le Postiche** (✉ *Av. Prof. Ascendino Reis 965, Vila Mariana, 04027-000* ☏ *011/5082–4388* ⊕ *www.lepostiche.com.br*) has 81 shops around the country. You can find one in almost any mall in São Paulo.

An excellent chain store for travel and leather goods, **Comtesse** (✉ *Rua Treze de Maio 1947, Shopping Paulista, Paraíso, 01361-900* ☏ *011/3284–5726* ⊕ *www.comtesse.com.br* Ⓜ *Paraíso*) can also be found at major shopping malls. **Inovathi** (✉ *Rua Oscar Freire 497, Jardins, 01426-001* ☏ *011/3062–2692* ⊕ *www.inovathi.com.br*) has leather accessories at good prices. It's in nearly every mall in town.

MUSIC

★ **Baratos Afins** (✉ *Av. São João 439, 2nd fl., No. 314–318, Centro, 01035-000* ☏ *011/3223–3629* ⊕ *www.baratosafins.com.br* Ⓜ *República*) is heaven for music collectors. Opened in 1978, it's also a record label and was the brainchild of Arnaldo Baptista, guitar player in the influential 1960's Brazilian rock band Os Mutantes. The store sells all kinds of music, but specializes in Brazilian popular music (MPB). If you're looking for rare records, ask for the owner, Luiz Calanca.

In shopping malls the best option is **Painel Musical** (✉ *Av. Ibirapuera 3103, Shopping Ibirapuera, Jurupis fl., store 135, Moema, 04029-200* ☏ *011/5561–9981* ⊕ *www.painelmusical.com.br*), a small record shop that carries CDs and DVDs. It usually has a good selection of instrumental Brazilian music and local rock. Browse through more than 100,000 records at **Ventania** (✉ *Rua 24 de Maio 188, 1st fl., store 113, Centro, 01041-000* ☏ *011/222–6273* ⊕ *www.ventania.com.br*

M*República*), a huge store specializing in MPB. You can find old vinyls 78s, contemporary CDs, and everything in between.

SÃO PAULO ESSENTIALS

TRANSPORTATION

BY AIR

Nearly all international flights stop in São Paulo, so it's easy to get from São Paulo to everywhere else in Brazil. There are flights every half hour covering the short (around one hour) trip between Sao Paulo and Rio (around R$150 one-way). There are also multiple departures per day to other major cities such as Brasília and Belo Horizonte. *For airline information see By Air, in Brazil Essentials.*

AIRPORTS

São Paulo's international airport, Aeroporto Internacional de São Paulo/Guarulhos (GRU), is in the suburb of Guarulhos, 30 km (19 mi) and a 45-minute drive (longer during rush hour or on rainy days) northeast of Centro. Much closer to the Zona Sul region is Aeroporto Congonhas (CGH), 14 km (9 mi) south of Centro (a 15- to 45-minute drive, depending on traffic), which serves regional airlines, including the Rio–São Paulo shuttle.

Airports Aeroporto Internacional de Congonhas (*CGH* ✉ *Avenida Washington Luís s/n, Jabaquara, 04626-911* ☎ *011/5090–9000* ⊕ *www.infraero.gov.br*). **Aeroporto Internacional de São Paulo/Guarulhos** (*GRU* ✉ *Rod. Hélio Smidt s/n, Guarulhos, 07143-970* ☎ *011/6445–2945* ⊕ *www.infraero.gov.br*).

AIRPORT TRANSFERS

State government–operated EMTU buses (blue vehicles, with air-conditioning) shuttle between Guarulhos and Congonhas Airports every 30 minutes from 5:30 AM to 11:10 PM and every 90 minutes from midnight to 5:30 AM (R$27). Look for the EMTU stand near the private bus and cab stalls outside the arrivals terminal. You may also be able to arrange a free transfer with your airline as part of your ticket.

GROUND TRANSPORTATION

The blue, air-conditioned EMTU buses travel between Guarulhos and the Tietê bus terminal (which is also on the main metro line) 5 AM–11:10 PM, every 50–60 minutes; the downtown Praça da República (5:40 AM–11:10 PM, every 30 minutes); and the Hotel Maksoud Plaza (6:10 AM–11:10 PM, every 60–70 minutes), stopping at most major hotels around Avenida Paulista. There are also lines that connect Guarulhos to the Barra Funda terminal and the Shopping Eldorado. The cost is R$28.

The blue-and-white, air-conditioned Guarucoop radio taxis are by far the most common at the international airport and take you from Guarulhos to Centro for around R$75. It can cost up to R$120 to the southern parts of the Zona Sul region. Congonhas is much closer to downtown and the Zona Sul, so it usually costs no more than R$30. The price is set before the trip based on your drop-off address or suburb and can take from 45 minutes to 1 ½ hours in peak traffic. The line for the cabs is just outside the arrivals terminal and moves quickly.

> ## TICKETS PLEASE
>
> While you can buy tickets for the frequent Rio de Janeiro buses a few minutes before departure, it's best to purchase your fare for other destinations in advance, especially during holiday seasons.

Contacts **EMTU** (☎ 0800/19-0088 or 011/6221-0244 ⊕ www.airportbusser vice.com.br). **Guarucoop** (☎ 011/6440-7070 ⊕ www.guarucoop.com.br).

BY BUS

ARRIVING & DEPARTING

The three key bus terminals in the city of São Paulo are connected to metro stations and serve more than 1,100 destinations combined. The huge main station—serving all major Brazilian cities (with trips to Rio every 10 minutes during the day and every half hour at night, until 2 AM) as well as Argentina, Uruguay, Chile, and Paraguay—is the Terminal Tietê in the north, on the Marginal Tietê Beltway. Terminal Jabaquara, near Congonhas Airport, serves coastal towns. Terminal Barra Funda, in the west, near the Memorial da América Latina, has buses to and from western Brazil. All stations have their own metro stops.

Socicam, a private company, runs all the bus terminals in the city of São Paulo and lists schedules on its Web site. Click on "*consulta de partidas de ônibus.*"

Contacts **Socicam** (☎ 011/3235-0322 ⊕ www.socicam.com.br). **EMTU** (☎ 0800/19-0088 or 011/6221-0244 ⊕ www.airportbusservice.com.br). **Terminal Barra Funda** (✉ Rua Mário de Andrade 664, Barra Funda, 01154-060 ☎ 011/3235-0322 ⊕ www.socicam.com.br Ⓜ Barra Funda). **Terminal Jabaquara** (✉ Rua Jequitibás, Jabaquara, 04321-090 ☎ 011/3235-0322 ⊕ www.socicam. com.br Ⓜ Jabaquara). **Terminal Tietê** (✉ Av. Cruzeiro do Sul, Santana, 02030-000 ☎ 011/3235-0322 ⊕ www.socicam.com.br Ⓜ Tietê).

GETTING AROUND

Municipal bus service is frequent and covers the entire city, but regular buses are overcrowded at rush hour and when it rains. If you don't speak Portuguese, it can be hard to figure out the system and the stops. Stops are clearly marked, but routes are spelled out only on the buses themselves. Buses do not stop at every bus stop, so if you're waiting, you'll have to flag one down.

Bus fare is R$2.30. You enter at the front of the bus, pay the *cobrador* (fare collector) in the middle, and exit from the rear of the bus. To pay, you can use either money or the electronic card *bilhete único,* introduced in 2004. The card allows you to take three buses in two hours for the price of one fare. Cards can be bought and reloaded at special booths at major bus terminals or at lottery shops.

For bus numbers and names, routes, and schedules, go to the (Portuguese-language) Web site of Transporte Público de São Paulo, the city's public transport agency, or purchase the *Guia São Paulo Ruas*, published by Quatro Rodas and sold at newsstands and bookstores for about R$30.

POTHOLES

Even in the best of circumstances, São Paulo's roads aren't that great. They're riddled with potholes, and many of the quieter streets and lanes also have sharp dips, so take special care if you're driving.

Contacts Transporte Público de São Paulo (☎ *156* ⊕ *www.sptrans.com.br*).

BY CAR

ARRIVING & DEPARTING

The main São Paulo–Rio de Janeiro highway is the Via Dutra (BR 116 North), which has been repaved and enlarged in places. The speed limit is 120 kph (74 mph) in most places and there are quite a few tolls that range from $3 to R$8 for a car. There are also plenty of call boxes to use if your car breaks down. The modern Rodovia Ayrton Senna (SP 70) charges reasonable tolls (R$6–R$12), runs parallel to the Dutra for about a quarter of the way, and is an excellent alternative route. The 429-km (279-mi) trip takes five hours, and either route is considered relatively safe, although you may be stopped at certain police checkpoints for a random car inspection. If you have time, consider the longer, spectacular coastal Rio-Santos Highway (SP 55 and BR 101). It's an easy two-day drive, and you can stop midway at the colonial city of Paraty, in Rio de Janeiro State.

Other main highways are the Castelo Branco (SP 280), which links the southwestern part of the state to the city; the Via Anhanguera (SP 330), which originates in the state's rich northern agricultural region, passing through the university town of Campinas; SP 310, which also runs from the farming heartland; BR 116 south, which comes up from Curitiba (a 408-km/265-mi trip); plus the Via Anchieta (SP 150) and the Rodovia Imigrantes (SP 160), parallel roads that run to the coast, each operating one-way on weekends and holidays.

GETTING AROUND

Driving in the city isn't recommended because of the heavy traffic (nothing moves at rush hour, especially when it rains), daredevil drivers, and inadequate parking. You'll also need to get a temporary driver's license from *Detran*, the State Transit Department, which can be a very time-consuming endeavor. If you do opt to drive, there are a few things to keep in mind:

The high-speed beltways along the Rio Pinheiros and Rio Tietê rivers—called Marginal Tietê and Marginal Pinheiros—sandwich the main part of São Paulo. Avenida 23 de Maio runs south from Centro and beneath the Parque do Ibirapuera via the Ayrton Senna Tunnel. You can take avenidas Paulista, Brasil, and Faria Lima southwest to the Morumbi, Brooklin, Itaim, and Santo Amaro neighborhoods, respectively. The

Elevado Costa e Silva, also called Minhocão, is an elevated road that connects Centro with Avenida Francisco Matarazzo in the west.

In most commercial neighborhoods you must buy hourly tickets (called Cartão Zona Azul) to park on the street during business hours. Buy them at newsstands, not from people on the street. Booklets of 10 tickets cost R$20. Fill out each ticket—you'll need one for every hour you plan to park—with the car's license plate and the time you initially parked. Leave the tickets in the car's window so they're visible to officials from outside. After business hours or at any time near major sights, people may offer to watch your car. If you don't pay these "caretakers," there's a chance they'll damage your car (R$2 is enough to keep your car's paint job intact). But to truly ensure your car's safety, park in a guarded lot, where rates are R$5–R$7 for the first hour and R$1–R$2 each hour thereafter.

Invest in the *Guia São Paulo Ruas,* published by Quatro Rodas, which shows every street in the city. It's sold at newsstands and bookstores for about R$30.

Rental Agencies Avis (✉ *Rua da Consolação 335, Centro, 01301-000* ☎ *011/3259–6868 or 0800/19–8456*). **Hertz** (✉ *Rua da Consolação 439, Centro, 01301-000* ☎ *011/3258–9384 or 011/4336–7300*). **Localiza** (✉ *Rua da Consolação 419, Centro, 01301-000* ☎ *011/3231–3055 or 0800/99–2000*).

BY SUBWAY

When you buy 10 tickets at once, note that ticket sellers often can't change large bills. You insert the ticket into the turnstile at the platform entrance, and it's returned to you only if there's unused fare on it. Transfers within the metro system are free, as are bus-to-metro (or vice-versa) transfers. You can buy a *bilhete integração* (combination ticket) on buses or at metro stations for R$4. You can print maps from the English-language Web site of the Metrô, where you can also find ticket prices and schedules.

Contacts Metrô (☎ *011/3286–0111* ⊕ *www.metro.sp.gov.br*).

BY TAXI

Taxis in São Paulo are white. Owner-driven taxis are generally well maintained and reliable, as are radio taxis. Fares start at R$3.20 and run R$1.80 for each kilometer (½ mi) or R$0.40 for every minute sitting in traffic. After 8 PM and on weekends fares rise by 25%. You'll pay a tax if the cab leaves the city, as is the case with trips to Cumbica Airport. Good radio-taxi companies usually accept credit cards, but you must call ahead and request the service. Delta takes calls in English.

Contacts Coopertaxi (☎ *011/6195–6000*). **Radio Taxi Vermelho e Branco** (☎ *011/ 3146–4000*). **Ligue-Taxi** (☎ *011/2101–3030*).

BY TRAIN

Most travel to the interior of the state is done by bus or automobile. Still, a few places are served by trains. Trains from Estação da Luz, near 25 de Março, run to some metropolitan suburbs and small interior towns. Trains from Estação Barra Funda serve towns in the west of the state. Estação Júlio Prestes, in Campos Elíseos, has trains to the southeast and some suburbs. Estação Brás serves the suburbs only.

Contacts **Estação Barra Funda** (✉ *Rua Mário de Andrade 664, Barra Funda, 01154-060* ☎ *011/3392-3616* Ⓜ *Barra Funda*). **Estação Brás** (✉ *Praça Agente Cícero, Brás, 03002-010* ☎ *0800/55-0121* Ⓜ *Brás*). **Estação Júlio Prestes** (✉ *Praça Júlio Prestes 148, Campos Elíseos, 01218-020* ☎ *0800/55-0121*). **Estação da Luz** (✉ *Praça da Luz 1, Luz, 01120-010* ☎ *0800/55-0121* Ⓜ *Luz*).

CONTACTS & RESOURCES

BANKS & EXCHANGE SERVICES

Avenida Paulista is the home of many banks (generally open 10–4), including Citibank. For *casas de câmbio* (exchange houses) without any extra fees, try Action. In Centro you can exchange money at Banco do Brasil and at Banespa. Several banks have automatic-teller machines (ATMs) that accept international bank cards and dispense reais.

Some banks accept only cards with Visa/Plus logos and others accept only cards with MasterCard/Cirrus logos. Banco24horas ATMs usually accept all cards, including American Express. *See "Money Matters" in Brazil Essentials for more information.*

Contacts **Action** (✉ *Aeroporto Guarulhos, TPS2 arrival fl., Guarulhos, 07143-970* ✉ *Rua Augusta 2766, Jardins, 01412-100* ✉ *Shopping Paulista, Rua 13 de Maio 1947, Paraíso, 01327-001* ⊕ *www.actioncambio.com.br* Ⓜ *Brigadeiro*). **Banco do Brasil** (✉ *Av. Paulista 2163, Jardins, 01311-933* ⊕ *www.bancodobrasil.com.br* Ⓜ *Consolação*). **Bank Boston** (✉ *Av. Paulista 800, Jardins, 01310-100* ⊕ *www.bankboston.com.br* Ⓜ *Brigadeiro*). **Citibank** (✉ *Av. Paulista 1111, Jardins, 01311-920* ⊕ *www.citibank.com.br* Ⓜ *Trianon-Masp*). **Santander Banespa** (✉ *Av. Paulista 2064, Jardins, 01310-928* ⊕ *www.banespa.com.br* Ⓜ *Consolação*).

EMERGENCIES & MEDICAL ASSISTANCE

The three main pharmacies have more than 20 stores, each open 24 hours—Droga Raia, Drogaria São Paulo, and Drogasil. The police department in charge of tourist affairs, Delegacia de Turismo, is open weekdays 8–8.

Contacts **Ambulance** (☎ *192*). **Delegacia de Turismo (Tourism Police)** (✉ *Av. São Luís 91, Centro, 01046-001* ☎ *011/3214-0209* Ⓜ *República*). **Fire** (☎ *193*). **Police** (☎ *190*).

Hospitals **Albert Einstein** (✉ *Av. Albert Einstein 627, Morumbi, 05651-901* ☎ *011/3747-1233* ⊕ *www.einstein.br*). **Beneficência Portuguesa** (✉ *Rua Maestro Cardim 769, Paraíso, 01323-900* ☎ *011/3505-1001* ⊕ *www.beneficencia.org.br* Ⓜ *Vergueiro*). **Sírio Libanês** (✉ *Rua. D. Adma Jafet 91, Bela Vista, 01308-000* ☎ *011/3155-0200* ⊕ *www.hsl.org.br*).

24-Hour Pharmacies **Droga Raia** (✉ *Rua José Maria Lisboa 645, Jardim Paulistano, 01423-001* ☎ *011/3884-8235, 011/3237-5000 delivery* ⊕ *www.drogaraia.com.br*). **Drogaria São Paulo** (✉ *Av. Angélica 1465, Higienópolis, 01227-100* ☎ *011/3667-6291* ⊕ *www.drogariasaopaulo.com.br*). **Drogasil** (✉ *Av. Brigadeiro Faria Lima 2726, Cidade Jardim, 01451-000* ☎ *011/3812-6276, 011/3767-2222 delivery* ⊕ *www.drogasil.com.br*).

TOUR OPTIONS

You can hire a bilingual guide through a travel agency or hotel concierge (about R$15 an hour with a four-hour minimum), or you can design your own walking tour with the aid of information provided at Anhembi booths around the city. Anhembi also offers Sunday tours of museums, parks, and Centro that are less expensive than those offered in hotels. The tourist

board (⇨ Visitor Information, below) has three half-day Sunday bus tours, one covering the parks, one centered on the museums, and one focused on the historical downtown area. Officially, none of the board's guides speaks English; however, it may be able to arrange something on request.

Gol Tour Viagens e Turismo has custom tours as well as car tours for small groups. A half-day city tour costs about R$40 a person (group rate); a night tour—including a samba show, dinner, and drinks—costs around R$100; and day trips to the beach or the colonial city of Embu cost R$80–R$90. Easygoing has fly-and-dine tours that include a helicopter trip and dinner. If you prefer something down-to-earth, try the carriage tours with Carruagens São Paulo. They tour the Centro Novo (New Downtown) or Centro Velho, or (Old Downtown). Both are available in English if you reserve by phone. The price is R$40 per person, plus R$35 per group for an English-speaking guides. For general sightseeing tours, try Check Point, whose daily tours are R$400 for four people.

Contacts **Carruagens São Paulo** (☎011/3237–4976 or 011/3255–8155). **Check Point** (☎011/6091–1316 ⊕ www.checkpointtours.com.br). **Easygoing** (☎011/3801–9540 ⊕ www.easygoing.com.br). **Gol Tour Viagens e Turismo** (☎011/3256–2388 ⊕ www.goltour.com.br Ⓜ República). **Terra Nobre** (☎011/3662–1505 ⊕ www.terranobre.com.br).

BIKING TOURS

Night Biker's Club has tours of the city at night. Sampa Bikers has city tours and excursions outside town. A day tour starts at R$50, including transport and lunch.

Contacts **Night Biker's Club** (✉ Rua Pacheco de Miranda 141, Moema, 04503-080 ☎011/3871–2100 ⊕ www.nightbikers.com). **Sampa Bikers** (✉ Rua Baluarte 672, Vila Olímpia, 04549-012 ☎011/3045–2722 ⊕ www.sampabikers.com.br).

VISITOR INFORMATION

The most helpful contact is the São Paulo Convention and Visitors Bureau, open 9–6. The sharp, business-minded president, Orlando de Souza, speaks English flawlessly and is extremely knowledgeable. Branches of the city-operated Anhembi Turismo e Eventos da Cidade de São Paulo are open daily 9–6.

ATMS

Finding an ATM in São Paulo can be difficult at times. Most are only located in very secure areas of shopping centres, gas stations, or actual bank branches. There are special 24-hour ATMs, but they usually charge a hefty transaction fee of up to R$8.

The bureaucracy-laden Secretaria de Esportes e Turismo do Estado de São Paulo, open weekdays 9–6, is less helpful, but has maps and information about the city and state of São Paulo. SEST also has a booth at the arrivals terminal in Guarulhos airport; it's open daily 9 AM–10 PM.

Contacts **Anhembi Turismo e Eventos da Cidade de São Paulo** (✉ *Anhembi Convention Center, Av. Olavo Fontoura 1209, Santana, 02001-900* ☎ *011/6224–0400* ⊕ *www.cidadedesaopaulo.com* ✉ *Praça da República at Rua 7 de Abril, Centro, 01045-000* Ⓜ *República* ✉ *Av. Paulista, across from MASP, Cerqueira César, 01310-100* Ⓜ *Trianon-Masp* ✉ *Av. Brigadeiro Faria Lima, in front of Shopping Center Iguatemi, Jardim Paulista, 01452-002* ✉ *Bus station, Tietê, 01154-060* Ⓜ *Tietê* ✉ *Guarulhos Airport Terminals 1 and 2, Aeroporto de Guarulhos, 07143-970*). **São Paulo Convention and Visitors Bureau** (✉ *Alameda Ribeirão Preto 130, conjunto 121, Jardins, 01331-000* ☎ *011/3289–7588* ⊕ *www.visitesaopaulo.com*). **Secretaria de Esportes e Turismo do Estado de São Paulo** (✉ *Praça Antônio Prado, 9, Centro, 01010-904* ☎ *011/3241–5822* ⊕ *www.selt.sp.gov.br*).

Side Trips from São Paulo

4

WORD OF MOUTH

"On Sundays you should visit a town that is about 30–40 minutes from São Paulo called Embu das Artes. They have a nice handicraft market on that day."

–Lilica

"From São we spent a few days in Ilhabela and also in lovely Paraty. I highly recommend Paraty."

–Graziella5b

Updated by
Ana Cristina

SÃO PAULO'S SURROUNDINGS ARE PERFECT for all types of getaways. The state has the best highways in the country, making it easy to travel by car or bus to its many small, beautiful beaches, and even beyond to neighboring states (Paraná, Rio de Janeiro, and Minas Gerais). Although most sandy stretches require one- or two-hour drives, good side trips from the city can be as close as the 30-minute trip to Embu.

Embu is famous for its furniture stores, and artisans from throughout Brazil sell their wares at its enormous weekend crafts fair; expect to see all the sights in one afternoon. Also less than an hour away, 1500s Santana de Parnaíba mixes historical settings and regional attractions with good restaurants.

For a weekend of relaxation, soak up the healing properties of Águas de São Pedro's spas and springs. Farther away, in Brotas, you can go white-water rafting or hike past waterfalls. If you like mountains, head up in another direction: Campos de Jordão, where cafés and clothing stores are often crowded with oh-so-chic *paulistanos* (natives of São Paulo city; inhabitants of São Paulo State are called *paulistas*). Favor the state's North Shore and Ilhabela (the name means "beautiful island") if you prefer the beach. The island is part of the Mata Atlântica (Atlantic Rain Forest) and has many waterfalls, trails, and diving spots.

ORIENTATION & PLANNING

ORIENTATION

Most of the towns in this chapter can be done as day trips from São Paulo. Trips by bus almost can take anywhere from one to four hours. It's even possible to take a taxi from the city to Embu das Artes and Santana do Parnaíba.

THE SOUTH SHORE
Long known as a decadent little getaway Guarujá (87 km from São Paulo) has cleaned up its more salacious side and now attracts travelers of all ilks. Enseada, Pitangueiras, and Pernambuco are popular beaches and some of the cleanest around. For surfing, check out Praia do Tombo.

THE NORTH SHORE
A little farther flung than its southern neighbor, the North Shore (about 210 km from São Paulo) has beautiful beaches for every kind of sun or sports enthusiast. In the 1990s the area experienced a building boom, with condos popping up seemingly overnight. Luckily, the region still managed to maintain its pristine environment.

INLAND
Just a stone's throw from the São Paulo, Embu das Artes is famous for its big handicraft fair with paintings, toys, and candles, as well as scrumptious pastries and breads. Campos do Jordão, known as the Switzerland of Brazil, attracts hordes of chill-seekers in winter, when

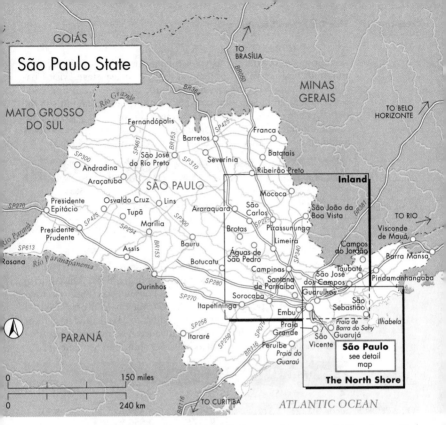

temperatures drop below tepid. In Brotas white-water thrill seekers will find their own little slice of heaven.

PLANNING

WHEN TO GO

The area around São Paulo is lovely year-round. Most places have a steady stream of visitors, so it's always wise to book hotels well in advance. Summers are hot and humid, and its rainy season, so it's good to have some indoor plans in the back of your mind. In winter, temperatures drop into the 40s F (5°C–10°C), so be sure to bring some warm clothing.

TOP REASONS TO GO

■ Bask on a range of beautiful beaches, from surfer paradises in Ubatuba to coastal islands and sandy rain-forest coves.

■ Witness Brazil's colonial and rural history in Embu and Santana de Parnaíba.

■ Luxuriant forests in Campos de Jordão combine with impressive bodies of water and wildlife in Águas de São Pedro, Brotas, and Ilhabela.

ABOUT THE RESTAURANTS & CUISINE

Restaurants in coastal towns tend to be of the rustic beach-café sort, and predictably serve lots of seafood. For a change of taste, visit Ubatuba, Maresias, Boiçucanga, and Camburi, where you can find good pizzerias and Japanese restaurants. Some of the best restaurants in the state, outside of São Paulo, are in Campos do Jordão, a popular paulistano mountain retreat. Here you can try a Brazilian version of Swiss fondue (both the chocolate and the cheese varieties are delicous).

WHAT IT COSTS IN REAIS					
	¢	$	$$	$$$	$$$$
AT DINNER	under R$15	R$15–R$30	R$30–R$45	R$45–R$60	over R$60

Prices are per person for a main course at dinner or for a prix-fixe meal.

ABOUT THE HOTELS

São Paulo has by far the best lodgings in the state. Elsewhere you can generally find basic *pousadas* (sort of like a bed-and-breakfasts), with the occasional gems like Maison Joly and Pousada do Hibiscus in Ilhabela and Hotel Estalagem Quinta das Cachoeiras in Brotas. Coastal towns are packed in summer (from December to March) and it's almost impossible to get anything without advance reservations. The same holds true for Campos do Jordão in winter (June and September).

WHAT IT COSTS IN REAIS					
	¢	$	$$	$$$	$$$$
FOR 2 PEOPLE	under R$125	R$125–R$250	R$250–R$375	R$375–R$500	over R$500

Prices are for a standard double room in high season, excluding tax.

GETTING AROUND

Bus travel to and from the towns around São Paulo can be a time-consuming affair, since they don't run too frequently. A better option is renting a car or taking a taxi. The roads are good and traffic isn't too chaotic.

THE NORTH SHORE

The cleanest and best *praias* (beaches) in São Paulo State are along what is known as the Litoral Norte (North Shore). Mountains and bits of Atlantic Rain Forest hug numerous small, sandy coves. Some of the North Shore's most beautiful houses line the Rio-Santos Highway (SP 055) on the approach to Maresias. On weekdays when school is in session the beaches are gloriously deserted.

The city of São Paulo rests on a plateau 72 km (46 mi) inland. If you can avoid traffic, getaways are fairly quick on the parallel Imigrantes (BR 160) or Anchieta (BR 150) highways, each of which becomes one-

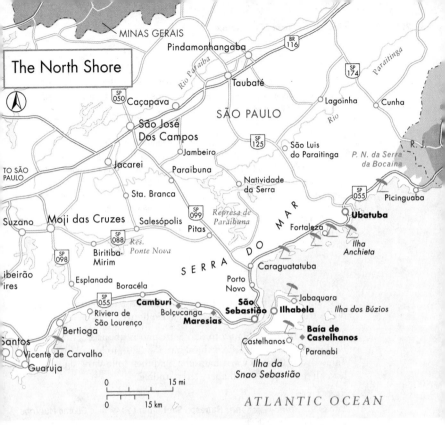

The North Shore

way on weekends and holidays. Buses from São Paulo's Jabaquara terminal, near the Congonhas Airport, run along the coast.

Beaches often don't have bathrooms or phones right on the sands, but several rent beach umbrellas or chairs, especially in summer and on holidays and weekends. They generally do have restaurants nearby, or at least vendors selling sandwiches, soft drinks, and beer.

SÃO SEBASTIÃO

204 km (127 mi) southeast of São Paulo

São Sebastião stretches along 100 km (62 mi) of the North Shore. Its bays, islands, and beaches attract everyone from the youngsters who flock to Maresias and Camburi to the families who favor Barra do Sahy. Boating enthusiasts, hikers, and wildlife-seekers also come here, especially on weekends, when hotels are often crowded. Nightlife is good here—the best is in Boiçucanga. The "beautiful island" of Ilhabela (⇨*below*) is a 15-minute boat ride away from downtown São Sebastião.

A BIT OF HISTORY

In the 19th century, farming, first of sugar cane, and then of coffee, was São Paulo's major industry, and brought prosperity to the region.

At the beginning of the 20th century, São Paulo became the center for industry in Brazil, as factories were built at a rapid pace, mostly by an immigrant workforce. By midcentury São Paulo was one of the largest industrialized centers in Latin America and the state with the highest population in Brazil, thanks in part to mass migration from within Brazil.

Today São Paulo is the richest and most multicultural state in the country. It has the largest Japanese community outside of Japan (an estimated 1 million people), about 1 million people of Middle Eastern descent, and about 6 million people of Italian descent.

TO & FROM

Litorânea buses travel five times daily to São Sebastião (to the ferry dock) from São Paulo and take about 2½ hours.

The drive from São Paulo to São Sebastião is about 2½ hours. Take Rodovia Ayrton Senna–Carvalho Pinto (SP 070), followed by Rodovia Tamoios (SP 099) to Caraguatatuba, and then follow the signs, which lead all the way to the Ilhabela ferry landing.

ESSENTIALS

Banks & Currency Exchange Banespa Santander (⊠ *Avenida Guarda Mor Lobo Viana, Centro 11600-000*).

Bus Contacts Litorânea (☎ *011/6221–0244* ⊕ *www.litoranea.com.br*). **Terminal Rodoviário** (⊠ *Praça Vereador Venino Fernandes Moreira, 10, 11600-000*).

Emergencies & Medical Assistance Ambulance (☎ *912*). **Fire** (☎ *193*). **Police** (☎ *190*).

Visitor & Tour Info Tourist Office Sectur (⊠ *Avenida Altino Arantes, 174, Centro, 11600-000* ☎ *12/3892–2620*) has trail maps that include descriptions of each trail's length and difficulty and, for the more popular routes, a listing of their unique features. Keep in mind that all trails require guides, which Sectur is happy to help arrange.

SAFETY & PRECAUTIONS

Leave jewelry, passports, and your money clip in your hotel safe, or at very least, don't leave your possessions unattended if decide to go for a dip.

WHAT TO SEE

★ Families with young children favor small, quiet **Barra do Sahy** (⊠ *Rio-Santos Hwy., SP 055, 157 km/97 mi southeast of São Paulo*). Its narrow strip of sand (with a bay and a river on one side and rocks on the other) is steep but smooth, and the water is clean and calm. Kayakers paddle about, and divers are drawn to the nearby Ilha das Couves. Area restaurants serve mostly basic fish dishes with rice and salad. Note that Barra do Sahy's entrance is atop a slope and appears suddenly—be on the lookout around marker Km 174.

The young and the restless flock to **Camburi** (⊠ *Rio-Santos Hwy., SP 055, 162 km/100 mi southeast of São Paulo*), to sunbathe, surf, and party. At the center of the beach is a cluster of cafés, ice-cream shops, and bars and the Tiê restaurant. The service may be slow, but Tiê's menu is extensive, and the open-air setup is divine. Camburi is just north of Barra do Sahy. If you're coming from the south, take the second entrance; although it's unpaved, it's usually in better shape than the first entrance, at Km 166.

Maresias (⊠ *Rio-Santos Hwy, Km 151, SP 055, 177 km/109 mi southeast of São Paulo*) is a 4-km (2-mi) stretch of white sand with clean, green waters that are good for swimming and surfing. Maresias is popular with a young crowd.

ILHABELA

7 km (5 mi)/15-min boat ride from São Sebastião.

Fodor's Choice
★ Ilhabela is favored by those who like the beach and water sports; indeed, many championship competitions are held here. This is the biggest sea island in the country, with 22 calm beaches along its western shore, which faces the mainland. The hotels are mostly at the north end, though the best sandy stretches are the 13 to the south, which face the open sea. Eighty percent of the island is in a state park area.

There are two small towns on the island: one is where the locals live; the other is where most visitors stay because of its hotels, restaurants, and stores. During the winter months most businesses that cater to tourists, including restaurants, are open only on weekends.

Scuba divers have several 19th- and early-20th-century wrecks to explore—this region has the most wrecks of any area off Brazil's coast—and hikers can set off on the numerous inland trails, many of which lead to a waterfall (the island has more than 300). ⚠ **Mosquitoes are a problem; bring plenty of insect repellent.**

TO & FROM
Balsas (ferries) from São Sebastião to Ilhabela run every 30 minutes from 6 AM to midnight and hourly during the night. The São Sebastião balsa transports vehicles as well as passengers. Fares range from R$10.70 (weekdays) to R$16 (weekends), including a car. To get to the ferry dock in São Sebastião, take Avenida São Sebastião from town to the coast. Make advance ferry reservations, particularly December–February.

GETTING AROUND THE ISLAND
The best way to get around Ilhabela is by car. There are no rental agencies on the island (or connecting bridges) so be sure to make arrangements beforehand. Public buses also cross the island from north to south daily.

ESSENTIALS

Banks & Currency Exchange Banespa (⊠ *Rua Dr. Carvalho 98, 11630-000*). **Bradesco** (⊠ *Praça Cel. Julião M. Negrão 29, 11630-000*).

Emergencies & Medical Assistance Ambulance (☎ *912*). **Fire** (☎ *193*). Hospital: **Pronto Socorro Municipal Governador Mário Covas⁄** (⊠ *Av. Prof. Malaquias de Oliveira Freitas 154* ☎ *012/3895–8789*). Pharmacy: **Drogaria Nova Esperança** (⊠ *Rua da Padroeira 73* ☎ *012/3896–1183*). **Police** (☎ *190*).

Ferry São Sebastião balsa (☎ *0800/704–5510*).

Visitor & Tour Info Ilhabela Secretaria do Turismo (⊠ *Rua Bartolomeu de Gusmão 140, 11630-000* ☎ *012/3896–1091* ⊕ *www.ilhabela.sp.gov.br*). **Maremar** (⊠ *Avenida Princesa Isabel, 90, 11630-000Ilhabela* ☎ *012/3896-3679* ⊕ *www. maremar.tur.br* ⌁ *Scuba-diving, jeep, horseback-riding, and hiking tours*).

SAFETY & PRECAUTIONS

Ilhabela is a safe little island. Nevertheless, be sure to take common-sense precautions. Don't carry large amounts of money on your person and don't leave your belongings unattended.

WHAT TO SEE

Praia Grande (⊠ *13 km/8 mi south of ferry dock, 11630-000*) has a long sandy strip with food kiosks, a soccer field, and a small church.

At night people gather at **Praia do Curral** (⊠ *6 km/4 mi south of Praia Grande, 16630-000*), where there are many restaurants and bars—some with live music—as well as places to camp. The wreck of the ship *Aymoré* (1921) can be found off the coast of this beach, near Ponta do Ribeirão, where you can also look for a waterfall trail.

A small church and many fishing boats add to the charm of **Praia da Armação** (⊠ *14 km/9 mi north of ferry dock, 11630-000*). The beach was once the site of a factory for processing blubber and other resources from whales caught in the waters around the island. Today windsurfers stick to capturing the wind and the waves.

To reach **Baía dos Castelhanos** (⊠ *22 km/14 mi east of the ferry dock, 11630-000*) you need a four-wheel-drive vehicle, and if it rains even this won't be enough. Consider arriving by sailboat, which demands a 1½- to 3-hour trip that can be arranged through local tour operators. With such an isolated location, you can see why slave ships once used the bay to unload their illicit cargo after slavery was banned in Brazil. If you're lucky, you might spot a dolphin off the shore of this 2-km (1¼-mi) beach—the largest on the island.

WHERE TO STAY & EAT

$–$$$$ ✕ **Ilha Sul.** The best option on the menu is the grilled shrimp with vegetables. Fish and other seafood are also available. ⊠ *Av. Riachuelo 287, 11630-000* ☎ *012/3894–9426* ⊟ *AE, DC, MC, V* ⊘ *Closed Mon.–Thurs. in the months of Apr.–June and Aug.–Nov.*

$$–$$$ ✕ **Viana.** *Camarão* (shrimp) is prepared in various ways at this tradi-
★ tional and petite restaurant with just a few tables. It's popular among locals, who come here to eat and enjoy the gorgeous view and sunsets. Grilled fish is also on the menu. ⊠ *Av. Leonardo Reale 1560, 11630-*

000 🕾*012/3896–1089* ⚓*Reservations essential* ▭*No credit cards* ⊗*Closed weekdays Apr.–June and Aug.–Nov.*

$$$$ ✕▣**Maison Joly.** Past guests of this exclusive hotel at the top of the
Fodor'sChoice Cantagalo Hill range from kings of Sweden to the Rolling Stones. Upon
★ arrival you're given a beach kit complete with mosquito repellent and a hat. Each of the rooms has distinctive furnishings that are part of its theme, such as a piano, a billiard table, or a telescope—and all have balconies facing the sea. The restaurant ($$$$), which now opens to nonguests, is excellent. ⊠*Rua Antônio Lisboa Alves 278, 11630-000* 🕾*012/3896–2213* 🖷*012/3896–2364* ⊕*www.maisonjoly.com.br* 🛏*9 rooms* ♿*In-room: safe. In-hotel: restaurant, bar, pool, spa, public Internet, no kids under 12, no elevator* ▭*DC, MC, V.*

$ 🛈**Pousada dos Hibiscos.** North of the ferry dock, this red house has mid-
★ size rooms, all at ground level. The friendly staff serves up a good breakfast and provides poolside bar service. Each room has its own unique decoration, but all have hardwood furnishings, and either tile or stone floors. ⊠*Av. Pedro de Paula Moraes 720, 11630-000* 🕾🖷*012/3896–1375* ⊕*www.pousadadoshibiscos.com.br* 🛏*13 rooms* ♿*In-room: safe. In-hotel: bar, pool, gym, refrigerator, no elevator* ▭*AE, V.*

SPORTS & THE OUTDOORS

BOATING & Because of its excellent winds and currents, Ilhabela is a sailor's mecca.
SAILING You can arrange boating and sailing trips through **Maremar Turismo** (⊠*Av. São João 574, 11630-000* 🕾*012/3896–3679* ⊕*www.maremar.tur.br*), one of the biggest tour agencies in Ilhabela. Maremar also has sailing courses and other activities, ranging from historical tours to off-road adventures.

For information on annual boating competitions that Ilhabela hosts, including a popular sailing week, contact **Iate Club de Ilhabela** (⊠*Av. Força Expedicionária Brasileira 299, 11630-000* 🕾*012/3896–2300*). **Ilha Sailing Ocean School** (⊠*Av. Pedro de Paula Moraes 578, 11630-000* 🕾*012/9766–6619* ⊕*www.ilhasailing.com.br*) has 12-hour sailing courses that cost about R$500.

HIKING The **Cachoeira dos Três Tombos** trail starts at Feiticeira Beach (a nude beach) and leads to three waterfalls. **Trilha da Água Branca** is an accessible, well-marked trail. Three of its paths go to waterfalls that have natural pools and picnic areas. You can arrange guided hikes through local agencies such as **Cia. Aventura** (⊠*Av. Princesa Isabel 809, 11630-000* 🕾*012/3896–2899*).

SCUBA DIVING Ilhabela has several good dive sites off its shores. In 1884 the British ship *Darth* sank near **Itaboca** (⊠*17 km/11 mi south of ferry dock, 11630-000*). It still contains bottles of wine and porcelain dishes. **Ilha de Búzios** (⊠*25 km/15 mi offshore; take boat from São Sebastião, 11630-000*), one of the three main Ilhabela islands, is a good place to see a variety of marine life, including dolphins. For beginners, the recommended diving and snorkeling spot is the sanctuary off the shore of islet **Ilha das Cabras** (⊠*2 km/1 mi south of ferry, 11630-000*). It has a statue of Neptune at a 22-foot depth.

You can rent equipment, take diving classes, and arrange for a dive-boat trip through **Colonial Diver** (⊠ *Av. Brasil 1751, 11630-000* ☏ *012/3894–9459* ⊕ *www.colonialdiver.com.br*). The basic course takes three to four days and costs around R$960, which includes underwater videos and photographs, course material, and an international certificate.

SURFING One of the best places to surf is **Baía de Castelhanos** (⊠ *22 km/14 mi east of ferry dock, 11630-000*). **Pacuíba** (⊠ *20 km/12 mi north of ferry dock, 11630-000*) has decent wave action.

KITE- & Savvy kite-surfers and windsurfers head to **Ponta das Canas,** at the
WINDSURFING island's northern tip. Side-by-side beaches **Praia do Pinto and Armação** (⊠ *12 km/7 mi north of ferry dock, 11630-000*) also have favorable wind conditions. You can take kite-surfing, windsurfing, and sailing lessons at **BL3** (⊠ *Av. Pedro Paulo de Moraes 1166, 11630-000* ☏ *012/3896–1034* ⊠ *Armação Beach, 11630-000* ☏ *012/3896–1271* ⊕ *www.bl3.com.br*), the biggest school in Ilhabela. A 12-hour course costs R$400–R$550.

UBATUBA

234 km (145 mi) southeast of São Paulo

Many of the more than 70 beaches around Ubatuba are more than beautiful enough to merit the long drive from São Paulo. Young people, surfers, and couples with and without children hang out in the 90-km (56-km) area, where waterfalls, boat rides, aquariums, diving, and trekking in the wild are major attractions. Downtown Ubatuba also has an active nightlife, especially in summer. Ubatuba can be reached from São Paulo via the Carvalho Pinto (SP 070) and Oswaldo Cruz (SP 125) highways.

TO & FROM

Litorânea buses travel six times a day to Ubatuba from São Paulo. The journey takes about four hours. By car from São Paulo, take Rodovia Ayrton Senna–Carvalho Pinto (SP 070), followed by Rodovia Tamoios (SP 099) to Caraguatatuba. Turn right and head north on SP 055.

ESSENTIALS

Bus Contacts Litorânea (☏ *011/6221–0244* ⊕ *www.litoranea.com.br*). **Rodoviária Litorânea** (*Rua Maria Victoria Gean* ⊠ *11680-000*).

Emergencies & Medical Assistance Ambulance (☏ *912*). **Fire** (☏ *193*). **Police** (☏ *190*).

WHAT TO SEE

Lively **Praia Grande** (⊠ *Off Tamoios [SP 099] and Rio-Santos intersection, 11680-000*) is one of Ubatuba's most popular beaches for its central location and loads of kiosks selling food and drink. The waters are good for swimming, though waves are big. Surfing is popular here.

In stark contrast to Praia Grande, isolated and peaceful **Praia do Prumirim** (⊠ *Off SP 055 at Km 23, 11680-000*) is surrounded by nature and doesn't see much tourist traffic. You can hire local fishermen to take you by boat to a small undeveloped island offshore.

INLAND

São Paulo's inland region has beautiful mountains, springs, rivers, and waterfalls perfect for outdoor activities like hiking and rafting. Historic attractions are generally fewer than in other states. Save some time for clothing and crafts shopping, and for the lavish regional cuisine.

Highways that lead to inland towns are some of the best in the state. To get to Águas de São Pedro and Brotas, take Anhangüera–Bandeirantes (SP 330/SP 348); to Santana de Parnaíba, take Castelo Branco (SP 280); and to Campos de Jordão, take Ayrton Senna–Carvalho Pinto (SP 70). Embu is the exception—it's a 30-minute drive from the capital on the not-so-well-maintained Régis Bittencourt (BR 116). To go by bus, choose between the daily departures from the Tietê and Barra Funda terminals in São Paulo. Both are next to subway stations, making access fairly easy.

ÁGUAS DE SÃO PEDRO

180 km (112 mi) northwest of São Paulo.

Although Águas de São Pedro is the smallest city in Brazil, at a mere 3.9 square km (1.5 square mi), its sulfurous waters made it famous countrywide in the 1940s and '50s. The healing hot springs were discovered by chance in the 1920s when technicians were drilling for oil.

Fonte Juventude is the richest in sulfur in the Americas and is often used to treat rheumatism, asthma, bronchitis, and skin ailments. The waters at Fonte Gioconda have minor radioactive elements (and, yes, they are reportedly good for you), whereas Fonte Almeida Salles's have chlorine bicarbonate and sodium (which are said to alleviate the symptoms of diabetes and upset stomachs).

You can access the springs at the Balneário Publico (public bathhouse) or through some hotels. Though a number of illnesses respond to the water, most visitors are just healthy tourists soaking in relaxation. Águas de São Pedro is compact, so it's easy to get around on foot.

TO & FROM
Piracicabana buses run daily from São Paulo to Águas de São Pedro. The trip takes three hours and costs R$ 33,10. Águas de São Pedro is about a 2½-hour drive north of São Paulo on Anhangüera-Bandeirantes (SP 330/SP 348) and then SP 304.

ESSENTIALS
Banks & Currency Exchange Bradesco (⊠*Av. Carlos Mauro 336, 13525-000*).

Bus Contacts Piracicabana (☎*011/6221–0032* ⊕*www.piracicabana.com.br*).

Emergencies & Medical Assistance Ambulance (☎*912*). **Fire** (☎*193*). **Hospital: Pronto Socorro Municipal** (⊠*Rua Antônio Feijó 52, 13525-000*

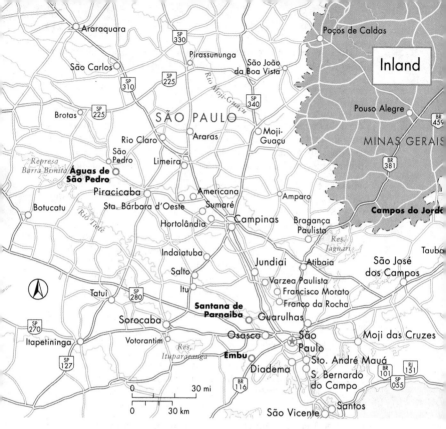

☎ 019/3482–1721). Pharmacy: **Drogaria Estância** (✉ *Av. Carlos Mauro 375, 13525-000* ☎ *019/3482–1347).* **Police** (☎ *190*).

Visitor & Tour Info **Águas de São Pedro Informações Turísticas** (✉ *Av. Carlos Mauro, in front of Balneário, 13525-000* ☎ *019/3482–2173 or 3482–1096* ⊕ *www. aguasdesaopedro.sp.gov.br).*

WHAT TO SEE

Balneário Municipal Dr. Octávio Moura Andrade has immersion baths in sulfurous springwater. You can swim in the pool or sweat in the sauna while you wait for your private soak, massage, or beauty appointment. A snack bar and a gift shop round out the spa services. ✉ *Av. Carlos Mauro, 13525-000* ☎ *019/3482–1333* ⊡ *R$8–R$33* ☽ *Mon.–Sun. 7–6.*

☽ A walk through the woods in **Bosque Municipal Dr. Octávio Moura Andrade** is a chance to relax. Horseback riding costs around R$10 for a half hour. It's part of the Balneário complex *(⇨below).* Saunas, baths, and massages cost R$8–R$33. ✉ *Av. Carlos Mauro, 13525-000* ☎ *019/3482–1333* ⊡ *Free* ☽ *Weekdays 7–noon, weekends 7–5.*

Built in the Swiss style, the 18th-century **Capela Nossa Senhora Aparecida** *(Our Lady of the Apparition Chapel)* perches atop the highest part of the city. Twelve pine trees were planted around the chapel to represent the 12 apostles. ⊠ *Rua Izaura de Algodoal Mauro, Jardim Porangaba, 13525-000* ☎*019/3482–1366* 💰*Free* ☉ *Weekends 1–5.*

☾ A good option if you have kids is **Thermas Water Park,** with its 11 pools, eight waterslides, and a small working farm. ⊠*Km 189, SP 304, 13525-000* ☎*019/3482–1011* 💰*R$32* ☉*Mon.–Sun. 8–6.*

WHERE TO STAY & EAT

$ ✕**Patagônia.** This restaurant with international cuisine owes its contemporary flavor to the city's gastronomy students who do internships here. Duck, lamb, trout, risotto, and salt cod are good choices. ⊠*Av. Presidente Kennedy 876, 13525-000* ☎*019/3482–2338* ▤*V* ☉*No lunch Thurs.–Sat. No dinner Sun.*

$$$–$$$$ ✕▦**Grande Hotel São Pedro.** The beautiful art deco building was a casino during the 1940s. Now it's a teaching hotel and restaurant ($$–$$$) with all the comforts of a full-service spa. Many of the friendly staff members are students—including those who prepare dishes such as salt cod in pistachio sauce. The property is in the middle of a 300,000-square-meter (3.2 million-square-foot) park with more than 1 million trees and local wildlife. ⊠*Parque Dr. Octávio de Moura Andrade, 13525-000* ☎*019/3482–7600* 🖷*019/3482–1665* ⊕*www.grande hotelsenac.com.br* ⇋*96 rooms, 16 suites* ⌂*In-hotel: 2 restaurants, room service, bar, tennis court, pool, gym, spa, refrigerator* ▤*AE, DC, MC, V.*

¢ ✕▦**Avenida.** This hotel with an arcaded veranda resembles a large ranch house. Rooms are plain and sparsely decorated, but they're spacious. The restaurant (¢–$$$) serves homestyle Brazilian fare like *filé cubana* (steak with fried bananas) and has live music on Friday and Saturday. ⊠*Av. Carlos Mauro 246, 13525-000* ☎*019/3482–1221* 🖷*019/3482–1223* ⊕*www.hotelavenida.com.br* ⇋*53 rooms* ⌂*In-room: no a/c. In-hotel: restaurant, room service, pool, public Internet, some pets allowed* ▤*No credit cards.*

$ ▦**Hotel Jerubiaçaba.** The rooms in this 30-year-old hotel are bathed in light colors and filled with simple furnishings. The 120 rooms are divided into four types, from standard to luxury, but all of them are in a 17,000-square-meter (183,000-square-foot) green area with springs and a bathhouse. ⊠*Av. Carlos Mauro 168, 13525-000* ☎*019/3482–7500* ⊕*www.hoteljerubiacaba.com.br* ⇋*120 rooms, 8 suites* ⌂*In-room: no a/c (some). In-hotel: restaurant, room service, bar, tennis court, pool, no-smoking rooms* ▤*AE, DC, MC, V.*

CAMPOS DO JORDÃO

184 km (114 mi) northeast of São Paulo.

In the Serra da Mantiqueira at an altitude of 5,525 feet, Campos do Jordão and its fresh mountain air are paulistas' favorite winter attractions. In July temperatures drop as low as 32°F (0°C), though it never snows; in warmer months temperatures linger in the 13°C–16°C (55°F–60°F) range.

In the past some people came for their health (the town was once a tuberculosis treatment area), others for inspiration—including such Brazilian artists as writer Monteiro Lobato, dramatist Nelson Rodrigues, and painter Lasar Segall. Nowadays the arts continue to thrive, especially during July's Festival de Inverno (Winter Festival), which draws classical musicians from around the world.

> ### SIGHTSEEING BY TRAIN
>
> A wonderful little train depart from **Estação Ferroviária Emílio Ribas** (⊠ *Av. Dr. Januário Miráglia, Vila Capivari*) for tours of the city and its environs, including the 47-km (29-mi) trip to Reino das Águas Claras, where there's a park with waterfalls and models from Monteiro Lobato's characters (Lobato is a well-loved children's-book author). Be sure to book in advance.

Exploring Campos do Jordão without a car is difficult. The attractions are far-flung, except for those at Vila Capivari.

TO & FROM
Expresso Mantiqueira buses leave São Paulo for Campos do Jordão every two hours daily. The journey takes three hours and costs R$29. To reach Campos do Jordão from São Paulo (a 2½-hour drive), take Rodovia Carvalho Pinto (SP 070) and SP 123.

ESSENTIALS
Banks & Currency Exchange **Bradesco** (⊠ *Av. Frei Orestes Girardi 1037, 12460-000*). **Itaú** (⊠ *Av. Frei Orestes Girardi 859, 12460-000*).

Bus Contacts **Expresso Mantiqueira** (☎ *011/6221–0244* ⊕ *www.expressoman tiqueira.com.br*). **Terminal Rodoviário** (⊠ *Av. Januário Miraglia,12460-000*).

Emergencies & Medical Assistance **Ambulance** (☎ *912*). **Fire** (☎ *193*). **Hospital São Paulo** (⊠ *Rua Agripino Lopes de Morais 1100, 12460-000* ☎ *012/3662–1722*). **Police** (☎ *190*).

Visitor & Tour Info **Campos do Jordão Tourist Office** (⊠ *At entrance to town, Campos do Jordão, 12460-000* ☎ *012/3664–3525* ⊕ *www.camposdojordao.com. br*).

WHAT TO SEE
The brand-new **Amantikir Garden,** created in August 2007, consists of 17 gardens that are inspired by famous international counterparts from around the world. On the grounds you can find a cafeteria and a learning center where there are courses on gardening. Plans are in the works for expanding the area and building a bird-watching center. Reservations are mandatory, as the place receives a limited number of guests per day. An English-speaking guide is available if booked in advanced. ⊠ *Estrada Paulo Costa Lenz César, km 2.8, 12460-000* ☎ *012/3662–2757* ⊕ *www.amantikir.com.br* ✄ *R$15, free on Tues.* ☼ *Mon.–Sun. 8–5.*

The bucolic **Baronesa Von Leithner** is a working berry farm where you can buy homemade jellies and jams. There's also a cafeteria and restaurant if you're in the mood for a snack. ⊠ *Av. Fausto Arruda Camargo,*

2.815, Alto da Boa Vista, 12460-000 ☎*012/3662–1121* ⊕*www.bar onesavonleithner.com.br* ✉*Free* ⊗*Tues.–Sun. 9 AM–10 PM.*

Boulevard Genéve, a mall in the busy Vila Capivari district, is lined with cafés, bars, and restaurants, making it a nightlife hub. You can also find plenty of clothing stores, and candy shops selling chocolate, the town's specialty.

Horto Florestal is a natural playground for *macacos-prego* (nail monkeys), squirrels, and parrots, as well as for people. The park has a trout-filled river, waterfalls, and trails—all set among trees from around the world and one of the last *araucária* (Brazilian pine) forests in the state. ⊠*Av. Pedro Paulo Km 13, 12460-000* ☎*012/3663–3762* ✉*R\$3– R\$4* ⊗*Daily 8–5.*

Outside town a chair-lift ride to the top of **Morro do Elefante** *(Elephant Hill)* is a good way to enjoy the view from a 5,850-foot height. ⊠*Av. José Oliveira Damas s/n, 12460-000* ☎*012/3663–1530* ✉*R\$7* ⊗*Tues.–Fri. 1–5, weekends 9–5:30.*

Palácio Boa Vista, the official winter residence of the state's governor, has paintings by such famous Brazilian modernists as Di Cavalcanti, Portinari, Volpi, Tarsila do Amaral, and Anita Malfatti. On the same property, the **Capela de São Pedro** (São Pedro Chapel) has sacred art from the 17th and 18th centuries. ⊠*Av. Dr. Adhemar de Barros 3001, 12460-000* ☎*012/3662–1122* ✉*R\$5* ⊗*Wed., Thurs., weekends 10– noon and 2–5.*

The athletically inclined can walk 3 km (2 mi) and climb the 300-step stone staircase to **Pedra do Baú,** a 6,400-foot trio of rocks inside an ecotourism park north of the city. A trail starts in nearby São Bento do Sapucaí, and it's recommended that you hire a guide. In the park you can also practice horseback riding, canopy walking, trekking, or mountain climbing and spend the night in a dormlike room shared with other visitors. Some of the activities are only available on weekends. ⊠*Km 25, Estrada São Bento do Sapucaí, 12460-000* ☎*012/3662– 1106* ✉*R\$5* ⊗*Wed.–Sun. 8–6.*

WHERE TO STAY & EAT

\$–\$\$\$ ✕**Baden-Baden.** One of the specialties at this charming German restaurant in the heart of town is sauerkraut *garni* (sour cabbage with German sausages). The typical dish serves two and is almost as popular as Baden-Baden's own brewery, which is open to visitors 10–5 on weekdays. ⊠*Rua Djalma Forjaz 93, Loja 10, 12460-000* ☎*012/3663– 3659* ▭*AE, DC, MC, V.*

\$–\$\$ ✕**Itália Cantina e Ristorante.** As its name suggests, this place specializes in Italian food. The pasta and the meat dishes are delicious, but you can also try trout, lamb, fondue, and even boar dishes. ⊠*Av. Macedo Soares 306, 12460-000* ☎*012/3663–1140* ▭*AE, DC, MC, V.*

¢–\$ ✕**Cyber Café.** Drink hot cocoa with crepes, fondue, or a slice of pie, while you browse the Internet at this downtown café. ⊠*Rua Djalma Forjaz 100, Loja 15, 12460-000* ☎*012/3663–6351* ⊕*www.cybercafe boulevard.com.br* ▭*MC, V.*

Os Bandeirantes

In the 16th and 17th centuries groups called *bandeiras* (literally, "flags," but also an archaic term for an assault force) set out on expeditions from São Paulo. Their objectives were far from noble. Their initial goal was to enslave Native Americans. Later, they were hired to capture escaped African slaves and destroy *quilombos* (communities the slaves created deep in the interior). Still, by heading inland at a time when most colonies were close to the shore, the bandeirantes inadvertently did Brazil a great service.

A fierce breed, *bandeirantes* (bandeira members) often adopted indigenous customs and voyaged for years at a time. Some went as far as the Amazon River; others only to what is today Minas Gerais, where gold and precious gems were found. In their travels they ignored the 1494 Treaty of Tordesillas, which established a boundary between Spanish and Portuguese lands. (The boundary was a vague north–south line roughly 1,600 km/1,000 mi west of the Cape Verde islands.) Other Brazilians followed the bandeirantes, and towns were founded, often in what was technically Spanish territory. These colonists eventually claimed full possession of the lands they settled, and thus Brazil's borders were greatly expanded.

Near Parque Ibirapuera in the city of São Paulo there's a monument, inaugurated in 1953, to honor the bandeirantes. It's a huge granite sculpture created by Victor Brecheret, a famous Brazilian artist. Protests are occasionally staged here by those who don't believe the bandeirantes deserve a monument.

$–$$$ ★ **Pousada Villa Capivary.** A stay at this cozy guesthouse puts you in the gastronomic and commercial center of Campos. The friendly staff is helpful and efficient. Most apartments have balconies, and the five suites have whirlpool baths. ⊠*Av. Victor Godinho 131, 12460-000* ☎*012/ 3663–1746* 🖷*012/3663–1736* ⊕*www.capivari.com.br* ⇆*10 rooms, 5 suites* ⚙*In-room: safe. In-hotel: bar* ▭*AE, DC, MC, V.*

SHOPPING

Casa de Chocolates Montanhês (⊠*Praça São Benedito 45, Loja 6, 12460-000* ☎*012/3663–1979* ⊕*www.chocolatemontanhes.com.br*) is a well-known chocolate shop whose prices start at R$48 per kilo. The best handmade embroidered clothing in town is at **Maison Geneve** (⊠*Rua Djalma Forjaz 100, Lojas 1 a 3, 12460-000* ☎*012/3663–2520* ⊕*www.geneve.com.br*), open weekdays 10–7 and weekends 10–10. For knits try **Paloma Malhas** (⊠*Rua Djalma Forjaz 78, Loja 15, 12460-000* ☎*012/3663–1218*), open weekdays 10–7 and weekends 10–10.

EMBU

27 km (17 mi) west of São Paulo.

Founded in 1554, Embu, or Embu das Artes, is a tiny Portuguese colonial town of whitewashed houses, old churches, wood-carvers' studios, and antiques shops. It has a downtown handicrafts fair every weekend. On Sunday the streets sometimes get so crowded you can barely walk.

Embu also has many stores that sell handicrafts and wooden furniture; most of these are close to where the street fair takes place.

On weekends it's difficult to find a place to park in Embu, and parking lots can be expensive. You can easily walk to all the main sights in town.

TO & FROM

EMTU runs an *executivo* (executive, or first-class) bus from São Paulo to Embu–Engenho Velho on Line 179, which departs hourly from Anhangabaú. Regular (intermunicipal) buses travel more often: every 20 minutes, Line 033 leaves from Clínicas to Embu. The ride is less comfortable, though: you might have to stand up.

To make the 30-minute drive from São Paulo to Embu, drive from Avenida Professor Francisco Morato to Rodovia Régis Bittencourt (BR 116) and then follow the signs.

ESSENTIALS

Banks & Currency Exchange **Bradesco** (⊠ *Rua Nossa Senhora do Rosario 29, 04603-000*).

Emergencies & Medical Assistance **Ambulance** (☎ *912*). **Fire** (☎ *193*). Hospital: **Pronto Socorro Municipal** (⊠ *Av. Elias Yazbek 1415, 04603-000* ☎ *011/4704–5744*). **Police** (☎ *190*).

Visitor & Tour Info **Embu Secretaria de Turismo** (⊠ *Largo 21 de Abril 139, Embu, 04603-000* ☎ *011/4704–6565* ⊕ *www.embu.sp.gov.br*). **Gol Tour Viagens e Turismo** (☎ *011/3256–2388* ⊕ *www.goltour.com.br* ☞ *Day trips from São Paulo to Embu R$80–R$90*).

WHAT TO SEE

Igreja Nossa Senhora do Rosário was built in 1690 and is a nice bet if you won't have a chance to visit the historic cities of Minas Gerais. The church contains baroque images of saints and is next to a 1730 monastery now turned into a sacred-art museum. ⊠ *Largo dos Jesuítas 67, 04603-000* ☎ *011/4704–2654* 🎫 *R$2* ⊙ *Tues.–Sun. 9–5.*

Ⓒ In the Mata Atlântica you can visit the **Cidade das Abelhas** *(City of the Bees)*, a farm with a small museum where you can watch bees at work. You can buy honey and other bee-related natural products while your kids climb the gigantic model of a bee. It's about 10 minutes from downtown; just follow the signs. ⊠ *Km 7, Estrada da Ressaca, 06803-000* ☎ *011/4703–6460* 🎫 *R$12* ⊙ *Tues.–Sun. 8:30–5.*

WHERE TO EAT

$–$$ ✕ **O Garimpo.** In a large room with a fireplace or around outdoor tables, choose between Brazilian regional dishes such as the house specialty, *moqueca de badejo* (spicy fish-and-coconut-milk stew), and German classics such as *eisbein* (pickled and roasted pork shank). ⊠ *Rua da Matriz 136, 06803-000* ☎ *011/4704–6344* ▤ *AE, DC, MC, V.*

¢–$$ ✕ **Os Girassóis Restaurante e Choperia.** A great variety of dishes is served at this downtown restaurant next to an art gallery. The *picanha brasileira* (barbecued steak) with fries and *farofa* (cassava flour sautéed in butter) is recommended. ⊠*Largo dos Jesuítas 169, 06803-000* ☎*011/4781–6671* ▤*AE, DC, MC, V* ⊗*Closed Mon.*

$ ✕**Casa do Barão.** In this colonial-style spot you find contemporary versions of country plates, but no salads or juices. Go for the exotic *picadinho jesuítico* (round-steak stew), served with corn, fried bananas, and farofa. Unlike most restaurants in the city, Casa do Barão serves single-person portions. ⊠*Rua Joaquim Santana 95, 06803-000* ☎*011/4704-2053* ▤*MC, V* ⊗*Closed Mon.*

SHOPPING

Cantão Móveis e Galeria (⊠*Largo dos Jesuítas 169, 06803-000* ☎*011/4781–6671*) is a good place to buy ceramics, paintings, sculptures, and antique decorations. **Fenix Galeria de Artes** (⊠*Rua Marechal Isidoro Lopes 10, 06803-000* ☎*011/4704–5634*) is a good place to find oil paintings as well as wood and stone sculptures.

Galeria Jozan (⊠*Rua Nossa Senhora do Rosário 59, 06803-000* ☎*011/4704–2600*) sells lovely antiques. **Guarani Artesanato** (⊠*Largo dos Jesuítas 153, 06803-000* ☎*011/4704–3200*) has handicrafts made of wood and stone, including sculptures carved from *pau-brasil* (brazilwood). **Embuarte Móveis Rústicos** (⊠*Av. Elias Yazbek 253, 06803-000* ☎*011/4704–2083*) is one of the many shops in town with colonial-style furniture.

SANTANA DE PARNAÍBA

42 km (26 mi) northwest of São Paulo.

With more than 200 preserved houses from the 18th and 19th centuries, Santana de Parnaíba is considered the "Ouro Preto from São Paulo"—a town rich with history and colonial architecture. Santana was founded in 1580; by 1625 it was the most important point of departure for the *bandeirantes*.

In 1901 the first hydroelectric power station in South America was built here. Throughout the 20th century, Santana managed to retain its houses and charm while preserving a local tradition: a rural type of *samba* called "de bumbo," in which the pacing is marked by the *zabumba* (an instrument usually associated with rhythms from the northeastern states of Brazil). The proximity to a couple of São Paulo's finest suburbs explains the region's fine dining. Outdoors lovers feel at home with the canopy-walking and trekking options. On weekends parking is scarce in Santana de Parnaíba, and parking lots can be expensive.

TO & FROM

EMTU's *executivo* (executive, or first-class) bus from Barra Funda in São Paulo to Pirapora do Bom Jesus (Line 385) stops in Santana de Parnaíba daily and takes one hour.

To reach Santana de Parnaíba from São Paulo—a 40-minute drive—take the express lane of Rodovia Castelo Branco (SP 280) and pay attention to the road signs.

ESSENTIALS

Banks & Currency Exchange Bradesco (⊠*Largo de S. Bento 30, 04600-000*).

Emergencies & Medical Assistance Ambulance (☎*912*). **Fire** (☎*193*). Hospital: **Hospital Santa Ana** (⊠*Rua Prof. Edgar de Moraes 707, 04600-000* ☎*011/4154–2234*). **Police** (☎*190*).

Visitor & Tour Info Santana de Parnaíba Secretaria de Cultura e Turismo (⊠*Largo da Matriz 19, 06500-000* ☎*011/4154–1874 or 011/4154–2377* ⊕*www. santanadeparnaiba.sp.gov.br*).

WHAT TO SEE

Begin your trip by appreciating the 17th- and 18th-century colonial architecture of the **Centro Histórico,** with its more than 200 well-preserved houses. All of them are concentrated around three streets: Suzana Dias, André Fernandes, and Bartolomeu Bueno—two of which are named after famous bandeirantes.

Museu Casa do Anhanguera provides an even sharper picture of the bandeirantes era. In a 1600 house (the second-oldest in the state) where Bartolomeu Bueno—nicknamed Anhanguera, or "old devil," by the Indians—was born, the museum displays objects and furniture from the past four centuries. ⊠*Largo da Matriz 9, 06500-000* ☎*011/4154–5042* ⊠*R$1* ⊙*Weekdays 8–4:30, weekends 11–5.*

Baroque **Igreja Matriz de Sant'Anna** was built in the same square as Casa do Anhanguera in 1610 and restored in 1892. It has terra-cotta sculptures and an altar with gold-plated details. ⊠*Largo da Matriz, 06500-000* ☎*011/4154–2401* ⊠*Free* ⊙*Daily 8–5.*

WHERE TO EAT

$$–$$$ ✕**Dom Afonso de Vimioso.** A place like this would have reminded Portuguese colonists of the motherland. Options include fine wines and more than 10 dishes made with salt cod. Don't miss out on typical sweets such as *pastéis de Santa Clara* (yolk and sugar-filled pastries). ⊠*Km 36, Estrada dos Romeiros, 06500-000* ☎*011/4151–1935* ▤*AE, DC, MC, V.*

$–$$$ ✕**Aldeia Cocar.** This restaurant and outdoor complex was built in a former indigenous village. It occupies a 86,111-square-foot Mata Atlântica (Atlantic Forest) area with wildlife, and hosts indigenous exhibits in a reconstructed native tent. Aldeia serves more than 30 Brazilian specialties from all over the country, as well as a few typical dishes from countries that helped shape Brazil, like Italy, Japan, and, of course, Portugal. *Arrumadinho* (sundried beef with mashed pumpkin and collard greens) is an excellent choice. After the meal, take some time to rest on the hammocks. ⊠*Estrada do Belo Vale 11, Km 32, SP-280, 06500-000* ☎*011/4192–3073* ⊕*www.aldeiacocar.com.br* ▤*AE, DC, MC, V* ⊙*Closed Mon.–Wed.*

$–$$ ✕**São Paulo Antigo.** In a century-old ranch-style house, taste *caipira* (rural) dishes such as *dobradinha com feijão branco* (intestines and white-bean stew) or *galinha atolada* (rural-style hen stew). The grand finale is a free carriage ride around the town's main square. ⊠*Rua*

Álvaro Luiz do Valle 66, 06500-000 ☎*011/4154–2726* ▭*DC, MC, V* ⊘*No dinner weekdays.*

$ ✕**Bartolomeu.** In a 1905 house, this restaurant serves regional specialties like feijoada and *picadinho* (steak stew served with rice and beans, farofa, fried banana, and fried egg). Salmon and boar ribs are some additional choices. ✉*Praça 14 de Novembro 101, 06500-000* ☎*011/4154–2679* ▭*DC, MC* ⊘*Closed Mon.*

SPORTS & THE OUTDOORS

Head back to the 21st century by participating in the weekend activities organized by the restaurant **Aldeia Cocar** (✉*Estrada do Belo Vale 11, Km 32, SP-280, 06500-000* ☎*011/4192–3073*), which include walks through the forest canopy and trekking. A half-hour canopy tour costs R$30. Activities take place Friday and Saturday 11–11 and Sunday 11–5.

Travessia do Caminho do Sol (☎*011/4154–2422*) is a 240-km (150 mi) trail that passes by 13 villages and crosses small rivers and cane plantations. The trail is considered the local version of the famous Camino de Santiago, in Spain. Call to join a group hike.

The South

WORD OF MOUTH

"Lucky you—going to Iguaçu Falls. I strongly rec-ommend the trip as the falls are spectacular (as impressive as Niagara Falls)."

—Lorraine Prieto

Updated by
Carlos G.
Tornquist

EXPECT THE UNEXPECTED IN THE southern states of Paraná, Santa Catarina, and Rio Grande do Sul. The climate is remarkably cooler (the highest elevations even get a couple of inches of snow every year) and the topography more varied than in the rest of Brazil. You're also just as likely to find people of German and Italian ancestry as Portuguese. And as Brazil's breadbasket, the Região Sul (southern region) has a standard of living comparable to that of many developed nations.

The southern section of the Serra do Mar, a mountain range along the coast, stretches well into Rio Grande do Sul. It looks like one green wall—broken only by the occasional canyon or waterfall—separating the interior from the shore. Most mountainsides are still covered with the luxuriant Mata Atlântica (Atlantic Rain Forest), which is as diverse and impressive as the forest of the Amazon. The Serra do Mar gives way to hills that roll gently westward to the valleys of the *rios* (rivers) Paraná and Uruguay. Most of these lands were originally covered with dense subtropical forests interspersed with natural rangelands such as the Campos Gerais, in the north, and the Brazilian Pampas, in the south.

ORIENTATION & PLANNING

ORIENTATION

Touring the three states of this region—roughly the size of France—in a short time is a challenge, despite a relatively efficient transportation network. The South can be divided into two major areas—the coast and the interior. Coastal attractions, along a 700-km (450-mi) line from Curitiba south to Porto Alegre, include fantastic beaches, forested slopes, canyons, and the Serra do Mar mountains. In the interior, Foz do Iguaçu, far to the west, should not be missed.

PARANÁ

The state of Paraná has a very short coastline of about 100 km (62 mi), with islands and historical cities. Curitiba, the capital, known internationally as a green city for its innovative urban planning and many parks, is about 90 km (56 mi) from the coast, on a plateau. West of Curitiba lies the vast interior, which incorporates Vila Velha State Park, with its ancient sandstone formations, and stretches all the way to the Paraguayan border and Foz do Iguaçu.

FOZ DO IGUAÇU

The grandeur of this vast sheet of white water cascading in constant cymbal-banging cacophony makes Niagara Falls and Victoria Falls seem sedate. Allow at least two full days to take in this magnificent sight, and be sure to see it from both the Argentine and Brazilian sides

SANTA CATARINA

Geographically, Santa Catarina is the opposite of Paraná: a long coastline of about 500 km (310 mi) and narrow interior. Most of the attractions are on or near the coast. Santa Catarina has some of the best beaches in South Atlantic. The capital, Florianópolis, an ideal hub for exploring the state's attractions, is on the Ilha de Santa Catarina (Santa Catarina Island).

RIO GRANDE DO SUL

Most tourist attractions in this state, with equal parts coast and interior, are in the heavily populated northeastern corner, including the capital, Porto Alegre, about 100 km (62 mi) from the coast. One highlight in the west are the Jesuit mission ruins in São Miguel.

> ## TOP REASONS TO GO
>
> - Seeing the mighty Iguaçu Falls.
> - Taking a train through Paraná coast's virgin rain forest.
> - The beaches of Santa Catarina.
> - Drinking wine on the slopes of Vale dos Vinhedo.
> - Hiking on the impressive green-clad canyons in northeastern Rio Grande do Sul.

PLANNING

WHEN TO GO

November through March is normally hot and humid. Rainfall is quite frequent, but less intense than in northern Brazil. Some years might have extremely rainy El Niño–related summers or, conversely, quite dry La Niña–affected years. January and February are top vacation months, so expect crowded beaches, busy highways, and higher prices. Winter (April–November) brings much cooler temperatures, sometimes as low as the upper 20s in the higher elevations at night. Major cold fronts blowing in from Patagonia can bring some gray, blustery days, usually followed by chilly days with deep blue skies.

ABOUT THE RESTAURANTS & THE CUISINE

One of the most famous foods of Brazil, *churrasco* (slow-grilled and -roasted meat), originated in Rio Grande do Sul. But cuisine is eclectic here in cowboy country, and rice and beans sit on southern tables beside Italian and German dishes, thanks to the South's many European immigrants. Look for *barreado,* a dish from coastal Paraná made by stewing beef, bacon, potatoes, and spices for hours in a clay pot made airtight with moistened manioc flour. *Café colonial* is the elaborate 5 PM tea—with breads, pies, and German kuchen—popular among the Germans in the South.

WHAT IT COSTS IN REAIS					
	¢	$	$$	$$$	$$$$
AT DINNER	under R$15	R$15–R$30	R$30–R$45	R$45–R$60	over R$60

Prices are per person for a main course at dinner or for a prix-fixe meal.

ABOUT THE HOTELS

The south has a great variety of hotels and inns, though upscale facilities are limited. Except for in the smallest towns and most remote areas, however, you shouldn't have a problem finding comfortable accommodations. Pousadas in historic buildings are common, particularly in beach towns. Hotel-fazendas are popular in rural areas. (*For descriptions of lodging types in Brazil see Accommodations in Brazil Essen-*

tials.) Southern beaches attract many South American tourists, and seaside cities might become crowded and highway traffic nightmarish from December through March. Make advance reservations.

WHAT IT COSTS IN REAIS					
	¢	$	$$	$$$	$$$$
FOR 2 PEOPLE	under R$125	R$125–R$250	R$250–R$375	R$375–R$500	over R$500

Prices are for a standard double room in high season, excluding tax.

GETTING AROUND

Avoid long trips in rental cars, as roads are busy with heavy truck traffic and pavement isn't always in good condition; take flights or bus trips instead. You can always rent a car or take taxis or local buses when you arrive. Organized tours are highly recommended for visiting remote attractions.

BORDER CROSSINGS AT FOZ DO IGUAÇU

U.S., Canadian, and British citizens need only a valid passport for stays of up to 90 days in Argentina, so crossing the border at Iguaçu isn't a problem. Crossing back into Brazil from Argentina, however, is a thorny issue. In theory, *all* U.S. citizens need a visa to enter Brazil, so make sure your paper work is in order before you depart.

Many local taxis (both Argentine and Brazilian) have "arrangements" with border control and can also get you across with no visa. Most charge 150–200 pesos for the return trip. Though the practice is well-established (most hotels and travel agents in Puerto Iguazú have deals with Brazilian companies and can arrange a visa-less visit), it *is* illegal. Enforcement of the law is generally lax, but sudden crack-downs and on-the-spot fines of hundreds of dollars have been reported.

PARANÁ

The state of Paraná is best known for the Foz do Iguaçu, a natural wonder, and the Itaipú Dam, an engineering marvel. But also worth a visit is Vila Velha, a series of strange sandstone formations in the center of Paraná that might remind you of the eerily moving landscapes of the western United States. At one time the rolling hills of the state's plateau were covered with forests dominated by the highly prized Paraná pine, an umbrella-shape conifer. Most of these pine forests were logged by immigrants half a century ago, and the cleared land of the immense interior is now where soybeans, wheat, and coffee are grown. (Still, be on the lookout for the occasional Paraná pine.) The state has a very short coastline, but the beaches are spectacular, as is the Serra do Mar, which still has pristine Atlantic forest and coastal ecosystems. Curitiba, the upbeat capital, ranks as a top Brazilian city in efficiency, innovative urban planning, and quality of life.

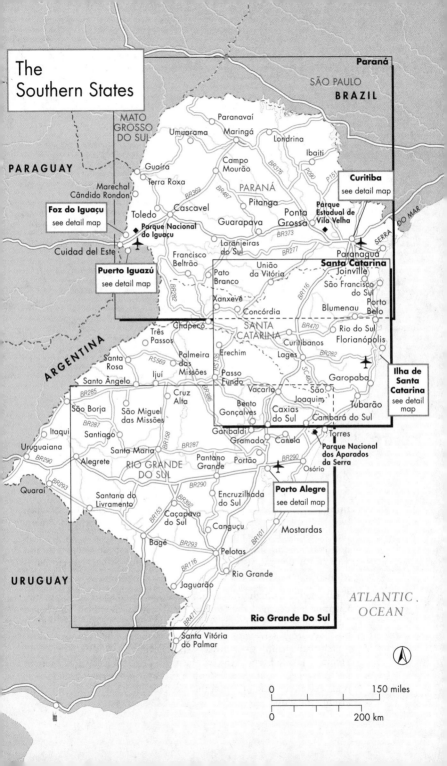

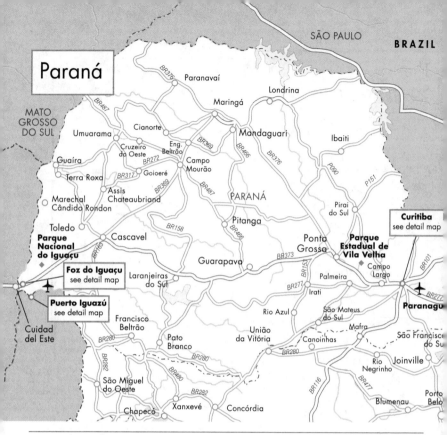

CURITIBA

408 km (254 mi) south of São Paulo, 710 km (441 mi) north of Porto Alegre.

A 300-year-old city, Curitiba is on the Paraná plateau, at an elevation of 2,800 feet. It owes its name to the Paraná pinecones, which were called *kur-ity-ba* by the native Guaranis. In a region that already differs considerably from the rest of the country, the city of 1.5 million is unique for its temperate climate (with a mean temperature of 16°C/61°F) and the 50% of its population that is of non-Iberian European ancestry.

With one of the highest densities of urban green space in the world, Curitiba is known as the environmental capital of Brazil. This is not only because of its array of parks but also because since the 1980s it has had progressive city governments that have been innovative in their urban planning—a process spearheaded by former mayor and architect Jayme Lerner. The emphasis on protecting the environment has produced an efficient public transportation system and a comprehensive recycling program that are being used as models for cities around the globe.

TO & FROM

The flight from São Paulo to Curitiba is about an hour. Curitiba's Aeroporto Internacional Afonso Pena is 21 km (13 mi) east of downtown. A cab ride to downtown is around R$50. A minibus service (R$8) provides transportation between Rua 24 Horas and Estação Rodoferroviária, passing by several downtown hotels on its way to the airport.

GETTING AROUND

Curitiba is internationally renowned for its modern and efficient public transportation system. Buses take you quickly to any place in the city. There are regular lines (R$1.90) and *ligeirinho* express lines (R$3.50). Moreover, tourists have a special service to get to the attractions, the 2½-hour Linha Turismo tour (⇨ *"The Tourism Line," below*. Taxis are easy to find in Curitiba. A ride from downtown to the Jardim Botânico costs about R$30.

ESSENTIALS

Airport **Aeroporto Internacional Afonso Pena** (*CWB* ⊠*Av. Rocha Pombo s/n, São José dos Pinhais, 83010-900* ☎*041/3381–1515*).

Banks & Currency Exchange **Banco do Brasil** (⊠*Praça Tiradentes 410, Centro, 80020-100* ⊠*Aeroporto Internacional Afonso Pena, Av. Rocha Pombo, s/n, São José dos Pinhais, 83010-900*). **SoViagem Cambio** (⊠*Av. Mal. Deodoro 344, 15th fl., Centro, 88010-010*).

Bus Contacts **Estação Rodoferroviária (Bus Station)** (⊠*Av. Pres. Afonso Camargo 330, 80051-980* ☎*041/3320–3000*).

Emergencies & Medical Assistance ■**TIP➔For any emergency in Curitiba, dial** ☎**100. Ambulance** (☎*192*). **Fire** (☎*193*). Hospital: **Hospital Cajuru** (⊠*Av. São José 300, Cajuru, 80050-350* ☎*041/3360–3000*). Pharmacy: **HiperFarma** (⊠*Rua P. Antonio Polito 1028, Alto Boqueirão, 81770-260* ☎*041/3018–5551*). **Police** (☎*190*).

Taxi **Radio taxi** (☎*0800/600–6666 or 0800/41–4646*).

Visitor & Tour Info **BWT** (⊠*Estação Rodoferroviária, Av. Afonso Camargo 330, Gate 8, Centro, 80051-980* ☎*041/3323–4007* ⊕*www.bwtoperadora.com.br* ⌖*Tours include: city of Curitiba, Paranaguá, Parque Nacional Superaguí, Serre Verde Express train*). **Paraná Turismo** (*State Tourism Board* ⊠*Rua Dep. Mário de Barros 1290, Centro Cívico, 80530-913* ☎*041/3331–3500, 041/3354–1516 24-hr hotline* ⊕*www.pr.gov.br/turismo* ⌖*Weekdays 1–7* ⊠*Aeroporto Internacional Afonso Pena, Av. Rocha Pombo s/n, São José dos Pinhais, 83010-900* ☎*045/3381–1153* ⌖*Daily 8–10*).

SAFETY & PRECAUTIONS

Although Curitiba is generally a safe city, in particular around tourist attractions, use your best judgment when venturing into unknown neighborhoods and avoid them at night.

EXPLORING

Numbers in the text correspond to numbers in the margin and on the Curitiba Setor Histórico map.

MAIN ATTRACTIONS

Jardim Botânico. Although not as old and renowned as its counterpart in Rio, the Botanical Garden has become a Curitiba showplace. Its most outstanding feature is the tropical flora in the two-story steel greenhouse that resembles a castle. The Municipal Botanical Museum, with its library and remarkable collection of rare Brazilian plants, is also worth visiting. There are several paths for jogging or just wandering. ⊠*Rua Eng. Ostoja Roguski s/n, Jardim Botânico, 80210-390* ☎*041/3364–7365* ⊠*Free* ☉*Gardens daily 6 AM–8 PM. Museum weekdays 8–5.*

THE TOURISM LINE

The **Linha Turismo** (☎*041/156*) is a bus line maintained by the city that follows a 2½-hour circular route, allowing five stops along the way for one fare. Buses depart every 30 minutes from 9 to 5:30 (Tuesday–Sunday) from the Praça Tiradentes, stopping at 25 attractions. Plan to spend an entire day on this route. There are taped descriptions of the sights (available in English), and the fare is R$16.

---

❶ **Museu Paranaense.** Founded in 1876, the State Museum of Paraná moved several times before installing its collections in this imposing art nouveau building, which served as city hall from 1916 to 1969. The permanent displays contain official documents, ethnographic materials of the native Guarani and Kaigang peoples, coins and photographs, and archaeological pieces related to the state's history. ⊠*Rua Kellers 289, Setor Histórico, 80410-100* ☎*041/3304–3300* ⊠*R$2* ☉*Weekdays 10–5, weekends 11–3* ⊕*www.pr.gov.br/museupr.*

❺ **Museu Oscar Niemeyer.** Pictures of Oscar Niemeyer's projects throughout the world are on display at this museum designed by the architect himself. The museum also incorporates a collection of the works of Paraná's artists from the former Museu de Arte do Paraná with temporary modern art exhibits. Niemeyer's futuristic building design includes a long rectangular building, formerly a school. The main building, a suspended eye-shape structure overlooking the adjacent John Paul II Woods, has the major modern art exhibit. ⊠*Rua Marechal Hermes 999, Centro Cívico, 80530-230* ☎*041/3350–4400* ⊕*www.museuos carniemeyer.org.br* ⊠*R$4* ☉*Weekdays 10–5, weekends 11–3.*

★ **Parque das Pedreiras.** This cultural complex was built in the abandoned João Gava quarry and adjacent wooded lot. The quarry itself was converted to an amphitheater that can accommodate 60,000 people. The 2,400-seat **Opera de Arame** (Wire Opera House), also on the grounds here, is built of tubular steel and wire mesh, built above a water–field quarry pit. National and international musical events have given this facility world renown. ⊠*Rua João Gava s/n, Pilarzinho, 82130-010* ☎*041/3355–6071* ⊠*Free* ☉*Tues.–Sun. 8–10.*

OFF THE BEATEN PATH

Santa Felicidade. What was once an Italian settlement, dating from 1878, is now one of the city's most popular neighborhoods. It has been officially designated as Curitiba's "gastronomic district," and, indeed, you'll find some fantastic restaurants—as well as wine, antiques, and handicrafts shops—along Via Veneto and Avenida Manuel Elias. The

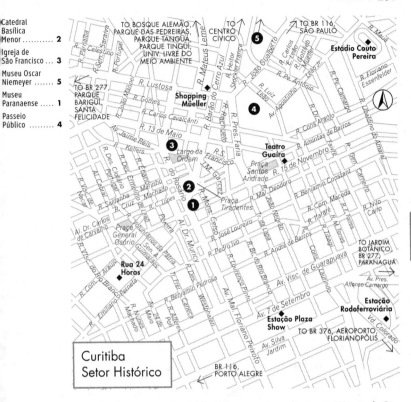

Curitiba
Setor Histórico

area also has some colonial buildings, such as the Igreja Matriz de São José (St. Joseph's Church).

IF YOU HAVE TIME

Bosque Alemão. The 8-acre German Woods, a park honoring German immigration, is on a hill in the Jardim Schaffer neighborhood. On its upper side is the Bach Oratorium, a small concert hall that looks like a chapel; it's the site of classical music performances. The park also has a viewpoint with a balcony overlooking downtown, a library with children's books, and a path through the woods called Hans and Gretel Trail, which depicts the Grimm Brothers' tale in 12 paintings along the way. The trail ends at the Mural de Fausto, where there's a stage for music shows. ⊠*Rua Nicolo Paganini at Rua Francisco Schaffer, Jardim Schaffer, 90820-200* ☎*041/3338–6835* ⊠*Free* ⊙*Park daily dawn–dusk. Library Mon.–Sat. 8–6.*

② **Catedral Basílica Menor.** The cathedral, also called Igreja de Nossa Senhora da Luz dos Pinhais, is on the site where the city was founded in 1693. The present neo-Gothic structure was finished in 1893 and was built according to the plan of a cathedral in Barcelona, Spain. ⊠*Praça Tiradentes s/n, Setor Histórico, 80020-100* ☎*041/3222–1131* ⊠*Free* ⊙*Daily 7 AM–9 PM.*

3 **Igreja de São Francisco.** St. Francis, Curitiba's oldest church, was built in 1737 and fully restored in 1981. Check out its gold-plated altar before ducking into the attached **Museu de Arte Sacra** (Sacred Art Museum), with its baroque religious sculptures made of wood and terra-cotta. ✉*Largo da Ordem s/n, Setor Histórico, 80510-010* ☎*041/3223–7545 church, 041/3321–3265 museum* 💲*Free* ☉*Tues.–Fri. 9–6, weekends 9–2.*

NEED A BREAK?

To satisfy your hunger, head for Rua 24 Horas (✉*Rua Coronel Mena Barreto, between Rua Visconde de Rio Branco and Rua Visconde de Nacar, Centro, 90020-100* ☎*041/3225–1732*), a short downtown alley sheltered by a glass roof. You'll find souvenir shops and newsstands as well as coffeehouses and bars whose tables spill out onto the walkway. Most are open 24 hours a day, seven days a week. Rua 24 Horas is closed for renovation until 2009.

4 **Passeio Público.** Opened in 1886, the Public Thoroughfare was designed as a botanical and zoological garden and soon became a favorite place for the affluent to spend their weekend afternoons. The main gate is a replica of that at the Cimetière des Chiens in Paris. Although it's no longer the official city zoo, you can observe several Brazilian primates and birds still kept in the park, as well as majestic sycamores, oaks, and the *ipê amarelo,* a striking Brazilian tree with vibrant yellow flowers found from the Amazon to the South. ✉*Main Gate: Rua Pres. Faria at Pres. Carlos Cavalcanti, Setor Histórico, 80020-290* ☎*041/3222–2742* 💲*Free* ☉*Tues.–Sun. 6* AM*–8* PM.

Parque Tangüá. The most-visited park in the city, Tangüá shows creative landscaping in an abandoned quarry with its pond, tunnel (dug 160 feet into the rock wall), artificial waterfall, and walkway over the water, all surrounded by woods, with many imposing Brazilian pines. ✉*Rua Eugenio Flor s/n, Pilarzinho, 82130-290* ☎*041/3335–2112* 💲*Free* ☉*Daily dawn–dusk.*

Parque Tingüí. Designed to protect the upper basin of the Rio Barigüí from urban encroachment, this pleasant park has trails through the woods and barbecue areas. It's best known as the site of the **Ukranian Memorial,** which includes a reproduction of a wooden church with onion domes built by Ukrainian Catholic immigrants in 1900 in the town of Prudentópolis, 250 km (155 mi) away. There is also a shop with traditional Ukrainian handicrafts. ✉*Rua Dr. Bemben s/n, Pilarzinho, 82115-030* ☎*041/3240–1103* 💲*Free* ☉*Daily 6–8.*

Universidade Livre do Meio Ambiente. The main objective of the Free University of the Environment, in the Bosque Zaninelli (Zaninelli Woods), is to promote environmental awareness. It opened in 1992 during the UN Conference on the Environment and Development being held in Rio. The impressive main structure is built of eucalyptus wood and has a scenic overlook on its top level. Several paths through the woods make the Bosque Zaninelli a popular place to wander. ✉*Rua Victor Benato 210, Pilarzinho, 82120-110* ☎*041/3254–3734* ⊕*www.unili vre.org.br* 💲*Free* ☉*Daily 7–6.*

CLOSE UP

The Mata Atlântica

The Amazonian rain forest is so famous that most tourists are amazed to learn that Brazil's southern states were once covered by an equally lush humid forest, teeming with animal and plant biodiversity. The Mata Atlântica (Atlantic Forest), really a series of forests, originally covered about a fourth of Brazil, mostly along the southeastern seaboard. One of the most complex ecosystems on earth, these evergreen forests contained about 7% of all known vertebrates and more than 20,000 plant species.

The major difference between the Amazon and the Mata Atlântica is the flora. In the Amazon plants are essentially lowland types adapted to the humid climate; those in the Atlantic forests have adapted to mountainous terrain, less rainfall, and lower mean annual temperatures. Unique Mata Atlântica fauna includes primates like the *mico-leão dourado* (golden-lion tamarin) and the *muriqui* (spider monkey), parrots, toucans, *arapongas* (bell birds), and the *anta* (tapir).

The flora is rich *pau-brasil* (brazilwood) and, at higher elevations, *araucária* (Brazilian pine). The hundreds of orchid species, the yellow flowers of the *ipê* (Brazil's national flower), and the flowers of the *manacá* (princess flower tree) that turn from white to purple to violet within days, compose a colorful spectacle.

The Mata Atlântica has been seriously overexploited since the 16th century, and is threatened by human encroachment and agricultural land conversion. Recent estimates indicate that only 8% of the original remains. Preservation, conservation, and recovery efforts by the national government and private organizations are ongoing. "Bright spots" include Foz do Iguaçu, Superagüí National Park (near Paranaguá), a golden tamarin reserve in southern Bahia State, and organizations that train farmers in sustainable agriculture practices.

WHERE TO STAY & EAT

As one of the major centers of industry, commerce, and tourism in Brazil, Curitiba has wide a variety of lodging and dining options that caters to hurried and demanding business travelers. The Santa Felicidade neighborhood carved a name for affordable restaurants that serve locally influenced Italian cuisine.

$$$$ ✕**Boulevard.** A sophisticated restaurant with an excellent wine selection (including a long list of imports), Boulevard has a sober decor, with impeccably white-linen table cloths and dark wood. The fare by renowned chef Celso Freire doesn't fail to impress. Try the wild boar ribs with herbs, truffles, and mustard sauce or the chef's take on grilled tenderloin with mustard sauce. ✉*Rua Voluntários da Pátria 539, Setor Histórico, 80020-000* ☎*041/3023–8244* ⊕*www.restau ranteboulevard.com.br* ⌑*Reservations essential* ▤*AE, DC, MC, V* ☾*Closed Sun.*

$$–$$$$ ✕**Durski.** This family-run restaurant has brought traditional Polish and
Fodor'sChoice Ukrainian food center stage. Occupying a renovated house in the his-
★ torical district, the restaurant has a rustic yet sleek look with tile floors

and exposed-brick walls. The impeccable service by staff in traditional attire, as well as the borscht, pierogi, and *bigos* (a round loaf of bread stuffed with sausages and sauerkraut), transport you to central Europe. There's also an alternative international menu that has many pasta, beef, and fish options. ⊠*Rua Jaime Reis 254, Largo da Ordem, 80510-010* ☎*041/3225–7893* ⊕*www.durski.com.br* ⌂*Reservations essential* ⊟*AE, DC, MC, V* ⊙*Closed Mon. No dinner Sun.*

$$–$$$ ✕**Bombordo.** This small but highly regarded restaurant serves the best seafood in town. The nautical decor, with model boats, ships' wheels, and fish figurines, creates the perfect ambience. Try the *congrio grelhado com molho de camarão* (grilled conger eel in shrimp sauce). At lunchtime a prix-fixe seafood buffet is served. ⊠*Av. 7 de Setembro 2275, Shopping Estação, Rebouças, 80230-010* ☎*041/3233–2350* ⊟*AE, DC, MC, V.*

$–$$ ✕**Estrela da Terra.** On weekends this restaurant in a grand colonial house is *the* place to try the local *barreado* (a long-simmered stew of beef, bacon, potatoes, and spices). On weekdays a buffet is served with several other regional choices including *frango com pinhão* (grilled chicken breast with cream sauce and Brazilian pine nuts). ⊠*Rua Jaime Reis 176, Largo da Ordem, 80510-140* ☎*041/3225–5007* ⊕*www.estreladaterra.com.br* ⊟*DC, MC, V* ⊙*No dinner.*

$–$$ ✕**Schwarzwald.** One of the city's most popular German bar–restaurants, Schwarzwald has carved a name for itself with great draft beer, including some imported brands and local bocks (German-style dark beers), which are hard to find in Brazil. Highly recommended entrées are the house version of *eisbein* (pig's leg served with mashed potatoes), *kassler* (beef fillet with a cream sauce), and duck with red cabbage. The restaurant is quite small and packed with tables, but there's plenty more space on the sidewalk in front. ⊠*Rua Claudino dos Santos 63, Centro Histórico, 80020-170* ☎*041/3223–2585* ⊟*AE, DC, MC, V.*

$ ✕**Madalosso.** One of the best-known restaurants in Curitiba, Madalosso is also quite possibly the largest restaurant in Brazil: the hangarlike building seats 4,800. The prix-fixe Italian menu includes a large selection of pastas and sauces, chicken dishes, and salads. Noteworthy are the gnocchi and the lasagna. The restaurant keeps a large wine cellar, with many renowned Brazilian and international wines, as well as house wine, made for the restaurant in the vineyards of Rio Grande do Sul. ⊠*Av. Manoel Ribas 5875, Santa Felicidade, 82020-000* ☎*041/3372–2121* ⊟*AE, DC, MC, V* ⊙*No dinner Sun.*

$$–$$$ ☷**Four Points Sheraton.** A new addition (opened 2005) to the roster of fine hotels in Curitiba, the Four Points aims at the business traveler. The lobby is spacious and modern, and room decor is a mix of modern and classic, with pastel colors and sleek wood furniture. The restaurant serves Italian fare. **Pros:** Great business facilities, central location. **Cons:** Expensive, few amenities for leisure travelers. ⊠*Av. Sete de Setembro 4211, Batel, 80250-210* ☎*041/3340–4000 or 0800/55–5855* ⊕*www.starwood.com.br* ⇌*165 rooms* ⌂*In-room: safe, ethernet. In-hotel: restaurant, bar, pool, gym, public Internet, Wi-Fi, parking (fee), airport shuttle* ⊟*AE, DC, MC, V* ❑*BP.*

$$ ⌂**Grand Hotel Rayon.** A spacious lobby welcomes you to Curitiba's most
★ sophisticated hotel. Superbly furnished standard rooms have sound-proof windows, LCD televisions, and two phone lines. Service is impeccable, and the location—in the heart of the financial district and right next to Rua 24 Horas—is convenient. Weekend stays get complimentary Linha Turismo bus-tour tickets. **Pros:** Prime location, friendly and attentive staff. **Cons:** Some rooms need updating. ⊠*Rua Visconde de Nacar 1424, Centro, 804116-201* ☎041/2108–1100 *or 0800/41–8899* ⊕*www.rayon.com.br* ⮑*136 rooms, 11 suites* ⌕*In-room: safe, ethernet. In-hotel: 2 restaurants, room service, bar, pool, gym, public Internet, Wi-Fi, parking (fee)* ⊟*AE, DC, MC, V* ⦿*CP.*

$ ⌂**Duomo Park Hotel.** Everything is shiny and comfortable at this small hotel. The rooms and suites are unusually spacious. All have large beds, blond-wood furniture, and carpeting. Bathrooms are heated—hard to find in Brazil, but welcome in the cold Curitiba winters, and the hotel has a sauna in the gym. Another draw is the location, steps from Rua 24 Horas. **Pros:** Great service, great location. **Cons:** Furniture needs updating, small commons area. ⊠*Rua Visconde de Rio Branco 1710, Centro, 80420-200* ☎041/3321–1900 *or 0800/41–1816* 🖷*041/3224–1816* ⮑*40 rooms, 8 suites* ⌕*In-room: safe. In-hotel: restaurant, bar, gym, airport shuttle, public Internet, parking (fee)* ⊟*AE, DC, MC, V* ⦿*CP.*

$ ⌂**Slaviero Braz Hotel.** In a landmark building overlooking the walkway of Rua das Flores, Slaviero Braz has large rooms with wood paneling and matching furniture. Beds are king-size, with colorful spreads and cushions that invite you to relax. Rooms in the east wing are smaller and oddly shaped, and elevators there are cramped because of the original building plan. The second-floor Getúlio bar-café is a popular gathering spot for businesspeople. **Pros:** Central location, good value for the better rooms. **Cons:** Some rooms small, few amenities. ⊠*Av. Luiz Xavier 67, Centro, 80020-020* ☎041/3017–1037 *or 0800/704–3311* ⊕*www.hotelslaviero.com.br* ⮑*89 rooms, 2 suites* ⌕*In-room: safe. In-hotel: restaurant, bar, gym, airport shuttle, public Internet, parking (fee)* ⊟*AE, DC, MC, V* ⦿*CP.*

¢ ⌂**Íbis Curitiba.** The Íbis leads the city's roster of budget lodgings. Room decor is undistinguished and bland, but beds are comfortable. The hotel is no-frills: be prepared to carry your own luggage. The reception desk and the restaurant are in restored historic houses that are detached from the main building. Íbis is one of the few hotels in Curitiba that has wheelchair-accessible rooms. **Pros:** Very affordable. **Cons:** Small bathrooms, few amenities. ⊠*Rua Comendador Araújo 730, Batel, 80020-050* ☎041/2102–2000 *or 0800/703–7000* ⊕*www.accorhotels.com.br* ⮑*150 rooms* ⌕*In room: safe. In-hotel: restaurant, bar, public Internet, parking (fee)* ⊟*AE, DC, MC, V.*

NIGHTLIFE & THE ARTS

Curitiba has a bustling cultural scene, a reflection of the European background of many of its citizens. Complete listings of events are published in the *Gazeta do Povo*, the major daily newspaper.

Asgard (⊠*Rua Brigadeiro Franco 3416, Rebouças, 80250-030* ☎*041/3333–8847*) is a popular microbrewery and live music venue. The beer is brewed to a lower alcohol content. **Aos Democratas** (⊠*Rua Dr. Pedrosa 485, Centro, 80250-030* ☎*041/3024–4496*) is a traditional *boteco* (small bar) that caters to soccer fans. It's a great place to watch games and hear the fans.

In what was once a railway terminal, the **Shopping Estação** (⊠*Av. 7 de Setembro 2775, Centro, 80230-010* ☎*041/2101–9101*) is a 700,000-square-foot covered area with a colorful and noisy collection of bars and restaurants, amusement parks, exhibits, a railway museum, a cineplex, daily live music shows, and more than 100 shops. The complex is open daily 10 AM–2 AM. The **Teatro Guaíra** (⊠*Rua 15 de Novembro 971, Centro, 88060-000* ☎*041/3304–7900*), formerly the Teatro São Teodoro (circa 1884), was totally rebuilt in its present location and reopened in 1974. It has a modern, well-equipped 2,000-seat auditorium, as well as two smaller rooms. Shows include plays, popular music concerts, and the occasional full-fledged opera.

SPORTS & THE OUTDOORS
Curitiba has three professional soccer clubs: Coritiba, Atlético Paranaense, and Paraná Clube. Check local newspaper listings for upcoming game times and locations. Many of the area's parks have paths for jogging and bicycling.

Arena da Baixada (Kyocera Arena) (⊠*Rua Eng. Rebouças 3113, Água Verde, 80250-170* ☎*041/3333–4747*) is home for Atlético Paranaense Club. It's the most modern sports facility in the country, with a 32,000-seat capacity, to be expanded to 50,000 in the future. **Estádio Couto Pereira** (⊠*Rua Ubaldino do Amaral 37, Alto da Glória, 80060-190* ☎*041/3362–3234*) is the 60-year-old home of Coritiba FC and holds 40,000 fans. **Parque Barigüi** (⊠*Av. Candido Hartmann at Av. Gen. Tourinho, off Km 1, BR 277, 82015-100* ☎*041/3335–2112*) contains soccer fields, volleyball courts, and paths spread throughout 310 acres.

SHOPPING
Curitiba Outlet Center (⊠*Rua Brigadeiro Franco 1916, Batel, 80420-200* ☎*041/3224–1900*) has a large array of clothing shops with rock-bottom prices. This government-sponsored shop offers a variety of wicker, clay, wood, and leather crafts as well as Ukrainian *pessankes* (painted eggshells), indigenous ornaments, and other traditional items and handmade toys. **UNIART Artesanato do Paraná** (⊠*Alameda Dr. Muricy 950, Centro, 80020-040* ☎*041/3234–1118*). Interact directly with the artisans every Sunday from 9 to 3 at the **Feira de Artesanato** (⊠*Largo da Ordem and Praça Garibaldi, Setor Histórico, 80510-210*), a popular fair with paintings from local artistis, pottery, tapestry, handicrafts, and antiques.

SIDE TRIP FROM CURITIBA

Parque Estadual de Vila Velha. The 22 towering rock formations of the 7,670-acre Vila Velha State Park, 97 km (60 mi) northwest of Curitiba, stand in sharp contrast to the green rolling hills of the Campos Gerais, Paraná's high plains. Three hundred million years of rain and wind have carved these sandstone formations, whose names—the Lion, the Cup, the Mushroom, the Sphinx—reflect their shapes. After watching a 10-minute video about the geology and environment of the area at the visitor center, you're led to the attractions on guided minibus tours. ✉Km 514, BR 376 ☎042/3228–1539 ☒R$8 ⊘Closed Tues.

PARANAGUÁ

90 km (56 mi) east of Curitiba.

Most of Brazil's coffee and soybeans are shipped out of Paranaguá, the nation's second-largest port, which also serves as chief port for landlocked Paraguay. Downtown holds many examples of colonial architecture and has been designated an official historic area. The city, founded in 1565 by Portuguese explorers, is 30 km (18 mi) from the Atlantic on the Baía de Paranaguá. The bay area is surrounded by the Mata Atlântica, of which a great swatch on the northern side is protected; several islands in the bay also have rain forests as well as great beaches. You'll find other less scenic but popular sandy stretches farther south, toward the Santa Catarina border.

TO & FROM

Although you can reach Paranaguá from Curitiba on BR 277, consider taking the more scenic Estrada da Graciosa, which follows the route taken by 17th-century traders up the Serra do Mar. This narrow, winding route—paved with rocks slabs in some stretches—is some 30 km (18 mi) longer than BR 277, but the breathtaking peaks and slopes covered with rain forest make the extra travel time worthwhile. You can drive or take a Viação Graciosa bus (75 minutes; R$17), but most tourists take the scenic train as part of an organized tour.

ESSENTIALS

Currency exchange is difficult in the Paranaguá area. Exchange reais in Curitiba.

Bus Contacts Terminal Municipal Rodoviário (Municipal Bus Station) (✉*Rua João Estevam at Rua João Regis, 83203-100*). **Viação Graciosa** (☎*041/3423–1215, 041/3423–1049 in Paranaguá* ⊕*www.viacaograciosa.com.br*).

Emergencies & Medical Assistance Ambulance (☎*192*). **Fire** (☎*193*). Hospital: **Santa Casa** (✉*Rua dos Expedicionários 269, Centro, 83206-450* ☎*041/3423–1422*). Pharmacy: **Caiofarma** (✉*Rua Mal. Deodoro 162, Centro, 83203-040* ☎*041/3422–8075*). **Police** (☎*190*).

Taxi **Ponto de Taxi** (☎*041/3423–4122*).

Visitor & Tour Info Informações Turísticas (✉*Rua Gen. Carneiro 258, Setor Histórico, 83203-280* ☎*041/3425–4542* ⟲*Open Tues.–Sat. 9–5*).

SAFETY & PRECAUTIONS

Paranaguá has some difficult neighborhoods, but the historic district downtown, where most attractions are, is fairly safe. Just the same, be extra careful with valuables such as cameras.

WHAT TO SEE

Igreja Nossa Senhora do Rosário, the city's first church, was destroyed, sacked, and rebuilt several times, but its facade (circa 1578) is original. ⊠*Largo Monsenhor Celso s/n, 83203-060* ☎*041/3423–2293* ⛛*Free* ⊙*Daily 7 AM–9 PM.*

Fodor's Choice ★ The 10-km-long (6-mi-long) **Ilha do Mel** *(Honey Island)*, a state park in the Baía de Paranaguá, is the most popular destination on Paraná's coast. It's crisscrossed by hiking trails—cars aren't allowed, and the number of visitors is limited to 5,000 at any one time—and has two villages, Encantadas and Nova Brasília, and several pristine beaches. Local lore has it that the east shore's Gruta das Encantadas (Enchanted Grotto) is frequented by mermaids. On the south shore check out the sights around Farol das Conchas (Lighthouse of the Shells) and its beach. From Forte de Nossa Senhora dos Prazeres (Our Lady of Pleasures Fort), built in 1767 on the east shore, take advantage of the great views of the forest-clad northern bay islands. The most scenic ferry rides leave from Paranaguá between 8 AM and 1 PM (2 hours; R$21). More convenient are the ferries that depart from Pontal do Sul, 49 km (30 mi) east of Paranaguá, every 30 minutes. Prices start at R$16. To ensure admission in the high season (December–March), book an island tour before you leave Curitiba. ⊠*Ferries depart from Alameda do Café s/n, Pontal do Sul, 83255-000* ☎*041/3455–2616.*

The northern shore of Baía de Paranaguá is home to the 92,000-acre **Parque Nacional de Superagüí** and its complex system of coves, saltwater marshes, and forested islands—including Ilha Superagüí and Ilha das Peças. Most of these pristine settings containing animal and bird species unique to the Mata Atlântica are closed to visitors. You can, however, see a lot of bird and animal species by basing yourself in the fishing village of Guaraqueçaba—reached by a three-hour ferry ride from Paranaguá's harbor—and then touring the bay and trails around the park. Your best bet for viewing wildlife and great views is to explore the islands on a guided boat tour. Ask for local boat operators and guides in the Paranaguá ferry dock. ⊠*Park administration: 2 km (1 mi) north of Guaraqueçaba. Ferry Dock: Rua da Praia s/n, Paranagú* ☎*041/3482–1262 park, 041/3455–2616 ferry informa-*

THE SERRA VERDE EXPRESS

The **Serra Verde Express** (☎*041/3323–4007* ⊕*www.serraverdeexpress.com.br*) tourist rail line runs from Curitiba to Paranaguá—a fabulous 110-km (69-mi) trip along the Serra do Mar slope, with views of peaks, waterfalls, and Atlantic rain forest and stops in historic towns. The regular train (4 hours; R$28–R$78) departs at 8 AM Tuesday–Sunday, returning at 2 PM; the faster *litorina* train (3 hours; R$118) departs at 9 AM weekends and returns at 2:30 PM. The full route is weekends only; weekday trips (3 hours) end at Morretes, the end of the scenic route. You can return , where you can return via van.

tion ⌨*Park free, ferry R$150–R$200* ☺*Park daily 9–6. Ferries to Guaraqueçaba at 9 and 1.* ·

WHERE TO STAY & EAT

$ ✕**Casa do Barreado.** In this small, homey family-run buffet-style restaurant the specialty is the traditional barreado. The prix-fixe menu includes a local chicken variety called *galinha na púcura*, chicken cooked in wine, tomato, and bacon sauce, several salads, and *cachaças* (Brazilian liquor distilled from sugarcane). Although the restaurant is officially open only on weekends, you can call ahead to arrange a dinner during the week. Barreado takes 24 hours to cook, so you must order it a day in advance. ✉*Rua José Antônio Cruz 78, 83206-452* ☎*041/3423–1830* ⌨*Reservations essential* ☰*DC, MC* ☺*Closed weekdays.*

$ ✕🏨**Camboa Resort Hotel.** In the historic district, Camboa has comfortable facilities, a long roster of activities, and a dedicated staff that can arrange for tours in the region. Modern architecture with red-tile roofs blends with the colonial surroundings. Rooms have a sleek design, with blond-wood furnishings and light colors. Ask to be on the north side for a bay view. Continental cuisine, with an emphasis on French, is served in the Camboa restaurant ($–$$). **Pros:** Close to historic district, many amenities. **Cons:** Very busy in summer months, poor Internet connection. ✉*Rua João Estevão s/n, 83203-020* ☎*041/3420–5200 or 0800/411–077* ⊕*www.hotelcamboa.com.br* ⇥*114 rooms, 6 suites* ⌨*In-room: safe, refrigerator. In-hotel: restaurant, bars, tennis courts, pool, gym, public Internet, parking (no fee)* ☰*AE, DC, MC, V* ⊙*CP.*

IGUAÇU FALLS

637 km (396 mi) west of Curitiba, 544 (338 mi) west of Vila Velha; 1,358 km (843 mi) north of Buenos Aires.

Iguazú consists of some 275 separate waterfalls—in the rainy season there are as many as 350—that plunge more than 200 feet onto the rocks below. They cascade in a deafening roar at a bend in the Iguazú River (Río Iguazú/Rio Iguaçu) where the borders of Argentina, Brazil, and Paraguay meet. Dense, lush jungle surrounds the falls: here the tropical sun and the omnipresent moisture make the jungle grow at a pace that produces a towering pine tree in two decades instead of the seven it takes in, say, Scandinavia. By the falls and along the roadside, rainbows and butterflies are set off against vast walls of red earth, which is so ubiquitous that eventually even paper currency in the area turns red from exposure to the stuff.

The falls and the lands around them are protected by Brazil's Parque Nacional do Iguaçu (where the falls go by the Portuguese name of Foz do Iguaçu) and the Argentina's Parque Nacional Iguazú (where the falls are referred to by their Spanish name, the Cataratas de Iguazú). The Brazilian town of Foz do Iguaçu and the Argentine town of Puerto Iguazú are the hubs for exploring the falls (the Paraguayan town of Ciudad del Este is also nearby).

GETTING HERE & AROUND

BRAZIL INFO

There are direct flights between Foz do Iguaçu and São Paulo (1 ½ hours; R$380), Rio de Janeiro (2 hours; R$440), and Curitiba (1 hour; $250) on TAM, which also has connecting flights to Salvador, Recife, Brasília, other Brazilian cities, and Buenos Aires. Low-cost airline Gol operates slightly cheaper direct flights on the same three routes.

The Aeroporto Internacional Foz do Iguaçu is 13 km (8 mi) southeast of downtown Foz. The 20-minute taxi ride should cost R$35–R$40; the 45-minute regular bus ride about R$3. Note that several major hotels are on the highway to downtown, so a cab ride from the airport to these may be less than R$30. A cab ride from downtown hotels directly to the Parque Nacional in Brazil costs about R$90.

Via bus, the trip between Curitiba and Foz do Iguaçu takes 9–10 hours with Catarinense (R$90; R$180 for sleeper service). The same company operates the 17-hour route to Florianópolis (R$120). Pluma travels to Rio de Janeiro, which takes 11½ hours (R$130), and São Paolo, which takes 14 hours (R$130; R$205 for sleeper). The Terminal Rodoviário in Foz do Iguaçu is 5 km (3 mi) northeast of downtown. There are regular buses into town, which stop at the Terminal de Transportes Urbano (local bus station, often shortened to TTU) at Avenida Juscelino Kubitschek and Rua Mem de Sá. From here, buses labeled Parque Nacional also depart every 15 minutes (7–7) to the visitor center at the park entrance; the fare is R$4. The buses run along Avenida Juscelino Kubitschek and Avenida Jorge Schimmelpfeng, where you can also flag them down.

There's no real reason to rent a car in Foz do Iguaçu: it's cheaper and easier to use taxis or local tour companies to visit the falls, especially as you can't cross the border in a rental car. There are taxi stands (*pontos de taxi*) at intersections all over town, each with its own phone number. Hotels and restaurants can call you a cab, but you can also hail them on the street.

BRAZIL ESSENTIALS

Airline Contacts GOL (☎300/115–2121 toll-free, 45/3521–4230 in Foz do Iguaçu ⊕www.voegol.com.br). **TAM** (☎800/570–5700 toll-free, 45/3528–8500 in Foz do Iguaçu ⊕www.tam.com.br).

Bus Contacts Catarinense (☎300/147–0470 toll-free, 45/3522–2050 in Foz do Iguaçu ⊕www.catarinense.net). **Pluma** (☎800/646–0300 toll-free, 045/3522–2515 in Foz do Iguaçu ⊕www.pluma.com.br).

Banks & Currency Exchange Banco do Brasil (⊠Av. Brasil 1377 ⊕www.bb.com.br).

Medical Assistance FarmaRede (pharmacy) (⊠Av. Brasil 46 ☎45/3572–1363). **Hospital e Maternidade Cataratas** (⊠Rua Santos Dumont 714 ☎45/3523–5200).

Post Office (⊠Praça Getúlio Vargas 72).

Taxis Ponto de Taxi 20 (☎45/3523–4625).

Visitor Info Foz do Iguaçu Tourist Office (✉Praça Getúlio Vargas 69, Brazil ☎45/3521-1455 ⊕www.iguassu.tur.br ⏱7 AM–11 PM).

ARGENTINA INFO

Aerolíneas Argentinas flies four to six times daily between Aeroparque Jorge Newbery in Buenos Aires and the Aeropuerto Internacional de Puerto Iguazú (20 km/12 mi southeast of Puerto Iguazú); the trip takes 1¾ hours. LAN does the same trip three to four times daily. Normal rates are about 350–400 pesos each way. Four Tourist Travel runs shuttle buses from the airport to hotels in Puerto Iguazú. Services leave after every flight lands and cost 12 pesos. Taxis to Puerto Iguazú cost 40 pesos.

> ## THE CROSS-BORDER BUS
>
> **Tres Fronteras** (☎3757/42-0377 in Puerto Iguazú ⊕www.tresfronteras.com.ar) runs an hourly cross-border public bus service between the centers of Puerto Iguazú and Foz do Iguaçu. Locals don't have to get on and off for immigration but be sure you do so. To reach the Argentine falls, change to a local bus at the intersection with RN 12 on the Argentine side. For the Brazilian park, change to a local bus at the Avenida Cataratas roundabout.

Vía Bariloche operates several daily bus services between Retiro bus station in Buenos Aires and the Puerto Iguazú Terminal de Omnibus in the center of town. The trip takes 16–18 hours, so it's worth paying the little extra for *coche cama* (sleeper) or *cama ejecutivo* (deluxe sleeper) services, which cost 200–240 pesos one-way (regular semi-cama services cost around 180 pesos). You can travel direct to Rio de Janeiro (22 hours) and São Paolo (15 hours) with Crucero del Norte; the trips cost 250 and 200 pesos, respectively.

From Puerto Iguazú to the falls or the hotels along RN 12, take El Práctico from the terminal or along Avenida Victoria Aguirre. Buses leave every 15 minutes 7–7 and cost 8 pesos round-trip.

There's little point in renting a car around Puerto Iguazú: daily rentals start at 150–200 pesos, more than twice what you pay for a taxi between the town and the falls. A rental car is useful for visiting the Jesuit ruins at San Ignacio, 256 km south of Puerto Iguazú on RN 12, a two-lane highway in excellent condition.

ARGENTINA ESSENTIALS

Airline Contacts Aerolíneas Argentinas (☎800/222-86527 ⊕www.aerolineas.com.ar). **LAN** (☎810/999-9526 ⊕www.lan.com).

Bus Contacts Crucero del Norte (☎11/5258-5000 in Buenos Aires, 3757/42-1916 in Puerto Iguazú ⊕www.crucerodelnorte.com.ar). **Four Tourist Travel** (☎3757/42-2962 at airport, 3757/42-0681 in Puerto Iguazú). **Vía Bariloche** (☎11/4315-7700 in Buenos Aires, 3757/42-0854 in Puerto Iguazú ⊕www.viabariloche.com.ar).

Banks & Currency Exchange Argencam (✉Av. Victoria Aguirre 1162). **Banco de la Nación** (✉Av. Victoria Aguirre 179 ⊕www.bna.com.ar).

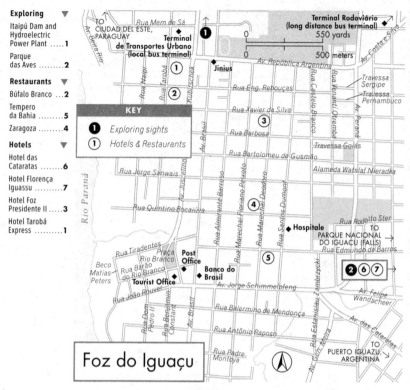

Foz do Iguaçu

Internet Telecentro (⊠Av. Victoria Aguirre 300 ☎3757/42-2864).

Medical Assistance Farmacia Bravo (⊠Av. Victoria Aguirre 423 ☎3757/42-0479).
Hospital Samic (⊠Av. Victoria Aguirre 131, Puerto Iguazú ☎3757/42-0288).

Post Office (⊠San Martín 384).

Taxis Remises Iguazú (⊠Puerto Iguazú ☎3757/42-2008).

Visitor Info Cataratas del Iguazú Visitors Center (⊠Park entrance ☎3757/42-0180 ⊕www.iguazuargentina.com ☯Apr.–Sept. 8 AM–6 PM; Oct.–Mar. 7:30 AM–6:30 PM). **Puerto Iguazú Tourist Office** (⊠Av. Victoria Aguirre 311, Puerto Iguazú ☎3757/42-0800 ☯Daily 7–1 and 2–9).

EXPLORING

To visit the falls, you can base yourself in the small Argentine city of Puerto Iguazú, or its sprawling Brazilian counterpart, the city of Foz do Iguaçu. The two cities are 18 km (11 mi) and 25 km (15 mi) northwest of the falls, respectively, and are connected by an international bridge, the Puente Presidente Tancredo Neves. Another bridge links Foz do Iguaçu with Ciudad del Este in Paraguay. Together, the three cities form the *Triple Frontera* (Tri Border).

5

KEY

⛴ *Cruise ship dock*

① *Exploring sights*

① *Hotels & Restaurants*

Originally a port for shipping wood from the region, Puerto Iguazú now revolves around tourism. This was made possible in the early 20th century when Victoria Aguirre, a high-society porteña, funded the building of a road to the falls to make it easier for people to visit them. Despite the constant stream of visitors from Argentina and abroad, Puerto Iguazú is small and sleepy: there are only 32,000 inhabitants, and many of its roads still aren't paved.

The same was once true of Foz de Iguaçu, but the construction of the Itaipú dam (now the second largest in the world) in 1975 transformed it into a bustling city with 10 times more people than Puerto Iguazú. Many have jobs connected with the hydroelectric power station at the dam, while others are involved with trade (both legal and illegal) with the duty-free zone of Ciudad del Este, in Paraguay.

In general it makes more sense to stay in tourism-oriented Puerto Iguazú: hotels and restaurants are better, peso prices are lower, and it's much safer than Foz do Iguaçu, which has a bad reputation for violent street crime. There's also more to do and see on the Argentine side of the falls, which take up to two days to visit. The Brazilian side, though impressive, only warrants half a day.

Many travel agencies offer packages from Buenos Aires, São Paulo, or Curitiba that include flights or bus tickets, transfers, accommodation, and transport to the falls. These packages are usually more expensive than booking everything yourself, but you do get round-the-clock support.

If you're staying in town, rather than at the hotels in the parks, you can easily reach the falls on your side of the border by public bus, private shuttle (most hotels work with a shuttle company), or taxi. Travel agencies and tour operators in Puerto Iguazú and Foz de Iguaçu also offer day trips to the opposite sides of the border. Most are glorified shuttle services that save you the hassle of changing buses and get you through immigration formalities quickly. Use them to facilitate getting to the park, but avoid those that include in-park tours: most drag you around with a huge group of people and a megaphone, which rather ruins the fabulous natural surroundings.

Both parks are incredibly well organized and clearly signposted, so most visitors have no trouble exploring independently. Once in the park, be sure to go on a boat trip, an unmissable—though drenching—experience that gets you almost under the falls. You can reserve these through tour operators or hotels, or at booths inside the parks.

THE OTHER SITES TO SEE
Surprisingly, Iguaçu is not the only site to see in these parts, though few people actually have time (or make time) to go to see them.

IN BRAZIL
❷ Flamingos, parrots, and toucans are some of the more colorful inhabitants of the privately run **Parque das Aves** *(Bird Park)*. Right outside the Parque Nacional Foz do Iguaçu, it's an interesting complement to a visit to the falls. A winding path leads you through untouched tropical forest and walk-through aviaries containing hundreds of species of birds. Iguanas, alligators, and other nonfeathered friends have their own pens. ⊠*Km 17, Rodovia das Cataratas* ☎*045/3529–8282* ⊕*www.parquedasaves.com.br* ⊠*$10* ☉ *Apr.–Sept., Daily 8:30–5:30; Oct.–Mar., Daily 8:30–6.*

❶ **Itaipú Dam and Hydroelectric Power Plant.** It took more than 30,000 workers eight years to build this 8 km (5 mi) dam, voted one of the Seven Wonders of the Modern World by the American Society of Civil Engineers. The monumental structure produces 25% of Brazil's electricity and 78% of Paraguay's, and will be the largest hydroelectric power plant on earth until China's Three Gorges (Yangtze) Dam is completed. You get plenty of insight into how proud this makes the Brazilian government—and some idea of how the dam was built—during the 30-minute video that precedes hour-long guided panoramic bus tours of the complex. Although commentaries are humdrum, the sheer size of the dam is an impressive sight. To see more than a view over the spillways, consider the special tours, which take you inside the cavernous structure and include a visit to the control room. Night tours—which include a light-and-sound show—begin at 8:30 Friday and Saturday. At the **Ecomuseu de Itaipú** *(Itaipú Eco-Museum)* (⊠*Km 10, Av. Tan-*

credo Neves ⬛*R$8* ⏱*Daily 8–5:30)* you can learn about the geology and archaeology of the area, and efforts to preserve its flora and fauna since the dam was built. Note that it's funded by the dam's operator Itaipú Binacional; information isn't necessarily objective. ✉*Km 11, Av. Tancredo Neves* ☎*800/645–4645* ⊕*www.itaipu.gov.br* ✉*Panoramic tour R$13, special tour R$30* ⏱*Panoramic tours Mon.–Sat. 8, 9, 10* AM, *2, 3, 3:30* PM. *Special tours Mon.–Sat. 8, 8:30, 9:30, 10* AM, *2, 2:30, 3:30* PM.

IN ARGENTINA

❸ **Gúira Oga.** Although Iguazú is home to around 450 bird species, the parks are so busy these days that you'd be lucky to see so much as a feather. It's another story at Gúira Oga, which means 'house of the birds' in Guaraní, although 'bird rehab' might be more appropriate. Injured birds, birds displaced by deforestation, and birds confiscated from traffickers are brought here for treatment. The large cages also contain many species on the verge of extinction, including the harpy eagle and the red macaw, a gorgeous parrot. The sanctuary is in a forested plot just off RN 12, halfway between Puerto Iguazú and the falls. ✉*RN 12, Km 5, Puerto Iguazú* ☎*3757/42–3890* ✉*Free* ⏱*Daily.*

❷ **La Aripuca.** It looks like a cross between a log cabin and the Pentagon, but this massive wooden structure—which weighs 551 tons—is a large-scale replica of a Guaraní bird trap. La Aripuca officially showcases different local woods, supposedly for conservation purposes—ironic, given the huge trunks used to build it, and the overpriced wooden furniture that fills the gift shop. ✉*RN 12 Km 5, Puerto Iguazú* ☎*3757/42–3488* ⊕*www.aripuca.com.ar* ✉*10 pesos* ⏱*Daily 9–7.*

❶ **Hito Tres Fronteras.** This viewpoint west of the town center stands high above the turbulent reddish-brown confluence of the Iguacú and Paraná rivers, which also form the *Triple Frontera,* or Tri Border. A mini pale-blue-and-white obelisk reminds you you're in Argentina; across the Iguazú river is Brazil's green-and-yellow equivalent; farther away, across the Paraná, is Paraguay's, painted red, white, and blue. A row of overpriced souvenir stalls stands alongside it. ✉*Av. Tres Fronteras, Puerto Iguazú.*

WHERE TO EAT

Booming tourism is kindling the restaurant scenes of Puerto Iguazú and Foz do Iguaçu, and each has enough reasonably priced, reliable choices to get most visitors through the two or three days they spend there. Neither border town has much of a culinary tradition to speak of, though most restaurants at least advertise some form of the local specialty *surubí* (a kind of catfish), although it's frequently out of stock. Instead, parrillas or churrascarias abound, as do pizza and pasta joints.

FOZ DO IGUAÇU

$$–$$$$ ✕**Tempero da Bahia.** If you're not going as far as Bahia on your trip, you can at least check out its flavors at this busy tangerine-painted restaurant. It specializes in northeastern fare like *moquecas* (a rich seafood

stew made with coconut milk and palm oil); their delicious versions are unusual for mixing prawns with local river fish. Spicy panfried sole and salmon are lighter options. The flavors aren't quite so subtle at the all-out seafood (and riverfood) buffets they hold several times a week, but tasty and cheap enough to pull in crowds. ⊠*Rua Marechal Deodoro 1228, 85851-030* ☎*45/3025–1144* ⊟*AE, MC, V* ⊘*No dinner Sun.*

$$–$$$$ ✕**Zaragoza.** On a tree-lined street in a quiet neighborhood, this traditional restaurant's Spanish owner is a dab hand at matching Iguaçu's fresh river fish to authentic Spanish seafood recipes. Brazilian ingredients sneak into some dishes—the *surubi á Goya,* catfish in a tomato and coconut-milk sauce—definitely merits a try. ⊠*Rua Quintino Bocaiúva 882, 85851-130* ☎*45/3028–8084* ⊟*AE, DC, MC, V.*

$$ ✕**Búfalo Branco.** The city's finest and largest churrascaria does a killer *rodizio* (all-you-can-eat meat buffet). The picanha stands out from the 25 meat choices, but pork, lamb, chicken, and even—yum—bull testicles find their way onto the metal skewers they use to grill the meat. The salad bar is well stocked, a boon for vegetarians. ⊠*Av. Rebouças 530, 85851-190* ☎*45/3523–9744* ⊟*AE, MC, V.*

PUERTO IGUAZÚ

$$–$$$ ✕**La Rueda.** This parrilla is so popular with visitors that they start serving dinner as early as 7:30 PM—teatime by Argentine standards. The local beef isn't quite up to Buenos Aires standards, but La Rueda's bife de chorizo is one of the best in town. Surubí is another house specialty, but skip the traditional Roquefort sauce, which rather eclipses the fish's flavor. They've stayed true to their rustic roots, however: hefty tree trunks hold up the bamboo-lined roof, and the walls are adorned by a curious wooden frieze carved by a local artist. ⊠*Av. Córdoba 28, 3370* ☎*3757/42–2531* ⚐*Reservations essential* ⊟*AE, DC, MC, V.*

$$ ✕**Aqva.** Locals are thrilled: finally, a date-night restaurant in Puerto Iguazú. Although the high-ceilinged split-level cabin seats too many to be truly intimate, they make up for it with well-spaced tables, discreet service, and low lighting. Softly gleaming timber from different local trees lines the walls, roof, and floor. Local river fish like *surubí* and *dorado* are the specialty: have them panfried, or, more unusually, as empanada fillings. Forget being romantic at dessert time: the chef's signature dessert, fresh mango and pineapple with a torrontés sabayon, is definitely worth keeping to yourself. ⊠*Av. Córdoba and Carlos Thays, 3370* ☎*3757/42–2064* ⊟*AE, MC, V.*

$$ ✕**El Gallo Negro.** A gaucho in full regalia mans the barbecue, which has
★ pride of place outside the hefty wooden cabin that houses this classy parrilla. The rustic-looking trestle tables on the wide veranda afford a great view of your sizzling steak; at night they get the white tablecloth and candle treatment. It's not all barbecued beef: caramelized suckling pig in an apple and honey sauce or lamb slow-cooked in red wine are some of the standouts from the kitchen. Their tempting take on Iguazú's only regional specialty, *surubi* (a local catfish), which they sauté in coconut milk, is sadly rarely available. ⊠*Av. Victoria Aguirre 773 at Curupí, 3370* ☎*3757/42–2465* ⊟*AE, MC, V.*

$ ✕**Puerto Bambú.** Iguazú's warm evenings make this popular pizzería's outdoor tables perfect for a casual meal. Their thin-crust pizzas are cooked *a la parrilla* (on a barbecue), so there's a pleasantly smoky edge to them. Reggae plays quietly in the background until around midnight, when they crank up the volume and bring out the cocktails as Puerto Bambú turns into a bar. ✉*Av. Brasil 96, 3370* ☎*3757/42–1900* ✍*Reservations not accepted* ▤*No credit cards.*

WHERE TO STAY

Once you've decided which country to base yourself in, the next big decision is whether to stay in town or at the five-star hotel inside each park. If you're on a lightning one-night visit and you only want to see one side of the falls, the convenience of staying inside the park might offset the otherwise unreasonably high prices for mediocre levels of luxury. Otherwise, you get much better value for money at the establishments in town or on highways BR 489 (Rodavia das Cataratas) in Brazil, or RN 12 in Argentina. During the day you're a 20-minute bus ride from the falls and the border, and at night you're closer to restaurants and nightlife (buses stop running to the park after 7 or 8; after that, it's a 70-peso taxi ride into town from the park). Hotels in Argentina are generally cheaper than in Brazil. During low season (late September–early-November and February–May, excluding Easter), rooms are often heavily discounted.

⚠**Staying on the Brazilian side (apart from at the Hotel das Cataratas in the park) is not recommended. It's dangerous, especially after dark, more expensive, and the hotels are worse.**

FOZ DO IGUAÇU

$$$$ ★ **Hotel das Cataratas.** Not only is this stately hotel *in* the national park, with views of the smaller falls from the front-side suites, but it also provides the traditional comforts of a colonial-style establishment: large rooms, terraces, vintage furniture, and hammocks. The main building, surrounded by verandas and gardens, is almost 100 years old and is a National Heritage Site. Although the rooms are comfortable, it's the setting and atmosphere that you pay for, rather than luxury fittings. Still, for many, the chance to wander the paths to the falls before and after the hordes of day visitors arrive is priceless. The Itaipú restaurant serves traditional Brazilian dinners, including feijoada and a variety of side dishes. There's also an all-you-can-eat barbecue and salad buffet each night in the Ipê grill near the pool. The hotel is undergoing extensive renovations through 2009: it will remain open, but with fewer rooms. **Pros:** Right inside the park, a short walk from the falls; serious colonial-style charm; friendly, helpful staff. **Cons:** Rooms aren't as luxurious as the price promises; far from Foz do Iguaçu so you're limited to the on-site restaurants; only the most expensive suites have views of the falls. ✉*Km 28, Rodovia das Cataratas, 85853-000* ☎*045/2102–7000 or 0800/726–4545* ⊕*www.hoteldascataratas.com. br* 🛏*198 rooms, 5 suites* ⚒*In-room: safes, refrigerator. In-hotel: 2 restaurants, tennis courts, pool, gym, laundry service, Internet, airport shuttle* ▤*AE, MC, V* ⋈*CP.*

$$ 🛏️**Hotel Florença Iguassu.** In a sprawling wooded lot on the road to the national park, Florença combines budget rates with excellent service. The rooms are nothing special but are spacious and clean, with walk-in closets and views of the gardens. The huge outdoor pool is perfect for post-falls lounging and for getting in some laps. **Pros:** Peaceful, natural surroundings; close to Brazilian park and to the border with Argentina; good value for money. **Cons:** Far from town center and restaurants; bland on-site restaurant; dead zone at night. ⊠*Km 13.7, Rodovia das Cataratas, 85863-000* 🕾*045/3529–7755* ⊕*www.hotelflorenca.com* ⮝*63 rooms* ⌂*In-room: refrigerator. In-hotel: restaurant, bar, tennis court, pool* ⊟*AE, MC, V* ⍾❘*CP.*

$ 🛏️**Hotel Foz Presidente II.** The main draw of this rather ugly budget hotel is the downtown location, which is useful if you need easy access to Foz's shopping malls, restaurants, and the business district. Rooms are small and nondescript, with generic motel-like furniture. They do have queen-size beds, however, and look out onto downtown Foz. **Pros:** Close to restaurants; big beds; decent breakfast spread. **Cons:** Basic rooms; not very convenient for the falls; area can be dangerous after dark. ⊠*Av. Marechal Floriano 1851, 85851-020* 🕾*045/3572–4450* ⮝*115 rooms* ⌂*In-room: refrigerator. In-hotel: pool, bar, laundry service, public Internet* ⊟*AE, MC, V* ⍾❘*CP.*

$ 🛏️**Hotel Tarobá Express.** Bright, modern-looking rooms set this hotel apart from most of the budget offerings in downtown Foz. Some are rather cramped, but all are kept spotless and make a fine base to return to after all-day falls visits. A pleasant roof deck with a small but attractive pool, a tiny gym, and Wi-Fi make the low prices even more appealing. Foz's shopping malls, restaurants, and business district are close by. **Pros:** Clean and cheerful rooms; relaxing pool area; good value for money. **Cons:** Street noise; area can be dangerous after dark; not particularly convenient for visiting either park. ⊠*Rua Tarobá 1048, 85851-221* 🕾*045/2101–7770* ⮝*82 rooms* ⌂*In-room: refrigerator, Wi-Fi. In-hotel: restaurant, room service, pool, gym, laundry facilities* ⊟*AE, MC, V* ⍾❘*CP.*

PUERTO IGUAZÚ

$$$$ 🛏️**Sheraton International Iguazú.** That thundering you can hear in the distance lets you know how close this hotel is to the falls. The lobby opens right onto the park trails and half the rooms have big balconies with fabulous falls views—be sure to reserve one of these well in advance (note that they're about 30% more expensive). The proximity is what you pay for: the rooms are perfectly serviceable, but the dated furniture, worn bathrooms, and drab linens aren't up to the price. And although the spa is a step in the right direction, with a gorgeous hot tub and treatment tents on an outdoor deck, you have to pay extra to use it. You can see the rising mist over the falls from the beautiful swimming pool, which is surrounded by palm trees and jungle. **Pros:** The falls are on your doorstep; great buffet breakfasts; well-designed spa. **Cons:** Drab rooms are in need of a complete makeover; mediocre food and service at dinner; other restaurants are an expensive taxi ride away. ⊠*Parque Nacional Iguazú, Argentina 3370* 🕾*3757/49–1800* ⊕*www.sheraton.com* ⮝*176 rooms, 4 suites* ⌂*In-room: refrigerator,* *safe.* In-hotel: 2 restaurants, room service, 2 pools, gym, spa, tennis courts, laundry service, airport shuttle, public Internet, no-smoking rooms ⊟AE, DC, MC, V.

$$$ ⚀**Panoramic Hotel Iguazú.** The falls aren't the only good views in Iguazú:
★ half the rooms of this chic hotel look onto the churning, jungle-framed waters of the Iguazú and Paraná rivers. The view inside the rooms is lovely, too. Taupe throws and ocher pillow shams offset the clean lines of the contemporary dark wood furniture. You don't miss out on luxury by booking a standard, as all have king-size beds, flat-screen TVs, and hot tubs. Even the pool, set on a large terrace, looks over the river. The view gets seriously panoramic from the top-floor bar, one of the best sundowner spots in town. **Pros:** River views; great attention to detail in the beautifully designed rooms; the gorgeous pool. **Cons:** The in-house casino can make the lobby noisy; indifferent staff aren't up to the price tag; it's a short taxi ride to the town center and in-house transport is over-priced. ⊠*Paraguay 372, 3370* ☎*3757/49–8133* ⊕*www. panoramic-hoteliguazu.com* ⚟*91 rooms* ⌂*In-room: safe, refrigerator, Wi-Fi. In-hotel: 3 restaurants, bar, pool, public Internet, no-smoking rooms* ⊟*AE, MC, V* ��*CP.*

$ ⚀**Secret Garden Iguazú.** Dense tropical vegetation overhangs the wooden walkway that leads to this tiny guesthouse's three rooms, tucked away in a pale blue clapboard house. There's nothing fancy about them, but the wood and wicker furniture and brightly painted paneling are cheerful and welcoming. So is the owner, John Fernandes. He's full of information and advice about Iguazú, which he shares with you over high-octane caipirinhas at the nightly cocktail sessions. **Pros:** Wooden deck overlooking the back-to-nature garden; knowledgeable owner John's charm and expert mixology; home-from-home vibe. **Cons:** The three rooms book up fast; no pool; comfortable but not luxurious. ⊠*Los Lapachos 623, 3370* ☎*3757/42–3099* ⊕*www.secretgar deniguazu.com* ⚟*3 rooms* ⌂*In-room: Wi-Fi, no phone, no TV* ⊟*No credit cards* ⓞ*CP.*

¢ ⚀**Hostel-Inn Iguazú.** An enormous turquoise pool surrounded by classy wooden loungers and well-kept gardens lets you know this hostel is far from typical. Spacious double rooms with private bathrooms, huge windows and lots of light attract couples and families. Partying backpackers love the great-value dorm accommodations (but be sure to book one with a/c) and organized weekend bar expeditions. The Hostel-Inn is on the road halfway between Puerto Iguazú and the falls so you can get to the park early, but you're only a short bus or taxi ride from the restaurants and bars in town. You can sort out excursions, including visa-less visits to the Brazilian side, through the in-house travel agency. The kitchen churns out simple sandwiches, salads, and burgers, and there's an all-out asado several times a week. **Pros:** Beautiful pool area; rooms are simple but clean and well designed; location between town and the falls gives you the best of both worlds. **Cons:** Impersonal service from indifferent staff; lounge and kitchen are rundown; very basic breakfast. ⊠*Ruta 12, Km 5, 3370* ☎*3757/42–1823* ⊕*www.hostel-inn.com* ⚟*52 rooms* ⌂*In-room: Wi-Fi, no phone, no*

5

TV (some), no a/c (some). In-hotel: dining room, pool, bar, laundry service, public Internet, no elevator ⊟*No credit cards* ⦿|CP.

¢ ⬚Río Tropic. Friendly owners Rémy and Romina give you a warm wel-
★ come at this rootsy B&B, which is surrounded by a lush garden. Rooms open onto a shady veranda that runs all the way along the wooden building; from there it's a few more steps to the pool. Pine paneling gives the rooms a country vibe, and though simple, they're spotlessly clean and have firm beds. **Pros:** The wonderfully helpful and attentive owners; peaceful surroundings; abundant homemade breakfasts served on a terrace in the garden. **Cons:** Too far from the town center to walk to; the rooms with no a/c are stuffy in summer; low on luxury. ⊠*Montecarlo s/n, at Km 5, RN 12, 3370* ☎*3757/15–41–6764* ⊕*www.rio tropic.com.ar* ⬚*10 rooms* ⬥*In-room: no a/c (some), no phone, no TV. In-hotel: bar, pool, bicycles* ⊟*No credit cards* ⦿|CP.

SANTA CATARINA

The state of Santa Catarina, the South's smallest state, has almost 485 km (300 mi) of coastline (with many gorgeous beaches). The capital, Florianópolis, is on Ilha de Santa Catarina, an island with 42 beaches and many world-class hotels and resorts that has become a major travel destination in Brazil. North and south of Florianópolis along the coast are other great destinations, where thousands of Brazilian and foreign tourists flock every summer. Santa Catarina is also home to the German settlements of Blumenau and Joinville, in the northern valleys. These highly industrialized cities still retain some of their German flavor, including a popular Oktoberfest.

BLUMENAU

250 km (156 mi) northwest of Florianópolis.

The cradle of the prosperous Vale do Itajaí region, Blumenau is a pleasant city of more than 260,000, with clean streets and friendly people. Its name is indicative of its German origins. Downtown has been restored to preserve the early German *enxaimel* architectural style of half-timber and half-brick construction, which is called *Fachwerk* in German (it resembles the Tudor style).

TO & FROM

The closest major airport is in Florianópolis. Regular buses by Catarinense to Blumenau from Florianópolis take two hours (R$30) and from Curitiba take four hours (R$44). By car, Blumenau can be reached from north (Curitiba) or south (Porto Alegre and Florianópolis) by BR 101. Once you reach the port city of Itajaí, go west for about 60 km (37 mi) either on BR 470 (wide, but with heavy traffic) or on SC 470 (narrow, but safer, with lights all the way).

ESSENTIALS

Banks & Currency Exchange Banco do Brasil (⊠*Rua XV de Novembro 1305, Centro, 89010-003*).

Continued on page 258

IGUAZÚ FALLS

By Victoria Patience

Big water. That's what *y-guasu*—the name given to the falls by the indigenous Guaraní people—means. As you approach, a thundering fills the air and steam rises above the trees. Then the jungle parts. Spray-soaked and speechless, you face the Devil's Throat, and it's clear that "big" doesn't come close to describing this wall of water.

Taller than Niagara, wider than Victoria, Iguazú's raging, monumental beauty is one of nature's most awe-inspiring sights. The Iguazú River, on the border between Argentina and Brazil, plummets 200 feet to form the Cataratas de Iguazú (as the falls are known in Spanish) or Foz do Iguaçu (their Portuguese name). Considered to be one waterfall, Iguazú is actually made up of around 275 individual drops, that stretch along 2.7 km (1.7 mi) of cliff-face. Ranging from picturesque cascades to immense cataracts, this incredible variety is what makes Iguazú so special. National parks in Brazil and Argentina protect the falls and the flora and fauna that surround them. Exploring their jungle-fringed trails can take two or three days: you get right alongside some falls, gaze down dizzily into others, and can take in the whole spectacle from afar. You're sure to come across lizards, emerald- and sapphire-colored hummingbirds, clouds of butterflies, and scavenging raccoonlike coatis. You'll also glimpse monkeys and toucans, if you're lucky.

GEOLOGY 101

Over 100 million years ago, lava surged up through cracks in the earth's crust near Iguazú. It spread out over the surrounding area, forming three layers of basalt (a dark, fine-grained rock) tens of meters high. The Iguazú River, which starts 1,200 km (745 mi) east, flowed over this. Later, the movement of tectonic plates raised parts of the surface, which became stepped. As the river flowed over these steps it eroded the rock surface it fell on even more, and over the next few million years, the waters carved out what are now the falls.

WHEN TO GO

Time of year	Advantages	Disadvantages
Nov.—Feb.	High rainfall in December and January, so expect lots of water.	Hot and sticky. December and January are popular with local visitors. High water levels stop Zodiac rides.
Mar.—Jun.	Increasingly cooler weather. Fewer local tourists. Water levels are usually good.	Too cold for some people, especially when you get wet. Occasional freak water shortages.
Jul.—Oct.	Cool weather.	Low rainfall in July and August—water levels can be low. July is peak season for local visitors.

WHERE TO GO: ARGENTINA VS. BRAZIL

Argentines and Brazilians can fight all day about who has the best angle on the falls. But the two sides are so different that comparisons are academic. To really say you've done Iguazú (or Iguaçu), you need to visit both. If you twist our arm, we'll say the Argentine side is a better experience with lots more to do, but (and this is a big "but") the Brazilian side gives you a tick in the box and the best been-there-done-that photos. It's also got more non-falls-related activities (but you have to pay extra for them).

	ARGENTINA	BRAZIL
Park Name	Parque Nacional Iguazú	Parque Nacional do Iguaçu
The experience	Up close and personal (you're going to get wet).	What a view!
The falls	Two-thirds are in Argentina including Garganta del Diablo, the star attraction.	The fabulous panoramic perspective of the Garganta do Diablo is what people really come for.
Timing	One day to blitz the main attractions. Two days to explore fully.	Half a day to see the falls; all day if you do other activities.
Other activities	Extensive self-guided hiking and Zodiac rides.	Organized hikes, Zodiac rides, boat rides, helicopter rides, rafting, abseiling.
Park size	67,620 hectares (167,092 acres)	182,262 hectares (450,379 acres)
Animal species	80 mammals/450 birds	50 mammals/200 birds

VITAL STATISTICS

Number of falls: 160—275*	Total length: 2.7 km (1.7 mi)	Average Flow: 396,258 gallons per second Peak Flow: 1,717,118 gallons per second
Major falls: 19	Height of Garganta del Diablo: 82 m (270 feet)	Age: 120—150 million years

*Depending on water levels

IGUAZÚ FALLS

5

IGUAZÚ ITINERARIES

LIGHTNING VISIT. If you only have one day, limit your visit to the Argentine park. Arrive when it opens, and get your first look at the falls aboard one of Iguazú Jungle Explorer's Zodiacs. The rides finish at the Circuito Inferior: take a couple of hours to explore this. (Longer summer opening hours give you time to squeeze in the **Isla San Martín**.) Grab a quick lunch at the Dos Hermanas snack bar, then blitz the shorter Circuito Superior. You've kept the best

for last: catch the train from **Estación Cataratas** to **Estación Garganta del Diablo**, where the trail to the viewing platform starts (allow at least two hours for this).

BEST OF BOTH SIDES. Two days gives you enough time to see both sides of the falls. Visit the Brazilian park on your second day to get the panoramic take on what you've experienced up-close in Argentina. If you arrive at 9 AM, you've got time to walk the entire trail, take photos, have lunch in the Porto Canoas service area, and be back at the park entrance by 1 PM. You could spend the afternoon doing excursions and activities from Macuco Safari

and Macuco EcoAventura, or visiting the Itaipú dam. Alternatively, you could keep the visit to Brazil for the afternoon of the second day, and start off with a lightning return visit to the Argentine park (half-price entrance on second visit) and see the **Garganta del Diablo** (left) with the sun rising behind it.

SEE IT ALL. With three days you can explore both parks at a leisurely pace. Follow the one-day itinerary, then return to the Argentine park on your second day. Make a beeline for the Garganta del Diablo, which looks different in the mornings, then spend the afternoon exploring the **Sendero Macuco** (and Isla San Martín, if you didn't have time on the first day). You'll also have time to visit Güira Oga bird sanctuary or La Aripuca (both on RN 12) afterwards. You could spend all of your third day in the Brazilian park, or just the morning, giving you time to catch an afternoon flight or bus.

IGUAZÚ FALLS

5

Estación Cataratas

Estación Central

Circuito Superior

Parque Nacional Iguazú

Circuito Inferior

Dos Hermanas

KEY

♿ *Wheelchair-accessible*
🍽 *Restaurant*
🌿 *Scenic Viewpoint*
--- *Walking/Hiking Trails*
⛴ *Ferry Lines*
┼┼┼ *Rail Lines*

VISITING THE PARKS

Visitors gaze at the falls in Parque Nacional Iguazú.

Argentina's side of the falls is in the **Parque Nacional Iguazú**, which was founded in 1934 and declared a World Heritage Site in 1984. The park is divided into two areas, each of which is organized around a train station: Estación Cataratas or the Estación Garganta del Diablo. (A third, Estación Central, is near the park entrance.)

Paved walkways lead from the main entrance past the **Visitor Center,** called *Yvyrá Retá*—"country of the trees" in Guaraní (☎ 3757/49-1469 ⊕ www.iguazuargentina.com ✉ 40 pesos; 20 pesos on second day ⊘ Apr.–Sep 8–6; Oct.–Mar. 7:30–6:30). Colorful visual displays provide a good explanation of the region's ecology and human history. To reach the park proper, you cross through a small plaza containing a food court, gift shops, and ATM. From the nearby Estación Central, the gas-propelled Tren de la Selva (Jungle Train) departs every 20 minutes.

In Brazil, the falls can be seen from the **Parque Nacional Foz do Iguaçu** (☎45/3521–4400 ⊕ www.cataratasdoiguacu.com.br ✉ R$20.50 ⊘ Apr.–Sep 9–5; Oct.–Mar. 9–6). Much of the park is protected rain forest—off-limits to

visitors and home to the last viable populations of panthers as well as rare flora. Buses and taxis drop you off at a vast, plaza alongside the park entrance building. As well as ticket booths, there's an ATM, a snack bar, gift shop, and information and currency exchange. Next to the entrance turnstiles is the small **Visitor Center,** where helpful geological models explain how the falls were formed. Double-decker buses run every 15 minutes between the entrance and the trailhead to the falls, 11 km (7 mi) away; the buses stop at the entrances to excursions run by private operators Macuco Safari and Macuco Ecoaventura (these aren't included in your ticket). The trail ends in the **Porto Canoas** service area. There's a posh linen-service restaurant with river views, and two fast-food counters the with tables overlooking the rapids leading to the falls.

VISAS

U.S. citizens don't need a visa to visit Argentina as tourists, but the situation is more complicated in Brazil. ⇨ See the planning section at the beginning of the chapter.

IGUAZÚ FALLS

5

EXCURSIONS IN AND AROUND THE PARKS

A Zodiac trip to the falls.

Iguazú Jungle Explorer (☎ 3757/42–1696 ⊕ www.iguazujungleexplorer.com) runs trips within the Argentine park. Their standard trip, the Gran Aventura, costs 100 pesos and includes a truck ride through the forest and a Zodiac ride to San Martín, Bossetti, and the Salto Tres Mosqueteros (be ready to get soaked). The truck carries so many people that most animals are scared away: you're better off buying the 50-peso boat trip—Aventura Nautica—separately.

You can take to the water on the Brazilian side with **Macuco Safari** (☎ 045/3574–4244 ⊕ www.macucosafari.com.br). Their signature trip is a Zodiac ride around (and under) the Salto Tres Mosqueteros. You get a more sedate ride on the Iguaçu Explorer, a 3½ hour trip up the river.

It's all about adrenaline with **Iguazú Forest** (☎ 3757/42–1140 ⊕ www.iguazuforest.com). Their full day expedition involves kayaking, abseiling, waterfall-climbing, mountain-biking, and canopying all within the Argentine park.

In Brazil, **Cânion Iguaçu** (☎ 045/3529–6040 ⊕ www.campodedesafios.com.br) offers rafting and canopying, as well as abseiling over the river from the Salto San Martín. They also offer wheelchair-compatible equipment.

Argentine park ranger Daniel Somay organizes two-hour Jeep tours with an ecological focus through his Puerto Iguazú–based **Explorador Expediciones** (☎ 3757/42–1632 ⊕ www.hotelguia.com/turismo/explorador-expediciones). The tours cost 50 pesos and include detailed explanations of the Iguazú ecosystem and lots of photo ops. A specialist leads the birdwatching trips, which cost 215 pesos and include the use of binoculars.

Macuco Ecoaventura (☎ 045/3529–6927 ⊕ www.macucoecoaventura.com.br) is one of the official tour operators within the Brazilian park. Their Trilha do Pozo Negro combines a 9-km guided hike or bike ride with a scary boat trip along the upper river (the bit before the falls). The aptly-named Floating trip is more leisurely; shorter jungle hikes are also offered.

ON THE CATWALK

You spend most of your visit to the falls walking the many trails and catwalks, so be sure to wear comfortable shoes.

Bus Contacts **Terminal Rodoviário (Bus Terminal) Herciolio Deeke** (⊠*Rua 2 de Setembro 1222, 89052-000*).

Emergencies & Medical Assistance **Ambulance** (☎*192*). **Fire** (☎*193*). Hospital: **Hospital Santa Catarina** (⊠*Rua Amazonas 301, Garcia, 89020-900* ☎*047/3036–6004*). Pharmacy: **Drogaria Capilé** (⊠*Rua XV de Novembro 895, Centro, 89010-001* ☎*047/3035–5903*). **Police** (☎*190*).

> ### PROST!
>
> During Blumenau's annual three-week-long Oktoberfest, attended by hordes of southerners, almost 100,000 gallons of beer and matching amounts of wurst and sauerkraut are consumed, to the sound of German folk music.

Taxi **Ponto de Taxi Ingo Hering** (☎*047/3322–6639*).

Visitor & Tour Info **Central de Informações Turíisticas** (⊠*Rua XV de Novembro 420, Centro, 89010-000* ☎*047/3322–6933* ⊕*www.blumenau.com.br* ⌖*Open daily 9–5*).

SAFETY & PRECAUTIONS

Bluemenau is generally safe, but avoid walking around downtown at night. During the Oktoberfest festival weekends, when town is packed with tourists, mugging and pickpocketing might be an issue, especially late at night.

WHAT TO SEE

For insight into the history of German immigration, check out the **Museu da Família Colonial** (*Colonial Family Museum*). The house, which was built in 1864 for the Gaertner family, some of the first settlers to the area, contains a collection of everyday objects that belonged to the city's first residents; its garden has many examples of regional flora. ⊠*Rua Duque de Caxias 78, Centro, 89015-010* ☎*047/3322–1676* ⊡*R$2* ⊗*Tues.–Fri. 8–6, Sat. 9–4, Sun. 9–noon.*

The Blumenau area is home to an important glassware industry, whose high-quality products are aimed at the discriminating customer. At **Glaspark** you can see artisans at work, learn about the industry at a museum, and buy designer glassware at reasonable prices. ⊠*Rua Rudolf Roedel 147, Salto Weisbach, 89032-080* ☎*047/3327–1261* ⊡*Free* ⊗*Mon.–Sat. 9–6.*

WHERE TO STAY & EAT

$$–$$$ ✕**Frohsinn.** On the outskirts of town is one of the best German restaurants in the region, in an enxaimel-style building constructed in 1968. The big windows allow a grand view of the city below. The *marreco com repolho* (stuffed duck served with mashed potatoes, cassava, and red cabbage) is a regional specialty. Dessert options include German pastries such as apple strudel. ⊠*Rua Gertrud Sierich 940, Morro do Aipim, 89015-210* ☎*047/3322–2137* ⊟*AE, DC, MC, V.*

$ ✕🖬**Plaza Blumenau.** Check in if you're looking for great facilities and convenient location. Rooms have a sober decor, with dark-wood furnishings and bluish carpeting. Some bathroms have whirlpool baths. The Terrace restaurant ($–$$) serves international cuisine with an emphasis on things German. **Pros:** Close to downtown, comfortable facilities. **Cons:** Some bathrooms are small, some rooms need upgrading. ⊠*Rua 7 de Setembro 818, Centro, 89010-200* ☎*047/3231–7000 or 0800/47–1213* ⊕*www.plazahoteis.com.br* ⌂*123 rooms, 8 suites* &*In-room: safe, refrigerator, Wi-Fi. In-hotel: restaurant, bar, pool, gym, public Internet, no-smoking rooms* ☰*AE, DC, MC, V* ❙◎❙*CP.*

SHOPPING

H Shopping (⊠*Rua 15 de Novembro 759, Centro, 89010-000* ☎*047/3326–2166*) has an outlet of the Hering textile and apparel company, a traditional brand of casual cottonwear in Brazil. Other shops sell locally produced glassware and china.

PORTO BELO

69 km (43 mi) north of Florianópolis.

The seafront town of Porto Belo lies at the base of a peninsula dotted with beaches, bays, and coves, and it has a great reputation among Argentine and Paraguayan tourists for its natural beauty, nice beaches, and many water sports. It's a port of call for some of the Buenos Aires–Rio cruise lines. The calm waters of the Porto Belo bay are a haven for scuba diving, snorkeling, sailing, and fishing. Porto Belo is an ideal base for exploring the paradisiacal landscapes of the region.

TO & FROM

Porto Belo can be reached by car or bus from Florianópolis. If driving, take BR 101 north for about 60 km (37 mi) to the intersection with SC 412. From there it's about 6 km (4 mi) west to Porto Belo. Catarinense (contact the bus terminal for tickets) operates the bus line between Porto Belo and Florianópolis (1 hour; R$25).

ESSENTIALS

Carry local currency to Porto Belo, as there's no exchange in the area.

Bus Contacts Terminal Rodoviário (Bus Terminal) (⊠*Rua Cap. Gualberto Leal Nunes 93, 88210-000*).

Emergencies & Medical Assistance Ambulance (☎*192*). **Fire** (☎*193*). Hospital: **Hospital Santa Inês** (⊠*Av. Estado 1690, Centro, 88339-060* ☎*047/3367–4411*). Pharmacy: **Farmais** (⊠*Av. Gov Celso Ramos 2384, Centro, 88210-000* ☎*047/3369–4522*). **Police** (☎*190*).

Taxi Ponto de Táxi Rodoviaria (☎*047/3369-4513*).

Visitor & Tour Info Get tourist information in Florianópolis before coming to Porto Belo. Hotel staff can also be helpful in providing information on the area.

WHERE TO STAY & EAT

$$$ ✕▢**Refúgio do Estaleiro.** On a hill overlooking the sea, this hotel opened in 2004. Rooms are rustic, but comfortably furnished and spacious. All have verandas with lush wicker chairs. Both of its restaurants are highly regarded: Pizzeria do Refúgio ($$) and Estaleiro ($$$), which serves seafood. **Pros:** Prime location, extra-comfortable room furnishings. **Cons:** Far from beach. ⊠*Rua Flavia Martelini 400, 88210-000* ☎⌂*047/3369–8282* ⊕*www.refugiodoestaleiro.com.br* ⌂*14 apart-*

ments, 4 chalets ⌂*In room: safe, refrigerator, ethernet. In-hotel: 2 restaurants, bar, pool, gym, tennis court, parking (no fee)* ▭*AE, DC, MC, V* ⦿*MAP.*

$–$$ ⌨**Baleia Branca.** There are plenty of amenities to recommend this hotel, but the short distance to the beach is certainly the highlight. The hotel is on a 20-acre lot, groomed as a tropical garden. Accommodations include rooms in the main building and chalets of different sizes spread around the grounds, convenient for larger parties. The all-white rooms are small but beds are comfortable. Expect impeccable service from one of the first hotels to open in the area. **Pros:** Great service, great views, many amenities. **Cons:** Rooms are small, far from town. ✉*Alameda Nena Trevisan 100, 88210-000* ☎*047/3369–4011* ⊕*www.hotelbaleiabranca.com.br* ⇆*43 apartments, 11 chalets* ⌂*In room: safe, refrigerator. In-hotel: restaurant, bar, pool, playground, children's programs (ages 5–12), beachfront, public Internet, parking (no fee)* ▭*V* ⦿*MAP.*

ILHA DE SANTA CATARINA

300 km (187 mi) southeast of Curitiba, 476 km (296 mi) northeast of Porto Alegre.

Its nickname is "Magic Island," which is an appropriate moniker for this island with breathtaking shoreline, 42 easy-to-reach beaches—some with warm waters—and seemingly endless vacation activities. Every summer (December–March), thousands of Argentines arrive here, adding to the constant influx of Brazilians, making this one of the country's top tourist destinations. The island's northern *praias* (beaches) are considered the best—because of their warm waters—and are therefore the busiest. Impressive seascapes dominate the Atlantic beaches, and southern beaches have fewer sun worshippers and a more laid-back atmosphere. Scuba diving, surfing, sailing, and parasailing are among the many water sports. You can also go for nature walks along trails with the ocean as backdrop.

The city of **Florianópolis** played an important part in the history of the island of Santa Catarina. Settled by colonists from the Azore Islands, it was the southernmost post of the Portuguese empire for some time, and it was the site of several skirmishes with the Spanish before the border disputes were settled. You might be lured by the beaches—which rank among the most beautiful in Brazil—but downtown Florianópolis also has worthwhile attractions.

▣ **TIP→Note that Brazilians tend to refer to all of Santa Catarina island as "Florianópolis," and all the beaches and forts on the island are under the city's jurisdiction.**

TO & FROM

Flights from São Paulo to Florianópolis are about an hour in length. The Aeroporto Internacional Hercílio Luz is 12 km (8 mi) south of downtown Florianópolis. Taking a cab into town costs about R$45. In addition, there's *amarelinho* (minibus) service for R$10.

Several bus companies have regular service to and from Florianópolis's Terminal Rodoviário Rita Maria. For the 12-hour journey to São Paulo, the 2-hour trip to Blumenau, or the 14-hour trip to Foz do Iguaçu, use Catarinense. Pluma buses travel to Curitiba (5 hours). União Cascavel/Eucatur and Catarinense travel to Porto Alegre (6 hours).

To drive to Ilha de Santa Catarina from the mainland, take the BR 262 exit off BR 101. Downtown Florianópolis is 7 km (4½ mi) from the exit. The island is joined to the mainland by two bridges: the modern, multilane Ponte Colombo Sales and the now condemned 60-year-old Ponte Hercilio Luz.

GETTING AROUND

Attractions are spread about the island, so a rental car is recommended. A quick, convenient way to visit the beaches is by *amarelinho* (also called *executivo*), express minibuses that cost about R$8. They leave regularly from designated places around Praça XV and are convenient if you plan to spend the day in one beach. If you want to move about and see different beaches and attractions in one day, a car is your only viable option.

ESSENTIALS

Airport Aeroporto Internacional Hercílio Luz (*FLN* ⊠*Km 12, Av. Deomício Freitas 3393, Carianos, 88047-402 Florianópolis* ☎*048/3331–4000*).

Banks & Currency Exchange Amplestur (⊠*Rua Jerônimo Coelho 293, Loja 01, Centro, 88010-030 Florianópolis*). **Banco do Brasil** (⊠*Praça 15 de Novembro 321, Centro, 88010-400 Florianópolis* ⊠*Aeroporto Internacional Hercílio Luz, Av. Dep. Diomício Freitas 3393, Carianos, 88047-900 Florianópolis* ☞*24-hour ATM*).

Bus Contacts Catarinense (☎*048/3222–2260*). **Pluma** (☎*048/3223—1709 and 0300-789–1300*). **Terminal Rodoviário (Bus Terminal) Rita Maria** (⊠*Av. Paulo Fontes 1101, Centro, 88010-230 Florianópolis* ☎*048/212–3100*). **União Cascavel/Eucatur** (☎*048/3222–1468*).

Emergencies & Medical Assistance Ambulance (☎*192*). **Fire** (☎*193*). Hospital: **Hospital Universitário** (⊠*Av. Beira-Mar Norte, Trindade, 88040-970 Florianópolis* ☎*048/3271–9100*). Pharmacy: **Farmácia SES** (⊠*Av. Prof. Othon Gama Deca 900, Centro, 88015-240 Florianópolis* ☎*048/3222–5966*). **Police** (☎*190*).

Taxi Radio taxi (☎*3240–6009*).

Visitor & Tour Info Amplestur (⊠*Rua Jerônimo Coelho 293, Loja 01, Centro, 88010-030 Florianópolis* ☎*048/2108–9422* ⊕*www.amplestur.com.br* ☞*Van tours of city, beaches, and more*). **Portal Turístico** (⊠*Rua Eng. Max de Souza 236, Coqueiros, mainland side of Ponte Colombo Sales (Colombo Sales Bridge), 88080-000Florianópolis* ☎*048/3348–9439* ⊕*www.pmf.sc.gov.br/turismo* ⊠*Terminal Rodoviária Rita Maria, Av. Paulo Fontes 1101, Centro, 88010-230 Florianópolis* ☎*048/3328–1095*). **SanTur** (*State Tourism Authority* ⊠*Rua Felipe Schmidt 249, 9th fl., Centro, 88810-902 Florianópolis* ☎*048/3212–6300 or 048/3212–6315* ⊕*www.sol.sc.gov.br/santur*).

SAFETY & PRECAUTIONS

Florianópolis is essentially a safe city and the beaches around the island even more so. Theft is occasionally a problem on beaches and during the crowded New Year's and Carnaval celebrations.

EXPLORING

MAIN ATTRACTIONS

Museu Histórico de Santa Catarina.
This museum is in the 18th-century baroque-and-neoclassical Palácio Cruz e Souza; its stairways are lined with Carrara marble. The sidewalks around the building are still paved with the original stones brought from Portugal. Exhibits revolve around state history: documents, personal items, and artwork that belonged to former governors (this used to be the governor's home). ⊠*Praça 15 de Novembro 227, Centro, 88010-400 Florianópolis* ☎*048/3228–8091* ⚹*Free* ⊙*Tues.– Fri. 10–6, weekends 10–4.*

Beyond the museum is the picturesque, 100-year-old **Mercado Público** *(Public Market)*, a Portuguese colonial structure with a large central patio. The original market was destroyed in a fire in 2005. The now-renovated market—filled with stalls selling fish, fruit, and vegetables—still preserves its Arabian-bazaar atmosphere. ⊠*Rua Cons. Mafra 255, Centro, 88010-200 Florianópolis* ☎*048/3225–3200* ⚹*Free* ⊙*Mon.– Sat. 7 AM–9 PM.*

Praia dos Ingleses *(Englishmen Beach)*. Named for a British sailboat that sank here in 1700, this narrow beach has an unparalleled lineup of hotels and restaurants for all budgets, making it one of the most popular beaches on the island. In summer Spanish with an Argentine accent is the local language. ⊠*34 km (21 mi) northeast of Florianópolis, North Island.*

★ **Praia da Joaquina.** Surfers have staked claims to this beach, the site of several surfing events, including one round of the world professional circuit. ⊠*15 km (9 mi) east of Florianópolis, Center Island.*

★ **Praia Jurerê.** Home to an upscale resort and condominiums, Jurerê normally has bigger waves than its neighbors. The increased development of beachfront hotels, restaurants, and shops has attracted many out-of-state visitors. ⊠*24 km (15 mi) north of Florianópolis, North Island.* .

Secluded **Praia da Lagoinha do Leste.** This secluded mile-long beach, with breathtaking views of the Atlantic surrounded by hills covered with lush tropical vegetation can only be reached by boat or by a steep, 5-km (3-mi) path that starts at the entrance of the Pântano do Sul village. ⊠*18 km (11 mi) south of Florianópolis, South Island.*

Praia Mole. Nudism is tolerated at this white-sand beach that mostly attracts surfers and foreign tourists. You can paraglide here, and there are a number of beachfront bars. ⊠*14 km (8.5 mi) east of Florianópolis, Center Island.*

> GET THE SCOOP

A reliable and up-to-date independent source about what's going on in Florianópolis is *Guia Floripa,* which is free and can be obtained at newsstands or online at ⊕*www.guiafloripa.com.br.*

IF YOU HAVE TIME

NEED A
BREAK?

Although small and somewhat cramped, Box 32 (⊠*Mercado Público, Rua Cons. Mafra 255, Centro, 88010-200 Florianópolis* ☎*048/3224–5588* ⊕*www.box32.com.br*) relives its tradition of being the meeting place for everyone from businesspeople to students. It has more than 800 kinds of liquor, including cachaça. Try the house specialty, *bolinho de bacalhau* (minced cod, formed into balls and fried) and the salmon carpaccio.

Praia do Canasvieiras. You're strongly advised to explore this sophisticated beach, which has calm, warm waters and great services and facilities. ⊠*27 km (17 mi) north of Florianópolis, North Island.*

Riberão da Ilha. One of the oldest Portuguese settlements on the island, this little fishing village with colonial houses overlooking the balmy ocean and the forest-clad mountains on the continent beyond is a rare find in this otherwise bustling island. There are several oyster farms in the area, the produce of which the visitor can try at beachfront restaurants ⊠*SC 401, 20 km (12.5 mi) south of Florianópolis, South Island.*

Praia do Pântano do Sul. This small beach community surrounded by hills has good restaurants and fishing-boat rides to other beaches and smaller islands nearby. ⊠*SC 406, 24 km (15 mi) south of Florianópolis, South Island. .*

WHERE TO STAY & EAT

$$–$$$

FodorśChoice
★

✕**Chef Fedoca.** This restaurant on the second floor of the Marina Ponta da Areia complex has a grand view of the Lagoa da Conceição, with surrounding green hills as the backdrop. The fare, carefully created by Chef Fedoca, a diver himself, includes a wide variety of seafood and pasta options. Fedoca's *moqueca* (a fish, shrimp, octopus, and mussel stew), inspired by the famed Bahian dish, is the house specialty. ⊠*Marina Ponta da Areia, Rua Sen. Ivo D'Aquino Neto 133, Lagoa da Conceição, Center Island, 88062-050* ☎*048/3232–0759* ▭*AE, DC, MC, V* ⊗*Closed Mon.*

$$–$$$ ✕**La Pergoletta Trattoria.** The variety of fresh pasta dishes is the highlight here. Try the pasta with shrimp, *kani kama* (ground crabmeat), and white-wine sauce. ⊠*Travessa Carreirão 62, Centro, 88015-540 Florianópolis* ☎*048/3224–6353* ⌕*Reservations essential* ▭*DC, MC, V* ⊗*Closed Mon.*

$$ ✕**Gugu.** This off-the-beaten-path restaurant combines no-frills service and undistinguished decor with an outstanding seafood menu. You can have the steamed oysters as an

SCHOONER TOURS

Scuna Sul (⊠*Rua Antonio Heil 605, Room 01, Canasvieiras, 88054-160 Florianópolis* ☎*048/3266–1810* ⊕*www.scunasul.com.br*) operates several schooner tours that visit some of the historic forts and various beautiful islands and traverse the Baía dos Golfinhos (Dolphin Bay), home to hundreds of gray dolphins. Tours range from approximately four to six hours and cost R$28–R$45. Scuna Sul plans to start a longer trip to Porto Belo in 2008. English-speaking staff is sometimes on hand to take reservations; otherwise, make arrangements through your hotel.

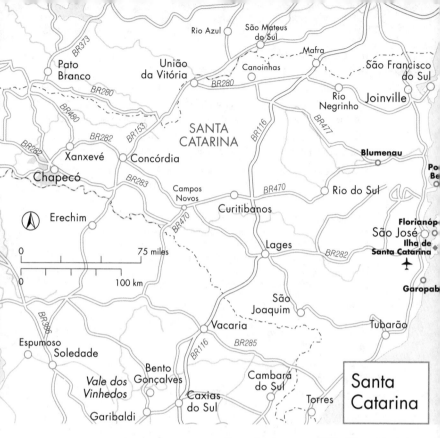

Santa Catarina

appetizer and move on to the seafood stew and fish fillet with shrimp sauce. ⊠*Rua Antonio Dias Carneiro 147, Sambaqui, North Island, 88051-200* ☎*048/3335–0288* ▬*DC, MC, V* ⊗*No lunch Mon.*

$ ✕**Ataliba.** You can expect nothing less than excellent service at this churrascaria in the business since 1977. The meat selections—more than 20 kinds, from beef to mutton and rabbit—and the salad bar are both outstanding. ⊠*Rua Irineu Bornhausen 5050, Agronomica, 88025-020 Florianópolis* ☎*048/3333–0990* ▬*AE, DC, MC, V* ⊗*No dinner Sun.*

$$$–$$$$ ✕▦**Jurerê Beach Village.** Renovated in 2006, this renowned hotel has **Fodor'sChoice** lush rooms with verandas, most of which give ample view of the beach. ★ Some are apartments with a small kitchen, perfect for longer stays. You're just steps from sophisticated Jurerê Beach. The efficient and attentive staff make you feel like a homeowner. The hotel is a prime destination for South American visitors, especially Argentines. The Z Perry restaurant ($$–$$$) serves international fare with seafood specialties. A minimum stay of one week is usually required in high season (December–March). **Pros:** Many amenities and sports, friendly staff. **Cons:** Expensive, some rooms small and cramped. ⊠*Alameda César Nascimento 646, Praia de Jurerê, North Island, 88053-000* ☎*048/3261–5100 or 0800/48–0110* ⊕*www.jurere.com.br/jbv* ⇱222

apartments ⟨In-room: safe, kitchen. In-hotel: 2 restaurants, bar, concierge, tennis court, pools, gym, beachfront, spa, water sports, airport
shuttle, beachfront ⊟AE, DC, MC, V †⊚MAP.

$$$$
Fodor'sChoice
★

⊞**Costão do Santinho Resort.** The ocean view from north-facing rooms
is one reason to stay at the island's most sophisticated resort; the surrounding 100-acre Atlantic Forest is another (there are several trails,
including one that leads to petroglyphs on the hill). The older buildings
have full apartments with mini kitchens, available for longer stays. A
new complex, opened in 2005, has traditional hotel rooms with modern decor. All have great ocean views. The list of activities is almost
unending: oriental martial arts, aerobics, surfing, sandboarding (like
snowboarding, but on sand), trekking. **Pros:** Many amenities, large
and comfortable rooms. **Cons:** Hectic when hosting conventions, service not as attentive in high season. ⊠*Rua Ver. Onildo Lemos 2505,
Praia do Santinho, North Island, 88001-970* ☏*048/3261–1000 or
0800/701–9000* ⊕*www.costao.com.br* ⤴*696 rooms* ⟨In-room: safe,
refrigerator. In-hotel: 6 restaurants, bars, tennis courts, pools, gym,
spa, beachfront, water sports, concierge, children's programs (ages 4–
6), public Internet, Wi-Fi, airport shuttle* ⊟AE, DC, MC, V †⊚MAP.

$$
⊞**Lexus Internacional Ingleses.** Although it has much to offer, this mid-
size hotel's main attraction is its location on the popular (and there-
fore crowded in high season) Praia dos Ingleses. The pool is one step
from the beach, making the Lexus a great place to enjoy the warm
northern waters. Choose the bay-facing apartments with balconies
where you can hang your hammock and feel the sea breeze. Rooms
are sleek, with colorful bedspreads and blond-wood furniture. **Pros:**
Great for extended stays, prime location. **Cons:** Crowded beach in
summer, rooms opposite the beach are noisy. ⊠*Rua Dom João Becker
859, Praia dos Ingleses, North Island, 88058-601* ☏*048/3269–2622*
⊕*www.hotellexus.com.br* ⤴*63 rooms* ⟨In-room: kitchen. In-hotel:
restaurant, bar, pool, beachfront* ⊟AE, DC, MC, V †⊚CP.

$–$$
⊞**Baía Norte.** Lush suites with hot tubs await discerning guests. Rooms
are meticulously furnished, and those facing west have a grand view of
the bay and Hercílio Luz Bridge. From here, quick access to the business district is guaranteed. Beaches are farther away, but access is easy.
Pros: Great service, great views. **Cons:** Cramped rooms, small bathrooms. ⊠*Av. Beira-Mar Norte 220, Centro, 88000-000 Florianópolis*
☏*048/3229–3144 or 0800/48–0202* ⊕*www.baianorte.com.br* ⤴*99
rooms, 9 suites* ⟨In room: safe, refrigerator. In-hotel: restaurant, bar,
pool, gym, bicycles, airport shuttle* ⊟AE, DC, MC, V †⊚CP.

¢
⊞**Íbis Florianópolis.** If you're looking for service and basic facilities like
those you can find back home, Íbis is a welcome retreat. Decor is undis-
tinguished, but almost all rooms have comfortable queen-size beds. It's
one of the few hotels in the area to offer rooms for people with disabilities. **Pros:** Modern facilities, convenient location for business travelers,
bargain price. **Cons:** Far from beaches, small common area. ⊠*Av. Rio
Branco 37, Centro, 88015-200 Florianópolis* ☏*048/3216–0000 or
0800/703–7000* ⊕*www.accorhotels.com.br* ⤴*198 rooms* ⟨In room:
safe, refrigerator. In-hotel: restaurant, bar, gym, public Internet* ⊟AE,
DC, MC, V.*

SPORTS & THE OUTDOORS

Sports lovers have much to keep them occupied on the island. Sandboarding, which is essentially snowboarding on sand, is practiced on the gigantic dunes at Praia da Joaquina. Windsurfing and jet skiing are popular on Lagoa da Conceição, but strict zoning rules are enforced and you must obtain a license by taking a course at an accredited outfitter or school—something most visitors won't have the time for.

Marina Ponta da Areia (⊠*Rua Sen. Ivo D'Aquino Neto 133, Lagoa da Conceição, Center Island, 88062-050* ☎*048/3232–2290*) is the place for boat rentals. Snorkeling and scuba diving are very popular on the northern beaches; check out **Parcel Dive Center** (⊠*Av. Luiz B. Piazza 3257, Cachoeira do Bom Jesus, 88056-000 Florianópolis* ☎*048/3284–5564* ⊕*www.parcel.com.br*) for internationally accredited diving lessons, diver's certification, and for equipment sale, maintenance, and rentals. The cost to rent basic gear is about R$275 a day. **OpenWinds** (⊠*Av. das Rendeiras 1672, Lagoa da Conceição, Center Island, 88062-400* ☎*048/3232–5004* ⊕*www.openwinds.com.br*) gives sandboarding, surfing, and windsurfing lessons; it also has a gear sales, rentals, and maintenance shop. A full course in windsurfing costs R$400. **Parapente Sul** (⊠*Rua João Antônio da Silveira 201, Lagoa da Conceição, Center Island, 88062-150* ☎☎*048/3232–0791* ⊕*www.parapentesul.com.br*), a center for parasailing—a popular sport on this mountainous, windy coast of Santa Catarina—leads tandem flights with an instructor for about R$150. For enthusiasts, a full course is available.

NIGHTLIFE

Florianópolis has an active night life, especially in summer. Listings of entertainment and cultural events can be found in the daily paper *Diario Catarinense*.

Just east of the city proper, the lively Lagoa da Conceição has popular bars and live-music venues. In summer expect heavy car and pedestrian traffic. **John Bull Pub** (⊠*Av. das Rendeiras 1046, Lagoa da Conceição, Center Island, 88062-400* ☎*048/3232–8535* ⊕*www.johnbullpub.com.br*) is *the* place for live music on the island. A roster of local and nationally known bands performs, from blues, rock and roll, and reggae to Brazilian popular music. It's also a great place for drinks and snacks. **Cachaçaria da Ilha** (⊠*Rua Osmar Cunha 164, Centro, 88015-100 Florianópolis* ☎*048/3224–0051*) is a popular bar at happy hour and a favorite meeting place for visitors. There are daily live-music performances (Brazilian and rock and roll) later in the evening.

GAROPABA

Fodor's Choice ★ 91 km (57 mi) south of Florianópolis, 380 (238 mi) northwest of Porto Alegre.

Around Garopaba you can find great beaches and sand dunes, green hills, and rocky cliffs that end right in the ocean. Praia do Rosa and Praia da Ferrugem have acquired national recognition for their awesome beauty and laid-back atmosphere. This is also prime sandboarding and surfing territory, but watching the *baleia-franca* (right whales) breeding grounds off the coast—scheduled to become a protected area—is quickly becoming popular. The warm waters here attract whales from Patagonia (especially from Peninsula Valdéz) July through November.

TO & FROM

To reach Garopaba, fly to Florianópolis and either drive or take a bus. PauloTur bus lines offers hourly service both ways, from 6 AM to 8 PM.

ESSENTIALS

Most hotels in Garopaba will provide public Internet access.

Banks & Currency Exchange **Banco do Brasil** (⌂*Rua João Orestes de Araújo 740, Centro, 88495-000* ☞*ATMs open 6 AM–10 PM*).

Bus Contacts **Estação Rodoviária (Bus Station)** (⌂*Praça Ivo Silveira 64, 88485-000*). **PauloTur** (☎*048/3244–2777* ⊕*www.paulotur.com.br*).

Emergencies & Medical Assistance **Ambulance** (☎*192*). **Fire** (☎*193*). Hospital: **Clinica Pronto Socorro GRB** (⌂*Rua 30 de Dezembro, Centro, 88485-000* ☎*048/3254–3275*). Pharmacy: **Farmax** (⌂*Rua Maria Antonia Santos 1, Centro, 88495-000* ☎*048/3354–1192*). **Police** (☎*190*).

Taxi **Ponto de Taxi** (☎*048/3254–3366*).

Visitor & Tour Info **Centro Atendimento ao Turista** (*Tourist Attention Center* ⌂*Praça Ivo Silveira 296, Centro, 88495-000* ☎*048/3254–2078* ☞*Open weekdays 8–noon and 1:30–5*).

WHERE TO STAY & EAT

$$ ✕⊞**PousadaVida, Sol e Mar.** This pousada combines easy access to the beach and several amenities, including OnoKaii ($–$$), one of the best seafood restaurants south of Florianópolis. A highlight here is the shrimp in squash and cheese sauce. There are rooms in the main building and in chalets spread out on the property, among palm trees and shrubbery. All chalets have grand views of the sea. Rooms are rustic, but very comfortable. An in-house operator works in conjunction with Instituto Baleia Franca (⇨Sports & Outdoors) to offer whale-watching boat trips (R$90/person on weekdays; R$140/person weekends). Surfing classes are also available. **Pros:** Great setting, close to beach, great for outdoor activities. **Cons:** Some bathrooms small, far from city. ⌂*Km 6, Estrada Geral da Praia do Rosa, 88780-0200Imbituba* ☎*048/3355–6111, 048/3254–4199 whale-watching* ⊕*www.vidasole mar.com.br* ⌐*26 rooms, 17 chalets* ⌂*In room: refrigerator. In-hotel: restaurant, bar, beachfront* ☰*MC, V.*

OFF THE BEATEN PATH

★ **Laguna.** The city of Laguna is the second-oldest Portuguese settlement in the state of Santa Catarina. Most downtown buildings reflect the early colonial days. Known for its many beaches, Laguna has one of the liveliest Carnival festivities of southern Brazil. Part of the city faces Lagoa Imaruí (Imaruí Lake), which connects to the Atlantic 5 km (3 mi) farther east. You can drive or hire a boat on the beaches to get to the Imaruí Lake delta, where exploring the imposing Santa Marta

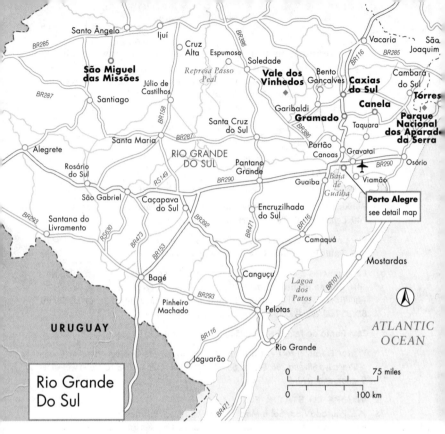

Rio Grande
Do Sul

Lighthouse and nearby beaches is well worth a day's outing. ✉ *62 km (38 mi) south of Garopaba on BR 101.*

SPORTS & OUTDOORS

Instituto Baleia Franca (*Right Whale Institute* ✉*Rua Manuel Álvaro de Araújo 186, Centro, 88495-000* ☎*048/3254–4198*) is a not-for-profit organization that provides whale-watching tours on Zodiacs from July to November, when right whales from Antarctica come to the warmer waters near Garopaba.

RIO GRANDE DO SUL

The state of Rio Grande do Sul is almost synonymous with the *gaúcho,* the South American cowboy who is glamorized as much as his North American counterpart. There's more to this state, however, than the idyllic cattle-country lifestyle of the early days. As it's one of Brazil's leading industrial areas, its infrastructure rivals that of any country in the northern hemisphere. Its mix of Portuguese, German, and Italian cultures is evident in the food and architecture. Indeed, to be gaúcho (which is a term for all people and things from this state) may mean to be a vintner of Italian heritage from Caxias do Sul or an entrepreneur of German descent from Gramado as much as a cattle rancher with Portuguese lineage out on the plains.

PORTO ALEGRE

476 km (296 mi) southwest of Florianópolis, 760 km (472 mi) southwest of Curitiba, 1,109 km (690 mi) southwest of São Paulo.

Porto Alegre's hallmark is the hospitality of its people, a trait that has been acknowledged over and over by visitors, earning it the nickname "Smile City." The capital of one of Brazil's wealthiest states, it has many streets lined with jacaranda trees that create violet tunnels when in full spring bloom.

The city was founded on the banks of the Rio Guaíba in 1772 by immigrants from the Azores. The Guaíba is actually a 50-km-long (31-mi-long) lagoon formed by four rivers that merge a few miles upstream from the city. The city has an important port, connected to the Atlantic by the Lagoa dos Patos.

> ### DOUBLE-DECKER CITY TOUR
>
> The Linha Turismo, a double-decker bus tour run by the Serviço de Atenção ao Turista departs from the Cidade Baixa SAT location. One ticket for the 80-minute ride, stopping at most of city's points of interest, costs about R$7. Service is available Tuesday through Friday, departing at 9 AM, 10:30 AM, 1:30 PM, 4 PM, and 4:30 PM. The schedule is reduced in winter (May–September).

TO & FROM

It takes about 90 minutes to fly from São Paulo to Porto Alegre. The Aeroporto Internacional Salgado Filho is one of Brazil's most modern air terminals. It's only 8 km (5 mi) northeast of downtown. The cost of a cab ride is around R$30. At a booth near the arrivals gate you can prepay your cab ride. There's also a minibus shuttle into town for about R$3.25.

Penha bus has service to São Paulo (19 hours); Pluma buses travel to Curitiba (12 hours); Florianópolis (6 hours) is served by Eucatur or Catarinense. To reach Foz do Iguaçu (14 hours), Unesul is the only option. Public bus service to São Miguel das Missões is painfully slow; instead, book a tour from Porto Alegre via flight or charter bus.

GETTING AROUND

Porto Alegre has an extensive bus system as well as the *lotação* (express minibuses).

Ask your hotel reception which lines to take. Alternatively, the Linha Turismo bus *(⇨"Double Decker City Tour," below)* stops at most tourist attractions. Another option is to take a cab downtown, where most sights are within walking distance of each other.

ESSENTIALS

Airport Aeroporto Internacional Salgado Filho (POA ✉Av. Severo Dulius 90010, Anchieta, 90200-910 ☎051/3358–2000).

Banks & Currency Exchange American Express (⊠*Av. Carlos Gomes 466, Mont Serrat, 90480-000* ☎*0800/702-0777*). **Banco do Brasil** (⊠*Rua Uruguai 185, Centro, 90010-140* ☎*051/3214-7500* ⊠*Aeroporto Internacional Salgado Filho, Av. Severo Dulius 90010, Anchieta, 90200-910* ☎*051/3371-1822*). **Citibank** (⊠*Praça Maurício Cardoso 176, Moinhos de Vento, 90570-010* ☎*051/3223-1000*).

Bus Contacts Catarinense (☎*051/3228-8900 or 0800/470-470*). **Estação Rodoviária (Bus Station)** (⊠*Largo Vespasiano Veppo 70, 90035-040* ☎*051/3210-0101* ⊕*www.rodoviaria-poa.com.br*). **Penha** (☎*051/3225-0933*). **Pluma** (☎*051/3224-9291*). **Unesul** (☎*051/3228-0029*).**União Cascavel/Eucatur** (☎*051/3228-8900*).

Emergencies & Medical Assistance Ambulance (☎*192*). **Fire** (☎*193*). Hospital: **Hospital Pronto Socorro** (⊠*Largo Theodor Herzl s/n, Bom Fim, 90040-194* ☎*051/3289-7999*). Pharmacy: **Farmácia PanVel** (⊠*Av. 24 de Outubro 722, Moinhos de Vento, 90510-000* ☎*051/3222-0188*). **Police** (☎*190*).

Taxi Radio taxi (☎*051/3334-7444 or 051/3266-7000*).

Visitor & Tour Info Cisne Branco (⊠*Port of Porto Alegre, Main Gate, Av. Mauá 1050, Centro, 90010-110* ☎*051/3224-5222* ⊕*www.barcocisnebranco.com. br* ☞*Day and night boat trips on Guaíba*). **Galápagos Tour** (⊠*Av. Senador Salgado Filho, 135, Room 202, Centro, 90010-221* ☎*051/3286-7094* ⊕*www. magoweb.com/sites/galapagostour* ☞*Tours of city, Serra Gaúcha, and off coast*). **Noiva do Caí** (⊠*Usina do Gasômetro, Av. João Goulart 551, Centro, 90010-120* ☎*051/3211-7662* ☞*Day and night boat trips on Guaíba*). **Secretaria de Turismo** (*State Tourism Authority, Serviço de Apoio ao Turista* ⊠*Centro Administrativo, Av. Borges de Medeiros 1501, 10th fl., Centro, 90119-900* ☎*051/3288-5400* ⊠*Aeroporto Internacional Salgado Filho, Av. Severo Dulius 90010, Anchieta, 90200-910* ☎*051/3358-2230* ⊠*Estação Rodoviária, Largo Vespasiano Veppo s/n, Centro, 90035-040* ☎*051/3288-5410* ⊕*www.turismo.rs.gov.br*). **Serviço de Atenção ao Turista** (*SAT* ⊠*Travessa do Carmo, 84, Cidade Baixa, 90050-210* ☎*0800/51-7686 or 051/3212-3464* ⊕*www.portoalegre.rs.gov.br/turismo* ⊠*Mercado Público, Store #99, Centro, 90020-070* ☎*051/3211-5705* ⊠*Mercado do Bom Fim, Store 12, Av. Osvaldo Aranha s/n, Bom Fim, 90040-194* ☎*051/3333-1873* ⊠*Usina do Gasometro, Av. João Goulart 551, Centro, 90010-120* ☎*051/3333-5979* ☞*Open daily 9–6*).

SAFETY & PRECAUTIONS

Some neighborhoods of Porto Alegre are sketchy at night—the central district being one; ask your hotel reception about the safety of your destination. During the day, pickpockets are generally the only concern.

EXPLORING

The heart of Porto Alegre lies within a triangle formed by Praça da Alfândega, the Mercado Público, and the Praça da Matriz. Not only is this the main business district, it's also the site of many cultural and historical attractions. Outside this area, Casa de Cultura Mário Quintana and Usina do Gasômetro are very active cultural centers, with movies, live performances, art exhibits, and cafés.

Numbers in the text correspond to numbers in the margin and on the Porto Alegre Centro map.

MAIN ATTRACTIONS

① Museu de Arte do Rio Grande do Sul. In the 1990s the old, neoclassical customs building was restored to house this art museum. German immigrant Theo Wiederspahn designed this and several other of the city's early buildings. You can also see paintings, sculptures, and drawings by gaúcho and other Brazilian artists from several periods. Two works of Di Cavalcanti—one of the country's most renowned painters—are exhibited as well as several pieces by local sculptor Xico Stockinger. ⌧*Praça da Alfândega s/n, Centro, 90010-150* ☎*051/3227–2311* ⊕*www.margs.org.br* ⌧*Free* ♁*Tues.–Sun. 10–7.*

② Memorial do Rio Grande do Sul. Built to house the post-office headquar-

> **BEAUTIFUL VIEWS**
>
> From Morro de Santa Teresa (Santa Teresa Hill), you get a grand view of the skyline as it confronts the expanse of the Rio Guaíba. From this spot and the numerous riverfront parks, the great spectacle of Porto Alegre's sunset is inspirational. As local poet Mário Quintana put it: "Skies of Porto Alegre, how could I ever take you to heaven?" For another great perspective of Centro, consider taking a riverboat tour of the Rio Guaíba and its islands (Galápagos Tur and Noiva do Caí do these tours), which are part of a state park.

ters at the turn of the 20th century, the building was declared a national architectural landmark in 1981. It now houses a state museum. Although overall the style is neoclassical, German baroque influences are strong; the asymmetrical corner towers with their bronze rotundas are said to resemble Prussian army helmets. A permanent exhibit focuses on the state's history and the lives of important gaúchos, and on the second floor there's one of Brazil's largest collections of documents and manuscripts about Brazilian society. ⌧*Praça da Alfândega s/n, Centro, 90010-191* ☎*051/3224–7210* ⊕*www.memorial.rs.gov.br* ⌧*Free* ♁*Tues.–Sun. 9–5.*

④ Mercado Público. The neoclassical Public Market was constructed in 1869. It has undergone repeated renovations, the last of which added the glass roof that now covers the central inner plaza. With these changes, some of the produce stalls have been replaced by souvenir shops, cafés, and restaurants, taking away a bit of the boisterous bazaar ambience but increasing the options for the visitor. One of the best restaurants in the city, Gambrinus, is here. ⌧*Largo Glenio Peres s/n, Centro, 90020-070* ⊕*www.mercadopublico.com.br* ♁*Mon.–Sat. 7 AM–11 PM.*

⑤ Museu Júlio de Castilhos. The small Júlio de Castilhos Museum is the oldest in the state. On display is an impressive collection of gaúcho documents, firearms, clothing, and household utensils. The home belonged to Governor Julio de Castilhos, who lived here at the turn of the 20th century, before the Palácio Piratini was built. ⌧*Rua Duque de Caxias 1231, Centro, 90010-293* ☎*051/3221–3959* ⌧*Free* ♁*Tues.–Fri. 10–5, weekends 1–5.*

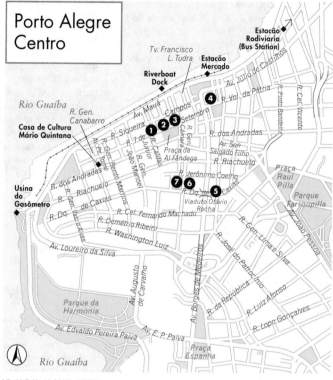

IF YOU HAVE TIME

⑥ Catedral Metropolitana Nossa Senhora Madre de Deus. Although its construction began in 1921, this cathedral wasn't completed until 1986. Its predominant style is Italian Renaissance, but note the twin bell towers, which were inspired by 17th-century Jesuit missions. The facade's mosaic panels were made in the Vatican ateliers. ⊠*Rua Duque de Caixas 1047, Centro, 90010-282* ☎*051/3228–6001* ☑*Free* ☉*Daily 7–noon and 2–7.*

③ Centro Cultural Santander. This stately building, constructed in 1927–32 and the former headquarters of various banks, is now owned by Banco Santander of Spain, which has transformed it into a cultural center and gallery (it's no longer a working bank). Guided tours (Portuguese only) show the intricate ironwork of the entrance door and second-floor balcony as well as the ceiling's neoclassical paintings. The massive bank vault now houses a café. ⊠*Rua Sete de Setembro 1028, Centro, 90010-975* ☎*051/3287–5500* ⊕*www.santandercultural.com. br* ☑*Free* ☉*Daily 9–5.*

⑦ Palácio Piratini. The Roman columns of the stately governor's mansion (which also houses executive offices) convey a solidity and permanence uncommon in official Brazilian buildings. In the main room murals by Aldo Locatelli depict gaúcho folktales. Guided 20-minute tours (Portuguese only) are given by appointment. ⊠*Praça da Matriz s/n, Centro, 90010-293* ☎*051/3210–4170* 🖃*Free* ⊙*Weekdays 9–5.*

OFF THE BEATEN PATH

Parque Estadual de Itapoã. Where the Rio Guaíba flows into Lagoa dos Patos, 57 km (35 mi) south of Porto Alegre, Itapoã State Park protects 12,000 acres of granitic hills and sandy beaches. Although the infrastructure is minimal, being able to bathe in the river, walk along marked trails, and watch magnificent sunsets attracts many visitors. Rare cacti, bands of *bugios* (howler monkeys), and a century-old lighthouse join the list of local highlights. Check with the listed travel agencies in Porto Alegre to hire boat tours to the park beaches and lighthouse. ⊠*Park entrance: Km 1, Estrada das Pombas, Viamão* ☎*051/3494–8083* 🖃*R$6* ⊙*Wed.–Sun. 9–6.*

WHERE TO STAY & EAT

$$–$$$
Fodor'sChoice ★

✕**Al Dente.** You may be surprised at the quality and authenticity of northern Italian cuisine at this small restaurant in Porto Alegre. Among many excellent choices: *garganelli* (a variety of pasta from Emilia-Romagna) with salmon in wine sauce and fettuccine *nere* (fettuccine with a black tinge from squid's ink) with caviar sauce. A house novelty is the Italian-gaúcho risotto, made with sundried meat, tomatoes, and squash. In a former residence, the decor is sober, with candlelit tables and cream drapes covering most of the walls. ⊠*Rua Mata Bacelar 210, Auxiliadora, 90540-150* ☎*051/3343–1841* 🖃*AE, D, MC, V* ⊙*Closed Sun. No lunch weekdays.*

$$–$$$
Fodor'sChoice ★

✕**Gambrinus.** Porto Alegre's best-known restaurant has been in business at the same spot, steps from city hall at the Mercado Público, since 1889. Walls are covered with azulejo tiles, antiques, and period photographs exalting those early days. The restaurant is a popular happy-hour spot for politicians and businesspeople. The menu varies daily from beef to fish dishes. One of the highlights is the large Brazilian anchovy stuffed with shrimp (served Fridays). ⊠*Rua Borges de Medeiros 85, Centro, 90020-020* ☎*051/3226–6914* 🖃*DC, MC, V* ⊙*No dinner weekends. Closes at 9 PM weekdays.*

$–$$

✕**Café do Porto.** One of the trendiest coffee shops in town, Porto serves several types of coffee, plus drinks, sandwiches, pies, and pastries. Try the *espetinho* (little skewer of meats and vegetables) combined with a glass of chardonnay or the house cappuccino. All coffee is Brazil's finest, from the Mogiana region in São Paulo. ⊠*Rua Padre Chagas 293, Moinhos de Vento, 90570-080* ☎*051/3346–8385* ⊕*www.cafedoporto.com.br* 🖃*AE, DC, MC, V.*

$–$$

✕**Galpão Crioulo.** One of Porto Alegre's largest churrascarias, Galpão Crioulo serves traditional *espeto-corrido*—a prix-fixe, never-ending rotation of roasted and grilled meats brought to the table, called *rodízio* elsewhere in Brazil—accompanied by a salad buffet, but its premium beef is more tender than that of most of its competitors. If a full espeto-corrido is too much for you, ask for the *miniespeto* (a small sampler skewer of all meats). Another option is the *comidas campeiras* (countryside food) buffet, which includes many recipes with rice, beans, and squash traditional to the South. Have a cup of *chimarrão* (an indigenous tea) at a tasting booth where the staff demonstrates the

5

traditional way to drink it. Gaúcho musical performances take place in the evening. ⊠*Rua Loureiro da Silva s/n, Parque da Harmonia, Centro, 91110-440* ☎*051/3226–8194* ═*AE, DC, MC, V.*

¢ ✕**Prato Verde.** This is the place to compensate for the likely excesses of espeto corrido–style churrasco. The very popular vegetarian buffet in the Bom Fim neighborhood, one step from Parque Farroupilha, serves a variety of salads and vegetable stews. Don't miss the eggplant parmigiana or the peanut patties (a nutty veggie burger). ⊠*Rua Santa Teresinha 42, Bom Fim, 90040-180* ☎*051/3388-6659* ⊕*www.pratoverde. com.br* ═*MC, V* ☾*No dinner.*

$$$$ ✕⊡**Sheraton Porto Alegre.** In the fashionable neighborhood of Moin-
Fodor's Choice hos de Vento, the Sheraton sets the city's standard of luxury. The level
★ of comfort is outstanding, from the lobby to the top-floor rooms. All rooms have plush king-size beds. Decor is subdued, with dark-wood furnishings. In the Brazil Suite you'll find 18th-century-style wooden furniture and copies of paintings by the French artist Debret, whose works depict rural scenes of colonial Brazil. The restaurant Porto Alegre Bistrô ($$–$$$) offers Mediterranean fare accompanied by live piano performances each weekday evening. The hotel is in the same complex as the Moinhos de Vento Mall. **Pros:** Top-notch service, prime location, many amenities. **Cons:** Can be hectic during business conferences. ⊠*Rua Olavo Barreto Viana 18, Moinhos de Vento, 90570-010* ☎*051/2121–6000 or 0800/891–3570* ⊕*www.sheraton-poa.com.br* ⇥*156 rooms, 22 suites* ♿*In-room: safe, dial-up, refrigerator. In-hotel: restaurant, bar, gym, pool, concierge, public Internet, Wi-Fi, parking (fee), no-smoking rooms* ═*AE, DC, MC, V* ⎡⎤*CP.*

$–$$ ✕⊡**Plaza San Rafael.** The Plaza has long been one of the city's most sophisticated hotels. The lobby and commons are clad in white marble and dark-wood paneling. The comfortable rooms are painted in light colors and have tasteful furnishings. All suites have whirlpool baths whose hot water is supplied by a thermal spring in the basement. The Plaza Grill ($$–$$$) serves international fare. The San Rafael convention center is just across the street. **Pros:** Excellent restaurant, spacious commons area, close to downtown. **Cons:** Very busy during conventions, neighborhood sketchy at night. ⊠*Rua Alberto Bins 514, Centro, 90030-040* ☎*051/3220–7000 or 0800/707–5292* ⊕*www.plazahoteis. com.br/sao_rafael.htm* ⇥*260 rooms, 24 suites* ♿*In-room: refrigerator, dial-up. In-hotel: restaurant, bar, pool, gym, no-smoking rooms, public Internet, Wi-Fi, parking (fee)* ═*AE, DC, MC, V* ⎡⎤*CP.*

$$ ⊡**Blue Tree Towers.** A haven for those seeking a peaceful night's rest, the
★ Blue Tree Towers is in the safe, scenic, and quiet residential Mont Serrat neighborhood. The spacious rooms have modern decor and king-size beds. Choose rooms in the back, which have superb views of downtown and the Guaíba. You can ask that a basic office be set up in your room. The Becco restaurant ($$$) serves Italian fare. **Pros:** Great for business travelers, attentive staff, spacious commons area. **Cons:** Far from downtown, small restaurant. ⊠*Rua Lucas de Oliveira 995, Mont Serrat, 90940-011* ☎*051/3019-8000 or 0800/15–0500* ⊕*www.blue tree.com.br* ⇥*130 rooms, 2 suites* ♿*In room: safe, refrigerator. In-*

hotel: restaurant, bar, pool, gym, no-smoking rooms, public Internet, Wi-Fi, parking (fee) ⊟*AE, DC, MC, V* ⦿|*CP.*

$ ⌂**Continental Business.** Tourists are lured to this downtown budget option despite its many business amenities, such as two phone lines for every room. Rooms are utilitarian, with plain and cheap-looking furnishings and carpeted floors, but the hotel is close to central attractions and the bus terminal, and access to the airport is quick and easy. **Pros:** Bargain price, good location. **Cons:** Blah decor, no restaurant, location sketchy at night. ⊠*Praça Otávio Rocha 49, Centro, 90010-000* ☎☐*051/3027–1600* ⊕*www.hotelcontinentalbusiness.com.br* ⟳*126 rooms* ⌂*In room: safe, refrigerator. In-hotel: bar, no-smoking rooms, public Internet, Wi-Fi, parking (no fee)* ⦿|*CP* ⊟*AE, DC, MC, V.*

$ ⌂**Everest.** This unassuming central hotel is close to the museums and cathedral. Rooms are spacious and decor is modern. The staff is well trained and can help you find tours and activities. The top-floor restaurant, popular with businesspeople, has a view of the Guaíba riverfront. **Pros:** Friendy staff, large rooms. **Cons:** Small bathrooms, area sketchy at night. ⊠*Av. Duque de Caxias 1357, Centro, 90010-283* ☎*051/3215–9500 or 0800/99–0095* ⊕*www.everest.com.br* ⟳*153 rooms* ⌂*In room: safe, refrigerator. In-hotel: restaurant, bar, gym, public Internet, Wi-Fi, concierge, parking (fee), no-smoking rooms* ⊟*AE, DC, MC, V* ⦿|*CP.*

NIGHTLIFE & THE ARTS

Porto Alegre has a very active cultural life. Complete listings of entertainment and cultural events are published in the daily papers *Zero Hora, Correio do Povo,* and *O Sul.*

The **Casa de Cultura Mário Quintana** (⊠*Rua dos Andradas 736, Centro, 90020-004* ☎*051/3221–7147* ⊕*www.ccmq.rs.gov.br*) occupies what was Porto Alegre's finest hotel at the turn of the 20th century. The building has two art-film cinemas, one theater, and several exhibit rooms. The popular Café Concerto Majestic, on the seventh floor, has regular jazz and classical music performances and is popular during happy hour.

Entertainment complex **Dado Bier** (⊠*Bourbon Country Center, Av. Túlio de Rose 100, Três Figueiras, 91340-110* ☎*051/3378–3000*) started off as the city's first microbrewery. Today local fashionistas and international tourists hang out at Dado Tambor, a live-music venue and dance club. The cover charge is R$20. **Rua Padre Chagas** in the Moinhos de Vento neighborhood is the place to find sophisticated bars and restaurants, such as Mulligan Irish Pub, Lilliput, and Z Café. **Barbazul** (⊠*Av. Itaqui, 57, Petropolis, 90470-010* ☎*051/3331–6180*) attracts the young and trendy for live music performances (mostly rock and roll) and dance.

The **Centro Cultural Usina do Gasômetro** (⊠*Av. João Goulart 551, Centro, 90010-120* ☎*051/3212–5979*), with its conspicuous 350-foot brick smokestack, was the city's first coal-fired powerplant—built in the early 1920s, when the city experienced rapid growth. Today it holds theaters, meeting rooms, and exhibit spaces on the banks of the Rio Guaíba. A terrace café overlooking the river is the perfect place to take in a sunset. The center is open Tuesday–Sunday 9–9.

SPORTS & THE OUTDOORS

Clube Veleiros do Sul (⊠*Av. Guaíba 2941, Asunção, 91900-420* ☎*051/3267–1733* ⊕*www.veleirosdosul.com.br*) takes advantage of the great expanse of the Guaíba waters to offer sailing classes and boat rentals. **Estádio Beir-Rio** (⊠*Av. Padre Cacique 891, Praia de Belas, 90810-240* ☎*051/3230–4600*), with a capacity of 56,000, is the home of Internacional—one of the city's major *futebol* (soccer) clubs.

SHOPPING

Brique da Redenção (⊠*Rua José Bonifácio, Bom Fim*), originally a flea market on the southeast side of Parque Farroupilha, has expanded into a full-blown antiques, crafts, and arts fair. All of **Rua José Bonifácio** is closed to vehicles and taken over by dealers and artisans every Sunday from 10 to 3.

Moinhos Shopping (⊠*Rua Olavo Barreto Vianna 36, Moinhos de Vento, 90570-901* ☎*051/2123–2000*) is the smallest of the city's malls and caters to the sophisticated consumer. It has a six-theater cineplex and is attached to a Sheraton. **Shopping Center Iguatemi** (⊠*Rua João Wallig 1831, Três Figueiras, 91349-900* ☎*051/3334–4500*) is the city's largest mall and includes branches of large chain stores as well as high-end specialty shops.

If you don't have the time to venture into Brazilian wine country, look for a sample to buy at **Vinhos do Mundo** (⊠*Rua João Alfredo 557, Cidade Baixa, 90050-230* ☎*051/3226–1911*).

VALE DOS VINHEDOS

124 km (77 mi) north of Porto Alegre

The Serra Gaúcha produces 90% of Brazilian wine. Grapevines grow throughout the hilly terrain, but the heart of the winemaking country is within the municipality of Bento Gonçalves, settled by Italian immigrants in the late 19th century. Because the best-known Brazilian wineries are within a few miles in this region, the name Vale dos Vinhedos (Vineyard Valley) has become synonymous with quality wines.

TO & FROM

To visit Vale dos Vinhedos, either rent a car or join an organized tour. From Porto Alegre, Bento Gonçalves is accessible by RS 240 and then RS 470 (exit in São Vendelino). The wineries on Vale dos Vinhedos are on RS 444, which intersects with RS 470 at Km 217.

ESSENTIALS

Make sure you have reais or credit cards when coming to Bento Gonçalves, as currency exchange is not readily available. All hotels and pousadas have public Internet acess, and most are adopting Wi-Fi connection.

Emergencies & Medical Assistance Ambulance (☎*192*). **Fire** (☎*193*). **Hospital:**

Hospital Dr. Bartholomeu Tacchini (⊠*Rua José Mario Monaco 358, Centro, 95700-000* ☎*054/3455–4333*). Pharmacy: **Droagaria Capilé** (⊠*Rua Marechal Floriano 30, Centro, 95700-000* ☎*054/3451–6188*). **Police** (☎*190*).

Visitor & Tour Info Valle Verde (⊠*Rua 13 de Maio 800, Centro, 95700-000* ☎*054/3451–4775* ⊕*www.valleverde.com.br* ☞*This travel agency can arrange 2-to-3-day tours in the Vale dos Vinhedos departing from Porto Alegre, which includes the major wineries, restaurants and other attractions.*).

WINERIES

Casa Valduga is run by Luiz Valduga and his sons. Together they produce premium wines (the cabernets are highly regarded). In summer you can take a tour of the family-owned vineyards and purchase other house products such as grape juice and fruit jellies. ⊠*Km 6, RS 444, 95700-000 Bento Gonçalves* ☎*054/2105–3154* ⊕*www.casavalduga. com.br* ☑*Free* ☉*Tours Dec.–Feb. by appointment; wine tastings weekdays 8–11 and 2–6, weekends 9–5.*

Guided tours of **Vinícola Cordelier** ends in a wine-tasting session. It's smaller than the other wineries in the area and gives more personal attention. Cordelier Reserva cabernet sauvignon and merlots have received awards. A restaurant serves international fare on-site. ⊠*Km 210, RS 470, 95700-000 Bento Gonçalves* ☎*054/2102–2333* ⊕*www. cordelier.com.br* ☑*Free* ☉*Weekdays 9–4, weekends 9–5.*

The Miolo family has carved a name for itself in the Brazilian wine industry with the **Vinícola Miolo.** Tours of the premises include the vineyards and tasting the award-winning wines, which include outstanding chardonnays, cabernet sauvignons, sauvignon blancs, and sparklers. ⊠*Km 9, RS 444, 95700-000 Bento Gonçalves* ☎*054/2102–1500 or 0800/541–4165* ⊕*www.miolo.com.br* ☑*Free* ☉*Tours daily 9–5.*

WHERE TO STAY & EAT

$$ ✕**Giuseppe.** Be ready for a luncheon: this highly regarded restaurant serves a prix-fixe Italian menu with *galeto al primo canto* (cripsy grilled chicken) and a large selection of pasta dishes. Accompaniments include cappelletti soup, polenta, and *radicci* (a green-leaf salad). ⊠*Km 221, RS 470, 95700-000 Bento Gonçalves* ☎*054/3463–8505* ☐*AE, DC, MC, V.*

$ ✕⊞**Pousada Valduga.** The Valduga winery maintains four redbrick houses with large, comfortable rooms overlooking the vineyards. Decor is contemporary, and each room is different. The breakfast is almost a full café colonial, served at the winery near the wine vats. The restaurant ($), which is open to nonguests on weekends, serves the best of Brazilian-Italian fare, such as cappelletti soup, roasted pork and chicken, and polenta. **Pros:** Great services, large and comfortable rooms. **Cons:** Few amenities, no children allowed. ⊠*Km 6, RS 444, 95700-000 Bento Gonçalves* ☎*054/2105–3154* ⊕*www.casavalduga. com.br* ⟳*21 rooms* ⌂*In room: refrigerator. In-hotel: restaurant, no elevator, pool, no kids under12* ☐*D, MC, V.*

Brazilian Wine

The first grapevines were brought to Brazil in 1532 by early Portuguese colonists, but it was the Jesuits, who settled in the South decades later, who were the first to establish true vineyards and wineries (to produce wine for the Catholic mass). Viticulture didn't gain importance in Brazil until Italian immigrants arrived, with the blessing of Italian-born empress Teresa Cristina, wife of Dom Pedro II, in 1875. In the next decades at least 150,000 Italians came to settle the mountainous region of Rio Grande do Sul—the Serra Gaúcha. They were the first to produce significant quantities of wine.

Although the South is suitable for growing grapes, the rainfall is often excessive from January to March—when the grapes reach maturity. This has traditionally made local winegrowers true heroes for being able to produce decent wines despite difficult conditions. Traditional grapes such as merlot and cabernet were grown to some extent, but most of the wine produced originated from less impressive American stock—Concord and Niagara grapes. These average wines are still produced for local markets.

New agricultural techniques and hybridization of grapes have brought modern viticulture to the area and allowed a dramatic expansion of higher-quality grapes. This has significantly improved wine quality and attracted such international industry heavyweights as Almadén, Moët et Chandon, and Heublein. In 1992 Almadén broke new ground and established vineyards in the hills near the city of Santana do Livramento—about 480 km (300 mi) southwest of Porto Alegre, on the Uruguay border—where, according to current agricultural knowledge, climate and soils are more apt to produce quality grapes.

Other wineries are following its steps. Today there are more than 100 *cantinas* (winemakers) in Rio Grande do Sul, primarily in the Vale dos Vinhedos (Vineyard Valley) near Bento Gonçalves. The wine producers' association of the Vale dos Vinhedos, IBRAVIN (⊕*www.ibravin.com.br)*, has registered a government-certified system similar to that used in European countries for controlled-origin wines to promote and warrant the quality of their products.

GRAMADO

115 km (72 mi) northeast of Porto Alegre.

No doubt it was Gramado's mild mountain climate that attracted German settlers to the area in the late 1800s. They left a legacy of German-style architecture and traditions that attract today's travelers. Ample lodging options and a seemingly endless choice of restaurants have given this city a reputation with conventioneers and honeymooners.

TO & FROM

Gramado is easily reached from Porto Alegre by car. Take BR 116 north for about 40 km to the intersection with RS 115. Then it's 97 km (60 mi) northeast to Gramado. Regular buses run by Citral depart from Porto Alegre every other hour during the day; the trip is 90 minutes and costs R$20. Although you might appreciate the independence of a rental car, most attractions are not too far apart and taxiing about is convenient.

ESSENTIALS

Nearly all hotels and pousadas have Internet for guest use.

Banks & Currency Exchange Banco do Brasil (⊠*Rua Madre Veronia 100, 95670-000*).

Bus Contacts Estaçao Rodoviária (Bus Station) (⊠*Av. Borges de Medeiros 2100* ☎*054/3286–1302*).

Emergencies & Medical Assistance Ambulance (☎*192*). **Fire** (☎*193*). Hospital: **Hospital São Miguel** (⊠*Rua Madre Verônica 396, 95670-000* ☎*054/3286–4594*). Pharmacy: **Farmacia Lider** (⊠*Rua Sao Pedro 664, Centro,* ☎*054/3286–2126*). **Police** (☎*190*).

Taxi Taxi Rodoviária (☎*054/3286-1320*).

Visitor & Tour Info Centro de Informações Turísticas (⊠*Rua Borges de Medeiros 1667, Centro, 95760-000* ☎*054/3286–1475* ⊕*www.gramado.rs.gov.br* ☞*Open daily 9–6*).

Vida Livre Turismo Expedições (⊠*Rua Madre Veronica 30, Suite 302, Centro, 95760-000* ☎*054/3286–7326* ⊕*www.vidalivreturismo.com.br* ☞*Sightseeing tours in and around Gramado; trips to Cambará do Sul canyons and Parque Nacional dos Aparados da Serra*).

SAFETY & PRECAUTIONS

Be more alert for theft during busy events like the movie festival and Christmas functions.

WHERE TO STAY & EAT

$$$ ╳**Gasthof Edelweiss.** With its veranda that overlooks pine trees and gardens, this German restaurant creates a relaxing atmosphere and an ideal setting for duck *à la viennese* (with an orange-flavor cream sauce)—the house specialty. Some tables are in the wine cellar, which has more than 1,000 bottles. It is one of the most traditional restaurants in town, in business since 1995. ⊠*Rua da Carriere 1119, Lago Negro, 95760-000* ☎*054/3286–1861* ⊟*AE, DC, MC, V.*

$ ╳**Casa di Pietro.** This Italian cantina-style restaurant has a unique, prix-fixe salad-and-five-soup buffet at dinner. Surefire soup choices include the cappeletti—best topped with grated Parmesan cheese—and the Serrano (a local vegetable soup). If this light fare doesn't suit you, opt for the grilled beef or other meats. Choose the cuts that you like directly from the grill. ⊠*Rua Garibaldi 305, Suite 01, Centro, 95760-000* ☎*054/3036–0331* ⊟*AE, DC, MC, V.*

¢ ╳**Stuttgart.** This homey prix-fixe restaurant has great dining at a budget price. Choose from a varied selection of salads and grilled-meat options, with the ubiquitous rice, beans, and potatos as accompaniments. ⊠*Rua Garibaldi 305, Suite 01, Centro, 95760-000* ☎*054/3036–0331* ⊟*AE, DC, MC, V.*

$$$–$$$$ ╳⛱**Serrano Resort.** Surrounded by Brazilian pines, everything at the Serrano is set to make your stay enjoyable and unforgettable: superb restaurants, plenty of sports and leisure options, and all just a few blocks

Fodor's Choice

★

from downtown Gramado. Rooms are plush and spacious, overlooking the city and forested hills beyond. Among the activities and amenities are a guided morning walk on the trail that circles the grounds, aerobics in the pool, massage, and a sauna. The Fronteras del Sur restaurant ($$–$$$) serves South American fare, with an emphasis on beef dishes. Another restaurant, Maggiore, has a dance floor and live music performances several nights a week. The resort has one of the best-regarded convention centers in Brazil on its grounds. **Pros:** Excellent facilities, great services, multiple dining options. **Cons:** Expensive. ⊠*Av. das Hortensias 1480, 95670-000* ☏*054/3286–8005* ⊕*www.serranoresort. com.br* ⌿*244 rooms, 28 suites* ⚒*In room: refrigerator, safe. In-hotel: 5 restaurants, bar, tennis court, pools, gym, spa, public Internet, Wi-Fi* ☰*AE, DC, MC, V* †◎*MAP.*

$–$$$ 🏨**Serra Azul.** This prestigious downtown hotel is almost synonymous
Ⓒ   with fine lodging in the region. Its architecture is German Bavarian
★   style, which is a trademark of Gramado. Room decor is elegant and sober, with dark-wood furnishings. At the *recanto* (lounge area) in the evenings guests can experience gaúcho traditions like chimarrão paired with the sound of folkloric rhythms played by local musicians. The location is prime for browsing the myriad shops, cafés, and restaurants of the city. **Pros:** Close to downtown, good service. **Cons:** Hectic when hosting business meetings, small bathrooms. ⊠*Rua Garibaldi 152, 95670-000* ☏*054/3286–1082* ⊕*www.serraazul.com.br* ⌿*151 rooms, 18 suites* ⚒*In room: safe, refrigerator. In-hotel: restaurant, bar, pool, public Internet, Wi-Fi* ☰*AE, DC, MC, V.*

¢   🏨**Pousada Zermatt.** This charming inn has a homey atmosphere, especially in the rooms with Brazilian-pine floors and wall panels, fireplaces, and colorful locally made bedspreads. Rates are reasonable and it's peaceful—3 km (2 mi) from the noisy downtown district; a handful of good restaurants is nearby. **Pros:** Good service, great price. **Cons:** No restaurant, small rooms, few amenities. ⊠*Rua da Fé 187, Bavaria, 95670-000* ☏*054/3286–2426* ⊕*www.pousadazermatt.com. br* ⌿*9 rooms* ⚒*In-room: no a/c, refrigerator. In-hotel: bar, no elevator* ☰*MC, V.*

SHOPPING

Gramado is well known for high-quality leather, cotton, and woolknit clothing. There are dozens of shops throughout the city. Shops vie for customers with frequent promotions, so shopping around can net bargains.

Kouro Arte (⊠*Largo Claudio Pasqual 65, Centro, 95670-000* ☏*054/ 3226–1835*) has a great variety of leather apparel. **Maríchen** (⊠*Rua Garibaldi 180, Centro, 95670-000* ☏*041/3234–1118*), a traditional name in apparel, carries a selection of fine wool and cotton knit apparel, manufactured at their own shops.

CANELA

8 km (5 mi) east of Gramado, 137 km (85 mi) north of Porto Alegre.

Gramado's "smaller sister" is quieter and more low-profile. Brazilians immediately associate this city of 35,000 with the Caracol Waterfall, but it also has great shopping, for cotton and wool-knit apparel, handmade embroidered items, and handicrafts. The impressive views of the forest-clad valleys with meandering rivers also bring many tourists.

Most visitors stay in Gramado, which has many more accommodations, and visit the attractions in Canela as a day trip.

TO & FROM
The route from Porto Alegre to Canela is the same to Gramado; from there drive or a take a taxi via RS 235 east for about 20 minutes to Canela.

ESSENTIALS
Take care of services and essentials in Gramado, 8 km (5 mi) west.

WHAT TO SEE
The **Parque Estadual do Caracol** *(Caracol State Park)* has an impressive 400-foot waterfall that cascades straight down into a horseshoe-shape valley carved out of the basaltic plateau. For the best views try the lookout atop the 100-foot tower (R$3). The park also includes 50 acres of native forests with several well-marked paths, dominated by Paraná pine and an environmental education center for children. The entrance area is somewhat overcrowded with souvenir shops and snack tents. ⊠*Km 9, Estrada do Caracol, 95680-000* ☎*054/3278–3035* 🖾*Park R$8, elevator to lookout tower R$5* ☉*Daily 9–7.*

Parque da Ferradura is a private nature preserve that has three lookouts to the Vale da Ferradura (Horseshoe Valley), formed by Rio Santa Cruz. You can walk trails in more than 500 acres of pine forests through hilly countryside. A strenuous two-hour trek reaches Rio Caí near its source. Spotting deer, anteaters, and badgers is quite common. ⊠*Km 15, Estrada do Caracol, 95680-000* ☎*054/9972–8666* 🖾*R$7* ☉*Daily 9–6.*

WHERE TO STAY & EAT
$$ ✕**La Charbonnade.** In a picturesque wooden chalet surrounded by herb and cactus gardens, La Charbonnade has two large fireplaces to keep guests warm in the cool winters of Serra Gaúcha. This is the place to try gaúcho-style "fondue," a local gastronomic invention in which you grill lean beef and poultry cuts on a charcoal minigrill on your table, then season your meat with one of 21 sauces. You can also select the wine yourself from the cellar, stocked with a large variety of imported and Brazilian wines. ⊠*Av. Dom Guanella 53, 95680-000* ☎*054/3282–4313* ⊟*No credit cards* ☉*No lunch.*

$ ✕**Castelinho Caracol.** The lofty two-story building surrounded by flower gardens is the oldest enxaimel house in the region, built in 1913 by the Franzen family, which ran a woodworking shop on the property for many years. Now this is the place for a hearty café colonial when

returning from the Caracol Falls. The specialty here is the apple stru-
del. Behind the house there's a small museum with woodworking tools
and farming equipment from the early days of German immigration.
⊠*Km 6, Estrada do Caracol, 95680-000* ☎*054/3278–3208* ▭*No
credit cards* ⊘*No dinner.*

$$ ▦**Laje de Pedra Mountain Village.** Part of the Laje de Pedra Resort com-
plex, added in 2005, this hotel has large apartmentlike rooms, each
with a living room and kitchenette. Decor is sleek and modern, with
granite countertops, brushed-steel accents, lush bedding, and gleaming
wood furnishings. The wooden floors have a heating system for the
cold winters. West-facing rooms have views of the Quilombo Valley.
Guests can use the amenities of the resort, like the swimming pools and
the tennis courts. ⊠*Km 3, Av. Pres. Kennedy, 95680-000* ☎*054/3278–
9900, 0800/51–2153 reservations* ⊕*www.mountainvillage.com.br*
⤵*24 rooms* ⌂*In room: safe, refrigerator. In-hotel: restaurant, bar,
tennis court, pool, gym, spa, children's programs (ages 4–8), public
Internet* ▭*AE, DC, MC, V.*

PARQUE NACIONAL DOS APARADOS DA SERRA

Fodor'sChoice   *47 km (29 mi) north of Gramado, 145 km (91 mi) north of Porto
★   Alegre.*

One of Brazil's first national parks, Aparados da Serra was created to
protect Itaimbezinho, one of the most impressive canyons dissecting the
plateau in the north of Rio Grande do Sul State. In 1992 the Parque
Nacional da Serra Geral was established to protect the other great
canyons farther north, the Malacara, Churriado, and Fortaleza. Winter
(June–August) is the best time to take in the spectacular canyon views,
as there's less chance of fog. The main entrance to the park, the Portaria
Gralha Azul, is 20 km (13 mi) southeast of Cambará do Sul, the small
town that serves as the park's hub. A visitor center provides informa-
tion on regional flora and fauna, as well as the region's geology and
history. Beyond the entrance you come to grassy meadows that belie
the gargantuan depression ahead. A short path (a 45-minute walk, no
guide necessary) takes you to the awesome Itaimbezinho Canyon rim,
cut deep into the basalt bedrock to create the valley 2,379 feet below.
The longest path requires a hired guide and trekking gear to traverse
the strenuous descent into the canyon's interior. The local tourist office
can also make arrangements for other trekking tours in the region. The
park allows only 1,500 visitors each day, so it's best to arrive early,
especially in the summer months.

▪**TIP**➔The best way to visit the park is to join an organized tour in Porto
Alegre (⇨**Visitor & Tour Info,** *below)* **that includes an overnight stay in one
of the region's pousadas.** Those visiting Gramado can join a day tour to
visit the canyons *(⇨Visitor & Tour Info in Gramado).*

⊠*20 km (12 mi) southeast of Cambará do Sul on unpaved road,
95480-000* ☎*051/3251–1277, 051/3251–1320 for tour guides (Cam-
bará Ecotourism Guides Association)* ▦*R$6 per person, R$5 parking
ticket* ⊘*Wed.–Sun. 9–5.*

TO & FROM

Cambará can be reached by car via RS 020. About half of the route is steep, winding single-lane road. The green mountain scenery, good pavement and signage recommend it.

ESSENTIALS

Emergencies & Medical Assistance **Ambulance** (☎*192*). **Fire** (☎*193*). Hospital: **Municipal** (⊠*Rua Pe. João Pazza 197, Centro, 95480-000* ☎*054/3251-1167*). Pharmacy: **Farmácia São José** (⊠*Av. Júlio de Castilhos 752, Centro, 95480-000* ☎*054/3244-5000*). **Police** (☎*190*).

Visitor & Tour Info **Caá-Etê Ecoturismo & Aventura** (⊠*Av. Protásio Alves 2715, Suite 905, Petrópolis, 90410-002 Porto Alegre* ☎*051/3338-3323* ⊕*www.caa-ete. com.br* ⊂*Guided overnight tours to Rio Grande do Sul canyons and Aparados da Serra national park*). **Serviço Informação ao Turista** (*Municipal Tourist Information Service* ⊠*Rua Adail de Lima Valim 31, Centro, 95480-000* ☎*054/3251-1320* ⊂*Open Tues.–Sat. 9–noon and 2–5*).

WHERE TO STAY & EAT

¢ ✕**Fogão Campeiro.** This churrascaria in a picturesque wooden bungalow has the ubiquitous southern Brazilian espeto-corrido, in addition to a fixed-price buffet with less advertised gaúcho dishes such as *arroz de carreteiro* (rice with dried beef), *farofa* (sautéed cassava flour), and cooked cassava. Traditional-music performances take place on Friday and Saturday. ⊠*Rua São Perdo 1044, 95480-000* ☎*051/3251-1012* ☰*No credit cards* ⊘*Closed Mon.*

$$$ ⌂**Pedra Afiada Refúgio.** The most comfortable lodging at the end of the canyon valleys, this pousada has established its niche among adventure tourists, who depart from here to explore the Malacara and other canyons beyond. All northwest-facing rooms have balconies with views of the canyon walls. Every room has a different color scheme, and all have comfortable, queen-size beds. **Pros:** Unique location, great for adventure tourism. **Cons:** Basic amenities, far from city. ⊠*Estrada da Vila Rosa s/n, Praia Grande, 88990-000* ☎*048/532-1059 or 051/3338-3323* ⊕*www.pedraafiada.com.br* ⤶*11 rooms* ⌖*In-room: no a/c, no phone, no TV. In-hotel: bar, no elevator* ☰*DC, MC* ⦿*MAP.*

$ ⌂**Pousada das Corucacas.** Step into the region's rugged world by staying at this inn on a working gaúcho horse-and-cattle farm: the 1,200-acre Fazenda Baio Ruano. This pousada is a wooden building made with Paraná pine wood. Rooms are no-frills and downright rustic, but beds are comfortable, and there's central heating (rare in these parts). The ample lounge with a fireplace, and a great view of the surrounding hills covered with native grass meadows and dotted with Paraná pine trees recommend a stay here. There are waterfalls and woods in the area: consider exploring them on horseback and perhaps trekking into the canyons beyond. **Pros:** Great for experiencing local traditions, bargain price. **Cons:** Far from downtown, small bathrooms. ⊠*Km 1, RS 020 (Estrada do Ouro Verde), 95481-970* ☎*054/3251-1123* ⊕*www. guiatelnet.com.br/pousadacorucacas* ⤶*11 rooms* ⌖*In-room: no a/c, no phone, no TV. In-hotel: no elevator* ☰*MC* ⦿*MAP.*

TORRES

205 km (128 mi) northeast of Porto Alegre.

The beaches around the city of Torres are Rio Grande do Sul's most exciting. The sophistication of the seaside areas attracts international travelers, particularly Argentines and Uruguayans. Some of the best beaches are Praia da Cal, Praia da Guarita, and Praia Grande. The Parque Estadual da Guarita (Watchtower State Park), 3 km (2 mi) south of downtown, was set aside to protect the area's unique vegetation as well as the basalt hills that end abruptly in the Atlantic. Locals like to fish from these cliffs. A mile offshore, Ilha dos Lobos (Seawolf Island) is a way station for sea lions in their annual migrations along the south Atlantic coast. South of Torres, and extending well into Uruguay, the coastline is a 650-km-long (400-mi-long) sandy stretch interrupted only by a few river deltas and lagoons.

TO & FROM

In the northeastern corner of Rio Grande do Sul, right on the border with Santa Catarina, Torres is easily reached by car or bus via the roads to the coast of Rio Grande do Sul (BR 290 to Osório and then North BR 101 or RS 389). The bus trip, with Unesul lines, takes about 2½ hrs and costs R$40. From Florianópolis, drive about 280 km (175 mi) south on BR 101.

ESSENTIALS

Banks & Currency Exchange **Banco do Brasil** (⊠*Rua XV de Novembro 236, Centro, 95560-000*).

Bus Contacts **Estação Rodoviária (Bus Station)** (⊠*Av. José Bonifácio 524, 95560-000*).**Unesul** (⊠*Rua Coronel Pacheco 3996–7600, 95560-000* ☎*051/3996-7600*).

Emergencies & Medical Assistance **Ambulance** (☎*192*). **Fire** (☎*193*). Hospital: **Hospital Nossa Senhora dos Navegantes** (⊠*Rua Manoel José Pereira 260, Centro, 95560-000* ☎*051/3664-1100*). Pharmacy: **Panvel** (⊠*Av. Rio Branco 258, Centro, 95560-000* ☎*051/3664-1040*). **Police** (☎*190*).

Taxi **Ponto de Taxi Central** (☎*051/3626-2441*).

Visitor & Tour Info **Casa do Turista** (*Municipal Tourist Ofice* ⊠*Av. Barão do Rio Branco, 315, Centro, 95560-000* ☎*051/3364-1129* ⏰*Open daily 9–7*).

SAFETY & PRECAUTIONS

Take extra precautions against theft during Carnaval, when the city is overwhelmed by visitors.

WHERE TO STAY & EAT

$$–$$$ ✕**Anzol.** The decor is not distinguished, but the ample windows overlooking Rio Mampituba create the perfect setting for a fine dinner. Seafood, either grilled or stewed, is the specialty here. Try the *camarão na moranga* (shrimp in a squash purée). ⊠*Rua Cristovão Colombo 265, 95560-000* ☎*051/3664–2427* ▭*DC, MC, V.*

$ ⊡**Guarita Park.** Guarita joined the town's lodging roster in 2005. The hotel is within walking distance from Watchtower State Park and its beaches. Rooms have balconies either facing the sea or the park. The all-white rooms are sleek, with colorful bedding and decoration. **Pros:** Prime location, great views, good service. **Cons:** Far from downtown, small common areas. ⊠*Rua Alfiero Zanardi 1017, Guarita, 95560–000* ☎*051/3664–5200* ⊕*www.guaritaparkhotel.com.br* ⇆*67 rooms* △*In room: safe, Wi-fi. In-hotel: restaurant, bar, pools, no elevator, public Internet* ⊟*AE, DC, MC, V.*

SÃO MIGUEL DAS MISSÕES

482 km (300 mi) northwest of Porto Alegre.

Of seven large missions in the area dating from the late 1600s to mid-1700s, São Miguel is the best preserved and the only one that has tourism infrastructure and allows visitors. The 120-acre Parque Histórico de São Miguel was created around the mission, which is a UNESCO World Heritage site. A nondescript town of about 7,000 has grown around the mission site and shares its name. Joining an organized, Porto Alegre–based tour with an English-speaking guide is the recommended option for visiting the mission.

TO & FROM

Most of the 482-km (300-mi) route from Porto Alegre to São Miguel das Missões is via toll roads (BR 386 and BR 285), which are single-lane but generally in good condition. Expect heavy truck traffic. São Miguel is 11 km (7 mi) off BR 285, via BR 466.

Ouro e Prata bus lines runs daily service to São Miguel (6 hours; R\$77) from Porto Alegre. The closest airport to São Miguel das Missões is 60 km (38 mi) away, in Santo Angelo. It's served daily by NHT, with daily flights from Porto Alegre.

ESSENTIALS

Air Contacts **Aeroporto Municipal de Santo Angelo** (⊠*Km 13, RS 218, 98801-000 Santo Angelo* ☎*055/3312–9779*). **NHT Airlines** (☎*0300/143–4343*).

Bus Contacts **Estação Rodoviária (Bus Station)** (⊠*Av. Antunes Ribas 1525, 98865-000*). **Ouro e Prata** (⊠*Rua Frederico Mentz 1419, Porto Alegre, 98240-111* ☎*0800/51–6216*).

Emergencies & Medical Assistance **Ambulance** (☎*192*). **Fire** (☎*193*). Hospital: **Hospital Caridade** (⊠*Rua Santo Angelo 519, Centro, 98865-000* ☎*055/3381–1136*). Pharmacy: **Farmácia Vida e Saúde** (⊠*Rua 29 de Abril 55, Centro, 98865-000* ☎*055/3381–1534*). **Police** (☎*190*).

Taxi **Ponto de Taxi Catedral** (☎*055/3312–2592*).

Visitor & Tour Info **Galápagos** (⊠*Av. Senador Salgado Filho, 135, Room 202, Centro, 90010-221 Porto Alegre* ☎*051/3286–7094* ⊕*www.magoweb.com/sites/galapagostour* ☞*Package tours to the São Miguel mission, and other mission sites in Brazil, Argentina, and Paraguay*).

WHAT TO SEE

★ **São Miguel das Missões** is the best-preserved and best-organized Jesuit mission in Brazil. It was an impressive, circa-1745 church built with reddish basalt slabs brought by the Guaranis from quarries miles away. The ruins are now a UNESCO World Heritage Site.

Jesuit missionaries moved into the upper Uruguay River basin around 1700. In the following decades the local Guarani peoples were converted to Christianity, leading them to abandon their seminomadic lifestyle and to congregate around the new missions—locally known as *reduções* (missionary communities). Seven of these existed in what is now Brazil, and several more were in Argentina and Paraguay—all linked by a closely knit trade and communication route. Historians have claimed that at the peak of their influence, the Jesuits actually created the first de facto country in the Americas, complete with a court system and elections. After the Treaty of Madrid granted rights over the lands and native peoples in the area to the Portuguese crown, the Jesuits were under pressure to leave. Recurrent clashes with Portuguese militia precipitated the breakdown of the mission system, but the final blow came with the decree of expulsion of Jesuit order from Portuguese territory. Most of the Guaranis dispersed back into unexplored country.

Across the border in Argentina, there's a larger and better preserved mission site, **San Ignácio Mini.** Tours of these missions and of São Miguel das Missões can be booked through Galápagos (⇨Visitor & Tour Info, *above*). ⊠*Parque Histórico de São Miguel, Rua São Miguel s/n, 98865-000* ☎*055/3381–1399* ⊠*R$5* ☉*Museum daily 8–6. Grounds daily 8* AM*–dusk.*

WHERE TO STAY & EAT

$ ✕**Churrascaria Barichello.** This simple, typical gaúcho restaurant is the best option in town. Savor the espeto-corrido, with more than a dozen cuts of beef, pork, and poultry. ⊠*Av. Borges do Canto 1567, 98865-000* ☎*055/3381–1275* ⊟*MC, V.*

¢ ✕🏨**Wilson Park Hotel Missões.** Not only the nicest accommodations in the region, the Wilson Park is a fine hotel by any standards. Large rooms have colonial-style furnishings and arched doorways echo the design of the mission a few blocks away. The well-trained staff is knowledgeable about the missions and other attractions in the region. The restaurant serves standard Brazilian fare. **Pros:** Attentive staff, great service, close to mission. **Cons:** Some rooms need updating. ⊠*Rua São Miguel 664, 98865-000* ☎*055/3381–2000* ⊕*www.wilsonparkhotel.com.br* ⟿*78 rooms* ⌂*In room: refrigerator. In-hotel: restaurant, no elevator, bar, pool, public Internet, no-smoking rooms* ⊟*AE, DC, MC, V* ⊺⊙|*CP.*

Minas Gerais

WORD OF MOUTH

"Please go to Ouro Preto and stay in a pousada overlooking the valleys and mountains. The tranquillity of Ouro Preto, plus the magic of the city, will forever remain in your memory."

—A. Lukosky

"The small, charming, historic, colonial Tiradentes is 325 km away from Rio de Janeiro, approx. 75 km closer to Rio de Janeiro than Ouro Preto. Fully restored, a precious gem, I love it much more than Ouro Preto."

—Dilermando

Updated
by Anna
Katsnelson

THOUGH IT'S FAR FROM THE CIRCUIT of Brazil's most visited places, the state of Minas Gerais holds unforgettable historical, architectural, and ecological riches. Minas has more UNESCO World Heritage sites that any other state in Brazil. This mountainous state's name, which means "general mines," was inspired by the area's great mineral wealth. Prior to the 18th century the region was unexplored due to its difficult terrain, but in the late 17th century *bandeirantes,* or adventurers, forged into the interior, eventually discovering vast precious-metal reserves. As a result, the state, and particularly the city of Ouro Preto, became the de facto capital of the Portuguese colony. That period of gold, diamond, and semiprecious-stone trading is memorialized in the historic towns scattered across the jagged blue mountain ridges and remains a tremendous source of pride for *mineiros* (inhabitants of the state).

Minas Gerais is one of the calmest and most conservative Brazilian states. Many say that it's because of the mountains that surround the state, which are also said to make the mineiro an introspective and friendly person. Yet Minas Gerais has also been a hotbed for movements that have triggered political, economic, and cultural development. Minas reared Brazil's first revolutionaries, the group of men in charge of the Inconfidência Mineira, the name for the Minas revolt against the monarchy in 1789. Later, other strong proponents of change would hail from Minas Gerais as well. Juscelino Kubitschek, president from 1956 to 1961, was born in Diamantina and a former mayor of Belo Horizonte. He reshaped the country by moving the capital from Rio de Janeiro to Brasília in the 1960s. Tancredo Neves, who helped restore Brazilian democracy in the 1980s was born in São João del Rey.

Though the Gold Towns—Ouro Preto, Mariana, Tiradentes, and Congonhas—are awe-inspiring, Minas Gerais has other attractions. Roughly six hours south of the state capital of Belo Horizonte, several mineral-spa towns form the Circuito das Águas (Water Circuit). Thought to have healing powers, the natural springs of places like São Lourenço and Caxambu have attracted the Brazilian elite for more than a century. Close by is the unusual town of São Tomé das Letras—a place where UFOs are said to visit and where mystics and bohemians wait for the dawn of a new world.

ORIENTATION & PLANNING

ORIENTATION

A landlocked state in the southeast of Brazil, Minas is approximately the size of France (588,384 square km/227,176 square mi). It borders six other Brazilian states. The Serra da Mantiqueira range creates a natural boundary between Minas and Rio de Janeiro, it encircles to the south the Paraíba Valley an area between the states of São Paulo, Rio de Janeiro, and Minas Gerais. The Serra da Canastra mountain range is a source of the São Francisco River; the longest river in the country flows

TOP REASONS TO GO

■ Walking on the *paralelepípedos* (cobblestones) in Ouro Preto, Diamantina, and Tiradentes, all magnificently preserved baroque towns of white and pastel houses and churches.

■ Seeing the baroque gems of architect and sculptor Alejaidinho, whom an ex-curator of the Louvre called the "Michelangelo of the Tropics."

■ Indulging your tastebuds in every Brazilian's favorite culinary state—if only for the *pão de queijo* (cheese bread) and the *doce de leite* or the

sweet of milk, a boiled version of condensed milk.

■ Minas Gerais produces most of the world's colored gemstones, including amethysts, aquamarines, tourmalines, emeralds, and the imperial topaz, which can only be found in Ouro Preto and in the Ural mountains in Russia.

■ Hiking, horseback riding, and swimming in and around the beautiful national parks and natural springs tapped by numerous spa towns.

down from the mountains through most of Minas Gerais and Bahia, and enters the ocean between the states of Sergipe and Alagoas. Minas is one of the most populous states, with a population of 19.4 million. The state has approximately 16% of the country's paved roads, making it one of the easiest states to navigate. Although Minas is large, its major attractions, including Belo Horizonte, Ouro Preto, and the mineral-spa towns, are in the state's southeast, within driving distance of one another.

BELO HORIZONTE

Belo Horizonte is the third-largest city in the country, with more than 2.5 million inhabitants. At an elevation of 2,815 feet, the city lies in a valley encircled by a ring of mountains, the Serra do Curral. The city center was planned for carriages, and the streets crisscross each other at 45-degree angles, making modern-day traffic absolutely impossible. Social and cultural activity is concentrated along three main plazas in the center: Praça Sete, Praç a da Liberdade, and Praç a da Savassi.

THE COLONIAL & GOLD TOWNS

The historic cities of Ouro Preto, Tiradentes, and Diamantina lie in the Serra do Espinhaço range, with Ouro Preto at 4,000 feet. This central region of Minas Gerais is the most populous, with more than 7 million inhabitants. The towns are typically very hilly, with narrow winding streets that are more easily navigated on foot than in a car.

THE MINERAL SPA TOWNS

The Circuito das Águas (Water Circuit) of Minas Gerais is concentrated in the southeastern regions (essentially counties) of Sul de Minas (2.6 million inhabitants) and Mata (population 2.2 million). The small cities of Caxambu and São Lourenço sit at an elevation of about 4,000 feet and have less than 50,000 inhabitants each. They're equidistant from the cities of São Paulo, Rio de Janeiro, and Belo Horizonte (400 km).

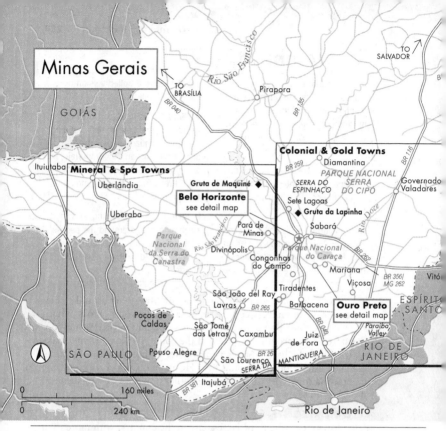

PLANNING

WHEN TO GO

The busiest and most expensive time to travel is during Christmas, Easter, Carnaval, and the month of July—because most Brazilians take their vacations at this time. The most exciting time to be in the colonial towns is during the Semana Santa (the Holy Week of Easter), when there are colorful processions of joyous locals in the streets, and everyone celebrates. Temperatures are usually around 24°C (75°F) in summer and 17°C (63°F) in winter. Summer is the rainy season, winter is dry but cooler; sturdy shoes and jackets are highly recommended at all times. To avoid crowds and rain, travel from April to June or August to November. Discounts may be available during these months, although fewer services will be offered.

YELLOW FEVER VACCINATIONS

A yellow fever outbreak in Brazil's interior was announced in early 2008; Belo Horizonte as well as the rest of the state are in the medium-risk category. A yellow fever vaccine, administered at least 10 days before your trip, is advisable.

A Bit of History

Exploration of Minas began in the 17th century, when *bandeirantes* (bands of adventurers) from the coastal areas came in search of slaves and gold. What they found in the area was a black stone that was later verified to be gold (the coloring came from the iron oxide in the soil). In 1698 the first capital of Minas was founded and called Vila Rica de Ouro Preto (Rich Town of Black Gold), and some 13 years later Brazil's first gold rush began. Along with the fortune seekers came Jesuit priests, who were later exiled by the Portuguese (for fear they would try to manipulate the mineral trade) and replaced by *ordens terceiros* (third, or lay, orders). By the middle of the century the Gold Towns of Minas were gleaming with new churches built first in the baroque-rococo style of Europe and later in a baroque style unique to the region.

By the end of the 18th century the gold had begun to run out, and Ouro Preto's population and importance decreased. The baroque period ended at the start of the 19th century, when the Portuguese royal family, in flight from the conquering army of Napoléon Bonaparte, arrived in Brazil, bringing with them architects and sculptors with different ideas and artistic styles. Ornate twisted columns and walls adorned with lavish carvings gave way to simple straight columns and walls painted with murals or simply washed in white.

Today Minas Gerais is Brazil's second most industrialized state, after São Paulo. The iron that darkened the gold of Ouro Preto remains an important source of state income, along with steel, coffee, and auto manufacturing. The traffic that the mines brought here in the 17th century thrust Brazil into civilization, and now, well into the wake of the gold rush, a steady sense of progress and a compassion for the land remain.

ABOUT THE RESTAURANTS & CUISINE

Probably the most popular cuisine in the country, Mineiran food is a mixure of Portuguese, Indian, and African flavors. Famous foods include *lombo de porco* (pork loin) often served with sausage on the side, and for dessert, *goiabada* (guava paste). *Pão de queijo*, chewy cheese bread in roll form, is the culinary hallmark of the state—mineiro bakeries get the consistency just right. The *cachaça* (sugarcane rum) from the northern region of Salinas is considered the best in the country. Mineiros tend to eat dinner after 8. Many restaurants close on Monday. Reservations may be required, especially on weekends.

WHAT IT COSTS IN REAIS				
¢	$	$$	$$$	$$$$
AT DINNER under R$15	R$15–R$30	R$30–R$45	R$45–R$60	over R$60

Prices are per person for a main course at dinner or for a prix-fixe meal.

ABOUT THE HOTELS

In the interior of Minas Gerais, especially in the historic cities and state parks, there are two types of traditional accommodations for tourists: *pousadas* (inns), with simple rooms, and *fazendas* (Texan-ranch-style farms), which can be a fun option. Most hotels outside of Belo Horizonte are small, lack English-speaking staff, and have few of the amenities common in American and European chains. In Belo Horizonte you can find large hotels and chain hotels equivalent to those found in U.S. cities that cater to the regular and business traveler. When you book, you'll likely be given a choice between an *apartamento standard* (standard room) and an *apartamento de luxo* (luxury room), which may be slightly larger, with a/c and nicer bathroom. Significant weekend discounts are common in Belo Horizonte.

WHAT IT COSTS IN REAIS				
	¢	$	$$	$$$	$$$$
FOR 2 PEOPLE	under R$125	R$125–R$250	R$250–R$375	R$375–R$500	over R$500

Prices are for a standard double room in high season, excluding tax.

GETTING AROUND

It's feasible to visit all the highlights of the state on a two-week vacation. If you have a week you could spend three days in Ouro Preto, two in Tiradentes, and two in Belo Horizonte. For a smaller three-day trip Ouro Preto comes highly recommended as one of the most beautiful and culturally rich places in Brazil. The buses in Minas are comfortable and inexpensive, and travel regularly between Belo Horizonte, Diamantina, Ouro Preto, Tiradentes, and other historic towns. The only reason to rent a car is to take in some of the national and state parks that are not easily accessed by bus. The city buses in Belo Horizonte are safe and easy to use.

BELO HORIZONTE

444 km (276 mi) northwest of Rio, 586 km (364 mi) northeast of São Paulo, 741 km (460 mi) southeast of Brasília.

Since the planned uprising of the Inconfidentes in 1789, the residents of the state had dreamed of a capital that would open a new historical chapter. The initiative to wipe the slate clean of Portuguese influence came at the end of the 19th century with the proclamation of the republic. The first planned modern city in Brazil modeled its streets on the wide avenues of Paris and Washington, and on their circular city centers. In 1893 the head of the state, Afonso Pena, proclaimed the site for the new capital. The Cidade de Minas (city of Minas) was established in 1897, when Ouro Preto, because of its mountainous geography, could no longer afford a population expansion. The city planning was overseen by the engineer Aarão Reis. In 1906 the city assumed its current name of Belo Horizonte.

Today Belo Horizonte, the third-largest city in Brazil after Rio and São Paulo, is distinguished by its politics and its contributions to the arts. In the early 20th century the Brazilian political system was referred to as Café com Leite ("coffee with milk"), because the presidency was alternately held by natives of São Paulo (where much of Brazil's coffee is produced) and natives of Minas Gerais (the milk-producing state). The current system is more diverse, but mineiros are still influential in the country's politics. Minas Gerais is home to some of the most respected Brazilian theater and dance companies and some of Brazil's most famous pop bands. The artistic tradition is emphasized by the many festivals dedicated to all forms of art, from comic books to puppet theater and short movies to electronic music. The arts and nightlife scene, along with the stunning modern architecture, are reasons to visit Belo Horizonte before or after traversing Minas Gerais's peaceful countryside.

> **RANCH STAYS**
>
> **AMETUR** (✉ *Rua Paraíba 1317, loja 15, Savassi, 30130-141 Belo Horizonte* ☎ *031/3227-0006 or 031/3227-6886* ⊕ *www.ametur. tur.br*), the Association of Rural Tourism, is a group of respected, trustworthy ranch owners who have converted their *fazendas* (farms, or ranches) into accommodations with luxurious yet down-home surroundings. You can visit one or more of these ranches, where relaxation, swimming, horseback riding, walks in the woods, and home-cooked meals are the order of the day.

TO & FROM

Flights from Rio de Janeiro or São Paulo to Belo Horizonte are less than an hour and can be quite inexpensive. The same trip by bus or car takes approximately six to eight hours. Roads can be bad and truck traffic is constant—flying is by far the easier option.

Belo Horizonte's main airport, which serves most domestic and international flights, is a half-hour taxi ride (about R$75) north of the downtown. *Executivo* (air-conditioned) buses leave every 45 minutes and cost R$10–R$15. Aeroporto Pampulha is 9 km (5 mi) northwest of downtown and serves some domestic flights. Taxis from here to downtown cost about R$25.

Frequent buses connect Belo Horizonte with Rio (R$60–R$83; 7 hours), São Paulo (R$70–R$126; 8 hours), and Brasília (R$93–R$105; 12 hours). All buses have a/c. Get advance tickets at holiday times. All buses arrive at and depart (punctually) from the Terminal Rodoviária Israel Pinheiro da Silva. Bus companies include Cometa for Rio and São Paulo; Gontijo, for São Paulo; Itapemirim, for Brasília, Rio, and Sao Pāulo; and Útil, for Rio.

Driving to BH from major cities is safe, the roads are in good condition, although exits aren't always clearly marked. BR 040 connects Belo Horizonte with Rio (6.5 hours), to the southeast, and Brasília (10 hours), to the northwest. BR 381 links the city with São Paulo (7.5 hours).

Belo Horizonte

GETTING AROUND

Minas Gerais is a mountainous state, so be prepared for lots of hills when walking around Belo Horizonte. The central and original section of the city, planned in the 19th century, is surrounded by Avenida Contorno. The city's main attractions are downtown (the center) and in the southern zone. On a map the center looks easily walkable, but the blocks are a lot larger than they seem and sometimes taking a bus is advisable. During the day these areas are not too crowded. To get to other neighborhoods, like Pampulha, you should take a bus or a taxi.

> ### BEAUTIFUL HORIZONS
>
> Belo Horizonte assumed its name in 1906. Its name means "beautiful horizons," so called because of the striking panoramic view of the mountains that used to dominate the city when it was just a village. The horizon is no longer visible because of pollution and skyscrapers. Brazilians will be impressed if you refer to the city as BH, (pronounced bei ah-*gah*), its affectionate nickname.

Belo Horizonte's municipal bus system is safe and efficient, although buses are crowded during rush hour. Bhtrans, the city's transit authority, has route information. Fares depend on the distance traveled but are always less than R$3.

Belo Horizonte's rush-hour traffic can be heavy, and parking can be difficult (for on-street parking you must buy a sticker at a newsstand or bookshop). Taking the bus in Belo Horizonte is recommended over driving because of the traffic and the city's diagonal grid, which is hard to navigate.

Taxis in Belo Horizonte are white and can be hailed or called. The meter starts at about R$3.30 and costs about R$1.84 for every kilometer traveled (slightly higher at night and on weekends).

ESSENTIALS

Airports Aeroporto Internacional Tancredo Neves (*Aeroporto de Confins* ✉ *MG 10, Confins, 39 km (24 mi) north of Belo Horizonte, 33500-972* ☎ *031/3689–2557*). **Aeroporto Pampulha** (✉ *Praça Bagatelle 204, Pampulha, 31270-705* ☎ *031/3490–2001*).

Banks & Currency Exchange Agência Belo Horizonte (✉ *Rua Espírito Santo 871, Centro, 30160-031* ⊕ *www.citibank.com.br*). **Banco do Brasil** (✉ *Rua Rio de Janeiro 750, Centro, 30160-040* ⊕ *www.bb.com.br*). **HSBC Savassi** (✉ *Rua Alagoas 1029, Savassi, 30130-160* ⊕ *www.hsbc.com.br*).

Bus Contacts Bhtrans (☎ *031/3277–6500* ⊕ *www.bhtrans.pbh.gov.br*). **Cometa** (☎ *031/4004–9600* ⊕ *www.viacaocometa.com.br*). **Gontijo** (☎ *0800/311–312* ⊕ *www.gontijo.com.br*). **Itapemirim** (☎ *0800/723-2121* ⊕ *www.itapemirim.com. br*). **Terminal Rodoviária Israel Pinheiro da Silva** (✉ *Av. Afonso Pena at Praça Rio Branco s/n, Centro, 30111-970* ☎ *031/3271–3000 or 031/3271–8933* ⊕ *www. pbh.gov.br/rodoviaria*). **Útil** (☎ *031/3271–6115 or 031/3907–9000* ⊕ *www.util. com.br*).

Emergencies & Medical Assistance Ambulance (☎ *192*). **Fire** (☎ *193*). **Police** (☎ *190*).

Hospital: **Hospital Semper** (⊠ *Av. Alameda Ezequiel Dias 389, Centro, 30130-110* ☎ *031/3248–3000 or 3248–3061*). Pharmacy: **Drogaria Araújo** (⊠ *Rua Curitiba 327, Centro, 30170-120* ☎ *031/3270-5577*).

Taxis Cooperbh Taxi (☎ *0800/35-3939 or 031/3251-8081*). **Unitaxi** (☎ *0800/283-0399 or 31/3418-3434*).

Visitor & Tour Info AMO-TE (⊠ *Rua Monte Verde 125, São Salvador, 30881-410* ☎ *031/3477-7757*). **Belotur** (⊠ *Rua Aimorés 981, 6th fl., Funcionários, 30140-071* ☎ *031/3277-9777* ⊕ *www.belotur.com.br* ⊠ *Mercado das Flores at Av. Afonso Pena 1055, Centro, 30130-003* ☎ *031/3277-7666* ⊠ *Rodoviária, Av. Afonso Pena at Praça Rio Branco, Centro, 30111-970* ☎ *031/3277-6907* ⊠ *Mercado Central at Av. Augusto de Lima 744, Centro, 30190-001* ☎ *031/3277-4691* ⊠ *Confins Airport, MG 10, Confins, 33500-972* ☎ *031/3689-2557* ☞ *Open daily 8 AM–10 PM at airport and bus station; weekdays 8-6 or 7 elsewhere*). **Setur** (⊠ *Praça da Liberdade s/n, 2nd fl., Funcionários, 30140-010* ☎ *031/3270-8501 or 031/3207-8502* ⊕ *www.turismo.mg.gov.br* ☞ *Info on historic cities and other attractions. Open weekdays 8-6*). **YTUR Turismo** (⊠ *Av. do Contorno 8000, loja 2, Lourdes, 30160-040* ☎ *031/2111-8000* ⊕ *www.ytur.com.br* ☞ *Tours of Belo Horizonte and beyond; hotel and transportation bookings*).

NIEMEYER & PORTINARI

Two great Brazilian artists, both renowned communists, Oscar Niemeyer and Candido Portinari collaborated on the Pampulha complex. Portinari grew up in São Paulo, the son of Italian immigrants, and was famous for his neorealism style. He died at the age of 34 from lead poisoning from his paints. Niemeyer is considered one of the world's most important architects due to his singular designs of reinforced concrete; many of his works can be found in Minas. The entire country celebrated his centennial birthday in 2007.

SAFETY & PRECAUTIONS

Avoid areas around Parque das Mangabeiras after dark.

EXPLORING

MAIN ATTRACTIONS

⑫ **Conjunto Arquitetônico da Pampulha.** This modern complex designed by
Fodor's Choice Oscar Niemeyer and built in the 1940s on the banks of Lagoa da Pam-
★ pulha cannot be missed. Opened in 1943, the **Casa do Baile** (*Ballroom House* ⊠ *Av. Otacílio Negrão de Lima 751, Pampulha, 31365-450* ☎ *031/3277–7443*)) was a popular dance hall. It closed its doors shortly after the casino that is now the Pampulha Art Museum. Today the Casa do Baile is an art gallery. It's open Tuesday through Sunday 9–7, and admission is free. The **Igreja de São Francisco de Assis** (*Church of St. Francis of Assisi* ⊠ *Av. Otacílio Negrão de Lima s/n, Pampulha, 31365-450* ☎ *031/3427–1644*) has 14 panels on the life of the saint that are moving riffs of the azulejos (decorative blue Portuguese tiles) found in many colonial churches in Brazil. The church is open Monday though Saturday 9–5 and Sunday 9–1; tickets are R$2. One of Niemeyer's first projects was the **Museu de Arte da Pampulha** (*Pampulha Art Museum* ⊠ *Av. Otacílio Negrão de Lima 16585, Pampulha, 31365-450* ☎ *031/3277–*

7996 *or 031/3277–7946*), which has landscaped gardens by Burle Marx. The building was a casino until 1946, when gambling was prohibited in Brazil. Transformed into a museum in 1957, the building also has multimedia rooms, a small theater, a library, and a coffee shop. It's open only for guided visits Tuesday through Sunday 9–9; admission is free.

> **KUBITSCHEK**
>
> In 1940 Juscelino Kubitschek became the mayor of Belo Horizonte, and in 1956 became president of Brazil. While he was responsible for the creation of Brasília, his years in office resulted in the devaluation of currency and corruption scandals. After the military took power in 1964, Kubitschek went into self-imposed exile, but returned three years later to the fight for democracy. He died in a car accident in 1976, but conspiracy theorists claim that he was assassinated by the military regime.

⑪ **Mercado Central** *(Central Market).*
★ In the more than 400 stores in this beautiful old market dating from 1929 you can find almost everything—from groceries to typical products from Minas Gerais, such as cheese, guava and milk sweets, arts and crafts, medicinal herbs and roots, and even pets. Many people (including local celebrities) stop by the popular bars inside the market to drink beer and sample the famous appetizers, such as liver with onions. ⊠ *Av. Augusto de Lima 744, Centro, 30190-922* ☎ *031/3277–4691* ⊕ *www.mercadocentral.com.br* ☜ *Free* ⊗ *Mon.–Sat. 7–6, Sun. 7–1.*

⑦ **Palácio das Artes.** Designed by Oscar Niemeyer and built in 1970, the **Fodor's Choice** Palace of the Arts is the most important cultural center in Belo Horizonte, comprising three theaters, three art galleries, a movie theater, a ★ bookstore, a coffee shop, and the Centro de Artesanato Mineiro (Mineiro Artisan Center), which has such contemporary Minas handicrafts as wood and soapstone carvings, pottery, and tapestries—all for sale. The main theater, Grande Teatro, stages music concerts, plays, operas, ballets, and other productions by Brazilian and foreign artists. ⊠ *Av. Afonso Pena 1537, Centro, 30130-004* ☎ *031/3236–7400* ⊕ *www. palaciodasartes.com.br* ☜ *Free* ⊗ *Tues.–Sat. 10–9, Sun. 2–8.*

⑧ **Parque Municipal Américo Renné Giannetti.** With 45 acres of luscious ☾ tropical plants and magical winding walkways, the Parque Municipal (municipal park) was inspired by the landscaping of French gardens and inaugurated in 1897. It shelters an orchid house, a school, a playground, and the Francisco Nunes Theater, a beautiful modern building designed by the architect Luiz Signorelli in the 1940s that still presents theatrical plays and musical performances. With more than 50 tree species, the Municipal Park is highly recommended for walks. ⊠ *Av. Afonso Pena s/n, Centro, 30130-004* ☎ *031/3277–4161 park, 031/3277–6325 theater* ☜ *Free* ⊗ *Tues.–Sun. 6–6.*

④ **Praça da Liberdade** *(Liberty Square).* When the city was founded, this square was created to house public administration offices. Today, in addition to centenarian palm trees, fountains, and a bandstand, the square also has neoclassical, art deco, modern, and postmodern buildings. ⊠*Between avs. João Pinheiro and Cristóvão Colombro, Funcionários, 30140-010.*

IF YOU HAVE TIME

5 **Basílica de Lourdes.** Conceived when the capital was founded but only inaugurated in 1923, Our Lady of Lourdes Church was elevated to the category of basilica by Pope Pius XII in 1958. Its Gothic architecture has received some adaptations, but it's still a magnificent building. ⊠*Rua da Bahia 1596, Lourdes, 30160-011* ☎*031/3213-4656* ⊠*Free* ⊙*Daily 7 AM–8 PM.*

> ### FIGHTING POVERTY
>
> The state of Minas Gerais is a frontrunner in seeking novel ways to help fight hunger. Tickets to many artistic performances at the Palácio das Artes and other venues can be bought at half price if the audience member brings one kilogram of nonperishable goods like oats or rice to the performance.

10 **Museu de Artes e Ofícios.** In the main building of the Praça da Estação, in the center of the city, this museum houses almost 2,000 rudimentary tools and other items from the 17th to the 20th centuries used by Brazilian laborers. Saturday admission is free. ⊠*Praça Rui Barbosa s/n, Estação Central, Centro, 30160-000* ☎*031/3248–8600* ⊠*R$4* ⊙*Tues., Thurs., and Fri. noon–7, Wed. noon–9, weekends 11–5.*

9 **Museu de História Natural e Jardim Botânico.** Although it has an area of nearly 150 acres with Brazilian fauna, flora, archaeology, and mineralogy, the museum's main attraction is the Presépio do Pipiripau (Pipiripau Crèche). This ingenious work of art narrates Christ's life in 45 scenes, with 580 moving figures. It was built by Raimundo Machado de Azevedo, who began assembling it in 1906 and finished in 1984. The Instituto do Patrimônio Histórico e Artístico Nacional (National Institute of the History and Arts) deemed it artistic patrimony in 1984. ⊠*Rua Gustavo da Silveira 1035, Santa Inês, 31080-010* ☎*031/3461–5805 or 031/3482–9723* ⊠*R$3* ⊙*Tues.–Fri. 8–11:30 and 1–4, weekends 10–5.*

3 **Museu de Mineralogia Professor Djalma Guimarães.** More than 3,000 pieces extracted from sites all over the world are on display in the mineralogy museum, which is housed in a postmodern steel-and-glass building. ⊠*Av. Bias Fortes 50, Funcionários, 30170-010* ☎*031/3271–3415* ⊕*www.pbh.gov.br* ⊠*Free* ⊙*Tues.–Sun. 9–5.*

1 **Museu Histórico Abílio Barreto.** Attached to an old colonial mansion, the Abílio Barreto Historical Museum (MHAB) has permanent and temporary exhibitions about the city of Belo Horizonte. Its comfortable coffee shop is open until midnight. ⊠*Av. Prudente de Morais 202, Cidade Jardim, 30380-000* ☎*031/3277–8573* ⊠*Free* ⊙*Tues.–Sun. 10–5.*

2 **Palácio da Liberdade.** Built in 1898, the French-style Liberdade Palace is the headquarters of the Minas Gerais government and is the official residence of the governor. Of note are the gardens by Paul Villon, the Louis XV–style banquet room, the paintings in Noble Hall, and a panel by Antônio Pereira. The palace is open to the public only on the last Sunday of every month. ⊠*Praça da Liberdade s/n, Funcionários, 30140-912* ☎*031/3250–6011* 🎫*Free* 🕑*Last Sun. of month, 8:30–2.*

WHERE TO EAT

\$\$–\$\$\$\$ ✕**Splêndido Ristorante.** The food and the service at this cosmopolitan restaurant are exceptional. The kitchen blends French and northern Italian cuisines to produce a menu with a mix of pasta, seafood, and meat dishes. It's assured that anyone who's anyone will show up here at some point during a visit to Belo Horizonte. The restaurant has the best wine cellar in town, with about 200 labels on the menu. ⊠*Rua Levindo Lopes 251, Funcionários, 30140-170* ☎*031/3227–6446* ▤*AE, DC, MC, V* 🕑*No lunch Sat. No dinner Sun.*

\$\$–\$\$\$\$ ✕**Vecchio Sogno.** What is widely considered Belo Horizonte's best Ital-
★ ian restaurant attracts a well-heeled clientele. Tuxedo-clad waiters serve selections from the extensive wine list as well as steak, seafood, and pasta dishes. Consider the grilled fillet of lamb with saffron risotto in a mushroom-and-garlic sauce; the gnocchi *di mare,* with spinach and potatoes, topped with a white clam and scallop sauce; or the *badejo,* a local white fish baked and dressed in a seafood sauce. The restaurant allows its diners into its kitchen to see the preparation of food; there are some no-smoking rooms. The interior, with its beautiful wood paneling and an extensive bar, mirrors a 1940s jazz club. ⊠*Rua Martim de Carvalho 75, Santo Agostinho, 30190-090* ☎*031/3292–5251* ⊕*www.vecchiosogno.com.br* 🍴*Reservations essential* ▤*AE, V* 🕑*No lunch Sat. No dinner Sun.*

\$–\$\$\$ ✕**Chalezinho.** There's only one reason to come here: romance. The
★ dimly lighted chalet, with its elegant piano music (accompanied by the occasional saxophone), is a magical retreat in the hills above town. The specialty is fondue; the filet mignon cooked in a bowl of sizzling oil and paired with any of eight delicious sauces is a treat. Afterward, order a chocolate fondue, which comes with a mouthwatering selection of fruits waiting to be dipped. When you finish, step outside to the Praça dos Amores (Lovers' Plaza) for a kiss under the moonlighted sky. ⊠*Alameda da Serra 8, Vale do Sereno, 34000-000* ☎*031/3286–3155* ⊕*www.chalezinho.com.br* ▤*DC, MC, V* 🕑*No lunch.*

\$–\$\$\$ ✕**Restaurante Varandão.** On the 25th floor of the Othon Palace hotel, this romantic restaurant has spectacular urban vistas. Start off with a cocktail at one of the outdoor candlelighted tables before coming inside for dinner, where a generous buffet serves as the dining room's centerpiece. Feijoada, pastas, salads, and various meats are on the buffet daily. The feijoada on Saturday is a special meal that centers mainly on

Eating Like a Mineiro

Some gastronomic critics say there are only three native Brazilian cuisines: the cuisine from the North (particularly from Pará); the Capixaba cuisine from Espírito Santo; and *comida mineira,* the cuisine from Minas Gerais. Purportedly, all other Brazilian cuisines are originally from outside Brazil. Since Minas Gerais is one of the few states without access to the sea, its cuisine is strongly based on pork and chicken, and legumes and cereals (most notably beans and corn).

The mainstay of comida mineira is *tutu,* a tasty mash of beans with roast pork loin, pork sausage, chopped collard greens, manioc meal, and boiled egg served with meat dishes. Another favorite is *feijão tropeiro,* a combination of beans, manioc meal,

roast pork loin, fried egg, chopped collard greens, and thick pork sausage. Among meat dishes, pork is the most common, in particular the famed *lingüiça* (Minas pork sausage) and *lombo* (pork tenderloin), which is often served with white rice and/or corn porridge. The most typical chicken dish is *frango ao molho pardo,* broiled chicken served in a sauce made with its own blood. Another specialty is *frango com quiabo,* chicken cooked in broth with chopped okra. The region's very mild white cheese is known throughout Brazil simply as *queijo Minas* (Minas cheese). Pão de queijo (bread baked with Minas cheese) is irresistible, and popular throughout Brazil. You'll realize very quickly that Minas Gerais isn't the place to start a diet.

the meat and beans portion of the usual buffet and is accompanied by live music. ⊠ *Av. Afonso Pena 1050, Centro, 30130-003* ☎ *031/2126–0000 or 031/2126–0090* ⊕ *www.othon.com.br* ▤ *AE, DC, MC, V.*

\$\$
FodorśChoice
★
× **Amigo do Rei.** The first Persian restaurant of Brazil appeared in Paraty, Rio de Janeiro, but moved to the capital of Minas Gerais in 2002. This homey place has 23 seats. The owner, Cláudio, is the host, and his wife, Nasrin, is the chef. Before your order is ready, the waiter will be happy to inform you about Iranian culture. A recommended dish is the *fessenjhuhn,* small meat spheres with walnuts and pomegranate, white rice with saffron, and the typical *borani* zucchini-and-yogurt dip. ⊠ *Rua Quintiliano Silva 118, Santo Antônio, 30350-040* ☎ *031/3296–3881* ⊕ *www.amigodorei.com.br* ⌁ *Reservations essential* ▤ *No credit cards* ☉ *Closed Mon. and Tues. No lunch Wed.–Sat. No dinner Sun.*

\$\$
× **Dona Lucinha.** Roughly 32 traditional Minas dishes, like feijão tropeiro, frango com quiabo, and frango ao molho pardo, are available at this reasonably priced buffet restaurant. The food is the only reason to go, as the place—in an old house devoid of taste—lacks charm. Children get significant discounts. ⊠ *Rua Padre Odorico 38, São Pedro, 30330-040* ☎ *031/3227–0562* ▤ *AE, DC, MC, V* ☉ *No dinner Sun.* ⊠ *Rua Sergipe 811, Funcionários, 30130-171* ☎ *031/3261–5930* ⊕ *www.donalucinha.com.br* ▤ *AE, DC, MC, V* ☉ *No dinner Sun..*

\$–\$\$
★
× **Memmo Pasta & Pizza.** This casual Italian eatery is popular with Brazilians celebrating the end of the workday for appetizers like the *champignon Recheado* (mushroom stuffed with shrimp and prosciutto), and entrées like *tournedo Amici Miei* (filet mignon wrapped in bacon

and marinated in garlic and olive oil). The pizza is arguably the best in town. The restaurant is often packed both inside and on the large outdoor patio; you may need to wait for the staff to find you a table. ⊠ *Rua Tome de Souza 1331, Funcionários, 30140-130* ☎ *031/3282– 4992* ⊕ *www.memmo.com.br* ☰ *AE, DC, MC, V* ☉ *No dinner Sun.*

¢–$$　✕ **Casa dos Contos.** A popular gathering place for local journalists, artists, and intellectuals, Casa dos Contos has an unpretentious and varied menu with choices ranging from fish and pasta to typical mineiro dishes. In keeping with its bohemian clientele, Casa dos Contos serves well past midnight. ⊠ *Rua Rio Grande do Norte 1065, Funcionários, 31130-131* ☎ *031/3261–5853* ☰ *AE, DC, MC, V.*

WHERE TO STAY

$$–$$$ 🏨 **Ouro Minas Palace Hotel.** The only five-star hotel in Belo Horizonte,
Fodor'sChoice the palatial Ouro Minas has rooms with large beds and well-appointed
★ bathrooms. The largest of the three presidential suites is more 300 square meters (3,229 square feet). A pillow menu with 10 different kinds of pillows, hydromassage bathtubs, CD players, a pool with waterfalls, and a multilingual staff are a few of the many amenities here that are otherwise hard to find in Belo Horizonte. **Pros:** The city's most luxurious hotel, with lots of extras. **Cons:** Not centrally located. ⊠ *Av. Cristiano Machado 4001, Ipiranga, 31910-810* ☎ *031/3429– 4001* ⊕ *www.ourominas.com.br* ⇆ *298 rooms, 45 suites* ☖ *In-room: safe, refrigerator, dial-up. In-hotel: restaurant, room service, bar, pool, sauna, gym, laundry service, public Internet, no-smoking rooms* ☰ *AE, DC, MC, V* ⍟ *BP.*

$$ 🏨 **Mercure Lourdes.** On a main city avenue, close to the Savassi area and not far from Belo Horizonte's central region, the Mercure hotel is popular among executives and artists. Its seven convention rooms occasionally stage music concerts. The restaurant's menu includes French, Italian, and international dishes. **Pros:** At a central location, rooms on higher floors have wonderful views of the city. **Cons:** Standard apartments do not get free Internet. ⊠ *Av. do Contorno 7315, Lourdes, 30110-046* ☎ *031/3298–4100* ⊕ *www.accorhotels.com.br* ⇆ *374 rooms* ☖ *In-room: safe, refrigerator. In-hotel: 2 restaurants, room service, bar, pool, gym, laundry service, public Internet, no-smoking rooms* ☰ *AE, DC, MC, V* ⍟ *BP.*

$–$$ 🏨 **Othon Palace.** Across the street from the vividly beautiful and exotic
★ Parque Municipal, the Othon has comfortable rooms with incredible city and park views. The rooftop pool and bar are the best in town, and the on-site Restaurante Varandão (⇨ *above)* is excellent. **Pros:** Best location of any hotel in Belo Horizonte. **Cons:** Rooms lack character. ⊠ *Av. Afonso Pena 1050, Centro, 30130-003* ☎ *031/2126–0000 or 0800/725–0505* ⊕ *www.hoteis-othon.com.br* ⇆ *266 rooms, 19 suites* ☖ *In-room: safe, refrigerator, broadband. In-hotel: restaurant, room service, bar, pool, gym, laundry service, executive floor, Wi-Fi, no-smoking rooms* ☰ *AE, DC, MC, V* ⍟ *BP.*

$ 🏨 **Ibis.** This neat and comfortable option has spacious rooms with
★ white oak furniture and large beds. Constructed in 2003, it has all the

modern amenities and a well-trained and professional staff. Ibis hosts a number of conventions, and is able to accommodate disabled visitors. It's in the backyard of an old mansion that has been well maintained. **Pros:** Best budget hotel in town, in the best part of the city. **Cons:** Minimalist rooms with sparser furnishings than those of most hotels in this price range. ⊠*Rua João Pinheiro 602, Lourdes, 30130-180* ☎*031/2111–1500* ⊕*www.accorhotels.com.br* ⇋*130 rooms* ⌂*In-room: safe, refrigerator, dial-up. In-hotel: bar, public Internet* ⊟*AE, DC, MC, V* ⧖*EP.*

$ 📺**Minas Hotel.** The lobby of this centrally located hotel, one of the city's oldest, is often crowded with conventioneers. Rooms are clean and in fine working order, but are inexpensively furnished and outdated style-wise. **Pros:** Many rooms have the same view of the city and surrounding mountains that you'll find from the small rooftop pool and bar. **Cons:** Rooms that don't have this view tend to be a bit dark. ⊠*Rua Espírito Santo 901, Centro, 30160-031* ☎*031/3248–1000* ⊕*www.dayrell.com.br* ⇋*230 rooms* ⌂*In-room: safe, refrigerator, dial-up. In-hotel: restaurant, room service, bar, pool, gym, laundry service* ⊟*AE, DC, MC, V* ⧖*BP.*

¢–$ 📺**Hotel Amazonas Palace.** This downtown hotel has clean, simple rooms that are reasonably priced. The 11th-floor restaurant is good and has a nice view of the city. **Pros:** Has a solarium, where you can get a tan to compete with the bronzed Brazilians. **Cons:** Hotel often used for conventions and lacks character. ⊠*Av. Amazonas 120, Centro, 30180-001* ☎*031/3201–4644 or 031/3309–4650* ⊕*www.amazonaspalace.com.br* ⇋*76 rooms* ⌂*In-room: refrigerator. In-hotel: restaurant, room service, bars, pool, laundry service, public Internet, no-smoking rooms* ⊟*AE, DC, MC, V* ⧖*BP.*

¢–$ 📺**Hotel Wimbledon.** A central location and a pleasant mix of elegance and warmth set this hotel above others in its price range. Rooms have polished hardwood floors, local artwork, and modern bathrooms. The rooftop bar, next to the pool, is the perfect spot for an afternoon drink. **Pros:** Charming and with attentive service that makes it feel like a bed-and-breakfast. **Cons:** Only luxury *apartamentos luxo* rooms have whirlpool baths. ⊠*Av. Afonso Pena 772, Centro, 30130-002* ☎*031/3222–6160* ⊕*www.wimbledon.com.br* ⇋*69 rooms, 1 suite* ⌂*In-room: safe, refrigerator, dial-up. In-hotel: restaurant, room service, bar, pool, laundry service, public Internet, no-smoking rooms* ⊟*AE, DC, MC, V* ⧖*BP.*

NIGHTLIFE

No other city in Brazil has as many bars and coffee shops as Belo Horizonte—there are 14,000, or one for every 150 inhabitants. This isn't a recent trend: the first bar appeared in 1893, four years before the city was founded. The bar culture is the core of the city's nightlife. There's even a contest every year in April, the Comida di Buteco, or Bar Food Contest (⊕*www.comidadibuteco.com.br*), to reward the bar with the best appetizers and the coldest beer.

BARS

Fodor'sChoice
★
For some of Brazil's best cachaças and one of the city's best views, try **Alambique Cachaçaria e Armazém** (⌗*Av. Raja Gabáglia 3200, Chalé 1D, Estoril, 30350-540* ☎*031/3296–7188* ⊕*www.alambique.com.br*). **Arrumação** (⌗*Av. Assis Chateaubriand 524, Floresta, 30150-101* ☎*031/3088–3952 or 031/3222–9794* ⊕*www.saulolaranjeira.com.br*) is a traditional bar in a colonial building that's owned by Brazilian comedian and actor Saulo Laranjeira; it specializes in cachaças.

> ### MINING WEALTH
>
> Brazil's mining wealth was almost completely exported to Portugal. The gold and diamonds mined in the colonial towns were used to build Lisbon. This tremendous infusion of wealth into the European economy led to the Industrial Revolution in Britain.

Bolão (⌗*Rua Mármore 689, Santa Tereza, 31010-220* ☎*031/3461–6211* ⊕*www.restaurantebolao.com.br*) is a bar and restaurant functioning in the bohemian disctrict of Santa Tereza, which is worth wandering itself. Its clientele includes bohemians, musicians, and poets. The bands Sepultura and Skank have been known to hang out here. A good house draft beer and an excellent feijoada are served Saturday at **Botequim Maria de Lourdes** (⌗*Rua Bárbara Heliodora 141, Lourdes, 30180-130* ☎*031/3292–6905* ⊕*www.mariadelourdes.com.br*).

Established in 1962, **Cantina do Lucas** (⌗*Av. Augusto de Lima 233, Loja 18, Centro, 30190-000* ☎*031/3226–7153*) is a Belo Horizonte cultural landmark. One of the best bars in town is **Mercearia do Lili** (⌗*Rua São João Evangelista 696, Santo Antônio, 30330-140* ☎*031/3296–1951*), which operates in a small grocery store in a bohemian area. During the day the shop sells eggs, cereals, and soap. When night comes, tables are placed on the sidewalk, and the owner serves iced beer and incomparable appetizers.

CAFÉS

Fodor'sChoice
★
The intellectual beau monde of BH collects at the **Café com Letras** (⌗*Rua Antônio de Albuquerque 781, Funcionários, 30112-010* ☎*031/3225–9973* ⊕*www.cafecomletras.com.br*) to eat dainty salads and drink imported wine in a beautiful interior surrounded by books and art. There are DJs most nights and live jazz others. One of the best spaces for great live music during the week and the perfect place to hide from the occasional showers right on Savassi is the **Status Café Cultura e Arte** (⌗*Rua Pernambuco 1150, Funcionários, 30130-151* ☎*031/3261–6045*). This large, warm space houses a bookstore a café/bar and a great stage for its many performers.

DANCE CLUBS

★
Inside the mall Ponteio Lar Shopping **Na Sala** (⌗*BR 356 no. 2500, Loja 120D, Santa Lúcia, 30320-055* ☎*031/3286–4705* ⊕*www.nasala.com.br*) is the most modern and well-equipped nightclub in the city. It's the premier club for house music in Belo Horizonte.

Fodor'sChoice
★
A hip and young crowd ranging in age from 18 to mid-30s gathers at **A Obra** (⌗*Rua Rio Grande do Norte 1168, Funcionários, 30130-131*

☎*031/3261–9431 or 3215–8077* ⊕*www.aobra.com.br*), a basement-level pub with a dance floor. Music styles vary from indie rock to classic rock and more, but it's always the best place to go for something other than mainstream music.

Josefiné (⊠*Rua Antônio de Albuquerque 729, Savassi, 30112-010* ☎*031/3225–2307 or 031/3225–2353* ⊕*www.josefine.com.br*) is a popular nightclub for GLS, which stands for *gays, lésbicas, e simpatizantes* (gays, lesbians, and sympathizers).

LIVE MUSIC

FodorsChoice Find typical Brazilian rhythms ★ such as samba and forró at **Lapa Multshow** (⊠*Rua Álvares Maciel 312, Santa Efigênia, 30150-250* ☎*031/3241–2074* ⊕*www.lapamultshow.com.br*). Belo's best and most authentic live-music venue is **Pedacinhos do Ceu** (⊠*Rua Belmiro Braga 774, Alta Caiçara, 30770-550* ☎*031/3462–2260* ⊕*www.pedacinhosdoceu.com.br*), literally, "little pieces of heaven." This small dive bar is known mostly for *choro*, an instrumental version of samba, with guitars dominating the sound. Groups of musicians that gather here for jam sessions with their *cavaquinhos* (small four-string guitars), *violãos* (guitars), and flutes until late in the night. The bar is named after a song by composer Waldir Azevedo (1923–80) and provides access to his archive. **Utópica Marcenaria** (⊠*Av. Raja Gabáglia 4700, Santa Lúcia, 30360-670* ☎*031/3296–2868* ⊕*www.utopica.com.br*) is a furniture store and an architecture office during the day, but from Tuesday to Saturday nights it's a venue for jazz, blues, and Brazilian and Cuban rhythms.

> ### MAGICAL REALISM FROM MINAS
>
> João Guimarães Rosa could be compared to Gabriel García Márquez in his use of magic and spiritualism to weave stories in rural settings. Rosa infused readers with the sounds and legends of Minas Gerais, and created a mystical landscape not unlike Faulkner's South. He became a member of the Brazilian Academy of Letters, the premier literary institution and authority on the Portuguese language in 1963, During WWII Rosa assumed a diplomatic post in Europe and was instrumental in helping many people fleeing the Holocaust with visas to Brazil.

THE ARTS

Belo Horizonte has produced some of the most creative artists in the country. One of the 20th century's most literary writers, João Guimarães Rosa (1908–67) was born near BH, and attended high school and college here. As a young architect, Oscar Niemeyer was chosen to design parts of the city, and his designs dominate the Pampulha district and the Praça da Liberdade. Rock and metal groups like Skank, Pato Fu, Jota Quest, and Sepultura all started their musical careers in BH. Numerous art festivals take place here year-round, including the Savassi Jazz Festival. One of Brazil's famous theater groups, Grupo Galpão, is based in BH, as are a number of other theaters and a dozen children's theater companies.

Information about cultural programs can be found online and in print in the daily *Estado de Minas* newspaper ⊕*www.estaminas.com.br*, the *Pampulha* paper that comes out on Saturday.

CONCERT HALLS

Inaugurated in 2003 the **Chevrolet Hall** (⊠*Av. Nossa Senhora do Carmo 230, Savassi, 30320-000* ☎*031/2191–5700* ⊕*www.chevrolethallbh. com.br*), with 3,700 seats, presents concerts by famous Brazilian and foreign musical artists. The place is also a venue for volleyball and basketball games and has awful acoustics. The center of cultural life in Belo Horizonte is the downtown **Palácio das Artes** (⊠*Av. Afonso Pena 1537, Centro, 30130-004* ☎*031/3237–7399* ⊕*www.palaciodasartes. com.br*), an intimate concert hall where symphony orchestras, ballet, opera, theater companies, and famous Brazilian acts like singer Caetano Veloso perform.

FILM

Espaço Unibanco Belas Artes Liberdade (⊠*Rua Gonçalves Dias 1581, Lourdes, 30140-092* ☎*031/3252–7232*) screens foreign and art films. Art movies and European films are the main attractions of **Usina Unibanco de Cinema** (⊠*Rua Aimorés 2424, Santo Agostinho, 30140-072* ☎*031/3337–5566*).

SPORTS & THE OUTDOORS

Information on sports events and tickets can be found in the daily *Estado de Minas* newspaper ⊕*www.estaminas.com.br*, the *Pampulha* paper, which comes out on Saturday. Shaded lawns and a sparkling lake make the **Parque Municipal** *(⇨ Main Attractions, above)* a good place to jog. Most city parks have good, short jogging paths, and running is common during the day. In the mountains surrounding the city, the 568-acre **Parque das Mangabeiras** (⊠*Av. José do Patrocínio Pontes 580, Mangabeiras, 30210-090* ☎*031/3277–9697*) is one of the largest urban parks in the country. It has jogging paths and hiking trails. It's closed Monday.

For outdoor activities near the city, *see* Side Trips from Belo Horizonte.

SOCCER

The huge, 75,000-seat **Estádio Mineirão** (⊠*Av. Antônio Abrahão Caram 1001, Pampulha, 31275-000* ☎*031/3499–1154* ⊕*www.ademg. mg.gov.br*) is Brazil's third-largest stadium and the home field for Belo's two professional *futebol* (soccer) teams: Atlético Mineiro and Cruzeiro. Admission to the stadium for a look around (there are no guided tours) is R$2; it's open daily 8–5, except when there's a match. Expect to pay R$10–R$30 or more for tickets to a big game.

SPELUNKING

For amateur spelunkers the mountains of Minas are replete with caves to be explored, though they must be seen with a tour guide who is available at the entrance booth. The most popular cavern, with six large chambers, is the **Gruta de Maquiné** (☎*031/3715–1078* ⊕*www. cordisburgo.mg.gov.br*), 113 km (70 mi) northwest of Belo Horizonte near Cordisburgo. Admission is R$10, and the cavern is open daily 8–5. The **Gruta da Lapinha** (☎*031/3689–8422* ⊕*www.lagoasanta.*

mg.gov.br) is 36 km (22 mi) north of Belo, near the city of Lagoa Santa, on the road leading from Confins Airport. You can tour the cave Tuesday–Sunday 8:30–4:30 for R$10.

SHOPPING

The fashionable Savassi and Lourdes neighborhoods have the city's best antiques, handicrafts, and jewelry stores. For clothing, head to one of the major shopping centers. On Saturday morning Avenida Bernardo Monteiro (between Rua Brasil and Rua Otoni) is the site of an antiques fair and food market, offering a taste of mineiro cuisine. On Sunday morning a large (nearly 3,000 vendors) arts-and-crafts fair is held in front of the Othon Palace hotel, on Avenida Afonso Pena.

ANTIQUES

Fodor'sChoice
★ **Arte Sacra Antiguidades** (⊠ *Rua Alagoas 785, Funcionarios, 30130-160* ☎ *031/3261–7256 or 031/3261–8158*) has a fine selection of Minas antiques.

CLOTHING

★ For a range of fashions, hit the malls and shopping centers (⇨ *below*). For clothes influenced by Minas Gerais culture, pay a visit to the store of designer **Ronaldo Fraga** (⊠ *Rua Raul Pompéia 264, São Pedro, 30330-080* ☎ *031/3282–5379 or 031/3282–5347* ⊕ *www.ronaldofraga.com*). **Brechó Santíssima** (⊠ *Rua Tomé de Souza 815, Funcionários 30140-131* ☎ *031/3261–9487*) sells secondhand clothing and accessories.

HANDICRAFTS

★ **Serjô** (⊠ *Rua Antônio de Albuquerque 749, Loja 2, Funcionários, 30112-010*
Fodor'sChoice
★ ☎ *031/3227–5251*) sells handicrafts from different Minas Gerais regions. The **Centro de Artesanato Mineiro** (⊠ *Palácio das Artes, Av. Afonso Pena 1537, Centro, 30130-004* ☎ *031/3272–9513 or 031/3272–9516*), has a wide range of regional crafts. In the main hall of the theater **Espaço Unibanco Belas Artes Liberdade** (⊠ *Rua Gonçalves Dias 1581, Lourdes, 30140-092* ☎ *031/3252–7232*) there's a small store with aboriginal arts and crafts, plus a coffee shop and a bookstore.

For jewelry and gemstone shops, see "Finding a Gem" CloseUp in Ouro Preto, below.

MALLS & CENTERS

Bahia Shopping (⊠ *Rua da Bahia 1022, Centro, 30160-011* ☎ *031/3222–1265 or 031/3247–6940*) is a good place to shop for men's and women's clothing. In the downtown area, **Shopping Cidade** (⊠ *Rua Tupis 337, Centro, 30190-060* ☎ *031/3279–8300*) is one of the most frequented malls. You can buy almost anything, from clothes to electronics. Many shops sell designer togs for men and women in Belo Horizonte's most exclusive mall, **BH Shopping** (⊠ *BR 356 no. 3049, Belvedere, 30320-055* ☎ *031/3228–4001*).

SIDE TRIP TO SABARÁ

19 km (12 mi) east of Belo Horizonte.

Sabará's churches drive home the enormous wealth of Minas Gerais during the gold-rush days. In this former colonial town, today a sprawling Belo Horizonte suburb of 140,000, historic buildings are scattered about, but signs at Praça Santa Rita point to all the major attractions. The interiors of the baroque churches are rich with gold-leaf paneling. As in most colonial towns all the churches are closed on Monday. This makes for a fun half-day trip from Belo.

TO & FROM

Buses for Sabará (Viação Cisne #5509) leave behind the Belo bus station from the local part of the station. There are several buses an hour and the ride takes less than 30 minutes. Via car, Sabará is slightly east of Belo, just off BR 262; it's a 30-minute ride.

WHAT TO SEE

In the main square sits the unfinished **Igreja de Nossa Senhora do Rosário dos Pretos** (*Church of Our Lady of the Rosary of the Blacks*), circa 1767, which was built, like its counterpart in Ouro Preto, by slaves. Here, however, they ran out of gold before the project could be completed. When slavery was abolished in 1888, the church was left as a memorial. ✉*Praça Melo Viana s/n, 34505-300* ☎*031/3671–1523* 💲*R$1* 🕙*Tues.–Sun. 9–noon and 1–5.*

Fodor'sChoice
★ The ornate **Igreja de Nossa Senhora da Conceição** (*Church of Our Lady of the Immaculate Conception*) , though small, is Sabará's main church and an outstanding example of Portuguese baroque architecture combined with elements of Asian art. Its simple exterior gives no indication of the wealth inside, typified by its luxurious gold altar and lavishly decorated ceiling. At this writing the church is undergoing renovations but is still open for public visits. ✉*Praça Getúlio Vargas s/n, 34505-730* ☎*031/3671–1724* 💲*R$1* 🕙*Weekdays 9–noon and 2–5.*

Igreja de Nossa Senhora do Ó (*Our Lady of Ó Church*), one of Brazil's oldest and smallest churches, contains paintings said to have been completed by 23 Chinese artists brought from the former Portuguese colony of Macau. Other signs of Asian influence include the Chinese tower and the gilded arches. ✉*Largo de Nossa Senhora do Ó s/n, 34505-730* ☎*031/3671–1724* 💲*R$1* 🕙*Weekends 9–noon and 2–5.*

★ In the **Igreja de Nossa Senhora do Carmo** (*Church of Our Lady of Carmel*) are pulpits, a choir loft, and a doorway all designed by the famed Aleijadinho. This is one of several Minas churches that were the result of a collaboration between Aleijadinho and painter Manuel da Costa Ataíde, a brilliant artist in his own right. ✉*Rua do Carmo s/n, 34505-460* ☎*031/3671–2417* 💲*R$2* 🕙*Tues.–Sat. 9–11:30 and 1–5:30, Sun. 1–6.*

THE COLONIAL & GOLD TOWNS

Two hours southeast of Belo is Ouro Preto, a UNESCO World Heritage Site. The country's de facto capital during the gold-boom years, it was also the birthplace of Brazil's first independence movement: the Inconfidência Mineira. Today a vibrant student population ensures plenty

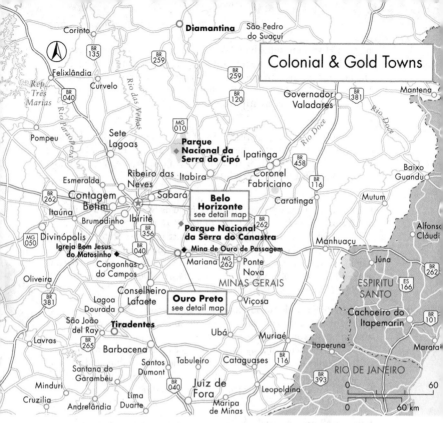

of year-round activity, and lodging, dining, and shopping options abound.

All the Gold Towns—Ouro Preto, Mariana, Tiradentes, and Congonhas—are characterized by winding cobblestone streets, brilliant baroque churches, impressive mansions and museums, and colorful markets. Tiradentes is smaller than Ouro Preto but no less charming; this town truly seems to have stopped in time about midway through the 18th century. Between Ouro Preto and Tiradentes lies Congonhas, whose Basilica do Bom Jesus de Matosinhos and its famous Prophets sculpted by Alejaidinho is a UNESCO World Heritage Site. Diamantina rivals Ouro Preto in its scope and the beautiful scenery of the mountains around it; the rich cultural history here sheds considerable light on colonial Brazil.

DIAMANTINA

290 km (180 mi) northeast of Belo Horizonte.

Diamantina took its name from the diamonds that were extracted in great quantities here in the 18th century. Perhaps because of its remote setting in the barren mountains close to the *sertão* (a remote arid region), Diamantina is extremely well preserved, although its churches lack the grandeur of those in other historic towns. Its white-wall structures stand in pristine contrast to the iron red of the surrounding mountains. The principal attraction in Diamantina is the simple pleasure of walking along the clean-swept cobblestone streets lined with colonial houses—note the overhanging roofs with their elaborate brackets.

> **THE SERENADE TOWN**
>
> Diamantina has the distinction of being Brazil's center of serenading. At night, particularly on weekends, romantics gather in a downtown alley called Beco da Mota, the former red-light district and now home to several popular bars. Strolling guitarists also gather on Rua Direita and Rua Quitanda.

The city was the home of two legendary figures of the colonial period: diamond contractor João Fernandes and his slave mistress, Chica da Silva, one of Brazilian history's first powerful Afro-Brazilian women. Two area attractions are linked with her; to see them, you should contact the Casa da Cultura to arrange a guided tour.

TO & FROM

Six daily Pássaro Verde buses leave the rodoviária in Belo Horizonte for Diamantina. The trip is five hours and costs about R$55. Via car, there's no ideal direct route from Belo Horizonte to Diamantina; your best bet is north on BR 040 and then east on BR 259 (5 hours).

ESSENTIALS

Banks & Currency Exchange ITAU (✉ *Praça Correa Rabelo 137, Centro, 39100-000*).

Bus Contacts Pássaro Verde (☎ *031/3280–9410 or 0300/789–4400* ⊕ *www.passaroverde.com.br*). **Rodoviária** (✉ *Largo Dom João 134, 39100-000*).

Emergencies & Medical Assistance Ambulance (☎ *192*). **Fire** (☎ *193*). Hospital: **Nossa Senhora da Saúde** (✉ *Praça Redelvim Andrade 564, Centro, 39100-000* ☎ *038/3531–1643*). Pharmacy: **Drogaria Diamante e Cia** (✉ *Praç Corréa Rabelo 109, Centro, 39100–000* ☎ *038/3531–1027*). **Police** (☎ *190*).

Taxi Pontos de Taxi Largo Dom João (☎ *038/3531–1413*).

Visitor & Tour Info Secretaria Municipal de Cultura e Turismo (✉ *Praça Antônio Eulálio 53, 39100-000* ☎ *038/3531–9530 or 038/3531–9532* ☞ *Open weekdays 8–6, Sat. 9–5, Sun. 9–noon*).

WHAT TO SEE

The **Casa de Chica da Silva** was the official residence of João Fernandes and Chica da Silva from 1763 to 1771, and contains colonial furniture and Chica's private chapel. A permanent art exhibit shows Chica in torrid poses and tawdry clothes as a personifaction of the Seven Deadly Sins. ✉ *Praça Lobo de Mesquita 266, 39100-000* ☎ *038/3531–2491* 🎟 *Free* ⊙ *Tues.–Sat. noon–5:30, Sun. 9–noon*.

Fodor's Choice ★ The **Igreja Nossa Senhora do Carmo** is a church built in 1751 as a gift from Fernandes to his mistress. Supposedly, Chica ordered that the bell tower be built at the back of the building so the ringing wouldn't disturb her. The altar has gold-leaf paneling, and the organ has 514 pipes. ⊠ *Rua do Carmo s/n, 39100-000* ☎ *No phone* 🖃 *R$2* 🕙 *Tues.–Sat. 9–noon and 2–6, Sun. 9–noon.*

🕙 ★ The **Museu do Diamante,** the city's diamond museum, in a building that dates from 1789, displays equipment used in colonial-period mines. It's in the former house of Padre Rolim, one of the Inconfidentes (supposedly Chica had once belonged to Rolim as well). Other items on exhibit include instruments made to torture slaves and sacred art from the 16th to the 19th centuries. There are guided tours of the rooms where diamonds were classified and separated. ⊠ *Rua Direita 14, 39100-000* ☎ *038/3531–1382* 🖃 *R$2* 🕙 *Tues.–Sat. noon–5:30, Sun. 9–noon.*

> **FROM RAGS TO RICHES**
>
> Chica (or Francisca) da Silva was a beautiful mulatto slave of African and Portuguese descent. As a young woman, she was bought by, and eventually married, diamond contractor and appointee of the Portuguese crown João Fernandes de Oliveira. He eventually returned to Portugal, but not before Chica bore 13 of his children. With her husband's wealth, and the freedom from slavery that came with the marriage, Chica climbed the social ladder and eventually became one of the wealthiest women in colonial Brazil. Da Silva is buried in the diocese of São Francisco de Assis, the stronghold of wealthy Diamantians.

The **Casa de Juscelino Kubitschek** was the childhood home of one of Brazil's most important 20th-century presidents, responsible for the construction of Brasília. ⊠ *Rua São Francisco 241, 39100-000* ☎ *038/3531–3607 or 038/3531–1970* 🖃 *R$1* 🕙 *Tues.–Sat. 9–5, Sun. 9–1.*

WHERE TO STAY & EAT

$ ✕ **Cantina do Marinho.** This well-respected restaurant specializes in comida mineira. Favorites are pork steak with tutu and pork tenderloin with feijão tropeiro. There's an à la carte menu as well as a self-service buffet. ⊠ *Rua Direita 113, 39100-000* ☎ *038/3531–1686* 🖃 *AE, DC, MC, V.*

¢–$ 🏨 **Tijuco.** This historic-district inn is housed in a sleek Oscar Niemeyer–designed structure. The gorgeous rooms are huge and have interesting furniture that does justice to Niemeyer's interior design. **Pros:** Considered the best hotel in town, views of the hills from some of the rooms are amazing. **Cons:** 1950s-modern structure doesn't fit with the historic ambience of Diamantina and has few facilities. ⊠ *Rua Macau do Meio 211, 39100-100* ☎ *038/3531–1022* ⊕ *www.hoteltijuco.com.br* 🛏 *27 rooms* 🖔 *In-room: refrigerator. In-hotel: room service, laundry service, no elevator* 🖃 *AE, DC, MC, V* 🍽 *BP.*

OURO PRETO

97 km (60 mi) southeast of Belo Horizonte.

The former gold-rush capital is the best place to see the legendary Aleijadinho's artistry. Now a lively university town, it's been preserved as a national monument and a World Heritage site. The surrounding mountains, geometric rows of whitewashed buildings, cobblestone streets, red-tile roofs that climb the hillsides, morning mist and evening fog---all give Ouro Preto a singular beauty.

In its heyday Ouro Preto (also seen as Ouro Prêto, an archaic spelling) was one of Brazil's most progressive cities and the birthplace of the colony's first stirrings of independence. Toward the end of the 18th century the mines were running out, all of the gold and jewels being sent to Portugal. The residents were unhappy with the corruption of the governor, and the Inconfidência Mineira was organized to overthrow the Portuguese rulers and establish an independent Brazilian republic. It was to have been led by a resident of Ouro Preto, Joaquim José da Silva Xavier, a dentist nicknamed Tiradentes ("tooth-puller").

THE TOOTH-PULLER

The Inconfidência Mineira was to have been led by Tiradentes and 11 followers. But Joaquim Silvério dos Reis, a Judas Mineiran who was in on the conspiracy, betrayed the movement in exchange for the pardon of his debt to the crown. Tiradentes assumed responsibility for the planned uprising and was sentenced to death. The Empress Dona Maria I documented in detail how he was to be killed: drawn and quartered, with his body parts (specified by name) hung around Ouro Preto until time turned them to ash. The date of Tiradentes's execution, April 21, is a national holiday.

TO & FROM

Pássaro Verde has 10 daily buses connecting Belo Horizonte with Ouro Preto (R$19; 1 hour, 45 minutes). From Rio, Útil makes one trip per day (R$60–R$100; 8 hours). By car from Belo you can take BR 040 south and BR 356 (it becomes MG 262) east to Ouro Preto (1½–2 hours).

GETTING AROUND

All the town's sights are within easy walking distance of the central square, Praça Tiradentes, a seven-minute walk from the bus station. There are taxis all around town; a taxi from the bus station to the center costs R$11. A small bus travels around town every 10 to 15 minutes.

The main streets of Ouro Preto have two names: one from the 18th century, still used by the city's inhabitants, and the other an official name, used on maps but not very popular. Therefore, Rua Conde de Bobadela is better known as Rua Direita, Rua Senador Rocha Lagoa as Rua das Flores, and Rua Cláudio Manoel as Rua do Ouvidor. Street signs sometimes use the official name and sometimes both. We use the official names in this guide.

ESSENTIALS

Banks & Currency Exchange Banco do Brasil and hotels exchange U.S. dollars, but in general, you'll get better rates in Belo Horizonte. **Banco do Brasil** (⊠ *Rua São José 189, Centro, 35400-970*). **HSBC** (⊠ *Rua São José 201, Centro, 35400-970*). **Itaú** (⊠ *Rua São José 105, Centro, 35400-970*).

Bus Contacts Pássaro Verde (☏ *031/3241–5191 or 0300/789–4400* ⊕ *www. passaroverde.com.br*). **Útil** (☏ *031/3551–3166 or 021/3907–9000* ⊕ *www.util.*

com.br). **Rodoviária Ouro Preto** (✉ *Rua Padre Rolim 661, São Cristóvão, 35400-971* ☎ *031/3559-3252*).

Emergencies & Medical Assistance Ambulance (☎ *192*). **Fire** (☎ *193*).

Hospital: **Unidade Pronto Atendimento** (✉ *Rua Padre Rolim s/n, São Cristóvão, 35400-971* ☎ *031/3559-3255*). Pharmacy: **Drogaria Itacolomi** (✉ *Rua Conde de Bobadela, 88, Centro, 35400-970* ☎ *031/3551-1624*). **Police** (☎ *190*).

Taxi Ponto de Táxi (☎ *031/3551-2123 or 031/3551-1977*).

Visitor & Tour Info Associação de Guias (✉ *Rua Padre Rolim s/n, São Cristóvão, 35400-971* ☎ *031/3551-2655 or 031/3551-2504* ☞ *Open weekdays 8–6. Association of professional tour guides; excellent 6-hr historic walking tours [in English], plus general info.*)**Grandtour Ouro Preto** (✉ *Rua Barão de Camargos 126, Loja 11, Centro, 35400-000* ☎ *031/3552-1100* ✉ *cln@ouropreto.com.br* ☞ *Historic cities tours; airport pickup and other transportation*). **Posto de Informação Turística** (✉ *Praça Tiradentes 04, Centro, 35400-000* ☎ *031/3559-3269* ☞ *Open daily 8:15–6:15. Has cultural and theater info, an art gallery, beautiful café, bookstore*).

ESTRADA REAL

The Royal Road was constructed by slaves, linking the colonial towns with the port of Paraty and the ships waiting to transport the mineral wealth to Portugal. Huge stone slabs are still present in parts of this historical trail. Thousands of slaves died building this road and taking the wealth to the coast. Parts of the road can be traversed by horse, on foot, and by car. Set up trips through the Instituto Estrada Real ☎ *031/3241-7166* .

SAFETY & PRECAUTIONS

The steep hills in Ouro Preto are very hard on cars—and legs. And when it rains, cobblestones are very slippery; sturdy footwear and warm clothing are recommended year-round. Hire only certified guides and buy gemstones only from stores, not at outdoor locations because they can be fakes, glass colored to look like gemstones, and if real they can also be overpriced.

MAIN ATTRACTIONS

Numbers in the text correspond to numbers in the margin and on the Ouro Preto map.

❺ Igreja de Nossa Senhora do Carmo. Completed in 1776, the impressive Our Lady of Carmel Church contains the last works of Aleijadinho. It was originally designed by Aleijadinho's father, an architect, but was later modified by Aleijadinho, who added additional rococo elements, including the soapstone sculptures of angels above the entrance. The church contains the only examples of azulejos (decorative Portuguese tiles) from this period in Minas Gerais. ✉ *Praça Brigadeiro Musqueira s/n, Centro, 35400-000* ☎ *031/3551-2601* ✉ *R$2* ⊙ *Tues.–Sun. 9–11 and 1–4:45.*

❿ Igreja de Nossa Senhora da Conceição. The charming Our Lady of the Conception church is decorated in unique rose and blue pastels and was completed in 1760, it contains the tomb of Aleijadinho as well as a small museum dedicated to the artist. On the same street is the artist's house, now in private hands. ⊠*Praça Antônio Dias s/n, Centro, 35400-000* ☎*031/3551–3282* ⊠*R$6* ⊙*Tues.–Sun. 9–11:45 and 1:30–5.*

② **Igreja de Nossa Senhora do Pilar.** This heavily gilded church was consecrated in 1733, built on the site of an earlier chapel. This is the most richly decorated of Ouro Preto's churches—it's said that 400 pounds of gold leaf were used to cover the interior. The church building also houses the Museu de Arte Sacra (Museum of Sacred Art). ⊠*Praça Monsenhor João Castilho Barbosa s/n, Centro, 35400-000* ☎*031/3551–4736* ⊠*R$4* ⊙*Tues.–Sun. 9–10:45 and noon–4:45.*

⑪ **Igreja de Santa Efigênia.** On a hill east of Praça Tiradentes, this interesting slave church was built over the course of 60 years (1730–90) and was funded by Chico-Rei. This African ruler was captured during Brazil's gold rush and sold to a mine owner in Minas Gerais. Chico eventually earned enough money to buy his freedom—in the days before the Portuguese prohibited such acts—and became a hero among slaves. The clocks on the facade are the city's oldest, and the interior contains cedar sculptures by Francisco Xavier de Brito, Aleijadinho's teacher. ⊠*Rua de Santa Efigênia s/n, Centro, 35400-000* ☎*031/3551–5047* ⊠*R$2* ⊙*Tues.–Sun. 9–4:30.*

⑨ **Igreja de São Francisco de Assis.** Considered Aleijadinho's masterpiece, Fodor'sChoice this church was begun in 1766 by the Franciscan Third Order and ★ not completed until 1810. Aleijadinho designed the structure and was responsible for the wood and soapstone sculptures on the portal, high altar, side altars, pulpits, and crossing arch. The panel on the nave ceiling representing the Virgin's glorification was painted by Ataíde. Cherubic faces, garlands of tropical fruits, and allegorical characters carved into the main altar are still covered with their original paint. ⊠*Largo de Coimbra s/n, Centro, 35400-000* ⊠*R$6* ⊙*Tues.–Sun. 8.30–11:45 and 1:30–5.*

⑥ **Museu da Inconfidência.** One of the best historical museums in Brazil, this Fodor'sChoice former 18th-century prison and onetime city hall has great interactive ★ computer and television screen displays devoted to the history of the failed uprising of the Inconfidêntes, life in colonial Tiradentes, slavery, and a number of other interesting topics. Other displays include period furniture, clothing, slaves' manacles, firearms, books, and gravestones, as well as works by Aleijadinho and Ataíde. The museum also holds the remains of revolutionaries, some brought back from exile in Portugal's African colonies, and the document in which Maria I details the fate of Tiradentes's body parts. ⊠*Praça Tiradentes 139, Centro, 35400-000* ☎*031/3551–1121* ⊠*R$6* ⊙*Tues.–Sun. noon–5:30.*

⑧ **Museu de Ciência e Técnica.** Opposite the Museu da Inconfidência in the ★ former governor's palace the Museum of Science and Technology contains an enormous collection of stunning precious and semiprecious gems (including diamonds), gold, and crystals. The museum has several sections including a section on the geology of the region, explanations of the mining process, and an entire floor devoted to gems organized

CLOSE UP

Finding a Gem

Gems vary widely in quality and value; don't buy them on the streets, and be wary about buying them from smaller shops. Do your research. Know that gold topaz, smoky topaz, and some other types of "topaz" are really quartz. It's very difficult to tell the difference between well-crafted synthetic lookalikes and the real deal. Get references for a jeweler before you buy.

Imperial topaz, sometimes called precious topaz, comes in shades of pink and tangerine. In general, the clearer the stone, the better the quality. The topaz can, at first glance, easily be confused with citrine quartz, found elsewhere in Brazil, but is harder, denser, and more brilliant.

WHERE TO BUY
Ouro Preto has a reputation for the best selection and prices in Brazil.

One of the best shops for gems, especially the rare imperial topaz, is **Ita Gemas** (✉ *Rua Conde de Bobadela 139, Centro, 35400-000* ☎ *031/3551-4895*). An excellent store for authenticated gems—including imperial topazes, emeralds, and tourmalines—is **Luiza Figueiredo Jóias** (✉ *Rua Conde de Bobadela 48, Centro, 35400-000* ☎ *031/3551-2487*). At **Brasil Gemas** (✉ *Praça Tiradentes 74, 35400-000* ☎ *031/3551-2976*) you can visit the stone-cutting and-setting workshop

Although not as upscale as the stores in Ouro Preto, **Artstones** (✉ *Rua Ministro Gabriel Passos 22, Tiradentes 36325-000* ☎ *032/3355-1730*) carries imperial topazes, emeralds, quartz, and tourmalines and also has some finished jewelry

according to their chemical families. ✉ *Praça Tiradentes 20, Centro, 35400-000* ☎ *031/3559-3118* 🖃 *R$4* ⊙ *Tues.–Sun. noon–5.*

❼ Museu do Oratório. Established in the historic house of the St. Carmel novitiate, once a home to Aleijadinho, this museum celebrates 18th- and 19th-century sacred art. Some of the oratories, which reflect ideas of religious beauty from the period, have been displayed at the Louvre. ✉ *Rua Adro do Carmo, 28, Centro, 35400-000* ☎ *031/3551-5369* ⊕ *www.oratorio.com.br* 🖃 *R$2* ⊙ *Daily 9:30–5:30.*

IF YOU HAVE TIME
❸ Casa dos Contos. This colonial coinage house dating from 1782–87 had many uses, one as a prison for some of the Inconfidentes, two of whom—Padre Rolim and Claudio Manuel da Costa—died here. It contains the foundry that minted coins of the gold-rush period and examples of coins and period furniture. The building is considered one of the best examples of Brazilian colonial architecture. ✉ *Rua São José 12, Centro, 35400-000* ☎ *031/3551-1444* 🖃 *R$3* ⊙ *Tues.–Sat. 10–6, Sun. 10–4, Mon. 2–6.*

❶ Igreja de Nossa Senhora do Rosário dos Pretos. The small, intriguing Church of Our Lady of the Rosary of the Blacks was inaugurated by slaves in 1785, some of whom bought their freedom with the gold they found in Ouro Preto. According to legend, the church's interior is bare because the slaves ran out of gold after erecting the baroque building. In the unusual oval interior the church houses sculptures of Santa Helena, Santo Antônio, and Sao Benedito. ⊠ *Largo do Rosário s/n, Centro, 35400-000* ☎ *031/3551–4735* ☒ *Free* ☾ *Tues.–Sun. noon–4:45.*

❹ **Teatro Municipal.** Billed as the oldest operating theater in Latin America, this former opera house opened in 1770. The Associação de Guias (⇨ *Essentials, above)* has information on events. ⊠ *Rua Brigadeiro Musqueira s/n, Centro, 35400-000* ☎ *031/3559–3224* ☒ *R$2* ☾ *Tues.–Fri noon–6, Sat. 9–6.*

ALEIJADINHO

Brazil's most famous baroque artist was the son of a Portuguese architect and a former slave. Antônio Francisco Lisboa was born in 1738 in the vicinity of present-day Ouro Preto. In adulthood, a disease left his arms and feet deformed (the cause is disputed: leprosy, syphilis, and Parkinson's are possibilities). Unable to hold his instruments Aleijadinho ("little cripple") worked with chisel and hammer strapped to his wrists. His work, primarily in cedarwood and soapstone, is profoundly moving. His sculptures have a singular look, many of his angels have curly hair, and enormous, humble eyes.

WHERE TO EAT

$-$$$
★ ✗**Café Geraes.** This beautiful Parisian-like café in an 18th-century building has a burgundy interior and marbletop tables, and feeds its regulars delicious sandwiches, soups, and pastries. It's especially appealing on a rainy day for a cup of coffee or a glass of wine, and to the accompaniment of a good novel. ⊠ *Rua Conde de Bobadela 122, Centro, 35400-000* ☎ *031/3551–5097* ▤ *DC, MC, V.*

$-$$$
Fodor'sChoice
★ ✗**Casa do Ouvidor.** This large and welcoming restaurant above a jewelry store has won numerous awards for its regional dishes like tutu, feijão tropeiro, and frango com quiabo. The portions are generous and the restaurant often gets crowded, try to sit by the windows with a view of the street below. The owner restored this once-crumbling 18th-century building to its former appearance. Since the restaurant's opening in 1972, it has hosted such luminaries as former President of France François Mitterand, Richard Dreyfuss, Henry Kissinger, and John Updike. ⊠ *Rua Direita 42, Centro, 35400-000* ☎ *031/3551–2141* ⊕ *www. casadoouvidor.com.br* ▤ *AE, DC, MC, V.*

$-$$$
✗**O Profeta.** The friendly staffers at this cozy restaurant serve up mineiran and international dishes, which are all for two people. On weekends there's also live MPB (Brazilian pop music). ⊠ *Rua Conde de Bobadela 65, Centro, 35400-000* ☎ *031/3551–4556* ▤ *DC, MC, V.*

$-$$
Fodor'sChoice
★ ✗**Le Coq d'Or.** The finest restaurant in Minas Gerais and one of the best in Brazil is in Ouro Preto's Solar Nossa Senhora do Rosário hotel. An elegant atmosphere with formal place settings, attentive service, and soft Brazilian music makes it ideal for a quiet, romantic dinner. The executive chef trained in Paris at the Cordon Bleu institute before introducing creative French-inspired cuisine to Brazilian gourmands. The ever-changing menu always includes an innovative selection of meat and fish dishes, and the wine list is excellent. ⊠ *Rua Getúlio Vargas*

6

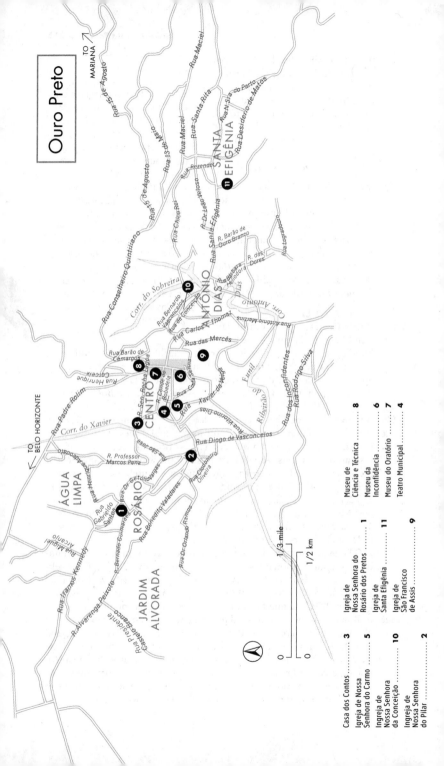

Ouro Preto

TO MARIANA

TO BELO HORIZONTE

SANTA EFIGÊNIA

ÁGUA LIMPA

JARDIM ALVORADA

ROSÁRIO

CENTRO

ANTÔNIO DIAS

Rua de 16 de Agosto
Rua Maciel
Rua Santa Rita
Rua N. Sra. do Parto
Rua Desidério de Matos
Rua 13 de Maio
Rua Maciel
Rua Conselheiro Quintiliano
Rua Chico Rei
Rua de 16 de Agosto
Rua Rezende
Rua Santa Efigênia
R. Barão de Ouro Branco
R. das Dores
Corr. do Sobreira
Rua Barão de Camargos
Rua Henrique Corcixa
Rua Padre Rolim
Corr. do Xavier
R. Professor Marcos Pena
Rua Dr Getúlio Vargas
Rua Miquel Arcanjo
Rua Gabriela Sá
Rua Benedito Valadares
Rua Dr Orlando Ramos
Rua Arcanjo
Rua Bernardo Guimarães
Rua Bernardo Vasconcelos
Rua da Conceição
Rua Carlos Thomaz
Rua das Mercés
Rua Antônio Martins
Corr. Antônio Dias
Rua Bárbara Heliodora Dias
Rua Henrique Dias
Rua Costa Senna
Rua Xavier da Veiga
Rua Victor Dias
Rua Diogo de Vasconcelos
Rua Clodomiro Oliveira
Rua dos Inconfidentes
Rua Rodrigo Silva
Ribeirão do Funil
R. Seis Rocha Lagoa
R. Conde de Bobadela
Rua São José
Casa Presidente
R. Alvarenga Peixoto
R. Tiradentes-Kennedy
R. Bernardo Guimarães

0   1/3 mile
0   1/2 km

270, Rosário, 35400–000
☏031/3551–5200 ⊟AE, DC,
MC, V ⊗No lunch Sun.–Fri.

$$ ✕**Chafariz.** The best place for a min-
★ eiran buffet in Ouro Preto is in this
vividly decorated eatery near the Casa
dos Contos. The large dining room
has beautiful furniture designed by
Oscar Niemeyer, and the cupboards
are decorated with antiques and
candles. On the gorgeous balcony in
the back you can sip jaboticaba (a
purple grapelike fruit) drinks look-
ing out over the countryside. ⊠Rua
São José 167, Centro, 35400-000
☏031/3551–2828 ⊗No dinner ⊟AE, DC, MC, V.

$ ✕**Piacere.** If you want to escape from the typical comida mineira, the
Piacere is an excellent option. This Italian restaurant is housed in a
stone grotto, but the metal chairs, sleek wooden tables, and winged
metal staircase give it a breezy 21st-century air. The menu is made
up of antipasti, cheese plates, and numerous homemade pastas.
⊠Rua Getúlio Vargas 241, Rosário, 35400-975 ☏031/3551–4297
or 031/3552–2422 ⊕www.restaurantepiacere.com.br ⊗Closed Mon.
No lunch Tues.–Sat. No dinner Sun.

WHERE TO STAY
Some families in Ouro Preto rent rooms in their homes, although usu-
ally only during Carnaval and Easter, when the city's hotels fill up. For
a list of rooms to rent, contact the Associação de Guias (⇨Essentials,
above).

$–$$ 🏨**Pousada do Mondego.** This intimate inn is next to the Igreja de São
Fodor'sChoice Francisco de Assis in a merchant's mansion that dates to 1747. You'll
★ find period furnishings, a gorgeous veranda and dining room for an
exceptional Minas breakfast, and the same modern conveniences one
expects from a high-class hotel. The hotel gives two-hour city tours in
a 1930s minibus, and it has an antiques store and art gallery. **Pros:** Nice
mix of modern amenities (marble bathrooms, TVs) and 18th-century
charm. **Cons:** When hotel is full they rent additional rooms in another
period house down the hill. ⊠Largo de Coimbra 38, Centro, 35400-
000 ☏031/3551–2040, 021/2287–1592 Ext. 601 reservations in Rio
🖳031/3551–3094 ⊕www.roteirosdecharme.com.br ➘24 rooms
⚒In-room: safe, refrigerator. In-hotel: restaurant, room service, no
elevator, concierge, laundry service, airport shuttle, public Internet
⊟AE, DC, MC, V �ⓘ⊗BP.

$$ 🏨**Estalagem das Minas Gerais.** As it's near a nature preserve, this place
is perfect for those who like to hike or walk in the woods. Rooms are
modern, and those in front have wonderful views of the valley. The lux-
ury chalets have two floors and granite details. Each can accommodate
as many as five people, with a double bed upstairs, single beds down-
stairs, and two bathrooms. The restaurant serves regional fare. **Pros:**

Beautiful setting and views. **Cons:** Not in the center of town. ⊠ *Rodovia dos Inconfidentes, Km 87, Centro, 35400-000* ☎ *031/3551–2122* 🖷 *031/3551–2709* 📠 *114 rooms, 32 chalets* 🛆 *In-room: no a/c, refrigerator. In-hotel: restaurant, room service, bar, pools, gym, no elevator, laundry service, Internet* ☰ *AE, DC, MC, V* ⦿ *BP.*

$$
★
$$

🏨 **Luxor Ouro Preto Pousada.** This fashionable hotel in a house with stone walls that date back 200 years, dark wooden floors, and gracious antique furnishings has the feeling of a rustic 19th-century lodge. Rooms enjoy incredible views of the city, some have original paintings by famous Minas artist Chanina, and are decorated with beautiful replicas of 18th-century furniture. The Igreja de Nossa Senhora da Conceição is just across the street. **Pros:** Gorgeous hotel, unparalleled service. **Cons:** Lobby leads to a small, romantic restaurant that is often filled with guests who are staying at the hotel. ⊠ *Rua Dr. Alfredo Baeta 16, Antônio Dias, 35400-000* ☎🖷 *031/3551–2244* ⊕ *www.luxorhoteis.com.br* 📠 *19 rooms* 🛆 *In-room: refrigerator, dial-up. In-hotel: restaurant, room service, no elevator, laundry service, public Internet, some pets allowed* ☰ *AE, DC, MC, V* ⦿ *BP.*

$-$$
★

🏨 **Pousada Minas Gerais.** Inaugurated in 2004, this wonderful hotel is in a new building that replicates Ouro Preto's colonial exteriors. All rooms are enormous, with sweeping views of the countryside, beautiful king-size beds, flat-screen TVs, and marble bathrooms. This is the perfect pousada for the ultramodern traveler or the business traveler seeking amenities like fluffy robes and telephones in the bathrooms. Three luxury suites have whirlpool bathtubs. **Pros:** On a quiet street, good for families because it's quiet and safe, good for business people because of its facilities. **Cons:** It's farther from the churches and restaurants than most other places. ⊠ *Rua Xavier da Veiga 303, Centro, 35400-000* ☎ *031/3551–5506* 📠 *17 rooms* 🛆 *In-room: safe, refrigerator, Wi-Fi. In-hotel: restaurant, bar, room service, no elevator, laundry service, concierge, public Internet, some pets allowed, parking (no fee)* ☰ *AE, DC, MC, V* ⦿ *BP.*

$

🏨 **Colonial.** Close to the main square, this is a good example of the typical mid-range inn with basic rooms and a hearty breakfast that can be found in most historic cities. Room 1 has a loft and can sleep up to five people. **Pros:** Clean rooms, low price. **Cons:** Small, no-frills. ⊠ *Rua Padre Camilo Veloso 26, Centro, 35400-000* ☎ *031/3551–3133* 🖷 *031/3551–3361* 📠 *18 rooms* 🛆 *In-room: refrigerator, Wi-Fi. In-hotel: room service, no elevator, laundry service, concierge, some pets allowed, parking (no fee)* ☰ *AE, DC, MC, V* ⦿ *BP.*

$

🏨 **Grande Hotel de Ouro Preto.** As its name suggests, the Grande is Ouro Preto's largest hotel, a curving two-story building on concrete pillars—it's immense by local standards, though room sizes are comparable to those at other hotels. All the suites have views on the historic center, the other rooms look out on the garden. **Pros:** Designed by Brazil's most famous living architect, Oscar Niemeyer, and Ouro Preto's premier modernist structure. **Cons:** Heavy on concrete and light on ambience. ⊠ *Rua Senador Rocha Lagoa 164, Centro, 35400-000* ☎ *031/3551–1488* 🖷 *031/3551–5028* ⊕ *www.hotelouropreto.com.br* 📠 *35 rooms* 🛆 *In-room: safe, refrigerator. In-hotel: restaurant, room service, bar,* pool, no elevator, laundry service, public Internet, parking (no fee) ⊟AE, DC, MC, V ⎟○⎟BP.

$ ⊞**Pousada Clássica.** Opened in 2000, this pousada is in an elegant house a few yards from the main churches and museums. One of the suites, in the front of the building, has a hydromassage bathtub. The breakfast is lavish and delicious, as is the afternoon tea. Apartments in the back are the most tranquil, but the views are not as good. **Pros:** City view from the balconies is spectacular, reception and breakfast room are stylish and comfortable. **Cons:** Rooms are boring and the furniture in them is not up to the standard of the lobby and dining room, noise from Rua Direita's bars can be a bother. ⊠*Rua Conde de Bobadela 96, Centro, 35400-000* ☎*031/3551–3663* ⎙*031/3551–6593* ⊕*www. pousadaclassica.com.br* ⇱*25 rooms, 2 suites* ⬠*In-room: refrigerator. In-hotel: restaurant, room service, laundry service, some pets allowed, public Internet, parking (no fee)* ⊟*DC, MC, V* ⎟○⎟*BP.*

¢ ⊞**Pousada Ouro Preto.** Popular with backpackers, this pousada has
★ small rooms filled with beautiful dark-wood beds and local art; some have incredible views of the city with a mountainous backdrop. Its open-air halls have flowers and paintings of Ouro Preto; the terrace in front of the lobby offers a peaceful view of the city center. **Pros:** Afternoon tea served in dining room, furniture, and setting commendable. **Cons:** Steep staircase up from street. ⊠*Rua Jose dos Anjos Costa 72, Centro, 35400-000* ☎⎙*031/3551–3081* ⇱*17 rooms* ⬠*In-room: no a/c, refrigerator. In-hotel: room service, no elevator, laundry service, some pets allowed* ⊟*MC, V* ⎟○⎟*BP.*

¢ ⊞**Pousada Recanto das Minas.** Its hilltop location at the edge of town is both a blessing and a curse: its location away from noise of the center is great for people seeking a relaxing and quiet stay, but it's not a comfortable location for nocturnal explorations of the city. The rooms are large and comfortable, with large windows and ample fresh air. It's a popular place with families and other groups. For more privacy and peace, opt for a simple but cozy chalet instead of a room in the main building. **Pros:** Lovely views, peaceful, and quiet. **Cons:** Walk to and from pousada is somewhat strenuous. ⊠*Rua Manganês 287, São Cristóvão, 35400-000* ☎⎙*031/3551–3003* ⇱*11 rooms, 25 chalets* ⬠*In-room: no a/c, refrigerator. In-hotel: room service, pools, no elevator, laundry service, public Internet* ⊟*AE, DC, MC, V* ⎟○⎟*BP.*

NIGHTLIFE & THE ARTS

★ The incredibly high ceilings, the stone walls, and the gorgeous garden with tropical plants at **Acaso 85** (⊠*Largo do Rosário 85, Rosário, 35400-975* ☎*031/3551–2397*) are impressive; the food and the service
FodorsChoice less so. There's live MPB Tuesday–Sunday. **Bardobeco** (⊠*Trv. Arieira*
★ *15, Centro, 35400-975* ☎*031/3551–1429*) is the city's best *cachaçaria,* or cachaça bar (cachaça is a rumlike sugarcane liquor) with more than 65 brands of cachaça, including the owner's own Milagre de Minas and an incredible variety of delicious cachaça cocktails. The interior is made of stone and reminiscent of an old Central European wine cellar.

The best place for information about theater, arts, and musical performances is the **Posto de Informações Turísticas** (⊠*Praça Tirandentes 4,*

Centro, 35400-000 ☏031/3559–5220). **Fundação de Artes de Ouro Preto** *(FAOP ✉Rua Alvarenga, 794, Cabec[ac]as, 35400-000 ☏031/3551–2014 ⊕www.faop.mg.gov.br),* the local arts foundation, hosts various art and photographic exhibitions throughout the year.

SHOPPING

HANDICRAFTS   There are numerous handicrafts stores on Praça Tiradentes and its surrounding streets. At the daily **handicrafts fair** in front of the Igreja de São Francisco de Assis, vendors sell soapstone and wood carvings, paintings, and other goods.

★   **Gomides** *(✉Beco da Mãe Chica 29, Barra, 35400-000 ☏031/3551–2511 or 031/3551–4571)* has a good selection of unique sculptures.

Fodor'sChoice   **Z Nelson** *(✉Rua Randolpho Bretas 67, Centro, 35400-000 ☏031/3551–*
★   *6434)* sells crafts and makes beautiful wood objects in mineiran baroque style: angels, oratories, and other sacred art.

For information about jewelry and gemstone shops, see the "Finding a Gem" CloseUp, above.

SIDE TRIP TO MARIANA

11 km (7 mi) east of Ouro Preto, 110 km (68 mi) southeast of Belo Horizonte.

The oldest city in Minas Gerais (founded in 1696) is also the birthplace of Aleijadinho's favorite painter, Manuel da Costa Ataíde. Mariana, like Ouro Preto, has preserved much of the appearance of an 18th-century gold-mining town. Its three principal churches showcase examples of the art of Ataíde, who intertwined sensual romanticism with religious themes. The faces of his saints and other figures often have mulatto features, reflecting the composition of the area's population at the time. Today Mariana is most visited for the weekly organ concerts at its cathedral.

TO & FROM

By bus from Belo Horizonte, there are seven Pássaro Verde buses a day to Mariana (R$20; 2½ hours). Buses from Ouro Preto to Mariana depart every 30 minutes (R$3; 30 minutes). If you're driving, take BR 040 south and BR 356 (it becomes MG 262) east to Ouro Preto and continue on 11 km (7 mi) to Mariana (30 minutes).

EN ROUTE   Between Ouro Preto and Mariana lies **Mina de Ouro de Passagem,** Brazil's oldest gold mine. During the gold rush thousands of slaves perished here because of its dangerous, backbreaking conditions. Although the mine is no longer in operation, you can ride an old mining car through 11 km (7 mi) of tunnels and see exposed quartz, graphite, and black tourmaline. Buses travel here from Ouro Preto (catch them beside the Escola de Minas) and cost about R$3; taxis are about R$25. *✉Road to Mariana, 4 km (3 mi) east of Ouro Preto, 35420-000 ☏031/3557–5001 ☞R$18 ☉Daily 9–5.*

WHAT TO SEE

The **Catedral Basílica da Sé,** completed in 1760, contains paintings by Ataíde, although it's best known for its 1701 German organ built by Arp Schnitger. Transported by mule from Rio de Janeiro in 1720, the instrument was a gift from the Portuguese court to the first diocese in Brazil. This is the only Schnitger organ outside Europe, and one of the best-preserved in the world. Concerts take place Friday at 11 AM and Sunday at 12:15. ✉ *Praça Cláudio Manoel s/n, 35420-000* ☎ *031/3557–1216* 💲 *R\$1 donation* ⊙ *Tues.–Sun. 8–noon and 2–6:30.*

Behind the cathedral is the **Museu Arquidiocesano de Arte Sacra de Mariana,** which claims to have the largest collection of baroque painting and sculpture in the state, including wood and soapstone carvings by Aleijadinho and paintings by Ataíde. ✉ *Rua Frei Durão 49, 35420-000* ☎ *031/3557–2516* 💲 *R\$3* ⊙ *Tues.–Sun. 8:30–noon and 1:30–5.*

★ Although the 1793 **Igreja de São Francisco de Assis** *(Church of St. Francis of Assisi)* has soapstone pulpits and altars by Aleijadinho, its most impressive works are the sacristy's ceiling panels, which were painted by Ataíde. They depict, in somber tones, the life and death of St. Francis of Assisi and are considered by many to be the artist's masterpiece. Sadly, they've been damaged by termites and water. ✉ *Praça Minas Gerais, 35420-000* ☎ *031/3557–1023* 💲 *R\$2* ⊙ *Tues.–Sun. 9–noon and 1–5.*

★ The **Igreja da Nossa Senhora do Carmo** *(Our Lady of Carmel Church),* with works by Ataíde and Aleijadinho, is noteworthy for its impressive facade and sculpted soapstone designs. Ataíde is buried at the rear of the church. At this writing, it's closed for renovations following a huge fire. ✉ *Praça Minas Gerais, 35420-000* ☎ *031/3558–1979* ⊙ *Tues.–Sun. 8–11 and 1–5.*

EN ROUTE
★ Dominating the small Gold Town Congonhas do Campo is Aleijadinho's crowning effort, the hilltop pilgrimage church **Igreja Bom Jesus do Matosinho.** Built in 1757, it's the focus of great processions during Holy Week. At the churchyard entrance are Aleijadinho's 12 life-size Old Testament prophets carved in soapstone, a towering achievement and one of the greatest works of art from the baroque period. The prophets appear caught in movement, and every facial expression is unforgettable. Leading up to the church on the sloping hillside are six chapels, each containing a scene of the stations of the cross. The 66 figures in this remarkable procession were carved in cedar by Aleijadinho and painted by Ataíde. From Mariana, Congonhas is about 50 km (31 mi) west; take BR 356 to MG 440 to MG 030, then go north on BR 040. It's also a fairly easy trip by bus or car from Belo Horizonte (94 km/58 mi) or Tiradentes (130 km/81 mi). ✉ *Praça da Basílica 180, Congonhas do Campo 36415-000* ☎ *031/3731–1591* 💲 *Free* ⊙ *Tues.–Sun. 6–6.*

TIRADENTES

210 km (130 mi) southwest of Belo Horizonte.

Probably the best historic city to visit after Ouro Preto and Diamantina, Tiradentes was the birthplace of a martyr who gave the city its name (it was formerly called São José del Rei) and retains much of its 18th-century charm. Life in this small town—nine streets with eight churches set against the backdrop of the Serra de São José—moves slowly. It attracts wealthy residents of Belo Horizonte, Rio, and São Paulo, who have sparked a local real-estate boom by buying up 18th-century properties for weekend getaways or to transform them into pousadas or restaurants.

TO & FROM

From Belo Horizonte there are six buses every day, you must first travel to São João del Rei on the Viação Sandra bus line (R$35; 3½ hours), then to Tiradentes on a Vale do Ouro bus. From São João del Rei, buses run every 1½ hours and the trip is about R$3.

To reach Tiradentes from Belo by car, take BR 040 south (Congonhas do Campo, with its Igreja Bom Jesus do Matosinho, is on this route) and then BR 265 west. It takes approximately 3½ hours.

ESSENTIALS

Banks & Currency Exchange Itáu (⊠ *Rua Ministro Gabriel Passos 43B, Centro, 36325-000*).

Bus Contacts Rodoviária (Terminal Turístico) (⊠ *Praça Silva Jardim, near Igreja São Francisco de Paula, 36325-000*). **Vale do Ouro** (☎ *032/3371–5119*). **Viação Sandra** (☎ *031/3201–2927*).

Emergencies & Medical Assistance Ambulance (☎ *192*). **Fire** (☎ *193*).

Hospital: **Posto de Saúde** (⊠ *Rua do Chafariz 10, Centro, 35325-000* ☎ *032/3355–1422*). **Police** (☎ *190*).

Visitor & Tour Info Cidinho Barbosa (☎ *032/3335–1267* ☞ *Individual guide with fluent English, very knowledgeable about the area*). **Tiradentes Secretaria de Turismo** (⊠ *Rua Resende Costa 71, 36325-000* ☎ *032/3355–1212* ☞ *Open weekdays 8–6. Horseback and hiking trips.*).

WHAT TO SEE

In addition to the excellent selection of handicrafts—some 20 shops line Rua Direita in the town center—the principal attraction is the **Igreja de Santo Antônio**. Built in 1710, it contains extremely well-preserved gilded carvings of saints, cherubs,

---

MARIA FUMAÇA

The Smoking Mary, a little red steam train in operation since the 19th century, is an authentic and fun way to get from São João del Rei to Tiradentes. The 13-km (8-mi) ride goes up the valley and through the oldest mining area in the state in 35 minutes (round-trip R$25, one-way R$15; twice daily Friday—Sunday and holidays). The train leaves from São João del Rei's Estação Ferroviária (Av. Hermilio Alves) tickets do not need to be bought in advance. The train leaves Sã João del Rei at 10 AM and 3 PM and returns from Tiradentes at 1 PM and 5 PM.

CLOSE UP

Brazilian Baroque

When gold was discovered in Minas Gerais in the 17th century, the Portuguese, to ensure their control of the mining industry, exiled the traditional religious orders, which led to the formation of third orders. Attempts by these lay brothers to build churches based on European models resulted in improvisations (they had little experience with or guidance on such matters) and, hence, a uniquely Brazilian style of baroque that extended into the early 19th century. Many churches from this period have simple exteriors that belie interiors whose gold-leaf-encrusted carvings are so intricate they seem like filigree.

As the gold supply diminished, facades became more elaborate—with more sophisticated lines, elegant curves, and large round towers—and their interiors less so, as murals were used more than carvings and gold leaf. Many sculptures were carved from wood or soapstone. Today Minas Gerais has the largest concentration of baroque architecture and art of any state in Brazil. You can see several outstanding examples of baroque architecture, many of them attributed to the legendary Aleijadinho ($\Rightarrow$ see box), in Ouro Preto (where there are 13 such churches) and the other Gold Towns of Minas: Mariana, Tiradentes, and Congonhas.

and biblical scenes. The church's soapstone frontispiece—a celebration of baroque architecture—is attributed to Aleijadinho. ⊠ *Rua Padre Toledo s/n, 36325-000* ☎ *032/3355–1238* ⊠ *R$5* ☉ *Daily 9–5.*

WHERE TO STAY & EAT

$$$–$$$$ ✕ **Teatro da Villa.** On the site of an old Greek-style amphitheater, this gorgeous restaurant with an extensive wine and champagne list offers dinner theater; most performances involve local folk music and dance. The menu is filled with international fare, including meat and fish dishes. ⊠ *Rua Padre Toledo 157, 36325-000* ☎ *032/3355–1275* ⊟ *AE, DC, MC, V* ☉ *Closed Mon. No lunch Thurs. and Fri.*

$$$ ✕ **Estalagem do Sabor.** The Estalagem draws rave reviews for its feijão
★ tropeiro and frango ao molho pardo, just two of the dishes that are part of the self-service buffet. Although it's small, it has an elegant atmosphere. Light music and a quiet, attentive staff make for a relaxing meal. ⊠ *Rua Ministro Gabriel Passos 280, Centro, 36325-000* ☎ *032/3355–1144* ⊟ *No credit cards* ☉ *No dinner on Sun.*

$$–$$$ ✕ **Tragaluz.** This mix of store, coffee shop, and restaurant serves unusual dishes, like jaboticaba ice cream. Caetano Veloso, Brazil's top musical export, popped in last year to play for an hour and eat the amazing chorizo beef. Try the gnocchi, Argentine meat, *frango de* Angola (marinated chicken), and for dessert, the *goiabada frita* (fried goaiba fruit jam). ⊠ *Rua Direita 52, 36325-000* ☎ *032/3355–1424* ⊟ *DC, MC, V* ☉ *Closed Tues.*

$ ✕ **Viradas do Largo.** One of the best restaurants in the country for typi-
FodorśChoice cal comida mineira, the Viradas do Largo (also known as Restaurante
★ da Beth) serves dishes such as chicken with *ora pro nobis* (a Brazilian cabbage) and feijão tropeiro with pork chops. Some of the ingredients, such as the *borecole* (kale), are cultivated in the restaurant's backyard.

The portions are generous, enough for three or four people, but you can ask for a half order of any dish. The restaurant is also a market, with typical arts and crafts from Minas Gerais. Reservations are essential on weekends. ☒*Francisco Candido Barbosa 180, 36325-000* ☎*032/3355–1111 or 032/3355–1110* ☐*AE, DC, MC, V.*

$$$–$$$$
Fodor'sChoice
★

🏨**Solar da Ponte.** In every respect—from the stunning antiques to the comfortable beds to the elegant place settings—this inn is a faithful example of regional style. With advance notice, the English owner and his Brazilian wife can arrange historical, botanical, and ecological tours on foot or horseback. **Pros:** Breakfast and afternoon tea (included in the rate) are served in the dining room, overlooking well-tended gardens. **Cons:** Two-night minimum stay in high season. ☒*Praça das Mercês s/n, 36325-000* ☎*032/3355–1255, 021/2287–1592 for reservations in Rio* ⇆*18 rooms* ♨*In-room: no a/c, refrigerator. In-hotel: room service, bar, pool, no elevator, laundry service, no kids under 12* ☐*AE, DC, MC, V* ⦿*BP.*

$–$$

🏨**Pousada Três Portas.** This pousada is in an adapted colonial house with hardwood floors and locally made furniture and artwork in the historic center of Tiradentes. The owner runs a small puppet theater adjacent to the breakfast room. **Pros:** Rooms are clean and modern. **Cons:** Prices jump dramatically on weekends. ☒*Rua Direita 280A, 36325-000* ☎*032/3355–1444* 🖷*032/3355–1184* ⊕*www.pousadatresportas.com.br* ⇆*8 rooms, 1 suite* ♨*In-room: no a/c, refrigerator, dial-up. In-hotel: room service, bars, pool, no elevator, laundry service* ☐*MC* ⦿*BP.*

$
★

🏨**Pouso Alforria.** Alforria enjoys a quiet, peaceful location with a fabulous view of the São José Mountains. The light-filled lobby—with its stone floors, high ceilings, and beautiful Brazilian artwork (some of it from Bahia)—leads to a charming breakfast space and courtyard. Rooms have considerable natural light and are individually decorated; mattresses are firm. **Pros:** Very nice, light-filled rooms; modern bathrooms. **Cons:** Only a few rooms, so reservations are required well ahead of time. ☒*Rua Custódio Gomes 286, 36325-000* ☎🖷*032/3355–1536* ⊕*www.pousoalforria.com.br* ⇆*8 rooms* ♨*In-room: no a/c, safe, refrigerator. In-hotel: room service, bar, pool, no elevator, laundry service, concierge, public Internet, no kids under 16* ☐*MC* ⦿*BP.*

THE ARTS

Cultural life in Tiradentes revolves around the **Centro Cultural Yves Alves** (☒*Rua Direita 168, 36325-000* ☎*032/3355–1503 or 031/3355–1604* ⊕*www.centroculturalyvesalves.org.br*), which has theatrical performances, films, concerts, and art exhibitions. On weekends the **Theatro da Villa** (☒*Rua Padre Toledo 157, 36325-000* ☎*032/3355–1275*) has musical shows that accompany dinner.

SHOPPING

Local artwork is the biggest draw here, with painters and sculptors famous throughout Brazil working in their gallerylike studios. The main street for galleries and antiques shops is Rua Direita.

Atelier Zé Damas (☒*Rua do Chafariz 130, 36325-000* ☎*032/3355–1578*) belongs to Tiradentes's most famous artist. He paints local scenes—such as a train winding through the mountains or a dusty afternoon street—on canvas and on stones. The small and quiet city **Bichinho** (⊠ *6 km/4 mi northeast of Tiradentes, 36325-000*) is recognized in the region for the quality of its arts and crafts.

For jewelry and gemstone shops, see "Finding a Gem" CloseUp in Ouro Preto, above.

> **PHYSICAL GEOGRAPHY**
>
> There are four different types of vegetation in Minas Gerais, the cerrado 50% (semi-dry land surrounding the rivers), the Mata Atlântica (what is left of the first-growth forest), the alpine vegetation, and the mata seca (dry forest) characterized by dry wood with spines and needles.

MINAS'S PARKS

Less that three hours from Belo Horizonte are some wild, wonderful national parks—worth a day or an overnight trip if you have the time. While not a national park, at the Parque Natural do Caraça you can stay at a lovely monastery and have monks cook for you, while during the day you hike the peaks surrounding it. In Parque Nacional do Serra do Cipo you can enjoy wonderful waterfalls, see monkeys, go horseback riding, and enjoy meals on a fazenda.

PARQUE NATURAL DO CARAÇA

123 km (76 mi) southeast of Belo Horizonte.

Waterfalls, caves—like Gruta do Centenário, one of the world's largest quartzite caves—and natural pools fill this rugged park whose name means "big face," in homage to its main mountain. The park also has some historic buildings, including an 18th-century convent and the Igreja de Nossa Senhora Mãe dos Homens (Church of Our Lady, Mother of Men), built at the end of the 19th century. It has French stained-glass windows, a rare organ, baroque altars, and a painting of the Last Supper by Ataíde. There was once a seminary in the park as well, but it caught fire in 1968. After the accident the building was transformed into an inn and small museum. The park's most famous inhabitant is the *lobo guará,* a beautiful orange wolf threatened by extinction. ⊠ *35960-000* ☎ *031/3837–2698* 💲 *R$10 per vehicle* ⊙ *Daily 7–9 for those staying at inn, otherwise 8–5.*

TO & FROM

From Belo Horizonte you can either drive or take a bus to Santa Barbara. Eight Pássaro Verde buses (R$20) per day go to Santa Barbara (2½ hours); from there it's a taxi ride (R$50) 25 minutes to the park. If you're driving from Belo Horizonte, take BR 262 to Santa Barbara in the direction of Victoria until you get to Barão de Cocais; from there continue for 5 km (3 mi) toward Santa Barbara until you see a sign on your right for Caraça, a road you take until you reach the entrance to the park—about 20 km (12 mi).

ESSENTIALS

Banks & Currency Exchange Take money out before leaving Belo Horizonte—the park accepts only cash.

Bus Contacts Pássaro Verde (⊠ *Rua Itapetinga 200, 31130-100* ⊕ *www.passaroverde.com.br*).

Emergencies & Medical Assistance Ambulance (☎ *192*). **Fire** (☎ *193*). **Police** (☎ *190*).

Visitor & Tour Info Guided tours—walking, spelunking, and other activities—can be arranged at the administration office once you arrive. The Catholic priests who run the park administer the tourist booth inside the park. They run guided day hikes up to the tallest peaks, some of which rise to about 6,000 feet; lunch is included.

> ## THE LEGEND OF CARAÇA
>
> There are many legends about the founder of the park, Carlos Mendonsa. The most famous is that he belonged to a prominent Jesuit family in 18th-century Portugal, at a time when Jesuits were being persecuted by the royal family. In 1758 there was an assassination attempt against King D. Jose. When suspicion fell on his family, the Tavoras, Carlos Mendonsa fled to Brazil and joined the Franciscan Order, using the name Father Lourenço. He later founded the sanctuary of Caraça.

SAFETY & PRECAUTIONS

When hiking, drink lots of water and wear sunscreen.

WHERE TO STAY

¢–$ ⊞ **Hospedaria do Caraça.** The park's hotel and restaurant are in an old school that was destroyed in the 1968 fire. The rooms are simple—some can accommodate five people—and are divided between two floors. Choose one on the second floor, with a view of the park and the mountain, or one of the three standard apartments. Groups of 15 to 40 people can rent one of the three houses in the park. Meals, which are served in the convent by priests, have very tight schedules: breakfast is 7–8:30, lunch noon–1:30, and dinner 6:30–7:30. **Pros:** Food is absolutely delicious, breakfasts have endless helpings and you can fry your own at a long wood-fired stove. **Cons:** Necessary to make reservations at least three weeks in advance (or longer), as there are often weddings and other celebrations. ⊠ *Km 25, Parque Natural do Caraça, 35960-000* ☎ *031/3837–2698* ☞ *51 rooms* ⏤ *In-room: no phone. In-hotel: restaurant, pool, no elevator, laundry service* ⊟ *MC, V* ⊙ *FAP.*

PARQUE NACIONAL SERRA DO CIPÓ

Highlights of the Serra do Cipó National Park include the roaring Cachoeira da Farofa (a waterfall) and the sprawling Canyon das Bandeirantes. Numerous bird species as well as wolves, jaguars, anteaters, monkeys, and the poisonous *sapo de pijama* (pajama frog) make up the park's wildlife. Although it's difficult to reach and is lacking in infrastructure, the park has a beautiful landscape and ecological wealth that make it worth the trip. Facilities are poor, so consider visiting the area as part of an organized tour with Cipó Aventuras (⇨ *Essentials, above*). The park can only be visited with a guide. ⊠ *MG 10, Km 97, Santana do Riacho 35847-000* ☎ *031/3718–7228 visitor center*

✉ *R$3* ⊙ *Daily 8–2, only with an authorized guide.*

TO & FROM
To get to Parque Nacional Serra do Cipó you can either hire a guide or rent a car—there are no buses. If driving, take MG 010 to Lagoa Santa (73 km) and then take the signs to Conceiçao do Mato Dentro (3 km), you will then reach the entrance to the park.

ESSENTIALS
Banks & Currency Exchange Take money out before leaving Belo Horizonte—the parks accept only cash.

Emergencies & Medical Assistance
Ambulance (☎192). **Fire** (☎193). **Police** (☎190).

Visitor & Tour Info Brasil Aventuras (☎031/3284–9828 ⊕ www.brasilaventuras.com.br ☞ Various park tours). **Tropa Serrana** (☎031/3344–8982, 031/9983–2356, or 031/9163–9063 ⊕ www.tropaserrana.zip.net ☞ 2-day fazenda tours on horseback with knowledgeable guide).

ON HORSEBACK

Tullio Marques at **Tropa Serrana** (✉ *Rua Gentios 55, apto. 1041, Luxemburgo, 30380-490* ☎ *031/3344–8982, 031/9983–2356, or 031/9163–9063* ⊕ *www.tropaserrana.zip.net*) runs some of the best horseback-riding tours in the country. His English is perfect (he claims to have hung out with Jimi Hendrix in Greenwich Village), and his stories about the surroundings insightful. Tullio's two-day *passeios* (jaunts) take you to the Parque Nacional Serra do Cipó, where you stay on a fazenda, eat the hearty meals of the interior, and enjoy the silence.

6

SAFETY & PRECAUTIONS
When hiking, drink lots of water and wear sunscreen. In Serra do Cipó make sure to stay covered and check yourself for ticks: they're widespread in the area around the park and especially on horses. These ticks do not carry Lyme disease but are nonetheless unpleasant.

WHERE TO STAY
Expect basic and rustic (no a/c), though clean, accommodations near the park.

$$ 🏨 **Cipó Veraneio.** The area's best hotel has dozens of activities for adults and children. The hotel is smack dab in the middle of some of the country's most beautiful nature and it's right next to a river. The rooms have king-size beds and views of the forest. **Pros:** Located in the park, beautiful pool area. **Cons:** Rooms are small, plain, and dark. ✉*MG 10, Km 95, 3 km (1 mi) south of park entrance, Jaboticatubas 33400-000* ☎*031/3718–7000* ▤*AE, DC, MC, V* ↩*32 rooms* ⚿*In-room: phone, refrigerator, a/c (some). In-hotel: restaurant, bar, pool, public Internet, bar, no elevator* ⚭*FAP.*

$
★ 🏨 **Fazenda Monjolos Pousada.** Bed down and board at this working farm where horseback tours are available. The fazenda serves a typical country breakfast, afternoon tea, and an evening meal. The large guest rooms have breathtaking views and are flooded with natural light. Our favorites are the ones with balconies. The spacious dining room is crisscrossed with a wooden ceiling beams and has a wraparound veranda. This is such a relaxing place that you'll hardly notice

the lack of facilities. **Pros:** Good views, excellent local cuisine. **Cons:** Few facilities. ☒*Km 95, Rodovia MG 10, 7 km (2½ mi) south of park entrance, Cardeal Mota 35847-000* ☏*031/3221-4253 or 031/3284-1914* ⊕*www.fazendamonjolos.com.br* ☜*21 rooms* ⌂*In-room: no a/c, refrigerator. In-hotel: pool, bar, no elevator* ▤*MC, V* ⦶*FAP.*

PARQUE NACIONAL DA SERRA DO CANASTRA

320 km (199 mi) southwest of Belo Horizonte.

Serra do Canastra National Park was created to preserve the springs of Rio São Francisco, one of the most important rivers in South America, which cuts through five Brazilian states. Its main attractions are its waterfalls, including the 610-foot Casca D'Anta. The park is in the city of São Roque de Minas, almost on the border with São Paulo State. The Brazilian Institute of the Environment (IBAMA) manages the park from its headquarters in São Roque de Minas. ☒*Off road to São Roque de Minas, 37925-000* ☏*037/3433–1840, 037/3433–1195 for IBAMA* ☞*R$3* ⊙*Daily 8–6.*

TO & FROM

From Belo Horizonte take the MG 050 southwest to Piumhi, then take the road to São Roque de Minas. The entrance to the park is 35 km (21 mi) west of São Roque de Minas (320 km from Belo Horizonte). By bus, take the Gardenia line from Belo to Piumhi—there are four buses a day (R$30; 5 hours)—then take the Transunião bus to São Roque de Minas (1.5 hours).

ESSENTIALS

Bus Contacts Gardênia (☒*Rodoviaria de Piumhi, 37925-000* ⊕*www.expresso gardenia.com.br*).

Emergencies & Medical Assistance Ambulance (☏*192*). **Fire** (☏*193*). **Police** (☏*190*).

Visitor & Tour Info Os Canastras Aventuras (☒*São Roque Minas, 37925-000* ☏*037/3433–1791* ⊕*www.canastra.com.br* ☞*Rapelling, hiking, canoeing, rafting, and other adventure tours; good Portuguese-language Web site about park*).

SAFETY & PRECAUTIONS

Bring lots of water and sunscreen.

WHERE TO STAY

The park has a camping area, but nearby towns have some simple inns.

$$ ⊞ **Paraíso da Serra.** Just ½ km from the main attraction at Parque Nacional da Serra do Canastra—the Casca D'Anta waterfall—this pousada has beautiful views from its rooms. There are also gorgeous natural pools that one can swim in. **Pros:** Trails lead straight from the pousada. **Cons:** Proximity to one of the park's main attractions means it's not as secluded as it could be otherwise. ☒*Serra da Canastra, Portaria 4, 37929-000* ☏*037/3433–2062 or 037/9988–8004* ⊕*www.pousadaparaisodaserra.com.br* ☜*8 rooms* ⌂*In-room: no a/c,* *no phone (some), refrigerator. In-hotel: restaurant, room service, bar, pools, bicycles, no elevator, laundry service, some pets allowed, no-smoking rooms* ☰*No credit cards* ⭐�‖*FAP.*

¢ 🏠**Pousada da Limeira.** On the bank of the São Francisco River, 15 km (9 mi) from the Casca D'Anta waterfall, this pousada has wonderful beamed ceilings, homey tablecloths, and comfortable wooden furniture, and feels like an authentic, humble farm. Rooms are large and have nice hammocks hanging on the porches for relaxation. **Pros:** Great price, owner provides attentive, thoughtful service. **Cons:** On a wide open plain. ✉*Estrada Cachoeira Casca D'Anta, Km 07, Vargem Bonita 37922-000* 📞📠*037/3435–1118* ⊕*www.pousadadalimeira.com.br* 🛏*13 rooms* ⚏*In-room: no a/c, no phone, refrigerator, no TV (some). In-hotel: restaurant, pool, no elevator, laundry service, public Internet* ☰*V* ⭐❖*BP.*

THE MINERAL SPA TOWNS

Known for the curative properties of their natural springs, a collection of mineral-spa towns in southern Minas Gerais forms the Circuito das Águas (Water Circuit). For more than a century people have flocked to these mystical towns, bathing in the pristine water parks and drinking from the bubbling fountains. Today the towns are especially popular among older, wealthier Brazilians.

⚠**Despite the purported curative properties of the mineral waters in the spa towns, don't drink too much when you first arrive unless you want to cleanse your system thoroughly.**

SÃO LOURENÇO

387 km (240 mi) south of Belo Horizonte.

This most modern of the mineral-spa towns is a good base from which to visit the other Circuito das Águas communities. From here taxis and tour operators happily negotiate a day rate for the circuit, usually around R$50.

TO & FROM

From Belo Horizonte, a bus to São Lourenço takes roughly seven hours and costs about R$52. The bus line is Gardênia. You must change buses in Três Corações.

If you're driving, take BR 381 south of Belo. You can also take BR 040 south to BR 267 west.

For R$50 you can get a taxi between São Lourenço and Caxambu (26 km/16 mi) or São Tomé das Letras R$100 (80 km/50 mi).

ESSENTIALS

Banks & Currency Exchange **Banco do Brasil** (✉*Av. D. Pedro II 266, Centro, 33321-049).* **Bradesco** (✉*Rua Dr. Olavo Gomes Pinto 313, Centro, 33324-176).* **HSBC** (✉*Rua Dr. Olaves Gomes Pinto 285, Centro, 33321-049).*

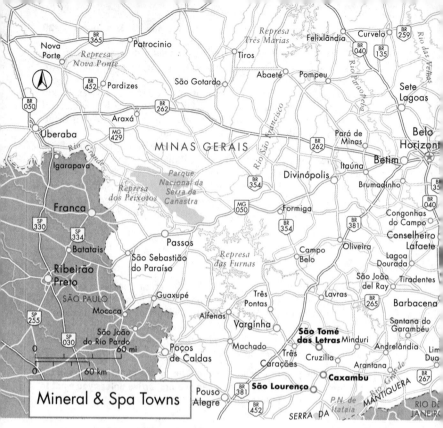

Mineral & Spa Towns

Bus Contacts Gardênia (☎ *0300/313–2020, 031/3495–1010, or 035/3423–3272 or 3423-3844* ⊕ *www.expressogardenia.com.br*). **Rodoviária-São Lourenço** (✉ *Rua Manoel Carlos 130, Centro, 37470-000* ☎ *035/3332–5966* ⊕ *www. rodoviaria-saolourenco.com.br*).

Emergencies & Medical Assistance Ambulance (☎ *192*). **Fire** (☎ *193*). Hospital: **Hospital da Fundação Casa de Caridade de São Lourenço** (✉ *Rua Ida Mascarenhas 310, Nossa Senhora de Fatima, 37470-000* ☎ *035/3332–2186*). Pharmacy: **Drogaria São Lourenço** (✉ *Ave. D. Pedro II, Centro, 37470-000* ☎ *035/3331–1224*). **Police** (☎ *190*).

Taxi Rodoviária (☎ *035/3332–4313*).

Visitor & Tour Info São Lourenço Tourist Kiosk (✉ *Praça João Lage s/n, 37470-000* ☎ *035/3332–4490* ⊕ *www.saolourenco.mg.gov.br* ☞ *Open weekdays 8–11 and 1–6*).

WHAT TO SEE

São Lourenço's **Parque das Águas** *(Water Park)* includes a picturesque lake with art deco pavilions, fountains, and gorgeous landscaping. The center of activity is its *balneário*, a hydrotherapy spa where you can immerse yourself in bubbling mineral baths and marble surroundings. There are separate bath and sauna facilities for men and women, and you can also get a massage. ✉ *Praça Brasil s/n, 37470-000* ☎ *035/3332–*

3066 or 035/3332–7111 ☜*R$4*
⊘*Park daily 8–5:20; Balneário daily 8–noon and 2–4:50.*

If your experience at the park fails to rid you of all ailments, head to the **Templo da Eubiose,** the temple of a spiritual organization dedicated to wisdom and perfection through yoga. The Eubiose, a group of New Age spiritualists, similar to European Theosophists, believe in living in harmony with nature. They also believe this will be the only place to survive the end of the world. ✉*Praça da Vitória s/n, 37470-000* ☎*035/3331–1333* ☜*Donations accepted* ⊘*Weekends 2–4.*

THE MINEIRAN BADEN-BADEN

While soaking in curative waters was a huge fad in early 19th-century Europe, Brazilians did not catch on until Princess Isabel came to partake of the waters in 1868 to find a cure for infertility. The Caxambu Water Company was founded in 1886, and other spa towns sprang up rapidly to form what is now one of the most extensive natural-spa regions in the world.

WHERE TO STAY & EAT

$$ ✕▥ **Emboabas Hotel.** This gracious fazenda is more like a private estate ★ than a rural farm. Its carefully decorated rooms have bucolic views; at night the only sounds you hear are those of various animals roaming the countryside. The restaurant ($) has prix-fixe buffets of at least three regional dishes as well as salads and dessert. **Pros:** Beautiful farm with nice rooms, occasional performances in the fazenda's theater. **Cons:** About a half-hour walk from the Parque das Águas. ✉*Alameda Jorge Amado 350, Solar dos Lagos, 37470-000* ☎*035/3332–4600* 🖷*035/3332–4392* ⊕*www.emboabashotel.com.br* ⟿*57 rooms, 3 suites* ⚲*In-room: no a/c, refrigerator, dial-up. In-hotel: restaurant, room service, bars, tennis court, pools, gym, no elevator, children's programs (ages 4–12), laundry service, public Internet, some pets allowed* ▤*AE, MC, V* ⊠*FAP.*

$$–$$$ ▥ **Hotel Brasil.** This luxury hotel is just across from the Parque das Águas at the Praça Duque de Caxias. It has its own pools, fountains, and mineral waters. The rooms are large and airy; ask for a room with a park view. **Pros:** Excellent facilities, good prix-fixe regional cuisine. **Cons:** Rooms lack sophistication and charm. ✉*Alameda João Lage 87, 37470-000* ☎*035/3332–2000* 🖷*035/3331–1536* ⊕*www.hotelbrasil.com.br* ⟿*142 rooms* ⚲*In-room: no a/c (some), refrigerator. In-hotel: restaurant, room service, bar, tennis court, pools, gym, children's programs (ages 2–12), laundry service, public Internet, some pets allowed* ▤*AE, DC, MC, V* ⊠*FAP.*

$ ▥ **Hotel Fazenda Vista Alegre.** The many activities and the low price of accommodations compensate for the lack of proximity to the water park. You can go boating on the lake or horsback riding, and there are thermal and regular pools, and tennis and football courts. If you're interested, the employees can even teach you how to milk a cow. The chalets fronting the lake can house up to five people. The hotel also has rooms for two or four people. **Pros:** Lots of facilities, good range of rooms. **Cons:** Around 4 km (3 mi) from the water park. ✉*Estrada*

6

São Lourenço-Soledade, Km 1, 37470-000 ☎*035/3332–4730* ⊕*www.* *hfvistaalegre.com.br* ⇆*9 chalets, 35 suites* ⚲*In-room: no a/c, no phone, refrigerator, TV. In-hotel: restaurant, room service, bar, pools, bicycles, no elevator, children's programs (ages 5–12), laundry service, public Internet, some pets allowed* ⊟*V* ⊙*FAP.*

CAXAMBU

30 km (19 mi) northeast of São Lourenço.

A 19th-century town once frequented by Brazilian royalty, Caxambu remains a favorite getaway for wealthy and retired *cariocas* (residents of Rio). Although most people spend their time here relaxing in bathhouses and drinking curative waters, you can also browse in the markets where local sweets are sold or take a horse-and-buggy ride to a fazenda.

> ### TAXI FOR HIRE
>
> There are plenty of taxis in both Caxambu and São Lourenço waiting to take you around the Circuito das Águas. The taxis wait at the Avenida Getúlio Vargas; for around a R$100 they'll tour the towns of Caxambu, Baependi, Cambuquira, Lambari, and Passo Quatro.

TO & FROM

Gardênia buses connect Belo Horizonte with Caxambu twice daily (7 hours; R$53). Caxambu is south of Belo off BR 381, parts of which are under construction. As an alternative, you can take BR 040 south to BR 267 west. A taxi between São Lourenço and Caxambu runs about R$50.

ESSENTIALS

Banks & Currency Exchange **Banco do Brasil** (⊠*Praça 16 de Setembro, Centro, 37440-000*).

Bus Contacts **Gardênia** (☎*031/3491–3300, 031/3495–1010, or 035/3231–3844*). **Rodoviária** (⊠*Praça Cônego José de Castilho Moreira s/n, 37440-000*).

Emergencies & Medical Assistance **Ambulance** (☎*192*). **Fire** (☎*193*). Hospital: **Casa de Caridade** (*São Vicente de Paulo* ⊠*Rua Princesa Isabel 92, Centro, 37440-000* ☎*035/3341–1553*). Pharmacy: **Drogaria Drogaminas** (⊠*Praça 16 de Setembro 2, 37440-000* ☎*035/3341–1402*). **Police** (☎*190*).

Internet **Estâncias Internet** (⊠*Av. Getúlio Vargas 235, 37440-000* ☎*035/3341–5198* ⊕*www.estancias.com.br*).

Taxi **Ponto de Táxi** (☎*035/3341–1730*).

Visitor & Tour Info **Caxambu Tourist Desk** (⊠*Rua João Carlos 100, 37440-000* ☎*035/3341–1298* ⊕*www.caxambu.mg.gov.br* ⌖*Open weekdays 8–6*).

WHAT TO SEE

Fodor'sChoice Towering trees, shimmering ponds, and fountains containing various
★ minerals—each believed to cure a different ailment—fill the **Parque das Águas.** Lavish pavilions protect the springs, and the balneário, a beautiful Turkish-style bathhouse, offers saunas and massages. In addition, hundreds of thousands of liters of mineral water are bottled here

daily and distributed throughout Brazil. ✉*Town center, 37440-000* ☎*035/3341–3999* ⊕*www.cax ambu.mg.gov.br* ✉*R$5* ☉*Park daily 7–6. Balneário Tues.–Sun 8:30–noon and 2–5.*

Overlooking the springs is the **Igreja Isabel da Hungria.** The small Gothic church was built by Princess Isabel, daughter of Dom Pedro II, after the springs were believed to have restored her fertility. She was infertile for many years, gave birth to a stillborn baby, but ultimately bore three boys. ✉*Rua Princesa Isabel s/n, 37440-000* ☎*035/3341–1582* ✉*Donations accepted* ☉*Daily 8–noon.*

You could take a chairlift (daily 9–5; R$15) from near the bus station to the peak of the **Cristo Redentor** (☎*035/9983–2223*) of, a smaller version of the one in Rio. The summit has a small restaurant and an impressive city view.

WHERE TO STAY & EAT

$-$$
★ ✕**La Forelle.** Inside the Fazenda Vale Formoso hotel, La Forelle is the best restaurant in town. Besides typical food from Minas Gerais, it also serves Danish cuisine. The specialty of the house is baked trout with potatoes. The filet mignon, the salmon, and the shrimp are among the extensive menu's stellar entrées. You can also find delicious fondues and freshly made breads. ✉*Estrada do Vale Formoso Km 8, 37440-000* ☎*035/3343–1900 or 035/3343–2556* ▤*DC, MC* ⚓*Reservations essential* ☉*Closed Mon.–Thurs. No lunch Sun.*

$$$$
Fodor'sChoice
★ 🏨**Hotel Glória.** Although it's just across from Caxambu's Parque das Águas, this luxury resort has its own rehabilitation pool and sauna as well as a variety of sports amenities. Rooms are well equipped and have marble baths. **Pros:** Gorgeous resort, meals served in an antiques-filled dining room. **Cons:** Full-size beds only in luxury rooms. ✉*Av. Camilo Soares 590, 37000-440* ☎*035/3341–3000* ⊕*www.thessho teis.com.br* ➥*120 rooms* ⚿*In-room: no a/c (some), safe, refrigerator. In-hotel: restaurant, room service, bars, tennis court, pools, gym, spa, children's programs (ages 5–12), laundry service, public Internet* ▤*MC, V* ⑩*FAP.*

$$
★ 🏨**Fazenda Vale Formoso.** A 19th-century coffee plantation transformed into a hotel, this fazenda hotel sits on more than 740 acres and is surrounded by mountains, lakes, and virgin forest. The original plantation machinery is on display and some of it, like the 19th-century water-operated sawmill and a cachaça distillery, is still working. **Pros:** Beautiful evirons, walking and riding trails. **Cons:** Rooms are comfortable but not luxurious. ✉*Estrada do Vale Formoso, Km 8, 37440-000* ☎*035/3343–1900* ⊕*www.hotelvaleformoso.com.br* ➥*17 rooms* ⚿*In-room: no a/c, refrigerator. In-hotel: restaurant, room service, bars, pools, bicycles, laundry service, public Internet, no kids under 12, some pets allowed* ▤*MC, DC* ⑩*FAP.*

6

SÃO TOMÉ DAS LETRAS

54 km (34 mi) northwest of Caxambu.

With its tales of flying saucers, its eerie stone houses that resemble architecture from outer space, and its 7,500 inhabitants who swear to years of friendship with extraterrestrials, São Tomé das Letras may be one of the oddest towns on earth. In a stunning mountain setting, it attracts mystics, psychics, and flower children who believe they've been spiritually drawn here to await the founding of a new world. Most visitors make São Tomé a day trip from Caxambu, smartly escaping nightfall's visiting UFOs.

TO & FROM

To reach São Tomé das Letras by bus from Belo Horizonte (six buses/day), take the Expresso Gardênia to Três Corações; from there, take the Viação Trectur (three buses daily). The entire journey from Belo Horizonte takes 5½ hours and costs about R$60. São Tomé das Letras can be reached from Belo via BR 381 south or BR 040 south to BR 267 west. A taxi between São Lourenço and São Tomé das Letras costs about R$70.

ESSENTIALS

Banks & Currency Exchange **Itaú** (⊠ *Av. Alameda Virgilio Andrade Martins 6, Loja B, Centro, 37418-000*).

Bus Contacts **Rodoviária** (⊠ *Av. Tomé Mendes Peixoto s/n, 37418-000*). **Viação Trectur** (⊠ *Av. Tomé Mendes Peixoto s/n, 37418-000*).

Emergencies & Medical Assistance **Ambulance** (☎ *192*). **Fire** (☎ *193*). **Police** (☎ *190*).

WHAT TO SEE

A center of religious activity and one of the few nonstone buildings in São Tomé, **Igreja Matriz** is in São Tomé's main square and contains frescoes by Brazilian artist Joaquim José de Natividade.

Next to the Igreja Matriz is the **Gruta de São Tomé**, a small cave that, in addition to its shrine to São Tomé, features some of the mysterious inscriptions for which the town is famous.

Just 3 km (2 mi) from São Tomé, two **caverns**, Carimbado and Chico Taquara, both display hieroglyphs. A short walk from the caves puts you in view of Véu da Noiva and Véu da Eubiose, two powerful waterfalls.

Brasília & the West

WORD OF MOUTH

"I've been to the Pantanal and you will absolutely love it. It is such an amazing place! We were in the small town of Bonito for two days and went on various tours in the area, in addition to staying at a fazenda in the middle of the Pantanal for two days. We went on many excursions—piranha fishing, night jungle tours, snorkeling in pristine rivers where we saw a lot of wildlife, exotic birds, monkeys, and you could maybe even see an anaconda or panther (which I was hoping not to!). I hope you have a great trip!"

–AngelaS

Updated
by Carlos
Tornquist

VISITING BRASÍLIA IS LIKE LEAPING into the future. Rising from the red earth of the 3,000-foot *Planalto Central* (Central Plateau) is one of the world's most singular cities. Its structures crawl and coil along the flat landscape and then shoot up in shafts of concrete and glass that capture the sun's rays.

All around this icon of modernity nestles the old and present Brazil—the *cerrado* (Brazilian savanna), intersected by sluggish rivers, now the land of soybean and sugarcane plantations and cattle ranches. Nevertheless, those who flock to the rugged yet beautiful west have their eyes on the future. The surreal collection of migrants includes opportunists with get-rich-quick schemes; frontier folk with hopes of a solid, stable tomorrow; mystics and prophets who swear by the region's spiritual energy; and dreamers who are convinced that extraterrestrials visit here regularly. For most earthly visitors, however, the high point of the west is the Pantanal, a flood plain the size of Great Britain that's home to an amazing array of wildlife and the ever-present possibilities for adventure.

ORIENTATION & PLANNING

ORIENTATION

The states that make up the western part of Brazil cover an area larger than Alaska, extending from the heart of the country—where Brasília is located—to the borders of Paraguay and Bolivia. Brasília, Cuiabá, and Campo Grande (the latter two the capitals of Mato Grosso and Mato Grosso do Sul states), form a massive triangle with roughly equal sides of about 700 mi. These large distances through agricultural areas mean that the best way to explore this region is by air.

BRASÍLIA
Brasília sits on the flat plateau known as the Planalto Central. The capital is actually part of the *Distrito Federal* (Federal District), a 55,000-square-km (21,000-square-mi) administrative region. Also within this district are the *cidades-satélite* (satellite cities), which originated as residential areas for Brasília workers but are now communities in their own right.

GOIÁS STATE
Surrounding the Federal District, Goiás State shares the same landscape—flat terrain now mostly covered by agricultural fields and cattle pastures. But it also has attractions of its own, such as tranquil colonial towns such as Goiás Velho or Pirenópolis. Many people visit the Chapada dos Veadeiros, one of the country's top hiking destinations, for its impressive hills and valleys. To the west, the Araguaia River forms the border with Mato Grosso.

THE PANTANAL

Several rivers in the west of Brazil and from neighboring Bolivia and Paraguay run through the sprawling lowlands in the area known as the Pantanal. The region is a vast alluvial plain that covers most of the southwest of the state of Mato Grosso and northwest of Mato Grosso do Sul. The Paraguay River, which runs roughly north–south, is the backbone of the Pantanal, providing the one outlet to the enormous amounts of water that fall during the rainy season. The city of Corumbá, at its southern edge, is about 1,300 km (800 mi) from the Atlantic.

> ### TOP REASONS TO GO
>
> ■ Brasília's remarkable architectural style is unique even among the world's other planned cities.
>
> ■ The wildlife of the Pantanal, the immense wetlands in the heart of South America, is amazing.
>
> ■ The historical districts of Goiás Velho and Pirenópolis take you right back to Brazil's colonial times.
>
> ■ The mountains, valleys, and waterfalls of Chapada dos Veadeiros or Chapada dos Guimarães highlands stand out against the plains.

PLANNING

WHEN TO GO

In Brasília and much of the west you can count on clear days and comfortable temperatures from March to July (the mean temperature is 22°C/75°F). The rainy season runs from November to February; in August and September the mercury often rises to 38°C [100°F]). When congress adjourns (July, January, and February), the city's pulse slows noticeably and hotel rooms are easier to come by. It's nearly impossible to get a room during major political events. On the other hand, popular holidays such as New Year's and Carnival are much less hectic than in other cities.

The best season to visit the Pantanal depends on what you intend to do. If the plan is to take photos of wildlife, the ideal time is the dry season running from June to October. As the waters dwindle, animals are concentrated in a smaller area, making them easier to spot. For fishing, the best time to visit is from August to October, before the onset of the rainy season, when most fish move upstream to spawn.

ABOUT THE RESTAURANTS & CUISINE

As the capital, Brasília attracts citizens from throughout the country as well as dignitaries from around the world. You can find a variety of regional cuisines as well as international fare. Brasília also has plenty of "per kilo" restaurants, usually decently priced cafeterialike places where you pay according to the weight of your plate. Except for fish dishes in the Pantanal, the food here is neither as interesting or as flavorful as that found elsewhere in the country. That said, the food is hearty, and the meals are large; affordable all-you-can-eat buffets are everywhere.

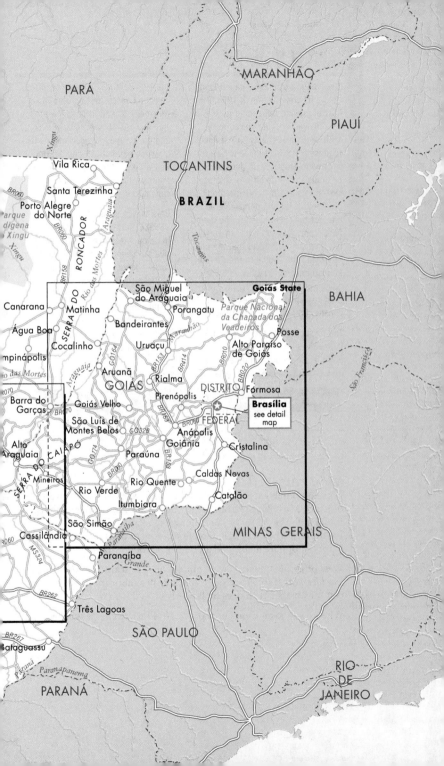

CLOSE UP

A Bit of History

The creation of Brasília began long before its construction in 1956. The idea of moving the capital to the countryside was first voiced in the 18th century, allegedly by the Portuguese Marquis of Pombal. Several sites were proposed, in different central states. A team was commissioned to study the climatic conditions of inland Brazil and demarcate an area for the future capital. The team's final report was submitted in 1894, but it wasn't until 1946 that the plan of moving the capital to the Central Plateau became a reality with the advent of a new Constitution. President Juscelino Kubitschek ordered the construction of Brasília in 1956.

The mystic part of the history of Brasília revolves around bishop Dom Bosco and the prophetic dream he had in the 19th century, 75 years before the construction of the city. Dom Bosco dreamed about Brasília being the "promised land, flowing with milk and honey and inconceivable riches" between parallels 15 and 20. Dom Bosco's dream was used as one of the mottos to justify the moving of the capital to the interior of the country.

Brasília was unveiled in 1960. In 1987 UNESCO declared the city a World Heritage Site. Since its founding, Brasília has seen important political and social changes, such as the enactment of the current Brazilian Constitution in 1988 (the first after the military dictatorship stepped down) and rallies against President Fernando Collor de Mello, the only Brazilian president to be impeached, in 1992.

WHAT IT COSTS IN REAIS				
	¢	$	$$	$$$	$$$$
AT DINNER	under R$15	R$15–R$30	R$30–R$45	R$45–R$60	over R$60

Prices are per person for a main course at dinner or for a prix-fixe meal.

ABOUT THE HOTELS

Brasília's hotels cater primarily to business executives and government officials. Most hotels, from the upscale resorts to the budget inns, are found in the Hotel Sectors and along Lago Paranoá. For ease in exploring the city, try to stay in Plano Piloto, close to most architectural landmarks, shopping malls, and a number of good restaurants.

West of Brasília, deluxe accommodations are scarcer. In the Pantanal, the *fazendas* (farms) are quite spartan. But there are a few extremely comfortable jungle lodges with nearly everything you could need.

When you book a room, note that a 10% service charge will be added.

WHAT IT COSTS IN REAIS					
	¢	$	$$	$$$	$$$$
FOR 2 PEOPLE	under R$125	R$125–R$250	R$250–R$375	R$375–R$500	over R$500

Prices are for a standard double room in high season, excluding tax.

GETTING AROUND

Exploring this region is no small feat. Given the great distances, you should fly between the large cities of Brasília, Cuiabá, and Campo Grande. To visit the interior you must either drive, take a bus, or join a tour. If you only have a week or so, its best to concentrate on Brasília and the surrounding area. The mighty Pantanal and its many natural wonders justify an extended trip.

BRASÍLIA

The idea of moving Brazil's capital to the interior dates from the early days of the country's independence, but it wasn't until 1955 that the scheme became more than a pipe dream. Many said Brasília couldn't be built; others simply went ahead and did it. The resolute Juscelino Kubitschek made it part of his presidential campaign platform. On taking office, he organized an international contest for the city's master plan. A design submitted by urban planner Lúcio Costa was selected, and he and his contemporaries—including architect Oscar Niemeyer and landscape artist Roberto Burle Marx—went to work. The new capital was built less than five years later, quite literally in the middle of nowhere.

Costa once mused, "The sky is the sea of Brasília." He made sure that the city had an unhindered view of the horizon, with buildings whose heights are restricted, wide streets and avenues, and immense green spaces. The sky here is an incredible blue that's cut only by occasional clusters of fleecy clouds. The earth is such an amazing shade of red that it seems to have been put here just for contrast. At night it's hard to tell where the city lights end and the stars begin. The renowned contemporary architect Frank O. Gehry said of Brasília, "It's a different city. I call it holy land, an untouchable icon of architecture."

Brasília is a great place for those interested in architecture and in a different city experience from Rio, Salvador, or São Paulo. Everything is divided into sectors (hotels, residences, swimming places, etc.), and the streets were designed without sidewalks—it's said that Brasília is a driver's paradise, but a pedestrian's nightmare. Because of this, Brasília has long been known as "the city without corners."

7

Brasília

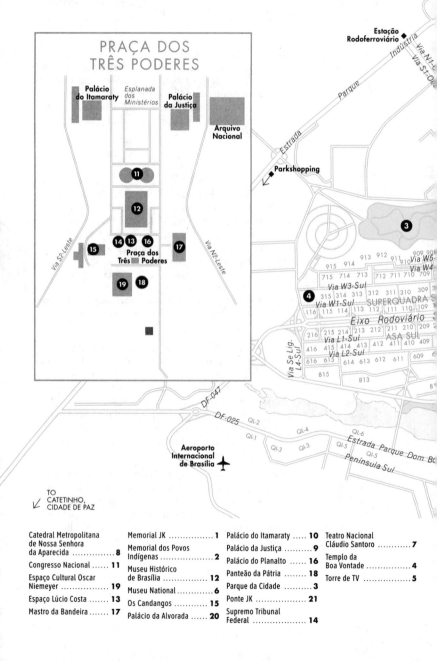

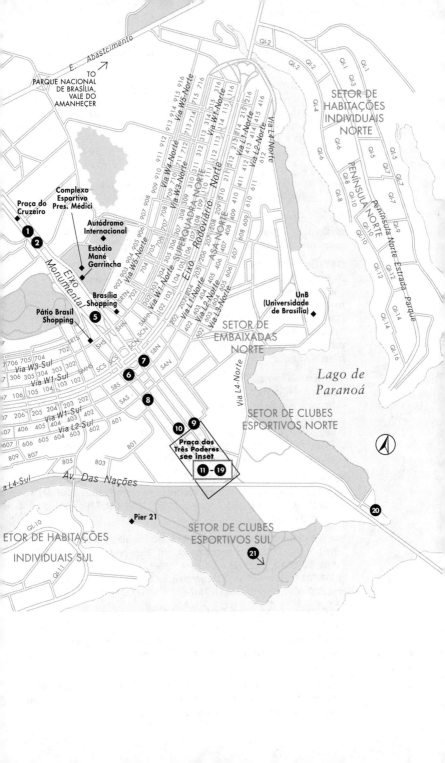

1,015 km (632 mi) north of São Paulo, 1,200 km (750 mi) northwest of Rio de Janeiro.

TO & FROM

Brasília's international airport, Aeroporto Juscelino Kubitschek (BSB), is one of the busiest in Brazil. To get to the city center, taxis are your only real option. Trips to the hotel sectors along the Eixo Monumental take roughly 15 minutes and cost about R$40. City buses, which cost about R$3, make many stops and don't have space for luggage.

Brasília is connected with the rest of the country by several major highways. BR 050 is the shortest way south to São Paulo. BR 040 goes to Rio, and BR 020 runs northeast to Salvador.

Interstate buses arrive and depart from the Estação Rodoviária. Real makes the 14-hour trip between Brasília and São Paulo. Itapemirim buses run to and from Rio de Janeiro (17 hours).

GETTING AROUND

As in most cities in Brazil, the public transportation system is based on commuter buses. Most bus lines depart from Estação Rodoviária, and from there you can go to virtually any part of the city. Rides within the Plano Piloto cost about R$3. Although Brasília does have a subway, it has currently only one line connecting the Estação Rodoviária to the suburb of Tabatinga. The few stations along the Plano Piloto are closed for renovation.

The best way to get around is by car—either taxi or rental car. Taxi fares in Brasília are a bit lower than in the rest of the country, and most cabs are organized as cooperatives with dispatchers ("radio taxis"). It's best to tackle the Eixo Monumental and then to visit the Praça dos Três Poderes first, and then choose other sights farther away. For this, hire a cab or join an organized tour. Alternatively, combine walking and bus rides with lines 104 and 108, which run by the Eixo Monumental.

ESSENTIALS

Airport Aeroporto Internacional Juscelino Kubitschek (*BSB* ✉ *DF-047 s/n, 12 km (7 mi) west of Eixo Monumental, 71608-900* ☎ *061/3364–9000* ⊕ *www.aeroportodebrasilia.gov.br*).

Banks & Currency Exchange Banco do Brasil (✉ *SBS, Bl. A, Lt. 23, 70073–900* ☎ *061/3310–4845* ✉ *Aeroporto Internacional Juscelino Kubitschek, DF-047 s/n, 71608-900* ☎ *061/3365–1183*). **Citibank** (✉ *SHL/Sul, Q. 716, Cj. N, Bl. A, Lj. 81/72, 70390-700* ☎ *061/4009–6001*). **Confidence Câmbio** (✉ *Patio Brasil Shopping Mall, SCS, Q. 07, Bl. A, 1st level, 70307-902* ☎ *061/3034–4999*).

Bus Contacts Estação Rodoferroviária (✉ *Setor Ferroviário, westernmost tip of Eixo Monumental), 70631-900* ☎ *061/3363–4045 or 061/3363–2281*). **Estação Rodoviária** (✉ *Eixo Monumental, at intersection of Asa Norte and Asa Sul, 72705-900* ☎ *061/3224-0376*). **Itapemirim** (☎ *061/3361–4505 or 0800/99–2627* ⊕ *www.itapemirim.com.br*). **Real** (☎ *061/2106–7199* ⊕ *www.realexpresso.com.br*).

Emergencies & Medical Assistance Ambulance (☎ *192*). **Fire** (☎ *193*).**Hospital: Hospital de Base do Distrito Federal** (✉ *Setor Médico Hospitalar Sul, Area Especial, 70335-900* ☎ *061/3225–5050*).

The Method to the Madness

Addresses in Brasília's Plano Piloto can make even surveyors scratch their heads. Although the original layout of the city is very logical, it can be hard to get chapter-and-verse addresses, making them seem illogical. Some necessary vocabulary, with abbreviations:

Superquadras (SQ): Supersquares

Setores (S.): Sectors

Quadra (Q.) Block within a Supersquare or Sector

Quadra Interna (QI.) Internal block

Bloco (Bl.): A large building within a *superquadra* or *setor*

Lote (Lt.): Lot, subdivision of a block

Conjunto (Cj.): A building subdivision

Loja (Lj.): Part of a larger building.

The Eixo Rodoviário has a line of superquadras made up of two (usually) quadras numbered from 100 to 116, 200 to 216, or 300 to 316 and consisting of six-story blocos. Quadras numbered 400 and above have been added outside the initial plan.

In addresses, compass points are sometimes added: *norte* (north), *sul* (south), *leste* (east), *oeste* (west). So an address might include SQN, meaning "superquadra norte." The Lago (Lake) region of the city is divided into the Lago Sul and Lago Norte districts. The residental areas on the shores of the lake include the Setores de Habitações Individuais (SHI) and the Setores de Mansões (SM).

Some important neighborhoods are:

Setor Comercial Local (SCL): for commercial areas within the Superquadras.

Setor Hoteleiro Norte (SHN): for hotels in the northern part of the city.

Setor Hoteleiro Sul (SHS): for hotels in the southern part of Brasília.

Setor de Diversões Sul (SDS): where the malls are located

Pharmacy: 24-Hour Pharmacy Hotline (☎*160*). **Drogaria Rosário** (✉*SHCS 102, Bl. C, Lj. 05, 70035-000* ☎*061/3323–5901 or 061/3212–1000*).

Internet Neon Lights (✉*Patio Brasil Shopping Mall, SCS, Q. 07, Bl. A, 2nd level, Lj. 321, 70307-902* ☎*061/3022–8060* ⊕*www.neonlights.com.br*).

Taxi Rádio Táxi Maranata (☎*061/3323–3900*). **Rádio Táxi Brasília** (☎*061/3323–3030*).

Visitor & Tour Info AirBrasil (✉*Galeria Hotel Nacional, SHS, Q. 1, Bl. A, Lj. 33-34, 70322-970* ☎*061/3322–8822*) offers trips around Brasília and the western states. **ESAT Aerotáxi** (✉*Eixo Monumental, 70000-300* ☎*061/3323–8777* ⊕*www.esataerotaxi.com.br*) offers 10-minute city helicopter tours of the city for R$400. **SETUR** (✉*SCN, Q. 4, Bl. B, S. 505, 70714-906* ☎*061/3429–7600* ⊕*www.setur.df.gov.br*), the Brasília Tourism Agency, is open weekdays 9 to 5. A branch at the airport is open weekdays 7 to 11, and a branch at the Eixo Monumental is open daily 9 to 6. The Brasília-based **VoeTur** (✉*Brasília Shopping, SCN, Q. 05, Bl. A, Lj. 41W, 70710-500* ☎*061/3327–5509* ⊕*www.voeturoperadora.com.br*) is a well-regarded travel agency with plenty of tours of the region and of the rest of Brazil.

SAFETY & PRECAUTIONS

Brasília, especially the Plano Piloto, is safe. In the residential blocks and their commercial subsectors you can wander in the evening without much concern. One exception is the commercial area around Estação Rodoviária, which can be sketchy at night. Watch out for pickpocketing, counterfeit items, and con artists.

> ### BRASÍLIA TOURS
>
> Most hotels can arrange tours. Popular excursions include basic daytime trips along the Eixo Monumental, shorter nighttime versions with stops at bars and clubs, and a "mystical tour" to cult communities around town.

EXPLORING

Numbers in the text correspond to numbers in the margin and on the Brasília map.

Shaped like an airplane when seen from above, the Plano Piloto (Pilot Plan) is the name of the original design for the city conceived by Lúcio Costa. The plan had four basic features: well-ventilated housing near green spaces; work spaces that were separate from housing; spaces for cultural activities near residential space; and the separation of vehicle and pedestrian pathways.

The Eixo (pronounced *eye*-shoo) Monumental, the "fuselage" portion of the plan, is lined with government buildings, museums, monuments, banks, hotels, and shops. It runs roughly from the Praça do Cruzeiro to the "cockpit," or the Praça dos Três Poderes. Intersecting the Eixo Monumental to form the Plano Piloto's "wings" is the Eixo Rodoviário. In and around the two main axes are streets and avenues that connect still more residential and commercial areas, parks and gardens, and the Lago Paranoá, formed by a dam built about 16 km (10 mi) southeast of the Plano Piloto. Along the outer shores of this lake, new neighborhoods are sprouting at a fast pace.

EIXO MONUMENTAL

Most of the Plano Piloto's major sights are along or just off the grand 8-km-long (5-mi-long) Eixo Monumental and its multilane boulevards. The distances are quite long, so if you want to explore on your own rather than as part of a organized tour, combine walking with riding the buses or taking taxis.

MAIN ATTRACTIONS

❽ Catedral Metropolitana de Nossa Senhora da Aparecida. The city's cathedral, considered one of Niemeyer's masterpieces, was finished in 1967. From outside, what is visible is a circular structure—a bundle of 16 concrete "fingers" arching skyward. For some, it resembles a crown of thorns. Large panes of stained glass supported by the concrete structure shelter the nave, leaving it awash in natural light. Inside, *Os Anjos* (*The Angels*)—an aluminum sculpture by Brazilian artist Alfredo Ceschiatti—hovers above the altar. The city's first mass was held at the Praça do Cruzeiro, on May 3, 1957; the *cruz* (cross) used is now here at the

Fodor'sChoice
★

cathedral. The building's entrance is guarded by four majestic bronze statues, also by Ceschiatti, *Os Evangelistas* (*The Evangelists*). The outdoor carillon is a gift of the Spanish government. ⊠*Esplanada dos Ministérios, SGAS, Q. 601, 70200-610* 🕾*061/3224–4073* 🎫*Free* ⊘*Daily 8–6.*

WHERE BIG RIVERS ARE BORN

Thanks to the abundant rainfall and favorable geologic conditions, the high plateaus of Central Brazil give birth to massive rivers. Some rank among the longest in the world. Rio Paraná, which runs southwest, ends up forming Rio de La Plata in Argentina; Rio Araguaia and Rio Tocantins run northward and are among the main tributaries to the Amazon.

🔟 **Palácio do Itamaraty.** For the home ★ of the Foreign Ministry, Niemeyer designed a glass-enclosed rectangular structure with a series of elegant arches on the facade. A reflecting pool augments the sense of spaciousness. The building and the water create a perfect backdrop for the *Meteoro* (*Meteor*), a round, abstract Carrara-marble sculpture by Brazilian-Italian artist Bruno Giorgi. A guided tour shows a collection of modern art—including paintings by Brazilian artists like Cândido Portinari—and the impressive tropical gardens by Brazilian landscape designer Burle Marx. Reserve ahead for tours. ⊠*Esplanada dos Ministérios, 70170-900* 🕾*061/3411–6159* 🎫*Free* ⊘*English tours weekdays 2–4:30, weekends 10–3:30.*

9️⃣ **Palácio da Justiça.** The front and back facades of Niemeyer's Justice Ministry have waterfalls that cascade between its arched columns. Besides the administrative offices, there's a library with more than 80,000 books, including a rare collection on German author Johann Wolfgang von Goethe, and one of the few complete original sets of Shakespeare's works—a gift from Queen Elizabeth. On the third floor there's a garden by Burle Marx. ⊠*Esplanada dos Ministérios, 70064-900* 🕾*061/3429–3000* 🎫*Free* ⊘*English tours weekdays 10–noon and 3–5.*

1️⃣ **Memorial JK.** This Niemeyer structure is a truncated pyramid and has a Fodor'sChoice function similar to its Egyptian counterpart: it's the final resting place ★ of former president Juscelino Kubitschek, the city's founding father, who died in 1981. The mortuary chamber has a lovely stained-glass roof by local artist Marianne Peretti. JK's office and library from his apartment in Rio have been moved to the memorial's north wing. The bronze statue of JK—his hand raised as if in blessing—surrounded by a half-shell (a trademark of Brasília) looks down upon the Eixo Monumental and makes this one of the capital's most moving monuments. Permanent and changing exhibits here document the city's construction. ⊠*Praça do Cruzeiro, at Eixo Monumental Oeste, 70070-300* 🕾*061/3225–9451* 🎫*R\$2* ⊘*Tues.–Sun. 9–6.*

IF YOU HAVE TIME

6️⃣ **Museu Nacional.** After more than 40 years in the planning stages, the National Museum opened in late 2006. The round building, which

7

resembles a helmet, was inspired by the *oca*, the round palm-covered hut of the country's native peoples. The space is mainly used to display frequently changing art exhibits. ✉*Setor Cultural Sul, at Eixo Monumental Leste, 70301-000* ☎*061/3225–6410* ⚑*Free* ⏱*Tues.–Sun. 9–6.*

❷ **Memorial dos Povos Indígenas.** Another Niemeyer project, this cylindrical structure was inspired by the huts built by the Bororo people. A spiraling ramp leads to a central plaza where collections of

> ### WE BUILT THIS CITY
>
> To build a city in just five years, thousands of laborers were brought here from the country's poor, drought-ridden interior. They often worked in 15-hour shifts, shrouded by red dust in the dry season and sloshing in mud during the rainy season. The nickname *candangos*, once a derisive term, today is proudly used by the workers and their descendants.

indigenous crafts are displayed. Highlights among the items: pottery, headdresses, and feather ornaments made by the Kayapó, the Xavante, and other indigenous peoples. ✉*Praça do Buriti, Eixo Monumental Oeste, 70075-900* ☎*061/3266–5206* ⚑*Free* ⏱*Tues.–Sun. 10–4.*

❸ **Parque da Cidade.** A few blocks from the Instituto Histórico and Geográfico is City Park, a collaborative effort by Costa, Niemeyer, and Burle Marx. Recent improvements include a state-of-the-art lighting system and more security guards, making an evening walk, run, or bike ride along a path more agreeable than ever. ✉*Entrances at Q. 901 S and Q. 912 S* ☎*061/3225–2451* ⏱*Daily 24 hrs.*

❼ **Teatro Nacional Cláudio Santoro.** Another of Niemeyer's "pyramid projects," this theater is adorned with an array of concrete cubes and rectangles designed by Brazilian architect Athos Bulcão. Its three stages host a variety of performances, and its several small art galleries offer rotating exhibits. ✉*SCN, via N2, 70070-200* ☎*061/3325–6239* ⚑*Free* ⏱*Daily 3–8.*

❺ **Torre de TV.** From the *Salão Panorâmico* (Observation Deck) of this 670-foot TV tower, you'll have a 360-degree view of the city. At night the view of the Congress building is spectacular. The small **Museu Nacional das Gemas** has an impressive collection of more than 3,000 Brazilian gems and semi-precious stones, a shop that sells crafts, and a café. ✉*Eixo Monumental, 70070-300* ☎*061/3323–1881* ⚑*Free, museum R$3* ⏱*Mon. 2–9, Tues.–Sun. 9–9; museum weekdays 1–6.*

PRAÇA DOS TRÊS PODERES

The buildings housing the government's three branches symbolically face each other in the Plaza of the Three Powers, the heart of the Brazilian republic. Here both power and architecture have been given balance as well as a view of Brasília and beyond. Indeed, the cityscape combined with the Planalto's endless sky have made the plaza so unusual that Russian cosmonaut Yuri Gagarin once remarked, "I have the impression of landing on a different planet, not on Earth!"

MAIN ATTRACTIONS

⑮ Os Candangos. This 25-foot-tall bronze sculpture by Giorgi has become the symbol of Brasília. It pays homage to the *candangos,* the workers who built the city from scratch. The statue, depicting two gracefully elongated figures holding poles, is across from the Palácio do Planalto.

> **DRESS FOR SUCCESS**
>
> Although Brazilians tend to be informal, remember that you'll be visiting government buildings and national monuments. Officials frown on shorts, tank tops, and the like, so dress comfortably but conservatively.

⑪ Congresso Nacional. One of Niemeyer's most daring projects consists of two 28-story office towers for the 500 representatives of the Câmara dos Deputados (House of Representatives) and the 80 members of the Senado (Senate). The convex dome is where the Câmara meets, and the concave bowl-like structure is where the Senado convenes. The main building is connected by tunnels to several *anexos* (annexes) located at the sides of Eixo Monumental. The complex contains works by such Brazilian artists as Di Cavalcanti, Bulcão, and Ceschiatti, as well as French designer Le Corbusier. A guided tour takes you through major sites within the building. Tours in English are available by request. ⊠ *Praça dos Três Poderes, 70160-900* ☎ *061/3216–1771 tours* 🖾 *Free* ⊙ *Daily 9:30–5.*

⑲ Espaço Cultural Oscar Niemeyer. This branch of the Oscar Niemeyer Foundation—which is based in Rio and was created to preserve and present the architect's work—houses a collection of sketches and drafts as well as a database with texts and images from Niemeyer's archives. ⊠ *Praça dos Três Poderes, Lt. J, 70070-010* ☎ *061/3226–6797* ⊕ *www.niemeyer.org.br* 🖾 *Free* ⊙ *Weekdays 10–5.*

⑬ Espaço Lúcio Costa. As a tribute to the urban planner who masterminded Brasília, this underground complex was added to the plaza in the late '80s. It has a 1,500-square-foot display of the city's blueprint, and you can read Costa's original ideas for the project (the text is in Portuguese and English). ⊠ *Praça dos Três Poderes, 70100-000* ☎ *061/3321–6163* 🖾 *Free* ⊙ *Daily 9–6.*

⑫ Museu Histórico de Brasília. Brasília's first museum has a small collection of pictures of the city and writings about it by such luminaries as Pope Pius XII, Kubitschek, and Niemeyer. The statue of Kubitschek on its facade is a 1960 work of Brazilian sculptor José Pedrosa. ⊠ *Praça dos Três Poderes, 70100-000* ☎ *061/3325–6244* 🖾 *Free* ⊙ *Tues.–Sun. 9–6.*

⑯ Palácio do Planalto. Niemeyer gave this highly acclaimed structure an unusual combination of straight and slanting lines, a variation of the design of Palácio da Alvorada. The access ramp to the main entrance is part of the national political folklore, because it represents the rise to power (presidents go up the ramp when inaugurated). ⊠ *Praça dos Três Poderes* ☎ *061/3411–2317* 🖾 *Free* ⊙ *Sun. 9:30–1.*

⑰ Mastro da Bandeira. This 300-foot steel flagpole supporting a 242-square-foot Brazilian flag is the only element of Praça dos Três Poderes not designed by Niemeyer. At 4 PM on the first Sunday of the month, members of the armed forces take part in a *troca da bandeira* (flag changing) ceremony, to the sound of the Brazilian Army band.

⓲ ★ **Panteão da Pátria.** Niemeyer designed this building to resemble a dove taking flight. Opened in 1986, the building honors such national heroes as Tancredo Neves, whose untimely death prevented him from being sworn in as Brazil's first democratically elected president after years of military dictatorship. Inside the curved structure are murals and stained-glass panels by Athos Bulcão, Marianne Peretti, and João Camara. One set of panels, *Os Inconfidentes,* depicts the martyrs of the 18th-century republican movement. ⊠ *Praça dos Três Poderes, 70100-000* ☎ *061/3325–6244* ☒ *Free* ☉ *Tues.–Sun. 9–6.*

> ## THE BRAZILIAN FLAG
>
> The Brazilian flag's green background symbolizes the forests that once spanned much of the country. The yellow diamond represents the gold-mining period that so influenced the nation's history. The blue circle in the center is homage to the great blue skies that dominate the territory; inside it are 27 stars, one for each state and the Federal District. The white band curving across the circle displays the national motto, *"Ordem e Progresso"* ("Order and Progress").

⓮ **Supremo Tribunal Federal.** The Brazilian Supreme Court building is classic Niemeyer—an otherwise ponderous structure seems lighter than air because of the curving lines of the columns that support the roof. The top floor houses a 70,000-volume legal library. In front of the Supreme Court is one of the city's best-known monuments, the 10-foot granite statue *The Justice,* by Ceschiatti. ⊠ *Praça dos Três Poderes, 70175-900* ☎ *061/3217–3000* ☒ *Free* ☉ *Weekends 10–5:30.*

IF YOU HAVE TIME

⓴ **Palácio da Alvorada.** At the tip of a peninsula projecting into Lago Paranoá, the president's official residence was Niemeyer's first project in the new capital. The architect used slanting support columns, here clad in white marble. The 1958 palace is not open to visitors, but you can appreciate the grand view from the reflecting pool next to the gate. To get here, take a cab from Plaza of the Three Powers. ⊠ *SHTN, Via Presidencial s/n.*

BEYOND THE PLANO PILOTO

If you have the time, head beyond the Plano Piloto and explore Lago Paranoá's outer perimeter, which has parks, gardens, and residential neighborhoods. Since its inception, the city has attracted a variety of religious groups; several of these "cult communities" have headquarters here. They reflect Brasília's mystical side, the origin of which can be traced to a vision by an Italian priest named Dom Bosco. In 1883 he dreamed of a new civilization rising around a lake between the 15th and 20th parallels. Many believe the city is "the promised land" in Bosco's vision. (Bosco never actually set foot in Brazil, making his vision seem even more mysterious.).

MAIN ATTRACTIONS

★ **Catetinho.** While the new capital was being built, the president's tempo-rary quarters was called the *Catetinho,* meaning a smaller version of the grand Palácio do Catete in Rio. The wooden edifice was built in 10 days during the summer of 1956. A nearby landing strip allowed the presi-dent to fly in from Rio for his frequent inspections. The building is a must-see museum for those interested in the city's history. It's surrounded by woods with a small spring where the president and his entourage once bathed. ⊠*Km 0, BR 040, 16 km (10 mi) southeast of Estação Rodoviária, 71745-000* ☎*061/3338–8694* ☜*Free* ☉*Daily 9–5.*

Parque Nacional de Brasília. Because of its many springs, locals often refer to the 60,000-acre Brasília National Park as Água Mineral (Min-eral Water). There are two spring-fed pools where people can cool off, dressing rooms, and picnic areas. Created to protect the water supply of Lago Paranoá, the park also preserves a bit of the region's *cerrado,* or grassy plains interspersed with thickets and woods. An informative trail runs through mostly flat terrain starts at the visitor center, where you can pick up maps and brochures. ⊠*EPIA, at Setor Militar Urbano, 9 km (6 mi) from Eixo Monumental, 70700-000* ☎*061/3465–2103* ☜*R$3* ☉*Daily 8–4.*

IF YOU HAVE TIME

Vale do Amanhecer. If you're interested in the mystical, occult, and eso-teric, Brasilía is the place to be. Valley of the Dawn was one of the first of the city's so-called cult communities, and is well prepared to receive visitors. The ellliptical temple at the center of the compound is one of the attractions. The religious community was founded in 1969 by Neiva Zelay, a onetime truck driver who reportedly had extrasensory powers. About 20,000 people live here. ⊠*Km 10, DF 015, Planaltina, DF* ☎*061/3389–7220* ☜*Free* ☉*Grounds daily 10* AM*–midnight.*

㉒ Ponte JK. Opened in late 2002, the third bridge crossing Lake Paranoá is consistent with the city's modernist aesthetic. The bridge—a project by Alexandre Chan from Rio de Janeiro—is held aloft by three diagonal arcs that crisscross the deck. Its lakeshore location and pleasant prom-enade attract many people to stroll across and enjoy the sunset. ⊠*Via L4, after SCES, south of Eixo Monumental* ☜*Free* ☉*Daily 24 hrs.*

❹ Templo da Boa Vontade. This temple is adjacent to the national headquar-ters of the Legião da Boa Vontade (Goodwill Legion), a religious and philanthropic organization. The building is a 60-foot-tall pyramidal structure with seven sides. At the apex sits a 21-kilogram (46-pound) quartz crystal, the largest ever found in Brazil. Inside, several thematic spaces—such as the Egyptian Room and Noble Room—are open to all denominations for worship or meditation. ⊠*SGAS 915, Lt. 75/6, 8 km (5 mi) south of Eixo Monumental, 70390-150* ☎*061/3245–1070* ☜*Free* ☉*Daily 10–6.*

CLOSE UP

The Making of a Capital

As far back as 1808 Brazilian newspapers ran articles discussing Rio's inadequacies as a capital (Rio became the capital in 1763, following Brazil's first capital, Salvador), the argument being that contact with Pará and other states far from Rio was difficult. Also, Rio was right on the water, and an easy target for enemy invasion. In 1892 congress authorized an overland expedition to find a central locale where "a city could be constructed next to the headwaters of big rivers" and where "roads could be opened to all seaports." Within three months the expedition leaders had chosen a plateau in the southeastern Goiás region.

But it was not until the mid-1950s that Juscelino Kubitschek made the new capital part of his presidential campaign agenda, which was summarized in the motto "Fifty Years in Five." When he was elected in 1956, he quickly set the wheels in motion. Within a few days the site was selected (in Goiás, as proposed by the 1892 expedition), work committees were set up, and Niemeyer was put in charge of architectural and urban development. The design, called the Plano Piloto (Pilot, or Master, Plan), was the work of Lúcio Costa, chosen from an international contest. The concept was simple and original: "Brasília was conceived by the gesture of those who mark a place on a map: two axes intersecting at a right angle, that is, the sign of a cross mark." The Plano Piloto's most important gardens were to be created by famed landscape designer Roberto Burle Marx.

Among Costa's objectives were to do away with a central downtown, design highways that were as accident-free as possible, and ensure that the vast horizon would always be visible. Construction officially began in February 1957—with 3,000 workers on-site.

Building a modern seat of power for Latin America's largest nation was a monumental undertaking. Before paved roads were built, supplies had to be flown in from the eastern cities. The majority of the workers were immigrants from the Northeast, and unskilled. They learned fast and worked hard, however. Settlements of shacks and tents sprang up around the construction site. The largest, Freetown (now the suburb Nucleo Bandeirante), was home to close to 15,000 workers and their families.

In Rio, opposition to the new capital was heated. Debates in the senate turned into fistfights. Government employees feared that Rio's business would decline and its real-estate values would drop, and were reluctant to leave Rio's comforts and beaches. Kubitschek's government induced them with 100% salary increases, tax breaks, early retirement options, ridiculously low rents, and even discounts on home furnishings.

On April 21, 1960, the city was inaugurated. The day began with mass in the uncompleted cathedral and ended with a fireworks display, where the president's name burned in 15-foot-high letters. A new era of pioneering and colonization followed the realization of Kubitschek's vision of a "nation of the future," looking westward from the coast.

Copacabana, Rio.

(top left) Buggies on the cliff at Morro Branco, near Fortaleza. (bottom left) Recife. (top right) São Paulo. (bottom right) Amazon River.

(top left) Christ the Redeemer statue at Corcovado, Rio. (top right) Foods at a market in Rio. (bottom) Brasília.

(top) Ipanema, Rio. (bottom) Carnival in Rio.

(top left) The Foz do Iguaçu cascades. (top right) Golden lion tamarin. (bottom) Spinning Brazilian samba.

(top) Salvador. (bottom) Farmworkers playing music in the Pantanal.

(top left) Toucan. (top right) Carnival in Recife. (bottom) A favela outside Rio.

WHERE TO EAT

$$$–$$$$　✕ **Universal Diner.** The kitchsy decor is one of the main attractions of this restaurant—bulldog statuettes, miniature porcelain dolls, used vinyl LPs, and other antiques cover the walls and hang from the ceiling. The chef-owner, Mara Alckamin, is always on hand, asking whether you liked the food. Try the lamb served with a lemongrass and cardamom sauce. On Friday night the place is transformed into a club that attracts a lively crowd of different ages. ✉*CLS 210, Bl. B, Lj. 30, 70273-520* ☎*061/3443–2089* ⊕*www.universaldiner.com.br* ▭*AE, DC, MC, V* ⊘*No lunch Mon. No dinner Sun.*

$$$–$$$$　✕ **La Chaumière.** For more than 40 years, this small but cozy restau-
★　rant has been the mainstay of fine dining *à la française* in the capital. Incredible as it may seem, the friendly owner and chef is a Brazilian who promised the original French owners to keep the original fare and ambience. His resolution still pays off: try the *filet au poivre* (steak with a green peppercorn and mushroom sauce). ✉*SCLS, Q. 408, Bl. A, Lt. 13, 70527–510* ☎*061/3242–7599* ▭*AE, DC, MC, V* ⊘*Closed Mon. No lunch Sat. No dinner Sun.*

$$$–$$$$　✕ **La Torreta.** In business for almost a decade, this highly regarded restau-rant's success can be attributed to the personalized service and the variety of authentic Spanish dishes prepared by chef Isaac Corcias. The Cata-lan-style *paella* has become a Saturday tradition. For appetizers, choose between several kinds of tapas, including the great ham and prawns. The wine list, with excellent choices from Spain, Argentina, Chile, and Bra-zil, doesn't go unnoticed. ✉*CLS 402, Bl. A, Lj. 9, Asa Sul, 70236-500* ☎*061/3321–2516* ▭*AE, DC, MC, V* ⊘*No dinner Sun.*

$$$–$$$$　✕ **Villa Borghese.** The quiet cantina ambience and fantastic cuisine make you feel as if you're in Italy. The *tagliatelli di Taormina* (pasta with squid ink), served with a garlic, herb, and shrimp sauce, is divine. If you're not too concerned about your weight, try the *agnello della nonna* (roasted lamb shank). ✉*SCLS, Q. 201, Bl. A, Lj. 33, 70232-510* ☎*061/3226–5650* ▭*DC, MC, V.*

$$$　✕ **Fogo de Chão.** A recent addition to the roster of fine-dining options
Fodor'sChoice　in Brasília, this *churrascaria* (steak house) has quickly become one of
★　the most popular. The sleek ambience of this spacious restaurant adds to the lure. It's famous for its *rodízio* service, in which waiters bring various types of meat on the spit to your table, where they'll carve off as much as you like. The prix-fixe meal includes a large and varied salad bar. ✉*SHS Q. 5, Bl. E, 70322-909* ☎*061/3322–4666* ▭*AE, DC, MC, V.*

$$–$$$　✕ **Fritz.** This longtime favorite is the place to go for German cuisine. The laid-back atmosphere and no-frills decor draw those looking for authen-tic food and a great selection of imported beer and wine. Savor the *roll-mops* (rolled thinly cut herring fillets) while you wait for your entrée. Good choices include the *Eisbein* (pig's leg with mashed potatoes) or *Ente mit Blaukraut und Apfelpurée* (duck cooked in wine served with red cabbage and applesauce). ✉*SCLS, Q. 404, Bl. D, Lj. 35, 70238-540* ☎*061/3223–4622* ▭*AE, DC, MC, V* ⊘*No dinner Sun.*

$$–$$$　✕ **O Convento.** With whitewashed walls, 18th-century furnishings, and waiters dressed as monks, this restaurant does indeed call to mind a

monastery. The fare leans toward Italian, with French and Brazilian accents—the *penne de camarão flambado* (flambéed shrimp with a broccoli sauce) is highly recommended. Weather permitting, you can sit outside on the patio surrounded by bougainvillea. ⊠*EQS 208/209, Cj. 8, 70254-400* 🖀*061/3443–3104* 🖃*AE, DC, MC, V* ⊗*Closed Mon. No dinner Sun.*

$$–$$$ ✕**Patú Anú.** On a steep hill in a residential neighborhood, this restaurant has an ample view of Paranoá Lake. This probably accounts for the name, which means "good spirits of the water," in the Tupi-Guarani language. The sophisticated stone-and-wood decor calls to mind tropical forests. For the proper romantic dinner, some of the tables are lighted by flickering candles. The meat and seafood dishes are excellent, but many people come for a chance to sample wild game. Try the boar fillet with rum and honey sauce, served with cinnamon-and-cashew rice. ⊠*Setor de Mansões do Lago Norte, trecho 12, Cj. 1, Casa 7, 71540-125* 🖀*061/3369–2788* ⊕*www.patuanu.com.br* 🖃*AE, DC, MC, V* ⊗*Closed Mon.*

$$ ✕**Carpe Diem.** If you're a bibliophile or a fan of the arts, you might enjoy the frequent book parties and art exhibits at this restaurant. On weekdays the lunch buffet is very popular with the business crowd. On weekends people flock here for the *feijoada* (meat stew with black beans). Among the regular entrées, the shrimp risotto is one of the most popular. There are five other locations in Brasília, but the original stands out because of its greenery-filled verandas. ⊠*SCLS 104, Bl. D, Lj. 1, 70343-540* 🖀*061/3225–5301* 🖃*AE, DC, MC, V.*

$–$$ ✕**Feitiço Mineiro.** Live Brazilian music, from bossa nova to contemporary, is a nightly feature at this restaurant. But the *comida mineira* (food from the state of Minas Gerais) is the best reason to come. One of the most popular dishes is the *costelinha ao Véio Chico* (fried pork ribs with cassava). ⊠*CLN 306 Bl. B, Lj. 45 and 51, 70847–520* 🖀*061/3272–3032* 🖃*DC, MC, V* ⊗*No dinner Sun.*

$–$$ ✕**Oca da Tribo.** The place might as well be in the middle of the rain forest. It was built to resemble an Amazonian *oca* (hut), complete with a palm-leaf roof. A firepit is set ablaze in the middle of the dining room, adding warmth to the exotic setting. At lunchtime there's an excellent vegetarian buffet with an array of well-seasoned dishes. The long list of dinner entrées includes beef as well as such wild game as boar, duck, quail, and emu. ⊠*SCES, Section 2, near Meditation Club, 70200-002* 🖀*061/3226–9880* 🖃*DC, MC, V* ⊗*No dinner Sun. and Mon.*

WHERE TO STAY

$$$–$$$$

Fodor'sChoice

★

🏨**Naoum Plaza Hotel.** Brasília's most sophisticated hotel, this longtime favorite has a faithful clientele that includes heads of state. (Prince Charles, Nelson Mandela, and Fidel Castro have all stayed in the Royal Suite.) The rooms are elegant, done up in soothing pastels. Little extras like fresh flowers in every room let you know the high level of service you can expect. Two fine restaurants, the Falls (serving international cuisine) and Mitsubá (with Japanese fare), add to the hotel's appeal. **Pros:** Luxurious rooms, gorgeous tropical-wood furniture, impeccable service. **Cons:** Neighborhood sketchy at night. ⊠*SHS, Q. 05, Bl. H/I, 70322-914* ☏*061/3322–4545 or 0800/61–4844* ⊕*www.naoumplaza. com.br* ⌧*171 rooms, 14 suites* ♿*In-room: safe, Ethernet. In-hotel: 2 restaurants, room service, concierge, bars, pool, gym, public Internet, public Wi-Fi, no-smoking floors, parking (no fee), airport shuttle* ▤*AE, DC, MC, V* ⍠*BP.*

$$$ 🏨**Bonaparte Bluepoint.** A sober granite lobby with wood paneling and sophisticated lighting welcomes you to this modern hotel. Its best feature is the rooms, large enough to be suites and filled with amenities like plush carpeting, king-size beds, kitchenettes, and oversize bathtubs. The on-site restaurant, Pitanga, is popular for its Brazilian fare. **Pros:** Perfect for longer stays, plush furnishings. **Cons:** Neighborhood sketchy at night, small commons area. ⊠*SHS, Q. 02, Bl. J, 70322-900* ☏*061/2104–6600 or 0800/701–9990* ⊕*www.bonapartehotel.com.br* ⌧*97 rooms* ♿*In-room: safe, refrigerator, Ethernet. In-hotel: 2 restaurants, room service, bar, pool, gym, public Internet, parking (no fee), airport shuttle* ▤*AE, DC, MC, V* ⍠*BP.*

$$$ ✗🏨**Kubitschek Plaza.** Owned by descendants of Brasília's founding father, Juscelino Kubistchek, this hotel is decorated with some of his own antiques. Original paintings on the walls are by renowned Japanese-Brazilian artist Tomie Otake. Rooms have a modern decor, with pastel color schemes and wood accents. The Diamantina restaurant has a varied menu that includes some of the president's favorite dishes from Minas Gerais State. **Pros:** Elegant decor, top-drawer restaurant. **Cons:** Small bathrooms, rooms rather drab. ⊠*SHN, Q. 02, Bl. E, 70702-904* ☏*061/3329–3333, 061/3319–3543 reservations* ⊕*www.kubitschek. com.br* ⌧*246 rooms* ♿*In-room: safe, refrigerator, dial-up. In-hotel: 2 restaurants, room service, bars, pool, gym, public Internet, parking (no fee)* ▤*AE, DC, MC, V* ⍠*BP.*

$$–$$$ 🏨**Blue Tree Park.** The building's massive scale and bright red facade
☽ might perplex visitors in tune with the city's low-slung and light-color
★ architecture. One of the lures of this hotel on the shore of Paranoá Lake is that it's far from the agitation of Eixo Monumental. The east-facing apartments have balcnonies with great views of the lake, while the rest look out onto greenery. The elegant rooms have contemporary designs. Large wall panels with sketches of Brasília's cathedral call to mind the city's heritage. Boats and water-sports equipment can be rented at a small pier on the lake. **Pros:** Quiet location, lovely lake views, plenty of water sports. **Cons:** Hectic during large conventions, far from city's center. ⊠*SHTN Trecho 01, Cj. 1B, Bl. C, 70800-200* ☏*061/3424–7000* ⊕*www.bluetree.com.br* ⌧*355 rooms, 60 suites*. ♿*In-room: safe. In-hotel: restaurant, room service, bar, tennis courts, pool, gym, water sports, public Internet, parking (no fee), airport shuttle* ▤*AE, DC, MC, V* ⍠*BP.*

$$–$$$ 🏨**Meliá Brasil 21.** One of the city's newest hotels, Meliá Brasil 21 has an enviable location on the Eixo Monumental. It's adjacent to the Brasil XXI convention center and just steps from the Parque da Cidade, so you often see guests heading out to enjoy the park. Catering to business travelers, the hotel has sleek rooms that are comfortable enough for longer stays. The hotel has made a commitment to going green,

and one floor is made entirely of wood from sustainable forestry. The hotel restaurant, Norton, has carved out a niche for itself because of its menu of grilled meats. **Pros:** Near city's main park, attentive staff. **Cons:** Neighborhood sketchy at night, can be too busy during conventions. ⊠*SHS, Q. 6, Bl. D, 70316-100* ☎*061/3218–4700, 0800/703–3399 reservations* ⊕*www.solmelia.com* ⬐*334 rooms* ⌂*In-room: safe, refrigerator, Ethernet. In-hotel: bar, restaurant, pool, gym, public Internet, no-smoking rooms* ▱*AE, MC, V* ⦿|*BP.*

$$
⦿
Fodor'sChoice
★

▢ Academia de Tênis Resort. What was once merely a tennis club on the shore of Lago Paranoá has, over the course of 30 years, grown into a sprawling resort. Accommodations, ranging from standard rooms to duplex suites, are in a two-story, semi-circular building that embraces the beautifully landscaped grounds. Faithful to its roots, the resort has 21 tennis courts, as well as four pools with waterfalls. There are six restaurants offering Brazilian, French, Chinese, and Japanese fare. **Pros:** Great for sports, spacious common areas. **Cons:** Can have a hectic feel, some rooms need refurbishing. ⊠*SCES, Trecho 4, Cj. 5, Lt. 1-B, 70200-000* ☎*061/3316–6161* ⊕*www.academiaresort.com.br* ⬐*226 rooms* ⌂*In-room: refrigerator. In-hotel: 6 restaurants, room service, concierge, bars, tennis courts, pools, gym, spa, public Internet, public Wi-Fi, parking (no fee), airport shuttle, no-smoking rooms* ▱*AE, DC, MC, V* ⦿|*BP.*

$–$$ **▢ Hotel Nacional.** One of Brasília's older hotels, the Nacional is still very highly regarded. The building reflects the modernist, almost minimalist, design principles of the city planners. In the early days of the capital, the Nacional welcomed many distinguished guests, including Queen Elizabeth. The Taboo Grill is a great place for grilled meat and seafood, and Belle Epoque serves international fare. **Pros:** Central location, good price considering what you get. **Cons:** Slightly dated decor, some rooms have small bathrooms. ⊠*SHS, Q. 01, Bl. A, 70322-900* ☎*061/3321–7575* ⊕*www.hotelnacional.com.br* ⬐*350 rooms* ⌂*In-room: safe, refrigerator, dial-up. In-hotel: 2 restaurants, room service, bar, pool, gym, public Internet, public Wi-Fi, parking (no fee), no-smoking floors* ▱*AE, DC, MC, V* ⦿|*BP.*

$ **▢ Brasília Plaza.** Brasília's first hotel, designed by Otto Niemeyer, ★ reopened in 2007 after a top-to-bottom renovation. The building, designated a national landmark, reflects Niemeyer's concept of promoting openness and functionality. Two wall-size panels by Athos Bulcão adorn the lobby. In the Lago Paranoá area, the hotel attracts those looking for quieter surroundings. The restaurant Oscar Jazz & Cucina serves Italian fare. Jazz musicians take to the stage Wednesday to Friday. **Pros:** Historic building, lovely furnishings, great restaurant. **Cons:** Small rooms, some staff is in training. ⊠*SHTN, Tr. 01, Cj. 01, 70800-200* ☎*061/3306–9100* ⊕*www.brasiliapalace.com.br* ⬐*156 rooms* ⌂*In-room: safe, refrigerator, dial-up. In-hotel: restaurant, room service, bar, pool, public Internet, parking (no fee)* ▱*AE, DC, MC, V* ⦿|*BP.*

$ **▢ SIA Park Executive Hotel.** If you're looking for a budget price and a convenient location near the airport, this hotel is a good option. Sleek rooms have laminated wood floors, the bathrooms are modern and clean, and facilities are up-to-date. **Pros:** Bargain rates, attentive staff, hearty breakfast. **Cons:** Few amenities, far from city center. ⊠*SIA, Q. 2, Bl. D, 70200-025* ☎*061/3403–6650* ⊕*www.siapark.com.br* ⤶*50 rooms* ♿*In-room: refrigerator. In-hotel: no elevator, parking (no fee)* ▭*AE, DC, MC, V* ⎓*BP.*

NIGHTLIFE & THE ARTS

NIGHTLIFE

BARS

If you want to experience a typical Brazilian happy hour, go to **Bar Brasília** (⊠*SCL, Q. 506, Bl. A, Lj. 15, Parte A, Asa Sul, 70350-515* ☎*061/3443–4323*), known for having the best draft beer in town. Traditional appetizers such as *bolinho de bacalhau* (cod cake) round out the offerings. **Beirute** (⊠*SCLS 109, Bl. A, Lj. 02/04, 70372-510* ☎*061/3244–1717*), an eclectic bar-restaurant with an Arab flair, has been in business since 1966. During its first decade it drew politicians making deals; today the gay-friendly place attracts a wide range of people. It's known for its ice-cold beer.

DANCE CLUBS

In Brasília, clubs play some international music, but many nights are devoted to such Brazilian rhythms as *forró*—the result of the large number of *nordestinos* (northeasterners) that settled here. **Café Cancun** (⊠*Liberty Mall, SCN, Q. 02, Bl. D, Lj. 52, 70712-903* ☎*061/3202–4466*) is known for playing a variety of musical styles. Each day of the week is dedicated to a certain type, such as *axé* (music from Bahia). **Gates Pub** (⊠*SCLS 403, Bl. B, Lj. 34, 70237-250* ☎*061/3325-4576*) is dance club that's been around for almost 30 years—a rarity in the city.

THE ARTS

The **Clube do Choro** (⊠*SDC, Eixo Monumental, 70070-350* ☎*061/3327–0494* ⊕*www.clubedochoro.com.br*) is where devotees of *chorinho*, a traditional Brazilian music, perform Wednesday to Friday. The main building of the **Fundação Brasileira de Teatro** (*Brazilian Theatrical Foundation* ⊠*SDS, Bl. C, Lj. 30, 70392-902* ☎*061/3226–0182*) has two theaters for plays and concerts: the Teatro Dulcina de Moraes and the Teatro Conchita de Moraes. The **Teatro Nacional Cláudio Santoro** (⊠*SBN, Via N2, 70040-010* ☎*061/3325–6239*) has three stages used by the Orquestra Sinfônica do Teatro Nacional, which performs here from March through November. The **Centro Cultural Banco do Brasil** (*CCBB* ⊠*SCES Trecho 2, Cj. 22, 70200-002* ☎*061/3310–7087*) hosts art exhibits, dance shows, and plays.

SPORTS & THE OUTDOORS

AUTO RACING

The **Autódromo Internacional Nelson Piquet** (⊠*70070-710* ☎*061/3273–6586*), named after three-time Formula I champion and Brasília native Nelson Piquet, has a 5-km (3-mi) racetrack that hosts such events as Formula III and stock car races.

GOLF

At the tip of Eixo Monumental, not far from the Palácio da Alvorada, you can golf on the 18-hole course at the **Clube de Golfe de Brasília** (⊠*SCES, Trecho 2, Lt. 2, 70200-002,* ☎*061/3224–2718* ⊕*www. golfebrasilia.com.br*). Greens fees are R$120 weekdays and R$180 weekends.

SOCCER

The modern, 66,000-seat **Estádio Mané Garrincha** (☎*061/3225–9860*) is the home stadium for Gama FC, Brasília's soccer team that plays in the second division of the Brazilian Soccer Federation.

SHOPPING

There are two major shopping districts along the Eixo Monumental: the Setor Comercial Norte (SCN, Northern Commercial Sector) and the Setor Comercial Sul (SCS, Southern Commercial Sector). In addition, almost every *superquadra* has its own commercial district.

CENTERS & MALLS

Housed in an odd arch-shape building, **Brasília Shopping** (⊠*SCN, Q. 05, 70715-900* ☎*061/3328–2122*), the most sophisticated mall in the city, has several international chain stores, as well as movie theaters, restaurants, and snack bars. The mall is close to both hotel sectors and is open Monday–Saturday 10–10 and Sunday 2–10. **Pátio Brasil Shopping** (⊠*SCS Quadra 07, Bl. A, 70307-902* ☎*061/2107–7400*) often has free concerts and is close to most hotels in SHN. It has a full range of shops and movie theaters and is open Monday–Saturday 10–10:30. **Parkshopping** (⊠*SAI/Sudoeste, Q. A-1, 71219-900* ☎*061/4003–4137*), Brasília's largest shopping center, has 183 shops as well as a Burle Marx–designed central garden, the site of many cultural events. It's open Monday–Saturday 10–10.

MARKETS

The **BSB Mix and Feira da Lua (Moon Fair)** (⊠*Centro Comercial Gilberto Salomão, SHIS, QI. 5, 71615-180*) are held alternately every other weekend 8–4. In more than 100 stalls you can find reasonably priced arts and crafts, furniture, jewelry, clothing, homemade food, and much more. The **Feira de Antiguidades** (*Antiques Fair* ⊠*Centro Comercial Gilberto Salomão, SHIS, QI. 5, 71615-180*) is held on the last weekend of each month from 8 to 6 and offers a great variety of decorative objects. At the **Feira de Artesanato** (*Artisans' Fair* ⊠*Foot of Torre de TV, Eixo Monumental Oeste*) you can find semiprecious-stone jewelry, bronze items, wood carvings, wicker crafts, pottery, and dried flowers. It's held weekends and holidays 8–6.

GEMSTONES

For gemstones from all over Brazil, head to the **Museu Nacional das Gemas** (⊠*Torre de TV, Eixo Monumental* ☎*061/3323–1881*). The shop is open Monday–Saturday 10–6.

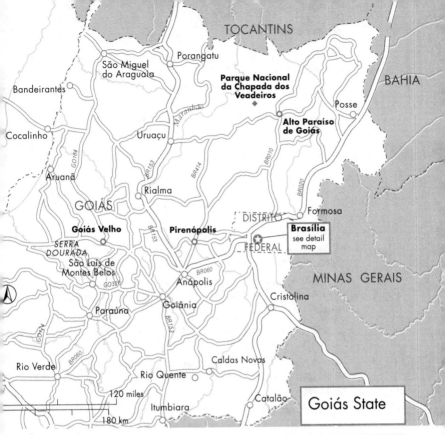

GOIÁS STATE

Brasília's Distrito Federal is surrounded completely by Goiás State, in the geographical heart of Brazil. Exploring Goiás means getting to know some of its historic cities, which started as settlements around gold mines, such as Goiás Velho and Pirenópolis, examples of colonial Brazil in their architecture and local culture. North of Brasília are the highlands of Chapada dos Veadeiros, with its impressive hills, canyons, and waterfalls. The largest town in the region is Alto Paraíso (High Paradise).

ALTO PARAÍSO DE GOIÁS

230 km (143 mi) north of Brasília.

This city is known throughout Brazil as a center of unexplained phenomena. The remoteness of the region—paved roads arrived about 20 years ago—gave birth to many stories about flying saucers and extraterrestrial beings. Many residents were attracted by the city's otherworldly vibe. Others came for the spectacular landscape. In sharp contrast to most of the central parts of the country, the area around

Alto Paraíso is made up of oddly shaped hills. It's a fairly modern town, with none of the colonial-era buildings found elsewhere in the state.

TO & FROM

Visitors usually drive to Alto Paraíso. From Brasília, the most logical route is to take BR 020 northeast for 40 km (25 mi), then take head north on the GO-118 for 190 km (118 mi). The roads are paved and in good condition. Real Expresso runs several buses here each day. The four-hour ride costs about R$29.

It's a 37-km (23-mi) drive from Alto Paraíso to Parque Nacional da Chapada dos Veadeiros. The road is gravel, but is wide and generally safe at moderate speeds. Many people opt for guided tours to the park.

ESSENTIALS

Banks & Currency Exchange Banco do Brasil (⊠ *Rua Ary Valadão Filho, 690, Centro, 73770-000*) has ATMs that are available 6 AM to 10 PM.

Bus Contacts Estação Rodoviária (⊠ *Rua Ary Valadão Filho s/n, 73770-000* ☎ *062/3446-1359*). **Real Expresso** (☎ *061/2106-7109* ⊕ *www.realexpresso. com.br*).

Emergencies & Medical Assistance Hospital Municipal (☎ *062/3446-1159*). **Fire** (☎ *193*). **Police** (☎ *190*).

Visitor & Tour Info Centro de Atendimento ao Turista (⊠ *Av. Ary Ribeiro Valadão Filho, 1100, Centro73770-000* ☎ *061/3446-1359*), the municipal tourist office, is open daily 9 to 5.

Travessia Ecoturismo (⊠ *Av. Ary R. Valadão Filho 979, Centro73770-000* ☎ *062/3346-1595* ⊕ *www.travessia.tur.br*) specializes in trekking expeditions, but also offers mountain-bike tours and other outdoor activities.

SAFETY & PRECAUTIONS

Alto Paraíso is a safe place to explore. However, as with most small towns in Brazil, petty theft can be occasionaly be a problem. Always keep an eye on your valuables.

WHERE TO STAY & EAT

$–$$ ✕ **Jambalaya.** Chef Nives Gardini runs the most refined restaurant in town. Jambalaya has a superb view of the county from its hilltop location. There's a self-service vegetarian buffet at lunchtime, à la carte European-style dishes (with an emphasis on Italian fare) for dinner, and a long wine list—a rarity outside of the major cities. The *ricotta rondelle* made with nuts and raisins is a must. ⊠ *Rua 7, Q. 06, lt 1, Estância Paraíso, 73770-000* ☎ *062/8438-5352* ⊟ *V* ⊗ *Closed Mon.*

$–$$ ✕ **Oca Lila.** One of the most popular restaurants in town, Oca Lila has a lively atmosphere. A vegetarian buffet is a great deal at lunchtime. Dinners are à la carte, with many types of pastas and pizzas on the menu. On weekend nights, live music (usually Brazilian pop or American blues) draws appreciative crowds. ⊠ *Av. João Bernardes Rabelo 449, 73770-000* ☎ *062/3446-1006* ⊟ *No credit cards.*

¢ ✕ **Jatô.** This spacious restaurant has been attracting artists and intellectuals for more than 15 years. Lunch is a self-service buffet, with traditional Goiás dishes such as *carne de sol com mandioca* (sundried beef with cassava) and *arroz integral* (whole-grain rice). ⊠*Rua Coleto Paulino 522, 73770-000* ☎*061/3446–1339* ▤*V* ⊘*No dinner.*

¢–$ ⛉**Camelot Inn.** As the name suggests, this inn's ramparts and parapets ☾ are supposed to call to mind the knights of the Round Table. The rooms, named for characters in the King Arthur legend, are spacious and comfortable. The grounds include a creek with waterfalls. **Pros:** Great for kids, hearty breakfast. **Cons:** A bit over the top, tile floors can be chilly in winter. ⊠*Km 168, GO 118, 73770-000* ☎*062/3446–1581* ⊕*www.pousadacamelot.com.br* ↪*20 rooms* ⟁*In-room: safes. In-hotel: bar, pools, public Internet, parking (no fee)* ▤*AE, MC, V* ⊚*BP.*

¢–$ ⛉**Pousada Alfa & Ômega.** Surrounded by neatly kept gardens, this inn has more to offer than others in the region. It has a heated pool and a room for meditation and massage. Each of the brick buildings is divided into four rooms decorated with Indian motifs. Standard but comfortable rooms have verandas, while suites have inner gardens. Breakfast includes a slew of pastries, jellys and jams, and tropical fruits. **Pros:** Soothing ambience, attentive staff. **Cons:** Few amenities, small and basic bathrooms. ⊠*Rua Joaquim de Almeida 15, 73770-000* ☎*062/3446–1225* ⊕*www.veadeiros.com.br* ↪*10 rooms, 2 suites* ⟁*In-room: no phone, refrigerator. In-hotel: pool, parking (no fee)* ▤*MC, V* ⊚*BP.*

PARQUE NACIONAL DA CHAPADA DOS VEADEIROS

Famous for its plunging waterfalls, deep canyons, and towering mountains, Parque Nacional da Chapada dos Veadeiros is breathtaking. The dramatic terrain is one of oldest surface formations on the planet, and therefore has been exposed to climate changes and constant erosion for about 1.8 billion years. Only a small portion of the park, which covers about 23,000 square mi, is open to tourists, and only then with a licensed guide. You can hire a guide at the park's entrance in Vila São Jorge, but it's better to find one in Alto Paraíso.

The climate is comfortable year-round. The flora is more exuberant in the dry season (May and October), when several trees and shrubs are in full bloom. ⊠*GO 327, Km 34, 40 km (25 mi) from Alto Paraíso de Goiás, 73770-000* ☎*062/3455–1166 for park, 062/3346–1159 for guides* ▤*R$3* ⊘*Tues.–Sun. 8–5; no admission after noon.*

PIRENÓPOLIS

159 km (99 mi) west of Brasília.

Settled in the 18th century at the height of the Goiás gold rush, Pirenópolis was abandoned by the early 19th century after most of its gold was mined. Some locals say the years of isolation were a blessing, as they've helped to preserve the town's historic character: several streets retain the original pavement, which has slivers of quartzite, an abundant mineral that's still quarried in the nearby hills. On weekends many people flee from the modern concrete and glass of Brasília to immerse themselves in Pirenópolis's colonial flavor. The town has several blocks of historic houses, churches, charming restaurants, and quaint resorts, along with several well-respected jewelers.

TO & FROM

From Brasília, take BR 070 west, then BR 414 south.Viação Goianésia buses make the trip in about 3 hours and cost R$20.

ESSENTIALS

Banks & Currency Exchange **Banco do Brasil** (⊠ *Av. Sizenando Jayme 15, Centro, 72980–000* ☞ *ATMs available 6 AM–10 PM*).

Bus Contacts **Estação Rodoviária** (⊠ *Av. Neco Mendonça, Centro, 72980–000* ☎ *061/3331–1248*). **Viação Goianésia** (☎ *062/3331–2765* ⊕ *www.viacaogoianesia.com.br*).

Emergencies & Medical Assistance **Ambulance** (☎ *192*). **Fire** (☎ *193*).**Hospital: Hospital Ernestina Lopes Jayme** (⊠ *Rua dos Pirineus s/n, 72980–000* ☎ *062/3331–1666*).**Pharmacy: 24-Hour Pharmacy Hotline** (☎ *132*). **Drogaria Santa Barbara** (⊠ *Rua Benjamim Constant 26, Centro, 72980–000* ☎ *062/3331–1578*). **Police** (☎ *190*).

Taxi **Leo Taxi** (⊠ *Av. Neco Mendonça s/n, Centro* ☎ *062/3331–1461*).

Visitor & Tour Info **Padilha Ecoturismo** (⊠ *Rua Juscelino Kubitschek 34, 72980–000* ☎ *062/3331–2998* ⊕ *www.pirenopolis.tur.br/padilhaecoturismo*) offers guided hiking tours to the national park. Rappelling and trekking expeditions are also available. **Secretaria Municipal de Cultura e Turismo** (⊠ *Rua do Bom Fim s/n, 72980–000* ☎ *062/3331–2633* ⊕ *www.pirenopolis.tur.br* ☉ *Daily 8 to 5.*).

WHAT TO SEE

The **Praça da Matriz** is part of the old neighborhood of the city. The oldest cathedral in the state (Igreja Matriz) and the Teatro de Pirenópolis (Pirenópolis Theater) are here. ⊠ *Rua do Rosário at Rua Direita*.

Igreja Nossa Senhora do Rosário–Matriz, the oldest church in Goiás, was completed in 1732. The foundation was made of stone and mortar, the walls (more than 40 inches thick) used adobe and a clay stucco technique called *taipa*. A fire almost destroyed the church in 2002. After extensive renovation, the church reopened in 2006. ⊠ *Praça da Matriz, Rua do Rosário, at Rua do Bonfim, 72980-000* ☎ *No phone*.

The **Museu das Cavalhadas** displays the outlandish medieval-style costumes worn by participants in the Festa do Divino Espírito Santo. Among the roster of activities are parade and a mock battle between Moorish and Christian mounted knights in a public field that resembles a bullring. (The Christians win every year.) The museum is in a private home—Dona Maria Eunice, the owner, is a descendant of early settlers. She gives a lively explanation of the annual festivities. ⊠ *Rua Direita 39, 72980-000* ☎ *062/3331–1166* ☞ *R$2* ☉ *Fri.–Sun. 9–5.*

Cachoeiras Bonsucesso is the most popular of the several waterfalls and swimming holes in the Rio das Almas. ⊠ *Rua do Carmo, 7 km (4 mi) north of town, 72980-000* ☎ *062/3321–1217* ☞ *R$7* ☉ *Daily 8–6.*

Santuário da Vida Silvestre Vagafogo (Vagafogo Wildlife Sanctuary) is a private wildlife preserve. There are plenty of things to do, including hiking trails through the grasslands and visiting a waterfall where you can cool off. If you want an adrenaline rush, try the Tree Canopy Ride, a rope course through the woods. On weekends locals come for a brunch of fruits and farm produce. ⊠*Rua do Carmo, 6 km (4 mi) north of town center, 72980-000* ☎*062/3335–8515* ⊠*R$11* ☉*Tues.–Sun. 8–5.*

WHERE TO STAY & EAT

$–$$ ✕**Pireneus Restaurante.** Housed in a colonial residence, this outstanding eatery serves traditional food from Goiás, including *churrasco goiano,* a barbecue over hot coals, and *arroz com pequi* (rice with souari nuts). ⊠*Praça da Matriz 31, 72980-000* ☎*062/3331–1577* ▭MC, V ☉*Closed Sun.*

¢–$ ✕**Aravinda.** This small restaurant was one of the first to open on the Rua do Rosário. The raspy-voiced owner, Edna Lucena, is the town's mother figure. The food is colorful and tasty, with an emphasis on vegetarian fare. The fish dishes are also delicious, particularly the *peixe na telha* (fish cooked in earthenwaren dish with spices). On weekends the live music could be anything from rock to blues to New Age. ⊠*Rua do Rosário 25, 72980-000* ☎*062/3331–2409* ▭*No credit cards* ☉*Closed Mon. and Tues.*

¢–$ ✕**Caffe & Tarsia.** One of the most popular restaurants in town, Caffe & Tarsia is run by an Italian man and his Brazilian wife. A wide variety of quality Mediterranean dishes are served; there's a self-service buffet on Saturday. Sit at the far end and enjoy the vines on the roof, which are covered with ice each day so they can endure the hot climate of the cerrado. Live music accompanies meals on weekend evenings. ⊠*Rua do Rosário 34, 72980-000* ☎*062/3331–1274* ▭V ☉*Closed Mon.–Thurs.*

$–$$ 🏨**Pousada dos Pireneus.** The main building of this bustling hotel is an adobe Spanish Colonial–style house. It looks out at the pools, tennis courts, and beyond the landscaped grounds toward the town. Rooms are in what could be described as a 17th-century condo complex, with two-story units scattered throughout the area. The all-white rooms have contrasting colorful fabrics and dark-wood furnishings. Most first-floor rooms have verandas hung with hammocks. **Pros:** Great amenities, many activities. **Cons:** Far from downtown, hectic when there are conventions. ⊠*Chácara Mata do Sobrato, 72980-000* ☎*062/3331–1345* ⊕*www.pousadadospireneus.com.br* ⮑*105 rooms, 6 suites* ⚘*In-room: refrigerator. In-hotel: restaurant, bar, tennis court, pools, spa, gym, no elevator, public Internet, parking (no fee)* ▭AE, DC, MC, V ⑩MAP.

© FodorsChoice ★

$ 🏨**Pousada Casa Grande.** In a converted 80-year old residence, this inn has lots of charm. Rooms tend to be small, but are cheerfully decorated in yellow pastel tones. Choose one with a veranda opening to the well-trimmed garden. **Pros:** Tasteful decor, attentive staff. **Cons:** Small bathrooms, small common areas. ⊠*Rua Aurora 41, 72980-000* ☎*062/3331–1758* ⊕*www.casagrandepousada.com.br* ⮑*23 rooms* ⚘*In room: refrigerator. In-hotel: pool* ▭DC, MC, V ⑩CP.

7

$ 🔃**Pousada Walkeriana.** If you appreciate tropical flowers or antiques, this inn is for you. An antiques shop in the main building specializes in furniture, and a large collection of Brazilian orchids is on display in the garden, including the inn's namesake. The main building housed different city government offices over the years before it was declared an architectural heritage site in 1990. A recent expansion and renovation preserved the historic flavor. The whitewashed rooms are spacious, with antique furnishings that give each its own character. **Pros:** Unique setting, hearty breakfasts. **Cons:** Inattentive staff, some antique beds not very comfortable. ⊠*Rua do Rosário 2, Centro, 72980-000* ☎*062/3331–1260* ⊕*www.pousadawalkeriana.com.br* ⤙*16 rooms* ♨*In-room: refrigerator. In-hotel: pool* ⊟*V* �|○|*BP.*

NIGHTLIFE

Most nightlife is along or just off the **Rua do Rosário** *(Rua do Lazer)*, which is closed to vehicular traffic on weekends, when bar and restaurant tables take over the narrow sidewalks and the street proper. The liveliest bars are Bar da Chiquinha, Pizzas Trotamundus, and Juca Pato.

SHOPPING

Pirenópolis is a well-known center for jewelry. There are several independent jewelers around the town's central district. **Galleria Shop Artes & Jóias** (⊠*Rua do Bom Fim 18, 72980-000* ☎*062/3331–1483*) has jewelry made from gold, silver, and semiprecious stones. **Pica Pedra** (⊠*Praça Bernardo Sayão 01, 72980-000* ☎*No phone*) specializes in ornaments made with quartzite obtained from the surrounding hills.

GOIÁS VELHO

320 km (200 mi) west of Brasília.

The city of Goiás, better known as Goiás Velho, was founded in 1727 by the *bandeirantes* (explorers whose initial goals were to enslave the indigenous peoples and, later, to capture African slaves who had escaped into the interior), who settled here when they found gold and diamonds. By order of the king of Portugal, a mint was built here in 1774 to process the large amounts of gold found in the Serra Dourada (Golden Sierras)—a mountain range surrounding the city. The town kept growing well into the 1800s but became stagnant as the gold, silver, and gemstones disappeared.

It was the state's capital until 1937, when the government moved to a more central location in the new planned city of Goiânia. Goiás seemingly lost its importance overnight, but most of the baroque colonial architecture was preserved, and today it's a UNESCO World Heritage Site.

Much like Pirenópolis, Goiás is an important handicrafts center. It's also known for being the hometown of Cora Coralina, one of Brazil's most renowned poets. The house where she lived *(⇨below)* has become a museum.

TO & FROM

From Brasília, drive west on BR 070. The paved road is generally in fair condition. Buses from Brasília, run by Transbrasiliana, take about five hours. The fare is about R$50.

ESSENTIALS

Banks & Currency Exchange Banco do Brasil (✉ *Av. Sebastiao Fleury Curado 250, Centro, 76600-000*) has ATMs available 6 AM to 10 PM.

Bus Contacts Estáão Rodoviária (✉ *Av. Dario De Paiva Sampaio s/n* ☎ *061/3371–1510*).

Emergencies & Medical Assistance Ambulance (☎ *192*). **Fire** (☎ *193*).**Hospital: Hospital São Pedro de Alcantara** (✉ *Rua Couto Magalhães 1, Setor Santana, 76600-000* ☎ *061/3371–1026*).**Pharmacy: Drogaria Brasil** (✉ *Rua Damiana Cunha 41, Centro, 76600-000* ☎ *061/3371–1898*). **Police** (☎ *190*).

Internet World Lan House (✉ *Rua Marechal Abrantes 14A, 76600-000* ☎ *061/3371–2418*).

Taxi Ponto de Taxi Rodoviária (☎ *061/3371–2017*).

Visitor & Tour Info Secretaria de Turismo (✉ *Praça da Bandeira 01, 76600-000* ☎ *062/3371–1968*) has information on lodging, restaurants, and upcoming events. The municipal tourism office is open weekdays 8 to noon and 1:30 to 5:30.

SAFETY & PRECAUTIONS

When thousands of visitors flock to Goiás for the Holy Week celebrations, it's time to watch out for pickpockets.

WHAT TO SEE

The **Chafariz de Cauda,** a baroque fountain, was built around 1778 to provide water for the population. Water was drawn from the Chapéu de Padre mine and carried by pipes carved in stone blocks—some are on display at the Palácio Conde dos Arcos. ✉ *Praça Brasil Caiado, Largo do Chafariz s/n, 76600-000.*

The handsome baroque **Igreja São Francisco de Paula,** built in 1761, is the oldest church in Goiás. The murals, depicting the life of St. Francis, were painted by local artist André da Conceição in 1870. ✉ *Praça Zacheu Alves de Castro s/n, 76600-000* 🎟 *Free* ⊙ *Weekdays 9:30–11 and 1–5, weekends 9–noon.*

The imposing two-story **Museu das Bandeiras** (circa 1766) housed the regional government, court, and jail for almost 200 years. Inside you can see vintage furniture, typical household items, and tools used by gold miners. ✉ *Praça Brasil Caiado s/n, 76600-000* ☎ *062/3371–1087* 🎟 *R$3* ⊙ *Tues.–Sat. 9–5, Sun. 8–1.*

The **Palácio Conde dos Arcos** housed the Goiás executive government from 1755 until the capital moved to Goiânia in 1937. Now the gov-

---

TRIAL BY FIRE

Cidade de Goiás is the site of the Procissão do Fogaréu (Fire Procession), a popular Holy Week celebration. Participants wearing hoods and robes walk in a procession that starts at Igreja da Boa Morte at midnight of Holy Thursday. More than 10,000 people, many of them toting burning stakes, now take part.

7

ernment returns here for three days every July in recognition of the city's historical importance. ⊠*Praça Tasso Camargo 1, 76600-000* ☎*062/3371–1200* 🖅*R$2* ⊙*Tues.–Sat. 9–5, Sun. 9–1.*

Goiás's most important poet, Cora Coralina (1889–1985), started writing at 14 but published her first book when she was 75. The **Casa de Cora Coralina** is the house owned by her family since 1784, now a museum. Her bedroom and the house's kitchen are kept exactly the way she left them when she died. ⊠*Rua D. Cândido 20* ☎*062/3371–1990* 🖅*R$3* ⊙*Tues.–Sat. 9–5, Sun. 9–4.*

WHERE TO STAY & EAT

$ ✕**Flor do Ipê.** This simple, homey restaurant may be nondescript when it comes to decor, but it's the best place to experience *comida goiana* (food from the state of Goiás). At lunchtime a buffet includes such dishes as *arroz com pequi* (rice with souari nuts) and *galinhada* (chicken cooked with rice and berries). The dinner menu includes fish dishes such as *peixe na telha* (fish cooked in earthenware bowl). ⊠*Rua Boa Vista 32-A, 76600-000* ☎*062/3372–1133* ▤*MC* ⊙*Closed Mon. No dinner Sun.*

$–$$ 🏨**Fazenda Manduzanzan.** The odd name comes from the rivers Mandu and Zanzan, both of which run through the property. This pousada is also a working farm where you can milk cows or go horseback riding. On the property are crystal-clear pools (one fed with water from the rivers) and a hiking trail to some pretty waterfalls. Rooms are plain and the decor rustic, but the place is more than comfortable. **Pros:** Impressive location, laid-back atmosphere, friendly staff. **Cons:** Few amenities, outside city limits. ⊠*Rodovia Municipal Goiás, Km 7, 76600-000* ☎*062/9982–3373* ⊕*www.manduzanzan.com.br* ➷*16 rooms* ⌂*In room: refrigerator. In-hotel: restaurant* ▤*No credit cards* ⦿*MAP.*

¢–$ 🏨**Vila Boa.** On a hillside, this inn has great views of the Serra Dourada. Rooms are adorned with colorful prints and tiled floors. Apartment-like suites have wood-paneled walls. **Pros:** Competent staff, good views. **Cons:** Meager breakfast, some rooms need refurbishing. ⊠*Av. Dr. Deusdete Ferreira de Moura s/n, Morro do Chapéu de Padre, 76600-000* ☎*062/3371–1000* ⊕*www.hotelvilaboa.com.br* ➷*29 rooms, 4 suites* ⌂*In-room: refrigerator. In-hotel: restaurant, bar, pool, gym, no elevator, parking (free)* ▤*AE, DC, MC, V* ⦿*CP.*

SPORTS & THE OUTDOORS

The hills of Serra Dourada are covered with dense forest and are a great place to hike. There are also waterfalls and swimming holes in the creeks and the Rio Vermelho. **Balneário Santo Antônio** (⊠*Km 125, GO 070*) is a popular bathing spot near town. The Rio Vermelho also has rapids and a first-come, first-served free camping site.

SHOPPING

Ponto Mirante (⊠*GO 070, Km 123, 76600-000* ☎*062/9238–5504*) sells pottery, wood, and wicker handicrafts.

THE PANTANAL

Smack in the middle of South America, the **Pantanal Wetlands** cover a gigantic alluvial plain of the Rio Paraguay and its tributaries. Its area is about 225,000 square km (96,500 square mi), two-thirds of which are in Brazil. Much of the land is still owned by ranching families that have been here for generations. The Portuguese had begun colonizing the area by the late 18th century; today it's home to more than 21 million head of cattle and some 4 million people

> ## THE MIGHTY SWAMP
>
> Pantanal literally means "land of swamps." Although the exact size of the Pantanal is a matter of debate among geologists and cartographers, 225,000 square km (96,500 square mi) is a common figure. This is about 3% of all the world's wetlands in one continuous area about 17 times the size of the Florida Everglades. All the water ends up draining through the Paraguay River.

(most of them living in the capital cities). Yet there's still abundant wildlife in this mosaic of swamp, forest, and savanna. From your base at a *fazenda* (ranch) or lodge—with air-conditioning, swimming pools, and well-cooked meals—you can experience the *pantaneiro* lifestyle, yet another manifestation of the cowboy culture. Folklore has it that pantaneiros can communicate with the Pantanal animals.

It's widely held that the Pantanal is the best place in all of South America to view wildlife. (It's slated to become a UNESCO Biosphere Reserve.) More than 600 species of birds live here during different migratory seasons, including *araras* (hyacinth macaws), fabulous blue-and-yellow birds that can be as long as three feet from head to tail; larger-than-life rheas, which look and walk like aging modern ballerinas; the *tuiuiú*, known as the "lords of the Pantanal" and one of the largest birds known (their wingspan is 5–6 feet), which build an intricate assemblage of nests (*ninhais*) on trees; as well as cormorants, ibis, herons, kingfishers, hawks, falcons, and egrets, to name a few. You're also sure to spot *capivaras* (capybaras; the world's largest rodents—adults are about 60 cm/2 feet tall), tapirs, anteaters, marsh and jungle deer, maned wolves, otters, and one of the area's six species of monkeys.

The amphibian family is well represented by *jacarés* (caiman alligators), whose population of 200 per square mi is a large increase from the 1970s, when poaching had left them nearly extinct. (The skin of four animals made just one pair of shoes.) Jacarés are much more tranquil than their North American and African relatives—they don't attack unless threatened. Almost blind and deaf, and lacking a sense of smell, caimans catch the fish they eat by following vibrations in the water. It's hard to spot jaguars and pumas during the day; a night photographic safari is the best way to try your luck. Native guides (some are actually converted hunters) take you safely to the animals' roaming areas. Sightings are not uncommon in the fazendas that go the extra mile to protect their fauna. Don't let scary tales about *sucuri* (anacondas), which can grow to 30 feet in length, worry you. Sightings of the snakes are extremely rare and instances of them preying on humans are even rarer.

GETTING AROUND THE PANTANAL

The Pantanal is accessible by car and boat, but flights are the most popular—and easiest—way to reach the the gateway cities. The main airports are in Campo Grande (Pantanal South), and Cuiabá (Pantanal North). Cuiabá is also the starting point for trips to Chapada dos Guimarães.

CUIABÁ

1,130 km (700 mi) west of Brasília, 1,615 km (1,000 mi) northwest of São Paulo.

The northern gateway to the Pantanal Wetlands, Cuiabá is also the southernmost gateway to the cerrado and the Amazon beyond. You can visit one of several museums while you're waiting for a tour into the wetlands or take a jaunt to Chapada dos Guimarães, a mountain range with impressive gorges, waterfalls, and vistas. The capital of Mato Grosso, Cuiabá is well known for being the hottest city in Brazil: mean annual temperature is a sizzling 27°C (81°F). Daily highs surpass 45°C (113°F) several times during the year. The city name comes from the Bororo native people, who lived in the area—it means "place where we fish with spears." It was originally settled in the 18th century, when gold was found in the nearby rivers.

> ### GO FISH
>
> The Pantanal is a freshwater fishermen's paradise. *Piraputanga* and *dourado* are the most prized catches in the Pantanal, but the abundant *pacú, pintado,* and *traíra* are also popular. Piranhas are endemic to the area. Although not the most sought-after catch, locals have some tasty recipes to prepare them. Beginning in November, most fish swim upstream to spawn, a phenomenon called *piracema.* That's why fishing is prohibited November to February.

TO & FROM

Cuiabá is best reached by air from São Paulo, Rio, or Brasília. Cuiabá's Aeroporto Marechal Rondon is about 10 km (6 mi) from downtown. Taxis from the airport cost R$40.

Andorinha buses travel to Cuiabá from Campo Grande (10 hours, R$70), and Chapada dos Guimarães (2 hours, R$15).

ESSENTIALS

Airport Aeroporto Marechal Rondon (*CGB* ☒*Av. João Ponce de Arruda s/n, Varzea Grande, 78110-900* ☏*065/3614–2500*).

Banks & Currency Exchange Banco do Brasil (☒*Av. Getúlio Vargas and Rua Barão de Melgaço, 78005-500*) has an ATM available 6 AM–10 PM.

Bus Contacts Andorinha (☏*065/3621–3201*). **Rodoviária de Cuiabá** (☒*Rua Jules Rimet 10, 78048-610* ☏*065/3621–3629*).

Emergencies & Medical Assistance Ambulance (☏*192*). **Fire** (☏*193*). **Hospital: Hospital Santa Casa** (☒*Praça Seminário 141, 78015-140* ☏*065/3322–3796*). **Pharmacy: 24-Hour Pharmacy Hotline** (☏*132*). **Drogaria Avenida** (☒*Rua da Arará 1933, Centro* ☏*065/3529–6108*). **Police** (☏*190*).

Taxi Rádio Táxi Cuiabana (☏*065/3322–6664*).

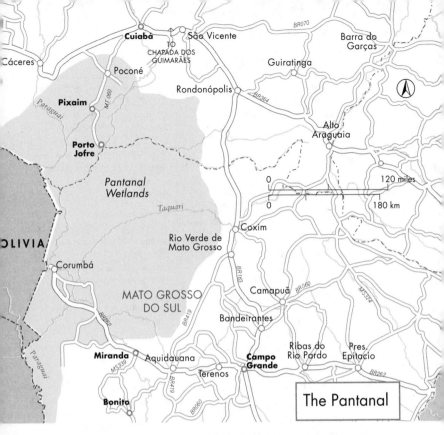

The Pantanal

Visitor & Tour Info *For information about tours in the Pantanal see "Pantanal Tours" box, above.* **SEDTUR** (✉*Praça Rachid Jaudy s/n, 78020-901* ☎*065/3613–9340* 🌐*www.sedtur.mt.gov.br*) *is open weekdays 8–8, Saturday 9–5, and Sunday 9–3.*

SAFETY & PRECAUTIONS

Take care in Cuiabá, which has a higher crime rate than other cities. Avoid straying too far from the hotel at night, as mugging can be a problem.

WHAT TO SEE

The **Museu História Natural e Antropologia** displays everything from ancient Indian artifacts to contemporary art. ✉*Palácio da Instrução, Praça da República, 78005-240* ☎*065/3321–3391* 💲*R$5* ⏰*Weekdays noon–6, Sat. 8–noon.*

The **Museu de Pedras Ramis Bucair** has a stunning collection of old maps, local fossils, and interesting stones, including what's purportedly a meteorite. ✉*Rua Galdino Pimentel 155, Calçadão, northeast of main square, 78005-020* 💲*R$5* ⏰*Weekdays 7–11 and 1–4.*

⏱ **Museu do Rio Cuiabá**, on the west bank of Cuiabá River, has maps and models of the river and photos of its history. The building, constructed in 1899, was once the public fish market. The **Aquário Municipal** (Municipal Aquarium), with typical fish of the Pantanal, is part of the

PANTANAL TOURS

When visiting the Pantanal it's essential to have a guide, as you'll be traversing a remote border region. Before you choose a travel agency, ask questions about the planned route, the kind of vehicle that will be used, and the accommodations. Also ask about the guides, especially about their level of experience and their English-language skills. To avoid being overcharged, compare prices at more than one agency.

In the southern Pantanal you may choose to book tours out of Bonito, where more than a dozen establishments vie for your business—you'll need to contact local agents, because all local attractions are on private property. **Pant Tour** (⊠ *Rua Senador Felinto Müller 578, Bonito, 72290-000* ☎ *067/3255–1000*) is a reliable local operator with good knowledge of the best spots in the region.

For tours deeper into the north or south Pantanal, **Impacto Turismo** (⊠ *Rua Padre João Crippa*

496, *Campo Grande, 79002-380* ☎ *067/3325–1333* ⊕ *www.impactotour.com.br*) is a good choice. **Agência AR** (⊠ *Rua Cel. Pilad Rebuá 1184, Bonito, 79290-000* ☎ *067/3225–1008* ⊕ *www.agenciaar.com.br*) is another popular option among travelers to the Pantanal.

You can book longer tours—including river trips in luxurious riverboats (locally known as "hotel-boats") equipped with comfortable air-conditioned cabins. There are several kinds of these boat tours. Some are fishing expeditions on the Paraguay River and its tributaries. Others may combine treks into the wetlands by horseback, 4x4 vehicle, or on foot—whatever it takes to get the best animal sightings. The cost is variable, depending on length, type of accommodation, and equipment, but you can budget between R$200 and R$500 per day, with everything included. Most tours last four to seven days. If you're pressed for time, there are shorter two-day tours.

complex. ⊠ *Av. Beira Rio s/n, Porto, 78125-090* ☎ *065/3617–0928 or 65/3617–0929* ☉ *Tues.–Sun. 9–5.*

WHERE TO STAY & EAT

$$$ ✕ **Morro de St. Antônio.** This surf-and-turf place with a Polynesian vibe caters to a yuppie crowd. The Brazilian buffet is varied and changes daily, but will certainly include roasted meats and pasta dishes, as well as a huge choice of salads. Dinner is served nightly until 1 AM. It's a good place to drink and be merry into the wee hours on weekends. ⊠ *Av. Isaac Póvoas 1167, Centro, 78045-340* ☎ *065/3622–0502* ⊟ *AE, DC, MC.*

$$ ✕ **Boi Grill.** If you've had your fill of fish, try this *churrascaria* (steak house) for as many beef dishes as you can imagine. Two of the most popular cuts are *picanha* (rump) and *costela* (ribs). Another recommended dish is *paleta de cordeiro* (lamb's rib). ⊠ *Av. Miguel Sutil 6711, 78048-000* ☎ *065/3624–9992* ⊟ *AE, DC, MC, V* ☉ *Closed Mon.*

$$ ✕ **O Regionalíssimo.** In the same building as the Casa do Artesão, this self-service eatery has regional cuisine and Brazilian staples such as rice and beans. Try the *mojica de pintado*, a stew made from a local freshwater

fish. ⊠*Av. 13 de Junho 38, Porto, 78005-250* ☎*065/3623–6881* ⊟V ⊙*Closed Mon. No dinner.*

$$ ✕**Peixaria Popular.** This is the place to try local fish; don't miss the delicious *piraputanga*, a local fish prepared in a stew or fried. Other options are the *pintado* (a large freshwater fish) and *pacu* (a small piranhalike fish). All orders include a side serving of *pirão* (a thick fish gravy with cassava flour) and *banana frita* (fried bananas). ⊠*Av. São Sebastião 2324, Goiabeiras, 78045-400* ☎*065/3322–5471* ⊟*DC, MC, V* ⊙*No dinner Sun.*

$–$$ ⊞**Paiaguás Palace.** The standard rooms at Paiaguás Palace are simple and small, but the large and luxuriously furnished suites suit the rather grandiose name. The top-floor restaurant, with its buffet of international fare, has good views—on clear evenings you can see the plains. Location is one of the main draws of this hotel; it's right in the business district. **Pros:** Central location, cozy rooms. **Cons:** Neighborhood sketchy at night, very busy during conventions. ⊠*Av. Rubens de Mendonça 1718, Bosque da Saúde, 78050-230* ☎*065/3642–5353* ⊕*www.hotelpaiaguas.com.br* ⤷*110 rooms, 11 suites* ⌂*In room: safe, refrigerator, dial-up. In-hotel: restaurant, bar, pool, gym, public Internet, public Wi-Fi, parking (no fee)* ⊟*AE, DC, MC, V* ⊺⊙*CP.*

$ ⊞**Deville.** This hotel has a lot to offer, including large rooms with queen-size beds. Ventanas restaurant offers international fare and is popular with businesspeople. **Pros:** Attentive staff, big breakfast. **Cons:** Hard beds, noisy nightclub nearby. ⊠*Av. Isaac Povoas 1000, 78045-200* ☎*065/3319–3000* ⊕*www.deville.com.br* ⤷*188 rooms* ⌂*In room: refrigerator, dial-up. In-hotel: restaurant, bar, pool, gym, public Internet, no-smoking rooms, parking (fee)* ⊟*AE, DC, MC, V* ⊺⊙*CP.*

NIGHTLIFE

Entretanto (⊠*Av. 31 de Março s/n, 78040-000* ☎*065/3623–3786*) has tables in a tree-lined garden and has daily performances of Brazilian and international pop music.

SHOPPING

For Indian handicrafts try the shop sponsored by the Brazilian Indian agency FUNAI: **Artíndia** (⊠*Rua Pedro Celestino 301, 78005-010* ☎*065/3623–1675*). For wicker, cotton, and ceramic crafts from local artists, go to **Casa do Artesão** (⊠*Rua 13 de Junho 315, Porto, 78005-450* ☎*065/3316–3151*). The shop inside the **Museu de Pedras Ramis Bucair** (⊠*Rua Galdino Pimentel 155, Calçadão, 78005-020* ☎*No phone*) sells precious and semiprecious stones, such as emeralds, tourmalines, and agates.

HEALTH CONCERNS IN THE PANTANAL

Malaria is quite rare in tourist areas, but yellow fever has been of greater concern in recent years. If you're traveling to the Pantanal, ask to your doctor about getting an inoculation before you leave on your trip. Dengue fever, for which there is no vaccination available, is a worry from November to March. The best way to prevent it is to avoid being bitten by mosquitoes. Lodgings in the Pantanal have screened windows, doors, and verandas. Use strong insect repellent at all times.

7

**EN
ROUTE**

Along the road to Chapada dos Guimarães from Cuiabá, you pass the **Portão do Inferno** (*Hell's Gate* ✉*MT 251, 48 km/30 mi northeast of Cuiabá*), a scenic viewpoint over the chasm that was created as Rio Cuiabá's waters eroded the mesa.

SIDE TRIPS FROM CUIABÁ

Besides the Patantanal, the areas in and around the **Parque Nacional Chapada dos Guimarães** are the region's most popular attractions. Traveling northeast of Cuiabá, you see the massive sandstone formations from miles away, rising 3,000 feet above the flat cerrado landscape. The **Cachoeira Véu de Noiva** (Bridal Veil Falls), with a 250-foot freefall, is the most impressive of the five falls in the park. You can enjoy lunch at the nearby open-air restaurant. Beyond this point there are hills, caves, more falls, and archaeological sites. The **Circuito das Cachoeiras** (Waterfalls Circuit) is a set of seven waterfalls 2 mi (3.5 km) from the visitor center.

If you have time, arrange a guided visit to **Caverna Aroe Jari** (✉*MT 251, 40 km from Guimarães*). The cave's name means "home of souls" in the Bororo language. This mile-long sandstone cave (one of Brazil's largest) can only be reached after a 4.8-km (3-mi) hike through the cerrado. Walk about 30 minutes beyond the Caverna Aroe Jari to **Gruta da Lagoa Azul** (Grotto of Blue Lagoon), a crystal-clear lagoon (bathing is prohibited). Visits are limited to 50 people a day. At the **Cidade de Pedra** (Stone City) is a huge formation of rocks and canyons carved by wind and rain inside the park. There are two great red walls that echo at each other. To get here, take MT 251 northeast of Guimarães Town.

Contact **Ecoturismo Cultural** (✉*Praça Dom Wunibaldo 464, 78195-000* ☎*065/3301–1393*) to arrange for a tour guide in the park. Packages start at R$100 per person. Book in advance if you plan on going in July, during summer, or on holidays. ✉*MT 251 at Km 51, 74 km (40 mi) north of Cuiabá* ☎*065/3301–1113* 🎫*R$3* ⊙*Daily 8–5.*

After navigating the steep and winding MT 251 through breathtaking canyons to reach the top of the mesa, you discover the pretty town of **Chapada dos Guimarães** (✉*MT 251, 8 mi/13 km east of national park, 78195-000*), which still retains some of its colonial charm. If you're going to Chapada dos Guimarães around the second fortnight of June, don't miss the **Winter Festival,** with art and music workshops and various concerts with local artists. The **Igreja de Nossa Senhora de Santana do Sacramento** (✉*Praça D. Wunibaldo, 78195-000* ☎*No phone*) is a handsome colonial church (circa 1779) with some exceptional gold-plated interior flourishes. It's open daily 7–9. In 1972 satellite images proved that the continent's true center was not in Cuiabá, where a monument had been built, but at **Mirante do Centro Geodésico** (✉*8 km/5 mi southwest of town*) on the mesa's edge. If the geodesic center doesn't hold spiritual meaning for you, come for the fantastic view—on a clear day you can see as far as the Pantanal.

Otherworldly Visitors

Many people believe that the cerrado and the Chapada dos Guimarães are landing spots of choice for UFOs. This assertion goes back to Brasília's early days, when an Air Force officer claimed that his weekend home just outside the city was one such spot. A popular story in the Chapada tells of a bus left powerless for several minutes after being encircled by beams of colorful light.

In 1996 officials in Barra do Garças, 420 km (260 mi) northwest of Brasília on the Goiás–Mato Grosso border, designated 12 acres for the world's first UFO "airport"—the Interspace Aerodrome. Though the aerodrome was never built, the publicity it received fueled the notion that the cerrado is a hotbed of UFO activity.

In mid-1997 members of a small farming community 258 km (160 mi) northeast of Cuiabá were convinced that a local farmer and his son were hiding aliens after a fiery ball was seen to crash on their property. The next year people all over the west, from Campo Grande to Cuiabá, reported seeing a large shiny cylinder pass silently overhead. Other mass and individual sightings have been reported, as have alien abductions. Many cerrado residents will warn you to beware of nighttime attacks—not by jaguars, but by aliens.

Many people and religious fanatics of the Osho Lua sect believe that Alto Paraíso de Goiás will be the capital of the world after the apocalypse. They claim the region hides the world's biggest diamond, which attracts "energetic vibrations."

7

WHERE TO STAY & EAT

$-$$ ★ ✕**Morro dos Ventos.** Perched on the edge of a cliff, this restaurant has fantastic views. The palm-shaded building and surrounding gardens add to the atmosphere. This is the place for fantastic regional dishes such as *vaca atolada* (literally "cow stuck in the mud"). The strange-sounding dish is actually beef ribs served in cooked cassava chunks. The restaurant is in a condominium complex; parking is R$5. ⊠ *Estrada do Mirante Km 1, ½ mi/1½ km east of town, 78195-000* ☎*065/3301–1030* ▤ *DC, MC* ⊗ *No dinner.*

¢-$ ✕**Nivio's.** True to its motto, QUALIDADE: INGREDIENTE FUNDAMENTAL DE BOA COZINHA, which translates as "quality: the basic ingredient of good cooking," this restaurant has delicious fish entrées cooked with care and skill. Entrées are always served with pirão and *farofa de banana* (cassava flour with bananas). ⊠ *Praça Dom Wunibaldo 63, 78195-000* ☎*065/3301–1203* ▤ *V* ⊗ *Closed Mon. No dinner.*

$ ▦**Pousada Penhasco.** Clinging to the mesa's edge, this small resort may be far from the Chapada dos Guimarães, but it has tremendous views of the cerrado. The sunny rooms are in cabins scattered about the grounds. All rooms have access to verandas with great vistas. Hiking tours and rappelling trips available. **Pros:** Many amenities, great sports options. **Cons:** Far from downtown, hectic during conventions. ⊠ *Av. Penhasco s/n, Bom Clima, 78195-000* ☎*065/3624–1000 in Cuiabá* ☎*065/3301–1555* ⊕*www.penhasco.com.br* ➪*45 rooms* ⌂*In room:*

safe, refrigerator. In-hotel: restaurant, bar, pools, bicycles, public Internet, public Wi-Fi ⊟*DC, MC, V* ⌶⃝⎮*CP.*

$ ⌘**Solar do Inglês.** Great care is taken with the decor at this charming hotel full of antiques and with a nice garden; the hotel's motto is "Enjoy Chapada dos Guimarães with an English touch." A delicious afternoon tea is served at 5 PM. Some rooms have fireplaces. **Pros:** Homey atmosphere, tasteful furnishings. **Cons:** Small bathrooms, few amenities. ⊠*Rua Cipriano Curvo 142, 78195-000* ☎*065/3301–1389* ⊕*www.solardoingles.com.br* ⌖*7 rooms* ⌂*In-room: safe. In-hotel: bar, pool, parking (no fee), no kids under 14* ⊟*V.*

PIXAIM

236 km (147 mi) south of Cuiabá.

The hotels here are some of the closest to the Pantanal Wetlands. There are many well-trained guides in town, who have lived here all their lives. (Be sure to specify if you need an English-speaking guide.) The Rodovia Transpantaneira (MT 080) was originally planned to cut a north–south line through the Pantanal. Lack of funds and opposition from environmentalists resulted in a stalemate. Today the road dead-ends at the banks of the Cuiabá River, in a village called Porto Jofre, about 150 km (93 mi) south of the town of Cuiabá. Still, the Transpantaneira makes it possible to observe the abundant fauna and lush vegetation of the northern part of the wetlands. A large number of fazendas and pousadas organize popular activities such as fishing and photo safaris.

TO & FROM

This "highway" is actually a dirt road with some 125 log bridges, some of which have caved in when cars passed over them. Traversing the Transpantaneira is time-consuming and relatively dangerous. It's best to join an organized tour; leave the driving to experienced guides in four-wheel-drive vehicles.

WHERE TO STAY

$$$ ⌘**Pousada Araras EcoLodge.** Rooms are impeccably clean at this
★ ecolodge, which has comforts unexpected in an area this remote. All have verandas where you can sit, relax, and enjoy the views. The restaurant serves great Pantanal fish. Environmental education and awareness is the motto here: this pousada goes the extra mile to keep the environmental impact of tourism to a minimum and explains why and how they do it. One highlight is the 3,000-foot wooden walkway over the wetlands. There are two observation towers extending well above the treetops. From there you have a bird's-eye view of the surroundings. There's a three-day minimum stay, which leaves you time to join the trekking, canoeing, and horseback riding. **Pros:** Superb location for wildlife-spotting, great amenities. **Cons:** Long distance from nearest airport, few English-speaking guides. ⊠*Km 33, Rodovia Transpantaneira, Pixaim* ☎*065/3682–2800 or 065/9603–0529* ⊕*www.araraslodge.com.br* ⌖*19 rooms* ⌂*In-room: no phone, no TV. In-hotel:*

The Brazilian Savanna

Brazil's vast *cerrado* (savanna) is the most biologically rich grassland in the world. More than 100,000 species of plants are found in this 500-million-acre (200-million-hectare) territory that covers about 25% of Brazil, and nearly 50% of them are endemic to Brazil. Its small trees, shrubs, and grasses are adapted to the harshness of the dry season, when temperatures in some parts rise well above 38°C (100°F) and humidity drops to a desert low of 13%. Palm species usually stand out among the shrubby vegetation—thick bunches of *buriti* usually grow around springs and creeks. Cacti and bromeliads are also abundant. Look also for the *pequi*, a shrub that produces berries used in local cuisine, which are called souari nuts.

Unfortunately, only about 2% of the cerrado is protected. Since development—mostly in the form of soy and corn farming and cattle ranches—it has become harder to spot such species of cerrado wildlife as deer, jaguars, and giant anteaters. Emus, however, can be seen wandering through pastures and soybean plantations.

restaurant, bar, pool, airport shuttle, public Internet $\equiv$*AE, DC, MC, V* ⭑○⭑*FAP.*

$$ ⬚**Pantanal Mato Grosso Hotel.** Rooms here may be sparsely decorated, but are more than comfortable enough to make your stay pleasant. The hotel arranges fishing expeditions, guided horseback tours and hikes, and visits to the Campo Largo ranch, an adjoining working ranch owned by the hotel. ⊠*Km 65, Rodovia Transpantaneira, Pixaim* ☎*065/9968–6205* ⊕*www.hotelmatogrosso.com.br* ⊅*35 rooms* ⭑*In-room: no TV. In-hotel: restaurant, pool, bicycles, airport shuttle* $\equiv$*DC, MC* ⭑○⭑*FAP.*

CAMPO GRANDE

1,025 km (638 mi) west of São Paulo, 694 km (430 mi) south of Cuiabá.

Campo Grande is the gateway to the southern Pantanal and to the water-sports-rich areas around Bonito. Nicknamed the Cidade Morena (Brunette City) because of the reddish-brown earth on which it sits, this relatively young city (founded in 1899) was made the capital of Mato Grosso do Sul in 1978, when the state separated from Mato Grosso. Campo Grande's economy traditionally relied on ranching, but in the 1970s farmers from the south settled in the region, plowed the plateaus, and permanently changed the landscape. Today ecotourism is gaining on agriculture as the main industry.

TO & FROM

Most tourists coming to the southern part of the Pantanal will fly to Campo Grande. Taxi fare from the Campo Grande airport to the town is about R$25. Andorinha has frequent bus service connecting Campo Grande with Cuiabá (10 hours, R$70), and daily service to and from São Paulo (16 hours, R$129).

ESSENTIALS

Airport **Aeroporto International de Campo Grande** (*CGR* ⊠ *Av. Duque de Caxias s/n, 7 km (4 mi) west of downtown, 79101-901* ☎ *067/3368–6000*).

Banks & Currency Exchange Banco do Brasil (⊠ *Av. Afonso Pena at Rua 13 de Maio, 79002-908*) is open weekdays 10–5.

Bus Contacts Andorinha (☎ *067/3382–3420*). **Rodoviária de Campo Grande** (⊠ *Rua Joaquim Nabuco 200, 79008-900* ☎ *067/3383–1678*).

> ### SEEING CAMPO GRANDE
>
> A double-decker bus whisks travelers past several points of interest, such as historic buildings and museums. A guide gives details of what's to see—only in Portuguese. There's one daily tour, beginning at 3 at the Centro de Informaçao Turística. Tickets for the 2½-hour tour cost R$8.

Emergencies & Medical Assistance Ambulance (☎ *192*). **Fire** (☎ *193*). **Hospital: Hospital Santa Casa** (⊠ *Rua Eduardo Santos Pereira 88, 79002-251* ☎ *067/3322–4000*).**Pharmacy: 24-Hour Pharmacy Hotline** (☎ *132*). **Drogaria Afonso Pena** (⊠ *Av. Afonso Pena 2326, Centro, 79002-024* ☎ *067/3324-8986*). **Police** (☎ *190*).

Internet Orbit Cyber Caf[ac] (⊠ *Rua Padre João Crippa 996, 79004-540* ☎ *No phone*).

Taxi Radio Taxi (☎ *067/3361–1111*).

Visitor & Tour Info *For information about tours in the Pantanal see "Pantanal Tours" box, above.* **Morada dos Baís** (⊠ *Av. Noroeste, 79008-520* ☎ *067/3324–5830* ⊕ *www.turismo.ms.gov.br*), the municipal tourism office, is open Tuesday to Saturday 8 to 7, Sunday 9 to noon.

SAFETY & PRECAUTIONS

Campo Grande is a relatively peaceful city. But you should beware of pickpockets, especially in markets and other crowded places. Take care at night, especially in areas away from downtown. When in doubt, ask your hotel staff.

WHAT TO SEE

The 70-year old **Mercado Municipal** (⊠ *Rua Mercado Municipal, 79002-040*) is a great place to try *sopa paraguaia* (Paraguayan soup), which, despite its name, is a corn pie with cheese, onions, and spices. There are many shops selling handicrafts from native peoples of Mato Grosso. The market is open daily 8–6.

To get acquainted with Mato Grosso's indigenous population, which includes more than 50,000 Terenas, Kaiowas, Guaranis, and Kadiweu, visit the **Memorial da Cultura Indígena**, a 25-foot-high bamboo *maloca* (traditional hut) built in the middle of an urban Indian reservation called Aldeia Marçal de Souza. You can shop for pottery and tapestries. The reservation is in the Tiradentes neighborhood. ⊠ *BR 262, exit to Tres Lagoas* ☎ *067/3341–6729* ⊡ *Free* ☉ *Daily 8:30–11:30 and 1–5:30.*

The **Museo Dom Bosco**, known as the Museu do Índio, has more than 5,000 indigenous artifacts of the Bororo, Kadiweu, and Carajás tribes.

Noteworthy are the taxidermy exhibits of the Pantanal fauna and the formidable seashell collection (with 12,000 pieces). Don't miss the collection of 9,000 butterflies from all over the world, and the bug room, whose walls are covered from floor to ceiling with insects. ⊠*Rua Barão do Rio Branco 1843, 79002-173* ☎*067/33126491* ᗌ*R$3* ⏲*Tues.–Sat. 8–6, Sun. 8–noon and 2–6.*

WHERE TO STAY & EAT

$–$$
Fodor'sChoice
★

✕**Fogo Caipira.** This is *the* place for regional cuisine, especially grilled and stewed fish dishes. The standout here is the *picanha grelhada na pedra* (grilled picanha steak). To try something more out of the ordinary, try *moqueca de jacaré* (stewed cayman meat with cassava). ⊠*Rua José Antônio Pereira 145, Centro, 79010-300* ☎*067/3324–1641* ▤*AE, DC, MC, V* ⏲*Closed Mon. and Tues. No dinner Sun.*

¢

✕**Soba Shimada.** This popular Japanese restaurant is known for its delicious *soba* (wheat-noodle soup with pork or chicken, eggs, and coriander). This soup became quite popular in the region after Japanese immigrants moved to Campo Grande in the early 19th century to work on the railway. Other Japanese specialties such as *yakitori* (grilled chicken pieces on skewers) are also tasty. ⊠*Av. Mato Grosso 621, 79002-030* ☎*067/3321–5475* ⏲*No lunch* ▤*MC, V.*

$$

▨**Jandaia.** This hotel is so thoroughly modern that it almost seems out of place in this Wild West town. Though it has little character—it's geared toward business travelers, so convenience wins over aesthetics—it does have all the facilities and amenities you'd expect at a deluxe hotel. The upscale Imperium restaurant, on the second floor, serves international fare with Brazilian options. **Pros:** Great business amenties, attentive staff. **Cons:** Neighborhood sketchy at night, hectic when conventions are held. ⊠*Rua Barão do Rio Branco 1271, 79002-174* ☎*067/3321–7000* ⊕*www.jandaia.com.br* ⤶*128 rooms, 12 suites* ⌂*In-room: refrigerator, dial-up. In-hotel: 2 restaurants, bar, pool, gym, public Wi-Fi, parking (no fee)* ▤*AE, DC, MC, V* ⏿*CP.*

$

▨**Metropolitan.** Near Avenida Afonso Pena, this hotel is popular with travelers on a budget. Rooms are basic, decorated all in white. The tile floors make the rooms feel extra cool—you might even forget to turn on the air-conditioning. **Pros:** Attentive staff, hearty breakfast. **Cons:** Drab rooms, small common areas. ⊠*Av. Pres. Ernesto Geisel 5100, 79008–410* ☎*067/3389–4600* ⊕*www.hotelintermetro.com.br* ⤶*75 rooms, 5 suites* ⌂*In-room: dial-up. In-hotel: bar, pool, public Internet, parking (no fee)* ▤*AE, DC, MC, V.*

$

▨**Novotel.** A red-tile roof gives this hotel a rustic appeal. Although not terribly sophisticated, the comfortable rooms have tile floors and blond-wood furnishings. **Pros:** Good location, sleek rooms. **Cons:** Neighborhood sketchy, small commons areas. ⊠*Av. Mato Grosso 5555, Jardim Copacabana, 79021-150* ☎*067/2106–5900* ⊕*www.accorhotels.com.br* ⤶*87 rooms* ⌂*In room: safe, refrigerator, dial-up. In-hotel: bar, restaurant, pool, tennis court, public Internet, parking (no fee), no-smoking rooms* ▤*AE, MC, V* ⏿*CP.*

7

NIGHTLIFE

Campo Grande is wilder than Cuiabá; parts of town (particularly the area near the bus station) are downright dangerous and best avoided at night. On the better side of the tracks is **Choperia 4 Mil** (⊠ *Av. Afonso Pena 4000, 79020-001* ☎*067/3325–9999*), a microbrewery that caters to an eclectic crowd of all styles and ages. It's open for drinks and snacks Wednesday–Sunday from happy hour until after midnight.

SHOPPING

For baskets of all shapes, beautiful wood handicrafts, and interesting ceramics made by Pantanal Indians, head to **Casa do Artesão** (⊠*Rua Calógeras 2050, at Av. Afonso Pena, 79002-005* ☎*067/3383–2633*). It's open weekdays 8–6 and Saturday 8–noon. The **Feira Indígena,** adjacent to the Mercado Central and just across Avenida Afonso Pena from the Casa de Artesão, is a good place to shop for locally made crafts. It's open Tuesday–Sunday 8–5. The massive **Shopping Campo Grande** (⊠*Av. Afonso Pena 4909, 79031-900* ☎*067/3389–8000*) has everything you'd expect in an American- or European-style mall, but the many boutiques are what makes it shine.

BONITO

277 km (172 mi) southwest of Campo Grande.

The hills around this small town of 15,000, whose name rightly means "beautiful," are on the southern edge of the Pantanal, not too far from the Bodoquena mountain range. The route to the Pantanal is longer than from Campo Grande, but you are well compensated with top-notch hotels that starkly contrast with the rustic Pantanal lodgings. In Bonito you can swim and snorkel among schools of colorful fish in the headwaters of several crystal-clear rivers. Fishing, rafting, rappelling, hiking, and spelunking are popular activities in this area. Tour guides can be hired on Bonito's main avenue.

TO & FROM

The paved roads to Bonito follow a circuitous route, but they're better than the more direct route on unpaved roads. Take BR 262 west to the town of Anastacio, then head south on BR 419 for about 100 km (66 mi) to Guia Lopes. From there it's about 56 km (35 mi) northwest to Bonito on MS 178. Viação Cruzeiro do Sul buses run here from Campo Grande (5 hours, R$ 25).

ESSENTIALS

Banks & Currency Exchange **Banco do Brasil** (⊠*Rua Luiz Da Costa Leite 2279, Centro, 79290-000* ☎*No phone*).

Bus Contacts **Estaçao Rodoviária** (⊠*Rua Pedro Álvares Cabral s/n, 79290-000* ☎*067/3255–1606*).

Emergencies & Medical Assistance **Ambulance** (☎*192*). **Fire** (☎*193*). **Hospital: Hospital Darcy Begaton** (⊠*Rua São Pedro Apóstolo 201, Jardim Andrea, 79290-000* ☎*67/3255-3455*).**Pharmacy: 24-Hour Pharmacy Hotline**

(☎*132*). **Farmacia Popular** (✉*Rua Santana Paraíso 812, Centro, 79290-000* ☎*67/3255–1094*). **Police** (☎*190*).

Internet Rhema LAN House (✉*Rua Pilad Rebuá 1626, 79290-000* ☎*067/3255–4271*).

Taxi Taxi Ponto 1 (☎*67/3255–1270*).

Visitor & Tour Info *For information about tours in the Pantanal see "Pantanal Tours" box, above.* **Centro Atendimento ao Tursista** (✉*Praça Central s/n, 79290-000* ☎*067/3255–1850*), the "tourist attention center," is open daily 8 to 6. It has information on hotels, restaurants, and tour companies.

WHAT TO SEE

At **Parque Ecológico Baía Bonita** you can go snorkeling along in the 1-km-long (½-mi-long) *Aquario Natural,* or "Natural Aquarium." The crystal-clear waters reveal an incredible array of colorful fish. Equipment rental is included in the admission price. A small museum describes the region's ecosystems. ✉*Road to Jardim, at Km 7, 79290-000* ☎*067/3255 1193* 💳*R$125* 🕐*Daily 9–5.*

The 160-foot-deep **Gruta do Lago Azul** *(Blue Lagoon Grotto)* has a crystal-clear freshwater lake at the bottom and smaller side caves in the calcareous rock. The best time to visit is from mid-November to mid-January at around 8:30 AM, when sunlight beams down the entrance, reflecting off the water to create an eerie turquoise glow. See stalagmites and stalactites in various stages of development. ✉*Fazenda Jaraguá, Rodovia Três Morros, 12 mi (20 km) west of Bonito, 79290-000* ☎*No phone* 💳*R$25* 🕐*Daily 9–5.*

The approximately 1½-hour rafting trip on the **Rio Formoso** takes you through clear waters and some rapids while you observe the fish and the birds of the Pantanal. You might also see and hear bands of *macaco-prego* (nail monkeys), the region's largest primates. The tour ends at Ilha do Padre (Priest's Island), where there's a complex of rapids emerging through thick riverine vegetation. There's a snack bar where you can relax after the tour. To best appreciate this attraction, make sure there hasn't been any rain in the previous days—the river gets quite muddy. ✉*Fazenda Cachoeira, 11 km (7 mi) east of Bonito on road to Ilha do Padre, 79290-000* ☎*067/3255–1213* 💳*R$50* 🕐*Tours by appointment.*

WHERE TO STAY & EAT

$–$$ ✕**Cantinho do Peixe.** Despite its modest appearance, this establishment is your best choice for local fish. The highlight is *pintado,* which is prepared in two dozen different ways. The cheese sauce is a good accompaniment to any of the fish dishes. ✉*Rua 31 de Março 1918, 79290-000* ☎*067/3255–3318* ▭*AE, DC, MC, V* 🕐*No dinner Sun.*

$ ✕**Castellabate.** This restaurant at the entrance to Bonito offers an array of pizza and pasta dishes. The highlights are the caiman or wild boar steaks. These are from farm-raised animals, as hunting is forbidden. ✉*Rua Pilad Rebuá 2168, 79290-000* ☎*067/3225–1713* ▭*DC, MC, V* 🕐*Closed Wed.*

$$$ ✕▥ **Zagaia Eco-Resort Hotel.** With decorations inspired in the Kadi-
☾   weu people's traditional crafts, this ecolodge has an authentic feel.
Fodor's Choice   The rooms—in single-story bungalows—are spacious, with colorful
★   furnishings, tile floors, and wood paneling. Most rooms have great
views of the gardens and the nearby forest-covered hills. The restaurant
serves international fare, but local fish is always available. Tours to the
region's attractions can be arranged through on-site travel agency. **Pros:**
Great amenities for families, unique decor, spacious common areas.
Cons: Hectic during conventions, away from downtown. ⊠*Km 0,
Rodovia Bonito–Três Morros, 79290-000* ☎*067/3255–5500* ⊕*www.
zagaia.com.br* ⟳*100 rooms, 30 suites* ⟳*In-room: safe, refrigerator.
In-hotel: restaurant, bar, tennis courts, pools, gym, bicycles, airport
shuttle* ▭*AE, DC, MC, V* ▯❙*MAP.*

$$ ▥ **Wetiga Hotel.** Large, luxurious, and expertly designed and land-
★   scaped, the Wetiga Hotel is the best in downtown Bonito. Rooms are
large, with tile floors, and decor inspired by indigenous peoples. Most
rooms have small living rooms, and some have verandas. The design is
dramatic, with rustic elements like log beams and rough-cut rocks interspersed with modern lighting and stainless steel. **Pros:** Great amenities,
sophisticated decor. **Cons:** Some bathrooms are small, busy neighborhood. ⊠*Rua Pilad Rebuá 679, 79290-000* ☎*067/3255–1699* ⊕*www.
wetigahotel.com.br* ⟳*63 rooms, 4 suites* ⟳*In-room: safe, refrigerator.
In-hotel: restaurant, bar, pool, gym, laundry facilities, public Internet,
public Wi-Fi, parking (no fee)* ▭*DC, MC, V.*

$ ▥ **Marruá.** The modern design of this hotel contrasts with others in
town, which lean toward rustic looks. The cream-color rooms have
a sleek design and are comfortably furnished. The best ones face the
impressive tropical gardens surrounding the pool. The restaurant serves
regional fare for dinner. **Pros:** Competent staff, soothing atmosphere.
Cons: Few amenities, bland decor. ⊠*Rua Joana Sorta 1173, 79290-
000* ☎*067/3255–1040* ⊕*www.marruahotel.com.br* ⟳*56 rooms, 30
suites* ⟳*In-room: refrigerator. In-hotel: restaurant, bar, pools, gym,
public Internet, public Wi-Fi, parking(no fee)* ▭*AE, DC, MC, V.*

$ ▥ **Pousada Rancho Jarinú.** A family-run business, Pousada Rancho Jarinú
has friendly owners who go to great lengths to make you feel at home.
The brick building helps keep the air cool—a boon in the heat of the
tropics. You're just steps from the main business district in Bonito.
Pros: Attentive owners, simple but tastful decor. **Cons:** Some rooms
are dark, small bathrooms. ⊠*Rua 24 de Fevereiro 1965, 79290-000*
☎*067/3255–2094* ⊕*www.pousadaranchojarinu.com.br* ⟳*9 rooms*
⟳*In-room: refrigerator. In-hotel: pool, public Internet* ▭*DC, MC, V.*

SHOPPING

The town's main avenue has great handicraft shops with native art and
other pieces by local artists. **Além da Arte** (⊠*Rua Pilad Rebuá 1966,
79290-000* ☎*067/3255–1597*) has beautiful bamboo and feather handicrafts and colorful ceramics made by the Kadiweu and Terena peoples.
Garimpo Pedras Naturais (⊠*Pilad Rebuá 1971, 79290-000* ☎*067/3255–
1597*) specializes in handicrafts made with semiprecious stones.

MIRANDA

205 km (128 mi) west of Campo Grande.

This tiny settlement on the Miranda River grew into a city after the construction of the railway linking São Paulo to Corumbá and on to Bolivia. In its heyday the railway was called Ferrovia da Morte (Death Railway) because of the many cattle thieves, train robbers, and smugglers that rode the rails. Since the 1980s the railway has been closed to passengers. A portion of the railway between Campo Grande and Corumbá is scheduled to open for tourist travel in 2009.

Ecotourism is Miranda's main source of revenue. Comfortable pousadas and farms allow you to get acquainted with the *pantaneiro* lifestyle. The Rio Miranda area has abundant fauna, including a sizable population of jaguars. Here's a great opportunity to practice *focagem*, a local version of a photographic safari: as night falls, guides take you into the Pantanal in 4x4 pickup trucks with powerful searchlights that mesmerize the animals for some time, so you can get a really close look.

TO & FROM

You must either drive or take a bus to Miranda from Campo Grande. The direct bus line from Campo Grande is run by Expresso Mato Grosso (4 hours, R$36).

ESSENTIALS

Banks & Currency Exchange Banco do Brasil (⊠ *Rua Tiradentes 364, Centro, 79380-000*).

Bus Contacts Estaçao Rodoviaria (⊠ *BR 262 s/n, 79380-000* 🕾 *No phone*). **Expresso Mato Grosso** (🕾 *067/3324–2263*).

Emergencies & Medical Assistance Ambulance (🕾 *192*). **Fire** (🕾 *193*).**Hospital: Hospital Ricardo Albuquerque** (⊠ *Rua Nicola Candia, Centro, 79380-000* 🕾 *067/3242-3600*).**Pharmacy: 24-Hour Pharmacy Hotline** (🕾 *132*). **Farmácia Avenida** (⊠ *Av. Afonso Pena 275, Centro, 79380-000*). **Police** (🕾 *190*).

Visitor & Tour Info *For information about tours in the Pantanal see "Pantanal Tours" box, above.*

WHERE TO STAY & EAT

$ ✕ **Rojo e Rojo.** This buffet-style restaurant serves regional fare, including grilled or stewed local fish. There's a large and varied salad bar. ⊠ *Rua Barão do Rio Branco 1146, 79380-000* 🕾 *067/3242–1330* ▭ *MC, V.*

$$$$ 🏨 **Caiman Ecological Refuge.** This 100,000-plus-acre ranch pioneered the
Fodor'sChoice concept of ecotourism in the Pantanal. Part of the working ranch is a
★ 10,000-acre private nature preserve. Lodges are spread out over the property. The main lodge has the longest list of amenities. The smaller lodges—Baiazinha, on the shores of a small lake, and Cordilheira, built on stilts next to a forest—provide close contact with Pantanal wonders. Guests can enjoy activities such as horseback rides through the wetlands, bird-watching tours, photo safaris, and canoe trips on the refuge's vast holdings. **Pros:** Excellent service, great ecotourism options. **Cons:** Few English-speaking guides, long distance from air-

port. ✉ *23 mi (37 km) north of Miranda, 146 mi (235 km) west of Campo Grande, 79380-000* ⚐ *Av. Brigadeiro Faria Lima 3015, Cj. 161, 04536-010 São Paulo* ☎ *067/3242–1450* ⊕ *www.caiman.com.br* ⏎ *25 rooms* ⚒ *In-room: no TV. In-hotel: restaurant, bar, pool, bicycles, public Internet, airport shuttle* ⊟ *AE, DC, MC, V* ⦾ *FAP.*

$$$$ ⬚ **Refúgio da Ilha.** This pousada is nestled on a 2,000-acre island in the Rio Salobra delta. Connected by a bridge to the mainland, it can be reached even during the high waters of the rainy season. The lodge, once a farmhouse, has comfortable apartments with tiled floors and pastel color schemes. Among the activities offered, snorkeling on the river and bird-watching are most porpular. Large wildlife (especially mammals) are best seen on the evening and dawn tours in a four-wheel-drive vehicle. **Pros:** Prime location for wildlife sightings, cozy rooms. **Cons:** Few English-speaking guides, far from airport. ✉ *22 mi (31 km) west of Miranda, 146 mi (235 km) west of Campo Grande, 79380-000* ☎ *067/3384–3270* ⊕ *www.refugiodailha.com.br* ⏎ *7 rooms* ⚒ *In-room: no phone, no TV. In-hotel: restaurant* ⊟ *No credit cards* ⦾ *FAP.*

¢–$ ⬚ **Pousada Águas do Pantanal.** A great budget choice, this inn is in a historic house with lots of antiques. You'll receive a warm welcome by the friendly staff and the owner, Fátima Cordella, who also runs a travel agency next door. The hearty breakfasts, with several kinds of pastries, are a rarity in a region where buttered bread is the norm. **Pros:** Good bargain, attentive staff. **Cons:** Few amenities, small bathrooms. ✉ *Av. Afonso Pena 367, Centro, 79380-000* ☎ *067/3242–1242* ⊕ *www. aguasdopantanal.com.br* ⏎ *17 rooms* ⚒ *In-room: no phone. In-hotel: bar, pool* ⊟ *MC, V* ⦾ *BP.*

SPORTS & THE OUTDOORS

The last reluctant ranchers are beginning to see tourism as a viable economic alternative in this region, which means you can visit a working ranch or farm for a day. **Fazenda San Francisco** (✉ *BR 262, 36 km/22 mi west of Miranda on BR 262* ☎ *067/3242–1088* ⊕ *www.fazendasanfrancisco.tur.br*) is a 37,000-acre working ranch where you can go on a photo safari in the morning and a boat tour on Rio Miranda in the afternoon, when you'll have the chance to fish for piranha. The R$95 fee includes a lunch of rice and beans with beef and vegetables. **Reserva das Figueiras** (✉ *BR 262, 20 km/12 mi west of Miranda* ☎ *067/9988–4082 Miranda, 062/3384–9862 Campo Grande* ⊕ *www.reservadasfigueiras.com.br*) has guided wildlife-sighting trips via canoe on the Rio Salobra for R$60.

Salvador & the Bahia Coast

WORD OF MOUTH

"Salvador is my favorite city in Brazil. The Pelourinho area is really nice at night with bands playing live Brazilian music."

—Lilica

"I visited Brazil in July 2007 and Salvador was the top highlight for me. Of course, it really depends on your interests. I personally love Spanish and Portuguese colonial architecture and Salvador is great for me!"

—Bencito

Updated
by Carlos
Tornquist
& Anna
Katsnelson

IN "THE LAND OF HAPPINESS," as the state of Bahia is known, the sun shines almost every day. Its Atlantic Ocean shoreline runs for 900 km (560 mi), creating beautiful white-sand beaches lined with coconut palms—while inland is Parque Nacional da Chapada Diamantina (Chapada Diamantina National Park), with 152,000 hectares (375,000 acres) of mountains, waterfalls, caves, natural swimming pools, and hiking trails. And in Bahia's capital, Salvador, the beat of bongo drums echoing through the narrow cobblestone streets is a rhythmic reminder of Brazil's African heritage.

Bahia's Costa do Coqueiros (Coconut Coast), north of Salvador up to the village of Mangue Seco, on the border of Sergipe State, has 190 km (118 mi) of beautiful beaches. South of Salvador, from Baía de Todos os Santos and its islands (Itaparica and Tinharé) to Itacaré is the Dendê Coast, where you find the African palms that produce the dendê oil used in Bahian cooking. The midsection of Bahia's coast is known as the Cocoa Coast, because cocoa plantations dominate the landscape and the economy.

Farther south, the Discovery Coast, from Santa Cruz de Cabrália to Barra do Caí, has many sites linked with the first Portuguese explorers to arrive in Brazil. The last bit of Bahia's coast heading south is the Whale Coast, near the towns of Caravelas and Alcobaça, where humpback whales mate and give birth from June to November.

ORIENTATION & PLANNING

ORIENTATION

Covering nearly 570,000 square km (220,000 square mi) of eastern Brazil, the state of Bahia is is hilly and dry. The vibrant capital of Salvador sits on the Atlantic Ocean about 1,649 km (1,024 mi) north of Rio de Janeiro and 1,962 km (1,219 mi) north of Saõ Paulo. The coastline, with its beautiful beaches, gets most of the attention. The 900 km (560 mi) of coastline is about a third of that in the entire country.

SALVADOR

On the southern tip of a triangular peninsula, Salvador sits at the mouth of the Bahia de Todos os Santos. The peninsula forms a natural harbor and shelters the city from the open waters of the Atlantic Ocean. Salvador is a hilly city, with the Cidade Alta (Upper Town) quite a bit higher than the Cidade Baixa (Lower Town).

THE COCOA COAST

Ilhéus and Comandatuba are the main attractions of the Cocoa Coast, which begins about 460 km (286 mi) south of Salvador. The region is famous as the setting for Jorge Amado's romantic novels of Bahian life. Ilhéus is where you'll find kilometers of beaches, forest reserves, and mineral springs. Comandatuba has one of the most luxurious resorts in South America.

TOP REASONS TO GO

- Warm waters year-round and a continuous lineup of beautiful beaches from south to north make Bahia one of the premier destinations in Brazil for soaking up the sun.

- Bahia's African influence on Portuguese and native Brazilian food has resulted in a distinct regional cuisine.

- Many argue that Rio's Carnival has become commercial and excessively elaborate, and Salvador is where people *really* know how to party.

- Salvador, the capital of Afro-Brazilian culture, and a World Heritage site with stunning monuments.

- The top names in Brazilian music, Gilberto Gil, Caetano Veloso, Gal Costa, Maria Bethânia, who were some of the musicians nicknamed Novo Baianos (New Bahians), are de facto ambassadors of Bahian music.

THE DISCOVERY COAST

Located 723 km (450 mi) south of Salvador, Porto Seguro is one of the country's most popular destinations. With the construction of new roads, the villages of Arraial d' Ajuda and Trancoso are now more accessible. Also popular destinations in the Discovery Coast are Atlantic Forest Reserves protecting the natural habitat.

PLANNING

WHEN TO GO

Peak seasons for Brazilians to travel are from December to March (South American summer) and the month of July, when schools have winter breaks. Most international visitors come in the months of August and September. Make reservations far in advance for stays during these months, especially if you plan to visit during Carnival (February or March). As the weather is sunny and warm year-round, consider a trip in the off-season, when prices are lower and the beaches less crowded. Mean temperatures are about 25°C (77°F) in winter (July and August), when there's usually more rainfall, including the occasional tropical downpour. Summer temperatures are a few degrees higher (28°C/82°F), but humidity is somewhat lower.

ABOUT THE RESTAURANTS & CUISINE

The laid-back lifestyle of Bahians is reflected in their food. In urban areas, breakfast is a minor meal—maybe just a cup of coffee with a lot of sugar (typical throughout Brazil) and a sandwich. Lunches are usually casual and not strictly defined by the clock, as the hottest part of the day is not the best for large meals. Dinner is the main meal, and starts late, usually after 9. Bahian cuisine is unique and delicious, and a definite reason to visit. The ever-present *oleo de dendê* (palm oil) is one ingredient that sets it apart from other Brazilian cuisines.

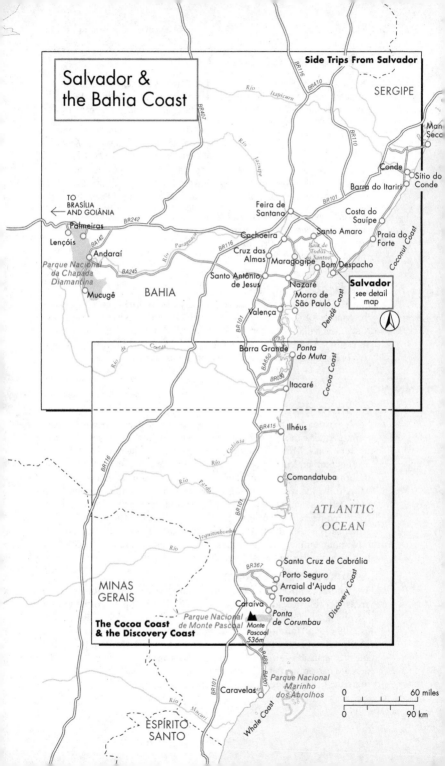

A Bit of History

In 1549 Tomé de Sousa was appointed Brazil's first governor-general, with orders to establish the colony's capital in Bahia. The deep waters at the mouth of Baía de Todos os Santos (All Saint's Bay) and the nearby hills, which provided a commanding view of the region and protection in case of attack by pirates, indicated a favorable site. Within a few decades the city of Salvador had become one of the most important ports in the southern hemisphere, and remained so until the 18th century. In 1763 the capital was moved to Rio de Janeiro, and the city lost part of its economic importance and prestige.

Due to its continental dimensions, Brazil's diverse culture is sometimes a mosaic, more often a blend of European, African, and indigenous backgrounds. But in Bahia the historical and cultural influence is predominately African. The demeanor of the large African-Brazilian population (comprising more than 70% of the population), the rhythms with mesmerizing percussion line, the scents on the streets of Salvador immediately evoke the other side of the Atlantic.

Until slavery ended officially in 1888, it's estimated that more than 4 million slaves were brought to Brazil from Africa, and the port of Salvador was a major center of the slave trade. By contrast, only around 600,000 slaves where brought to the United States. This large African slave population and generally lenient attitude of Portuguese masters and the Catholic Church led to greater preservation of African customs there than in other countries. The indigenous tribes, forced to work with the Portuguese to harvest pau-brasil trees, either fled inland to escape slavery or were integrated into the European and African cultures.

Today Bahia faces several challenges. As Brazil's fourth-largest state, it's struggling to juggle population growth and the economic boom that started 50 years ago when oil was found in its territory. The race is on to preserve its way of life and its landscapes, especially the remaining patches of Atlantic Rain Forest, coral reefs, mangroves, and interior sierras.

	¢	$	$$	$$$	$$$$
WHAT IT COSTS IN REAIS					
AT DINNER	under R$15	R$15–R$30	R$30–R$45	R$45–R$60	over R$60

Prices are per person for a main course at dinner or for a prix-fixe meal.

ABOUT THE HOTELS

Lodging options in Salvador range from modern high-rises with an international clientele and world-class service to cozy, often family-run *pousadas* (inns). The one place you can find big resorts is Costa do Sauípe. Pousadas are usually the only option in remote beaches or in fishing villages. Apartment hotels, where guest quarters have kitchens and living rooms as well as bedrooms, are available in some places. Low-end pousadas may not have air-conditioning or hot water; be sure to ask before you book.

WHAT IT COSTS IN REAIS					
	¢	$	$$	$$$	$$$$
FOR 2 PEOPLE	under R$125	R$125–R$250	R$250–R$375	R$375–R$500	over R$500

Prices are for a standard double room in high season, excluding tax.

GETTING AROUND

Most destinations around Salvador can be easily reached by car. To visit the Discovery Coast, fly to Porto Seguro (723 km/450 mi south of Salvador), and then rent a car to explore other beaches and attractions. For the Cocoa Coast, you can fly directly to Ilhéus, 460 km (286 mi) south of Salvador.

SALVADOR

Though the city of Salvador, founded in 1549, lost its status as capital of Brazil in 1763 when that honor was given to Rio (and later to Brasília), it remains the capital of Bahia. At least 70% of its 2,250,000 population is classified as Afro-Brazilian. African rhythms roll forth everywhere—from buses and construction sites to the rehearsals of percussion groups. The scents of coriander, coconut, and palm oil waft around corners.

Salvadorians may tell you that you can visit a different church every day of the year, which is almost true—the city has about 300. Churches whose interiors are covered with gold leaf were financed by the riches of the Portuguese colonial era, when slaves masked their traditional religious beliefs under a thin Catholic veneer. And partly thanks to modern-day acceptance of those beliefs, Salvador has become the fount of Candomblé, a religion based on personal dialogue with the *orixás,* a family of African deities closely linked to nature and the Catholic saints. The influence of Salvador's African heritage on Brazilian music has also turned this city into one of the musical capitals of Brazil, with many of its exponents like Gilberto Gil, Caetano Veloso, and Daniela Mercury acquiring international exposure.

Salvador's economy today is focused on telecommunications and tourism. The still-prevalent African culture draws many tourists—this is the best place in Brazil to hear African music, learn or watch African dance, and see *capoeira,* a martial art developed by slaves. In the district of Pelourinho, many colorful 18th- and 19th-century houses remain, part of the reason why this is the center of the tourist trade.

TO & FROM

Salvador's Aeroporto Deputado Luís Eduardo Magalhães (SSA) is one of the busiest in Brazil. In the last few years several international carriers have opened direct service from abroad, especially from Europe. TAM is the only airline with direct flights from the United States. Most international flights require a change of plane in São Paulo. The airport is quite far from downtown—37 km (23 mi) to the northeast. Taxis to central hotels should cost about R$60. To avoid being overcharged, pay your fare in advance at the booth inside the terminal.

Long-distance buses arrive at Salvador's Terminal Rodoviário. The trips are tortuously long (22 hours from Sao Paulo, 24 to 28 hours from Rio de Janeiro) and may be more expensive than flying.

GETTING AROUND

Regular buses (R$2) serve most of the city, but they're often crowded and rife with pickpocketing. Fancier executivo buses (R$3.50 to R$4) are a better option.

Comum taxis (white with a blue stripe) can be hailed on the street or at designated stops near major hotels, or summoned by phone. Taxis are metered, and fares begin at R$2.50. Unscrupulous drivers sometimes "forget" to turn on the meter and jack up the fare. In Salvador tipping isn't expected. A company called Cometas runs taxis that are spacious, air-conditioned, and equipped with modern security devices. Although more expensive than regular taxis, these are a good choice for foreign travelers.

Itaparica and the other harbor islands can be reached by taking a ferry or a *lancha* (a small boat carrying up to five passengers), by hiring a motorized schooner, or by joining a harbor schooner excursion—all departing from two docks. Boats depart from the Terminal Turístico Marítimo or Terminal São Joaquim close to the Feira São Joaquim.

ESSENTIALS

Airport **Aeroporto Deputado Luís Eduardo Magalhães** (*SSA* ⊠ *Praça Gago Coutinho s/n, São Cristovão, 41520-570* ☏ *071/3204–1214 or 071/3204–1444*).

Banks & Currency Exchange **Banco do Brasil** (⊠ *Largo do Cruzeiro de São Francisco 9, Pelourinho, 40025-060*). **Citibank** (⊠ *Rua Miguel Calmon 555, Comércio, 40015-010*).

Boat Contacts **Terminal Marítimo São Joaquim** (⊠ *Av. Oscar Ponte 1051, São Joaquim, 40015-270*). **Terminal Turístico Marítimo** (⊠ *Av das Naus s/n, Comércio, 40015-270*).

Bus Contacts **Terminal Rodoviário** (⊠ *Av. Antônio Carlos Magalhães 4362, Iguatemi, 41800-700* ☏ *071/3450–3871*).

Emergencies & Medical Assistance **Farmácia Drogadelli** (⊠ *Avenida Adhemar de Barros 59, 40170-110* ☏ *071/3237–3270*). **Hospital Espanhol** (⊠ *Av. 7 de Setembro 4161, Barra, 40148-900* ☏ *071/3264–1500*). **Hospital Português** (⊠ *Av. Princesa Isabel 2, Santa Isabel, 40146-900* ☏ *071/3203–5555*). **Tourist Police** (☏ *071/3116-6817*).

Internet **Internet Café** (⊠ *Av. 7 de Setembro 3713, Porto da Barra, 41100-000* ☏ *071/3264–3941*).

Taxi **Cometas** (☏ *071/3646–6304*). **Rádio-Táxi** (☏ *071/3243–4333*).

Visitor & Tour Info **Bahia Bella Viagens e Turismo-Iguatemi** (⊠ *Centro Empresarial Redenção, Av. Tancredo Neves 1063, Pituba, 41820-021* ☏ *071/3273–8200*) has excellent bus and van tours of Salvador and the surrounding area. **Bahiatursa**

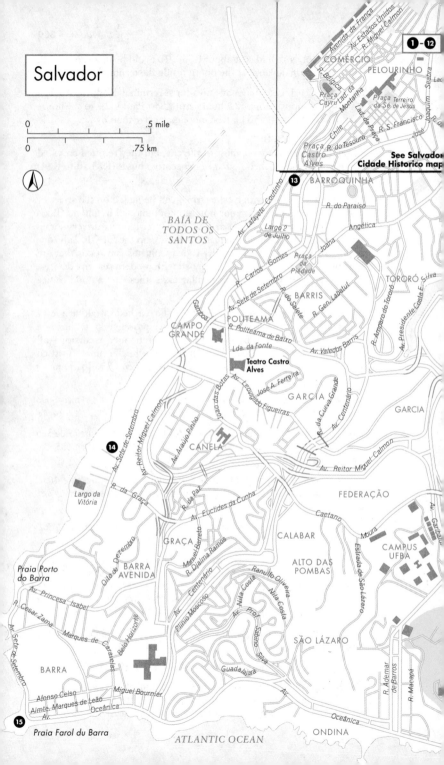

8

(⊠ *Centro de Convenções da Bahia, Jardim Armação s/n, Armação, 41750–230* ☎ *071/3117–3000* ⊠ *Aeroporto Internacional Luís Eduardo Magalhães s/n, 41510-055* ☎ *071/3204–1244* ⊠ *Terminal Rodoviária, Av. Antônio Carlos Magalhães 4362, 41800-700* ☎ *071/3460–8300* ⊠ *Rua das Laranjeiras 12, Pelourinho, 40026-230* ☎ *071/3321–2133* ⊠ *Mercado Modelo, Praça Visconde de Cayrú 250, Comércio, 40015-975* ☎ *071/3241–0242*) is one of the city's largest tour companies. **Tatur Tourismo** (⊠ *Centro*

> ### BAIANAS
>
> Salvadorian street food is prepared and sold by *baianas*, turbaned women in voluminous lace-trim white dresses who take great pride in preserving their Afro-Brazilian culture. Their outfits, an amalgam of African and Afro-Brazilian designs, symbolize peace in Yoruba culture.

Empresarial Iguatemi, Av. Tancredo Neves 274, Iguatemi, 41820-021 ☎ *071/3450–7216* ⊕ *www.tatur.com.br*) offers custom city tours and excursions outside the city. The company has great programs on the city's African heritage.

SAFETY & PRECAUTIONS

Salvador is no different from most big cities in Brazil—crime is a concern in most neighborhoods. The Centro Histórico area, especially Cidade Alta during daytime, is one of the safest places in Salvador. There are tourist police stationed on almost every corner. At night stick to the main tourist areas and don't walk down deserted streets. Elsewhere around the city, take a taxi between neighborhoods. Cidade Baixa and the Comércio neighborhood are notorious for petty crime, and pick-pocketing is common on buses and ferries and in crowded places.

EXPLORING

Salvador sprawls across a peninsula surrounded by the Baía de Todos os Santos on one side and the Atlantic Ocean on the other. The city has about 50 km (31 mi) of coastline. The original city, referred to as the Centro Histórica (Historical Center), is divided into the Cidade Alta (Upper City), also called Pelourinho, and Cidade Baixa (Lower City).

The Cidade Baixa is a commercial area—known as Comércio—that runs along the port and is the site of Salvador's largest market, Mercado Modelo. You can move between the upper and lower cities on foot, via the landmark Elevador Lacerda, behind the market, or on the Plano Inclinado, a funicular lift, which connects Rua Guindaste dos Padres on Comércio with the alley behind Cathedral Basílica.

From the Cidade Histórica you can travel north along the bay to the hilltop Igreja de Nosso Senhor do Bonfim. You can also head south to the point, guarded by the Forte Santo Antônio da Barra, where the bay waters meet those of the Atlantic. This area on Salvador's southern tip is home to the trendy neighborhoods of Barra, Ondina, and Rio Vermelho, with many museums, theaters, shops, and restaurants. Beaches such as Amaralina, Jardim dos Namorados, and Itapuã, north of Forte Santo Antônio da Barra and along the Atlantic coast, are among the city's cleanest. Many are illuminated at night and have bars and restaurants that stay open late.

Numbers in the text correspond to numbers in the margin and on the Salvador and Salvador Cidade Histórico map.

CIDADE HISTÓRICO

The heart of the original colonial city, the Cidade Alta section, incorporates the Comércio and Pelourinho neighborhoods and is a riveting blend of European and African cultures. More than 500 of the 2,982 buildings have been restored, earning Salvador the reputation of having the finest examples of baroque architecture in South America. Along the winding and sometimes steep streets,

TOUR SAVVY

Do not hire "independent" guides who approach you at churches and other sights, as they are usually not accredited and will likely overcharge you. Also avoid large group tours, which give little information about the sites and are targeted by hordes of street vendors. Private tours with accredited agencies such as Bahiatursa are your best bet. Prices vary depending on the size of the group; most include hotel pick-up and drop-off.

whose cobbles were laid by slaves, are restored 17th- and 18th-century buildings. Many of the restored buildings are now occupied by restaurants, museums, bars, and shops that sell everything from clothing, film, musical instruments, and handicrafts to precious stones. They are painted in bright colors, which, along with the sounds of vendors, street musicians, and capoeiristas, add to the festive atmosphere.

The Cidade Baixa (Lower City) is the section of historic Salvador that fronts the Atlantic Ocean. Its star attraction is the Mercado Modelo, one of Salvador's landmarks, with dozens of stalls that sell everything from Bahian lace dresses and musical instruments to amulets believed to ward off evil or bring good luck. Around the building gathers a mixed crowd of locals and visitors, impromptu entertainers, fortune tellers, and handicrafts vendors.

In the port of Salvador, the Forte de São Marcelo serves as a backdrop for cruise ships, schooners, and an assortment of small boats jockeying for space. Ferryboats and catamarans leave from different docks for Ilha de Itaparica (Itaparica Island), Morro de São Paulo, and other destinations within Baía de Todos os Santos. The area is busy during the day but is practically deserted at night, especially near the base of the Lacerda Elevator. Take a taxi at night.

MAIN ATTRACTIONS

❻ Catedral Basílica. The masonry facade of this 17th-century masterpiece ★ is made of Portuguese sandstone, brought as ballast in shipping boats; the 16th-century tiles in the sacristy came from Macau. Hints of Asia permeate the decoration, such as the facial features and clothing of the figures in the transept altars and the intricate ivory-and-tortoise shell inlay from Goa on the Japiassu family altar, third on the right as you enter. These are attributed to a Jesuit monk from China. The altars and ceiling have a layer of gold—about 10 grams per square meter. ⊠ *Praça 15 de Novembro, Terreiro de Jesus, 40020-210* ☏ *071/3321–4573* ⊠ *R$3* ⊙ *Daily 8–11 and 1:30–5:30.*

8

⑪ **Fundação Casa de Jorge Amado/ Museu da Cidade.** The Jorge Amado House contains photos and other momentos of the life of Bahia's best-known and most beloved writer. Amado set many of his books in this part of the city. Next door is the Museu da Cidade, with exhibitions on African culture. ⊠ *Largo do Pelourinho, Pelourinho, 40025-280* ☎ *071/3321–00070* ⊕ *www.fundacaojorgeamado.com.br* ☞ *R$3* ☉ *Fundação: Mon.–Sat. 10–6. Museum: Mon. and Wed.–Sat. 10–5.*

> **MAKE A WISH**
>
> At the Igreja de Nosso Senhor do Bonfim, vendors will try to tie printed ribbons around your wrist (and sell you 20 more to take home to friends). They'll tell you that each is good for one wish if you wear the ribbon until it falls off, then throw it into the ocean. Each color represents a Catholic saint and Candomblé deity.

⑯ **Igreja de Nosso Senhor do Bonfim.** North of the Centro Histórico, the Itapagipe Peninsula extends into the bay. Atop a hill is Salvador's iconic Igreja de Nosso Senhor do Bomfim. It's central to African religious traditions because of its patron saint, Oxalá, the father of all the gods and goddesses in Candomblé mythology. Here each Thursday before the third Sunday in January is the Lavagem do Bonfim ritual; a procession of *baianas*—women dressed in petticoat-puffed white dresses and adorned with turbans and ritual necklaces—comes here to wash the steps with holy water. Built in the 1750s, the church has many ex-votos (wax, wooden, and plaster replicas of body parts), left by those praying for miraculous cures. Outside the church, street vendors sell a bizarre mixture of figurines, such as St. George and the Dragon, devils, monks, sailors, and warriors. The morning mass on the first Friday of the month draws a huge congregation, most wearing white, with practitioners of Candomblé on one side and Catholics on the other. The church is 8 km (5 mi) north of Cidade Histórico. ⊠ *Praça do Senhor do Bonfim, Alto do Bonfim, 40240-090* ☎ *071/3176–4200* ☞ *Free* ☉ *Open for services Wed. and Thurs. 9* AM; *Fri. 6* AM, *9:30* AM; *Sat. 7 and 8* AM *and 5* PM; *Sun. 6, 7, 9, and 10:30* AM *and 5* PM.

⑫ **Igreja de Nossa Senhora do Rosário dos Pretos.** Built by and for slaves ★ between 1704 and 1796, the Church of Our Lady of the Rosary has finally won acclaim outside the local Afro-Brazilian community. After extensive renovation, it's worth a look at the side altars to see statues of the church's few black saints. African rhythms pervade the services. ⊠ *Largo do Pelourinho s/n, Pelourinho, 40025-280* ☎ *071/3327–9701* ☞ *Free* ☉ *Weekdays 8–5, Sat. 9–5, Sun. 10–5.*

⑧ **Igreja São Domingos de Gusmão da Ordem Terceira.** The baroque Church ★ of the Third Order of St. Dominic (1731) houses a collection of carved processional saints and other sacred objects. Such sculptures often had hollow interiors and were used to smuggle gold into Portugal to avoid taxes. Asian details in the church decoration are evidence of long-ago connections with Portugal's colonies of Goa and Macau. Upstairs are two impressive rooms with carved wooden furniture used for church meetings. ⊠ *Praça 15 de Novembro s/n, Terreiro de Jesus, 40020-*

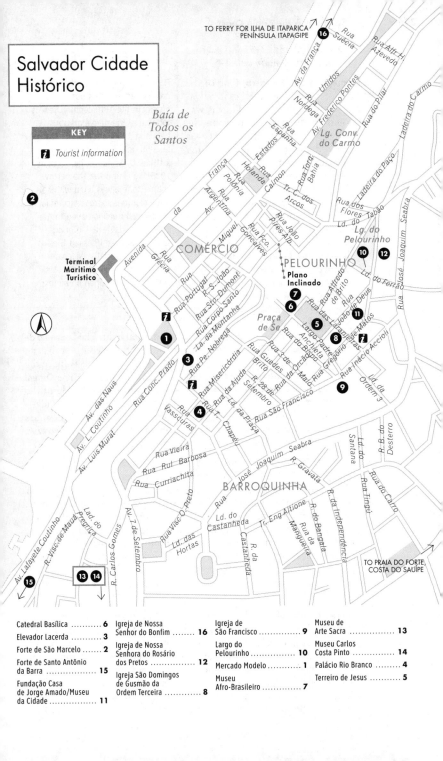

Salvador Cidade Histórico

KEY

🛈 *Tourist information*

Baía de
Todos os
Santos

TO FERRY FOR ILHA DE ITAPARICA
PENÍNSULA ITAPAGIPE

COMÉRCIO

Terminal
Maritimo
Turístico

PELOURINHO

Plano
Inclinado

Praça
de Se

BARROQUINHA

TO PRAIA DO FORTE,
COSTA DO SAUÍPE

210 ☎*071/3242–4185* ✉*Free* ☉*Sun.–Fri. 8–noon and 2–5.*

⑨ Igreja de São Francisco. One of the most impressive churches in Salvador, the Church of St. Francis was built in the 18th century on the site of an earlier church that was burned down during the Dutch invasion in early 1600s. The ceiling was painted in 1774 by José Joaquim da Rocha, who founded Brazil's first art school. The ornate cedar-and-rosewood interior is covered with images of mermaids and other fanciful creatures bathed in gold leaf. Guides say that there's as much as a ton of gold here, but restoration experts maintain there's much less. At the end of Sunday morning mass, the lights are switched off so you can catch the wondrous subtlety of the gold leaf under natural light. The **Convento de São Francisco** (☎*071/3322–6430*), part of the church complex, has an impressive series of 37 white-and-blue tile panels lining the walls of the cloister, each with a scene from Greco–Roman mythology. The **Ordem Terceira de São Francisco** (☎*071/321–6968*), on the north side of the complex, has an 18th-century Spanish plateresque sandstone facade—the only one in Brazil—that is carved to resemble Spanish silver altars made by beating the metal into wooden molds. ✉*Rua Ordem Terceira, Pelourinho, 40025-050* ☎*071/322–6430* ✉*R$3* ☉*Mon.–Sun. 8–5.*

⑩ Largo do Pelourinho *(Pelourinho Square).* This small plaza commemorates the day in 1888 when Princesa Isabel, daughter of Dom Pedro II, signed the decree that officially ended slavery. It was at this spot where runaway or uncooperative slaves were tied to a pillory and publicly beaten until the practice was forbidden in 1835. Today the plaza has one of the largest and most charming groupings of Brazilian colonial architecture. It's also a thriving cultural center, with four public stages named after characters in Jorge Amado novels. There's music nightly, and usually dancing on Tuesday and Sunday evenings. ✉*Intersection of Rua Alfredo de Brito and Ladeira do Ferrão, Pelourinho, 40025-050.*

⑦ Museu Afro-Brasileiro. Next to the Catedral Basílica, the Afro-Brazilian Museum has a collection of more than 1,200 pieces relating to the city's religious or spiritual history, including pottery, sculpture, tapestry, weavings, paintings, crafts, carvings, and photographs. There's an interesting display on the meanings of Candomblé deities, with huge carved-wood panels portraying each one. The two other museums that share the building are the Memorial de Medicina (Old School of Medicine Memorial) and the Museu Arqueologia e Etnologia (Archaeology and Eth-

Fodor's Choice
★

Spiritual Salvador

Evidence that Brazil is officially a Roman Catholic country can be found everywhere. There are beautiful churches and cathedrals—from the colonial to the baroque to the modern—across the nation. Most Brazilians wear a religious medal or two, bus and taxi drivers place pictures of St. Christopher prominently in their vehicles, and two big winter celebrations (in June) honor St. John and St. Peter. For many Brazilians, however, the real church is that of the spirits.

When Africans were forced aboard slave ships, they may have left their families and possessions behind, but they brought along an impressive array of gods. Foremost among them were Olorum, the creator; Yemanja, the goddess of the rivers and water; Oxalá, the god of procreation and the harvest; and Exú, a trickster spirit who could cause mischief or bring about death. Of lesser rank but still very powerful were Ogun, Obaluayê, Oxôssi, and Yansan, to name but a few.

The Catholic Church, whose spiritual seeds were planted in Brazil alongside the rows of sugarcane and cotton, was naturally against such religious beliefs. As a compromise, the slaves took on the rituals of Rome but kept their old gods. Thus, new religions— Candomblé in Bahia, Macumba in Rio, Xangó in Pernambuco, Umbanda in São Paulo—were born.

Yemanja had her equivalent in the Virgin Mary and was queen of the heavens as well as queen of the seas; the powerful Oxalá became associated with Jesus Christ; and Exú, full of deception to begin with, became Satan. Other gods were likened to saints: Ogun to St. Anthony, Obaluayê to St. Francis, Oxôssi to St. George, Yansan to St. Barbara. On their altars, crosses and statues of the Virgin, Christ, and saints sit beside offerings of sacred white feathers, magical beads, and bowls of cooked rice and cornmeal.

Salvadorans are eager to share their rituals with visitors, though often for a fee (you can make arrangements through hotels or tour agencies). The Candomblé temple ceremony, in which believers sacrifice animals and become possessed by gods, is performed nightly except during Lent.

Temples, usually in poor neighborhoods at the city's edge, don't allow photographs or video or sound recordings. You shouldn't wear black (white is preferable) or revealing clothing. The ceremony is long and repetitive, and there are often no chairs and there's no air-conditioning; men and women are separated.

A *pãe de santo* or *mãe de santo* (Candomblé priest or priestess) can perform a reading of the *búzios* for you; the small brown shells are thrown like jacks into a circle of beads—the pattern they form tells about your life. Don't select your mãe or pãe de santo through an ad or sign, as many shell readers who advertise are best not at fortune-telling but at saying "100 dollars, please" in every language.

nology Museum); both are closed for extensive renovation. ⊠*Praça 15 de Novembro s/n, Pelourinho, 40025-010* 🕾*071/3221–2013* 🖃*R$3* 🕙*Weekdays 9–5.*

❺ **Terreiro de Jesus.** This wide plaza lined with 17th-century houses sits in the heart of historic Salvador. Where nobles once strolled under imperial palm trees, there's a crafts fair on weekends. Occasionally a group of locals might practice *capoeira*—a stylized dancelike fight with African origins—to the sound of the *berimbau*, a bow-shape musical instrument. ⊠*Intersection of Rua das Laranjeiras and Rua João de Deus, Pelourinho, 40025-050.*

> ### SIGHTSEEING BUSES
>
> Double-decker tour buses run by **Salvador Bus** (⊕*www.salva dorbus.com.br*) travel around the upper and lower cities and to the beaches. A R$30 wristband lets you hop off and on as many times as you like.

IF YOU HAVE TIME

❸ **Elevador Lacerda.** For a few centavos, ascend 236 feet in about a minute in this elevator that runs between Praça Visconde de Cayrú in the Lower City and the Paço Municipal in the Upper City. Built in 1872, the elevator originally ran on hydraulics. It was electrified when it was restored in the 1930s. Bahians joke that the elevator is the only way to "go up" in life. Watch out for pickpockets when the elevator's crowded. ⊠*West side of Praça Visconde de Cayrú, Comércio, 40015-900* 🖃*R$0.05* 🕙*Daily 5 AM–midnight.*

❹ **Palácio Rio Branco.** The building dates to 1549, when it was the headquarters of the colonial government of Brazil. The current construction, completed in 1919, is the result of several renovations and expansions and has resulted in an eclectic style that leans toward neoclassical. Today it houses Salvador's Chamber of Commerce, the Cultural Foundation of the State of Bahia, and the state tourist office. On the first floor there's a small memorial to the state's governors, depicting the last two centuries of local history. Get a great view of Cidade Baixa and the bay from the east balcony. ⊠*Rua Chile s/n, Pelourinho, 40020-010* 🕾*071/3320-9300/9377* 🕙*Tues.–Sat. 10–6.*

CIDADE BAIXA (THE LOWER CITY)

This historic district was made up of the port of Salvador and adjoining warehouses and businesses. Because of poor planning, most of the original structures were demolished and replaced with private and government office buildings from the early 20th century.

Numbers in the text correspond to numbers in the margin and on the Salvador and Salvador Cidade Histórico map.

MAIN ATTRACTIONS

❷ **Forte de São Marcelo.** Jorge Amado jokingly called this doughnut-shape fortress near the Terminal Maritimo, the "belly button of the world." Bahia's economy essentially revolved around this spot, with the merchants, the market, and the port clustered practically within arm's reach. The fort, built between 1650 and 1680 in a mix of medieval and

FodorśChoice
★

colonial styles, housed the Imperial Army for more than 200 years. The troops staved off attacks from buccaneers and other invaders. Inside you can see the armory and soldier's quarters and get a great view of the bay from the lookouts. Hour-long tours in English depart from Terminal Maritimo. ⊠*Av. França s/n, Comércio, 40010-000* ☎*071/3321–5286* ✉*R$ 5* ☾*Call ahead for hrs.*

❶ ★ **Mercado Modelo.** From the 17th to the 19th century, slaves were kept in chains in the basement of this building upon arriving from Africa. The market has seen many changes since then. Today it's a convenient place to buy handicrafts. Bargaining is expected here for goods like *cachaça* (sugarcane liquor), cashews, pepper sauce, cigars, leather goods, hammocks, musical instruments, and semiprecious stones. *Repentistas* (impromptu folksingers) and fortune-tellers gather outside. The market is open Monday to Saturday 9–6, Sunday 9–2. ⊠*Praça Visconde de Cayrú 250, Comércio admission, 40015-170* ☎*071/3241–2893.*

IF YOU HAVE TIME

⓯ **Forte de Santo Antônio da Barra.** Since 1583 St. Anthony's Fort has stood guard for Salvador. The lighthouse atop the fort wasn't built until 1696, after many a ship wrecked on the coral reefs around Baía de Todos os Santos entrance. Inside the fort the **Museu Nautico** (☎*071/3264–3296*) has permanent exhibitions of old maps, navigational equipment, artillery, model vessels, and remnants of shipwrecks found by archaeologists off the Bahian coast. An eatery, Café do Farol, is open until 11 PM. ⊠*Praça Almirante Tamandaré s/n, Barra, 40060-240* ☎*071/3267–8881* ✉*R$4* ☾*Museum Tues.–Sun. 8–7.*

⓭ **Museu de Arte Sacra.** Housed in a former Carmelite monastery, the museum and the adjoining **Igreja de Santa Teresa** (St. Theresa Church) are two of Salvador's best-cared-for repositories of religious objects. An in-house restoration team has worked miracles that bring alive Salvador's golden age as Brazil's capital and main port. See the silver altar in the church, recovered from the fire that razed the original Igreja da Sé in 1933, and the blue-and-yellow-tile sacristy replete with a bay view. ⊠*Rua do Sodré 276, Centro, 40060-240* ☎*071/3243–6310* ⊕*www.mas.ufba.br* ✉*R$5* ☾*Weekdays 11:30–5:30.*

⓮ **Museu Carlos Costa Pinto.** A collection of more than 3,000 objects collected from around the world by the Costa Pinto family, including furniture, crystal, silver pieces, and paintings, is on display at this museum. Included in the collection are examples of gold and silver *balangandãs*, chains with large silver charms in the shapes of tropical fruits and fish, which were worn by slave women around the waist. ⊠*Av. 7 de Setembro 2490, Corredor da Vitória, 40080-001* ☎*071/3336–6081* ⊕*www.museucostapinto.com.br* ✉*R$12* ☾*Mon. and Wed.—Sun. 2:30–7.*

CITY BEACHES

In general the farther east and north from the mouth of the bay, the better the beaches. To avoid large crowds, don't go on weekends. Regardless of when you go, keep an eye on your belongings and take only what you need to the beach—petty thievery is a problem. There are no public bathrooms. You can rent a beach chair and sun umbrella for about R$10.

Beaches are listed in geographical order, beginning with Piatã, north of the city on the Baía de Todos os Santos, and then to Praia da Barra, near the peninsula's tip, and northeast to other Atlantic beaches.

MAIN ATTRACTIONS

Praia da Barra is a popular beach in Barra that's a convenient option if you're staying in the hotel districts of Ondina and Rio Vermelho, where rock outcroppings make swimming dangerous and pollution is often a problem. ⊠ *Av. Oceânica east of Santo Antônio da Barra, Barra, 40140-130.*

One of the nicest beaches along Avenida Oceánica is **Praia Corsário,** a long stretch popular with a younger crowd. There are kiosks where you can sit in the shade and enjoy seafood and ice-cold beer. ⊠ *Av. Oceánica, south of Parque Metropolitan de Pituaçu, Pituaçu, 41706-840.*

IF YOU HAVE TIME

Praia Piatã. Heading north and leaving the more built-up areas of the city behind, the first truly clean beach you'll come to is the wide Piatã. Its calm waters and golden sand attract local families. ⊠ *Northeast of Praia Corsário, along Av. Oceânica, Piatã, 41650-020.*

Praia Itapuã. Frequented by the artists who live in the neighborhood, the Itapuã beach has an eclectic atmosphere. There are food kiosks—including Acarajé da Cira, one of the best places to get *acarajé* (a spicy fried-bean snack). The area was once a whale cemetery, and bones are still an occasional find. Inland from Itapuã, a mystical freshwater lagoon, the **Lagoa de Abaeté,** and surrounding sand dunes are now a municipal park. Itapuã's dark waters are a startling contrast to the fine white sand of its shores. ⊠ *16 km/10 mi northeast of downtown, Itapuã, 41600-060.*

The northernmost beach in the Salvador municipality along the Avenida Oceánica is **Praia Stella Maris,** popular with surfers and the young crowd. There are myriad food-and-drink kiosks, more than at any other beach—it's the perfect place to sooth your thirst with *água de côco* (coconut water). ⊠ *20 km/12 mi north of downtown, after Itapuã, Stella Maris, 41600-010.*

OFF THE BEATEN PATH

★

Ilha de Itaparica. The largest of 56 islands in the Baía de Todos os Santos, Itaparica was originally settled because its ample supply of fresh mineral water was believed to have rejuvenating qualities. Its beaches are calm and shallow, thanks to the surrounding reefs, which are avidly sought by windsurfers, divers, and snorkelers. The main port of entry on the north of the island is the town of Bom Despacho, where the ferries from Salvador dock. The best beaches are near the villages of Vera Cruz, Mar Grande, and Conceição, the latter almost entirely owned by Club Med Itaparica.

Instead of buses or taxis, small Volkswagen vans (called *kombis*) provide the most convenient local transportation around the island. You can hail vans and hop from beach to beach along the 40 km (25 mi) of BA 001, the coastal highway that connects Itaparica village on the north part of the island to the mainland via Ponte do Funil (Funnel Bridge) on the southwest side. The drive from Salvador to the island takes about four hours. Bicycle rentals are readily available in the island's towns, so you don't really need a car.

> ### FAST FOOD
>
> Baianas typically make *acarajé*, a delicious street food made of bean dough fried with palm oil and filled with bean paste and shrimp. *Moqueca* is another specialty made with palm oil, coconut milk, and fish or shrimp cooked slowly over a low fire.

Ferries to the island run daily from the **Terminal Marítimo São Joaquim** (⊠ *Av. Oscar Ponte 1051, São Joaquim, 40015-270*). Tickets cost R\$3.35 during the week, R\$4.35 on the weekend. The ferries run from 5 AM to 11:30 PM and last 40 minutes.

WHERE TO EAT

You can easily find restaurants serving Bahian specialties in most neighborhoods. Pelourinho and Barra, full of bars and sidewalk cafés, are good places to start. There are also many good spots in bohemian Rio Vermelho and a slew of places along Orla, the beachfront drive beginning around Jardim de Alah. The regional cuisine leans toward seafood, but some meat dishes should be tried. And, like anywhere else in Brazil, there are *churrascarias* for beef lovers. One main course often serves two; ask about portions when you order. Beware that regional food is normally spicy and hot.

$$$–$$$$ ✕**Bargaço.** Great Bahian seafood dishes are served at this longtime favorite. *Pata de caranguejo* (vinegary crab claws) is hearty and may do more than take the edge off your appetite for the requisite moqueca *de camarão* (with shrimp) or moqueca *de siri mole* (with soft-shell crab); try the cocada for dessert, if you have room. ⊠ *Rua Antonio da Silva Coelho s/n, Jardim Armação, 41750-040* ☎*071/3231–3900* ⊕*www. restaurantebargaco.com.br* ▭*DC, MC.*

$$$–$$$$ ✕**Yemanjá.** A bubbly underwater theme—replete with aquariums full
★ of colorful fish and sea-goddess murals—sets the tone for the fabulous seafood here. Small portions of acarajé can be ordered as appetizers. The service is somewhat slow, but most patrons don't seem to mind, concentrating instead on plowing through enormous portions of moqueca, or *ensopado,* seafood cooked in a light sauce. Reservations are essential on weekends. ⊠ *Av. Otávio Mangabeira 4655, Jardim Armação, 41750-240* ☎*071/3461–9010* ⊕*www.restauranteyemanja. com.br* ▭*AE, DC, MC, V.*

8

$$-$$$$ ✕ **Trapiche Adelaide.** It's almost impossible to have a bad meal in this
FodorśChoice city, but this restaurant along the harbor and near the Mercado Mod-
★   elo still stands out for its unique blend of Italian, French, and Bahian
cuisines. Try the seafood risotto or quail in *farofa* (cassava flour). Hav-
ing drinks before dinner on the deck overlooking the Todos os San-
tos Bay is a pleasant way to wind down after a day of sightseeing.
⊠*Praça dos Tupinambás, Av. Contorno 02, Comércio, 40240-090*
☎*071/3326–0443* ⊕*www.trapicheadelaide.com.br* ▤*DC, MC, V*
☾*No dinner Sun.*

$$$ ✕ **Boi Preto.** Beef is cooked to perfection at one of the best barbecue
places in Salvador. Seafood, including lobster, crab, and sushi, and more
exotic fare like alligator or wild boar are also on the menu. A piano
bar keeps the atmosphere light. ⊠*Av. Otávio Mangabeira s/n, Jardim
Armação, 41715-240* ☎*071/3362–8844* ⊕*www.grupoboipreto.com.
br* ▤*AE, MC, V.*

$$-$$$ ✕ **Maria Mata Mouro.** At this *sobrado* (colonial house) in the Pelourinho,
you almost feel as if you're at a friend's home for dinner. Bahian food
is lighter than in most restaurants. Try the *badejo* (grouper) in ginger
sauce. The roasted leg of lamb is a great choice if you want to depart
from seafood. Entrée servings are more than enough for two. ⊠*Rua a
Ordem Terceira 8, Pelourinho, 40026-270* ☎*071/3321–3929* ▤*AE,
DC, MC, V.*

$$-$$$ ✕ **Uauá.** The cuisine here is representative of many Brazilian regions,
making Uauá one of the most popular restaurant chains in Salvador,
and therefore almost always crowded. The cuisine is representative of
many Brazilian regions, with special attention to northeastern dishes.
Don't skip the *guisado de carneiro* (minced mutton), here with cala-
brese sausage. ⊠*R. Gregório de Matos 36, Pelourinho, 40025-060*
☎*071/3321–3089* ▤*AE, DC, MC, V* ☾*Closed Mon.*

$-$$ ✕ **Encontro dos Artistas.** This simple Bahian restaurant has both alfresco
and indoor dining. The fish-and-shrimp moqueca, a stew made with
coconut milk and *dendê* (a type of palm) oil, is a must here. The charm
of this neighborhood establishment lies in its casual ambience, surroundings in a centuries-old part of town, and local clientele, who
gather here after work. Service can be slow—order an appetizer or
salad and drinks as soon as you sit down. ⊠*Rua Francisco Muniz
Barreto 13, Pelourinho, 40025-100* ☎*071/3321–1721* ▤*AE, DC,
MC, V.*

$ ✕ **Escola Pelourinho.** This restaurant, which opened in 1975, is a cooking
school where new generations of Bahian chefs hone their skills under
supervision of experienced teachers. More than 40 typical Bahian and
Brazilian dishes are served buffet style in this old colonial house. It's
regarded as one of the best restaurants in town. The bargain prices
are an extra incentive. ⊠*Praça José de Alencar 13/19, Pelourinho,
40025-140* ☎*071/3324–4550* ⊕*www.ba.senac.br* ▤*AE, DC, MC,
V* ☾*No dinner Sun.*

Afro-Brazilian Heritage

Of all of Brazil's states, Bahia has the strongest links with its African heritage. There are few other countries with such a symphony of skin tones grouped under one nationality. This rich Brazilian identity began when the first Portuguese sailors were left to manage the new land. From the beginning Portuguese migration to Brazil was predominantly male, a fact that led to unbridled sexual license with Indian and African women.

The first Africans arrived in 1532, along with the Portuguese colonizers, who continued to buy slaves from English, Spanish, and Portuguese traders until 1855. All records pertaining to slave trading were destroyed in 1890, making it impossible to know exactly how many people were brought to Brazil. It's estimated that from 3 to 4.5 million Africans were captured and transported from Gambia, Guinea, Sierra Leone, Senegal, Liberia, Nigeria, Benin, Angola, and Mozambique. Many were literate Muslims who were better educated than their white overseers and owners.

It was common in the main houses of sugar plantations, which relied on slave labor, for the master to have a white wife and slave mistresses. In fact interracial relationships and even marriage was openly accepted. It was also fairly common for the master to free the mother of his mixed-race offspring and allow a son of color to learn a trade or inherit a share of the plantation.

When the sugar boom came to an end, it became too expensive for slave owners to support their "free" labor force. Abolition occurred gradually, however. It began around 1871, with the passage of the Law of the Free Womb, which liberated all Brazilians born of slave mothers. In 1885 another law was passed, freeing slaves over age 60. Finally, on May 13, 1888, Princess Isabel, while Emperor Dom Pedro II was away on a trip, signed a law freeing all slaves in the Brazilian empire.

The former slaves, often unskilled, became Brazil's unemployed and underprivileged. Although the country has long been praised for its lack of discrimination, this veneer of racial equality is deceptive. Afro-Brazilians still don't receive education on a par with that of whites, nor do they always receive equal pay for equal work. There are far fewer black or mulatto professionals, politicians, and ranking military officers than white ones.

Subtle activism to bring about racial equality and educate all races about the rich African legacy continues. For many people the most important holiday is November 20 (National Black Consciousness Day). It honors the anniversary of the death of Zumbi, the leader of the famous *Quilombo* (community of escaped slaves) de Palmares, which lasted more than 100 years and was destroyed by *bandeirantes* (slave traders) in one final great battle for freedom.

WHERE TO STAY

There are only a few hotels in the Cidade Histórico. Heading south into the Vitória neighborhood along Avenida 7 de Setembro there are many inexpensive establishments convenient to beaches and sights. In the fashionable Barra neighborhood, many hotels are within walking distance of cafés, bars, restaurants, and clubs. The resorts in the beach areas of Ondina and Rio Vermelho are a 20-minute taxi ride from downtown. High seasons are from December to March and the month of July. For Carnival, reservations must be made months in advance, and prices are substantially higher.

$$$–$$$$ ⊡**Pousada das Flores.** The Brazilian–French owners have made this inn,
★ within walking distance of the historical district, one of the city's best options. Rooms are large and have high ceilings and hardwood floors. For peace and quiet as well as an ocean view, opt for a room on an upper floor. If you feel like splurging, request the penthouse, which has a fantastic view of the harbor. Breakfast is served on the patio. **Pros:** Beautiful building, great decor, perfect location. **Cons:** Pricey during high season. ⊠*Rua Direita de Santo Antônio 442, Santo Antônio, 40301-280* ☎*071/3243–1836* ⊕*www.pflores.com.br* ➷*6 rooms, 3 suites* ⚅*In-room: Wi-Fi. In-hotel: no elevator* ☴*MC, V.*

$$$ ⊡**Bahia Othon Palace Hotel.** A short drive from most sights, nightspots, and restaurants, this busy, modern hotel sits on a cliff overlooking Ondina Beach. Top local entertainers often perform at the hotel's outdoor park, and in high season the friendly staff organizes poolside activities and trips to better beaches. **Pros:** Pleasant rooms, eye-catching location. **Cons:** Most attractions aren't within walking distance. ⊠*Av. Oceanica 2294, Ondina, 40170-010* ☎*071/800–725–0505* ⊕*www.othonhotels.com.br* ➷*300 rooms, 25 suites* ⚅*In-room: safe, refrigerator. In-hotel: restaurant, pool, gym, parking (no fee)* ☴*AE, DC, MC, V.*

$$$ ⊡**Catussaba Resort Hotel.** In a garden of flowers and palm trees, this
★ hotel has large rooms, some of which have beautiful wicker furniture, with balconies and ocean views. The resort complex opens directly onto Itapuã beach, one of the cleanest and most famous in Salvador. The hotel is 40 km (25 mi) from downtown, near the airport. If you tire of saltwater and sand, head for the large pool area. **Pros:** Spacious rooms, pleasant decor, plenty of amenities. **Cons:** A bit impersonal. ⊠*Alameda da Praia, Itapuã, 41600-460* ☎*0800–998010* ⊕*www.catussaba.com.br* ➷*186 rooms, 4 suites* ⚅*In-hotel: restaurant, room service, bar, tennis courts, pool, gym, public Internet, parking (no fee)* ☴*AE, MC, V.*

$$ ⊡**Hotel Mercure Salvador.** This high-rise hotel has a prime location in the business district. You're guaranteed a perfect view because all the apartments face the Atlantic Ocean. Furnishings are sleek and modern, and the baths have relaxing marble tubs. The Casarão restaurant has tables on a deck overlooking the ocean. **Pros:** Excellent views, great amenities for business travelers. **Cons:** Not in the historic district. ⊠*Rua Fonte de Boi 215, Rio Vermelho, 40210-090* ☎*071/3330–8200* ⊕*www.accorhotels.com.br* ➷*175 rooms* ⚅*In-room: safe, refrigera-*

tor. In-hotel: restaurant, bar, gym, public Internet, parking (no fee) ▤AE, DC, MC, V ⍟BP.

$$ ▥**Sofitel Salvador.** This branch of the international chain sits in a lushly landscaped park near Itapuã Beach and the Abaeté Lagoon, about 5 km (3 mi) from the airport. It's the only hotel in the city with its own golf course, albeit a 9-hole one. As this gleaming white high-rise aims for the business as well as the purely tourist clientele, rooms are more sober than at other beachfront hotels. The Oxum restaurant has an excellent regional menu. There's free transportation to the Centro Histórico. **Pros:** Amenities for business travelers, lovely grounds. **Cons:** Far from the center, Internet connections cost extra. ⊠*Rua da Passargada s/ n, Itapuã, 41620-430* ☎*071/3374–8500* ⊕*www.sofitel.com* ⟿*206 rooms* ⌂*In-room: safe, Ethernet. In-hotel: 2 restaurants, room service, bars, golf course, tennis courts, pools, gym, concierge, children's programs (ages 4–12), laundry service, public Internet, airport shuttle, parking (no fee)* ▤*AE, DC, MC, V.*

Fodor'sChoice ★

$$ ▥**Tropical Hotel da Bahia.** Owned by Varig Airlines, this hotel is often included in package deals. The centrally located property is a bit dated, but its location makes it a good choice for those interested in the city's history and culture. The hotel is away from the beaches, but there's a free beach shuttle. Some rooms overlook Largo de Campo Grande, one of the hubs of Carnival in Salvador. **Pros:** Good location for sightseeing. **Cons:** Basic decor, not on the ocean. ⊠*Praça 2 de Julho 02, Campo Grande, 40080-121* ☎*071/2105–2000* ⊕*www.tropicalhotel. com.br* ⟿*275 rooms* ⌂*In-room: refrigerator, safe. In-hotel: restaurant, room service, bar, pools, public Internet, concierge, parking (fee)* ▤*AE, DC, MC, V.*

$ ▥**Blue Tree Towers Salvador.** Although it doesn't have the best sea views, the local link of the Blue Tree chain has easy access to the historic center and the beaches. Rooms with king-size beds and other facilities are very comfortable. From here it's a short distance to the many restaurants and bars of the Barra district. **Pros:** Close to everything, nice amenities. **Cons:** Lacking views. ⊠*Rua Monte Conselho 505, Rio Vermelho, 41940-370* ☎*071/2103–2233* ⊕*www.bluetree.com.br* ⟿*200 rooms* ⌂*In-room: safe, refrigerator, dial-up. In-hotel: restaurant, room service, pool, gym, laundry service, public Internet, public Wi-Fi, parking (fee)* ▤*AE, DC, MC, V* ⍟BP.

$ ▥**Fiesta Bahia Hotel.** In the city's financial district beside the convention center, the Fiesta Bahia has amenities for business travelers that distinguish it from its competitors. It's also good for vacationing families, as there are nice touches like a pair of swimming pools. The accommodations are standard-issue chain hotel rooms. **Pros:** Good for business travelers. **Cons:** Not in the most scenic location. ⊠*Av. Antônio Carlos Magalhães 711, Itaigara, 41125-000* ☎*071/3352–0000* ⊕*www.fiesta hotel.com.br* ⟿*236 rooms, 8 suites* ⌂*In-room: safe, refrigerator, dial-up. In-hotel: restaurant, room service, bar, pools, gym, parking (no fee)* ▤*AE, DC, MC, V.*

$ ▥**Hotel Bahia do Sol.** The decor might be simple, but this budget hotel has a prime location close to museums and historic sights. Some rooms have a partial ocean view, but those in the back are quieter. Zarzuela

8

is somewhat eclectic, but you can certainly find some Bahian dishes on the menu. **Pros:** Good location for sightseeing. **Cons:** Basic decor, not the best views. ⊠ *Av. 7 de Setembro 2009, Corredor da Vitória, 40080-002* ☎*071/3338–8800* ⊕*www.bahiadosol.com.br* ↩*90 rooms, 2 suites* ⌂*In-room: refrigerator. In-hotel: restaurant, bar, parking (no fee)* ⊟*AE, DC, MC, V.*

$ **Hotel Catharina Paraguaçu.** Rooms and suites in this 19th-century
Fodor'sChoice   mansion are small but comfortable. If you're looking for space, ask
★   for one of the six split-level suites. Extra attention is devoted to the decor, with pottery and embroidery from local artisans. The pousada is family-run and in a neighborhood of many restaurants and bars. It has one room for guests with disabilities, including wheelchair access, unusual for a small hotel. **Pros:** Family-friendlly environment, near dining and nightlife. **Cons:** Not many amenties. ⊠*Rua João Gomes 128, Rio Vermelho, 41950-640* ☎*071/3334–0089* ⊕*www.hotelcath arinaparaguacu.com.br* ↩*31 rooms* ⌂*In room: refrigerator. In-hotel: public Internet, no elevator* ⊟*AE, MC, V* ❍*BP.*

$ **Ondina Apart Hotel Residência.** In the resort hotel district, a short drive
☾   from the sights, restaurants, and nightlife of downtown, this beachfront complex has simple modern furniture. Business travelers and families opt for this hotel when they're staying in Salvador for extended periods, as all rooms have small kitchens. **Pros:** Short drive to downtown, pleasant rooms, family-friendly environment. **Cons:** Not walking distance to sites. ⊠*Av. Oceânica 2400, Ondina, 40170-010* ☎*071/3203–8216* ⊕*www.ondinaapart.com.br* ↩*100 rooms* ⌂*In-room: safe, kitchen, dial-up. In-hotel: restaurant, bar, tennis court, pool, gym, laundry service, parking (fee)* ⊟*AE, DC, MC, V.*

$ **Pestana Bahia.** This hotel built atop a seaside cliff in the trendy Rio Vermelho neighborhood has carved itself a tradition of excellent services for tourists and conventioneers. It was thoroughly renovated a few years ago, so the rooms are completely modern. It's a short walk from the neighborhood's bars and restaurants. **Pros:** Close to nightlife, comfortable rooms. **Cons:** Can be crowded, impersonal feel. ⊠*Rua Fonte de Boi 216, Rio Vermelho, 40170-010* ☎*071/2103–8000 or 800/26–6332* ↩*430 rooms* ⌂*In-room: safe, refrigerator. In-hotel: restaurant, bar, pool, gym, laundry service* ⊟*AE, DC, MC, V.*

¢   **Âmbar Pousada.** The highlight of this small and simple pousada is the service—the staff is attentive to your needs. Location is a draw, too, as here you are just a couple of streets away from the eclectic Barra neighborhood. If you're braving Salvador at Carnival time, the parade passes noisily two blocks away on Avenida Oceânica. The rooms are kept impeccably clean. There's a nice terrace and courtyard. **Pros:** Intimate setting, pleasant rooms. **Cons:** Can be loud during Carnival. ⊠*Rua Afonso Celso 485, Barra, 40140-080* ☎*071/3264–6956* ⊕*www. ambarpousada.com.br* ↩*5 rooms* ⌂*In-room: no TV. In-hotel: public Internet* ⊟*MC, V* ❍*BP.*

NIGHTLIFE & THE ARTS

Pelourinho is filled with music every night and has more bars and clubs than you can count. Most bars serve food as well as drink. Activity also centers along the seashore, mainly at Rio Vermelho and between the Corsário and Piatã beaches, where many hotels have bars or discos.

Salvador is considered by many artists as a laboratory for the creation of new rhythms and dance steps. As such, this city has an electric performing arts scene. See the events calendar published by Bahiatursa or check local newspapers for details on live music performances as well as rehearsal schedules. In Pelourinho, groups often have practices open to the public on Tuesday and Sunday nights.

> ### THE SAMBA MAN
>
> Dorival Caymmi, one of the greatest Brazilian composers, was born in Salvador in 1914. With his beautiful Bahian sambas, Caymmi brought the sights, smells, and sounds of his native state into the popular imagination. One of his most beautiful compositions is called "Minha Jangada Vai Sair Pro Mar" ("My Boat Will Go Out to Sea").

NIGHTLIFE

After dark, Praça Terreiro de Jesus is a hot spot, especially on Tuesday and Saturday nights, when stages are set up here and at other squares around the city for live performances. This plaza is especially popular with tourists because it has been painted, cleaned up, and gentrified. Although there may be impromptu musical performances any night, you can always count on it on Tuesday.

BARS There are many bars in the Pelourinho area, as well as on the beachfront avenues. The shopping complex Aeroclube Plaza on Avenida Otávio Manguabeira has also become quite popular among the young crowd, with bars, restaurants, and nightclubs.

Sancho Panza (⊠ *Av. Otávio Mangabeira 122, Pituba, 41830-050* ☎ *071/3248–3571*) is a great place for sangria and typical Spanish fare. Sooner or later you must have a *caipirinha* (lime and sugarcane-liquor cocktail) at **Cantina da Lua** (⊠ *Largo Terreirro de Jesus 2, Pelourinho, 41820-020* ☎ *071/33241–7383*).

DANCE SHOWS There are Afro-Brazilian dinner shows at the **Solar do Unhão** (⊠ *Av. do Contorno 08, Comércio, 40025-060* ☎ *071/3321–5551*). The unforgettable Afro-Bahian show at the **Teatro Miguel Santana** (⊠ *Rua Gregório de Matos 49, Pelourinho, 40025-060* ☎ *071/3322–1962* ⊕ *www.bale folcloricodabahia.com.br*) has the town's best folkloric dance troupes. This is an entertaining way to learn about Afro-Brazilian culture.

NIGHTCLUBS **Rock in Rio Café** (⊠ *Av. Otávio Mangabeira 6000, Boca do Rio, 41740-000* ☎ *071/3461–0300*) is in the shopping-and-entertainment complex Aeroclube Plaza. The atmosphere here is more like Miami than Salvador.

THE ARTS

CARNIVAL
REHEARSALS

Afro-Brazilian percussion groups begin Carnival rehearsals—which are really more like creative jam sessions—around midyear. **Associação** ★ **Cultural Bloco Carnavalesco Ilê Aiyê** (⊠*Rua do Curuzu 288, Liberdade, 40365-000* ☎*071/3256–1013*), which started out as a Carnival bloco, has turned itself into much more in its 34-year history. It now has its own school and promotes the study and practice of African heritage, religion, and history. Public practices are held every Saturday night at Forte de Santo Antônio, and should not be missed.

★ **Olodum,** Salvador's best-known percussion group, gained international fame when it participated in Paul Simon's "Rhythm of the Saints" tour and recordings. The group has its own venue, the **Casa do Olodum** (⊠*Rua Maciel de Baixo 22, Pelourinho, 40026-240* ☎*071/3321– 5010* ⊕*www.narin.com/olodum*). Olodum also has a percussion school, **Escola Criativa Olodum** (⊠*Rua das Laranjeiras 30, Novo Horizonte, 41218-042* ☎*071/3322–8069*).

MUSIC,
THEATER &
DANCE

Teatro Casa do Comércio (⊠*Av. Tancredo Neves 1109, Pituba, 41820- 021* ☎*071/3273–8732*) hosts music performances and some theatrical productions. Classical and popular music performances, operas, and plays are all held at **Teatro Castro Alves** (⊠*Praça 2 de Julho s/n, Campo Grande, 40080-121* ☎*071/3339–8014* ⊕*www.tca.ba.gov.br*), Salvador's largest theater. The **Teatro Associação Cultural Brasil-Estados Unidos** (⊠*Av. 7 de Setembro 1883, Vitória, 40080-002* ☎*0800/284–2828 or 071/3337–4395* ⊕*www.acbeubahia.org.br*) has contemporary and classical music, dance, and theater performances by Brazilian and international artists.

SPORTS & THE OUTDOORS

CAPOEIRA

You can see capoeira in almost any beach or park in Salvador and Bahia. Some places are traditional gathering points for practitioners. One such place is the parking lot of Forte de Santo Antônio on Tuesday, Thursday, and Saturday early evenings. Two schools practice here, of which the Grupo de Capoeira Angola is the best known.

There are several capoeira schools in Salvador for anyone who wants to learn the art that trains both the mind and body for combat. Mestre Bamba (Rubens Costa Silva) teaches at **Bimba's Academy** (⊠*Rua das Laranjeiras 01, Pelourinho, 40025-230* ☎*071/3322–0639*). A single hour-long class costs R$15.

SOCCER

Bahia and Vitória are the two local teams that play in the first division of the Brazilian soccer federation. There are games year-round in the **Estádio Manuel Barradas** (⊠*Av. Artemio Valente s/n, Tancredo Neves, 41207-400*) Advance tickets sales are available, but games hardly ever sell out. The best seats are in the higher-priced *arquibancada superior* (upper-level section).

CLOSE UP

Carnival in Salvador: Brazil's Wildest Party

Forget Rio's commercialized spectacle. The most accessible and authentic large-scale Carnival in Brazil is in Salvador—an explosion of hundreds of thousands of revelers, all dancing in frenzied marching crews, called *blocos*, or hopping parade-side as *pipoca*, or popcorn. At the center of each bloco is the *trio elétrico*, a creeping stage whose towering speakers blare walls of energetic, ribcage-rattling *axé* music—a danceble and distinctly Bahian mix of African rhythms, rock, and reggae. Top pop stars like Daniela Mercury or Ivete Sangalo perform their party-stoking Carnival favorites.

To be part of the action, and to avoid the hordes of pickpockets that are unfortunately part of the "excitement," join a bloco, which is roped off from the general public. Each bloco has its own all-purpose beer, first-aid, and toilet truck—and you'll have instant camaraderie with your crewmates. (A warning: it's not unusual for women to be kissed by strangers. It might sound feeble, but having a male friend close may deter unwanted groping.)

Favorite bloco themes include Egyptian-garbed percussion band Olodum, and axé acts Are Ketu and Timbalada. Alternatively, there's the peaceful Filhos de Ghandy (Children of Ghandi),

a white sea of robes and jeweled turbans. Once you've chosen your bloco, all you have to do is lay down upward of US$100 to buy a crew-specific T-shirt, called an *abadá*, purchased at Central do Carnival kiosks, or at markets from scalpers.

Blocos travel along specific *circuitos* (routes) through the city. Seaside Dodô (about 1 mi, 5 hours) is the route of choice for Carnival's biggest stars and begins at Farol da Barra. Osmar (about 2 mi, 6 hours), beginning near Campo Grande, is large and traditional. The less-populated and calmer Batatinha, which clings to historic Pelourinho, allows an intimate look at smaller percussionist groups and is popular with families. Prepare by checking the maps at ⊕ *www. carnaval.salvador.ba.gov.br* (click on Mapas do Circuito).

Add to all of these fine reasons to patronize Salvador's Carnival the more than 20 pre-Carnival warm-up celebrations and its honor in the *Guinness Book of World Records* as the biggest street carnival on the planet, and it's hard to argue that, come Carnival season, true partiers shouldn't be anywhere but Salvador.

–Joe Gould

SHOPPING

AREAS & MALLS

Aeroclube Plaza Shopping (⊠*Av. Otavio Mangabeira 6000, Jardim Armação, 41706-900* ☎*071/3461–0300*) is a beachfront mall with live music venues, cinemas, restaurants, and jewelry shops. It has the only bowling alley in Salvador.

For paintings, especially art naïf, visit the many galleries in the Cidade Alta and around the **Largo do Pelourinho** (⊠*Rua Alfredo de Brito at Ladeira do Taboão, 40140-141*). **Shopping Barra** (⊠*Av. Centenário 2992, Barra, 40149-900*) is the best shopping mall in Salvador. It isn't far from the historic center and has cinemas, restaurants, and local

Capoeira: The Fight Dance

Dance and martial arts in one, *capoeira* is purely Brazilian. The early days of slavery often saw fights between Africans from rival tribes who were thrust together on one plantation. When an owner caught slaves fighting, both sides were punished. To create a smoke screen, the Africans incorporated music and song into the fights. They brought a traditional *berimbau* string-drum instrument (a bow-shape piece of wood with a metal wire running from one end to the other, where there's a hollow gourd containing seeds) to the battles. Tapped with a stick or a coin, the berimbau's taut wire produces a throbbing, twanging sound whose rhythm is enhanced by the rattling seeds. Its mesmerizing reverberations were accompanied by singing and chanting, and when the master appeared, the fighters punched only the air and kicked so as to miss their opponents.

The fights have been refined into a sport that was once practiced primarily in Bahia and Pernambuco but has now spread throughout Brazil. Today's practitioners, called *capoeristas,* swing and kick—keeping their movements tightly controlled, with only hands and feet touching the ground—to the beat of the berimbau without touching their opponents. The goal is to cause one's opponent to lose concentration or balance. Capoeira is traditionally performed in a *roda* (wheel), which refers both to an event of continuous capoeira and to the circle formed by players and instrumentalists. Strength, control, flexibility, artistry, and grace are the tenets of capoeira. In any exhibition the *jogadores,* or players, as they are called—with their backs bending all the way to the floor and their agile foot movements (to avoid an imaginary knife)—as well as the compelling music, make this a fascinating sport to watch.

boutiques, as well as branches of the major Rio, São Paulo, and Minas Gerais retailers. Many hotels provide transportation to the mall, but you can also take the Rodoviária bus line.

SPECIALTY STORES

ART Top local artists (many of whom use only first names or nicknames) including Totonho, Calixto, Raimundo Santos, Joailton, Nadinho, Nonato, Maria Adair, Carybé, Mário Cravo, and Jota Cunha have their crafts and paintings at **Portal das Artes** (⊠*Rua Gregório de Matos 20, Pelourinho, 40025-060* ☎*071/3222–9890*).

Livraria Siciliano (⊠*Shopping Barra, Av. Centenário 2992, 2nd fl., 40149-900* ☎*071/3332–3209*) is the local branch of a major Brazilian chain that has lots of foreign-language books and international magazines.

HANDICRAFTS Of Salvador's state-run handicrafts stores, the best is the **Instituto de Artesanato Visconde de Mauá** (⊠*Praça Azevedo Fernandes 2, Porto da Barra, 40140-110* ☎*071/3264–5440* ⊠*R. Gregorio de Mattos 27, Pelourinho, 40025-080* ☎*071/3321–5501*). Look for exquisite lace, musical instruments of African origin, weavings, and wood carvings. **Kembo** (⊠*Rua João de Deus 21, Pelourinho, 40025-080* ☎*071/3322– 1379*) carries handicrafts from Brazilian native peoples, such as the

Pataxós, Karajá, Xingú, Tikuna, Caipós, and Yanomami.

JEWELRY & GEMSTONES

Bahia is one of Brazil's main sources of gems, and amethysts, aquamarines, emeralds, and tourmalines are the most abundant. Prices for these stones are usually cheaper here than elsewhere in Brazil, but you should have an idea of what stones are worth before you enter a shop. The well-known, reputable **H. Stern** (⊠ *Ave. Centenario 2992, Chame Chame, 40155-150* ☎ *071/3264–3599*) has several branches in Salvador, most of them in malls and major hotels. **Bahia Preciosa** (⊠ *Rua Portas do Carom 17, Pelourinho, 40025-040* ☎ *071/3242–5218*), the city's most famous jeweler, allows you to peer through a window into the room where goldsmiths work.

> **MEET DONA FLOR**
>
> Prepare yourself for Bahia by reading *Dona Flor and Her Two Husbands,* a Jorge Amado novel steeped in the folklore of Bahia. At the center of the story is a passionate young widow who keeps having to choose between her new husband and the ghost of her dead husband. Sonia Braga starred in a film that was shot in the streets of Salvador.

SIDE TRIPS FROM SALVADOR

Although attractions in Salvador can keep you entertained for more than a week, there are great places for a one- or two-day break in more relaxing environs. On a two-day tour to Morro de São Paulo, you can enjoy the near-pristine beaches and tropical forest. Or plan a day trip to Praia do Forte or the other northern beaches; they're less crowded and more beautiful than those in and near Salvador.

MORRO DE SÃO PAULO

On Ilha de Tinharé, just south of Itaparica, Morro de São Paulo is the most popular place on the island, most of which is covered with thick Atlantic Forest protected by a state park. Private cars are not allowed here; you can walk to the beaches, take tractor-pulled trolleys, or hire a small boat to "beach-hop" about the island.

TO & FROM

To get here from Salvador, take either a *lancha* (small boat carrying up to five passengers) or larger *catamarã* (catamaran) from Salvador's Terminal Marítimo. Lanchas and catamarãs leave daily from 8 AM to 2 PM, and return from Morro de São Paulo from noon to 4 PM. Fares range from R$50 to R$60 and include food, drinks, and live music.

A handful of small flight operators, including AeroStar and Adey, have service to Morro de São Paulo from Salvador. The 20-minute flight costs about $R180. There's only a landing strip at Morro de São Paulo.

ESSENTIALS

Airline Contacts Adey (☎ *071/3652–1312*).

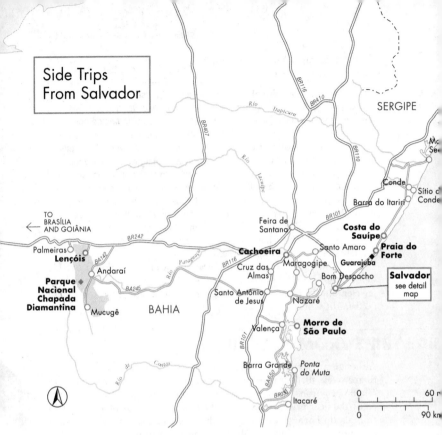

Banks & Currency Exchange There are no banks in Morro de São Paulo and only one ATM, so get plenty of cash before you arrive

SAFETY & PRECAUTIONS

Do not keep your belongings unattended when you're on the beach.

WHAT TO SEE

Popular beaches dot the 40-km (25-mi) Atlantic side of Tinharé. Starting at the village of Morro de São Paulo, beaches begin with Primeira (First) and go on to Segunda, Terceira, and so forth. Waters are calm thanks to the coral reef just off the surf, whose abundant marine life (mostly in the form of small fish) makes scuba diving or snorkeling worthwhile. The number of tourists nearly triples from December to February, when Brazilians on their summer vacation fill the pousadas for festival and Carnival season. The southernmost beaches near Boca da Barra are usually quieter even during peak season. The government has begun to charge a R$6.50 tourism tax per person.

NORTH COAST BEACHES

To reach some of Bahia's more pristine and less crowded beaches, head north of Salvador on the Estrada do Coco (Coconut Road), leaving the baroque churches and colonial dwellings behind in favor of miles of quiet road lined with coconut palms.

TO & FROM

At the fishing village and turtle haven of Praia do Forte, take the Linha Verde (Green Line) up the coast. Buses to this string of beaches are readily available, but the convenience of having your own car is justified here.

WHAT TO SEE

Barra do Jacuípe. A river runs down to the ocean at this long, wide, pristine beach lined with coconut palms. There are beachfront snack bars. The Santa Maria/Catuense bus company operates six buses here daily. ✉ *40 km (25 mi) north of Salvador, 42820-000.*

Guarajuba. With palm trees and calm waters banked by a reef, this is the nicest beach of them all, though it's lined with condos. The bus to Barra do Jacuípe continues on to Guarajuba, which has snack kiosks, fishing boats, surfing, dune buggies, and a playground. ✉ *60 km (38 mi) north of Salvador, 42820-991.*

PRAIA DO FORTE

72 km (45 mi) northeast of Salvador.

Praia do Forte was first settled in 1549 by Garcia D'Avila, a clerk for the Portuguese crown. For reasons lost in the mists of history, Garcia D'Avila had acquired a fortune and became a landowner. With foresight he introduced cattle ranching and coconut-palm cultivation in the area. To protect the coast, a medieval-style castle was built that served as a fort—hence the town's name, which means "Fortress Beach." All that remains from the castle is just the outer walls, and there isn't too much to see, but it now has a helpful visitor center. Today the area's biggest attraction is the headquarters of a sea-turtle preservation center called Projeto Tamar. Instead of earning their living by killing turtles for meat, eggs, and shells, local fishermen are now paid to protect them. Jobs have also been provided by the bars, restaurants, pousadas, and shops that now line the three brick-paved streets. Almost everything in town is on the main street, Alameda do Sol.

TO & FROM

To reach Praia do Forte by car from Salvador, take the Estrada do Coco (BA 099) north and follow the signs. From there on, it's called Linha Verde (Green Line), to Costa do Sauípe and the northern beaches all the way to the Sergipe border. Linha Verde has hourly bus service from Salvador to Praia do Forte. The two-hour trip on the un-air-conditioned bus costs R$8.

ESSENTIALS

Internet Café Connect (⊠Alameda das Estrelas s/n, 48280-000 ☎71/3676–
0431).

Taxi Valdécio Franco (☎71/9616–2712).

Visitor & Tour Info Centrotour (⊠Av. Do Farol, Térreo Praia do Forte, 48280-000
☎71/3676–1091 ⊕www.centrotour.com.br) is one of the area's most respected
tour companies. It specializes in ecotourism packages.**Bahia Adventure** (⊠Km 76,
Rodovia BA 099, Costa do Sauípe, Mata de São João, 48280-000 ☎712104–8600
⊕www.bahiaadventure.com) has jeep tours, white-water rafting, and other adventure treks. **Fly and Fun** (☎071/3676–1540 ⊕www.flyandfun.com.br) has charter
flights along the coast. **Odara Turismo** (⊠Praia do Forte Eco Resort Hotel, Praça
da Música s/n, Praia do Forte, Mata de São João, 48280-000 ☎071/676–1080)
has four-wheel-drive tours, horseback-riding excursions, and hiking trips.

WHAT TO SEE

Fodor'sChoice
★
Five of the seven surviving sea-turtle species in the world roam and
reproduce on Brazil's Atlantic coast, primarily in Bahia. The headquarters of **Projeto Tamar,** established in 1980, has turned what was once a
small, struggling fishing village into a tourist destination with a mission—to save Brazil's giant sea turtles and their hatchlings. During
the hatching season (September through March), workers patrol the
shore at night to locate nests and move eggs or hatchlings at risk of
being trampled or run over to safer areas or to the open-air hatchery
at the base station. Here you can watch adult turtles in the swimming
pools and see the baby turtles that are housed in tanks until they can
be released to the sea. Eighteen other Tamar base stations on beaches
along 1,000 km (621 mi) of coastline in five northeastern Brazilian
states protect about 400,000 hatchlings born each year. The headquarters also has educational videos, lectures, and a gift shop where
you can buy turtle-theme gifts. From December to February, you can
sign up for the "Tartaruga by Night" project to help release hatchlings
from the station hatchery to the sea. ⊠Alameda do Sol s/n, 48280-000
☎071/3676–1020 ⊕www.tamar.org.br ☞R$12 ☉Daily 9–7.

Swim or snorkel in the crystal-clear (and safe) waters of the **Papa
Gente,** a 3-meter-deep (10-foot-deep) natural pool formed by reefs at
the ocean's edge. Snacks are sold at little huts on the beach, but if
you're really hungry, a restaurant, in the Sobrado Da Vila pousada,
is nearby.

If you have a couple of days to visit Praia do Forte, spend one of them
on a jeep tour. These tours make their way through the **Reserva de Sapi-
ranga,** with 600 hectares (1,482 acres) of Atlantic Forest that contains
rare orchids and bromeliads. The reserve is a sanctuary for endangered
animals. White-water rafting is possible on the Rio Pojuca, which flows
through the park, and Lago Timeantube, where more than 187 species
of native birds have been sighted.

WHERE TO STAY & EAT

$$–$$$$ ✕**Sabor da Vila.** It isn't surprising that seafood fresh from the ocean is the specialty at this small modest restaurant on Praia do Forte's main street. After visiting Praia do Forte's attractions, stop here for a fish-and-shrimp moqueca. ⊠*Av. ACM 7, 48280-000* ☎*071/3676–1156* ▤*DC, MC, V.*

$$$$ ▥**Praia do Forte Eco Resort and Thalasso Spa.** Relax in a hammock and
      🕐 contemplate the sea from your private veranda at this sprawling beach-
Fodor's Choice front resort. You'll be within walking distance of the village in case you
      ★ need more action, but there's a full roster of activities available including horseback riding, volleyball, kayaking, sailing, and snorkeling. All rooms face the ocean, and a large part of the grounds still has the original Atlantic Forest vegetation that once covered the region. **Pros:** Close to everything, plenty of amenities, relaxing spa therapies. **Cons:** Restaurant open only to resort guests. ⊠*Av. do Farol s/n, Praia do Forte, Mata de São João, 48280-000* ☎*071/3676–4000 or 0800/71–8888* ⊕*www.ecoresort.com.br* ↪*293 rooms* △*In-room: safe, refrigerator. In-hotel: 2 restaurants, bars, tennis courts, pools, gym, beachfront, water sports, children's programs (ages 4–12), public Internet* ▤*AE, DC, MC, V* ⦿*MAP.*

$$ ✕▥**Pousada Sobrado Da Vila.** Leave your laptop and organizer at home—this laid-back pousada is a place to kick back and relax. Right on the main drag, this lodging has rooms that are plain but comfortable. The restaurant serves Bahian specialties. If you've never tried a *queijo de coalho frito* (roasted cheese ball), this is your chance. **Pros:** Relaxing environment, good restaurant. **Cons:** Few amenities. ⊠*Av. ACM 7, 48480-000* ☎*071/3676–1088* ⊕*www.sobradodavila.com.br* ↪*23 rooms* △*In-room: safe, refrigerator. In-hotel: restaurant, bar, public Internet* ▤*MC, V.*

SHOPPING

Pietra Rara (⊠*Av. ACM, 48280-000* ☎*71/3676–1437*) sells ceramics, wood carvings, paintings, clothing, and antiques.

COSTA DO SAUÍPE

114 km (71 mi) northeast of Salvador; 42 km (26 mi) northeast of Praia Do Forte.

An hour's drive north from Salvador along the Atlantic coast brings you to the Costa do Sauípe resort complex. Its five hotels, convention center, re-created local village with six pousadas, and sports center are all part of a 500-acre development in an environmental protection area bordered by rain forest.

If you prefer small lodgings to grand resorts, opt for a stay in one of the six pousadas in Vila Nova da Praia, a re-creation of a typical northeastern village, with cobblestone lanes lined with restaurants and bars. Vila Nova da Praia is also a great place to find souvenirs, especially ceramics.

TO & FROM

If you're driving, take the Linha Verde highway north from Salvador. Linha Verde buses to the village of Costa de Sauípe. If you're headed to the resort area, you'll have to take a taxi the rest of the way.

ESSENTIALS

Taxi Jossivaldo (☎ 71/9964–0826).

WHERE TO STAY

Regardless of where you stay in Costa do Sauípe, you have access to all the resort's amenities, including the 18-hole golf course, the tennis center, the equestrian center, water-sports facilities, and soccer field.

$$$$ 🏨 **Costa do Sauípe Conventions.** Replicas of early sailing ships hanging in the lobby hint at the hotel's themes: sailing and the discovery of Brazil. The Porão da Nau Pub & Club, off the lobby, is decorated in the style of a ship's hold, making it a unique place for drinks and dancing. If you prefer a cocktail in the sun, head for the enormous poolside bar. The main restaurant, the Île de France, serves fine French cuisine. Rooms look almost like the staterooms of an elegant ship with their dark-wood furniture and beige walls and drapes. Sliding-glass doors lead out to individual balconies with hammocks that overlook the gardens, with tall palm trees and the beautiful beach beyond. **Pros:** Lots of amenities, pleasant rooms. **Cons:** Impersonal feel. ✉ *Km 74, Rodovia BA 099, 48280-000* ☎ *071/2104–7600* ⊕ *www.costadosauipe.com.br* ➪ *404 rooms, 12 suites* ⟁ *In-room: safe, refrigerator. In-hotel: 3 restaurants, room service, bar, pool, gym, beachfront, water sports, bicycles, concierge, children's programs (ages 3–12), laundry service, airport shuttle* ▭ *AE, DC, MC, V* ⊚ *MAP.*

$$$$ 🏨 **Marriott Resort & Spa.** The view from your balcony is of the garden's swaying palm fronds and a clean sweep of beach. Inside your large room, the dark-wood furniture is offset by bright fabrics. Have a typical Brazilian meal at the poolside restaurant or retreat inside to the restaurant with an ocean view that serves Japanese tempura, Korean barbecue, and other Asian specialties. Dance the night away with the other guests in the ballroom. The spa has facial treatments and body treatments that include shiatsu massage and hot-stone therapy. **Pros:** Lovely garden, pretty beach. **Cons:** Chain-hotel feel. ✉ *Km 74, Rodovia BA 099, 48280-000* ☎ *071/2104–7000* ⊕ *www.marriott. com* ➪ *239 rooms, 17 suites* ⟁ *In-room: safe, refrigerator, dial-up. In-hotel: 3 restaurants, room service, bars, pool, gym, spa, beachfront, concierge, children's programs (ages 4–12), laundry service, airport shuttle* ▭ *AE, DC, MC, V* ⊚ *BP.*

$$$$ 🏨 **Renaissance Costa do Sauípe Resort.** The open-air lobby has a casual feel and a restaurant that looks out over sand dunes. If you opt to dine in the Mediterranean restaurant, your choices include specialties from Provence and southern Italy; some of the dishes are even cooked in a wood-burning oven. Tile-floor rooms are breezy and pleasant. With breakfast and dinner included and a beautiful beach right out your door, it's a nice place to stay. **Pros:** On the beach, lovely views. **Cons:** Internet access costs extra. ✉ *Km 74, Rodovia BA 099, 48280-000* ☎ *071/2104–7300* ⊕ *www.renaissancehotels.com/ssabr* ➪ *237* *rooms, 17 suites* ⚐*In-room: safe, refrigerator, Ethernet. In-hotel: 2 restaurants, room service, pool, gym, beachfront, concierge, laundry service, airport shuttle* ▭*AE, DC, MC, V* ⍟*MAP.*

$$$$ ⊡ **Sofitel Suites.** This hotel is evocative of the days when large coconut groves filled the Bahian landscape. Rooms are done in subdued shades of brown and gold, and wood and natural fibers are used throughout. From the lobby bar you can see the free-form pool, which surrounds small islands planted with coconut trees, and the Atlantic beyond. From the Tabuleiro bar-restaurant watch the chef prepare traditional Bahian dishes. The more sophisticated Casa Grande restaurant serves French and other international fare. **Pros:** Great landscaping, all rooms have verandas and hammocks. **Cons:** Chain-hotel feel. ✉*Km 74, Rodovia BA 099, 48280-000* ☎*071/2104–8000* ⊕*www.sofitel.com* ⌥*198 suites* ⚐*In-room: safe, dial-up. In-hotel: 2 restaurants, room service, bars, pool, children's programs (ages 4–12), laundry service, airport shuttle* ▭*AE, DC, MC, V* ⍟*BP.*

$$ ⊡ **Vila Nova da Praia.** The six pousadas in this planned village are nearly identical—all have the same amenities and are of equal quality—-though each has a different theme and number of rooms. All have access to an ecotourism agency, a car-rental agency, bars and restaurants, several kilometers of beaches, and shops selling clothing, jewelry, and handicrafts. Each has its own pool. **Pousada Gabriela** (20 rooms) resembles colonial architecture of downtown Ilhéus, south of Salvador. It's named after a character from a Jorge Amado novel. With its bright colors, **Pousada Carnaval** (39 rooms) captures the spirit of Bahia's pre-Lenten festivities. **Pousada do Agreste** (18 rooms) echoes the colonial architecture of the interior of northeastern Brazil. Art and antiques fill **Pousada da Torre** (28 rooms, 2 suites), which tries to re-create the Garcia D'Avila mansion at Praia do Forte. As its name implies, **Pousada do Pelourinho** (38 rooms) is a replica of a house in Salvador's historic district. **Pousada Aldeia** (20 rooms) makes you feel as if you're staying in a 16th-century coastal village. **Pros:** Pleasant rooms, interesting atchitecture. **Cons:** A sprawling complex. ✉*Km 74, Rodovia BA 099, 48280-000* ☎*071/2104–8200* ⊕*www.costadosauipe.com.br* ⚐*In-room: safe, refrigerator, Wi-Fi. In-hotel: pools, laundry service, airport shuttle, public Internet* ▭*AE, DC, MC, V* ⍟*BP.*

SPORTS & THE OUTDOORS

The **Costa do Sauípe Sports Complex** (☎*071/353–4544*) has an 18-hole golf course with a clubhouse, a tennis center, a water-sports center, an equestrian center, a soccer field, and squash courts. There's also a small "farm" where you can learn how to milk a cow or watch a hog burrow in the mud. Your hotel's staff can help you make arrangements to participate in either the active or spectator sports of your choice.

CACHOEIRA

109 km (67 mi) northwest of Salvador.

This riverside colonial town dates from the 16th and 17th centuries, when sugarcane was the economy's mainstay. It has been designated a national monument and is the site of some of Brazil's most authentic Afro-Brazilian rituals. After Salvador it has the largest collection of baroque architecture in Bahia. A major restoration of public monuments and private buildings was finished in 2003, and included revitalized streets and plazas in town. On an excursion to Cachoeira you can walk through the colorful country market and see architecture preserved from an age when Cachoeira shipped tons of tobacco and sugar downriver to Salvador.

> **OUR LADY OF GOOD DEATH**
>
> Devotion to Nossa Senhora da Boa Morte (Our Lady of Good Death) began in the slave quarters, where discussions on abolition of slavery took place. The slaves implored Our Lady of Good Death to end slavery and promised to hold an annual celebration in her honor should their prayers be answered. Brazil was the last country in the Western Hemisphere to abolish slavery, in 1888.

One of the most interesting popular events is the festival held by the Irmandade da Boa Morte (Sisterhood of Good Death). Organized by descendants of 19th-century slaves who founded an association of black women devoted to abolition, it's held on a Friday, Saturday, and Sunday in the middle of August.

TO & FROM

To drive from Salvador, take BR 324 north for about 55 km (34 mi), then head west on BR 420 through the town of Santo Amaro. The trip takes 1½ hours. Santana has daily service from Salvador to Cachoeira.

ESSENTIALS

Banks & Currency Exchange Banco Bradesco (⊠ *Aristides Milton 10, Centro, 44300-000*).

Bus Contacts Santana (☎ *071/3438–4303*).

WHAT TO SEE

The **Capela da D'Ajuda,** built in the 16th century, is one of the most remarkable examples of early baroque architecture in this part of Brazil. ⊠ *Largo D'Ajuda s/n, 44300-000* ☎ *No phone* 🖃 *R$3* ☉ *Inquire at Museu da Boa Morte to gain entrance to chapel.*

Museu da Boa Morte displays photos and ceremonial dresses worn by members of the Sisterhood of Our Lady of Good Death during their rituals and festivals. You may also meet some of the elderly but always energetic women whose ancestors protested slavery. The ladies at the museum will let you in to see the chapel and the church. ⊠ *Largo D'Ajuda s/n, 44300-000* ☎ *075/3425–1343* 🖃 *By donation* ☉ *Weekdays 10–1 and 3–5.*

WHERE TO STAY & EAT

¢ 🏨 **Pousada do Convento.** You can stay overnight in one of the large rooms or have a good lunch at this one-time Carmelite monastery that dates from the 17th century. The meeting room adjacent to the hotel main room was formerly a church. **Pros:** Recently remodeled rooms, beautiful colonial furniture. **Cons:** Simple accommodations, few amenities. ⊠*Praça da Aclamação s/n, 44300-000* ☎*075/3425–1716* ⤶*26 rooms* ♿*In-room: refrigerator. In-hotel: restaurant, pool* ▭*MC, V.*

LENÇÓIS

427 km (265 mi) west of Salvador; 1,133 km (704 mi) northeast of Brasília.

In 1822 a precious-stone frenzy began with the discovery of diamonds in riverbeds around the town of Mucugê. Hundreds of people hoping to make their fortune flooded into the region. This golden age lasted until late in the 1800s, when gems ran out. What remained were towns such as Lençóis, Igatu, and Mucugê, where cobblestone streets are lined with 19th-century colonial houses. Because of the historic and architectural importance of the region, buildings are being restored to give travelers a taste of what life was like in those heady days.

The largest community in the Chapada Diamantina area, as well as the gateway to Chapada Diamantina National Park, Lençóis arose from the hundreds of makeshift tents of white cotton fabric built by *garimpeiros* (gold- and precious stone–seekers). (*Lençóis* means "bedsheet"). The settlement quickly became an important trade hub for precious stones, attracting merchants from as far away as England, France, and Germany. Many fortunes were made, but the golden age ended in 1889, when most of the stones had been hauled away, and the city was forgotten.

The small town enjoyed a renaissance after it was designated a national monument in 1973. Several *sobrados* (houses) have been restored to their original grandeur. The *mercado municipal* (municipal market), where most of the diamonds were sold, has been completely renovated.

TO & FROM

When driving, the route to Chapada Diamantina from Salvador is fairly straighforward: take BR 342 west to Feira de Santana, then BR 242 to Lençóis. Both roads are in good condition, but expect irregular pavement in some spots. Real Expresso buses make the eight-hour trip from Salvador to Lençóis for about R$35, with departures at 11:30 PM daily and at 7 AM Tuesday, Thursday, and Saturday. Return is at 11:30 PM daily, with additional departures at 7:30 AM Monday, Wednesday, and Friday.

ESSENTIALS

Banks & Currency Exchange **Banco do Brasil** (⊠*Praça Horacio de Mattos 56, Centro, 46960-000).*

Bus Contacts **Estação Rodoviária** (⊠*Av. Senhor dos Passos s/n, Centro, 46960-000* ☎*075/3334–1595).* **Real Expresso** (☎*075/3334–1112 in Lençóis, 071/450–9310 in Salvador* ⊕*www.realexpresso.com.br).*

Emergencies & Medical Assistance **Farmacia Maciel** (⊠*Av. 7 de Setembro s/n, Centro, 46960–000* ☎*075/3334–1224).* **Municipal de Lençóis** (⊠*Rua Vai Quem Quer s/n, Centro, 46960-000* ☎*075/3334–1587).*

Internet **Café.com** (✉*Mercado Cultural, 46960-000* ☎*075/9114–7099*).

Taxi **Lençois Táxi** (☎*075/3334–1115*).

Visitor & Tour Info **Secretaria de Turismo** (✉*Mercado Cultural, Centro, 46960–000* ☎*075/3334–1117*) has a well-trained staff that will discuss tours and lodging and dining options. **LenTur Turismo Ecológico** (✉*Av. 7 de Setembro 10, Centro, 46960-000* ☎*075/3334–1224* ⊕*www.lentur.com.br*) pioneered trekking expeditions in the remote backcountry areas of the Chapada.

SAFETY & PRECAUTIONS

During festivals, when excessive drinking might occur, it's best to be on the safe side. Stay in groups and stick to the downtown area.

WHAT TO SEE

One of the region's most popular hiking trails runs along a section of Rio Lençóis called **Rio Serrano.** It's surrounded by exuberant forest, now protected as municipal park. The reddish-color water is due to organic matter from the forest floor. You can bathe and relax in several natural pools—they look a bit like hot tubs—formed on the rock-strewn river-bed. There are also three waterfalls along the way to a scenic overlook of the town and surrounding hills. The trailhead is about 1 km (½ mi) north of Lençóis, after the gate to Portal de Lençóis hotel. ✉*End of Rua Altina Alves.*

A steep 6-km (4 mi) cobblestone road connects the BA 142 highway with the community of **Igatú.** During the 19th century several thousand lived in this boomtown. Today the ruins of hundreds of abandoned homes can be explored. ✉*113 km (70 mi) south of Lençóis.*

A 30-minute hike takes you down to the mouth of the **Lapa Doce** cave. Along the easy walk through the cave you'll see a stunning collection of large stalagmites and stalactites. Because it's so accessible, Lapa Doce is especially recommended for children. ✉*From Lençóis, take BR 242 west 25 km (16 mi), then take BA 432, the road to Irecê for about 18 km (11 mi)* ☎*075/3229–4117* ✉*R$15* ⊙*Daily 9–6. .*

Torrinha. The cave's name, which means "Little Tower," refers to a rock formation outside the entrance. Here you can find a diverse collection of cave formations; besides the usual stalactites and stalagmites, arago-nite flowers, clusters of helectites, and chandeliers abound. There are three different guided tours ranging from 1 to 2½ hours that explore different sections of the cave. ✉*From Lençóis, take BR 242 west 25 km (16 mi), then take BA 432, the road to Irecê for about 13 km (8 mi)* ☎*075/3229–4117* ✉*R$20 per group, plus R$10 per person* ⊙*Daily 9–6.*

WHERE TO STAY & EAT

There are a growing number of hotels and pousadas in the area. Ranch-style accommodations, complete with hearty meals, appeal to many visitors.

$$ ✕ **Maria Bonita Casa de Massas.** Three sisters from Lençóis teamed up under the supervision of their Italian father to open this restaurant offering lasagna and other pasta dishes. Try the ravioli stuffed with ricotta and tomato sauce. ✉*Rua das Pedras s/n, 46960-000* ☎*075/8812–2186* ▤*No credit cards.*

$ ✕ **Neco's.** One of the oldest eateries in town, it's the place to taste some of the *garimpeiro* staples like *godó de banana,* a simple but tasty dish combining sun-dried meat and sliced green bananas. ✉*Praça Clarim Pacheco 15, 46960-000* ☎*075/3334–1179* ▤*No credit cards.*

$$–$$$ ✕▦ **Portal de Lençóis.** Overlooking Lençóis, this distinctive hotel has a Portuguese tile roof and stone facade. The stone-and-wood rooms and suites are the most luxurious choice in the region. West-facing accommodations have magnificent views of the forest-covered river valley. **Pros:** Interesting architecture, plush accommodations. **Cons:** Rather pricey. ✉*Av. Sr. dos Passos 1, 46960-000* ☎*075/3334–1154* ⊕*www.lencois.com.br* ⇌*44 rooms, 8 suites* ⌂*In-room: refrigerator. In-hotel: restaurant, bar, pool, no elevator, public Wi-Fi* ▤*AE, DC, MC, V.*

$–$$ ✕▦ **Hotel Canto das Águas.** One of the first hotels to open after the creation of the national park, Canto das Águas is inspired by the colonial architecture of the nearby historic district. Stone archways open to the garden that surrounds the main building. Nearby is the Rio Lençóis, whose soothing sound inspired the hotel's name, which means "Water Chant." Sleek rooms with balconies are equipped with modern amenities like flat-screen TVs and wireless Internet. **Pros:** Superb location, near the main plaza. **Cons:** Noisy during festivals. ✉*Av. Sr. dos Passos 1, 46960-000* ☎*075/3334–1154* ⊕*www.lencois.com.br* ⇌*44 rooms, 8 suites* ⌂*In-room: refrigerator, Wi-Fi. In-hotel: restaurant, bar, pool* ▤*AE, D, MC, V* ⦿*BP.*

$ ▦ **Pousada Casa da Geléia.** If you're seeking a home away from home, look no further. The English-speaking owners of this pousada will entertain you with tales of the history of the Chapada. The spacious white-walled rooms are clean and simple. The hearty breakfast will reveal the origin of the inn's name, Jelly House: dozens of homemade jams and jellys that include regional fruits such as umbú, seriguela, and cajú. The owner Zé Carlos is a bird-watching enthusiast, and has escorted tourists and biologists in tours of the Chapada. ✉*Rua General Viveiros 187, 46960-000* ☎*075/3334–1151* ⇌*6 rooms* ⌂*In-room: refrigerator. In-hotel: no elevator* ▤*AE, DC, MC, V* ⦿*BP.*

PARQUE NACIONAL CHAPADA DIAMANTINA

60 km (37 mi) west of Lençóis

The Chapada Diamantina (Diamond Highlands) in Central Bahia was once famous for its precious gems, but it's now recognized one of the country's best spots for ecotourism. In this chain of mountain ranges with an average altitude of 3,000 feet you'll find historic mining towns, rivers, and creeks with natural pools and waterfalls, and the largest number of caves in any part of Brazil.

Established in 1985, the 1,520-square-km (593-square-mi) national park is one of the most scenic places in Brazil. Here you can find crystal-clear creeks and rivers with abundant rapids and waterfalls and more than 70 grottos and caverns. There are also the tall peaks of the Sincorá Range, the highest point being Barbados Peak (2,080 meters, or 7,000 feet). The flora and fauna of the area, which include many varieties of cactus, orchids, and bromeliads and more than 200 bird species, have been the subject of two extensive studies by the Royal Botanical Gardens at Kew in England. The best time to visit the park is in the dry season from March to October, but expect high temperatures during the day (rarely above 36 C [100 F]). From May to July, temperatures might drop to near 10°C (45°F). The park does not have a visitor center, but there's a small ranger headquarters in the town of Palmeiras.

TO & FROM
The town of Lençóis by far the best gateway to the park.

ESSENTIALS
Visitor & Tour Info **Associação dos Condutores de Visitantes** (☎ 075/3334–1425), based in Lençóis, has certified guides to take you to the national park. Itineraries can be arranged to suit your interests and level of fitness.

SAFETY & PRECAUTIONS
Traversing the roads and especially the trails within the park definitely requires experienced guides, as trails are not well marked.

WHAT TO SEE
One of the most popular hikes in the national park leads to the country's tallest waterfall, 1,312-foot **Cachoeira da Fumaça** (Smoke Waterfall). Most of the falling water evaporates before reaching the ground, hence the odd name. A 4-km (2-mi) path from the village of Caeté-Açú takes you to the canyon's rim. The most scenic route is a longer trail that leaves Lençóis and reaches the gorge below the falls. The path goes past the impressive Capivara Falls. ⊠ *25 km (14 mi) west of Lençóis.*

Vale do Paty, one of the country's most scenic treks, takes you through towering sierras, through caves, and past waterfalls.The 70-km (43-mi) trail starts in Bomba, climbs to Candombá hills, follows a plateau at Gerais de Vieira, then goes alongside the steep Rio Paty toward Andaraí. ⊠ *20 km (12 mi) west of Lençóis.*

THE COCOA COAST

The best driving tour in this region is from Salvador south along the coast on the Estrada do Coco (Coconut Highway), picking up the Linha Verde (Green Highway) at Praia do Forte. Along the way are fishing villages, endless beaches, restaurants, and small hotels and pousadas, stretching to Mangue Seco at the Sergipe state border. Regional bus service to towns on the Cocoa Coast departs from Salvador's Terminal Rodoviário.

ILHÉUS

460 km (286 mi) south of Salvador.

In Brazil, Ilhéus (literally meaning "islanders") is synonymous with cocoa and Jorge Amado, one of Brazil's best-known 20th-century writers. Amado spent his childhood here, and the house he lived in is now a cultural center. Many of his world-famous novels are set in places in and around Ilhéus. Catedral de São Sebastião (San Sebastian Cathedral) is the heart of the central area—a plaza surrounded by colonial-period buildings akin to those in Pelourinho.

Ilhéus has many beaches and a small harbor at the mouth of the Rio Cachoeira. The palm-tree-covered beaches to the south of the city are the most scenic; you can get a good view of them from hills that surround the city, such as Morro de Pernambuco (Mount Pernambuco). Ilhéus experienced fast development earlier in the 20th century with the export of cacau (cocoa) from plantations nearby. The spread of a bacterial disease in the 1980s almost wiped out the plantations; in recent times improved agricultural techniques and higher cocoa market prices are leading the way to economic resurgence in the region, tourism being another of the main pillars. Throngs of tourists descend during Carnival—the street festivities last just as long as and are as lively as in Salvador.

TO & FROM

There are flights to Ilhéus from Rio de Janeiro, Saõ Paulo, and Salvador. AgiaBranca buses travel from Salvador to Ilhéus in about six hours. The cost is R$80 for a regular bus and R$125 for an executive bus. By car take Rodovia BR 101 south.

ESSENTIALS

Airport **Aeroporto Luiz Eduardo Magalhaes** (✉ *Rua Brigadeir o Eduardo Gomes s/n, Pontal, 45653-000* ☎ *73/3234–5256*).

Banks & Currency Exchange **Banco do Brasil** (✉ *Rua Marq. Paranaguá 112, Centro, 45653-000*).

Emergencies & Medical Assistance **Ambulance** (☎ *192*). **Police** (☎ *190*).

Taxi **Rádio Taxi** (☎ *73/3634–4213*).

Visitor & Tour Info **Associação de Turismo de Ilhéus** (✉ *Rodovia Ilhéus/Olivença km 2.5, 45690-000* ☎ *073/3234–1212*) has information on lodging and local attractions.

WHERE TO STAY

The Cocoa Coast has a few upscale resorts and hotels and many budget pousadas with good-quality, ranch-style accommodations, complete with hearty meals and a wide array of activities such as horseback riding, tennis, and swimming.

$$$$ **Transamérica Ilha de Comandatuba.** On an island with a giant coconut grove, this hotel has a private beach. The best accommodations are the bungalows—each has a balcony and a hammock. The many activities include fishing and various water sports. An airstrip has a weekly char-

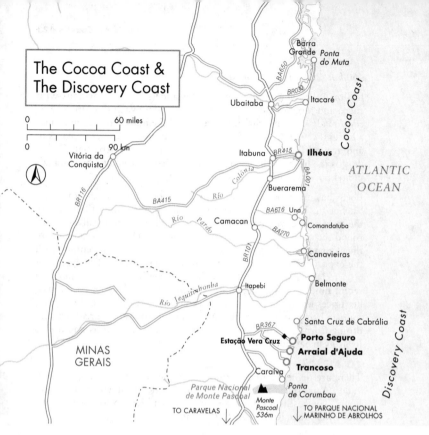

The Cocoa Coast &
The Discovery Coast

0   60 miles
0   90 km

ter jet landings from São Paulo. The hotel is 70 km (43 mi) south of Ilhéus. **Pros:** Beautiful building, nicely furnished rooms, lovely beach. **Cons:** Far from nightlife options. ✉*Ilha de Comandatuba s/n, 45690-000 Una* ☎*073/3686–1122 or 0800/012–6060* ⊕*www.transamerica. com.br* ⟿*239 rooms, 110 bungalows, 13 suites* ⚬*In-room: safe, refrigerator. In-hotel: 2 restaurants, room service, bars, golf course, tennis courts, pools, gym, spa, concierge, children's programs (ages 4–8), laundry service, airport shuttle* ▭*AE, DC, MC, V* ◍*FAP.*

$$ 🏨 **Ecoresort Tororomba.** This small beachfront resort is beside a beach
🕃 with turquoise waters. The resort's main attractions are the sports facilities, such as the climbing wall, sea kayaks, and mountain bikes. The hotel is 25 km (16 mi) south of Ilhéus. **Pros:** Gorgeous beach, inexpensive rates. **Cons:** Far from nightlife options. ✉*Rod Canavieras, 45653-970 Oliveça* ☎*073/3269–1200* ⊕*www.tororomba.com. br* ⟿*86 rooms, 4 bungalows* ⚬*In-room: safe, refrigerator, Wi-Fi. In-hotel: restaurant, room service, bars, tennis courts, pool, gym, beachfront, concierge, children's programs (ages 10–14), laundry service, airport shuttle* ▭*AE, MC, V* ◍*MAP.*

CLOSE UP

Beach Savvy

■ As a rule, the farther away from the downtown area, the better the beach in terms of water cleanliness and number of people, especially on weekends.

■ Beaches in Bahia, as in most of Brazil, tend not to have facilities like bathrooms or showers.

■ Pickpocketing and minor theft can be a problem. Bring as few items to the beach as possible, and just enough money for the day. Never leave anything unattended.

■ Vendors, no matter what age or gender, tend to be aggressive and overly persistent in Bahia, sometimes bordering on harassment. You might have to say no many times before they move on. Be patient or look for police officers (there are usually several on duty at Centro Historico for this reason alone).

■ Larger cities such as Salvador, Ilhéus, and Porto Seguro have quick and comfortable public transportation to beaches, like the ônibus executivo (executive bus; a minibus or van, usually labeled ROTEIRO DAS PRAIAS).

■ Be careful when entering the water for the first time—a few steps in can put you in deep waters.

■ Be aware of rock outcroppings and coral reefs that can cut your feet.

■ If you plan to snorkel, bring your own gear. Rentals are not always available.

■ Food and drink are available at almost every beach, except those you have to hike to. However, if you're squeamish about eating food from a beach vendor, bring your own.

8

THE DISCOVERY COAST

Protected areas where you can experience nature in its pristine state form the backdrop to the birthplace of Brazil.

PORTO SEGURO

730 km (453 mi) south of Salvador.

Not too long ago, Porto Seguro (Safe Harbor) was a serene fishing village. Now it's one of the prime tourist destinations in the country, with international flights from several Europeans cities. Hotels, inns, and restaurants have risen to please nearly every need or taste.

Porto Seguro has an intense atmosphere comparable only to Salvador in Bahia. Picture a city whose main drag is called "Passarela do Alcool" (Booze Walkway). Carnival is a major event here, drawing hundreds of thousands of tourists. The beaches north of the city, such as Mutá, are recommended for those looking for calmer grounds.

TO & FROM

From Salvador, Águia Branca offers daily overnight bus service to Porto Seguro (11 hours, R$120). There are daily flights from Salvador, Rio de Janeiro, and Saõ Paulo on Tam and GOL.

ESSENTIALS

Airport Aeroporto Porto Seguro (✉ *Estr. Aeroporto, 45810-000* ☎ *73/3288–1880*).

Banks & Currency Exchange Banco do Brasil (✉ *Av. Dos Navegantes 22, Centro, 45810-000* ☎ *no phone*).

Bus Contacts Águia Branca (☎ *071/3460–4400 or 0800/725–1211*). **Rodoviária** (✉ *Rua José Borges Souza 35, 45810-0000* ☎ *no phone*).

Emergencies & Medical Assistance Drogaria Plantão (✉ *Av 22 Abril, 18 lj 3, Centro, 45810-000* ☎ *73/3268–3370*). **Pronto Socorro** (✉ *Rua Cova Moca 551, Centro, 45810-000* ☎ *no phone*).

Taxi Porto Táxi (☎ *73/3288-1010*).

Visitor & Tour Info Glória Agênicia de Viagens e Turismo (✉ *Av 22 Abril 400 lj. 10, Centro, 45810-000* ☎ *73/3288-0758*) arranges trips in the region.

WHAT TO SEE

Fodor's Choice ★ One of the most biodiverse places on the planet, **Estação Vera Cruz** is a 6,000-hectare nature preserve. This is the largest private Atlantic Forest protected area in Brazil, owned by one of the world's largest paper pulp mills. The visitor center introduces you to the ecology of the area. From here knowledgeable guides lead you on a 2-km (1.2-mi) trail through the forest. Highlights are the *pau-brasil* (brazilwood) and *jatobá* (South American locust) trees, and birds—especially the colorful toucans and parrots. Call ahead to announce your visit. ✉ *BR 367, at Km 37.5, 45810-000* ☎ *073/9985–1808* 🎫 *Free* ⊗ *By appointment.*

WHERE TO STAY & EAT

$ ✕ **Recanto do Sossego.** This restaurant right on Mutá beach, is popular—on weekends you'll have to wait in line. But it's worth the wait. Fare is Italian—start with appetizers such fish carpaccio and move on to gnocchi with pesto sauce. ✉ *Praia do Mutá, Av. Beira Mar,* ☎ *073/3677–1266* ☲ *AE, D, MC, V.*

$$$ 🏨 **Hotel La Torre.** This hotel is popular with international visitors because of its location on quiet Mutá Beach. Rooms are run-of-the-mill, but spacious. The restaurant serves international fare with some Bahian dishes. **Pros:** All-inclusive property, on the beach. **Cons:** Basic rooms. ✉ *Praia do Mutá, Av. Beira Mar 9999, 45650-000* ☎ *073/3672–1243* ⊕ *www.latorreaparthotel.com.br* ⇱ *128 rooms* ⚿ *In-room: safe, kitchen, Ethernet. In-hotel: restaurant, room service, pool, gym, public Internet, airport shuttle* ☲ *AE, DC, MC, V.*

$$ 🏨 **Villagio Arcobaleno.** Porto Seguro's five-star choice is right on hip ★ Taperapuã Beach. Apartments are comfortable and decorated in tune with the tropical surroundings. The hotel maintains a large awning and wooden deck on the beach. **Pros:** Nicely furnished rooms, free Internet. **Cons:** A bit removed from the center. ✉ *Av. Beira Mar, at Km 6.5, 45810-000* ☎ *073/3679–1284* ⊕ *www.hotelarcobaleno.com. br* ⇱ *160 rooms, 5 suites* ⚿ *In-room: safe, refrigerator, Ethernet. In-hotel: restaurant, room service, bar, tennis courts, pools, gym, concierge, laundry service, public Internet, airport shuttle* ☲ *AE, DC, MC, V* ��⃝ *CP.*

CLOSE UP

Eating Bahian

When African slaves arrived in Bahia, they added coconut milk, palm oil, and hot spices into Portuguese and Indian dishes, transforming them into something quite new. Additional basic raw materials are lemon, coriander, tomato, onions, dried shrimp, salt, and hot chili peppers. Seafood is the thing in Bahia, and most regional seafood dishes are well seasoned, if not fiery hot. Bahia's most famous dish is *moqueca*, a seafood stew made with fish and/or shellfish, dendê oil, coconut milk, onions, and tomatoes, cooked quickly in a clay pot over a high flame. *Bobó* is equally tasty, but creamier version of moqueca, due to the addition of cassava flour. Other classics include *vatapá*, a thick puree-like stew made with fish, shrimp, cashews, peanuts, and a variety of seasonings; *caruru*, okra mashed with ginger, dried shrimp, and palm oil;

ximxim de galinha, chicken marinated in lemon or lime juice, garlic, and salt and pepper and then cooked with dendê and peanut oil, coconut milk, tomatoes, and seasonings; and *efo*, a bitter chicorylike vegetable cooked with dried shrimp. *Sarapatel* is a Portuguese dish, a stew of pig meat and inner organs, that has been incorporated seamlessly into Bahian cuisine.

A popular snack is *acarajé*, a pastry of *feijão fradinho* (black-eyed beans) flour deep-fried in dendê oil and filled with *camarão* (sun-dried shrimp) and *pimenta* (hot-pepper sauce). A variation is *abará*, peas or beans boiled in a banana leaf instead of fried. Note that palm oil is high in saturated fat and hard to digest; you can order these dishes without it. Restaurants in Bahia usually serve hot pepper sauce on the side of all dishes, which is unusual elsewhere in Brazil.

8

ARRAIAL D'AJUDA

The municipality of Arraial starts just across Rio Buranhém from Porto Seguro, a 10-minute ferry ride. The town is about 4 km (2.5 mi) south of the river. It was founded by Jesuits that arrived in 1549 with the Portuguese official Tomé de Souza, the first governor-general of Brazil. Its name is a tribute to Our Lady of Help, a much-revered saint in Portugal. The church and parish were the center of the Catholic church in Brazil for more than a century.

In the 1970s, laid-back Arraial d'Ajuda attracted Brazilian hippies, and then a slew of foreign adventurers moved here, giving the place an eclectic atmosphere and the nickname "Corner of the World."

Coroa Vermelha beach, to the south, is where the first mass in Brazil was celebrated. Other great beaches are Mucugê, Parracho, and Pitinga.

TO & FROM

Take one of the ferries that depart from Porto Seguro every half hour. The five-minute trip costs R$2.

ESSENTIALS

Emergencies & Medical Assistance **Ambulance** (☎*192*). **Police** (☎*190*).

WHERE TO STAY & EAT

$ ✕**A Portinha.** This popular buffet-style restaurant attracts many foreign visitors because of the many salad-bar and entrée options. The restaurant serves a different type of food every day, among them Brazilian, Italian, and Asian specialties. ⊠*Rua do Campo, 44816-000* ☎*073/3575–1289* ⊕*www.portinha.com.br* ☐*V.*

$$$$ ⊡**Arraial d'Ajuda Eco Resort.** This resort should be your choice if you're
☮ looking for a beachfront hotel with ample activities—besides lazing
★ on the beach. You can sail, windsurf, and dive; classes are offered for the neophyte. A water park next to the resort has many pools, water slides, and water games to keep children and adults entertained for the whole day. **Pros:** Water park admission included in rates. **Cons:** Can be crowded with day-trippers. ⊠*Ponta do Apaga Fogo, 45810-000* ☎*073/3575–8500* ⊕*www.arraialresort.com.br* ⇌*160 rooms* ☾*In-room: safe. In-hotel: restaurant, room service, bar, tennis court, pool, gym, concierge, children's programs (ages 4–10), laundry service, public Internet, airport shuttle* ☐*AE, DC, MC, V* ⦿*MAP.*

$ ⊡**Manacá Pousada Parque.** The main draw are the comfortable and well decorated rooms, all with king-size beds. Each room has a balcony with hammock. The pousada has a large garden surrounding its facilities, and is one step from the beach. **Pros:** Pleasant rooms, reasonable prices. **Cons:** No pool, no bar. ⊠*Estrada Arraial 500, 45816-000* ☎*073/3575–1442* ⊕*www.pousadamanaca.com.br* ⇌*20 rooms* ☾*In-rooms: safe, refrigerator. In-hotel: restaurant, public Internet, no elevator* ☐*MC, V* ⦿*CP.*

TRANCOSO

Smaller than its northern neighbors Arraial and Porto Seguro, Trancoso moves at a much slower pace. Founded by Jesuit missionaries in 1586, its first name was St. John Baptist of the Indians. Life here circles around the downtown plaza called "Quadrado" (the Square), where pedestrians have the right of way—no cars allowed. This is where everybody goes for shopping, dining, and people-watching. In recent years Trancoso has become a boomtown of sorts, and a haven for high-society Brazilians from São Paulo, especially. As a result, it now has several upscale developments, such as the Club Med and a US$90-million 18-hole golf course.

TO & FROM

Take a ferry to Arraial D'Ajuda. From here take a bus or van to Trancoso. If you're driving, take BA 101 from Arraial d'Ajuda to Trancoso.

ESSENTIALS

Emergencies & Medical Assistance **Ambulance** (☎*192*). **Police** (☎*190*).

Visitor & Tour Info **Trancoso Receptivo** (⊠*Rua Carlos Alberto Parracho, s/n, Centro, 45818-000* ☎*73/3668–1333*).

WHERE TO STAY & EAT

Compared to its northern neighbors, Trancoso has fewer lodging options, but you're sure to find a pousada that meets your taste. Or, if you prefer, go for the resort with a golf course. Some of the restaurants attract people from Porto Seguro and Arraial on weekends.

$$–$$$$ ✗**Capim Santo.** Capim Santo, right on the central square, is *the* place in Trancoso for seafood. Popular dishes are the fish fillet in shrimp sauce and the lobster. Servings are small. ⊠*Rua do Beco 55, 45818-000* ☎*073/3668–1122* ⊟*AE, MC, V* ⊗*Closed Sun.*

$$–$$$$ ✗**O Cacau.** Unique versions of Bahian dishes are served at this res-
★ taurant catering to international visitors. A must is the *arrumadinho,* with sun-dried meat, beans, cassava flour, and spicey *pico de gallo* sauce. ⊠*Praça São João 96, 45818-000* ☎*073/3668–1266* ⊟*MC, V* ⊗*Closed Mon.*

$$$$ 🏨**Club Med Trancoso.** Built on the beachfront hills south of Tranco-
★ so's village, this Club Med property went to great lengths to merge the sprawling resort with the landscape, with minimal environmental impact. Services are first-rate, as this is one of the higher ranking hotels in this worldwide chain. The spa is very good. The hotel is 6 km (4 mi) south of Trancoso. **Pros:** Beautiful hotel, great service. **Cons:** Not an intimate space. ⊠*Km 18, Estrada do Arraial, 45818-000* ☎*073/3575–8400* ⊕*www.clubmed.com.br* ↩*250 rooms, 50 suites* ⌂*In-room: refrigerator. In-hotel: 2 restaurants, room service, bars, tennis courts, pools, gym, spa, beachfront, concierge, laundry service, public Internet, airport shuttle* ⊟*MC, V* �❍*FAP.*

$$$–$$$$ 🏨**Pousada Etnia.** This small pousada is designed for the most demand-
FodorśChoice ing guest. The Italian owners also keep an art and antiques shop
★ nearby. Most of the furniture in the pousada's public areas comes from the shop. Each bungalow has a theme decor, like the Moroccan bunga-low. Among the draws here are the several massage options and artsy activities taught by art therapists that assist you with painting and pot-tery that are designed to help you reach the highest level of relaxation. **Pros:** Intimate feel, romantic spot, lovely furnishings. **Cons:** Not for families. ⊠*Av. Principal s/n, 45818-000* ☎*073/3668–1137* ⊕*www. etniabrasil.com.br* ↩*8 bungalows* ⌂*In-room: safe, refrigerator, Eth-ernet. In-hotel: restaurant, room service, pool, gym, public Internet, airport shuttle, no kids under 14, no-smoking rooms* ⊟*AE, DC, MC, V* ❍*FAP.*

$$ 🏨**Mata N'ativa Pousada.**Location is prime here, right on banks of Trancoso's river, three minutes from the beach and the downtown square. As the name implies—Mata Nativa means "native forest"—the pousada is virtually hidden under the canopy of Atlantic Forest. In the rooms, large beds with bedposts holding mosquito nets add to the rug-ged ambience. **Pros:** Pleasant rooms, ecofriendly environment. **Cons:** Rather rustic, very secluded. ⊠*Estrada do Arraial s/n, 45818-000* ☎*073/3668–1830* ⊕*www.matanativapousada.com.br* ↩*8 rooms* ⌂*In-room: DVD. In-hotel: gym* ⊟*AE, MC* ❍*CP.*

8

The Northeast

WORD OF MOUTH

"If you go to Recife, make sure and visit Olinda. Olinda is a wonderful colonial town, with cobble-stone streets, and a craft market."

—Tammy

"Recife has historical significance—the Golden Chapel is a sight to behold. I think the beach at Boa Viagem is better than Rio's and Olinda is a designated World Heritage site."

—CB

Updated by
Brad Weiss
& Anna
Katsnelson

LIKE THE WHOLE OF BRAZIL, the Northeast is a place of contrasts. Churches, villas, and fortresses in Recife, Natal, and Fortaleza tell the tale of Portuguese settlers who fought Dutch invaders and amassed fortunes from sugar. The beaches in and around these cities evoke Brazil's playful side and its love affair with sun, sand, and sea. West of the cities, the rugged, often drought-stricken *sertão* (bush) shows Brazil's darker side—one where many people struggle for survival. This warp and weave of history and topography is laced with threads of culture: indigenous, European, African, and a unique blend of all three that is essentially Brazilian.

Brazil's northeastern cities are experiencing a renaissance whose changes strike a balance between preservation and progress. Recife remains a place of beautiful waters, and nearby Olinda is still a charming enclave of colonial architecture—though bohemians have long since replaced sugar barons. On Ceará State's 570-km-long (354-mi-long) coast, Fortaleza continues to thrive against a backdrop of fantastic beaches with both new amenities and timeless white dunes. Although smaller and with a less storied past, Natal and the surrounding region are experiencing dizzying growth in tourism and other major industries.

ORIENTATION & PLANNING

ORIENTATION

The Northeast of Brazil includes the coastal states Bahia, Sergipe, Alagoas, Pernambuco, Rio Grande do Norte, Paraiba, Ceará, Maranhão and the landlocked state of Piauí. In the middle of this region are two large and vibrant cities, Recife and Fortaleza. The region, which covers an area of 1,554,257 square km (600,102 square mi), is home to a little less than a third of the population of the entire country.

RECIFE
In the state of Pernambuco, the sprawling city of Recife has a population of 3,646,204. It's bounded by the Beberibe and the Capibaribe rivers, which flow into the Atlantic. The city is known for the dozens of bridges linking its many boroughs. It is 2,392 km (1,486 mi) from Rio de Janeiro and 2716 km (1,688 mi) from São Paulo.

NATAL
The capital of Rio Grande do Norte, Natal has a population of 1,234,819. The city is surrounded by dunes on both sides, which gives it a unique appearance. It's 2,680 km (1,665 mi) from Rio de Janeiro and 3,011 km (1,871 mi) from São Paulo.

FORTALEZA
A thriving economic center, Fortaleza is the entry point for the state of Ceará. The population is 2,416,920, and is growing at a rapid pace. On the Atlantic Ocean, it's 2,808 km (1,744 mi) from Rio de Janeiro and 3,109 km (1,932 mi) from São Paulo.

TOP REASONS TO GO

■ Relaxing on some of Brazil's most beautiful beaches, with warm water all year and sand dunes high enough to ski down.

■ Wandering along the winding streets of Olinda as you gaze up at the beautiful colonial-era architecture.

■ Joining in the out-of-season Carnival celebrations in Natal and Fortaleza, two of the largest in Brazil.

■ The energetic Carnival in Olinda is considered to be among the best in Brazil, rivaling those in Rio and Salvador.

■ Try the amazing *carne de sol*, or sun-dried beef, as well as the other amazing Northeastern dishes using lobster, shrimp, and crabs.

FERNANDO DE NORONHA

An archipelago in the state of Pernambuco, the national marine park of Fernando de Noranha consists of 21 sparsely populated islands. About 354 km (219 mi) from the coast of Brazil, these islands have a population of roughly 2,000.

PLANNING

WHEN TO GO

High season corresponds to school vacations (July) and Carnival (late December–mid-March). Prices are better off-season, but if you've come to partake in festivities, Olinda has one of the best Carnival celebrations in the country. Also, the region has two of the most popular out-of-season Carnival celebrations: Carnatal in Natal, on the first weekend in December; and Fortal in Fortaleza, on the last weekend in July. Temperatures hover between about 20°C and 35°C (70°F and 95°F) year-round—temperatures get hotter the farther north you go. Rain is heaviest from May to August in Recife. In Fortaleza, March and April are the rainiest months. Natal sits at about 25°C (75°F) year-round; it sees much less rain than Fortaleza or Recife, but March–July are the wettest months.

ABOUT THE RESTAURANTS & CUISINE

The Northeast has little of the hustle and bustle you'll find in the southern cities of Rio de Janeiro and São Paulo. Residents enjoy a relaxed lifestyle, so in restaurants you'll find that casual attire is the norm. The many *batidas* (tropical fruit cocktails) are the highlights of the local cuisine, but many restaurants serve foods from other parts of Brazil. You'll also have many other options, including Italian, Dutch, and French favorites. Dinner begins around 8 PM. Most hotels include breakfast in the cost of your room. Restaurants not in hotels are usually not open for breakfast.

WHAT IT COSTS IN REAIS				
	¢	$	$$	$$$	$$$$
AT DINNER	under R$15	R$15–R$30	R$30–R$45	R$45–R$60	over R$60

Prices are per person for a main course at dinner or for a prix-fixe meal.

ABOUT THE HOTELS

Hotels are plentiful throughout the Northeast. Prices range from moderate to pricey, depending on season. Many hotels are sleek and modern, comparable to those you'd find in tourist destinations around the world. Pousadas tend to have a bit more charm and personalized service. Making reservations is advisable during high seasons. In low season better deals can often be negotiated at the front desk without a reservation.

WHAT IT COSTS IN REAIS				
	¢	$	$$	$$$	$$$$
FOR 2 PEOPLE	under R$125	R$125–R$250	R$250–R$375	R$375–R$500	over R$500

Prices are for a standard double room in high season, excluding tax.

GETTING AROUND

The distances between the cities in Northeast Brazil make flying the best way to get around. Even then, the times involved are not small. Flying to Fortaleza from Salvador, for example, takes 2½ hours. That's nothing compared to the 24 hours you'd spend on a bus. Once you've reached your destination, there's often no reason to rent a car. In Natal or Fortaleza you can easily get around by taxi or bus.

RECIFE

Just over 3.6 million people make their home in the capital of Pernambuco State. This vibrant metropolis 829 km (515 mi) north of Salvador has a spirit that's halfway between that of the modern cities of Brazil's south and of the traditional northeastern centers. It offers both insight on the past and a window to the future.

The city has beautiful buildings alongside the rivers that remind many visitors of Europe. Unfortunately, huge swathes of 19th-century buildings were razed to make way for modern structures. As a result, the center of the city has pockets of neocolonial splendor surrounded by gap-toothed modern giants. Today Recife is a leader in health care and design, among other things. It's also Brazil's third-largest gastronomic center—it's almost impossible to get a bad meal here.

Recife is built around three rivers and connected by 49 bridges. Its name comes from the *recifes* (reefs) that line the coast. Because of this unique location, water and light often lend the city interesting textures. In the morning, when the tide recedes from Boa Viagem Beach, the

The Northeast Coast

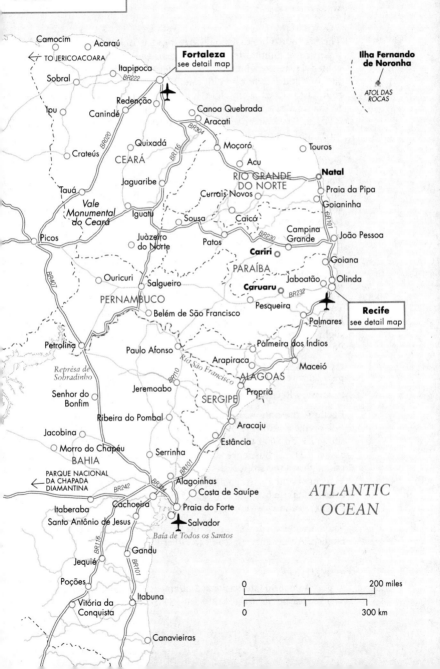

TO JERICOACOARA

Camocim
Acaraú
Itapipoca
BR222
Sobral
Ipu
Canindé
Redenção
Fortaleza
see detail map
Canoa Quebrada
Aracati
Quixadá
BR304
Moçoró
Touros
Acu
Crateús
CEARÁ
BR116
Natal
RIO GRANDE
DO NORTE
Praia da Pipa
Jaguaribe
Currais Novos
Goianinha
BR020
Tauá
Vale
Monumental
do Ceará
Iguatu
Sousa
Caicó
Campina
Grande
BR101
João Pessoa
Picos
Juàzeiro
do Norte
Patos
BR230
Cariri
Goiana
Ouricuri
Salgueiro
PARAÍBA
Caruaru
BR232
Jaboatão
Olinda
BR407
PERNAMBUCO
Belém de São Francisco
Pesqueira
Recife
see detail map
Petrolina
Paulo Afonso
Rio São Francisco
Palmeira dos Índios
Palmares
Maceió
Arapiraca
Represa de
Sobradinho
BR110
Jeremoabo
Propriá
ALAGOAS
Senhor do
Bonfim
Ribeira do Pombal
SERGIPE
Jacobina
Aracaju
Morro do Chapéu
Estância
BAHIA
Serrinha
PARQUE NACIONAL
DA CHAPADA
DIAMANTINA
BR242
BR324
Alagoinhas
BR101
Costa de Sauípe
Itaberaba
Cachoeira
Praia do Forte
Santo Antônio de Jesus
Salvador
BR116
Baía de Todos os Santos
Jequié
Gandu
BR101
Poções
Itabuna
Vitória da
Conquista
Canavieiras

Ilha Fernando
de Noronha
ATOL DAS
ROCAS

ATLANTIC
OCEAN

0   200 miles
0   300 km

rocks of the reefs slowly reappear. Pools of water are formed, fish flap around beachgoers, and the rock formations dry into odd colors. And if the light is just right on the Rio Capibaribe, the ancient buildings of Recife Antigo (Old Recife) are reflected off the river's surface in a watercolor display.

TO & FROM

The Aeroporto Internacional Guararapes is 10 km (6 mi) south of Recife, just five minutes from Boa Viagem, and 15 minutes from the city center. There are numerous daily flights between São Paulo, Rio de Janeiro, and Recife on GOL and TAM. In the airport lobby, on the right just before the exit door, is a tourist-information booth, and next to that is a taxi stand. You can pay at the counter; the cost is about R$23 to Boa Viagem and R$34 to downtown. There are also regular buses and microbuses (more expensive). The bus labeled AEROPORTO runs to Avenida Dantas Barreto in the center of the city, stopping in Boa Viagem on the way.

The Terminal Integrado de Passageiros (TIP), a metro terminal and bus station 14 km (9 mi) from the Recife city center, handles all interstate bus departures and some connections to local destinations. To reach it via metro, a 30-minute ride, enter through the Museu do Trem, opposite the Casa da Cultura, and take the train marked RODOVIÁRIA. Expresso Guanabara has several buses a day to Fortaleza (12 hours, R$130) and Natal (four hours, R$50) and frequent service to Caruaru (two hours, R$12). Itapemerim has buses to Rio de Janeiro (36 hours, R$235) and Salvador (14 hours, R$119).

The main north–south highway through Recife is BR 101. To the north it travels through vast sugar plantations; it's mostly straight, with only slight slopes. To travel south, you also can take the scenic coastal road, PE 060, which passes through Porto de Galinhas Beach.

GETTING AROUND

Because of horrible rush-hour traffic and careless drivers, it's best not to drive in Recife.

Recife is the only northeastern city with a subway system. A single ride on the metro is R$1.50. You can find a map at the Metrorec Web site (click on MAPA DA REDE). Transfer tickets and city bus tickets cost about R$1.75. Buses are clearly labeled and run frequently and past midnight. Many stops have signs indicating the routes. To reach Boa Viagem via the metro, get off at the Joana Bezerra stop (a 20-minute ride) and take a bus or taxi (R$20) from here. Buses are free when using the metro and vice-versa.

Taxis are cheap (fares double on Sunday), but drivers seldom speak English. All use meters. You can either hail a cab on the street or call for one.

ESSENTIALS

Airport Aeroporto Internacional Guararapes (*REC* ✉ *Praça Ministro Salgado Filho s/n, Imbiribeira, Recife, 51210-010* ☎ *081/3322–4188*).

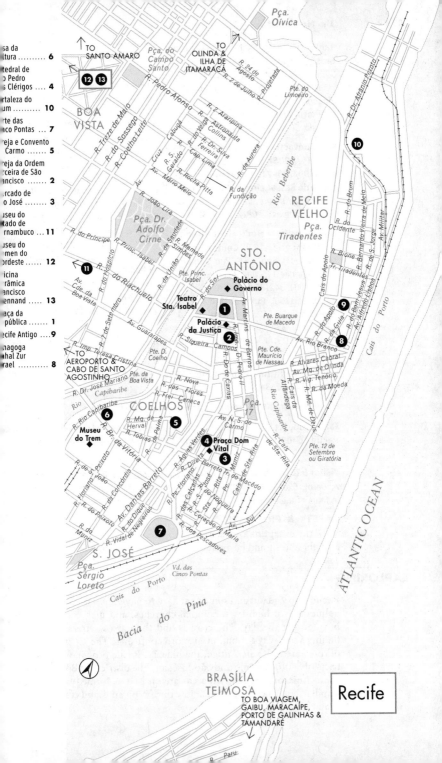

Banks & Currency Exchange Banco do Brasil (⊠ *Rua São Miguel 350, Afogados, 50770-720*). **Colmeia Câmbio & Turismo** (⊠ *Rua dos Navegantes 784, Loja 4, Boa Viagem, 51021-330*). **Mônaco Câmbio** (⊠ *Praça Joaquim Nabuco 159, Santo Antônio, 50010-480*).

Bus Contacts Expresso Guanabara (☎ *085/4005-1992*). **Itapemerim** (☎ *0800/723-2121*). **Terminal Integrado de Passageiros** (⊠ *Km 15, Rodovia BR 232, Curado, 50791-650, Jaboatão dos Guararapes* ☎ *081/3452-2824*).

Emergencies & Medical Assistance Ambulance (☎ *192*). **Centro Hospitalar Albert Sabin** (⊠ *Rua Senador José Henrique 141, Ilha do Leite, 50071-460* ☎ *081/3421-5411*). **Fire** (☎ *193*). **Police** (☎ *190*). **Puntual Med** (⊠ *Rua Real da Torre 570, Madalena, 50610-000* ☎ *081/3326-6498*). **Real Hospital Português** (⊠ *Av. Agamenon Magalhães s/n, Derby, 52010-900* ☎ *081/3416-1122*).

Internet Multilink Cyber Cafe (⊠ *Rua Futuro 516, Graças, 52050-010* ☎ *081/3426-2534*).

Subway Contacts Metrorec (⊕ *www.metrorec.com.br*).

Taxis Coopertáxi (☎ *081/3424-8944* ⊕ *www.coopertaxi.com.br*). **Radiotáxi Recife** (☎ *081/3423-7777*). **Teletáxi** (☎ *081/3429-4242* ⊕ *www.teletaxirecife.com.br*).

Visitor & Tour Info Agência Luck (⊠ *Rua Jornalista Paulo Bittencourt 163, Casa A, Derby, 52010-260* ☎ *08//3366-6222* ⊕ *www.luckviagens.com.br*) specializes in tours of the region.

SAFETY & PRECAUTIONS

With the exception of Recife Antigo, Recife's downtown area is dead at night and should be avoided as a safety precaution.

> ## RECIFE BY BOAT
>
> Catamaran cruises along the Rio Capibaribe take you past Recife's grand houses, bridges, and mangrove forests. **Catamaran Tours** (⊠ *Praça Marco Zero, Recife Antigo, 53020-170* ☎ *081/3424-2845 or 081/3424-8930*) offers two such excursions: the hour-long afternoon trip goes through the old rotating bridge and passes Recife Antigo and São José, the customs quay, the Santa Isabel Bridge, and the Rua da Aurora quays to the area near the Casa da Cultura. The two-hour-long night tour is aboard a slower—but more lively—vessel. It passes the quays of São José Estelita..

EXPLORING

Recife is spread out and somewhat hard to navigate. The Centro—with its mixture of high-rises, colonial churches, and markets—is always busy during the day. The crowds and the narrow streets can make finding your way around even more confusing. The Centro consists of three areas: Recife Antigo, the old city; Recife proper, with the districts of Santo Antônio and São José; and the districts of Boa Vista and Santo Amaro. The first two areas are on islands formed by the rivers Capibaribe, Beberibe, and Pina; the third is on an island created by the Canal Tacaruna.

Six kilometers (4 mi) south of Centro is the upscale residential and beach district of Boa Viagem, reached by bridge across the Bacia do Pina. Praia da Boa Viagem (Boa Viagem Beach), the Copacabana of Recife, is chockablock with trendy clubs and restaurants as well as many moderately priced and expensive hotels.

Numbers in the text correspond to numbers in the margin and on the Recife map.

MAIN ATTRACTIONS

❹ Catedral de São Pedro dos Clérigos. The facade of this cathedral, which was built in 1782, has fine wood sculptures; inside is a splendid trompe-l'oeil ceiling. The square surrounding the cathedral is a hangout for artists, who often read their poetry or perform folk music. It's lined with many restaurants, shops, and bars. A museum has exhibits on Carnival and an art gallery. ⊠ *Pátio de São Pedro, São José, 50020-220* ☎ *081/3224–2954* ⊠ *Free* ⊙ *Tues.–Fri. 8–11 and 2–4, Sat. 8–10:30.*

❺ Igreja e Convento do Carmo. The historic baroque-style church and convent are constructed of wood and white gold. The main altar has a life-size statue of Our Lady of Carmel. ⊠ *Praça do Carmo s/n, Santo Antônio, 50010-170* ☎ *081/3224–3341 or 081/3224–3174* ⊠ *Free* ⊙ *Weekdays 6:30 AM–8 PM, Sat. 7 AM–noon, Sun. 10–noon and 6 PM–9 PM.*

❷ Igreja da Ordem Terceira de São Francisco. Built in 1606, this church has beautiful Portuguese tile work. Don't miss the adjoining Capela Dourada (Golden Chapel), which was constructed in 1697 and is an outstanding example of Brazilian baroque architecture. The complex also contains a convent—the Convento Franciscano de Santo Antônio—and a museum displaying sacred art. ⊠ *Rua Imperador Dom Pedro II s/n, Santo Antônio, 50010-240* ☎ *081/3224–0530* ⊠ *R$2* ⊙ *Weekdays 8–11:30 and 2–5, Sat. 8–11:30.*

❸ Mercado de São José. In the city's most traditional market, vendors sell handicrafts, produce, and herbs. It's housed in a beautiful cast-iron structure that was imported from France in the 19th century. ⊠ *Trv. do Macêdo s/n, São José, 50050-280* ⊙ *Mon.–Sat. 6–6, Sun. 6–noon.*

⓫ Museu do Estado de Pernambuco. The state historical museum, in a mansion once owned by a baron, seems more like a home filled with beautiful antiques than a museum. There are a grand piano, a dining-room table set with 18th-century china, an ornate 19th-century crib, and many beautiful paintings. ⊠ *Av. Rui Barbosa 960, Graça, 52050-000* ☎ *081/3427–9322* ⊠ *R$2* ⊙ *Tues.–Fri. 9–5, weekends 2–5.*

⓬ Museu do Homem do Nordeste. With three museums under one roof—one has displays about sugar, another anthropological exhibits, and the third regional handicrafts—the Museum of Northeastern Man offers great insight into Brazil's history. There are utensils made by indigenous peoples, European colonizers, and African slaves; religious articles used in Catholic and Candomblé rituals; and ceramic figurines by such artists as Mestre Vitalino and Mestre Zé. At the time of this writing the building was closed for repairs, so call ahead. ⊠ *Av. 17 de Agosto*

2187, Casa Forte, 52061-540
☎081/3441–5500 or 081/3073–
6340 ☜R$5 ☉Weekdays 9–5,
weekends 1–5.

⑬ **Oficina Cerâmica Francisco Brennand.**
☽ In the old São José sugar refinery, this
★ museum houses more than 2,000
ceramic pieces by the great (and pro-
lific) Brazilian artist Francisco Brennand. Having studied in France, he
was influenced by Pablo Picasso
and Joan Miró, among others, and
his works also include paintings,
drawings, and engravings. About
15 km (9 mi) from Recife Antigo,
the museum's location amid forests
and fountains is almost as appealing as its displays. ⊠Km 16, Proprie-
dade Santo Cosme e Damião s/, Várzea, 50740-970 ☎081/3271–2466
⊕www.brennand.com.br ☜R$4 ☉Weekdays 8–5.

> **THE JEWS OF RECIFE**
>
> In the 17th century, Portuguese
> Jews living in Holland sailed to
> Recife in search of religious free-
> dom. By 1645 Jews made up half
> of the Dutch colony's European
> population. The community was
> prosperous until the Portuguese
> defeated the Dutch in 1654. Reli-
> gious persecution forced them
> to board another ship, this time
> bound for the Dutch colony of
> New Amsterdam.

① **Praça da República.** Republic Square was originally known as the Field
of Honor, a nod to those who were drawn and quartered here during
the Republican movement of 1817. The structures around the square
showcase the city's architecture from the 19th through the 20th centuries. Highlights include the Teatro Santa Isabel (St. Isabel Theater,
1850); the Palácio do Campo das Princesas, also known as the Palácio
do Governo (Government House, 1841); and the Palácio da Justiça
(Court House, 1930).

⑨ **Recife Antigo.** Most of Old Recife's colonial-era public buildings and
Fodor'sChoice houses have been restored. The area between Rua do Bom Jesus and
★ Rua do Apolo is full of shops, cafés, and bars, making it the hub of
downtown life both day and night; on some weekends there's dancing
in the streets. A handicrafts fair is held every Sunday from 1 to 10 on
Rua do Bom Jesus.

⑧ **Sinagoga Kahal Zur Israel.** Opened in 1641, this synagogue was the first
in the Americas. All that remains of the original sanctuary are the walls
and the ground, which can be viewed through glass floor panels. An
excellent museum provides explanations of the Jewish experience in
Brazil. Some guides speak English. ⊠Rua do Bom Jesus 197, Recife Antigo, 50030-170 ☎081/3224–7376 or 081/3224–2128 ⊕www.
arquivojudaicope.org.br ☜R$4 ☉Tues.–Fri. 9–5, Sun. 2–7.

IF YOU HAVE TIME

⑥ **Casa da Cultura.** In this 19th-century building, the old cells, with their
heavy iron doors, have been transformed into shops that sell clay figurines, wood sculptures, carpets, leather goods, and articles made from
woven straw. One of the cells has been kept in its original form to give
you an idea of how the prisoners lived. ⊠Rua Floriano Peixoto s/n,
Santo Antônio, 50020-905 ☎081/3224–4402 ☜Free ☉Weekdays
9–7, Sat. 9–6, Sun. 9–2.

⑩ Fortaleza do Brum *(Military Museum).* To safeguard their control, the Dutch wisely yet futilely built more than one fortress. In this one (c. 1629) you find reminders of those precarious days in the on-site **Museu Militar,** with its collection of old cannons, infantry weapons, and soldiers' utensils; there's even a skeleton of a soldier that dates from 1654. The fort also has a restaurant. ⊠ *Praça Comunidade Luso-Brasileiro s/n, Recife Antigo, 50030-280* ☎ *081/3224–4620 or 081/3224–7559* 🖃 *R$2* ⊗ *Tues.– Fri. 8–4:30, weekends 2–5.*

⑦ Forte das Cinco Pontas. The Dutch used mud to build the original five-sided fort in 1630. It was rebuilt in 1677 with stone and mortar; it now only has only four sides, but it has retained its original name. Inside is the **Museu da Cidade,** where maps and photos illustrate Recife's history. Before becoming a museum, it was used as a military headquarters and a prison. ⊠ *Praça das Cinco Pontas, São José, 50020-100* ☎ *081/3224–8492* 🖃 *R$2* ⊗ *Tues.–Fri. 9–6, weekends 1–5.*

> ### CARNIVAL IN RECIFE
>
> In Recife people attend *baile* (dance) and *bloco* (percussion group) practice for months prior to the main Carnival festivities. The beat of choice is *frevo* (a fast-pace rhythm accompanied by a dance performed with umbrellas). Galo da Madrugada, the largest of Recife's 500 blocos, opens Carnival and has included up to 20,000 costumed revelers. The blocos are joined by *escolas de samba* (samba schools or groups), *cabo-clinhos* (wearing traditional Indian garb and bright feathers), and *maracatus* (African percussionists).

BEACHES

★ **Boa Viagem.** Coconut palms line Recife's most popular beach, the 7-km-long (4-mi-long) Praia da Boa Viagem. A steady Atlantic breeze tames the hot sun, and reef formations create pools of warm water that are perfect for swimming. Sailors and fishermen beach their *jangadas* (handcrafted log rafts with beautiful sails), and vendors sell coconut drinks from kiosks. Avenida Boa Viagem separates a row of hotels and apartments from the beach, which is lined by a wide blue *calçadão* (sidewalk) that's perfect for runs, bike rides, or evening promenades. On weekend afternoons there's a handicrafts fair in Praça da Boa Viagem. Surfing and swimming beyond the reef are not recommended because of the presence of sharks. ⊠ *Boa Viagem, 51021-010.*

Cabo de Santo Agostinho. One of Pernambuco's finest beaches, Cabo de Santo Agostinho is good for swimming, though surfing has been banned due to the danger of shark attacks. In the town of Cabo de Santo Agostinho you can walk around the ruins of the Forte Castelo do Mar. ⊠ *35 km (22 mi) southeast of Recife, 54500-000.*

Gaibu. Quiet, beautiful Gaibu is surrounded by palm trees. Its blue waters are good for surfing, and it's also the site of volleyball competitions and fishing and sailing events. ⊠ *30 km (19 mi) south of Recife, 54505-000.*

↺ **Ilha de Itamaracá.** This island is off the coast of the historic city of Igarassu. The best beach is Forte Orange, next to Coroa do Avião, it has a historic fort that kids love to explore. Buses to Igarassu and Ilha de

9

Itamaracá leave from the center of Recife, at Avenida Martins de Barros, in front of the Grande Hotel. ⊠*39 km (24 mi) north of Recife, 53900-000.*

Maracaípe. Quiet Maracaípe Beach hosts surfing competitions; it hosted the World Surfing Games in 2000 (Brazil won first place in that competition). Maracaípe is a tiny hamlet with three dune buggies, two beach bars, and a small hotel. The beach's appeal is seclusion and surfing. ⊠*73 km (46 mi) southwest of Recife.*

★ **Porto de Galinhas.** This historic port has a tragic history. It was called Port of Chickens because of the chicken crates that African slaves were transported in across the Atlantic. You'll find cool, clean waves and several resorts at Porto de Galinhas. The beach, which follows the curve of a bay lined with coconut palms and cashew trees, gets crowded on weekends year-round. There are plenty of jangadas for rent; other boats can take you to the island of Santo Aleixo. ⊠*70 km (43 mi) south of Recife, 55590-000.*

Tamandaré. Although it's in the middle of an important nature reserve, developers have their eye on Tamandaré. Come quick, before its beaches—such as Praia dos Carneiros and Praia de Guadalupe—become one big resort area. ⊠*110 km (68 mi) south of Recife, 55578-000.*

WHERE TO EAT

$$-$$$$ ✕**Bargaço.** People come to this pleasant restaurant for the renowned dishes from the state of Bahia. If you don't mind a heavy dish, try the outstanding *moqueca baiana* (fish cooked with onion, tomatoes, peppers, parsley, and coconut milk). ⊠*Av. Boa Viagem 670, Pina, 51011-000* ☎*081/3465–1847* ▭*MC, V.*

$$-$$$$ ✕**Tasca.** The menu is more Portuguese than Brazilian, so, not surprisingly, one of the best dishes is *bacalhau a calí*—codfish cooked with olive oil, onion, garlic, tomatoes, potatoes, and white wine. ⊠*165 Rua Dom José Lopes, Boa Viagem, 51021-370* ☎*081/3326–6309* ▭*MC, V* ⊗*Closed Mon. No lunch Tues.–Sat., no dinner Sun.*

$$-$$$ ✕**Buongustaio.** This Italian restaurant has a diverse menu for all palates. Although the dishes often change, you cannot go wrong if you order the lamb or cod. ⊠*Av. Domingos Ferreira 467, Boa Viagem, 51020-040* ☎*081/3465–9922* ▭*AE, DC, MC, V* ⊗*No lunch weekdays.*

$ ✕**Parraxaxá.** Waiters wear the bent orange hats of Lampião, a Jesse James–like folk hero who made his way through the interior of the northeast during the early 20th century. The buffet has a wide selection of the regional specialties Lampião might have encountered back then. Food is priced per kilo. Try the amazing *escondinho* (a wonderful meat and cheese dish), *charque* (dried beef), and *carne sol* (brisket). ⊠*Rua Baltazar Pereira 32, Boa Viagem, 51011-550* ☎*081/3463–7874* ⊕*www.parraxaxa.com.br* ▭*MC, V.*

WHERE TO STAY

Most of Recife's top hotels are about 20 minutes from the airport, across from the Boa Viagem and Pina beaches or along Piedade Beach, in the municipality of Jaboatão dos Guararapes.

$$$ ⛛**Atlante Plaza Hotel.** Facing Recife's most popular beach, this high-rise's blue-glass windows make even the sky look pale. All rooms have sea views, but be sure to take a ride in the glass-enclosed elevator for a truly memorable ocean panorama. A buffet breakfast is served in the Brasserie restaurant, where you can also have an à la carte or buffet lunch. The Mirage restaurant serves international or Brazilian dinners. **Pros:** On the beach, great views. **Cons:** Carpeted rooms have faint mildew odor. ⊠*Av. Boa Viagem 5426, 51030-000* ☎*081/3302–3333* ⟲*241 rooms* ⚬*In-room: refrigerator. In-hotel: 2 restaurants, bars, pool, gym* ⊟*AE, DC, MC, V.*

$$ ⛛**Golden Beach.** These beachfront apartments are ideal for families or groups of friends traveling together. Each spacious unit has one or two bedrooms, a living room, and a fully equipped kitchenette. **Pros:** Great location, nice kitchenettes. **Cons:** Basic decor. ⊠*Av. Bernardo Vieira de Melo 1204, Piedade, 54410-001, Jaboatão dos Guararapes* ☎*081/2125–9300* ⊕*www.goldenbeach-pe.com.br* ⟲*125 apartments* ⚬*In-room: kitchen, Wi-Fi. In-hotel: restaurant, bars, pool, gym, public Internet* ⊟*AE, DC, MC, V.*

$$ ⛛**Recife Monte Hotel.** A block from Boa Viagem Beach, this hotel has all the amenities of a luxury hotel, including a lovely pool. A must during your stay here is the Sunday *feijoada* (Brazilian national dish consisting of black beans, smoked meats, oranges, and whatever else the chef may decide to throw in) in the Marruá restaurant. **Pros:** Pleasant rooms, great amenities, affordable rates. **Cons:** The hustle and bustle of a big hotel. ⊠*Rua dos Navegantes 363, Boa Viagem, 51021-010* ☎*081/2121–0909* ⊕*www.recifemontehotel.com.br* ⟲*152 rooms, 21 suites* ⚬*In-room: refrigerator. In-hotel: restaurant, bar, pool, public Internet* ⊟*DC, MC, V* ❢*BP.*

$ ⛛**Mar Hotel Recife.** Location is one of this hotel's main draws: it's a five-minute drive from the airport, a 20-minute drive from Recife Antigo, and very close to Boa Viagem. Rooms are nicely decorated and well equipped with desks that have swivel chairs, two phone lines, and fax and modem lines. When you're ready to call it a day, you can relax by the pool, which has a soothing waterfall. **Pros:** Great location, lovely pool area. **Cons:** Small rooms. ⊠*Rua Barão de Souza Leão 451, Boa Viagem, 51030-300* ☎*081/3302–4444* ⊕*www.marhotel.com.br* ⟲*207 rooms* ⚬*In-room: Ethernet. In-hotel: 2 restaurants, bar, pool, gym* ⊟*AE, DC, MC, V.*

¢   ⛛**Recife Plaza.** Overlooking the Rio Capibaribe, this simple downtown hotel emphasizes function over form. Some rooms have views of the river and the city; the pool has this view, too. **Pros:** Inexpensive rates, river views. **Cons:** Area is seedy at night. ⊠*Rua da Aurora 225, Boa Vista, 50060-000* ☎*081/3059–1200* ⊕*www.recifeplazahotel.com. br* ⟲*80 rooms* ⚬*In-room: refrigerator. In-hotel: restaurant, bar, pool* ⊟*AE, DC, MC, V.*

9

Brazil's National Dish

The first feijoada was reputedly made in Recife, and while the popular story of its origins is that it was a dish that slaves made for themselves with the scraps of meats from the masters' tables, some historians now believe that feijoada was, in fact, made *for* the masters. It has a semblance to the Portuguese dish *cozido* (a meat and vegetable stew), and the cuts of meat used—including pig's feet and ears—are thought to have been parts prized by the Portuguese elite.

Feijoada, served at most Brazilian restaurants on Saturday, is accompanied by rice, collard greens, *farofa* (finely ground manioc fried in butter), rice, aipîm frito (fried yuca), *torresminho* (pork rinds), and orange slices—the citrus supposedly counteracts the fat.

MAKING FEIJOADA

2 cups (1 pound) black beans, rinsed and picked over
¾ lb. pork butt or shoulder, trimmed of fat
6 ounces slab bacon
½ lb. smoked pork sausages
½ lb. hot Portuguese sausage such as *linguiça*
1 or 2 lbs. ham hock or shank, cut into 1-inch rounds
1 large yellow onion, chopped
3 garlic cloves, minced and sautéed in 1 tablespoon vegetable oil
6 green onions, including tops, chopped
1 yellow onion, chopped
½ cup chopped fresh parsley
2 bay leaves, crumbled
1½ tablespoons dried oregano, crushed
Salt and ground black pepper to taste
Chopped fresh cilantro or parsley

Directions:

Soak the beans overnight in enough water to cover by several inches.

Place the drained beans in a saucepan and add enough water to cover by 3 inches. Bring to a boil, reduce the heat to low, cover, and simmer until the beans are tender, 2–2½ hours. Add additional water as needed to keep the beans covered.

While the beans are cooking, prepare the meats. Preheat an oven to 375 degrees. Dice the pork butt or shoulder and the bacon into ½-inch cubes. Place the pork, sausages, and bacon in a large baking pan. Roast until well done. The sausages will be ready in 35–40 minutes and the other meats in 45–60 minutes.

Cook the ham hock at the same time as the meats are roasting. In a saucepan combine the ham hock rounds and onion with water to cover. Bring to a boil, reduce heat to a simmer, and cook until tender, about 1 hour. Remove the ham from the water and remove the meat from the bones; set aside. Or leave the rounds intact for serving alongside the beans. Strain the cooking liquid into a bowl. Add the strained onions to the beans. Add the cooking liquid to the beans if needed.

Once the beans are almost cooked, check to make sure there's plenty of cooking liquid in the pot. It should be rather soupy at this point. Cut the sausages into rounds and add them and all the other cooked meats to the pot. Then add all the seasonings. Simmer for another 30 minutes.

Taste and adjust the seasonings. Sprinkle with chopped cilantro or parsley just before serving.

NIGHTLIFE & THE ARTS

NIGHTLIFE

Pólo Pina, the calçadão in the Pina district, is a popular area near the beach for nighttime activities. Along the streets off Rua Herculano Bandeira you can find close to two-dozen bars and restaurants. Between Rua do Apolo and Rua do Bom Jesus (or Rua dos Judeus) in Recife Antigo, people gather in a seemingly endless variety of bars, cafés, and nightclubs. On Saturday the market in Praça de Boa Viagem comes alive with forró dancers.

BARS

O Biruta (⊠ *Rua Bem-te-vi 15, Brasília Teimosa, 51110-130* ☎ *081/ 3326–5151* ⊕ *www.birutabar.com.br*) is a great spot to watch the moon rise over the beach. There's live samba music every Saturday. Chilled draft beer, tasty snacks, and excellent service make **Boteco** (⊠ *Av. Boa Viagem 1660, Boa Viagem, 51111-000* ☎ *081/3327–4285*) one of the most popular bars in town. **Depois** (⊠ *Av. Rio Branco 66, Recife Antigo, 50030-310* ☎ *081/3424–7232* ⊕ *www.depoisdancingbar.com. br*) is in an old building in the heart of a bohemian neighborhood. Hits from the '60s and '70s are a hit with an over-30 crowd. **Galeria Joana D'Arc** (⊠ *Rua Herculano Bandeira 513, Pina, 51110-130*) is a cluster of small cafés and bars, among them Café Poire, Anjo Solto, Barnabé, and Oriente Médio. It's a favorite hangout for local gay men and lesbians.

DANCE CLUBS

Downtown (⊠ *Rua Vigário Tenório 105, Recife Antigo, 50030-010* ☎ *081/3424–6317* ⊕ *www.downtownpub.com.br*), a club with a London pub look, is a good place to be on Saturday night when local bands play. The club is popular with teenagers and twentysomethings.

THE ARTS

Built in 1850, lovely **Teatro Santa Isabel** (⊠ *Praça da República s/n, Santo Antônio, 50010-040* ☎ *081/3224–1020 or 081/3224–0005*), looks splendid after a major restoration. The neoclassical theater is the setting for operas, plays, and classical concerts.

9

SPORTS & THE OUTDOORS

SAILING

At Boa Viagem, fishermen with jangadas offer sailing or fishing trips. The waters are shallow and calm at Maria Farinha Beach, on the north coast at the mouth of the Rio Timbó. Here you can rent Jet Skis, take ultralight flights, and enjoy motorboat and catamaran rides.

UNDER THE SEA

More than a dozen shipwrecks make good destinations for underwater explorers of all experience levels. The *Vapor de Baixo* is one such dive site. Bombed by the Germans during World War II, it's 20 meters (65 feet) down and is crawling with lobsters and turtles.

SCUBA DIVING

For centuries the treacherous offshore reefs that gave Recife its name have struck fear into the hearts of sailors. Many a vessel has failed to navigate the natural harbor successfully. Though diving is practiced year-round, visibility is best between October and May, when the wind and water are at their calmest. The **Seagate** (⊠ *Av. Herculano Bandeira 287, Pólo Pina, 51110-130* ☎ *081/3328–4712* ⊕ *www.seagaterecife. com.br*) offers diving courses, rents equipment, and runs trips for certified divers.

SHOPPING

The **Feira Hippie** *(Hippie Fair)* , held in the seafront Praça da Boa Viagem on afternoons starting at 4, has handicrafts. Vendors at the **Mercado de São José** (⊠ *Praça Dom Vital s/n, São José, 50020-280* ☎ *081/3424– 4681*) sell clothes and handicrafts as well as produce. It's open weekdays 6–6, Saturday 6–4, and Sunday 6–noon.

Shopping Center Guararapes (⊠ *Av. Barreto de Menezes 800, Piedade, Jaboatão dos Guararapes, 54325-000* ☎ *081/2122–2211* ⊕ *www.shop pingguararapes.com.br*) has everything the Shopping Center Recife has but on a smaller scale. It's near Piedade Beach. The enormous **Shopping Center Recife** (⊠ *Rua Padre Carapuceiro 777, Boa Viagem, 51020-280* ☎ *081/3464–6000* ⊕ *www.shoppingrecife.com.br*) is the perfect place for a day of bargain-hunting. It's not far from Boa Viagem Beach.

SIDE TRIP TO OLINDA   ·

7 km (4 mi) north of Recife.

The name of Pernambuco State's original capital means "beautiful," and this must have been what came to mind when the first Europeans stood atop the forested hills and gazed at ocean and beach spread out before them. Today the town's natural beauty is complemented by colonial buildings painted in a rainbow of colors, making it a stunning slice of the old Northeast.

Founded by the Portuguese in 1535, Olinda was developed further by the Dutch during their brief turn at running Pernambuco in the 1600s. The narrow cobblestone streets of this UNESCO World Cultural Site curve up and down hills that, at every turn, offer spectacular views of both Recife and the Atlantic. The scenery is just as nice up close: many houses have latticed balconies, heavy doors, and stucco walls. The zoning laws are strict, resulting in a beautiful, compact city that artists, musicians, and intellectuals have made their own.

The city center is hilly but fairly easy to explore by foot. You may want to hire a guide to help provide some historical background on the city and its principal sites. Look for the official guides (they have ID cards) who congregate in the Praça do Carmo. They are former street children, and half the R$45 fee for a full city tour goes to a home for kids from the streets.

TO & FROM

A cab from the airport in Recife costs between R$40 and R$55. Alternatively, you can take the AEROPORTO bus to Avenida Nossa Senhora do Carmo in Recife and transfer to the CASA CAIADA bus bound for Olinda.

ESSENTIALS

Banks & Currency Exchange Banco do Brasil (✉ *Av. Antônio Costa Azevedo 540, 53220-130*).

Emergencies & Medical Assistance Ambulance (☎ *192*). **Fire** (☎ *193*).

Visitor & Tour Info SEPACCTUR (✉ *Rua de São Bento 160, Varadouro, 53020-081* ☎ *081/3439–1988* ⊕ *www.olinda.pe.gov. br*), the local tourism agency, is open weekdays 9 to 5.

SAFETY & PRECAUTIONS

To be on the safe side, don't hire sightseeing guides who approach you on the street. Hire one through the museum or sight you're visiting, a tour operator, the tourist board, your hotel, or a reputable travel agency.

> **OLINDA'S CARNIVAL**
>
> Many rate Carnival in Olinda as one of the best in Brazil, rivaling those in Rio de Janeiro and Salvador. It's considered Brazil's most traditional Carnival—meaning there's noticeably less skin exposed. Music is generally the slower-paced *forró*, in contrast to Rio's *samba* and Salvador's *axé*. Carnival here lasts a full 11 days. Highlights include the opening events—led by a bloco of more than 400 "virgins" (men in drag)—and a parade of *bonecos de pano* (huge dolls) and *mamulengos* (marrionettes) in the likenesses of famous Northeasterners. The dolls and puppets are made of Styrofoam, fabric, and papier-mâché.

WHAT TO SEE

The **Alto da Sé** is the most scenic spot for viewing Olinda, Recife, and the ocean. It's also a good place see some historic churches as well as to sample Bahia-style *acaraje* (black-eyed pea fritters) and Pernambuco's famous tapioca cakes. Have a seat at one of the outdoor tables here, or browse in the shops that sell handicrafts—including lace—and paintings. To get here, just walk up on Ladeira da Sé.

On Olinda's southern edge is the **Centro de Convenções Pernambuco,** one of the most modern convention centers in Latin America, which houses Empetur, the state tourism office. Cultural performances are often held in the center's theater and auditorium. ✉ *Complexo Viário Vice Governador Barreto Guimarães s/n, Salgadinho, 53110-000* ☎ *081/3427–8000* ⊕ *www.empetur.com.br.*

★ The **Convento de São Francisco,** built in 1577, was the first Franciscan convent built in Brazil. The floors are Portuguese tile work, ceilings are frescoed, and walls are made of ground-up local coral. ✉ *Rua São Francisco 280, Carmo Olinda, 53120-070* ☎ *081/3429–0517* ✑ *R$4* ⊙ *Weekdays 7–noon and 2–5, Sat. 7–noon.*

Built in 1540 and restored in 1654, the **Igreja da Misericórdia** *(Mercy Church)* has rich sculptures of wood, gold, and silver. It's atop the Alto da Sé. ✉ *Alto da Misericórdia s/n, Carmo, 53010-000* ☎ *081/3429–2922* ✑ *Free* ⊙ *Daily 9–1 and 2–6.*

9

The last of many renovations to the 1537 **Igreja da Sé**, on the Alto da Sé, was in 1983. It has now been restored as much as possible to its original appearance. From its side terrace you can see the Old City and the ocean. ⊠*Rua Bispo Coutinho s/n, 53010-000* ☎*Free* ⊙*Daily 8–11:30 and 2–5.*

Fodor'sChoice
★

The main chapel of the **Mosteiro de São Bento**, a Benedictine monastery, is considered one of Brazil's most beautiful. It once housed

---

TAPIOCA STANDS

While in Olinda, try out the food at the different stands selling *tapioca*, or patties made from shaved coconut. Many claim that the tapioca made here is the best in the country. Try the the savory chicken and catupiry tapioca, then follow it up with a sweet doce de leite tapioca for dessert.

---

the nation's first law school. Sunday's 10 AM mass features Gregorian chants. ⊠*Rua de São Bento s/n, 53020-080* ☎*081/3429–3288* ☎*Free* ⊙*Daily 8–11 and 2–5.*

At the **Museu do Mamulengo-Espaço Tiridá,** everyday life and northeastern folk tales are the stuff of shows, presented using some of the more than 300 puppets made of wood and cloth that are on display in this whimsical museum. ⊠*Rua do São Bento 344, 53020-170* ☎*081/3429–6214* ☎*R$2* ⊙*Tues.–Fri. 9–5, weekends 10–5.*

WHERE TO STAY & EAT

$$–$$$$ ✕**Oficina do Sabor.** Everything is tasty at this regional restaurant, but do try the *abóbora com camarão,* pumpkin stuffed with shrimp and served with a *pitanga* cherry sauce. ⊠*Rua do Amparo 335, 53020-190* ☎*081/3429–3331* ⊕*www.oficinadosabor.com* ☐*AE, DC, MC, V* ⊙*Closed Mon. No dinner Sun.*

$$–$$$
★

Pousada do Amparo. This lovely pousada is made up of two colonial houses with soaring ceilings. Wood and brick details, original artwork, and an indoor garden lend considerable warmth to the cavernous spaces. It's a member of the exclusive Brazilian Roteiros de Charme hotels group. **Pros:** Atmospheric buildings, lovely rooms. **Cons:** Restaurant not open for lunch. ⊠*Rua do Amparo 199, 53020-190* ☎*081/3439–1749* ⊕*www.pousadadoamparo.com.br* ◄*18 rooms* △*In-room: safe, refrigerator, Wi-Fi. In-hotel: restaurant, bar, pool, no elevator* ☐*AE, DC, MC, V.*

$$ **Hotel 7 Colinas.** This hotel sits in an off-street hollow amid the trees and flowers of a tangled garden. From here it's just a short hike up to Alto da Sé. Rooms are comfortably furnished, and all look out on the grounds. **Pros:** Cozy rooms, nice atmosphere. **Cons:** No Internet connections in the rooms. ⊠*Ladeira de São Francisco 307, 53120-070* ☎*081/3439–6055* ⊕*www.hotel7colinasolinda.com.br* ◄*44 rooms* △*In-room: refrigerator. In-hotel: restaurant, bar, pool, no elevator, public Wi-Fi* ☐*AE, DC, MC, V.*

$ **Hotel Pousada Quatro Cantos.** In a converted mansion, this pousada has rooms that vary considerably in size, quality, and price. The suites, with hardwood floors, rival those at the best hotels, but the standard rooms are just average. The individually decorated deluxe rooms are considerably nicer. Carnival decorations enliven the lobby. The Mercado da Ribeira is within walking distance. **Pros:** Wonderful suites, good rates. **Cons:** Not all rooms are equal. ⊠ *Rua Prudente de Morais 441, 53020-140* ☎*081/3429–0220* ⊕*www.pousada4cantos.com.br* ↩*16 rooms, 2 suites* ♿*In-rooms: refrigerator. In-hotel: restaurant, bar, no elevator* ▤*AE, DC, MC, V.*

¢ 🏨**Pousada Peter.** You may wonder whether this grand mansion is a pousada or an art gallery. Peter Bauer, whose paintings have hung in many galleries, is both the owner and the resident artist. The large guest rooms lead out to a terrace with views of Olinda and Recife. During Carnival, for which the pousada has special packages, revelers dance along the street out front. **Pros:** Lovely garden, great views. **Cons:** Noisy during Carnival. ⊠ *Rua do Amparo 215, 53020-170* ☎*081/3439–2171* ⊕*www.pousadapeter.com.br* ↩*13 rooms* ♿*In room: refrigerator. In-hotel: pool.*

SHOPPING

For crafts, head to the **Casa do Artesão** (⊠ *Rua de São Bento 170, 53120-000* ☎*081/3429–2979*). It's open weekdays 9–6 and Saturday 9–2.

SIDE TRIP TO CARUARU

134 km (83 mi) west of Recife.

Caruaru and its crafts center, Alto do Moura (6 km/4 mi south of Caruaru), became famous in the 1960s and '70s for clay figurines made by local artisan Mestre Vitalino. There are now more than 500 craftspeople working in Alto do Moura. All are inspired by Vitalino, whose former home is now a museum, open Monday–Saturday 8–noon and 2–6 and Sunday 8–noon. At the crafts center you can buy not only figurines, which depict Northeasterners doing everyday things, but also watch the artisans work.

TO & FROM

A shuttle bus runs between Recife and Caruaru every half hour. Caruaruense buses cost R$12. To reach Caruaru from Recife by car, take BR 232 west; the trip takes two hours

ESSENTIALS

Bus Contacts Caruaruense (☎*81/3721–1374*).

Emergencies & Medical Assistance Ambulance (☎*192*). **Fire** (☎*193*). **Police** (☎*190*).

WHAT TO SEE

In Caruaru a great open-air market, **Feira de Artesanato** (⊠ *Parque 18 de Maio, 55030-400*), is held every Saturday, when, as the songwriter Luis Gonzaga put it, "It is possible to find a little of everything that exists in the world." Look for pottery, leather goods, ceramics, hammocks, and baskets.

WHERE TO STAY

$ 🏨**Caruaru Park Hotel.** On the outskirts of town, the Caruaru Park's colorful rooms and chalets are sparsely decorated but neat and clean. Balconies have hammocks and decent views of town. **Pros:** Pleasant rooms.

Cons: Basic decor. ✉ *BR 232, Km 128, 55030-400* ☎ *081/3722–9191* ⊕ *www.caruaruparkhotelonline.com.br* 🛏 *68 rooms* 🔑 *In-room: refrigerator. In-hotel: restaurant, pool, no elevator, public Internet* 🖃 *MC, V.*

NATAL

Natal, with a population now exceeding 700,000, has been growing by leaps and bounds over the past decade. The capital of Rio Grande do Norte has become an important industrial center, yet no industry has had more effect on the economy than tourism. The past few administrations have invested heavily in the infrastructure and promotion, effectively placing it on the map as one of the prime tourism destinations in Brazil.

Although it has little in the way of historical or cultural attractions, the city's main asset is its location along one of the most beautiful stretches of coast in Brazil. In fact, Natal's foundation and much of its history have been all about location. In 1598 the Portuguese began construction of the Fortaleza dos Reis Magos in present-day Natal. Its location was strategic for two reasons. First, it was at the mouth of the Rio Potengi. Second, it was near the easternmost point of the continent and therefore was closest to Europe and Africa. On December 25, 1599, the city was founded and named Natal, Portuguese for "Christmas."

Because of its valuable location, Natal was a target for the Dutch, who ultimately seized control of the city in 1633 and renamed it New Amsterdam. The Portuguese repossessed Natal after the Dutch abandoned the city in 1654. Yet it was never a major colonial center for the Portuguese. The city had to wait nearly three centuries to regain importance, again due to its location. In World War II the United States built several military bases in and around the city that they deemed "the springboard to victory"—its position at the far-eastern point of the continent made it ideal for launching aerial attacks into Europe.

TO & FROM

Aeroporto Internacional Augusto Severo is 15 km (9 mi) south of the town center. Taxis to Ponta Negra or downtown Natal cost around R$30 to R$40. Vans from the airport to downtown costs R$2.

Natal has two bus stations. For most destinations you use the Rodoviário de Natal, 5 km (3 mi) from Ponta Negra. It's often referred to as the *terminal nova* (new terminal). Several buses daily go to Praia da Pipa (1½ hours; R$10), Recife (four hours; R$50), Fortaleza (eight hours; R$$65–R$120), and Rio de Janeiro (44 hours; R$200). Buses to Genipabu and Ponta Negra beaches leave from Natal's other bus station, the Rodoviário Velho (old bus station), downtown.

Natal lies at the northern end of BR 101, making it an easy trip by car from Recife, which is due south on BR 101. To reach Praia da Pipa, head south on BR 101 and then take RN 003 to the east. To Fortaleza, take BR 304 northwest and then head north on BR 116.

GETTING AROUND

Natal's few museums and historic buildings are mostly clustered in the Cidade Alta (Upper City) , within easy walking distance of each other. Ponta Negra is still small enough that it can easily be explored on foot—most hotels and restaurants are very close to the beach. All taxis have meters and are easy to locate in Ponta Negra and downtown.

ESSENTIALS

Airport **Aeroporto Internacional Augusto Severo** (*NAT ⊠ BR 101, Parnamirim, 59148-970 ☎ 084/3087–1270*).

Banks & Currency Exchange **Banco do Brasil** (⊠ *Natal Shopping, Av. Sen. Salgado Filho 2234, Loja 232, Candelária, 59064-900*). **Praia Câmbio** (⊠ *Praia Shopping, Av. Engenheiro Roberto Freire 8790, qd. 5, Ponta Negra, 59082-400*). **VIP Câmbio** (⊠ *Aeroporto Internacional Augusto Severo, BR 101, Parnamirim, 59148-970*).

Bus Contacts **Terminal Rodoviário de Natal** (⊠ *Av. Capitão Mor. Gouveia 1237, Cidade de Esperança, Natal, 59060-400 ☎ 084/3232–7312*). **Rodoviário Velho** (⊠ *Praça de Augusto Severo, Natal, 52012-580 ☎ No phone*).

Emergencies & Medical Assistance **Ambulance** (☎ *192*). **Fire** (☎ *193*). Hospital: **Hospital Memorial** (⊠ *Av. Juvenal Lamartine 979, Tirol, 59022-020 ☎ 084/3211–3636*). **Hospital Monsenhor Walfredo Gurgel** (⊠ *Av. Hermes Fonseca 817, Tirol, 59014-555 ☎ 084/3232–7536*). Pharmacy: **Farmácia Nobre** (⊠ *Av. Praia dos Búzios 9036, Ponta Negra, 59092-200 ☎ 084/3219–3381*). **Cooperfarma** (⊠ *Av. Praia de Ponta Negra 8936, Ponta Negra, 59094-100 ☎ 084/3219–3471*). **Police** (☎ *190*).

Internet **Interjato** (⊠ *Praia Shopping, Av. Roberto Freire 3796, Ponta Negra, 59090-000 ☎ 084/3219–5510*).

Taxis **Rádio Táxi** (☎ *084/3221–5666*). **Rádio Táxi Relámpago** (☎ *084/3223–5444*). **Rádio Cooptáxi** (☎ *084/3205–4455*).

Visitor & Tour Info **Aventura Turismo** (⊠ *Av. Prudente de Morais, 4262, Loja 3B, sala 1, Lagoa Nova, 59065-500 ☎ 084/3206–4949 ⊕ www.caririecotours.com.br*) offers trips to Praia da Pipa. **Natal Tur** (⊠ *Av. Praia de Ponta Negra 8884, Ponta Negra, 59092-100 ☎ 084/3236–2280 ⊕ www.nataltur.com.br*) has dune-buggy trips to Genipabu and other local beaches, as well as trip to Fernando de Noronha. **SETUR** (⊠ *Rua Mossoró 359, Petrópolis, 59020-090 ☎ 084/3232–2500 ⊠ Aeroporto Internacional Augusto Severo, BR 101, Parnamirim, 59148-970 ☎ 084/3643–1811 ⊠ Centro de Turismo, Rua Abedal de Figueiredo 980, Petrópolis, 59010-115 ☎ 084/3211–6149 ⊠ Praia Shopping, Av. Engenheiro Roberto Freire 8790, Ponta Negra, 59090-000 ☎ 084/3232–7248 ⊠ Terminal Rodoviário de Natal, Av. Capitão Mor. Gouveia 1237, Cidade da Esperança, 59060-400 ☎ 084/3232–7219 ⊕ www.setur.rn.gov.br*) is the local tourism agency. The airport branch is open weedays 7–1 and 2–6, while all the others are open daily 8 to 10.

9

EXPLORING

Few tourists stay in the city itself, and many do not even visit, and instead head straight to Ponta Negra, a rapidly developing beach area 10 km (6 mi) south of the city center.

MAIN ATTRACTIONS

FodorśChoice ★ **Genipabu.** Massive dunes have made this one of the best-known beaches in the country. The area is most commonly explored on thrilling, hour-long dune-buggy rides. You have two choices: *com emoção* (literally, "with emotion"), which rivals any roller-coaster, or *sem emoção* (without emotion), a little calmer but still fairly hair-raising. Buggy operators, who usually find you before you find them, charge around R$150 for five people. You can also explore the dunes on camels imported from southern Spain. Other activities include half-hour boat rides and sky-boarding (also called sky-surfing)—which is basically snowboarding down the dunes. The beach is attractive, although it gets very crowded during high season. Because Genipabu is close to Natal, it's primarily a day-trip destination. There are a few small pousadas and restaurants near the beach, but the town shuts down at night. Buses leave from the Rodoviário Velho every half hour or so for the half-hour trip, also the city bus costs R$1.75. Depending on where you are in the city, you might have to take two buses to get there. ⊠ *Take BR 101 north to Pitanguí access road; 10 km (6 mi) north of Natal, 59575-000.*

Museu Câmara Cascudo. This well-conceived museum has exhibits from a variety of disciplines: archaeology, paleontology, mineralogy, ethnography, and popular culture. A highlight is the collection of dinosaur fossils. ⊠ *Av. Hermes da Fonseca 1398, Tirol, 59015-001* ☎ *084/3212–2795* ⊠ *R$3* ۞ *Tues.–Sun. 8–11:30 and 2–5:30.*

Ponta Negra. Nearly all tourism development has focused on or around this beach in the past few years. It has a multitude of pousadas, restaurants, and shops and even a few large resorts at the northern end. The beach itself, around 2½ km (1½ mi) long, can no longer be called pristine, but is still attractive and reasonably clean. Large waves make it popular with surfers. Ponta Negra's distinguishing feature is the Morro da Careca (Bald Man's Hill), a 120-meter (390-foot) dune at the southern end. You can catch a taxi or a bus (look for buses marked PONTA NEGRA) at various stops along the Via Costeira south of Natal. Buses run fairly frequently. From Ponta Negra to downtown Natal, look for buses marked CENTRO or CIDADE ALTA. ⊠ *Via Costeira; 10 km (6 mi) south of Natal, 59090-420.*

Praça 7 de Setembro. The two most notable buildings around this center of old Natal are the Victorian-style governor's mansion, built in 1873, and the uninspiring cathedral, built in 1862. The square is rather lifeless except for in the month of December, when a play retelling the Christmas story is performed.

IF YOU HAVE TIME

Búzios. This beach has been endowed with great natural beauty, yet does not usually have many visitors. The barrier reef creates an area of clear, calm waters ideal for bathing, snorkeling, and scuba diving. In the background are some impressive dunes, covered with palm trees and other vegetation. The modest infrastructure consists of just a few small pousadas and restaurants. ⊠ *RN 063 (Rota do Sol); 35 km (21 mi) south of Natal, 59164.*

Maracajaú. The principal draw at Maracajaú is the large coral reef 6 km (4 mi) off the coast. Teeming with marine life, the sizable reef offers the best snorkeling in the Natal area. **Ma-noa Parque Aquático** (☎084/3211–2140 ⊕*www. ma-noa.com.br*) has all that day visitors require: a restaurant, water rides, a huge pool, boat trips to the reef with snorkeling equipment provided, and even transport to and from Natal hotels. Go now, as the ecosystem will not be able to

> **SANDY CLAUSE**
>
> The sand dunes of the Northeast are dangerous for digital cameras, as the fine sand can get into the lenses. Make sure to carry your camera not only in the case, but also in a plastic bags. Even one piece of sand can cause irreparable damage, and many companies will not cover sand damage even if the camera is under warranty.

handle the up to 1,000 daily visitors indefinitely. ⊠*Take BR 101 north to Maracajaú access road; 55 km (34 mi) north of Natal, (Ma-noa Aquatic Park) Enseada Pontas dos Anéis, Maracajaú, 59056-450.*

Pirangi do Norte. This long white-sand beach is an extremely popular summer vacation destination for residents of Natal. Boat rides to nearby coral reefs and beaches run frequently. Near the beach is the world's largest cashew tree, according to the *Guinness Book of World Records*. Its circumference measures 500 meters (1,650 feet), and it's as big as roughly 70 normal cashew trees. ⊠*RN 063, 28 km (17 mi) north of Natal, 59161-250.*

WHERE TO EAT

$$ ✕**Peixada da Comadre.** If you were wondering where locals go for the town's best fish, this is it. The decor is rather simple, but tables in the back have excellent views of the Praia dos Artistas through large glass windows. Dishes like the tasty fried fish fillets are easily large enough for two. ⊠*Rua Dr. José Augusto Bezerra de Medeiros 4, Praia do Meio, 59010-010* ☎*084/3202–3411* ▭*No credit cards* ⊙*Closed Tues. No dinner Sun.*

$–$$ ✕**Piazzale Itália.** During the high season (July and December–mid-March), make a reservation, or you'll be among the many waiting outside, salivating from smells of fresh tomato sauce and garlic. The restaurant's popularity is a result of reasonable prices, proximity to the Ponta Negra Beach, and skillful preparation of pasta and seafood dishes. Particularly recommended is the *tagliolini allo scoglio* (pasta with lobster, shrimp, and mussels). ⊠*Av. Deputado Antônio Florêncio de Queiroz 12, Ponta Negra, 59092-500* ☎*084/3219–5023* ▭*AE, DC, MC, V.*

$ ✕**Mangai.** Choose from more than 40 delicious regional specialties at Fodor's Choice this immensely popular buffet restaurant. Tourists and town residents ★ eat together at communal wood tables, which fit the typical rustic decor of the sertão. To top off your meal, consider ordering the *cartola*, a popular dessert made of caramelized banana, cheese, and cinnamon. ⊠*Av. Amintas Barros 3300, Lagoa Nova, 59062-250* ☎*084/3206–3344* ▭*AE, MC, V.*

9

Off-Season Carnivals

CARNATAL

When Natal's Carnatal began in 1991, it was the country's first *carnaval fora da epoca,* or out-of-season Carnival. (Off-season Carnivals are also sometimes called *micaretas.*) More than a dozen other cities have since instituted similar celebrations, but this remains one of the largest. Always on the first weekend in December, it unites party seekers from throughout the country and beyond. There are about 10 blocos, each with room for 3,000 revelers. They travel along a 2-km (1-mi) route that starts just outside the soccer stadium. Performances are given by some of the country's top acts. Tickets often sell out early, especially for the more popular blocos. You can reserve tickets online through ⊕ *www.carnatal.com.br.*

FORTAL

Fortaleza's Fortal, one of the country's foremost carnival fora da epoca celebrations, began in 1992. It's held the last week in July on a 4-km (2½)-mi stretch along the seaside Avenida Beira-Mar. Its scale is impressive: there are six blocos, each with 2,500 revelers. An average of 500,000 participate in the festivities each of the four days, 200,000 of them tourists. Like Carnatal, Fortal attracts top acts. For more information visit ⊕ *www.fortal.com.br.*

WHERE TO STAY

$$$ ✕🖾 **Manary Praia Hotel.** It's hardly surprising that this small hotel was
★   chosen as a member of the prestigious Roteiros de Charme group. Both the service and decor reflect tremendous attention to detail. The restaurant serves skillfully prepared dishes such as grilled seafood in the pretty pool area that overlooks the beach. The location is ideal, as it's just beyond the crowded portion of Ponta Negra. The owner also runs Natal's only ecotourism operation, which has top-flight trips to area beaches and fascinating inland destinations such as Cariri and Dinosaur Valley. **Pros:** Amazing location, beautiful building. **Cons:** All rooms don't have great views. ⊠ *Rua Francisco Gurgel 9067, Ponta Negra, 59090-050* ☎ *084/3204–2900* ⊕ *www.manary.com.br* 🛏 *20 rooms, 1 suite* ♨ *In-rooms: safe, refrigerator, Ethernet. In-hotel: restaurant, bar, pool, public Wi-Fi* ▤ *AE, DC, MC, V.*

$$$ 🖾 **Pestana Natal Beach Resort.** This attractive accomodation manages to avoid some of the problems associated with massive resort complexes: its beige color allows it to blend into its sandy surroundings, rooms have original artwork and other strokes of personality, and personalized service makes you feel like more than just a number. **Pros:** Pleasant atmosphere, doting service. **Cons:** A bit noisy. ⊠ *Av. Senador Dinarte Mariz 5525, Via Costeira, 6 km north of Ponta Negra, 59090-001* ☎ *084/3220–8900* ⊕ *www.pestana.com* 🛏 *188 rooms, 5 suites* ♨ *In-room: refrigerator, Wi-Fi. In-hotel: 3 restaurants, bars, pool, gym* ▤ *AE, DC, MC, V.*

$$$ 🖾 **Rifóles.** The eclectic architectural style of this all-inclusive resort is
☾   both attractive and confusing; pirate and cave-painting motifs are cultivated through the use of materials such as old driftwood, plaster, marble, and *tijolo aparente*—locally produced beige bricks. The beach

in front is uncrowded, as it's a mile or so from the busy part of Ponta Negra. You can also bathe in one of the two pools, but the nearby karaoke machine ruins any semblance of peace. Rooms are well equipped and adequately sized. **Pros:** On the beach, friendly atmosphere. **Cons:** Lacks personal service. ⊠ *Rua Cel. Inácio Vale 8847, Ponta Negra, 59090-040* 🕾*084/3646–5000* ⊕*www.rifoles.com.br* ⟿*204 rooms* ♻*In-rooms: refrigerator, safe, Wi-Fi. In-hotel: restaurant, bar, pool* ▤*AE, DC, MC, V.*

$ 🎬 **Divi-Divi.** One block from the beach, this small hotel is a great value if you're willing to forgo a beachside location. Apart from the elevator, the three-story hotel seems more like a guesthouse. Rooms are thoughtfully decorated, well equipped, and comfortable. The small, stylish pool in front helps compensate for the lack of beach. **Pros:** Affordable rates, friendly atmophere. **Cons:** Not on the beach. ⊠ *Rua Elias Barros 248, Ponta Negra, 59090-140* 🕾*084/4006–3900* ⊕*www.dividivi. com.br* ⟿*32 rooms, 2 suites* ♻*In-rooms: refrigerator, safe. In-hotel: bar, pool, public Internet.* ▤*AE, DC, MC, V.*

$ 🎬 **O Tempo e o Vento.** The four-star rooms at this hotel are highly incongruous with the two-star-quality lobby. Luckily, prices are more representative of the latter. The small hotel is a block from the beach, with a pool in front. All rooms have balconies; request those with direct sea views, since they cost the same. **Pros:** Pleasant rooms, great views. **Cons:** Shabby lobby, not on the beach. ⊠ *Rua Elias Barros 66, Ponta Negra, 59090-140* 🕾*084/3219–2526* ⊕*www.otempoeovento.com. br* ⟿*22 rooms* ♻*In room: refrigerator, safe, Ethernet. In-hotel: bar, pool, no elevator, public Wi-Fi* ▤*DC, MC, V.*

$ 🎬 **Residence Praia Hotel.** This modern hotel a block from Praia dos Artistas is a good option for those who want all major amenities but don't want to pay Ponta Negra prices. The hotel is easily recognizable by its blue-glass facade. Rooms are pleasant and colorful, with pastel-painted brick walls. **Pros:** Comfortable accommodations, affordable rates. **Cons:** Area is a bit sketchy at night. ⊠ *Av. 25 de Dezembro 868, Praia dos Artisas, 59010-030* 🕾*084/3202–4466* ⊕*www.residence praia.com.br* ⟿*118 rooms* ♻*In-room: refrigerator. In-hotel: restaurant, pool, public Internet* ▤*AE, DC, MC, V.*

SHOPPING

The best place to go for local crafts and artwork is the **Centro de Turismo** (⊠ *Rua Aderbal de Figueiredo 980, Petrópolis, 59010-780* 🕾*084/3211–6149*). Little shops are housed within the cells of the former prison. It's open daily 8–7. Natal also has several malls and shopping centers. The largest is **Natal Shopping** (⊠ *Km 02, Rodovia BR 101, Candelária, 59064-900* 🕾*084/3209–8199*). **Praia Shopping** (⊠ *Av. Engenheiro Roberto Freire 8790, Ponta Negra, 59052-380* 🕾*084/4008–0800* ⊕*www.praiashopping.com.br*) is the most convenient shopping mall for those staying in Ponta Negra.

NIGHTLIFE & THE ARTS

NIGHTLIFE

Natal has a fairly active nightlife, supported by nearly year-round tourists. Some of the most frequented bars and clubs are in Praia dos Artistas. Other popular spots are scattered downtown and in Ponta Negra. Every Thursday the Centro de Turismo hosts a live forró band as part of the long-running "Forró com Turista" program, which is aimed at acquainting tourists with this important piece of local culture.

BARS

A bar with character, **Taverna Pub** (⊠ *Rua Dr. Manuel Augusto Bezerra de Araújo 500, Ponta Negra, 59090-430* ☎ *084/3236-3696*) is in the basement of a stylized medieval castle. It's popular with locals in their twenties and tourists who stay in the hostel upstairs. A common nighttime destination for Ponta Negra tourists is **Praia Shopping** (⊠ *Av. Engenheiro Roberto Freire 8790, Ponta Negra, 59052-380* ☎ *084/4008–0800*), which has a cluster of small bars and restaurants.

DANCE CLUBS

Downtown (⊠ *Rua Chile 11, Bairro da Ribeira, 59012-250* ☎ *084/611–1950*), modeled after typical London clubs, has live rock music Thursday through Saturday. **Chaplin House Club** (⊠ *Rua Presidente Café Filho 27, Praia do Meio, 59010-000* ☎ *084/3202–1199*), near Praia dos Artistas, has three distinct environments, each with a different type of live music: *pagode* (a popular, mellow samba derivative), forró, and rock. A pricey cover charge doesn't prevent up to 1,500 young people from pouring in the doors.

COUNTRY MUSIC

Forró is the name of what was considered Northeast country music. It became a national favorite in the 1950s, and is still played and danced to up and down the coast. It features *zarumba* (African drum), accordion, and triangle accompaniments. As the story goes, U.S soldiers or British engineers stationed in the Northeast during World War II always invited the townsfolk to their dances, saying they were "for all." This term, when pronounced with a Brazilian accent, became "forró." But music historians trace the origin of the term to an abbreviation of an Indian word *forróbodo*, or craziness.

SIDE TRIP TO PRAIA DA PIPA

85 km (51 mi) south of Natal

Praia da Pipa was a small fishing village until it was "discovered" by surfers in the '70s. Word of its beauty spread, and it's now one of the most famous and fashionable beach towns in the Northeast. It's also rapidly gaining a reputation for having an extremely active nightlife. Praia da Pipa receives a truly eclectic mix of people: hippies, surfers, foreign backpackers, Brazilian youth, and, most recently, high-end visitors attracted by the increasingly upscale restaurants and pousadas.

On either side of the town is a string of beaches with amazingly varied landscapes created by stunning combinations of pink cliffs, black volcanic rocks, palm trees, and natural pools. You can spend hours exploring the various beaches, most of which are deserted because they fall within environmentally protected areas. Another recommended activity is the boat ride to see dolphins, which often frequent the surrounding waters. The 90-minute boat ride leaves regularly from the north end of the principal beach and costs R$15.

TO & FROM

Take BR 101 South from Natal. Buses leave from the Rodoviário de Natal several times daily (1½ hours; R$10).

ESSENTIALS

Bus Contacts **Oceano** (☎ 84/3205-3833).

Emergencies & Medical Assistance **Ambulance** (☎ 192). **Fire** (☎ 193). **Police** (☎ 190).

WHAT TO SEE

For active travelers a good option is the **Santuário Ecológico de Pipa** *(Pipa Ecological Sanctuary)*, a 120-hectare (300-acre) protected area. Sixteen short, well-maintained trails pass through Atlantic Forest vegetation and allow for some great views of the ocean. ⊠*Estrada para Tibau do Sul, 2 km (1 mi) northwest of town, 59178-000* ☎*084/3211–6070* ⊕*www.pipa.com.br/santuarioecologico* 🎟*Free* ☉*Daily 9–5.*

WHERE TO STAY & EAT

$$–$$$$
★
 🏨**Toca da Coruja.** Although many pousadas have been built since this one opened back in 1991, when Pipa was still a fishing village, none can top Toca da Coruja. The chalets are more spacious and expensive than the apartments, and feel more like jungle lodges—one even has an "outdoor" bathtub. But all units are beautifully furnished. This is a Roteiros de Charme hotel. **Pros:** Romantic setting, modern amenties. **Cons:** Some rooms are small. Not the place for families with small children. ⊠*Av. Baía dos Golfinhos 464, 59178-000* ☎*081/3246–2226* ⊕*www.tocad acoruja.com.br* 🛏*6 apartments, 17 bungalows* 🔑*In-hotel: restaurant, bar, pool, no elevator, public Wi-Fi* 🚭*AE, DC, MC, V.*

$ 🏨**Pousada da Ladeira.** Made from local wood and tijolo aparente, this simple pousada has clean rooms—some with balconies overlooking the pool. Because it's right on the main road, it may not be the best choice for those looking for peace and quiet. **Pros:** Affordable rates. **Cons:** A bit noisy. ⊠*Av. Baía dos Golfinhos 802, 59178-000* ☎*084/3246–2334 or 084/3502–2310* ⊕*www.pipa.com.br* 🛏*35 rooms* 🔑*In-room: refrigerator. In-hotel: bar, pool* 🚭*AE, DC, MC, V.*

FORTALEZA

Called the "City of Light," Fortaleza claims that the sun shines on it 2,800 hours a year. And it's a good thing, too, as the coastline stretches far beyond the city. To the east, along the Litoral Leste or the Costa Sol Nascente (Sunrise Coast) are many fishing villages. To the west, along the Litoral Oeste or the Costa Sol Poente (Sunset Coast), there are pristine stretches of sand. The shores here are cooled by constant breezes and lapped by waters with an average temperature of 24°C (72°F).

The city originally sprang up around the Forte de Schoonemborch, a Dutch fortress built in 1649. After the Portuguese defeated the Dutch, the small settlement was called Fortaleza Nossa Senhora da Assunção (Fortress of Our Lady of the Assumption). It didn't see significant growth until 1808, when its ports were opened to facilitate the export of cotton to the United Kingdom.

Today Fortaleza, a large, modern state capital with more than 2 million inhabitants, is Brazil's fifth-largest city. It's also on the move, with one of the country's newest airports, a modern convention center, a huge cultural center with a planetarium, large shopping malls, several museums and theaters, and an abundance of sophisticated restaurants. At Praia de Iracema there's a revitalized beachfront area of sidewalk cafés, bars, and dance clubs. But if you wander along the shore, you're still bound to encounter fishermen unloading their catch from traditional jangadas—just as they've done for hundreds of years.

TO & FROM

There are some direct flights to Fortaleza from the U.S., but most fights connect in São Paulo or Rio de Janeiro. Aeroporto Internacional Pinto Martins is 6 km (4 mi) south of downtown. After clearing customs, those headed downtown should take an *especial* (special) taxi that costs between R$38 and $50. For reliable taxis to Iracema, Aldeota, or Beira Mar, cross the street in front of the terminal. These taxis should cost about $28. City buses run frequently from the airport to the the main bus station, Terminal Rodoviário João Tomé, 6 km (4 mi) south of the Centro and Praça José de Alencar in the Centro.

The main bus station, Terminal Rodoviário João Tomé, is 6 km (4 mi) south of Centro. In low season you can buy tickets at the station right before leaving. São Benedito runs three daily to Aracati and Canoa Quebrada (3½ hours; R$185). Expresso Guanabara has five daily buses to Recife (12 hours; R$100–R$130). Itapemerim has one daily to Salvador (20 hours; R$164) and daily buses to Rio de Janeiro (43 hours; R$315). Penha runs buses to São Paulo.

The main access roads to Fortaleza are the excellent BR 304 to Natal and Recife; the BR 222 to Brasília, which has a few poor sections; and the BR 116 to Salvador, which has several stretches in poor condition. The CE 004, or Litoránea, links the coastal towns to the southeast as far as Aracati.

GETTING AROUND

The easiest way to get around the city is by bus and taxi. Taxis have meters, but you often have to negotiate a fare beforehand with the driver. Fares from Beira Mar to Fortaleza Centre and Praia Futuro will be between R$8 and R$15. Rides to Das Dunas will be between R$40 and R$50. The fare on city buses is R$1.60.

ESSENTIALS

Airport **Aeroporto Internacional Pinto Martins** (FOR ⌧ Av. Senador Carlos Jereissati, Serrinha, Fortaleza, 60741-900 ☎ 085/3392–1200).

Banks & Currency Exchange **Banco do Brasil** (⌧ Av. Duque de Caxias 560, Centro, 60035-110 ⌧ Av. Desembarcador Moreira 1195, Aldeota, 60170-001).

Bus Contacts **Expresso Guanabara** (☎ 085/4011–1992 ⊕ www.expres soguanabara.com.br). **Itapemirim** (☎ 085/3242–1182 ⊕ www.itapemerim. com.br). **Penha** (☎ 085/3256–4511). **São Benedito** (☎ 085/3444–9999). **Terminal Rodoviário Engenheiro João Tomé** (⌧ Av. Borges de Melo 1630, Fátima, 60415-510 ☎ 085/3256–2100).

Emergencies & Medical Assistance **Ambulance** (☎ 192). **Fire** (☎ 193). Hospital: **Hospital Antônio Prudente** (⌧ Rua Prof. Dias da Rocha 2530, Aldeota, 60170-311 ☎ 085/3269–3308). **Hospital Batista** (⌧ Rua Prof. Dias da Rocha 2530, Aldeota, 60170-311 ☎ 085/3268–3308).

Pharmacy: **Farmácia Aldesul** (⌧ Av. Abolição 2625, Meireles, 60165-000 ☎ 085/3242–7071). **Farmácia Portugal** (⌧ Av. Abolição 2950, Meireles, 60165-081 ☎ 085/3242–4422).

Police (☎ 190).

Internet **Alô Brasil** (⌧ Rua Alto Bonito 46, Santa Terezinha, Fortaleza, 60181-060 ☎ 085/3263–3309).

Taxis **Coopertáxi** (☎ 085/3295–8258). **Disquetáxi** (☎ 085/3287–7222). **Radio Táxi Fortaleza** (☎ 085/3254–5554).

Visitor & Tour Info **Ernanitur** (⌧ Av. Barão de Studart 1165, 1 andar, Aldeota, 60120-001 ☎ 085/3533–5333 ⊕ www.ernanitur.com.br) offers city tours and arranges transportation to Jericocoara, Canoa Quebrada, and a number of other beaches. **Funcet** (⌧ Rua Pereira Filgueiras 4, Centro, 60160-150 ☎ 085/3105-1392 ⊕ www.funcet.fortaleza.ce.gov.br), the local tourism agency, is open daily 8–noon and 2–6. **Lisatur Viagens e Turismo Ltda** (⌧ Av. Monsenhor Tabosa 1067, Praia Iracema, 60165-011 ☎ 085/3219–5400 ⊕ www.lisatur.com.br) has city tours and a wide range of other options. **OceanView Tours and Travel** (⌧ Av. Monsenhor Tabosa 1165, Meireles, 60165-011 ☎ 085/3219–1300 ⊕ www.oceanviewturismo.com. br) has trips to Flexeiras, Jericoacoara, or other beach areas outside Fortaleza. **SETUR** (⌧ Centro Administrativo Virgílio Távora, Cambeba, 60830-120 ☎ 085/3101–4688 ⌧ Aeroporto Internacional Pinto Martins, Av. Senador Carlos Jereissati, Serrinha, 60741-900 ☎ 085/3392–1200 ⌧ Centro de Turismo, Rua Senador Pompeu 350, Centro, 60025-000 ☎ 085/3101–5508 ⌧ Terminal Rodoviário João Tomé, Av. Borges de Melo 1630, Fátima, 60415-510 ☎ 085/3230–1111 ⊕ www.setur.ce.gov. br) has a branch in the airport open daily 6 AM–11 PM, one in the bus station open daily 6 AM–9 PM, one in the Centro open Monday to Saturday 8 to 6 and Sunday 8 to noon, and one in Cambeba open weekdays 8 to 5.

EXPLORING

Numbers in the text correspond to numbers in the margin and on the Fortaleza map.

Fortaleza is fairly easy to navigate on foot because its streets are laid out in a grid. Its business center lies above the Centro Histórico (Historic Center) and includes the main market, several shopping streets, and many government buildings. East of the center, urban beaches are lined with high-rise hotels and restaurants. Beyond are the port and old lighthouse, from which Praia do Futuro runs 5 km (3 mi) along Avenida Dioguinho. Be on guard against pickpockets—particularly in the Historic District.

MAIN ATTRACTIONS

⑤ Catedral Metropolitana. Inspired by the famous cathedral in Cologne, this one was built between 1937 and 1963 and has a dominant Gothic look. Its two spires are 75 meters (250 feet) high, and it can accommodate 5,000 worshipers, who are no doubt inspired by its beautiful stained-glass windows. ⊠*Rua Sobral s/n, Centro, 61055-151* ☎*085/3231–4196* ⊕*www.arquidiocesedefortaleza.org.br* ☞*Free* ⊗*Weekdays 8–5, weekends 8–11.*

⑩ Centro de Turismo. Originally a prison, this building was structurally changed in 1850 along simple, classical lines. It's now the home of the state tourism center, with handicraft stores as well as the Museu de Minerais (Mineral Museum) and the Museu de Arte e Cultura Populares (Popular Art and Culture Museum), whose displays of local crafts and sculptures are interesting. ⊠*Rua Senador Pompeu 350, Centro, 60025-000* ☎*085/3101–5508* ☞*R$2* ⊗*Weekdays 7–6, Sat. 8–5, Sun. 8–noon.*

⑧ Centro Dragão do Mar de Arte e Cultura. Not far from the Mercado
★ Central, this majestic cultural complex is an eccentric mix of curves, straight lines, and angular and flat roofs. What's inside is as diverse as the exterior. There's a planetarium as well as art museums with permanent exhibitions of Ceará's two most famous artists, Raimundo Cela and Antônio Bandeira. Another museum presents Ceará's cultural history, with exhibits of embroidery, paintings, prints, pottery, puppets, and musical instruments. When you need a break, head for the center's romantic Café & Cultura, which serves a variety of cocktails made with coffee as well as little meat or vegetarian pies. The center's bookstore has English-language titles as well as souvenirs and cards. ⊠*Rua Dragão do Mar 81, Praia de Iracema, 60060-390* ☎*085/3488–8600* ⊕*www.dragaodomar.org.br* ☞*Museums R$2, planetarium R$8* ⊗*Tues.–Sun. 2–9:30.*

⑥ Mercado Central. With four floors and more than 600 stores, this is *the* place to find handicrafts and just about anything else. It has elevators to take you from one floor to the next, but since it's built with an open style and has ramps that curve from one floor to the next, it's just as easy to walk up. ⊠*Av. Alberto Nepomuceno 199, Centro, 60055-000*

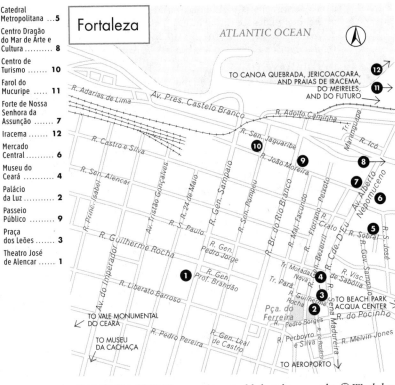

☎ *085/3286–5180* ⊕ *mercadocentraldefortaleza.com.br* ⊘ *Weekdays 7:30–6:30, Sat. 8–4, Sun. 8–noon.*

❾ **Passeio Público.** Also called the Praça dos Mártires, this landmark square
Fodor'sChoice dates from the 19th century. In 1824 many soldiers were executed here
★ in the war for independence from the Portuguese crown. It has a central
fountain and is full of century-old trees and statues of Greek deities.
Look for the ancient baobab tree.

❸ **Praça dos Leões (Praça General Tibúrcio).** Built in 1817, this square is offi-
★ cially named after a Ceará general who fought in Brazil's war against
Paraguay. However, it's commonly referred to as the Praça de Leões
because of its bronze lions, which were brought over from Paris in the
early 20th century.

❶ **Theatro José de Alencar.** The José de Alencar Theater is a rather shock-
Fodor'sChoice ing example (especially if you come upon it suddenly) of the eclectic
★ phase of Brazilian architecture. It's a mixture of neoclassical and art
nouveau styles. The top of the theater, which looks as if it was designed
by the makers of Tiffany lamps, really stands out against Ceará's per-
petually blue sky. It was built in 1910 of steel and iron (many of its
cast-iron sections were imported from Scotland) and was restored in
1989. It's still used for cultural events—including concerts, plays, and

dance performances—and houses a library and an art gallery. Some of the tour guides speak English; call ahead for reservations. ⊠*Praça do José Alencar s/n, Centro, 60030-160* ☎*085/3101–2583* ⊕*www.secult.ce.gov.br* ☜*R$4* ⊙ *Weekdays 8–5, Sat. 8–3.*

IF YOU HAVE TIME

Beach Park Acqua Center. Just 30 minutes from downtown on the idyllic Porto das Dunas Beach is this enormous water park. A 14-story-high waterslide dumps you into a pool at a speed of 105 kph (65 mph), or if you prefer slow-paced attractions, visit its museum, which has the country's largest collection of jangadas, the wooden sailing rafts used by fishermen. An open-air restaurant at the beach serves excellent seafood dishes. There is no bus from downtown, and a taxi costs around R$50. ⊠*Rua Porto das Dunas 2734, Aquiraz, 61700-000* ☎*085/4012–3000* ⊕*www.beachpark.com.br* ☜*R$85* ⊙ *Daily 11–5.*

⓫ Farol do Mucuripe. Erected by slaves and dedicated to Princess Isabel, the monarch who eventually put an end to slavery, this lighthouse was inaugurated in 1846. Surrounded by a system of battlements, it operated for 111 years and was not deactivated until 1957. In 1982 it underwent a restoration and was designated a municipal historic monument. It now houses the Museu de Fortaleza, better known as the Museu do Farol, with exhibits on the city's history. ⊠*Av. Vicente de Castro s/n, Mucuripe, 60180-410* ☎*085/3263–1115* ☜*Free* ⊙ *Mon.–Sat. 7–5, Sun. 7–11.*

❼ Forte de Nossa Senhora da Assunção. Built by the Dutch in 1649, this fort was originally baptized Forte Schoonemborch. In 1655 it was seized by the Portuguese and renamed after the city's patron saint, Nossa Senhora da Assunção. It was rebuilt in 1817 and is now a military headquarters. The city took its name from this fortress (*fortaleza*), which still has the cell where the mother of one of Ceará's most famous writers, José de Alencar, was jailed. ⊠*Av. Alberto Nepomuceno s/n, Centro, 60055-970* ☎*085/3255–1600* ☜*Free* ⊙ *Daily 8–4.*

Museu da Cachaça. It's a toss-up whether coffee or cachaça is Brazil's national drink. This museum just west of Fortaleza offers tastings of the latter. Of course, this happens after you tour the plant and learn the history of what has been a family business for four generations. In the tavern you see a 98,736-gallon wooden barrel, the largest in the world. ⊠*Turn left off CE 65 just before small town of Maranguape, 61940-000* ☎*085/3341–0407* ☜*R$8* ⊙ *Tues.–Sun. 8–5.*

❹ Museu do Ceará. Housed in the former Assembléia Provincial (Provincial Assembly Building), this museum's exhibits are devoted to the history and anthropology of Ceará State. ⊠*Rua São Paulo 51, Centro, 60030-100* ☎*085/3101–2610* ☜*Free* ⊙ *Tues.–Fri. 8:30–5, Sat. 8:30–noon, Sun. 2–5.*

❷ Palácio da Luz. What was originally the home of the Portuguese crown's representative, Antônio de Castro Viana, was built by Indian laborers. In 1814 it became the property of the imperial government and served as the residence of the provincial president. The next important occupant was painter Raimundo Cefa. It now houses a display of his work and has been designated a historic landmark. ⊠*Rua do Rosário 01, 60135-050* ☎*0853226–0326* ☞*Free* ☉ *Weekdays 8–2.*

BEACHES

Fortaleza's enchanting coast runs 22 km (14 mi) along the Atlantic between the Rio Ceará, to the west, and the Rio Pacoti, to the east. The feel of this great urban stretch of sand along with its scenery varies as often as its names: Barra do Ceará, Pirambu, Formosa, Iracema, Beira-Mar, Meireles, Mucuripe, Mansa, Titanzinho, Praia do Futuro, and Sabiazuaba.

In the city center and its immediate environs, feel free to soak up the sun and the ambience of the beaches, but stay out of the water—it's too polluted for swimming. However, you can find clean waters and amazing sands just a little way from Centro and beyond. Surfing is fine at several beaches, including those near the towns of Paracuru and Pecém, to the west of Fortaleza, and Porto das Dunas, to the east.

Fodor'sChoice
★ **Canoa Quebrada.** Hidden behind dunes, the stunning Canoa Quebrada Beach was "discovered" in the 1970s by French doctors working in the area. The spectacular scenery includes not only dunes but also jangadas, red cliffs, and groves of palm trees. Carved into a cliff is the symbol of Canoa: a crescent moon with a star in the middle. Although it was originally settled by Italian hippies, the village itself has moved on with the times and now has good roads, several comfortable pousadas, and bars and restaurants. The best way to get here is on a trip offered by one of Fortaleza's many tour operators, but bus companies also have daily departures from Fortaleza and Natal. ⊠*Take BR 116 to BR 304; 164 km (101 mi) east of Fortaleza, 62800-000.*

Iguape. The white-sand dunes at this beach are so high that people actually ski down them. The water is calm and clean. In the nearby village you find both fishermen and lace makers (lace is sold at the Centro de Rendeiras). There's also a lookout at Morro do Enxerga Tudo. Buses depart from Fortaleza for this beach several times daily. ⊠*CE 040, 50 km (31 mi) east of Fortaleza, 61752-000.*

Flexeiras. The ocean is always calm at this beach. Coconut trees, lagoons, and sand dunes surround it. During low tide the reefs surface, and you can see small fish and shells in the rocks. When the tide comes in and the natural pools form, you can grab your mask and go snorkeling. In a 5-km (3-mi) stretch between Flexeiras and Mundaú—another almost-deserted beach—there are several fishing villages and a working lighthouse. A river joins the ocean at Mundaú, forming a large S on the sand; on one side is a line of coconut trees and on the other, fishermen with their jangadas—the scene conveys the very essence of Ceará. Flexeiras is about a 90-minute drive from Fortaleza. You can take the Rendenção bus or arrange a trip here with a tour operator. As yet there are no luxury resorts here, but there are several simple, clean pousadas. ⊠*CE 085, 177 km (110 mi) northwest of Fortaleza, 62690-000.*

9

Porto das Dunas. Its water-sports options, including surfing, and its sand dunes are enough to draw many people to this beach. But it has much more, including an all-suites hotel and a water park and entertainment complex that might make Disney jealous. You can get here on the *jardineira* bus from Centro or from along Avenida Beira-Mar. ⊠ *Take Av. Washington Soares, then follow signs to Estrada da Cofeco and Beach Park; 22 km (14 mi) southeast of Fortaleza, 61700-000.*

WHERE TO EAT

■ TIP→ **Along Praia de Iracema and Praia do Mucuripe there are several good seafood restaurants.**

$$–$$$$ ✕**Cemoara.** A sophisticated decor with clean lines adds to the appeal
★   of this traditional seafood restaurant. Although the *bacalão* (salt cod) selections are fabulous, you can't go wrong with the grilled lobster in a caper sauce or any of the flambéed dishes. The piano in the corner is there for a purpose: a musician accompanies your dinner with nice, soft music. Cemoara has air-conditioning and a no-smoking area. ⊠ *Rua Joaquim Nabuco 166, Meireles, 60125-120* ☎ *085/3242–8500* ⊟ *AE, DC, MC, V* ⊗ *No dinner Sun.*

$–$$$ ✕**Pulcinella.** You can feast on this restaurant's classic Italian fare (sometimes given a regional twist) in either the air-conditioned dining room with a no-smoking section or in the alfresco seating area. Among the most popular dishes are spaghetti in garlic sauce with shrimp and pimiento and veal in a mushroom-and-herb sauce. ⊠ *Rua Osvaldo Cruz 640, Aldeota, 60125-150* ☎ *085/3261–3411* ⊟ *AE, DC, MC, V.*

$–$$ ✕**Colher de Pau.** Ana Maria Vilmar and her mother opened this restaurant more than a decade ago in a small rented house in the Varjota district. It became so popular that they had to open in a larger building down the street. The sun-dried meat is served not only with paçoca but also with banana and *baião-de-dois* (rice and beans). The shellfish dishes, many prepared using regional recipes, are also standouts. ⊠ *Rua Frederico Borges 204, Varjota, 60175-040* ☎ *085/3267–3773* ⊕ *www.restaurantecolherdepau.com.br* ⊟ *AE, DC, MC, V.*

$–$$ ✕**Santa Grelha.** The international fare with local accents smartly matches the attractive decor that employs traditional local materials. In a restored colonial house about a mile from the beach, Santa Grelha is off the tourist path. The specialty is grilled meat and grilled fish. ⊠ *Rua Vicente Leite 102, Aldeota, 60150-121* ☎ *085/3224–0249* ⊟ *AE, MC, V* ⊗ *Closed Mon.*

$ ✕**Caicó.** Locals come for arguably the city's most famous sun-dried meat and paçoca, though dishes of chicken and lamb are also recommended. Ambience is at a minimum in the simple, outdoor seating area on a busy road. ⊠ *Av. Engenheiro Santana Jr. 1002, Papicu, 60175-145* ☎ *085/3234–1915* ⊕ *www.restaurantecaico.com.br* ⊟ *AE, MC, V.*

WHERE TO STAY

Most hotels are along Avenida Beira-Mar (previously known as Avenida Presidente John Kennedy). Those in the Praia de Iracema are generally less expensive than those along Praia do Mucuripe. Iracema, however, is also a more interesting area to explore, and it's full of trendy restaurants and bars.

$$$$ ⚏**Beach Park Suites Resort.** There's ☾ very little this pleasant all-suites resort doesn't offer. It faces the beautiful Porto das Dunas Beach, and the Beach Park Acqua Center is a five-minute walk away (hotel guests get a discount). All the spacious suites have balconies, and the dozens of pots of flowers in the lobby give the whole place a cheerful atmosphere. **Pros:** Family-friendly environment, spacious accommodations. **Cons:** Anonymity of a large hotel. ⊠*Rua Porto das Dunas 2743, Aquiraz, 61700-000* ☎*085/4012–3000* ⊕*www.beachpark.com.br* ⊸*198 suites* ⟑*In-room: refrigerator, Wi-Fi. In-hotel: restaurant, bar, tennis courts, pool, gym, beachfront, children's programs (ages 4–12), public Internet* ▤*AE, DC, MC, V.*

$$–$$$ ⚏**Vila Galé Fortaleza.** This family-friendly resort is the most upscale hotel in the Praia do Futuro area. Extremely well run, it represents the Portuguese chain's foray into Brazil. Although the exterior lacks distinction, the grand lobby is impressive in its design and decor. Services and amenities are top-notch, which is fortunate since there's no nightlife to speak of in the area. **Pros:** Everything sparkles, great amenities. **Cons:** Far from the action, plain architecture. ⊠*Av. Dioguinho 4189, Praia do Futuro, 60182-001* ☎*085/3486–4400* ⊕*www.vilagale.com. br* ⊸*285 rooms, 15 suites* ⟑*In-room: refrigerator. In-hotel: restaurant, bar, pool, gym, public Internet* ▤*AE, DC, MC, V.*

$$ ⚏**Gran Marquise.** On Praia do Mucuripe, just a 15-minute drive ★ from the Centro, this luxury hotel can certainly trumpet its "convenient location." Marble and black granite give the building a modern, sleek look. One of the on-site restaurants serves Brazilian fare, while another focuses on French cuinsine. The third, Mariko, is noteworthy for Japanese food and buffets of lobster, shrimp, sushi, sashimi, and oysters. The view from the pool area on the 20th floor is fantastic. **Pros:** Great location, good dining choices, excellent amenities. **Cons:** Not all rooms have views. ⊠*Av. Beira-Mar 3980, Mucuripe, 60165-121* ☎*085/3466–5000* ⊕*www.granmarquise.com.br* ⊸*230 rooms, 26 suites* ⟑*In-room: safe, refrigerator. In-hotel: 3 restaurants, room service, bars, pool, gym* ▤*AE, DC, MC, V.*

$$ ⚏**Marina Park.** Designed to look like a huge ship, the resort overlooks a calm bay and is connected to a marina from which you can take boat trips. It's rather far from the center of everything, but it does have an uncrowded 5-km-long (3-mi-long) beach, as well as an enormous free-form pool. **Pros:** Beautiful beach, impressive pool area. **Cons:** Far from the action, tacky furnishings. ⊠*Av. Presidente Castelo Branco 400,*

9

Praia de Iracema, 60010-000 ☎*085/4006–9595* ⊕*www.marinapark. com.br* ⤴*305 rooms, 10 suites* &*In-room: safe, refrigerator, dial-up. In-hotel: 5 restaurants, bar, tennis courts, pool* ▤*AE, DC, MC, V.*

$$ 🏨**Mercure Fortaleza Golden.** These comfortable apartments are perfect for families and visitors in the city for a long stay. Each unit has one or two bedrooms, a living room, and a fully equipped kitchen. If you get tired of preparing your own meals, you can head for the restaurant or the coffee shop. **Pros:** Family-friendly environment. **Cons:** Plain decor. ⊠*Av. Beira-Mar 4260, Mucuripe, 60165-121* ☎*085/3466–1413* ⊕*www.accorhotels.com.br* ⤴*132 apartments* &*In-room: kitchen. In-hotel: restaurant, bar, pool* ▤*AE, DC, MC, V.*

$$ 🏨**Othon Palace Fortaleza.** The Othon Palace Fortaleza sits on a small hill right where the beach makes a big curve, affording guests a spectacular view of the beach and Mucuripe Bay. There's comfortable seating in the stylish lobby, where a spiral staircase leads up to meeting rooms. Tastefully decorated rooms are more like small suites. **Pros:** Spacious accommodations, excellent beach. **Cons:** Fewer amenties than at other hotels. ⊠*Av. Beira-Mar 3470, Mucuripe, 60165-121* ☎*085/3466– 5500* ⊕*www.othon.com.br* ⤴*121 rooms, 13 suites* &*In-room: refrigerator. In-hotel: restaurant, gym* ▤*AE, DC, MC, V.*

$$ 🏨**Seara Praia.** When you're in the mood for action, there's plenty of it across the street at Meireles Beach. The lobby is decorated with works by local artists. Rooms have tile floors, modern art, and furniture with clean, classic lines. For an ocean view, ask for a deluxe room or suite. Don't despair if such a room isn't available; simply head for the rooftop pool and deck and partake of the glorious sunsets. **Pros:** Pleasant rooms, nice rooftop pool. **Cons:** Noisy location, spotty service. ⊠*Av. Beira-Mar 3080, Meireles, 60165-121* ☎*085/4011–2200* ⊕*www.hotelseara. com.br* ⤴*217 rooms, 14 suites* &*In room: refrigerator, Ethernet. In-hotel: restaurant, bar, pool, public Internet* ▤*AE, DC, MC, V.*

$ 🏨**Ponta Mar Hotel.** This refined and modern hotel is across the street
★ from a popular beach. A handicrafts fair and a shopping plaza are nearby. Rooms are extra large, and those with great sea views cost just R$15 more than those without. **Pros:** Nice views, pleasant common areas. **Cons:** On a noisy street. ⊠*Av. Beira-Mar 2200, Meireles, 60165-121* ☎*085/4006–2200 or 085/4006–2222* ⊕*www.pontamar. com.br* ⤴*260 rooms, 12 suites* &*In-room: refrigerator, Ethernet. In-hotel: restaurant, bar, pool, gym* ▤*AE, DC, MC, V.*

$ 🏨**Praiano Palace.** This hotel is a surprisingly affordable option in the chic Praia do Meireles area. Its rooms are simple but comfortable, and nearly all have sea views. Windows alongside the lobby look out on a small garden and a waterfall. **Pros:** Great service, nice views. **Cons:** Rooms are small. ⊠*Av. Beira-Mar 2800, Meireles, 60165-121* ☎*085/4008–2200* ⊕*www.praiano.com.br* ⤴*189 rooms* &*In-room: a/c, refrigerator, Ethernet. In-hotel: restaurant, bar, pool, public Internet* ▤*AE, DC, MC, V.*

¢ 🏨**Malibu Praia Hotel.** Being six blocks from the beach means you do not pay a lot for a decent-size room with all major amenities. Its only major flaws are small beds and dim lighting. Tacky paintings and plastic flowers lend a comical touch to the lobby. **Pros:** Budget rates. **Cons:** Plain decor. ⊠*Av. Rui Barbosa, Iracema, 60115-220*

☎ *085/3261–5755 or 085/3261–8687* ↩ *29 rooms* ♻ *In-hotel: restaurant* 🖃 *AE, DC, MC, V.*

NIGHTLIFE & THE ARTS

NIGHTLIFE

Fortaleza is renowned for its lively nightlife, particularly along Avenida Beira-Mar and Rua dos Tabajaras in the vicinity of Praia de Iracema. The action often includes live forró, the traditional and very popular music and dance of the northeast.

BARS & CLUBS

A young crowd grooves to the latest music at **Boite Domínio Público** (⊠ *Rua Dragão do Mar 212, Praia de Iracema, 60060-390* ☎ *085/3219–3883*). **Mucuripe Club** (⊠ *Travessa Maranguape 108, Centro, 60546-200* ☎ *085/3254–3020* ⊕ *www.mucuripe.com.br*) houses two separate clubs, one with a nautical theme and one with an underwater theme. In Papicu Tuesday and Thursday nights are hottest at **Oásis** (⊠ *Av. Santos Dumont 6061, 61190-800* ☎ *085/3234–4970*), when live music from years past draws a crowd to the large dance floor.

> ### FATHER OF FORRÓ
>
> The originator of forró, Luiz Gonzaga was born in 1912 in the state of Pernambuco. In 1939 the musician moved to Rio de Janeiro, but could not play the music he grew up with because of prejudice against Northeasterners. Because of this he did not record his own compositions for years.
>
> Gonzaga's most famous song is called "Asa Branca," or "White Wing." This mournful tune refers to a white bird that was the last to leave the Northeast during a devastating drought. Once the bird leaves, the *sertanejos,* or people of the region, must either follow or die of thirst.

THE ARTS

The large **Centro Dragão do Mar de Arte e Cultura** (⊠ *Rua Dragão do Mar 81, Praia de Iracema, 60060-390* ☎ *085/3488–8625*), near the Mercado Central, has several theaters and an open-air amphitheater that host live performances. There are also classrooms for courses in cinema, theater, design, and dance. The **Centro Cultural Banco do Nordeste** (⊠ *Rua Floriano Peixoto 941, Centro, 60025-130* ☎ *085/3464–3108*) hosts plays, concerts, and art exhibitions. The early-19th-century **Theatro José de Alencar** (⊠ *Praça do José Alencar s/n, Centro, 60030-150* ☎ *085/3101–2596* ⊕ *www.secult.ce.gov.br*) is the site of many concerts, plays, and dance performances. Alongside the gorgeous main theater is a smaller venue for more intimate events. There's also a small stage in the theater's garden.

SPORTS & THE OUTDOORS

The sidewalk along Avenida Beira-Mar is a pleasant place for a walk, run, or bike, and there's usually a pickup volleyball or soccer game in progress on the beach—don't hesitate to ask the players whether you can join in. There are also running tracks and sports courts in the 25-km-long (16-mi-long) Parque do Cocó, on Avenida Pontes Vieira.

SCUBA DIVING

Off the coast of Ceará are some good dive sites with coral reefs, tropical fish, and wrecks. To rent equipment or arrange lessons, contact **Projeto Netuno** (✉ *Rua Osvaldo Cruz 2453, Dionísio Torres, 60165-151* ☎ *085/3264–4114* ⊕ *www.pnetuno.com.br*). If you're a novice, you can benefit from its courses, with presentations on equipment and dive techniques as well as marine biology.

SHOPPING

Fortaleza is one of the most important centers for crafts—especially bobbin lace—in the Northeast. Shops sell a good variety of handicrafts, and others have clothing, shoes, and jewelry along Avenida Monsenhor Tabosa in Praia de Iracema. Shopping centers both large and small house branches of the best Brazilian stores.

Markets and fairs are the best places to look for lacework, embroidery, leather goods, hammocks, and carvings. More than 600 artisans sell their work at the nightly **Feirinha de Artesanato** (✉ *Av. Beira-Mar, 60165-121* ☎ *No phone* ⊕ *www.ceart.ce.gov.br*).

For lace aficionados, a trip to the town of **Aquiraz** (✉ *30 km/19 mi east of Fortaleza, 61700-000*) is a must. Ceará's first capital (1713–99) is today a hub for the artisans who create the famous *bilro* (bobbin) lace. On the beach called Prainha (6 km/4 mi east of Aquiraz) is the Centro de Rendeiras Luiza Távora. Here, seated on little stools, dedicated and patient women lace makers explain how they create such items as bedspreads and tablecloths using the bilro technique.

SIDE TRIP TO VALE MONUMENTAL DO CEARÁ

158 km (98 mi) southwest of Fortaleza.

Ecological parks and huge monoliths fill the Vale Monumental do Ceará (Monumental Valley), an area of nearly 247,100 acres of sertão a two-hour drive over good roads from Fortaleza. Activities include mountain climbing, biking, hiking, horseback tours, paragliding, hang gliding, geology treks, and birding (400 species of birds have been identified).

TO & FROM

To get to Vale Monumental de Ceara, take CE 060 and CE 452 from Fortaleza. Expresso Guanabara or Redencão buses bound for Quixada leave daily from the main bus station in Fortaleza. They cost R$16 to R$20.

ESSENTIALS

Bus Contacts **Expresso Guanabara** (☎ *085/4005–1992* ⊕ *www.expressoguanabara.com.br*). **Empresa Redencão** (☎ *088/3412–2424* ⊕ *www.redencaoonline.com.br*).

Emergencies & Medical Assistance **Ambulance** (☎ *192*). **Fire** (☎ *193*). **Police** (☎ *190*).

SPORTS & THE OUTDOORS

You can hire guides to take you on hikes along the Trilha das Andorinhas (Andorinhas Trail). The valley is filled with giant rocks sculptured by the elements into unusual formations. Trails have been mapped out for moderate hikes to grottos, caves (some of which have prehistoric etchings), lagoons, canyons, and tunnels. Contact **Sertão & Pedras** (⊠ *Rua Basílio Pinto 365, Quixadá, 63900-000* ☎ *088/3412–5995*) to arrange canoeing or rock-climbing trips.

Thermal wind conditions are just right for paragliding off a mountaintop near the towns of Quixadá and Quixeramobim, about two hours southwest of Fortaleza. One person's excursion of 6½ hours in the air made it into the *Guinness Book of World Records*. Once you're harnessed up, it's just a short downhill run before the wind grabs you and off you go. The most popular month for competitions is November because it's dry. Chico Santos at **Go Up Brazil** (⊠ *Estrada das Canoas 722, Bloco 4, Apto. 207, São Conrado, Rio de Janeiro, 22610–210RJ* ☎ *021/3322–3165 or 021/9177–9134*) can help you make arrangements for paragliding trips in the Vale Monumental. If you'd like to learn to paraglide, contact Claudio Henrique Landim, an instructor with **Escola de vôo Livre** (☎ *085/9984–1330*). The course is R$680 for 30 hours.

SIDE TRIP TO JERICOACOARA

Fodor's Choice
★
300 km (186 mi) northwest of Fortaleza.

It could be the sand dunes, some more than 30 meters (100 feet) tall; it could be the expanse of ocean that puts no limits on how far your eyes can see; or it could be that in the presence of this awesome display of nature, everyday problems seem insignificant. Jericoacoara, a rustic paradise on Ceará State's northwest coast, affects everyone differently but leaves no one unchanged—just like the sand dunes that change their shape and even their colors as they bend to the will of the winds.

In Jericoacoara, or Jerí, time seems endless, even though in the back of your mind you know you'll be leaving in a day or two (or a week or two, if you're lucky). It's the ultimate relaxing vacation, and not because there isn't anything to do. You can surf down sand dunes or ride up and down them in a dune buggy. Also, you can take an easy hike to the nearby Pedra Furada, or Arched Rock, a gorgeous formation sculpted by the waves.

TO & FROM

From Fortaleza, Viacão Redenção buses depart at 5:30 PM and arrive in Jijoca at around 11 PM. From there an open-air bus drives you the rest of the way to Jericocoara. The journey costs R$35. Buy your return ticket as soon as you arrive in Jericoacoara, as they sell out quickly.

ESSENTIALS

Bus Contacts Empresa Redencão (☎ *85/3256-2728* ⊕ *www.redencaoonline. com.br*).

Emergencies & Medical Assistance
Ambulance (☎ *192*).

Visitor & Tour Info Hard Tour Ecotourismo (✉ *Rua Francisco Holanda 843, 60130-040 Fortaleza* ☎ *085/8800–0741* ⊕ *www.hardtour.com*) offers three-day trips to Jericoacoara that stop at all the beaches and hamlets along the way. **Heliance Turismo** (✉ *Av. Senador Virgílio*

> ### SAY BONGIORNO!
>
> If you make it to Jericoacoara, you might feel you're in the heart of Italy. It's a great place to practice your Italian, as it's spoken far more widely than Portuguese.

Távara 195, Meireles, 60170-250 ☎ *085/3066–9383* ⊕ *www.heliance.com.br*) can arrange the six-hour trip between Fortaleza and Jericoacoara. **OceanView Tours and Travel** (✉ *Av. Monsenhor Tabosa 1165, Meireles, 60165-970* ☎ *085/3219–1300* ⊕ *www.oceanviewturismo.com.br*) can arrange tours to Ceara's beaches.

WHERE TO STAY & EAT

$–$$ ✕ **Carcará.** This highly regarded restaurant has a wide variety of seafood dishes, from local specialties to international favorites such as sashimi and ceviche. You can choose between pleasant indoor and outdoor seating areas. ✉ *Rua do Forró 530, 62598-000* ☎ *088/3669–2013* ▭ *DC, MC, V* ☽ *Closed May. No lunch Sun.*

$ ▥ **Pousada Ibirapuera.** Wind chimes, candles, and mobiles help cre-
★ ate a sense of peace and tranquillity at this splendid pousada. Colorful duplex apartments have windows looking out into the garden and hammocks in front. The dining area is decorated with a mix of modern art and antiques. **Pros:** Pleasant rooms, lots of privacy. **Cons:** Few amenities. ✉ *Rua S da Duna 06, 62598-000* ☎ *088/3669–2012 or 088/9961–5544* ▭ *8 apartments* ☖ *In-room: no TV, refrigerator, safe. In-hotel: bar, no elevator, public Internet* ▭ *AE, DC, MC, V.*

SPORTS & THE OUTDOORS

Casa do Turismo (☎ *084/621–0211* ⊕ *www.jericoacoara.com*) can set you up for a 9-km (5-mi) self-guided hike through the dunes using a handheld GPS (global positioning system) monitor. When you arrive at the oasislike Lagoa do Paraiso, you are picked up in a canoe and taken to a restaurant where Italian chef Fred treats you to a divine five-course meal.

FERNANDO DE NORONHA

322 km (200 mi) off the coast of Recife.

This group of 21 islands is part of the Mid-Atlantic Ridge, an underwater volcanic mountain chain more than 15,000 km (9,315 mi) long. It was discovered in 1503 by the Italian explorer Amérigo Vespucci, but was taken over by Fernando de Noronha of Portugal. Its attackers have included the French, Dutch, and English, but the Portuguese built several fortresses and, with cannons in place, fought them off.

Brazil used these islands for a prison and as a military training ground. As word of its beauty and spectacular underwater wonders spread, it was designated a protected marine park. Today stringent regulations protect the archipelago's ecology.

The mountainous, volcanic main—and only inhabited—island of Fernando de Noronha is ringed by beaches with crystal-clear warm waters that are perfect for swimming, snorkeling, and diving. In summer surfers show up to tame the waves. There are shipwrecks to explore and huge turtles, stingrays, and sharks (14 species of them) with which to swim. Diving is good all year, but prime time is from December to March on the windward side (facing Africa) and from July to October on the leeward side (facing Brazil).

If you're an experienced diver, be sure to visit the *Ipiranga,* a small Brazilian destroyer that sank in 1987. It sits upright in 60 meters (200 feet) of water and is swarming with fish, and you can see the sailors' personal effects, including uniforms still hanging in closets. Another good site is the Sapata Cave, which has an antechamber so large that it has been used for marriage ceremonies (attended by giant rays, no doubt).

Well-maintained trails and well-trained guides make for enjoyable hikes. You can also enjoy the landscape on a horseback trek to the fortress ruins and isolated beaches where hundreds of seabirds alight. In addition, Projeto Tamar has an island base for its work involving sea turtles. One of the most fascinating exploring experiences, however, is an afternoon boat trip to the outer fringes of the Baía dos Golfinhos (Bay of the Dolphins), where dozens of spinner dolphins swim south each day to hunt in deep water.

There are two daily departures to Fernando de Noronha from both Recife and Natal; flight time from either is around an hour. Only 90 visitors are allowed here each day, and there's a daily tourist tax of R$35, including the day you arrive and the day you leave. Divers pay an additional R$20 a day. Bring enough reais to last the trip, as credit cards are not widely accepted and changing money is difficult. There is only one bank in Fernando de Noronha, so withdraw cash before your trip here.

TO & FROM
Flights on Varig from Recife and Natal usually cost around R$1,000.

GETTING AROUND
Taxis from the airport cost about R$30.

ESSENTIALS
Airport **Aeroporto de Fernando de Noronha** (☎*081/3619–1148*).

Banks & Currency Exchange **Banco Real** (✉*Vila dos Remedios s/n, 53990-000*).

Emergencies & Medical Assistance **Ambulance** (☎*192*). **Fire** (☎*193*). **Police** (☎*190*).

Visitor & Tour Info **Karitas Turismo Ltda** (✉*Rua Agenor Lopes 292, Boa Viagem, Recife51021-310* ☎*081/3466–4300* ⊕*www.karitas.com.br*) arranges tours and makes reservations at pousadas.

WHERE TO STAY & EAT

$$$$ ✕ **Ecologiku's.** This very small restaurant is known for its seafood,
especially lobster. If you can't decide
what to order, the *sinfonia ecologiku*
is a sampling of every type of seafood on the menu. ⊠*Estrada Velha
do Sueste, near airport, 53990-000*
☎*081/3619–1807* ▭*MC, V* ⊙*No
lunch.*

$$–$$$$ ✕ **Tartarugão.** One of island's best
restaurants also operates a little
rent-a-buggy business on the side.
The phenomenal steak is big
enough for two people and comes

> **AN ISLAND PRISON**
>
> Brazil took advantage of Fernando
> de Noronha's isolated location
> and built a prison on one of the
> islands. The vegetation on the
> island was cut down so that pris-
> oners wouldn't be able to build
> rafts on which to escape. In the
> 1930s and 1940s the prison was
> used to house political prison-
> ers, specifically communists and
> anarchists.

with rice and a salad. The restaurant is on the west side of the island.
⊠*Alameda do Boldró 238, 53990-000* ☎*081/3619–1331* ▭*MC, V.*

$$$$ ⌂ **Pousada Dolphin.** A five-minute walk from the beach, this pousada has
large, attractively decorated rooms. **Pros:** Lots of space. **Cons:** Not on
the beach. ⊠*Alameda Boldró s/n, BR 363, 53990-000* ☎*081/3366–
6601* ⊕*www.dolphinhotel.tur.br* ⟿*11 rooms* ⌂*In room: refrigerator,
Wi-Fi. In-hotel: restaurant, bar, pool, no elevator* ▭*MC* ⦿*MAP.*

$$$$ ⌂ **Pousada Zé Maria Paraíso.** Although this friendly, popular pousada
isn't on the beach, the ocean is a 15-minute walk away. It sits atop a
hill, surrounded by vegetation. **Pros:** Airy rooms. **Cons:** Plain decor.
⊠*Rua Nice Cordeiro 1, Floresta Velha, 53990-000* ☎*081/3619–
1258* ⊕*www.pousadazemaria.com.br* ⟿*6 rooms, 13 bungalows*
⌂*In-room: refrigerator. In-hotel: restaurant, pool, no elevator, public
Wi-Fi.*

SPORTS & THE OUTDOORS

For dive trips, **Atlantis Divers** (⊠*Fernando de Noronha, Caixa Postal
20, 53990-000* ☎*081/3619–1371* ⊕*www.atlantisnoronha.com.br*)
has excellent English-speaking staffers and good boats.

The Amazon

10

Updated by
Rhan Flatin
& Anna
Katsnelson

THE WORLD'S LARGEST TROPICAL FOREST seems an endless carpet of green that's sliced only by the curving contours of rivers. Its statistics are as impressive: the region covers more than 10 million square km (4 million square mi) and extends into eight other countries (French Guiana, Suriname, Guyana, Venezuela, Ecuador, Peru, Bolivia, and Colombia). It takes up roughly 40% of Brazil in the states of Acre, Rondônia, Amazonas, Roraima, Pará, Amapá, and Tocantins. The Amazon forest is home to 500,000 cataloged species of plants and a river that annually transports 15% of the world's available freshwater to the sea, yet it's inhabited by only 16 million people. That's less than the population of metropolitan São Paulo.

Although there are regular flights and some bus routes through the Amazon, many visitors opt for the area's primary mode of transportation—boat (⇨*The Amazon by Boat, below*). Though much slower, boats offer a closer look at Amazon culture, nature, and the river system, and they go just about everywhere you'd want to go.

ORIENTATION

A trip along the Amazon itself is a singular experience. From its source in southern Peru it runs 6,300 km (3,900 mi) to its Atlantic outflow and averages more than 3 km (2 mi) in width, but reaching up to 48 km (30 mi) across in the rainy season. Of its hundreds of tributaries, 17 are more than 1,600 km (1,000 mi) long. The Amazon is so large it could hold the Congo, Nile, Orinoco, Mississippi, and Yangtze rivers with room to spare. In places it is so wide you can't see the opposite shore, earning it the appellation Rio Mar (River Sea). Although there has been increasing urbanization in the Amazon region, between one-third and one-half of the Amazon's residents live in rural settlements, many of which are along the riverbanks, where transportation, water, fish, and good soil for planting are readily available.

BELÉM

Belém lies 60 mi upstream from the ocean at the confluence of several rivers. It was one of the first areas to be settled by the Portuguese. Its blend of river, ocean, and tropical forest makes for interesting geography and traveling. Buses run to landlocked villages northeast and southwest of the city, while boats run elsewhere. Boats are slow, so add extra time to your travel plans.

SIDE TRIPS FROM BELÉM

The river beaches of Mosqueiro lie an hour away by bus, and Salinópolis's expansive ocean beaches are three hours. Thirty minutes in a boat will get you to villages across the river. Interesting towns with beaches on the southeast coast of Marajó Island take three to four hours. Overnight boats will get you to communities like Macapá and Breves. Two days will get you to Santarém.

TOP REASONS TO GO

■ **The Rain Forest:** Experience the largest tropical forest in the world and one of the wildest places on the planet.

■ **The River:** Explore the largest river in the world (by volume) and the second-longest, spanning more distance than the continental U.S.; the Amazon is also the earth's biggest freshwater ecosystem, and home to more fish than the Atlantic Ocean.

■ **Exotic Foods:** Dig into water-buffalo steak, duck in manioc sauce (*pato no tucupí*), fried piranha, and other river fish with exotic Indian names such as *tucunaré* and *pirarucú*.

■ **Handicrafts:** Shop for traditional indigenous crafts, such as wood-crafted and woven items, bows, arrows, blowguns, and jewelry and headdresses of seeds and feathers.

BETWEEN BELÉM & MANAUS

As one would expect, distances between the major cities are huge. Traveling from one to another is done mostly by boat and plane, since there are no roads connecting them. Boats commonly run from Belém to Manaus and back, though the 1,150-mi journey takes four or five days. Large planes connect cities and larger towns. Small planes reach some smaller towns, though they are costly. While the Trans Amazônica highway is intended to connect the eastern and western regions, nature is still in control. Much of it is still dirt, mud, or dust. Consider it impassable and even dangerous in places.

MANAUS

Manaus is the Amazon's largest city as well as its main entrance. It was built largely on the good fortune of a couple of economic booms. The first was rubber. The second was the creation of a tax-free zone. Getting around the city or heading north to Venezuela is done by car or bus. To go anywhere else, you must use a boat or plane. Don't plan to drive south to Porto Velho or Bolivia. The road will be gone in a number of places.

10

PLANNING

Visiting outlying areas in the Amazon usually results in unforgettable adventures, but tropical environments can be hostile, so prepare well and go with a companion if possible. It's a good idea to hire a guide or go with a tour company specializing in backcountry adventures. To join a tour or to choose a destination, contact one of the tour companies we suggest, or consult with a state-run tour agency. Paratur in Belém and SEC in Manaus can also be helpful. Before departure make sure someone knows exactly where you are going and when you are returning. Tell them you will contact them as soon as you have phone access. Research important health and safety precautions before your trip. A small cut, for example, can turn into a bad infection, and a painful

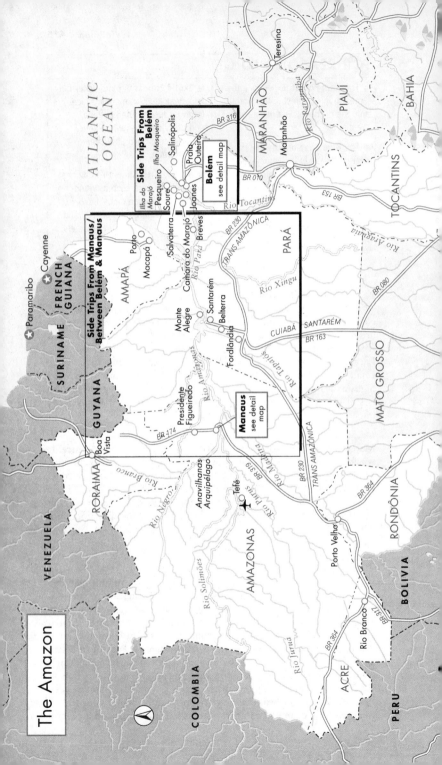

The Amazon

ATLANTIC OCEAN

Side Trips From Belém

Belém see detail map

Side Trips From Manaus/ Between Belém & Manaus

Manaus see detail map

Teresina

MARANHÃO

PIAUÍ

BAHIA

Rio Parnaíba

BR 316

Salinópolis

Praia
Outeiro

Ilha do
Marajó
Pesqueiro Ilha Mosqueiro
Soure
Joanes

Salvaterra

Câmara do Marajó

Breves

Rio Pará

BR 010

Rio Tocantins

BR 153

TOCANTINS

BR 230

TRANS AMAZÔNICA

PARÁ

Rio Xingu

BR 080

Macapá

Porto

AMAPÁ

Monte
Alegre

Santarém

Belterra

Fordlândia

CUIABÁ   SANTARÉM
BR 163

Rio Tapajós

MATO GROSSO

Cayenne

FRENCH
GUIANA

Paramaribo

SURINAME

GUYANA

Boa
Vista

RORAIMA

Rio Branco

BR 174

Presidente
Figueiredo

Rio Amazonas

Anavilhanas
Arquipélago

Tefé

Rio Negro

VENEZUELA

COLOMBIA

Rio Solimões

AMAZONAS

Rio Juruá

Rio Purus

BR 319

Rio Madeira

Porto Velho

TRANS AMAZÔNICA

BR 230

RONDÔNIA

BR 364

BR 364

Rio Branco

ACRE

BR 317

BOLIVIA

PERU

N

A Bit of History

Spaniard Vicente Pinzón is credited with being the first to sail the Amazon, in 1500. But the most famous voyage was undertaken by Spanish conquistador Francisco de Orellano, who set out from Ecuador on a short mission to search for food in 1541. Instead of gold or a lost kingdom, however, Orellano ran into natives, heat, and disease. When he emerged from the jungle a year later, his crew told a tale of women warriors they called the Amazons (a nod to classical mythology), and the story lent the region its name. In the late 19th century, rubber production transformed Belém and Manaus into cities. Rubber barons constructed mansions and

monuments and brought life's modern trappings into the jungle. Since the rubber era, huge reserves of gold and iron have been discovered in the Amazon. Land-settlement schemes and development projects, such as hydroelectric plants and major roadworks, have followed. In the process, vast portions of tropical forest have been indiscriminately cut; tribal lands have been encroached upon; and industrial by-products, such as mercury used in gold mining, have poisoned wildlife and people. The Brazilian government has established reserves and made some efforts to preserve the territory, but there is much more to be done.

encounter with a stingray's barb can result in a ruined vacation. The more remote your destination, the more seriously you should heed the travel advice and health precautions in this book. Your adventure can be wonderful, but you have to prepare well.

WHEN TO GO

The dry season (low water) between Belém and Manaus runs roughly from mid-June into December, and it's often brutally hot. Shortly before the new year, rains come more often and the climate cools a bit. The average annual temperature is 80°F (27°C) with high humidity. The early morning and the evening are always cooler and are the best times for walking around. The rainy season (high water) runs from December to June. "High water" means flooded forests and better boat access to lakes and wetlands for wildlife spotting. It also means flooded river beaches. Fishing is prime during low water, when fish move from the forest back into rivers and lakes, making them more accessible. Keep in mind that even the driest month has an average rainfall of 2 inches (compared with up to 13 inches during the wet season), so some kind of raingear is always recommended. Depending on where you are in the Amazon, during the rainy season it may rain every day, or three out of every four days, whereas during the dry season it may rain only one out of four days or less.

PACKING

For remote travel in the Amazon, a small backpack is the most efficient way to carry your gear. Plan for drenching downpours by bringing sufficient plastic bags, especially for important items. Specific things to consider packing for an off-the-grid Amazon vacation are: water bottle, filter, and purification tablets, sunscreen, insect repellent, hat, a good medical kit, knife, lightweight gold-miner's hammock (*rede de garimpeiro*), mosquito netting, sheet, 3 yards of ¼-inch rope, tent (if you're planning to camp), rain poncho, light shorts, pants (important for warding off pests while hiking), jacket, flashlight, batteries, matches, earplugs, sunglasses, and a waterproof camera case (good old plastic bags work, too!) *For more information on packing, see Packing in Brazil Essentials.*

ABOUT THE RESTAURANTS & CUISINE

Reservations and dressy attire are rarely needed in the Amazon (indeed, reservations are rarely taken). Tipping isn't customary except in finer restaurants. Call ahead on Monday night, when many establishments are closed.

WHAT IT COSTS IN REAIS				
¢	$	$$	$$$	$$$$
AT DINNER under R$15	R$15–R$30	R$30–R$45	R$45–R$60	over R$60

Prices are per person for a main course at dinner or for a prix-fixe meal.

ABOUT THE HOTELS

Amazon hotel prices tend to be reasonable and include breakfast. Services and amenities such as laundry, however, may cost quite a bit extra. Don't expect to be pampered. When checking in, ask about discounts (*descontos*). During the slow season and midweek, you may get a break. Cry a little, as the Brazilians say, and you may get a larger discount. Paying with cash may lower the price. Rooms have air-conditioning, TVs, phones, and bathrooms unless we indicate otherwise, but showers don't always have hot water. Jungle lodges and smaller hotels in outlying areas often lack basic amenities.

WHAT IT COSTS IN REAIS				
¢	$	$$	$$$	$$$$
FOR 2 PEOPLE under R$125	R$125–R$250	R$250–R$375	R$375–R$500	over R$500

Prices are for a standard double room in high season, excluding tax.

GETTING AROUND

Given the enormous size of the region and the difficulty of traveling large distances, most visitors only travel through one region. For example, you can visit Manaus and its surrounding area or choose the Belém region. If you fly into Manaus, see the Meeting of the Waters, walk through the Adolfo Lisboa market, and take a tour in Teatro Amazonas. Then take a boat to a jungle lodge for a few days for trekking, swimming, and wildlife viewing. Conversely, fly into Belém and explore historic sites for a couple of days and then take a boat and van to a ranch on Marajó Island for a cultural experience and to see some wildlife watching.

Health in the Amazon

Several months before you go to the Amazon, visit a tropical medicine specialist to find out what vaccinations you need. Describe your planned adventure, and get tips on how to prepare.

BITES & STINGS

Tropical forests are home to millions of biting and stinging insects and other creatures. Most are harmless and many, such as snakes, are rarely seen. Mosquitoes can carry malaria and dengue, so it's important to protect yourself (see the Health Tips below). To avoid snake bites, wear boots and pants in the forest and watch closely where you step. Escaping the Amazon without a few bites is nearly impossible—some anti-itch ointment will help you sleep at night.

FOOD & WATER

In rural areas, avoid drinking tap water and using ice made from it. In the cities most restaurants buy ice made from purified water. Beware of where you eat. Many street stands are not very clean. Over-the-counter remedies can ease discomfort. For loose bowels, Floratil can be purchased without a doctor's prescription. Estomazil and Sorrisal (which may contain asprin) are remedies for upset stomach.

INFECTIONS & DISEASES

Dehydration and infections from insect bites and cuts are common. Get plenty of (bottled or purified) water and treat infections quickly. Rabies, Chagas' disease, malaria, yellow fever, meningitis, hepatitis, and dengue fever are present in the Amazon. Research tropical diseases in the Amazon so you know the symptoms and how to treat them

should you fall ill. You shouldn't have any problems if you take precautions.

HEALTH TIPS

■ If you're allergic to stings, carry an adrenaline kit.

■ Use screens on windows and doors, and sleep in rooms with air-conditioning, if possible.

■ Apply strong repellents containing picaridin or DEET (diethyl toluamide) when hiking in rural or forested areas.

■ A *mosquiteiro* (netting for hammock or bed) helps tremendously at night—to be effective it must reach the floor and not touch your skin.

■ Cover up with long pants and a shirt at night indoors, and wear pants, a long-sleeve shirt, and boots in the forest.

■ Check inside your shoes every morning for small guests.

■ Do not leave water in sinks, tubs, or discarded bottles. Dengue mosquitoes thrive in urban areas and lay their eggs in clean water.

■ If you have dengue symptoms, *do not* take aspirin, which can impair blood clotting.

■ If you find a tick on your skin, carefully remove it, treat the site with disinfectant, and see a doctor as soon as possible.

■ To avoid hard-to-see chiggers, which inhabit grassy areas, spray repellent or sprinkle powdered sulfur on shoes, socks, and pants.

■ Don't bathe in lakes or rivers without knowing the quality of water and the risks involved.

10

AMAZON BY BOAT

Sleep in a hammock on the middle deck of a thatch-roof riverboat or in the air-conditioned suite of an upscale tour operator's private ship. Keep in mind that wildlife-viewing is not good on boats far from shore. Near shore, however, the birding can be excellent. Binoculars and a bird guide can help, and shorebirds, raptors, and parrots can be abundant. Common in many parts of the river system are *boto* (pink dolphins) and *tucuxi* (gray dolphins).

ADVENTURE CRUISES

Adventure cruises combine the luxury of cruising with exploration. Their goal is to get you close to wildlife and local inhabitants without sacrificing comforts and amenities. Near daily excursions include wildlife-viewing in smaller boats with naturalists, village visits with naturalists, and city tours. **G.A.P** (*Great Adventure People* ✉*19 Charlotte St., Toronto, ON, Canada, M5V 2H5* ☎*800/708–7761 or 416/260–0999* ⊕*www.gapadventures.com*) makes these trips, which run from 9 to 16 days.

OCEANGOING SHIPS

Some cruise ships call at Manaus, Belém, and Santarém as part of their itineraries. Most trips take place October through May. They range in length from 10 to 29 days, and costs vary. Two major lines making such journeys are Princess Cruises and Royal Olympic Cruises.

TOURIST BOATS

Private groups can hire tourist boats that are more comfortable than standard riverboats. They generally travel close to the riverbank and have open upper decks from which you can observe the river and forest. The better tour operators have an English-speaking regional expert on board—usually an ecologist or botanist. You can either sleep out on the deck in a hammock or in a cabin, which usually has air-conditioning or a fan. Meals are generally provided.

SPEEDBOATS

You can take a speedboat to just about anywhere the rivers flow. Faster than most options, speedboats can be ideal for traveling between smaller towns, a morning of wildlife-viewing, or visiting a place that doesn't have regular transportation, such as a secluded beach or waterfall. You design the itinerary, including departure and return times. Prices and availability vary with distance and locale. Contact tour agencies, talk with locals, or head down to the docks to find a boat willing to take you where you want to go. Work out the price, destination, and travel time before leaving. You may have to pay for the gas up front, but don't pay the rest until you arrive. For trips longer than an hour, bring water, snacks, and sunscreen.

MACAMAZON BOATS

Longer boat routes on the lower Amazon are covered by **MACAMAZON** (☎*091/3222–5604 or 091/3228–0774*). Regular departures run between Belém, Santarém, Macapá, Manaus, and several other destinations. The boats are not luxurious but are a step above regional boats. You can get a suite for two from Belém to Manaus with air-conditioning and bath for about R$800. *Camarote* (cabin) class gets you a tiny room for two with air-conditioning and a shared bath. *Rede* (hammock) class is the cheapest and most intimate way to travel, since you'll be hanging tight with the locals on the main decks. Hammocks are hung in two layers very close together, promoting neighborly chats. Arrive early for the best spots, away from the bar, engine, and bathrooms. Keep your valuables with you at all times and sleep with them. Conceal new sneakers in a plastic bag. In addition to a hammock (easy and cheap to buy in Belém or Manaus), bring two 4-foot lengths of 3/8-inch rope to tie it up. Also bring a sheet, since nights get chilly.

REGIONAL BOATS

To travel to towns and villages or to meander slowly between cities, go by *barco regional* (regional boat). A trip from Belém to Manaus takes about five days; Belém to Santarém is two days. The double- or triple-deck boats carry freight and passengers. They make frequent stops at small towns, allowing for interaction and observation. You might be able to get a cabin with two bunks (around R$400 for a two-day trip), but expect it to be claustrophobic. Most passengers sleep in hammocks with little or no space between them. Bring your own hammock, sheet, and two 4-foot sections of rope. Travel lightly and inconspicuously.

Booths sell tickets at the docks, and even if you don't speak Portuguese, there are often signs alongside the booths that list prices, destinations, and departure times. Sanitary conditions in bathrooms vary from boat to boat. Bring your own toilet paper, sunscreen, and insect repellent. Food is sometimes served, but the quality ranges from so-so to deplorable. Consider bringing your own water and a *marmita* (carry-out meal) if you'll be on the boat overnight. Many boats have a small store at the stern where you can buy drinks, snacks, and grilled *mixto quente* (ham-and-cheese) sandwiches. Fresh fruit and snacks are available at stops along the way. Be sure to peel or wash fruit thoroughly with bottled water before eating it.

10

BELÉM

The capital of Pará State, Belém is a river port of around 1.3 million people on the south bank of the Rio Guamá, 120 km (74 mi) from the Atlantic, and 2,933 km (1,760 mi) north of Rio de Janeiro. The Portuguese settled here in 1616, using it as a gateway to the interior and an outpost to protect the area from invasion by sea. Because of its ocean access, Belém became a major trade center. Like the upriver city of Manaus, it rode the ups and downs of the Amazon booms and busts. The first taste of prosperity was during the rubber era. Architects from Europe were brought in to build churches, civic palaces, theaters, and mansions, often using fine, imported materials. When Malaysia's rubber supplanted that of Brazil in the 1920s, wood and, later, minerals provided the impetus for growth.

Belém has expanded rapidly since the 1980s, pushed by the Tucuruvi hydroelectric dam (Brazil's second largest), the development of the Carajás mining region, and the construction of the ALBRAS/Alunorte bauxite and aluminum production facilities. Wood exports have risen, making Pará the largest wood-producing state in Brazil. As the forests are cut, pastures and cattle replace them, resulting in an increase in beef production. In 2000 the state government began construction of a bridge network connecting Belém

BIO-PIRACY

In the mid-19th century Manaus and Belém flourished because of the Pará rubber trees (*Hevea brasiliensis*). The sap (latex) was tapped and exported to Europe. Colonial Britain committed old-fashioned industrial espionage and managed to steal several rubber seedlings. Before long, England was growing rubber trees in Asia.

to outlying cities. The resulting increase in commerce has spurred economic growth in the region, though there's still considerable poverty and high unemployment. In the city, high-rise apartments are replacing colonial structures. Fortunately, local governments have launched massive campaigns to preserve the city's rich heritage while promoting tourist-friendly policies. This effort has earned state and federal government funds to restore historical sites in the Belém area. Tourism is on the rise in the city and is becoming increasingly important for the city's economic well-being.

TO & FROM

There are several daily flights to Belém from Rio and São Paulo. TAM offers heavily discounted flights every weekend, and GOL has frequent promotions. During the Brazilian summer flights to Belém can be cheap since this is the rainy season and most flock to the beaches instead. If time is not an issue, there are daily buses from Rio and São Paulo on Transbrasilia (45 hours).

All airlines arrive at the Aeroporto Internacional Val-de-Cans, 11 km (7 mi) northwest of the city. Varig and TAM sometimes offer direct flights from Miami. TAM and Gol fly regularly from Rio, São Paulo, Brasília, and Manaus. TAF flies from São Luis, Fortaleza, Cayena, and Macapá in the northeast of Brazil. Soure, Kovacs, and Renaissance airlines have charter flights to small regional airports, including rivers and grass strips. Prices vary, but a flight for four people to Marajó, for example, would be about R$2,000.

The easiest route from the airport is south on Avenida Julio Cesár and then west on Avenida Almirante Barroso. The 20-minute taxi ride from the airport to downtown Belém costs around R$30.

Most long-distance ships arrive and depart from the Terminal Hidroviário (Ave. Marechal Hermes). MACAMAZON and Bom Jesus (based in Macapá) have ships and standard riverboats to Macapá, Santarém, Manaus, and other places. The Belém to Santarem boat on MACAMAZON takes three days and costs R$120 for a hammock, and R$500 for a two-person cabin. The Belém to Manaus boat on

MACAMAZON takes five days and costs R$180 for a hammock and R$800 for a two-person cabin. A trip to Ilha de Marajo from Belém takes two hours and costs R$15. From Belém to Macapa the boat takes 24 hours and the hammock costs R$100, and R$350 for a two-person cabin.

GETTING AROUND

Belém's local bus service is safe (though you should keep an eye on your belongings) and comprehensive, but a little confusing. Ask a resident for guidance. The bus costs R$1.50.

Although Belém has the most traffic of any Amazon city and what seems like more than its fair share of one-way streets, in-town driving is relatively easy. Parking is only tricky in a few areas, such as Avenida Presidente Vargas and the Escadinha.

ESSENTIALS

Airlines (Local) **Kovacs** (☎091/3233–1509). **Soure** (☎091/3233–4986). **TAF** (☎0300/313–2000 ⊕www.voetaf.com.br).

Airport **Aeroporto Internacional Val-de-Cans** (✉Av. Julio Cesár s/n, 66115-970 ☎091/3210–6000 or 091/3257–3780 ⊕www.aeroportosdobrasil.com.br).

Banks & Currency Exchange **Banco Amazônia** (✉Av. Presidente Vargas 800, Comércio, 66017-901). **Banco do Brasil** (✉Aeroporto Internacional Val-de-Cans, Av. Júlio César s/n, 66115-970 ⚠A hefty commission is charged for cashing traveler's checks). **Casa Francesa Câmbio e Turismo** (✉Trv. Padre Prudêncio 40, Batista Campos, 66010-150 ☎No phone).

Boat Contacts **Bom Jesus** (☎091/3272–1423 or 3223-2342). **MACAMAZON** (☎091/3222–5604 or 091/3228–0774).

Bus Contacts **Rodoviário São Brás** (✉Av. Almirante Barroso s/n, São Brás, 66090-000 ☎091/3266–2625).

Emergencies & Medical Assistance **Ambulance** (☎192). **Fire** (☎193). **Hospital: Hospital e Maternidade Dom Luiz I** (✉Av. Generalíssimo Deodoro 868, Umarizal, 66055-904 ☎091/3241–4144). **Pharmacy: Big Ben** (✉Av. Gentil Bittencourt 1548, Nazaré, 66040-000 ☎091/3241–3000). **Police** (☎190).

Internet **Speednet** (✉Rua Gama Abreu 152, Campina, 66015-130 ☎091/3222–7506 or 091/8147–3937).

Taxi **Coopertáxi** (☎091/3257–1041 or 091/3257–1720). **Taxi Nazaré** (☎091/3242–7867).

Visitor & Tour Info Sightseeing boats leave from Estação das Docas Ave. Marechal Hermes, and from behind Hotel Beira Rio on Rua Bernardo Saião, 20-minutes southeast of town near the Federal University.

Amazon Star Tours (✉Rua Henrique Gurjão 236, Campina, 66055-360 ☎091/3212-6244 ☞Wide range of tours and transport options, trips on boats, and to different islands. They also have excursions to Ilha de Marajo (3 days, R$860), Ilha de Papagaios (R$80). Open weekdays 8–6, Sat. 8–noon.). **BELEMTUR** (✉Av. Governador José Malcher 592, Nazaré, 66060-230 ☎091/3242-0900 or 091/3242-0033 ☞Open weekdays 8–noon and 2–6). **Lusotur** (✉Av. Brás de

Aguiar 471, Nazaré, 66035-000 ☎*091/3241–1011* ⊕*www.lusotur.com.br* ⌕*City tours and ecotours).* **PARATUR** (⊠*Praça Maestro Waldemar Henrique s/n, Reduto, 66010-040* ☎*091/3212-0575* ⊕*www.paratur.pa.gov.br* ⌕*Open weekdays 8–6).* **Valeverde Turismo** (⊠*Ave. Alcindo Casela 104, Cremação, 66060-000* ☎ *091/3241-7333* ⌕*They offer city tours in Belém (4 hours), tours to the Island of Marajó, tours to Salinas 6–8 hours, tours to Mosquieros, and to ecological sites in the city. This company also offers Cultural Belém—a tour of the main points of interest in Belém.).*

SAFETY & PRECAUTIONS

In Belém watch out for pickpockets everywhere, but especially at Ver-o-Peso, on Avenida President Vargas, and in Comércio. Avoid walking alone at night or on poorly lighted streets, and don't wear jewelry, especially gold.

EXPLORING BELÉM

Belém is more than just a jumping-off point for the Amazon. It has several good museums and restaurants and lots of extraordinary architecture. Restored historic sites along the waterfront provide areas to walk, eat, and explore. Several distinctive buildings—some with Portuguese *azulejos* (tiles) and ornate iron gates—survive along the downtown streets and around the Praça Frei Caetano Brandão, in the Cidade Velha (Old City). East of here, in the Nazaré neighborhood, colorful colonial structures mingle with new ones housing trendy shops.

CIDADE VELHA

Cidade Velha (Old City) is the oldest residential part of Belém. Here you'll find colonial houses made of clay walls and tiled roofs, the tallest being only three stories high. However, there are more and more 15-floor apartment buildings invading from the north. Much of Cidade Velha is middle-income with a variety of hardware, auto-parts, and fishing-supply stores. On its northwestern edge, the Forte Presépio lies along the bank of the Rio Guamá.

MAIN ATTRACTIONS

❺ ★ Casa das Onze Janelas. At the end of the 18th century, sugar baron Domingos da Costa Barcelar built the neoclassical House of Eleven Windows as his private mansion. Today Barcelar's mansion is a gallery for contemporary arts, including photography and visiting expositions. The view from the balcony is impressive. Take a walk through the courtyard and imagine scenes of the past. This is where the aristocracy took tea and watched over the docks as slaves unloaded ships from Europe and filled them with sugar and rum. ⊠*Praç Frei Caetana Brandão, Cidade Velha, 66010-320* ☎*91/4009–8821* ⊠*R$2, free Tues.* ⊙*Tues.–Fri. 10–6, weekends 10–8.*

❷ ★ Estação das Docas. Next to Ver-o-Peso market on the river, three former warehouses have been artfully converted into a commercial–tourist area. All have one wall of floor-to-ceiling glass that provides a full river view when dining or shopping. The first is a convention center with a cinema and art exhibits. The second has shops and kiosks

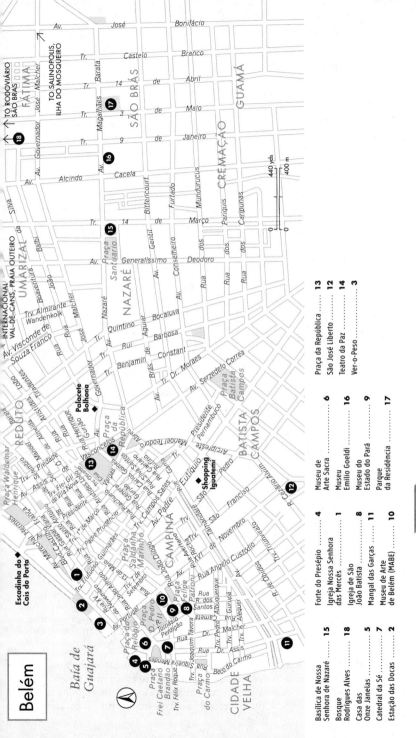

Belém

Baía de Guajará

Escadinho do Cais do Porto ◆

TO RODOVIÁRIO SÃO BRÁS →
↑ TO SALINÓPOLIS, ILHA DO MOSQUEIRO

FÁTIMA

SÃO BRÁS

GUAMÁ

CREMAÇÃO

UMARIZAL

Av. Visconde de Souza Franco

INTERNACIONAL VAL-DE-CANS, PRAIA OUTEIRO

Trv. Almirante Wandenkolk

NAZARÉ

Praça Santuário

Palacete Bolonha ◆

Praça da República

REDUTO

Praça Batista Campos

BATISTA CAMPOS

Av. Serzedelo Correa

Praça Batista Campos

CAMPINA

Shopping Iguatemi ◆

CIDADE VELHA

Praça do Carmo

440 yds
400 m

selling crafts and snacks, and the third has a microbrewery and six upscale restaurants. The buildings are air-conditioned and connected by glass-covered walkways and contain photos and artifacts from the port's heyday. A stroll outside along the docks provides a grand view of the bay. Tourist boats arrive and depart at the dock—a good place to relax both day and night. ⊠*Ave. Boulevard Castilho França s/n, Campina, 66010-020* ☏*091/3212–5525* ☑*Free* ⊘*Noon–midnight or later.*

> ## SNAKES IN BELÉM
>
> One of the most popular Amazon myths is about the *cobra grande* a huge snake, which lives underneath towns and once in a while comes out at night to feast on the inhabitants. Recently, deforestation has caused the myth to become reality. Last year alone 21 snakes were captured in Belém, among them a 10-foot anaconda. As the rain forest is destroyed by fires and logging, these Amazonian natives search for living space and food in the city.

4 **Forte do Presépio** *(Fort of the Crèche).* Founded January 12, 1616, this fort is considered Belém's birthplace. From here the Portuguese launched conquests of the Amazon and watched over the bay. The fort's role in the region's defense is evidenced by massive English- and Portuguese-made cannons pointing out over the water. They are poised atop fort walls that are 3 yards thick in places. Renovations completed in 2002 unearthed more than two dozen cannons, extensive military middens from the moat, and native Tupi artifacts. A small museum of prefort indigenous cultures is at the entrance. Just outside the fort, cobblestone walkways hug the breezy waterfront. ⊠*Praça Frei Caetano Brandão, Cidade Velha, 66020-210* ☏*91/4009–8828* ☑*R$4, Tues. free* ⊘*Tues.–Fri. 10–6, weekends 10–8.*

11 **Mangal das Garças.** City beautification efforts to increase tourism and encourage environmental conservation led to the creation of the Mangrove of the Egrets. A great place for a short stroll, it has an aviary, a tower with a view, a navigation museum, a boardwalk leading to a lookout over the Rio Guamá, a live butterfly exhibit, ponds with aquatic plants, food vendors, a gift shop, and a restaurant. ⊠*Passagem Carneiro da Rocha, Arsenal, 66020-160* ☏*91/8114–2828* ✉*encarregados@mangaldasgarcas.com.br* ☑*R$6* ⊘*Weekdays 9–5, Tues. free.*

6 **Museu de Arte Sacra.** A guided tour (call 48 hours in advance to reserve an English-speaking docent) begins in the early-18th-century baroque Igreja de Santo Alexandre (St. Alexander's Church), which is distinguished by intricate woodwork on its altar and pews. On the second half of the tour you see the museum's collection of religious sculptures and paintings. ⊠*Praça Frei Caetano Brandão, Cidade Velha, 66020-310* ☏*091/4009–8802* ☑*R$4, Tues. free* ⊘*Tues.–Fri. 1–6, weekends 9–1.*

9 **Museu do Estado do Pará.** The Pará State Museum is in the sumptuous Palácio Lauro Sodré (circa 1771), an Antônio Landi creation with Venetian and Portuguese elements. Consistently outstanding visiting exhibits are on the first floor; the second floor contains the permanent collection of furniture and paintings. ⊠*Praça Dom Pedro II, Cidade Velha, 66020-240* ☎*091/3241–2215* ⊠*R$4, Tues. free* ⊘*Tues.–Fri. 1–6, weekends 9–1.*

❸ **Ver-o-Peso.** Its name literally mean-
★ ing "see the weight" (a throwback to the time when the Portuguese weighed everything entering or leaving the region), this market is a hypnotic confusion of colors and voices. Vendors hawk tropical fruits, regional wares, and an assortment of tourist kitsch. Most interesting are the *mandingueiras,* women who claim they can solve any problem with "miracle" jungle roots and charms for the body and

> ### DANCE THE LAMBADA
>
> This musical form, popular among Brazilians in the '80s and early '90s, originated in the state of Pará in the 1970s. The first lambada was composed by the Pinduca, who had written a number of carimbós. The music swept the North, Northeast, and even become popular outside of the country. Two American movies popularized the genre but were made only after the craze began to wane—*Lambada* (1990) and *The Forbidden Dance* (1990).

soul. They sell jars filled with animal eyes, tails, and even heads, as well as herbs, each with its own legendary power. The sex organs of the pink river dolphin are a supposedly unrivaled cure for romantic problems. In the fish market you get an up-close look at pirarucu, the Amazon's most colorful fish and the world's second-largest freshwater species. Look for bizarre armored catfish species, such as the *tamuatá* and the huge *piraiba.* Across the street is a small arched entrance to the municipal meat market. Duck in and glance at the French-style pink-and-green-painted ironwork, imported from Britain. Be sure to visit Ver-o-Peso before noon, when most vendors leave. It opens around 6 AM. Leave your jewelry at home and beware of pickpockets. ⊠*Av. Castilhos França s/n, Comércio.*

IF YOU HAVE TIME

The many regional flavors at ice-cream shop **Cairu** include some unique to the Amazon, such as *taperebá, graviola,* and *cajá* (cashew fruit), as well as the more familiar *cocó* (coconut), mango, and chocolate. Juices, sandwiches, and soft drinks are also served. ⊠*Estação das Docas, Blvd. Castilhos França s/n, Umarizal, 66055-200.*

❽ **Igreja de São João Batista** *(St. John the Baptist Church).* Prodigious architect Antônio Landi finished this small octagonal church in 1777. It was completely restored in the late 1996 and is considered the city's purest example of baroque architecture and the country's first octagonal church. ⊠*Largo de São Joã on Rua João Diogo s/n, Cidade Velha, 66015-160* ☎*91/3223–2362* ⊠*Free* ⊘*Mon.–Sat. 6:30 AM–9 AM.*

❼ **Catedral da Sé.** In 1755 Bolognese architect Antônio José Landi, whose work can be seen throughout the city, completed the cathedral's construction on the foundations of an older church. Carrara marble adorns the rich interior, which is an interesting mix of baroque, colonial, and neoclassical styles. The high altar was a gift from Pope Pius IX. At this writing, the Catedral da Sé is under renovation until sometime in 2009.

10

✉*Praça Dom Frei Caetano Brandão s/n, Cidade Velha, 66010-320* ☎*91/3241–6282 or 91/3223–2362* 🖥*Free* ⊙*Daily 8–noon and 2–6.*

❶ Igreja Nossa Senhora das Mercês *(Our Lady of Mercy Church).* Another of Belém's baroque creations, the shell dates from the 17th century, the rest attributed to Antônio Landi's restoration, this church is notable for its pink color and convex facade. It's part of a complex that includes the Convento dos Mercedários, which has served both as a convent and a prison, though not simultaneously. ✉*Gaspar Viana e Frutuosa Guimarães, Comércio, 66013-010* ☎*91/3212–3102* 🖥*Free* ⊙*Mon.–Sat. 8–5:45, Sun. 8–10.*

❿ Museu de Arte de Belém (MABE). The permanent collection of furniture and paintings dates from the 18th century through the rubber boom. The museum is housed in the Palácio Antônio Lemos (circa 1883), a municipal palace built in the imperial Brazilian style with French influences. ✉*Praça Dom Pedro II s/n, Cidade Velha, 66020-240* ☎*091/3283–4687* 🖥*Free* ⊙*Tues. 9–5, weekends 9–1 PM.*

⓬ São José Liberto In 250 years Belém's old prison, which began as a monastery, became a brewery, then an armory, a nunnery, and eventually the final stop for many criminals. Today's museums and garden seem an attempt to redeem long years of tortuous conditions and bloody rebellions. Behind the enormously thick walls are a gem museum, a prison museum, and several shops. ✉*Praça Amazonas, Jurunas, 66023-075* ☎*91/3344–5300* 🖥*R$4* ⊙*Tues.–Sat. 10–10, Sun. 3–10.*

NAZARÉ

Just east of the Cidade Velha, Nazaré's mango tree–lined streets create the sensation of walking through tunnels. Among the historic buildings there's a tremendous variety of pastel colors and European styles. Many of the newer buildings house elegant shops.

MAIN ATTRACTIONS

⓯ Basílica de Nossa Senhora de Nazaré. It's hard to miss this opulent Roman-style basilica. Not only does it stand out visually, but there's an enormous *samauma* tree (kapok variety) filled with screeching white-winged parakeets in the plaza out front. The basilica was built in 1908 as an addition to a 1774 chapel, on the site where a *caboclo* (rural, riverside dweller) named Placido is said to have seen a vision of the Virgin in the early 1700s. The basilica's ornate interior is constructed entirely of European marble and contains elaborate mosaics, detailed stained-glass windows, and intricate bronze doors. ✉*Praça Justo Chermont, Nazaré, 66035-140* ☎*091/4009–8400, 091/4009–8407 museum* 🖥*Free* ⊙*Daily 6–7.*

Fodor'sChoice ★

⓰ Museu Emílio Goeldi. Founded by a naturalist and a group of intellectuals in 1866, this complex contains one of the Amazon's most important research facilities. Its museum has an extensive collection of Indian artifacts, including the distinctive and beautiful pottery of the Marajó Indians, known as *marajoara.* A small forest has reflecting pools with giant *vitória régia* water lilies. But the true highlight is the collection of Amazon wildlife, including manatees, anacondas, macaws, sloths,

☼ ★

Tales from the Mist

The immense Amazon region is fertile ground not only for flora and fauna but also for legends, which are an integral part of local culture and are remarkably consistent throughout the region. Many are based on strange creatures that inhabit the rivers and jungle.

One particulary creepy legend is that of Curupira, who appears as a nude and savage indigenous child, about six or seven years old, whose feet are turned backward. He is said to lure people into the jungle—causing them to become irreversibly lost. As the story goes, white men cut off his feet before killing him; a god sewed Curupira's feet on backward and returned him to the forest to exact revenge. Some people claim you can solicit Curupira's help for hunting and crop failures. As payment, you must bring him tobacco, matches, and a bottle of liquor—the latter of which he will down in one swig to seal the pact. If you ever tell anyone about the agreement, Curupira will hunt you down and stab you to death with his long, sharp fingernails.

Several tales explain the origins of important fruits and vegetables. Guaraná, for example, was the name of a young child beloved by all. As the story goes, he was killed by the jealous god Jurupari, who disguised himself as a snake. Lightning struck as the village gathered around Guaraná's body and wept. At that moment the lightning god, Tupã, ordered the villagers to bury the child's eyes. The guaraná fruit (which actually resembles eyes) sprouted from the burial spot.

In a legend explaining the origins of the açaí fruit (a rich, dark-purple fruit endemic to the Amazon), the chief of a starving tribe ordered all babies to be sacrificed to end the famine. The chief's daughter, Iaçá, had a beautiful baby. Before its sacrifice, she found the child holding a palm tree, and then he suddenly vanished. The tree then became full of açaí (which is Iaçá spelled backward), from which a wine was made that saved the tribe and ended the sacrifices. To this day, Amazonians call the cold soup made from the fruit vinho (wine).

The legend of the native water flower vitória régia begins with a beautiful girl who wished to become a star in the heavens. She trekked to the highest point in the land and tried in vain to touch the moon. Iaci—the god of the moon—was awed and enchanted by the girl's beauty. He knew that a mortal could never join the astral kingdom, so he decided to use his powers to immortalize the girl on earth instead. He transformed her into a stunning flower with an unmistakable, alluring scent. Realizing that he needed something fitting to help display this "star," he stretched a palm leaf and created a lily pad, and thus the vitória régia came to be.

10

---

and monkeys. ⊠*Av. Magalhães Barata 376, Nazaré, 66040-170* ☎*091/3249–0477* ☞*Park R$3, R$2 aquarium, R$2 museum, Tues. free* ♥*Tues.–Sun. 9–noon and 2–5.*

⓮ ★ **Teatro da Paz.** A complete renovation of this 1878 neoclassical theater was finished in 2001. Concert pianos were acquired to facilitate production of operas. Greek-style pillars line the front and sides; inside, note the imported details such as Italian marble pillars and French chandeliers. Classical music performances are also held in the theater, which seats more than 800 people. ⊠*Rua da Paz s/n, Praça da República, Campina, 66017-210* ☎*091/4009–8758 or 091/4009–8750* ⊠*R$4, Wed. free* ⊗*Tours on the hr Tues.–Fri. 9–6, Sat. 9–1.*

IF YOU HAVE TIME

⓲ Bosque Rodrigues Alves. In 1883 this 40-acre plot of rain forest was designated an ecological reserve. Nowadays it has an aquarium and two amusement parks as well as natural caverns, a variety of animals (some in the wild), and mammoth trees. ⊠*Av. Almirante Barroso, Marco, 66095-000* ☎*091/3276–2308* ⊠*R$1* ⊗*Tues.–Sun. 8–5.*

⓱ Parque da Residência. For decades this was the official residence of the governor of Pará. Now it provides office space for the Secretaria de Cultura (SECULT; Executive Secretary of Culture), as well as public space. Within the park are a 400-seat theater, an orchid conservatory, an ice-cream parlor, a restaurant, and shaded spots to relax and soak in the atmosphere. ⊠*Av. Magalhães Barata 830, São Brás, 66063-240* ☎*091/4009–8715* ⊠*Free* ⊗*Tues.–Sun. 9–9.*

⓭ Praça da República. At this square you'll find a large statue that commemorates the proclamation of the Republic of Brazil, an amphitheater, and several French-style iron kiosks. On Sunday vendors, food booths, and musical groups create a festival-like atmosphere that attracts crowds of locals. ⊠*Bounded by Av. Presidente Vargas, Trv. Osvaldo Cruz, and Av. Assis de Vasconcelos, 66017-060.*

> ### BIBLICAL NAMES
>
> Belém is the Portuguese name for Bethlehem. One of its main neighborhoods, Nazaré, is the Portuguese for Nazareth. The city was renamed three times before it assumed its current name: Feliz Lusitânia, Santa Maria do Grão Pará, Santa Maria de Belé do Grão Para.

WHERE TO EAT

$–$$$$ ✗**Boteco das Onze.** In the Casa das Onze Janelas *(⇨above)*, the Boteca das Onze has thick stone and mortar walls stylishly adorned with antique instruments. The full bar has a complete drink menu with one of the largest selections of wines in the city. The patio has a view of the garden and river. A house favorite is the seafood platter for two. ⊠*Praça da Sé, Cidade Velha, 66010-320* ☎*91/3224–8599 or 91/3241–8255* ⊘*boteca@nautilus.com.br* ▤*MC, V* ⊗*No lunch Mon.*

$–$$$ ✗**Hatoba Restauranté.** This is the best sushi in Belém, which is no small potatoes, since the city has a large Japanese community (second only to that of São Paulo), and many Japanese restaurants. A bonus: Hotoba is in the Estação das Docas, so you can dine along the waterfront. ⊠*Estação das Docas, Campina, 66055-200* ☎*091/3212–3143 or 091/3088–2900* ▤*AE, DC, MC, V.*

$–$$ ✗**Dom Giuseppe.** From gnocchi to ravioli, flawless preparation of the ★ basics distinguishes this Italian eatery from others. Everyone in town knows this, so reservations are a good idea—particularly on weekends. Don't leave without ordering a scrumptious *dolce Paula* (ice cream–and–brownie dessert). ✉*Av. Conselheiro Furtado 1420, Batista Campos, 66035-350* ☎*091/4008–0001* ⊕*www.domgiuseppe.com.br* ▭*AE, DC, MC, V* ⊗*No lunch Mon.–Sat.*

$–$$ ✕**Lá em Casa.** From inauspicious beginnings has emerged one of Belém's
Fodor'sChoice most popular restaurants. Regional cuisine, prepared to exacting speci-
★ fications, has earned Lá em Casa its good reputation. Consider trying Belém's premier dish, *pato no tucupi* (duck in a yellow manioc–herb sauce served with the mildly intoxicating *jambu* leaf). Crabs on the half-shell covered with *farofa* (finely ground manioc fried in margarine) is another good choice, as is *açaí* sorbet for dessert. Sitting on the patio fringed by tropical vines and bromeliads, you feel like you're dining in the middle of the forest. ✉*Trv. Dom Pedro Primeiro 546, Umarizal, 66050-100* ☎*091/3242–4222* ⊕*www.laemcasa.com* ▭*AE, DC, MC, V.*

$–$$ ✕**Palafita.** Excellent regional dishes with open-air dining over the river are why locals enjoy Palafita. Pirarucú fish balls and duck pastries are among the specialties. Palafita has music on weekend evenings and it's a one-minute walk from the Forte do Presépio. ✉*Praça da Sé, Rua Siquiera Mendes 264, Cidade Velha, 66020-310* ☎*091/3212–6302* ▭*V, MC.*

$ ✕**Garrote.** A traditional *churrascaria* (Brazilian barbecue restaurant), Garrote serves up as much grilled and roasted beef, pork, and other meat as you can eat for a reasonable fixed price. A salad buffet and dessert are also included. Service is excellent. ✉*Travessa Padre Eutíquio 1380, Batista Campos, 66023-110* ☎*091/3225–2776* ▭*AE, MC, V* ⊗*No dinner Sun.*

$ ✕**Mixtura Paulista.** A convenient location near the Hilton and the Praça da República makes this pay-per-kilo restaurant with *churrasco* a good choice for a quick lunch. The buffet table always has numerous main dishes and grilled meats, along with salads, beans, and rice. ✉*Rua Serzedelo Corrêa 15, Nazaré* ☎*091/3222–4309* ▭*DC, MC, V* ⊗*No dinner.*

¢ ✕**Casa do Caldo.** Eight soups (out of 36) are featured every night for family dining in the "House of Soup." One price covers the rodizio of unlimited soup, toast, and dessert porridge. Try the crab soup with cilantro and the cow's-foot soup. It's air-conditioned and casual, with superb service. ✉*Rua Diogo Moia 266, Umarizal, 66055-170* ☎*091/3224–5744* ▭*AE, DC, MC, V* ⊗*No lunch.*

10

WHERE TO STAY

$$$ ⊞**Hilton International Belém.** Centrally located on the Praça da República,
★ this Hilton is very similar to the others— comfortable rooms, good facilities and lots of amenities. Executive rooms have the nicest views as well as access to a lounge with a VCR, a meeting area, and complimentary food and drink. **Pros:** Great location and excellent facilities. **Cons:** Rooms have few decorations, and simple color schemes. ✉*Av. Presidente Vargas 882, Campina, 66017-000* ☎*091/4006–7000 in U.S.* ✉*belem@hilton. com* ⊕*www.belem.hilton.com* ⤏*361 rooms* ⌂*In room: Internet. In-hotel: restaurant, bars, pools, gym* ▭*AE, DC, MC, V.*

$ **Hotel Regente.** This hotel has excellent service and a prime location for a reasonable price. Stained-glass windows and soft leather couches welcome you in an attractive lobby as well as free Internet. Rooms on the 12th floor are nicer and more modern than those on other floors, yet they cost the same. **Pros:** Lovely views and a great location. **Cons:** Internet in the rooms costs R$10. ⊠*Av. Governador José Malcher 485, Nazaré, 66035-100* ☎*091/3181–5000* ☎*091/3181–5005* ✎*reserva@hregente.com.br* ⊕*www.hotelregente.com.br* ⬛*219 rooms, In room: refrigerator, Internet. In-hotel: restaurant, pool* ⊟*AE, DC, MC, V.*

> **SATERÊ MAUÉ**
>
> An indigenous language from the Amazon, *saterê Maué* has contributed many words to Brazil's language. For example, the root word for fish is "pira." The fish species that use this indigenous root are: piramutaba, piranambu, piranha, pirapitinha, and pirarara.

$ **Itaoca Hotel.** It comes as no surprise that this small, reasonably priced hotel has the highest occupancy rate in town. It's in the center of town, on the city's main street and right next to the Estação das Docas and Ver-o-Peso. Its rooms are extremely comfortable, modern, and most have a fantastic view of the dock area and river. **Pros:** Inexpensive hotel with great views, and well-equipped rooms. **Cons:** The furnishings in the rooms are outdated, for broadband Internet you have to use the lobby. ⊠*Av. Presidente Vargas 132, Campina, 66010-902* ☎*091/4009–2400 or 091/4009–2402* ⊕*www.hotelitaoca.com.br* ⬛*32 rooms, 4 suites In-room: refrigerator, dial-up, safe. In-hotel: restaurant, bar* ⊟*AE, DC, MC, V.*

¢   **Hotel Grão Pará.** The oldest hotel in town is also the best deal. Hotel Grão Pará has few amenities, but has the best price for a modern, clean room with the basics, sparsely furnished, but with marble sinks in the bathrooms. The hotel is across the street from the Praça da Republica and the Teatro da Paz. **Pros:** Inexpensive hotel in the best location. **Cons:** No-frill rooms, simply furnished. ⊠*Av. Presidente Vargas 718, Campina, 66017-000* ☎*091/3221–2121* ⊕*www.hotelgraopara.com.br* ⬛*150 rooms In-room: refrigerator* ⊟*DC, MC, V* ⊚*EP.*

NIGHTLIFE & THE ARTS

NIGHTLIFE

Umarizal is Belém's liveliest neighborhood at night, with a good selection of bars, clubs, and restaurants. Other nightlife hot spots are scattered around the city. *For information about Brazilian music, see the Brazilian Music essay in Understanding Brazil.*

BARS   **Água Doce** (⊠*Rua Diogo Móia 283, Umarizal, 66055-170* ☎*091/3222–3383*) specializes in *cachaça* (Brazilian sugar-cane liquor). Listed on its menu are 182 kinds of cachaça and 605 different drinks, along with appetizers and entrées. Softly lighted with lots of tables, this place gets busy on weekends. It's open Tuesday–Saturday 5 PM–3 AM. If you prefer your music in a relaxed environment, head to **Cosanostra Café** (⊠*Travessa Benjamin Constant 1499, Nazaré, 66035-060*

☎091/3241–1068), which has live MPB (*música popular brasileira*) and jazz. Catering to locals and expatriate foreigners alike, it serves food from an extensive menu until late in the night. **Roxy Bar** (✉*Av. Senador Lemos 231, Umarizal, 66050-000* ☎*091/3224–4514*) tops nearly everyone's list of hip places to sip a drink and people-watch.

> ### CARIMBÓ
>
> The carimbó is an indigenous dance and music form, originating in Belém and the island of Marajó that later gave way to the rhythms of the lambada. This music is steeped in the sounds of the Amazon and its folklore, but has also been influenced by African culture. It's accompanied by wooden tambourines. During the dance the woman passes her skirt over the man.

DANCE CLUBS The hot spots for dancing are open on Friday and Saturday nights and sometimes on Sunday; many are downtown. Mixed-age crowds frequent them no matter what the music. Prices vary depending on the show. Drinks are available but no food. All clubs except Signos have live music on occasion. Clubs open around 10 PM, though they don't get lively before 11 or midnight.

THE ARTS

For information about cultural events, contact the state-run **Secretaria de Cultura** (*SECULT* ✉*Av. Governador Magalhães Barata 830, São Brás, 66630-040* ☎*091/4009–8707 or 091/4009–8717* ⊕*www.secult. pa.gov.br*), which prints a monthly listing of cultural events throughout the city and has a great Web site with regular updates.

Bar do Gilson (✉*Travessa Padre Eutíquio 3172, Condor, 66023-230* ☎*913272–7306*) has excellent live choro and samba, Friday 11:30, weekends at 4. Live music is played nightly at the **Estação das Docas** (✉*Ave. Boulevard Castilho França s/n, Campina, 66010-020* ☎*091/3212–5525*). Weekday shows usually consist of acoustic singers and/or guitarists. On weekends rock, jazz, and MPB bands play on a suspended stage that moves back and forth on tracks about 8 meters (25 feet) above patrons of the microbrewery and surrounding restaurants. Outstanding theatrical productions in Portuguese are presented at the **Teatro Experimental Waldemar Henrique** (✉*Av. Presidente Vargas 645, Praça da República, Campina, 66017-000* ☎*091/4009–8757 or 4009–8758*).

Teatro da Paz (✉*Av. da Paz s/n, Praça da República, Campina, 66017-210* ☎*091/4009–8758, 091/4009–8759, or 091/4009–8750*) often hosts plays, philharmonic concerts, and dance recitals.

SPORTS & THE OUTDOORS

Belém's two *futebol* (soccer) teams are Payssandú and Remo. Payssandú has been in the premier league for several years and is highly popular. Attending a Brazilian match is a memorable experience. Do not go alone and do not wear the other team's colors. Beware of pickpockets. For Remo games head to **Estádio Evandro Almeida** (✉*Av. Almi-*

rante Barroso s/n, Marco, 66093-900 ☎*091/3223–2847*). Payssandú plays at **Estádio Leônidas de Castro** (✉*Av. Almirante Barroso s/n, Marco, 66093-020* ☎*091/3241–1726*).

SHOPPING

Indigenous-style arts and crafts are popular souvenir items in Belém. Some of them, however, can create problems with customs when returning home. Import regulations of Australia, Canada, New Zealand, the United Kingdom, and the United States strictly prohibit bringing endangered species (dead or alive) into those countries, and the fines can be hefty. Nonendangered wildlife and plant parts are also illegal to import, though there are some exceptions. Wooden and woven items, for example, are usually not a problem. Avoid headdresses and necklaces of macaw feathers and caiman teeth, and go for the marajoara pottery and the tropical fruit preserves (pack them carefully).

SHOPPING AREAS & MALLS

Belém's main shopping street is **Avenida Presidente Vargas,** particularly along the Praça da República. **Icoaraci,** a riverside town 18 km (11 mi) northeast of Belém, is a good place to buy marajoara pottery.**All Amazon pottery is soft and breaks readily. Be sure it's packed exceptionally well.** There are many boutiques and specialty shops in the neighborhood of **Nazaré.** To shop in air-conditioning, head for the upscale **Shopping Center Iguatemi** (✉*Trv. Padre Eutíquio 1078, Batista Campos, 66023-710*), a mall in the truest sense of the word. There are a few well-stocked music stores, a food plaza on the third floor, a bookstore on the first floor that has maps, and two department stores—Y. Yamada and Visão—with a bit of everything.

MARKETS

Ver-o-Peso (✉*Av. Castilhos França s/n, Campina, 66010-020*) is one of the most popular markets in town. It sells fresh fruits, vegetables, fish, and meats. The city's largest concentration of vendors of medicinal plants and various concoctions (love potions, anyone?) is clustered under a canvas roof in the outdoor section. Look for beautifully woven hammocks. **Praça da República** (✉*Bounded by Av. Presidente Vargas, Trv. Osvaldo Cruz, and Av. Assis de Vasconcelos, 66017-060*) is busy only on Sunday, when *barracas* (small shops) pop up to sell paintings, snacks, artisanal items, and regional foods. You can watch the action from a park bench while sipping a cold coconut or eating a slice of *cupuaçú* cake. It's a local favorite for morning family strolls.

SPECIALTY SHOPS

Artesanato Paruara (✉*Rua Serzedelo Correa 15, Nazaré, 66035-400* ☎*091/3248–4555*) specializes in oils, stones, and other "mystical" items. A great souvenir shop, **Canto do Uirapurú** (✉*Av. President Vargas 594, Campina, 66017-000*) is well stocked with medicinal plant concoctions, T-shirts, hats, pottery, and more. **Casa Amazônia Artesanatos** (✉*Av. President Vargas 512, Campina, 66017-000* ☎*091/3225–0150*), though small, is packed with natural soaps, regional fruit preserves, pottery, and wood carvings. A short walk from Av. President

Vargas, **Loja Jaguar** (⊠*Sen. Manoel Barata 298, Comércio, 66015-020* ☎*91/3224–9771*) sells hammocks and *mosquiteiros* (mosquito nets). For photo needs visit **New Color** (⊠*Av. President Vargas 356, Campina, 66010-000* ☎*091/3212–2355*), which is fast, friendly, and reliable.

São José Liberto (⊠*Rua 16 de Novembro s/n, Jurunas, 66023-075* ⊙*Tues.–Sat. 10–8*) is a combination museum *(⇨Cidade Velha in Exploring Belém, above)* and high-price jewelry and craft shops with Amazonian wares of gold, amethyst, and wood; pottery; and seeds and plant fibers.

SIDE TRIPS FROM BELÉM

If you're interested in beaches, fishing, forests, wildlife, or rural communities, there are some great spots to visit beyond the sidewalks of Belém. Buses and boats can take you to all of these spots and there's always a taxi driver willing to take you where you want to go.

PRAIA OUTEIRO

The closest ocean beach to Belém is Salinas, a four-hour drive. River beaches like Outeiro and those at Ilha Mosqueiro are much closer. Depending on the season and time of day, river beaches are either expansive stretches or narrow strips of soft sand. Currents are rarely strong, and there's usually a large area of shallow water. Outeiro is generally crowded. The shoreline is eroded and dirty in places, but the swimming is good if you can handle muddy water. Restaurants line the beach with tables under trees. These are great places to have a cold drink and snack on freshly boiled crabs, quail eggs, and salted shrimp.

30 km (19 mi) north of Belém; about 45 min by bus.

TO & FROM

Clearly marked buses travel from Belém to Praia Outeiro and the town of Icoaraci (23km). Bus tickets are R$2.20. ⊠*Buses depart from Rodoviário São Brás, Av. Almirante Barroso s/n, São Brás, 66090-000.*

ILHA DO MOSQUEIRO

Most Belém residents head for one of 18 beaches on Mosqueiro Island, along the Rio Pará. Mosqueiro is easily accessible by car or intermunicipal bus Beira-Dão.

60 km (36 mi) from Belém; about 2 hrs by bus or car.

TO & FROM

Beira-Dão buses leave every half hour from Belém and cost R$4. To reach the beaches at Ilha Mosqueiro from Belém, take BR 316 and then head north on PA 191.

10

Side Trips from Belém

ESSENTIALS

Bus Contacts Beira-Dão (☎091/3226–1162). **Estação Rodoviária Arthur Pires Teixeira** (✉Rua Juvênia Silva, 66915-000 ☎91/3771–3624).

WHAT TO SEE

One of Mosqueiro's most popular beaches, **Praia Farol,** is often crowded because it's close to **Vila,** the island's hub. At low tide you can walk to tiny, rocky Ilha do Amor (Love Island). In October and March the waves are high enough for river-surfing competitions. **Praia Morubira,** also close to Vila, has beautiful colonial houses and many restaurants and bars. The water is clear and the shore clean at **Praia Marahú,** but no bus from Belém travels here directly. You have to disembark in Vila and hop another bus. **Praia Paraíso** is lined with trees and has soft white sands and clear emerald waters. If you can't bear to leave at day's end, consider a stay at the Hotel Fazenda Paraíso. ✉*Buses depart from Rodoviário São Brás, Av. Almirante Barroso s/n, São Brás, 66090-000.*

WHERE TO STAY

$ 📷**Hotel Fazenda Paraíso.** Wood-and-brick chalets with red-tile roofs accommodate as many as five people. Similarly designed apartments, which house up to three people, are more economical for singles and couples. The pool is configured in the shape of a clover. Be sure to make reservations—the hotel is very popular on weekends. **Pros:** Beachside location. **Cons:** Simple rooms with little space. ⊠*Beira-Mar, Praia do Paraíso, Ilha Mosqueiro, 66915-000* ☎*091/3228–3950* ⊕*www.hotelfazendaparaiso.com.br* ⤴*28 rooms, 22 chalets* ⌂*In-room: refrigerator. In-hotel: restaurant, pool, beachfront, no elevator* ⊟*AE, DC, MC, V.*

SALINÓPOLIS

Commonly known as **Salinas,** this old salt port on the Atlantic coast is loaded with beaches. It lies south of the mouth of the Amazon River, three to four hours from Belém on good roads, making it accessible to weekend beachgoers.

200 km (120 mi) east of Belém.

TO & FROM

Buses run every couple of hours from the Belém *rodoviário* (bus terminal) and drop you off at the Salinas terminal. Boa Esperança makes the 220-km (125-mi) journey from Belém to Salinópolis every couple of hours daily and cost R$17.50. There are also many alternative vans that leave from the same terminal for R$20.

> ### ENGLISH NATURALISTS IN THE AMAZON
>
> Alfred Russel Wallace (1823–1913) is known in academic circles as a co-discoverer of the theory of natural selection along with Charles Darwin. Wallace spent four years in the Amazon and collected a trove of Amazonian species. When he left for England on the ship *Helen,* the ship caught fire and although the crew was saved, all of Wallace's notes and specimens—four years of work—were lost. However, he succeeded in resurrecting from the memory of his notes two books: *Palm Trees of the Amazon* and *Their Uses* and *Travels on the Amazon.*

Once there, take a taxi about a mile to Centro and Maçarico Beach, or travel 20 minutes to Atalaia. A rickety old bus travels between the beaches every hour, from around 6:30 AM to 10 PM. It takes some work to get to Salinas's more secluded beaches. Praia Maria Baixinha and Praia Marieta require a boat, as do island beaches. Ask your hotel to make arrangements for you. To reach Salinas Beach from Belém by car, take BR 316 to PA 324 and head north on PA 124.

ESSENTIALS

Banks & Currency Exchange Banco do Brasil (⊠*Av. Dr. Miguel Santa Brigida, 68721-000*).

Bus Contacts Boa Esperança (☎*091/3266–0033*). **Terminal Rodoviário** (⊠*Ave. Miguel Santa Brigada, 68721-00*).

Emergencies & Medical Assistance Ambulance (☎*192*). **Fire** (☎*193*). **Police** (☎*190*).

Taxi Ponto de Taxi do Terminal (☎*91/3423–1234*).

WHAT TO SEE

Praia Atalaia is Salinas's largest and most popular beach. The 14-km (9-mi) white-sand beach is expansive; the highest dunes have nice views. Behind them is the black-water pond Lago Coca Cola, which sometimes dries up between September and January. Also visible are dunes encroaching on hotels and businesses, signs of poor coastal management. Atalaia has numerous restaurant-bars with simple, low-price rooms for rent (R$50); expect no amenities, and bring your own towel and soap. The best places to eat and stay are in the middle of the beach, and some accept credit cards. Pampulha, David House, and Minha Deusa are good. They serve excellent seafood and other dishes at low prices (R$10–R$25). Beware of eating at other places. Shop around and choose a room with a secure window. A 10-minute walk from Atalaia is a quieter beach, **Praia Farol Velho,** which has few services. To get here, turn left at the entrance and walk around the point.

> ### ACTIVIST NUN
>
> Dorothy Stang, an American from Ohio, was one of the most famous activists in the Amazon. A Catholic nun, she had spent 30 years fighting for the protection of the rain forest. At 73 years old, she was an ambitious leader in the Amazon and an outspoken advocate for the poor and landless. In 2005 she was shot by two men who had been hired by a rancher. The killers were sentenced to more than 25 years in prison and the government eventually imposed a ban on logging in parts of the rain forest.

In the old section of downtown Salinas, known as **Centro,** life revolves around the Farol Velho (the old light tower). Just across from the tower on Rua João Pessoa is Mercado Marissol, with an excellent selection of fruits, vegetables, drinks, and convenience items. In the same vicinity are a pharmacy, an ice-cream parlor, and a restaurant. The street changes dramatically at the beginning of the **Praia Maçarico.** The Maçarico strip, which sits back from the beach, is broad, clean, and dotted with benches and coco palms. On the strip are a couple of playgrounds, exercise stations, and some restaurants and hotels. The beach can get crowded. Maçarico is about a 10-minute walk downhill on João Pessoa toward the water. As you walk toward the beach, beware of the sidewalk on the left that occasionally drops off and has deep exposed gutters. **Praia Corvina,** near Maçarico, is a calmer spot. Upon entering Maçarico Beach, turn left and round the point to Corvina.

Ecotours can be arranged to mangrove forests to see scarlet ibis and other species. Talk to your hotel manager *or see Tours in The Amazon Essentials.*

WHERE TO STAY & EAT

$$ ✕⬚**Hotel Clube Privé do Atalaia.** Just off the beach, this place has more amenities than any other in town. Breezy, spacious public areas, a wet bar, and water slides help you keep cool. The restaurant specializes in shrimp and crab, but serves lots of fish and other dishes. **Pros:** Beachside location, lots of water activities. **Cons:** Few amenities, no in-room Internet or phones. ✉*Estrada do Atalaia 10, 68721-000* ☎*91/3464–*

1244 ⊕*www.privedoatalaia.tur.br*
🛏*141 rooms* Ⓣ*In room: refrigerator. In-hotel: restaurant, bar, pools, no elevator* ⊟*AE, DC, MC, V.*

$ Ⓣ**Hotel Salinópolis.** Right above
★ Maçarico Beach, this hotel has the best location in town. You can look down the length of the beach from the pool. It's a 10-minute walk from the light tower. **Pros:** Rooms are pleasant, brightly colored, doors open onto water. **Cons:** Windows are small. ⊠*Av. Beira Mar 26, 68721-000* ☎*091/3423–3000 or 091/9114–5248* ⊕*www.hotel salinopolis.com.br* 🛏*35 rooms* ⓉIn-room: refrigerator. In-hotel: restaurant, bar, pool, no elevator* ⊟*MC, V.*

¢–$$ ✕Ⓣ**Rango do Goiano.** Well situated on the Maçarico strip, this family-run place has compact but comfortable rooms. The restaurant (¢–$) has full meals as well as soups and salads. Try the crab soup. **Pros:** Beachside location, good seafood menu. **Cons:** Small rooms, few amenities. ⊠*Rua João Pessoa 2165, 68721-000* ☎*091/3423–3572, 091/3788–2054, or 091/3241–1099* ✉*ruycarlosbarros@yahoo.com.br* 🛏*19 rooms* ⓉIn Room: refrigerator. In-hotel: restaurant, bar* ⊟ *MC, V.*

NIGHTLIFE

During the week nightlife is almost nonexistent apart from a few folks gathered in a hotel bar or restaurant. On the weekends, though, and especially during holidays, things get lively. Atalaia restaurant-bars serve drinks and crank the music. Beach bar **Marujo's** (⊠*Praia Farol Velho, 68721-000*) turns into a dance club at 10 PM on weekends.

SHOPPING

The high-end boutique at **Hotel Clube Privé do Atalaia** (⊠*Estrada do Atalaia 10, 68721-000* ☎*091/3464–1244*) has sunscreen, hats, crafts, T-shirts, and Salinas memorabilia. Otherwise, ask hotel staff for directions to Shopping Maçarico or Russi Russi.

PINK DOLPHINS

Legend has it that the *botos cor de rosa* (pink river dolphins) can take human form. As humans, they are always handsome men, dressed immaculately in white, and very seductive. After dancing with the youngest and most beautiful girls, they lure them outside, have their way with them, and then return to the water just before dawn. You can always tell a boto from its slightly fishy smell and the hole in the top of its head, which is covered by a hat. Or at least this is what the pregnant girls tell their parents.

BETWEEN BELÉM & MANAUS

The smaller communities between the Amazon's two major cities give the best picture of pure Amazonian culture. Life tends to be even more intertwined with the river, and the center of activity is the dock area in village after village. Even a brief stop in one of these towns provides an interesting window into the region's day-to-day life.

10

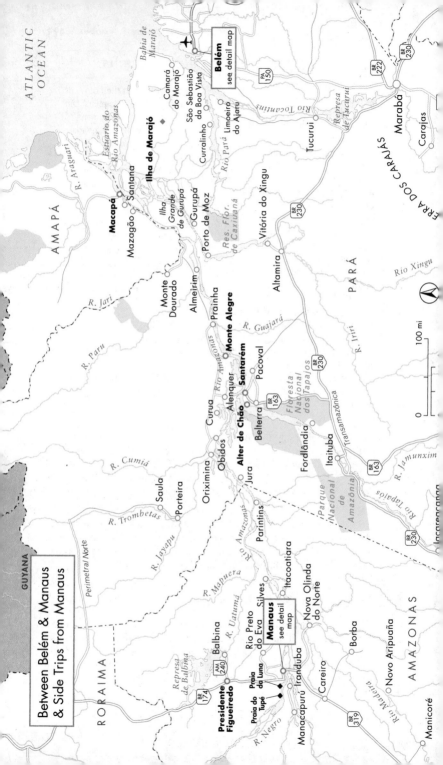

Between Belém & Manaus & Side Trips from Manaus

ATLANTIC OCEAN

GUYANA

AMAPÁ

RORAIMA

AMAZONAS

PARÁ

SERRA DOS CARAJÁS

Estuário do Rio Amazonas

Bahia de Marajó

Ilha de Marajó

Belém see detail map

Camará do Marajó
São Sebastião da Boa Vista
Curralinho
Limoeiro do Ajaru
Marabá
Carajás

Santana
Macapá
Mazagão

Ilha Grande de Gurupá
Gurupá
Porto de Moz
Res. Flor. de Caxiuanã
Vitória do Xingu
Tucuruí
Represa de Tucuruí

Monte Dourado
Almeirim
Prainha
Monte Alegre
Altamira

R. Jari
R. Paru
R. Guajará
Santarém
Alenquer
Pacoval
Fordlândia
Itaituba
Transamazônica

R. Cumiá
Curuá
Alter de Chão
Belterra
Floresta Nacional dos Tapajós
Rio Xingu

Oriximiná
Óbidos
Jura
Parque Nacional da Amazônia

Saulá
Porteira
R. Trombetas
R. Jayapu
Parintins
Itacoatiara
Rio Tapajós

Perimetral Norte

Silves
Nova Olinda do Norte
Borba

Balbina
Rio Preto do Eva
Manaus see detail map
Careiro
Novo Aripuaña

Represa de Balbina
R. Uatumã
Iranduba
Manacapuru
Manicoré

Presidente Figueiredo
Praia da Luna
Praia do Tupé
R. Negro
Rio Madeira

Rio Tocantins
Rio Pará
Rio Amazonas
R. Iriri
R. Iamunxim

100 mi

ILHA DO MARAJÓ

With an area of roughly 49,600 square km (18,900 square mi), Ilha do Marajó is reputedly the world's largest river island. Its relatively unspoiled environment and abundant wildlife make it one of the few accessible places in the Amazon that feel isolated. The Aruã tribes that once inhabited the island resisted invasion by the British and Dutch but were eventually conquered by the Portuguese through trickery. Ilha do Marajó's western half is dominated by dense forest and its eastern half by expansive plains, wetlands, and savannas. The island is ideal for raising cattle and water buffalo and has a half-million water buffalo and more than a million head of cattle; the human head count is about 250,000. According to local lore, the arrival of the water buffalo was an accident, the result of the wreck of a ship traveling from India to the Guianas. A day trip to a local ranch or a stay at Fazenda Carmo gives you a close-up look at the unique lifestyle of the island's people as well as the chance to view some of its animals, both domesticated and wild. You may see caiman, toco toucans, monkeys, and capybara, the world's largest rodent. Hiking is better in the dry season and boating in the rainy season.

> **VAMPIRES IN THE RIVER**
>
> A new species of fish was recently discovered in the Amazon. Related to the candiru (which is attracted to urine and lodges itself in the urinal tract of a swimmer) this little catfish clamps onto the host and sucks its blood. Always wear snug swimming trunks and bikinis to keep the little critter from going any farther.

Soure (the islands largest town) is 82 km (49 mi) northwest of Belém.

TO & FROM

Arapari operates boats between Belém and Camará, on Ilha do Marajó, twice daily Monday through Saturday (R$30 round-trip). A one-way trip from Belém to Ilha de Marajó takes two and hours costs R$15. A ferry takes cars to Ilha do Marajó. Vans run from Camará to Soure and cost about R$9.

GETTING AROUND

On Ilha do Marajó one of the best ways to reach the beaches or to explore towns is to use a bike. Rates are R$2 an hour. You can find motorcycles to rent for R$60–R$70, though you'll have to ask around, since they're not advertised. The locals usually know who has equipment for rent. Contact Pousada dos Guarás or Pousada Boto for more information.

10

ESSENTIALS

Boat Contacts Arapari (☎091/3242–1870 *or* 091/3241–4977). **Vans (Camará to Soure)** (☎091/3741–1441).

Emergencies & Medical Assistance Ambulance (☎192). **Fire** (☎193). **Hospital: Menino Deus** (✉*RuaOitava between 13 and 14 Trv., Soure, 66000-000* ☎091/3741–1307). **Pharmacy: Farmácia Salvador** (✉*Rua 2 s/n, Soure, 66000-000* ☎091/3765–1165). **Police** (☎190).

Taxi Soure Taxis (☎091/3741–1336).

Visitor & Tour Info **Iara Turismo** (✉*Rua Geronimo Pimentel 82, Umarizal, 66055-000 Belém* ☎*091/4006–3850* ⏱*Weekdays 8–6*) provides paquets to Ilha de Marajó, and passages from Belém to the island, it also makes reservations for the Hotel Ilha de Marajó. **Muiraquitã Turismo** (✉*Trav. São Pedro 566, Batista Campos, Belém66023-570* ☎*91/4006–1999* ⏱*Weekdays 9–5* ⊕*www.muiraquitan.com.br* ⏱*Muiraquitã have a three day package to Ilha de Marajó with hotel and transportation included*). **Secretaria Municipal de Turismo Marajó** (✉*Rua 2, between Trv. 14 and Trv. 15, Soure, 68870-000* ⊕*www.soure.tur.br* ⏱*Mon.–Sun. 7:30–6*).

SAFETY & PRECAUTIONS

Wear sandals on the beach, as the sand is known to hide worms, known locally as *bichos-do-pé,* which can burrow into the soles of your feet and breed.

WHAT TO SEE

Marajó is a huge island, but most human activity is clustered on its eastern coast, due to proximity to Belém. The western side of the island is beachless and floods during the rainy season.

The beach at **Caju Una,** a secluded fishing village, is breathtaking: a long strip of white sand with no vendors and few people. The village and its neighbor, Vila do Céu, are about a 45-minute drive (19 km/11 mi) north of Soure. Buses don't travel here, but you can hire a taxi (about R$30–R$50) or a mototaxi (about R$25) for an afternoon.

Camará, one of the island's most important ports, is where many boats from Belém dock. Buses to Camará pass by the riverside in Soure regularly.

Joanes, 23 km (14 mi) southwest of Soure, was the island's first settlement. Poke around the ruins of a 16th-century Jesuit mission, bask on a beach, and have a meal in one of the seafood restaurants. A taxi from Soure costs about R$60 round-trip.

Praia do Araruna is a red-mangrove forest about 20-minute (a 4-km/2-mi taxi ride) northeast of Soure. Here you may see flocks of scarlet ibis that appear out of nowhere.

Praia do Pesqueiro, 14 km (8 mi) north of Soure, is the island's most popular beach. When you stand on the white-sand expanse looking out at the watery horizon, the waves lapping at your feet, it's hard to believe you're not on the ocean. The beach has several thatch-roof restaurant-bars, making this an even more ideal place to spend an afternoon. You can travel here from Soure by taxi, by mototaxi (for one passenger), or by bike. Ask locals or hotel staff about bike rentals when you arrive in Soure.

Enchanting **river beaches** are a short (and cheap) taxi ride from both Soure and Salvaterra.

Salvaterra, a quarter-mile boat ride south across the narrow Rio Paracauari, is smaller than Soure but equally charming, and boats called *rabetas* cost R$1.

With almost 20,000 people, **Soure** (20 mi north of Camará) is Ilha do Marajó's largest town. Its many palm and mango trees, simple but brightly painted houses, and shore full of fishing boats make it seem more Caribbean than Amazonian.

WHERE TO STAY & EAT

Local cuisine invariably involves the water buffalo, whether in the form of a succulent steak or in cheeses and desserts made with buffalo milk. There's also an array of local fish to try. Bring cash in small bills, as breaking large ones can be a challenge and credit cards are rarely accepted. In a pinch, beer vendors can usually make change. Marajó has few hotels, and they are all quite rustic. Those we've listed are the best on the island.

$ ✕⊡**Hotel Ilha do Marajó.** Great verandas, solid creature comforts, and excellent facilities, including a lovely pool, make this hotel popular. The outdoor restaurant (¢–$) has good food and a view of the river. Saturday evening sometimes brings performances of *carimbó*, local music with African and native rhythms. Package deals, arranged at Belém travel agencies, include transport by bus to and from the dock in Camará and day trips to fazendas and beaches. English-speaking guides are available. **Pros:** Airy hotel, immaculate rooms, excellent amenities. **Cons:** During the rainy season (December–June) mosquitoes infiltrate rooms. ⊠*Trv. 2 No. 10, Soure 68870-000* ☎*091/4006–3850 or 091/3731–1315* ⊕*www.iaraturismo.com.br* ⟳*32 rooms* ⌂*In-room: refrigerator. In-hotel: restaurant, bar, tennis court, pool, bicycles, no elevator* ⊟*AE, MC, V.*

$ ⊡**Fazenda Carmo.** As a guest in this small antiques-filled farmhouse, you're privy to wonderful hospitality in a simple and rustic setting, and homestyle meals prepared with farm-fresh ingredients. Fazenda Carmo has fascinating activities like early-morning canoe trips in search of howler monkeys, horseback rides through wildlife-rich pastures, and muddy jeep rides to an archaeological site. The farmhouse is in rough condition and the menu is repetitious. The fazenda can accommodate 8 to 10 people, and stays are part of a package that includes meals, an English-speaking guide, and transportation to and from Camará (a 90-minute trip via van and boat). An English-speaking guide costs extra. If you speak Portuguese, call the Fazenda directly and you may get a better price. **Pros:** A bed-and–breakfast experience in such a remote location, fresh food, uniquely decorated rooms. **Cons:** Lacks basic creature comforts, like hot water, private bathrooms, and sometimes electricity. ⊠*Salvaterra, 68660-000* ⌂*Amazon Star Tours, Rua Henrique Gurjão 236, Belém66053-360* ☎*091/3241–1019* ⟳*8 rooms* ⌂*In-room: no a/c, no phone, no TV. In-hotel: no elevator* ⊟*AE, MC, V* ⊙*FAP.*

$ ⊡**Pousada & Camping Boto.** For a reasonable price you get lovely gardens, clean, modern rooms, friendly staff, and good food. The Boto is three minutes from the beach and is the only place in town with camping and hammock space. It rents motorcycles and bicycles—perfect for tooling around the island. The hotel also plans trips. **Pros:** Pleasant surroundings with well-kept rooms. **Cons:** The restaurant functions only on the weekend and the rooms are small. ⊠*Av. Alcindo Cacela, Sal-*

10

vaterra, 68870-000 ☎*091/3765–1539* ⊕*www.pousadaboto.com.br* 📞*9 rooms* ⌂*In-room: refrigerator, no phone. In-hotel: restaurant, bicycles, public Internet* ☷*V.*

NIGHTLIFE

On Friday or Saturday night there are usually live music and dancing at **Badalué** (✉*Trv. 14, Soure, 68870-000*). The most popular music in the region is accordion-heavy *brega*, which translates as "tacky." The name is appropriate, but don't be surprised if it grows on you. A **carimbó group** performs at the Hotel Ilha do Marajó on Saturday and sometimes in Soure on Wednesday or Friday. Ask at your hotel or ask a taxi driver for details.

SHOPPING

There are a few stores that sell sundries along Travessa 17 and Rua 3 in Soure. For marajoara pottery and ceramic figurines, try **Arte Caboclo** (✉*Trv. 5 between ruas 8 and 9, Soure, 68870-000*). You can even see how the ceramics are made in the workshop at the back of the store, which is open daily 8–6. For accurately re-created native pottery, ask anyone in Soure for **Carlos da ceramica** (Carlos of the ceramics). He'll show you how he makes pieces the native way. His work is the most authentic that we've seen. He usually has a few pieces for sale. **Soft marajoara pottery breaks easily. Pack it well.** For sandals, belts, and other leather goods, head to **Curtume Marajó** (✉*Rua 1, Bairro Novo, Soure, 68870-000*), a five-minute walk from downtown Soure and next to the slaughterhouse. The workers here can give you a tour of the tannery. The shop's hours are 7–11 and 1–5 Monday–Saturday. **Núcleo Operário Social Marilda Nunes** (✉*Rua 3 between Trv. 18 and Trv. 19, Soure 68870-000*) has stalls with everything from marajoara pottery and woven items to T-shirts and liquor. In theory, the hours are daily 7–noon and 2:30–6; the reality may be something else entirely.

For more information on local events and shopping, stop in at SECTUR (the Secretary of Culture) in downtown Soure.

BOI BUMBA

One of the largest festivals in the country is the Boi Bumba folklore festival in the Amazon. Called the Carnaval of the north, it takes place in Parintins, Amapá, during the last three days of June. Two schools put on a musical and theatrical extravaganza for three hours each night. The Caprichoso and the Garantido compete against each other in the Bumbodromó, a stadium that seats thousands.

MACAPÁ

Macapá is on the north channel of the Amazon Delta and, like Belém, was built by the Portuguese as an outpost. Today it's the capital of and the largest city in the Amapá State, with 150,000 people. It's also one of only five metropolises in the world that sit on the equator. Macapá's main lure is as a base for trips to see an extraordinary phenomenon—the *pororoca* (riptide).

330 km (198 mi) northwest of Belém.

TO & FROM

Domestic carriers TAM, and Gol (⇨*Brazil Essentials chapter)* have flights to Macapá. Aeroporto de Macapá is 4 km (2 mi) northwest of town. Take a taxi for the short, inexpensive ride.

Although Macapá is close to Ilha do Marajó's western side, most boats traveling to Macapá, including MACAMAZON and Bom Jesus, originate in Belém. Trips are 24 hours and you can get hammock space for around R$100, and two-person cabin for R$350. Boats dock in the nearby port town of Santana, where taxis await. The fare to Macapá is R$2–R$50, depending on how many other passengers the driver can gather. Buses in Macapá cost R$1.75 and taxi rides around major tourist points cost around R$50 maximum.

> ### THE GREATEST SURF ON EARTH
>
> The *pororoca* tidal bore is the most continuous wave in the world. From February to March, as the Atlantic currents meet the waters of the Amazon, the tide produces waves as high as 4 meters (15 feet) and can travel as far as 8 mi upstream. The indigenous tribes used the onomatopoeic word to describe the "big roar" that the wave produces. An endless wave is a surfers dream, and they flock here to participate in the yearly surf championship. It as dangerous as it is exciting; they're swimming in jungle debris, piranhas, anacondas, and alligators.

ESSENTIALS

Airport Aeroporto de Macapá (⊠*Rua Hildemar Maia s/n, 68909-490* ☏*96/3223-4087*).

Banks & Currency ExchangeBanco do Brasil (⊠*Rua Independência 250, 68900-090*). **Casa Francesa Câmbio e Turismo** (⊠*Rua Independência 232, 68900-090*).

Boat Contacts Bom Jesus (⊠*Av. Mendonça Junior 12, 68900-020* ☏*096/3223-2342*). **MACAMAZON** (☏*091/3222–5604 or 091/3228–0774*).

Bus Contacts Terminal Rodoviário (☏*96/3251-5045*).

Emergencies & Medical Assistance Ambulance (☏*192*). **Fire** (☏*193*). **Hospital: Hospital de Emergência** (⊠*Rua Hamilton Silva 1648, 68900-068* ☏*096/3212–6180*). **Pharmacy: Farmácia Globo** (⊠*Rua Hamilton Silva, 1585, 68900-068* ☏*096/3225–2525*). **Police** (☏*190*).

Taxi Rádio Taxi (☏*096/3223–2639*).

Visitor & Tour Info Casa Francesa Viagens e Turismo (⊠*Rua Independência, 236, 68900-090* ☏*096/3223–1902* ⊕*www.casafrancesa.tur.br* ↻*Weekdays 8–6, Sat. 8–noon*) Trips to the capital city of Macapá, ecological tours, and two day excursions to see the *pororoca* tidal bore.

10

WHAT TO SEE

Macapá's top man-made attraction is Brazil's largest fort, **Fortaleza de São José de Macapá.** Completed in 1782 after 18 grueling years, it's constructed of stones brought from Portugal as ship ballast. The well-preserved buildings house a visitor center, an art gallery, a meeting room, and a dance–music recital room. ⊠*Rua Cândido Mendes s/n, 68906-974* ☎*096/3212–5118* ⊠*Free* ☉*Tues.–Sun. 8–6.*

The **Marco Zero do Equador** is a modest monument to the equatorial line that passes through town. Although it consists of only a tall, concrete sundial and a stripe of red paint along the equator, there's a distinct thrill to straddling the line or hopping between hemispheres. The soccer stadium across the street uses the equator as its centerline. From Macapá's outdoor bus terminal on Rua Antônio Coelho de Carvalho, a block from the fort, catch the bus labeled B. NOVO/UNIVERSIDADE to the Marco Zero, a 20-minute ride. ⊠*Av. Equatorial 0288, 68903-110* ☎*096/3241–1951* ⊠*Free* ☉*Daily 9–noon and 2–8.*

WHERE TO STAY & EAT

$–$$ ✕**Cantinho Baiano.** To shake up the conservative cuisine scene here, the Salvador-born owner began cooking specialties from Bahia State. These dishes, especially the seafood *moqueca* (fried fish in vegetable, coconut milk, and dendê oil), are a highlight. The excellent river view, soft music, and colorfully clad waiters add to the ambience. ⊠*Av. Acelino de Leão 01, 68000-900* ☎*096/3223–4153* ⊟*AE, MC, V* ☉*No dinner Sun.*

¢–$$ ✕**Café Aymoré.** This is a local favorite for regional specialties such as *maniçoba* (stew with various cuts of pork—including feet and head—and cassava leaves) and *vatapá* (shrimp in flour and African palm oil). If you have more exotic taste, it's the only restaurant in town with government consent to serve *tartaruga* (turtle). There are also regional ice creams made from acai, tapioca, as well as many flavors from the Amazon. ⊠*Av. Iracema Carvão Nunes 92, 68900-099* ☎*096/3223–2328* ⊟*MC, V* ☉*No lunch.*

$ ☷**Hotel Atalanta.** Garishly pink and supported by towering Roman columns, there's nothing else in town that looks like the Atalanta. Inside are stained-glass windows, small pink columns, and cozy rooms. **Pros:** Comfortable guest rooms. **Cons:** Inconvenient location (10 blocks from the river in a residential neighborhood). ⊠*Av. Coaracy Nunes 1148, 68900-010* ☎*096/3223–1612* ⊕*www.atalantahotel.com.br* ⇥*33 rooms, 3 suites* ⌂*In-rooms: refrigerator. In-hotel: pool, gym, no elevator, public Internet* ⊟*AE, DC, MC, V.*

$ ☷**Macapá.** Partially obscured by palm trees, this three-story, white, colonial-style hotel is on well-manicured grounds. The hotel has many amenities, including hard-to-find wireless Internet in the rooms. **Pros:** Suites have balconies with exceptional river views. **Cons:** The interior is slightly worn, guest rooms aren't very impressive, despite modern amenities. ⊠*Av. Francisco Azarias Neto 17, 68900-080* ☎*096/3217–1350* ⊕*www.macapahotel.com.br* ⇥*74 rooms, 2 suites* ⌂*In-room: refrigerator, Wi-Fi, safe. In-hotel: bar, tennis court, pool, no elevator* ⊟*AE, DC, MC, V.*

¢ 🏨**Frota Palace Hotel.** Clean and spacious, rooms here even have phones, which aren't easy to come by in this area. It's conveniently located in Centro, and the staff is friendly. **Pros:** Inexpensive, modern facilities. **Cons:** No-frills rooms with little decoration. ⊠*Rua Tiradentes 1104, 68906-420* ☎*096/3223–3999* ⊕*www.hotelfrota.com.br* ↩*33 rooms* ⅏*In-rooms: Wi-Fi, refrigerator. In-hotel: restaurant, bar* ➾*AE, MC, V.*

NIGHTLIFE & THE ARTS

Macapá has a surprisingly active nightlife. If you like to bar-hop, head for the riverfront, where about 10 bars, some with music, are busy nearly every night. On weekends true night owls appreciate **Arena** (⊠*Rua Hamilton Silva s/ n, 68900-068*), which doesn't open until midnight. Most weekends and even sometimes during the week there's a play, a philharmonic concert, or a dance recital in the **Teatro das Bacabeiras** (⊠*Rua Cândido Mendes 368, 68905-670* ☎*096/3212–5272*). Tickets range from R$10 to R$20.

SHOPPING

Although Macapá has a free-trade zone, neither the prices nor the selection is anything special. The largest concentration of shops is on Rua Cândido Mendes and Rua São José. The **Casa do Artesão** (⊠*68904-030* ☎*96/3212–9158*), sells works by local craftspeople and artists—from tacky souvenirs to exquisite paintings and pottery—and is open 8–6 Monday–Sunday. Visa is accepted. The **Associação dos Povos Indígenas do Tumucumaque (APITU)** (⊠*68906-370* ☎*96/3224–2028*) has textiles, baskets, and other objects made by Amapá natives. It's open Monday–Saturday 8–noon and 2–6, Sunday 3–8.

> ### DEFORESTATION
>
> Every year huge tracts of land are logged and burned. Despite efforts to stop the illegal destruction of rain forest, the Amazon remains just too large to be policed. Brazil's federal environmental agency (IBAMA) has only one inspector per 4 million hectares (about the size of Switzerland) and estimates that they only track about 10% of logging. Most of these beautiful trees end up as cheap plywood for construction industries abroad; the major importing nations, such as the U.S., U.K., Spain, France, and Japan, have taken minimal steps to keep ill-gotten timber from their markets.

10

SANTARÉM

Since its founding in 1661, Santarém has ridden the crest of many an economic wave. First wood, then rubber, and more recently minerals have lured thousands of would-be magnates hoping to carve their fortunes from the jungle. The most noteworthy of these may have been Henry Ford. Although he never actually came to Brazil, Ford left his mark on this country in the form of two rubber plantations southwest of Santarém—Fordlândia and Belterra. Today this laid-back city of 242,000 has a new boom on the horizon—soybeans. As highway BR 163 from Mato Grosso State improves (a federal government priority is to pave the rest of this road closer to Santarém), it's becom-

508 < The Amazon

ing the fastest, cheapest route for hauling soybeans from Santarém to Atlantic seaports for international export. To meet the global demand for soybeans and to make enormous profits, Brazilian farmers are clearing vast tracts of forest south of town and all along the way to Mato Grosso. With this new boom, Santarém may change drastically in coming years.

Santarém-based trips can take you into a little-known part of the Amazon, with few foreign visitors, to places where the ecosystem is greatly different from those around Belém and Manaus. The area receives much less rain than upstream or downstream, and has rocky hills, enormous wetlands, and the Amazon's largest clear-water tributary, the Rio Tapajós.

> ## A MUSICAL GENIUS
>
> Maestro Wilson Dias da Fonseca resurrected the forgotten musical folklore of the Amazon. Mixing classical music with Amazonian rhythms and choro, he took his inspiration from the themes of the region and its natural splendors. Fonseca composed close to 1,600 works, among them the unique Amazonian opera *Vitória Regis, o Amor Cabano*. Recently the state of Paraiba has payed tribute to its self-taught musical genius by renaming the airport after him.

Perhaps the best place for walking is on the huge **riverfront sidewalk.** You can watch boat traffic and check out some of the shops along the way.

836 km (518 mi) west of Belém; 766 km (475 mi) east of Manaus.

TO & FROM

Domestic carriers TAM, Gol *(⇨Brazil Essentials chapter)* have flights to Santarém, and Santarém is easily accessible by air via Belém or Manaus. Aeroporto Maestro Wilson Fonseca is 14 km (23 mi) west of town, and buses and taxis from the airport are plentiful; a taxi ride costs around R$43.

MACAMAZON makes the two-day trip from Macapá to Santarém and onward to Manaus, R$70 for a hammock, and R$400 for a two-person cabin. The Belém to Santarém boat costs R$120 for a hammock, R$500 for a two-person cabin, and the ride takes three days. Sleeping arrangements are the same as on the Belém–Macapá route. Taxis are always at the docks in Santarém. The cost to any of the nearby hotels in town is less than R$10.

ESSENTIALS

Airport Aeroporto Maestro Wilson Fonseca (⊠*Rodovia Fernando Guilhon, Praça Eduardo Gomes s/n, 68035-000* ☎*093/3522–4328).*

Banks & Currency Exchange Banco do Brasil (⊠*Av. Rui Barbosa 794, 68005-080).*

Boat Contacts MACAMAZON (☎*091/3222–5604 or 091/3228–0774).*

Bus Contacts Rodoviário-SINART (⊠*Rod. Santarém, Cuiaba, 68030-000).*

Emergencies & Medical Assistance Ambulance (☎*192).* **Fire** (☎*193).*

Hospital: Hospital e Maternidade Sagrada Familia (⊠*Av. Presidente Vargas 1606, 68005-110* ☎*093/3523–84247*).
Pharmacy: Drogaria Droga Mil (⊠*Trv. Turiano Meira, 1828, 68020-590* ☎*093/3522–1000*). Police (☎*190*).

Internet **Amazon's Star Cyber** (⊠*Trv. dos Martires, 12lj 3, Central, 68005-540* ☎*093/3522—7720*).

Taxi **Rádio Táxi Piauí** (☎*093/3523–2725*).

Visitor & Tour Info **Amazon Tours** (⊠*Trv. Turiano Meira 1084, 68010-060* ☎*093/3522–6144* ⊕*www.amazonriver. com*) can help with airline tickets. **Santarém Tur** (⊠*Rua Adriano Pimentel 44, 68005-550* ☎*093/3522–4847* or *093/3522–1836* ⊕*www.santaremtur.com. br*)offer boat trips on the Amazon and Arapiuns rivers, day trips to Alter do Chão, and city tours. **SANTUR** (⊠*Rua Inácio Corrêa 22, 68005-260* ☎*093/3523–2434* ⊙*Weekdays 8–noon*).

> ### THE CONFLUENCE OF WATERS
>
> In Santarém, for about 5 ½ mi, the beautiful Rio Tapajós floats next to the murkier waters of the Amazon, until the larger river finally absorbs it. In Manaus a similar phenomenon can be seen when the slow-moving, muddy Amazon and the darker, quicker Río Negro flow side by side for 4 mi (6 km) without mixing. If you run your foot in the water from the boat, you can feel the difference in temperature—the Amazon is warm and the Negro is cold, the consistencies of the rivers are different, and the experience is magical.

WHAT TO SEE

The city is at the confluence of the aquamarine Rio Tapajós and the muddy brown Amazon. Seeing the **meeting of the waters** is second only to witnessing the pororoca (tidal bore) outside Macapá. It's best viewed from the **Praça Mirante do Tapajós,** on the hill in the center of town and just a few blocks from the waterfront.

To learn more about Santarém's culture and history, head for the **Centro Cultural João Fona** *(João Fona Cultural Center).* This small museum has a hodgepodge of ancient ceramics, indigenous art, and colonial-period paintings and a library for more in-depth studies. It also houses the Secretary of Tourism. ⊠*Praça Barão de Santarém, 68005-260* ☎*093/3523–2434* ✎*centur@netsan.com.br* ⊠Free ⊙*Weekdays 8–5.*

WHERE TO STAY & EAT

¢–$$ ✕**Santo Antônio.** Fill up on *churrasco* (grilled meat) or one of the regional specialties at this restaurant behind a gas station. The fish is always fresh, and a single portion serves two. The tucunaré (peacock bass), served on a searing-hot marble platter, is delectable. The restaurant also serves a reasonably priced beef churrasco. ⊠*Av. Tapajós 2071, 68040-500* ☎*093/3523–5069* ▭*No credit cards.*

$ ✕**Mascote.** Since 1934 this has been one of the most popular and famous restaurants in town. The indoor dining area is enchanting, but the palm-lined patio is well-lighted and inviting and has a good view of the river and the plaza. An extremely varied menu includes pizzas, sandwiches, steaks, and seafood. ⊠*Praça do Pescador s/n* ☎*093/3523–2844* ▭*AE, DC, MC, V.*

10

CLOSE UP

Ford's Impossible Dream

Henry Ford spent millions of dollars to create two utopian company towns and plantations to supply his Model T cars with rubber tires. In 1927 he chose an area 15 hours southwest of Santarém. A year later all the materials necessary to build a small town and its infrastructure were transported by boat from Michigan to the Amazon. Small Midwestern-style houses were built row after row. *Seringueiros* (rubber tappers) were recruited with promises of good wages, health care, and schools for their children. Fordlândia was born. Despite all the planning, the scheme failed. The region's climate, horticulture, and customs weren't taken into account. Malaria and parasites troubled the workers; erosion and disease plagued the trees.

Convinced that he had learned valuable lessons from his mistakes, Ford refused to give up. In 1934 he established another community in Belterra, 48 km (30 mi) outside Santarém. Although some rubber was extracted from the plantation, production fell far short of original estimates. World War II caused further disruptions as German boats cruised the Brazilian coast and prevented food and supplies from arriving. Advances in synthetic rubber struck the final blow. Today some rusted trucks and electric generators, a few industrial structures, and many empty bungalows are all that remain of Ford's impossible dream.

$ ✕**Mistura Brasileira.** Excellent sandwiches and a self-service buffet keep the MB hopping. Try the beef fillet sandwich or the lasagna. The restaurant is housed in a hotel of the same name. ⊠*Av. Tapajós 23, Centro, 68005-290* ☎*093/3522–4819* ▭*No credit cards.*

¢ ✕**Delícias Caseiras.** A constant stream of locals filters in to fill up at the buffet table of this restaurant whose name means, roughly, "homemade delectables." Salads aren't noteworthy, but the chicken *milanesa* (breaded and fried) and beef Stroganoff are very good. ⊠*Trv. 15 de Agosto 121, Centro* ☎*093/3523–5525* ▭*No credit cards* ☾*No dinner.*

¢ ▦**Rio Dourado.** Reasonable rates get you simple but attractive accommodations, a convenient location, and friendly service. The hotel has a nice view of an open market area and a bit of the waterfront from the dining area on the second floor (where you have breakfast). **Pros:** Good prices and pleasant rooms. **Cons:** Not many modern facilities. ⊠*Rua Floriano Peixoto 799, 68005-080* ☎*093/3522–4021* ☝*30 rooms* ⌂*In room: refrigerator. In-hotel: airport shuttle, public Internet, no elevator* ▭*AE, DC, MC, V* ⋈*BP.*

NIGHTLIFE

One of the best places in town to get a drink is **Mascotinho** (⊠*Praça do Pescador 10, Centro, 68000-000* ☎*093/3523–2844*). It has passable food and is usually breezy since it's on the river. There's MPB music all nights except when it rains, since the seats are outside.

SHOPPING

One of three artisan shops grouped together, **Loja Regional Muiraquitã** (⊠*Rua Senador Lameira Bittencourt 131, 68005-010* ☎*093/3522–7164*) sells an incredible variety of regional items including native musical instruments, locally mined minerals, and wood carvings. A reliable photo shop in town is **Foto Society** (⌧*Rui Barbosa 785, Centro, 68005-080* ☎*093/3522–1422*).

SPORTS & THE OUTDOORS

Santarém, at the hub of two different river systems and forests, has a lot of outdoor options. Secluded beaches for swimming, forest trails for hiking, boats for exploring backwater areas and wildlife-watching—they're all here. An American who knows the area particularly well is Steven Alexander, who has been living down here for nearly 30 years. He leads ecotours on occasion, especially to a forest preserve he has created outside town called **Bosque Santa Lúcia.** It has several trails with tree identification tags, troops of monkeys, and lots of birds and insects. Contact **Amazon Tours** (⌧*Trv. Turiano Meira 1084, Santarém, 68010-060* ☎*093/3522–1928* ⊕*www.amazonriver.com*) for information on Steven Alexander's ecotours, or check out his Web site.

> ### A BEAR IN THE AMAZON
>
> Having lost a presidential election to Woodrow Wilson in November 1912, Teddy Roosevelt decided to drown his sorrows in the Amazon River. He traveled with an expedition of renowned scientists and Amazon explorers to take a closer look at the River of Doubt (Rio de Duvida), an unexplored tributary. Though Roosevelt had always been an intrepid adventurer, the Amazon almost brought him to his end. The expedition lacked meat, lost boats in the whirling river, and was ravaged by disease.

ALTER DO CHÃO

The cruise down the Rio Tapajós to the village of Alter do Chão, on the Lago Verde (Green Lake), is one of the best excursions from Santarém. The area has been called "the Caribbean of the Amazon," and when you see its clear green waters and its white-sand beaches you understand why. Buses also make the journey from Santarém to Alter do Chão regularly. From the village it's a short canoe ride across a narrow channel to the beach. Note that from April to July, when the water is high, the beach shrinks considerably.

On weekends vendors and small restaurants set up on the beach. A hiking trail 100 meters beyond the vendors winds about 1 mi through scrub forest to **Serra Pelada** (Naked Hill). Wear good shoes and take water and a camera for the hike to the top. The trail can be slick and is eroded in places, but it's only a couple of hundred meters from the base to the top. **Lanche do Bené,** near the water, is a great stop for a cold drink under an Indian almond tree.

About 30 km (about 20 mi) south of Santarém.

TO & FROM

Buses from Santarém to Alter do Chão depart from Praça Tiradentes in the city center or from Avenida Cuiabá (near the Amazon Park Hotel). They make the journey back and forth five or six times a day and hourly on Sunday (32km, 45min). The bus costs R$1.80. A taxi to Alter do Chão costs R$30. It's close to Santarém, where banks and other essentials can be found.

WHERE TO STAY & EAT

Churrascaria e Pizzaria D'Italia has very good food at low prices. Try the grilled pirarucú or tambaqui. Two blocks up from the plaza on Rua Antônio Augustinho Lobato is **Restaurante Tribal.** Quiet, clean, and friendly, it has excellent homestyle grilled meat and grilled fish, and it's inexpensive.

$ ✕🖭**Beloalter.** A white-sand beach
★ is right outside the front door and there are an impressive range of room prices. Higher prices get you a better view or even a room in a treehouse. The restaurant (¢–$$) specializes in fish, but has a good variety of other dishes, such as pastas, salads, meats. **Pros:** Large and pleasantly decorated rooms, beachfront location. **Cons:** Lesser views in lower-priced rooms. ⊠*Rua Pedro Texeira s/n, 68105-000* ☎*093/3527–1247 or 093/3527–1230* ⊕*www.beloalter.com.br* ↩*24 rooms* ⌂*In-room: refrigerator, safe, Wi-Fi. In-hotel: restaurant, pool, no elevator* ▭*MC, V* ⊺*EP.*

¢ 🖭**Belas Praias Pousada.** Just up from the riverbank, Belas Praias is in a great location if you want to be where the action is. Rooms are modern, clean, and have lots of wood. Request one with a view of the bay and beaches. **Pros:** Pleasant rooms, great location for going out. **Cons:** Rooms are simply furnished. ⊠*Rua da Praia 509, 68109-000* ☎*093/3527–1365* ↩*5 rooms* ⌂*In-room: no phone, refrigerador* ▭*V* ⊺*EP.*

SHOPPING

Shops ring the central plaza in the village of Alter do Chão. On the same street as Restaurante Tribal, close to the plaza, is **Aráribá Arte e Artes,** which has the best selection of authentic native artisanal items in town.

Every year, anglers from around the world descend on the Amazon—peacock bass (*tucunare*) is a favorite. These fish can get to be over 3 feet long and weigh up to 30 pounds. They're predators and vocacious eaters, so fishing for them is very exciting. Tucunare will take just about any artificial lure, but anglers tell us that the surface plug bait fishing is the most fun.

MONTE ALEGRE

Wedged on a hillside between fertile Amazon wetlands and *cerrado* (dry scrub forest), the Monte Alegre area has long been a preferred site for human habitation. In the hills behind the town, carbon dating of middens below cave paintings indicates a human presence as many as 11,000 years ago, making them some of the earliest known in the Americas. A small band of Irish and English settled here in the 1570s, about 40 years before the Portuguese arrived in Belém. The site later became a missionary outpost—called Gurupatuba—for area natives. In 1758 it was incorporated as a village.

Today Monte Alegre is a city of around 80,000. Its economy relies mostly on ranching, farming, and fishing. The town obviously has a rich history, but it's not well organized for tourism. There's no town map, for example, and the streets are confusing. Also, visiting hours for the few historic sites change often if there are any. You can thoroughly enjoy Monte Alegre, however, if you walk around and talk to the locals. They're helpful and may go out of their way to assist you.

90 km (60 mi) northeast of Santarém.

TO & FROM
Both boats and buses depart from Praca Tiradentes in Santarém for R$30 one-way. Boat trips are six hours for the downriver trip and eight hours upriver. The bus takes four hours.

ESSENTIALS
This is a small town with only one bank. Other essentials can be found in Santarém.

Banks & Currency Exchange Banco do Brasil (✉ *Av. Maj. Francisco Mariano, 310, Cidade Alta, 68220-000).*

WHAT TO SEE
One of the largest sites for cave paintings dating 10- to 12,000 years ago is in Monte Alegre. Thousands of **cave paintings** can be seen in the hills behind town in the area called Serra da Lua. Hire a cab or a moto-taxi to take you to the closest ones, about an hour away.

WHERE TO STAY & EAT
¢ ✕🏠**Panorama I.** In the Cidade Alta and a little out of the way, these small chalets are quiet and private. A 100-yard walk takes you to an impressive overlook. The restaurant (¢–$) is rated by locals as the best in town. **Pros:** Rooms are pleasant and relaxing. **Cons:** Not in the center. ✉ *serra Oriental 100, 68220-000* ☎ *093/3533–1716* 🛏 *4 chalets* 🛋*In-room: no phone, refrigerator. In-hotel: restaurant, no elevator* 🚫*No credit cards* ❢⊙*EP.*

¢ 🏨**Hotel Panorama II.** Few hotels have a view as incredible as this one. Next to the plaza on top of the hill, the veranda looks out over the Lower City and the Amazon River. Rooms are clean, but not especially attractive. Music at the bar next door can get noisy on weekends. Wander over for a cold drink and catch the sunset, or get the same view from the hotel's veranda. **Pros:** Nice vistas and comfortable rooms. **Cons:** Can get noisy, the rooms have slightly worn furniture. ✉*Praça*

BEST GUIDE IN TOWN

Nelsi Sadeck (☎*093/3533–1430* or *093/3533–1215* ✉*nelsi@net-san.com.br)* is a local guide with a wealth of information on cave paintings. He's a civil engineer by trade, but has assisted archaeologists in the region. Nelsí doesn't speak English (though you can e-mail him in English), but he's still the best guide around. Contact him a few weeks in advance (R$400 for a group up to 8). Wear comfortable hiking clothes, sturdy shoes, sunscreen, and take lots of water, a light lunch, snacks. It's customary to tip the guide and driver. Plan to leave around 6:30 AM and until 8 PM.

10

Fernando Guilhon 500, 68220-000 ☎093/3533–1716 ➦6 rooms
&*In-room: no phone, refrigerator* ▤*No credit cards* ⍾EP.

MANAUS

Manaus, the capital of Amazonas State, is a hilly city of around 1.8 million people that lies 766 km (475 mi) west of Santarém and 1,602 km (993 mi) west of Belém on the banks of the Río Negro 10 km (6 mi) upstream from its confluence with the Amazon. Manaus is the Amazon's most popular tourist destination, largely because of the 19 jungle lodges in the surrounding area. The city's principal attractions are its lavish, brightly colored houses and civic buildings—vestiges of an opulent time when the wealthy sent their laundry to be done in Europe and sent for Old World artisans and engineers to build their New World monuments.

Founded in 1669, Manaus took its name, which means "mother of the Gods," from the Manaó tribe. The city has long flirted with prosperity. Of all the Amazon cities and towns, Manaus is most identified with the rubber boom. In the late 19th and early 20th centuries it supplied 90% of the world's rubber. The industry was monopolized by rubber barons, whose number never exceeded 100 and who lived in the city, and spent enormous sums on ostentatious lifestyles. They dominated the region like feudal lords. Thousands of *seringueiros* (rubber tappers) were recruited to work on the rubber plantations, where they lived virtually as slaves. A few of the seringueiros were from indigenous tribes, but most were transplants from Brazil's crowded and depressed northeast. Eventually conflicts erupted between barons and indigenous workers over encroachment on tribal lands. Stories of cruelty abound. One baron is said to have killed more than 40,000 native people during his 20-year "reign." Another boasted of having slaughtered 300 Indians in a day.

The 25-year rubber era was brought to a close thanks to Englishman Henry A. Wickham, who took 70,000 rubber-tree seeds out of Brazil in 1876. (Transporting seeds across borders has since been outlawed.) The seeds were planted in Kew Gardens in England. The few that germinated were transplanted in Malaysia, where they flourished. Within 30 years Malaysian rubber ended the Brazilian monopoly. Although several schemes were launched to revitalize the Amazon rubber industry, and many seringueiros continued to work independently in the jungles, the high times were over. Manaus entered a depression that lasted until 1967, when the downtown area was made a free-trade zone. The economy was revitalized, and its population jumped from 200,000 to 900,000 in less than 20 years.

In the 1970s the industrial district was given exclusive federal free-trade-zone status to produce certain light-industry items. Companies moved in and began making motorcycles and electronics. In the mid-1990s the commercial district lost its free-trade-zone status. Hundreds lost their jobs and businesses crumbled, but the light-industrial sector held strong and even grew. Today it employs 80,000, has the largest motorcycle factory in South America, and makes 90% of Brazilian-made TVs.

TO & FROM

Brigadeiro Eduardo Gomes Airport is 17 km (10 mi) north of downtown. Most flights connect in São Paulo. Varig and TAM have regular flights to and from Brasília, Rio, and São Paulo. TAM also has flights from Santarém and Belém.

> ### GOODYEAR THE INVENTOR
>
> The American inventor Charles Goodyear created a process called vulcanization, which made rubber tougher. It was Goodyear's invention in 1839 that led to the use of rubber in a variety of applications and indirectly caused the Brazilian rubber boom.

The trip to Manaus Centro from the airport takes 25 minutes and costs about R$49 by taxi. A trip on one of the city buses, which depart regularly during the day and early evening, costs R$2.

If you're looking for a boat from Manaus to another town, a lodge, or a beach, go to the Hidroviária Regional Terminal. At the ticket or tourist information booths you can get information about prices and departure times and days to all the locations. You can also walk down to Porto Flutuante via the bridge behind the terminal to take a look at the regional boats. Their destinations and departure times are listed on plaques.

MACAMAZON boats run from Manaus to Santarém on Wednesday and Friday from the Porto São Raimundo (west of downtown) or the Porto Flutuante. The journey takes two days and cost R$70 for a hammock and R$400 for a two-person cabin. Boats from Manaus to Belém run three times a week; the trip takes five days and costs R$180 for a hammock, and R$800 for a two-person cabin.

The bus station in Manaus, Terminal Rodoviário Huascar Angelim, is 7 km (4 mi) north of the city center. From Manaus, BR 174 runs north (471 mi) to Boa Vista in Roraima State. BR 319 travels south to Porto Velho in Rondônia State but involves a ferry crossing and is only paved for about 100 km (63 mi); the road is eventually invaded by rivers and lakes. Even if you're after adventure, don't think about driving to Porto Velho.

GETTING AROUND

The city bus system is extensive, easy to use, and inexpensive (R$2). Most of the useful buses run along Avenida Floriano Peixoto, including Bus 120, which goes to Ponta Negra and stops near the Hotel Tropical. From the airport a taxi to Hotel Tropical costs R$49; a trip from the Tropical to the center of town also costs R$49. The Fontur bus, which costs about R$14, travels between Centro and the Hotel Tropical several times a day. Manaus has its share of traffic and parking problems, but the driving is calmer than in Belém.

ESSENTIALS

Airlines (Local) **Rico** (☎092/4009-8333 ⊕www.voerico.com.br).

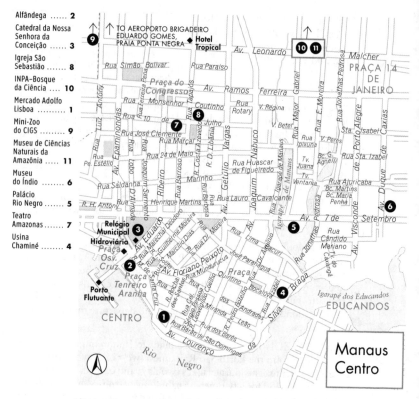

Manaus
Centro

Airport **Aeroporto Brigadeiro Eduardo Gomes** (✉*Av. Santos Dumont s/n, 69041-000* ☎*092/3652–1210*).

Banks & Currency Exchange

Amazonia Câmbio e Turismo Exchange (✉*Av. 7 de Setembro 1199, Centro, 69005-141*). **Banco Amazônia** (✉*Aeroporto Brigadeiro Eduardo Gomes, Av. Santos Dumont s/n, 69041-000*).

Boat Contacts **MACAMAZON** (☎*091/3222–5604 or 091/3228–0774*).

Bus Contacts **Terminal Rodoviário Huascar Angelim** (✉*Rua Recife 2784, Santo Antonio, 69029-520* ☎*092/3642–5805*).

Emergencies & Medical Assistance **Ambulance** (☎*192*). **Fire** (☎*193*). **Hospital: Hospital e Pronto Socorro** (✉*Av. Cosme Ferreira 3775, São Jose, 69083-000* ☎*092/3647–1750*). **Pharmacies: Drogaria Avenida** (✉*Av. Senador Alvaro Maia 748, Centro, 69025-070* ☎*092/3633–6761*). **Police** (☎*190*).

Internet **Amazon Cyber Café** (✉*Av. Getúlio Vargas 626, Centro, 69020-010* ☎*092/3232–9068*). **Internext** (✉*Rua 24 Maio, 220 sl 32, Centro, 69010-080* ☎*092/3633–4409*).

Taxi **Recife Rádio Táxi** (☎*092/3656–6121*). **Tucuxi** (☎*092/2123–9090*).

Visitor & Tour Info **Amazonastur** (⊠*Rua Saldanha Marinho 321, Centro, 69010-040* ☎*092/2123–3800* ⊕*www.amazonastur.am.gov.br* ☞*Open weekdays 8–5*). **Centro de Atendimento ao Turista (CAT)** (⊠*Av. Eduardo Ribeiro 666, Centro, 69010-001* ☎*092/3622-0767* ⊙*Weekdays 8–6*). **Fontur** (⊠*Hotel Tropical, Av. Coronel Teixeira 1320, Ponta Negra, 69037-000* ☎*092/3658–3052 or 092/3658–3438* ⊕*www.fontur.com.br* ⊙*Mon.–Sat. 7–7, Sun. 7–3*) has boat and city tours, as well airplane flights to various locations. They can also arrange trips to jungle lodges. **Selvatur** (⊠*Av. Djalma Batista 276, Carrefour, Flores, 69005-010* ☎*092/3642–3192 or 92/3642–8777* ⊕*www.selvatur.com.br*) gives good Manaus-area ecotours.

EXPLORING MANAUS

Manaus is a sprawling city with a couple of high-rise buildings. There are a lot of hotels and sights are in this small city center (Centro), but the area is congested and not very attractive.

CENTRO

Manaus's downtown area has a lot going on. The floating docks are here, with tourist shops nearby. Open markets sell fish, meats, and all sorts of produce, while general stores ply machetes, hoes, hardtack, cassava flour, and boat motor parts to those pursuing a livelihood outside the city. Centro is also the most important historic section of the city. The Teatro Amazonas, the Customs House (Alfândega), and the Adolfo Lisboa Market are here, along with old churches, government buildings, and mansions. The result is a mix of neoclassical, Renaissance, colonial, and modern architecture.

MAIN ATTRACTIONS

❻ Museu do Índio. The Indian Museum is maintained by Salesian Sisters, an order of nuns with eight missions in the upper Amazon. It displays handicrafts, weapons, ceramics, ritual masks, and clothing from the region's tribes. ⊠*Rua Duque de Caxias 296, Centro, 69020-140* ☎*092/3635–1922* ⊠*R$5* ⊙*Weekdays 8:30–11:30 and 2–4:30, Sat. 8:30–11:30.*

❺ Palácio Rio Negro. The extravagant Rio Negro Palace was built at the ★ end of the 19th century as the home of a German rubber baron. Later it was used as the official governor's residence. Today it houses some of the city's finest art exhibits and a cultural center. The Museu da Imagem e do Som, on the same property, has three daily screenings of art films and documentaries Tuesday through Friday and four screenings daily on weekends. Don't miss the cultural exhibits out back, which include a caboclo home, an indigenous home, and a cassava-processing house. ⊠*Av. 7 de Setembro 1546, Centro, 69005-141* ☎*No phone* ⊠*Free* ⊙*Weekdays 9–6.*

❼ Teatro Amazonas. Operas and other events are presented regularly. Monday-evening performances are free and usually feature local artists of FodorsChoice ★ various musical genres. The Amazonas Philharmonic Orchestra plays Thursday night and can be seen and heard practicing in the theater weekdays 9–2. A variety of foreign entertainers, from José Carreras to the Spice Girls, have performed here. Half-hour tours are conducted

10

daily 9–4. ⊠*Praça São Sebastião s/n, Centro, 69025-140* ☎*092/3232–1768* ⊠*R$10* ⊗*Mon.–Sat. 9–5.*

❹ **Usina Chaminé.** Transformed from a sewage-treatment plant that never functioned, this art gallery displays exhibits and holds dance and theater performances. Its neo-Renaissance–style interior, with hardwood floors and massive wood beams, is another reason to visit. ⊠*Av. Lourenço da Silva Braga, Centro, 69005-015* ☎*092/3633–3026* ⊠*Free* ⊗*Tues.–Fri. 10–5, weekends 4–8.*

IF YOU HAVE TIME

❷ **Alfândega.** The Customs House was built by the British in 1902 with bricks imported as ship ballast. It stands alongside the floating dock that was built at the same time to accommodate the annual 10-meter (32-foot) rise and fall of the river. It's now home to the regional office of the Brazilian tax department, and the interior is of little interest. ⊠*Rua Marquês de Santa Cruz s/n, Centro, 69005-050* ☎*No phone* ⊠*Free* ⊗*Weekdays 10–3.*

❸ **Catedral da Nossa Senhora da Conceição.** Built originally in 1695 by Carmelite missionaries, the Cathedral of Our Lady of Immaculate Conception (also called Igreja Matriz) burned down in 1850 and was reconstructed in 1878. It's a simple, predominantly neoclassical structure with a bright, colorful interior. ⊠*Praça da Matriz, Centro, 69005-390* ☎*92/3234–7821* ⊠*Free* ⊗*Usually Mon.–Sat. 9–5, but hrs vary.*

❽ **Igreja São Sebastião.** This neoclassical church (circa 1888), with its charcoal-gray color and medieval characteristics, seems foreboding. Its interior, however, is luminous and uplifting, with white Italian marble, stained-glass windows, and beautiful ceiling paintings. The church has a tower on only one side. No one is sure why this is so, but if you ask, you may get one of several explanations: the second tower wasn't built because of lack of funds; it was omitted as a symbolic gesture to the poor; or the ship with materials for its construction sank. As you stroll through the church plaza and the one in front of the Teatro Amazonas, note the black-and-white Portuguese granite patterns at your feet. They are said to represent Manaus's meeting of the waters. ⊠*Praça São Sebastião, Centro, 69010-240* ☎*092/3232–4572* ⊠*Free* ⊗*Usually Mon.–Sat. 9–5, but hrs vary.*

❶ **Mercado Adolfo Lisboa.** Vendors sell Amazon food products and handi-
★ crafts at this market. Built in 1882, it's a wrought-iron replica of the original Parisian Les Halles (now destroyed); the ironwork is said to have been designed by Gustave Eiffel himself. ⊠*Rua dos Barés 6, Centro, 69005-020* ☎*No phone* ⊗*Daily 6–6.*

ELSEWHERE IN MANAUS

Most of the area surrounding downtown Manaus is not very attractive to visit. The few places of interest include the Natural History Museum and INPA's Bosque da Ciência in Aleixo. The Bosque and nearby Parque Municipal do Mindu in Parque 10 are both forested and good for walks. A taxi will cost around R$30 one-way from downtown to these sites. The Mini-Zoo do CIGS is in São Jorge, and a taxi will

A Vanishing People

In 1500, when the Portuguese arrived in Brazil, the indigenous population was 4.5 million, with an estimated 1,400 tribes. From the beginning the Portuguese divided into two camps regarding the native people: the missionaries, who wanted to "tame" them and convert them to Catholicism, and the colonizers, who wished to enslave and exploit them. The missionaries lost, and when it became apparent that the indigenous people couldn't be enslaved, the infamous *bandeirantes* (assault forces) relentlessly persecuted them so as to "liberate" tribal lands. Many lost their lives defending their land and their way of life, but the greatest killers were smallpox and influenza—European diseases against which they had no immunity. Slow but steady integration into Portuguese society caused the native population to dwindle.

Today, of Brazil's 328,000 remaining indigenous people, about 197,000 live in the Amazon. Each of the 220 societies has its own religious beliefs, social customs, and economic activities. The larger groups include the Manaó, Yanomami, Marajó, Juma, Caixana, Korubo, and Miranha. Each speaks one of the 170 distinct languages spoken by the indigenous peoples of Brazil; Tupi (with seven in-use derivations, including Tupi-Guarani) is the most widely spoken, followed by Macro Jê, Aruák, Karíb, and Arawá.

Throughout Brazil's history sporadic efforts were made to protect indigenous people, but it was only in 1910 that the government established an official advocacy agency, the Service for the Protection of the Indians (SPI), to support Indian autonomy, ensure respect for traditional practices, and help indigenous peoples to acquire Brazilian citizenship. In 1930 the SPI was abolished due to corruption and lack of funds. It was replaced in 1967 by the current governmental advocacy group, FUNAI (Fundação Nacional do Indio, or the National Indian Foundation). Although it has been highly criticized, FUNAI helped to get the first (and, thus far, only) indigenous person elected into office: Mario Juruna, an Indian chief, served as federal deputy from 1983 to 1987. The foundation has also defended the rights of indigenous people to protect their lands (it allows only legitimate researchers to visit reservations), which are increasingly targeted for logging, rubber extraction, mining, ranching, or the building of industrial pipelines and hydroelectric plants.

The indigenous people of the Amazon have always respected and understood their environment; their plight and that of the rain forest are closely linked. Conservation efforts to preserve the rain forest have called attention to some of FUNAI's issues, but for the Brazilian government the issue is complicated: rain-forest conservation is often overshadowed by economic development. Further, the indigenous people still lack many basic human rights, and violence (such as the 1998 murder of prominent activist Francisco de Assis Araujó) still sporadically occurs as the indigenous people continue to defend their way of life against outsiders.

–Melisse Gelula and Althia Gamble

10

cost about R$20. Ponta Negra along the Río Negro has several restaurants and is super for evening strolls. Also, Hotel Tropical is on its upstream end. Taxis charge between R$49 from downtown.

MAIN ATTRACTIONS

⑩ **INPA–Bosque da Ciência.** Used as a research station for the INPA (Instituto Nacional de Pesquisa da Amazônia), this slice of tropical forest is home to a great diversity of flora and fauna. Some highlights include manatee tanks, caiman ponds, a museum, a botanical garden with an orchidarium, and nature trails. It's a great place for a walk in the shade. ⊠*Rua Otávio Cabral s/n, Petropolis, 69011-970* ☎*092/3643–3377* ⊴*R$2* ⊙*Tues.–Sun. 9–4.*

Meeting of the Waters. This natural phenomenon is one of the area's biggest tourist attractions. At the CEASA port you can rent a boat, or go with a tour company. It takes about an hour to go from CEASA to the Meeting of the Waters, spend some time there, and return. A taxi to CEASA from downtown is about R$30.

Fodor's Choice ★

❾ **Mini-Zoo do CIGS.** Dozens of animals native to the Amazon live at this 5-acre zoo. Pains have been taken to create natural habitats for some of the animals, but due to lack of funds, other animals are simply kept in cages. The Brazilian army operates a jungle-survival training school here, but it's not overrun with tanks and soldiers. ⊠*Estrada do São Jorge 750, São Jorge, 69033-000* ☎*No phone* ⊴*R$3* ⊙*Tues.–Sun. 8–4.*

IF YOU HAVE TIME

⑪ **Museu de Ciências Naturais da Amazônia.** The Natural History Museum of the Amazon has preserved specimens of insects, turtles, and fish on display. This is a great place to get acquainted with fish, reptiles, and insects that you might later see in the Amazon jungle or river. ⊠*Estrada Belém s/n, Aleixo, 69054-711* ☎*092/3644–2799* ⊴*R$12* ⊙*Mon.–Sat. 9–noon and 2–5.*

Praia da Ponta Negra. Known as the Copacabana of the Amazon, this beach is next to the Hotel Tropical and has restaurants, bars, sports, and nightlife facilities (including an amphitheater).

WHERE TO EAT

$–$$$$ ✕**Canto da Peixada.** When Pope John Paul II came to Manaus in 1981, ★ this restaurant was chosen to host him. The dining areas aren't elegant, but the fish dishes are outstanding, and there are 43 types of salad. One platter feeds two. ⊠*Rua Emilio Moreira 1677, Praça 14, 69020-040* ☎*092/3234–1066* ⊟*No credit cards* ⊙*Closed Sun.*

¢–$$$$ ✕**Chez Charufe.** On the banks of the Río Negro, Chez Charufe is in a lovely location for breezy, open-air dining. Fish dishes as well as beef and chicken are all very good, and it's a 10-minute walk from the Hotel Tropical. The most expensive dish on the menu is a paella for two, but there are plenty of tasty options for much less. ⊠*Estrada da Ponta Negra, Ponta Negra, 69037-000* ☎*092/3658–5101* ✐*charufenasser@hotmail.com* ⊟*AE, DC, MC, V* ⊙*No lunch.*

$$$ ✕**El Touro Loco.** Excellent regional
★ dishes, unusual and tasty appetizers, pizza, pasta, sushi, salads—El Touro Loco has it all. It also has a fascinating rustic-European decor, and great service in an open-air setting. There's one price for all the food; alcohol and service are separate. ⊠*Av. Do Turismo 215, Tarumã, 69037-000* ☎*92/3631–2557* ▤*AE, V.*

> ### CARBON SEQUESTRATION
>
> A recent study has shown that the Amazon trees have taken in through carbon sequestration all the emissions of logging and burning in the region since the 1980s. But scientists estimate that this trend is bound to stop soon.

$$ ✕**Churrascaria Búfalo.** Twelve waiters, each with a different cut of chicken, beef, or goat, scurry around this large, sparkling clean restaurant. As if the delectable meats weren't enough, tables are also stocked with side dishes, including manioc root, pickled vegetables, and caramelized bananas. ⊠*Rua Joaquim Nabuco 628-A, Centro, 69000-000* ☎*092/3633–3773* ⊕*www.churrascariabufalo.com.br* ▤*AE, DC, MC, V.*

FodorśChoice
★

$–$$ ✕**Fiorentina.** The green awning and red-and-white-check tablecloths are hints that this restaurant serves authentic Italian cuisine. Pasta dishes are delicious, especially the lasagna *fiorentina* (with a marinara and ground-beef sauce). ⊠*Praça da Polícia 44, Centro* ☎*092/3215–2233* ▤*AE, DC, MC, V.*

$ ✕**Filosóphicus.** Whole grains, textured vegetable protein, gluten, and soy are used in the dishes at this vegetarian buffet restaurant. It's on the second floor and tricky to find. From the street take the door between Belmiros and Marisa e Familia. ⊠*Av. 7 de Setembro 752, 2nd fl., Centro, 69005-140* ☎*092/3234–2224* ▤*No credit cards* ⊗*No dinner.*

$ ✕**Restaurante Aves Grill.** For a quick, cheap bite, you can't beat this pay-per-kilo restaurant. Most main courses contain some kind of bird, whether quail, turkey, duck, or chicken. Side dishes include lovely salads, fries, beans, and rice. ⊠*Rua Henrique Martins 366, Centro, 69010-010* ☎*092/3233–3809* ▤*DC, MC, V* ⊗*No dinner.*

WHERE TO STAY

Manaus has several decent in-town hotels, but the jungle lodges outside town are where you should base yourself if you're interested in Amazon adventures. Most jungle lodges have naturalist guides, swimming, caiman "hunts" (the animals are blinded with flashlights, captured, photographed, and released), piranha fishing, and canoe trips. Many jungle lodges (and all of those that we list) are near the Río Negro, where mosquitoes are less of a problem because they can't breed in its acidic black water. Unless otherwise noted, prices at jungle lodges are for two-day, one-night packages, which generally include transport to and from the lodge, meals (not drinks), and a variety of activities that depend on the length of your stay. These are essentially glorified camps that lack many amenities, so expect to rough it a bit. Air-conditioning, hot water, telephones, and televisions are rare amenities.

10

Chico Mendes: Rubber Tapper & Environmental Pioneer

Born in 1944 in the northwestern state of Acre, Chico Mendes was the son of a *seringueiro* (rubber-tree tapper) who had moved across the country in the early 20th century to follow the rubber boom. Chico followed in his father's footsteps as a seringuero in Xapuri, close to the Bolivian border. In the 1960s rubber prices dropped dramatically, and tappers began to sell forests to cattle ranchers who cut them for pastures. In the '70s, to protect forests and the tappers' way of life, Mendes joined a group of nonviolent activists who managed to prevent many ranch workers and loggers from clearing the rubber trees. On the local council of Xapuri, he promoted the creation of forest reserves for rubber and Brazil-nut production. He founded the Xapuri Rural Workers Union and the National Council of Rubber Tappers to educate tappers on forest issues.

In 1987 Mendes was invited to Washington, D.C., to help convince the Inter-American Development Bank to rescind its financial support of a planned 1,200-km (750-mi) road to be constructed through the forest. That same year, Mendes was awarded the Global 500 environmental achievement award from the United Nations, making him an international celebrity.

In 1988 Mendes stopped rancher Darly Alves da Silva from extending his ranch into a reserve. On December 22, 1988, da Silva and son Darcy murdered Mendes outside his home. Upon his death, Chico Mendes made the front page of the *New York Times* and numerous other publications worldwide. Subsequently, Brazil created the Chico Mendes Extractive Reserve near Xapuri, along with 20 other reserves covering more than 8 million acres.

IN-TOWN HOTELS

$$$$

Fodor's Choice

★

Hotel Tropical. Nothing in the Amazon can match the majesty of this resort hotel. It's 20 km (12 mi) northwest of downtown and overlooks the Río Negro, with a short path to the beach. In addition to a zoo, sports facilities, and two gorgeous pools, the Tropical has its own dock. The location is remote, far from Centro, but a 20-minute cab ride from the airport. The restaurant is a reliable choice for dinners of regional and international fare. **Pros:** Beautifully appointed rooms, luxurious furniture, all the amenities of a high-class resort. **Cons:** Far from all points of interest, expensive commute (R$49) by taxi. ⊠*Av. Coronel Teixeira 1320, Ponta Negra, 69029-120* ☎*092/2123–5000* ⊕*www. tropicalhotel.com.br* ↪*594 rooms, 8 suites* ⌂*In-room: safe, Wi-Fi, refrigerator. In-hotel: 2 restaurants, 2 bars, tennis courts, pools, gym, beachfront* ⊟*AE, DC, MC, V* ⊚*EP.*

$$

St. Paul Apart Service. If you're planning an extended stay, this apartment hotel in Centro is a good deal at around R$148 per day for a minimum of 20 days. The accommodations are pleasantly furnished in beiges and browns, and rooms are kept immaculate. **Pros:** Modern facilities. **Cons:** Not all apartments have living rooms and kitchens. ⊠*Av. Ramos Ferreira 1115, Centro, 69020-080* ☎*92/2101–3800* 🖷*092/2101–3838* ⊕*www. manaushoteis.com.br* ↪*70 apartments*

⛄*In-room: refrigerators, kitchens, Internet, safe. In-hotel: restaurant, bar, pool, gym* ☰*AE, DC, MC, V* ❑*EP.*

$$ ❑**Taj Mahal.** Much of the charming East Indian artwork of the original hotel disappeared in the last renovation, although you can still see some in the lobby. The Taj Mahal is a pleasant option, with a rooftop pool, a revolving restaurant with a view, and a convenient location. Request a room with a river view. **Pros:** Good location, pleasant rooms. **Cons:** Hotel is a bit unkempt. ✉*Av. Getúlio Vargas 741, Centro, 69020-020* ☎*092/3627–3737* ⊕*www.grupotajmahal.com.br* ➹*144 rooms, 26 suites* ⛄*In-room: Internet, refrigerator. In-hotel: restaurant, bar, pool* ☰*AE, DC, MC, V* ❑*EP.*

$ ❑**Central Hotel Manaus.** A good option if you're on a budget, this hotel has simple, clean rooms with standard amenities. It's near the market and the port, and is popular with businessmen on a tight budget. **Pros:** Inexpensive and pleasant. **Cons:** Rooms are plainly decorated. ✉*Rua Dr. Moreira 202, Centro, 69005-250* ☎*092/3622–2600* ⊕*www.hotel centralmanaus.com.br* ➹*50 rooms* ⛄*In-room: Internet, refrigerator. In-hotel: restaurant* ☰*AE, DC, MC, V* ❑*EP.*

$ ❑**Hotel Manaós.** Across from Teatro Amazonas and just up the street from the busy part of downtown, Hotel Manaós is in a great spot. Rooms are small but are clean and have nice woodwork. The staff are warm and friendly. **Pros:** One of best locations in town. **Cons:** Rooms are small. ✉*Av. Eduardo Ribeiro 881, Centro, 69010-001* ☎*092/3633–5744* ⊕*www.hotelmanaos.com.br* ➹*39 rooms* ⛄*In-room: Internet, refrigerator. In-hotel: restaurant, bar* ☰*AE, DC, MC, V* ❑*EP.*

$ ❑**Lider Hotel.** Although far from luxurious, this hotel is clean, comfortable, and conveniently located in Centro. It's a good base from which to branch out on city tours. **Pros:** Good location for sightseeing **Cons:** Basic furnishings. ✉*Av. 7 de Setembro 827, Centro, 69005-140* ☎*092/3621–9700* ⊕*www.liderhotelmanaus.com.br* ➹*60 rooms* ⛄*In-hotel: restaurant, bar* ☰*AE, DC, MC, V* ❑*EP.*

JUNGLE LODGES

Though most tour companies will pick you up at the airport and drop you off following your adventure, airport pickup should not be assumed in all situations. It's often included in tour packages, but ask while making arrangements. Local naturalist guides are often available at lodges. Though knowledgeable, they're neither biologists nor teachers. Do not expect accurate information and identification of species or interpretation of ecological relationships. The guides and companies in the Adventure & Learning Vacations chapter are those we recommend.

$$$$ ❑**Amazon Rainforest Adventure.** Rustic floating cabins with air-conditioning and baths make up this remote lodge. Monkey- and bird-watching is excellent. The English-speaking guides are knowledgeable and friendly. The minimum stay is two nights and the package includes transportation to and from Manaus. **Pros:** Beautiful cabins, close to nature. **Cons:** Steeply priced. ✉*74 km (50 mi) south of Manaus, Lago Juma* ⌂*Mango GuestHouse, Rua Flávio Espirito Santo 1, 69040-250 Manaus* ☎*092/3656–6033* ⊕*www.naturesafaris.com.br* ➹*16 rooms*

10

⟨⟩*In-room: no phone, no TV. In-hotel: restaurant, no elevator* ⊟*No credit cards* ⟨◯⟩*FAP.*

$$$$ 🏨**Ariaú Amazon Towers.** The most famous of the Amazon jungle lodges, Ariaú is made up of four-story wooden towers on stilts and linked by catwalks. The effect is more dramatic when the river floods the ground below from December to June. The feeling of being integrated with nature is a bit lost here due to Ariaú's size, and contact with wildlife is rare,

> ### THE AMAZON CANOPY
>
> Trees in the Amazon are not only connected at the roots, but they're linked at the branches as well. This creates an enormous ecosystem far above the ground. The canopy holds more species of insects than any other part of the rain forest. Research on the rain-forest ceiling only began around 20 years ago.

apart from brightly colored macaws and cute semiwild monkeys that visit and make mischief. One suite is the Tarzan House, 100 feet up in the treetops. The packet includes pick-up and drop-off. **Pros:** Excellent food, nicely furnished rooms. **Cons:** Large complex, small rooms. ⊠*60 km (40 mi)/2 hrs northwest of Manaus, Rio Ariaú* ⟨⟩*Rua Leonardo Malcher 699, 69010–170 Manaus* ☎*092/2121–5000* ⊕*www. ariautowers.com.br* ↩*300 rooms, 8 suites* ⟨⟩*In-room: refrigerator, no phone (some), no TV. In-hotel: 2 restaurants, bars, pools, public Internet* ⊟*AE, DC, MC, V* ⟨◯⟩*FAP.*

$$$$ 🏨**Jungle Othon Palace.** It's quite a sight to cruise down the Río Negro and see the neoclassical columns of this luxurious "flotel," built on a steel barge, looming on the horizon. Explore the region by day, and at night return to your air-conditioned cabin for a hot shower or to take a stroll on the observation deck. Packages include airport or hotel pick-up and drop-off in Manaus. **Pros:** Right on the river, all of the usual amenities. **Cons:** Furnishings not as nice as the other lodges. ⊠*35 km (20 mi)/1 hr west of Manaus, Río Negro* ⟨⟩*Joaquim Nabuco, 1133, 69020–031 Manaus* ☎*92/3622–2104 or 92/3212–5409* ⊕*www.jun glepalace.com.br* ↩*34 rooms* ⟨⟩*In-room: refrigerator. In-hotel: restaurant, bar, pool, gym, no elevator* ⊟*DC, MC, V* ⟨◯⟩*FAP.*

$$$ 🏨**Acajatuba Jungle Lodge.** Civilization seems hundreds of miles away at this thatch-hut lakeside lodge. Twenty individual screened round thach-huts are elevated 1 meter (3 feet) aboveground and connected to the rest of the lodge by walkways. Lighting is provided by 12-volt batteries and kerosene lamps (generators would keep wildlife away), and there's no hot water, but what it lacks in luxury, it more than makes up for by putting you in the middle of the tropical forest. They have many other arrangements including three- and four-night stays. **Pros:** Staying in beautiful large bungalows. **Cons:** Putting up with humidity and cold water. ⊠*60 km (35 mi)/4 hrs west of Manaus, Lago Acajatuba; boats to lodge leave from CEASA port near meeting of waters* ⟨⟩*Conj. Vila Municipal Rua 7 #87, 69057-750Manaus* ☎*092/3642–0358* ⊕*www. acajatuba.com.br* ↩*30 rooms* ⟨⟩*In-room: no a/c, no phone, no TV. In-hotel: bar, restaurant, no elevator* ⊟*V* ⟨◯⟩*FAP.*

$$ 🏨**Amazon Ecopark.** For a comfortable jungle experience, stay at this lodge with air-conditioned rooms, hot showers, and mosquito nets.

You can visit monkeys in rehabilitation, hike with a naturalist guide on 6 mi (10 km) of trails through several habitat types with enormous trees, and relax in streams and natural pools. It's not far from Manaus and easily accessible. The packet includes meeting the passengers in any airport or hotel. **Pros:** Elegant, well-appointed rooms, lots of activities. **Cons:** No TVs, refrigerators, or Internet. ⊠*Rio Tarumã* ☎*21/2547–7742 or 92/9146–0570* ⊕*www.amazonecopark.com.br* ⌷*60 rooms* ⌂*In-hotel: restaurant, bar, beachfront, no elevator* ═*MC, DC* ⏐⌷*MAP.*

THE RAREST BEER

Amazonian tribes have been making manioc and corn beers for about 2,000 years. The most popular of these is a hearty dark beer used during social and religious festivals. All types of celebrations are accompanied with beer drinking in the Amazon. The Tapajó tribe used to add the unique ingredient of cremated human bones to ensure that their ancestors would carry on in them. Try the Xingu beer that is sold all over.

Mamirauá Sustainable Development

OFF THE
BEATEN
PATH
Fodor'sChoice
★

Reserve. The largest wildlife reserve in Brazil, Mamirauá is about 1,050 km (650 mi) west of Manaus on the Rio Solimões. The reserve is known for its abundant wildlife, including the endemic, and endangered, red-faced uakari monkey. Guided tours (from Uakari Lodge) take you through the *várzea* (flooded forest) in canoes during the rainy season (January–April) and on foot the rest of the year. Plan to get muddy if you're hiking. Frequent animal sightings include three species of monkeys, colorful birds, and pink river dolphins. Dry season is the best time to see caimans and fish. Since Mamirauá encompasses several communities, cooperation and assistance of local inhabitants in the areas of research, ecotourism, maintenance, and fiscalization help make it successful as a sustainable development reserve.

To get to the reserve, you'll need to fly to Tefé (a one-hour flight from Manaus) and take Mamirauá's boat from there. It's a bit of an effort but well worth it. (⊕*www.mamiraua.org.br*)

$$ ⏢**Uakari Floating Lodge.** Nearly all visitors to Mamirauá stay at the nearby Uakari Floating Lodge, which has free transportation to and from the reserve. The lodge takes great pride in its efforts to exist in harmony with the local population and the environment—for instance, local guides are hired and most of the lodge uses solar power. Activities include river tours, fishing trips, and guided visits to a local village. Cabin-type rooms have few amenities but are clean and have large windows. Each has a small porch with a hammock. The minimum stay is three nights. Transport to and from the airport is included. **Pros:** Rustic rooms with lots of light. **Cons:** Few amenities. ⊠*30 min by boat from Tefé,* ☎*97/3343–4160 or 97/8116–1349* ⊕*www.mamiraua.org.br* ⌷*10 rooms* ⌂*In-room: no a/c, no phone, no TV. In-hotel: restaurant, bar, airport shuttle, no kids under 12, no elevator* ═*MC, V* ⏐⌷*FAP* ⌷*R$360 per person double occupancy, 4 days and 3 nights ($240 for 2 per night).*

10

BEACHES

Crescent-shape **Praia da Lua** is on the Río Negro, and is cleaner and less crowded than other beaches. **Praia do Tupé,** another Río Negro beach, is popular with locals and tends to fill up on Sunday and holidays. Both beaches can only be reached by boat and the trip lasts 30 minutes. Departures are from behind the Mercado Municipal every morning. You must bring your own food and drink.

To reach most Manaus-area beaches, catch a boat from Porto Flutu-ante. Sunday is the only day with regularly scheduled trips; boats will take a big crowd for about R$10 a head. You can hire smaller craft to the beaches. Look for people wearing the green vests of the Associação dos Canoeiros Motorizados de Manaus near the Porto Flutuante or in the Escadinha area closer to the market in Belém. They can set you up with local boat trips at reasonable prices.

Praia da Lua is 23 km (14 mi) southwest of Manaus; Praia do Tupé is 34 km (20 mi) northwest of Manaus.

NIGHTLIFE

Manaus em Tempo is a newspaper that lists nightlife events in Manaus; it's availabe at newsstands. *Boi bumbá* (ox legend) music and dance—native to the central Amazon region—tells stories with tightly choreographed steps and strong rhythms. The amphitheater at Praia da Ponta Negra holds regular boi-bumbá performances.

Botequim (⊠*Rua Barroso 279, Centro, 69010-050* ☎*092/3232–1030*), near the Teatro Amazonas, Thursday, Friday, and Saturday live bands play a mix of MPB (*música popular brasileira,* or Brazilian pop music), samba, bossa nova, and other Brazilian styles. Food, live music every night, and four varieties of homemade beer are made at microbrewery **Cervejaria Fellice** (⊠*Av. Rodrigo Otavio 3555,* ☎*92/3216–3401*).

THE ARTS

Secretaria da Estado de Cultura (SEC) (⊠*Av. 7 de Setembro 1546, Centro, 69020-120 Manaus* ☎*092/3633–3041* ☉*Weekdays 8–1, 2–5*) provides all the information on cultural activities and festivals in Manaus. **Teatro Amazonas** (⊠*Rua Tapajos 5, Centro, 69025-140* ☎*092/3622–2420*) draws some of the biggest names in theater, opera, and classical music. Monday-evening performances are free. The Amazonas Philharmonic Orchestra plays every Thursday night. The Teatro holds an opera festival every year in April and May.

SPORTS & THE OUTDOORS

JET SKIING
Clube do Jet (⊠*Rua Praiana 13, access through Av. do Turismo, Ponta Negra,* ☎*092/3657–5435*) rents equipment for R$100 an hour on the Río Negro.

Elusive El Dorado

The search for El Dorado (which means, in Spanish, "The Gilded Man") and his supposedly wealthy kingdom began with the arrival of the conquistadors to South America in the 1500s and continued into the 1900s. The suspected location of El Dorado (as the kingdom came to be called) changed depending on who was searching. The most captivating story placed it in Colombia, in a village where each year Chibcha natives rolled a chieftain in gold dust. The chieftain then paddled to the middle of sacred lake Gustavita and bathed. So powerful was the lure of finding riches there, that when conquistadors Gonzalo Pinzarro and Francisco de Orellana heard the story, they mounted an expedition of hundreds of men, horses, and dogs. They went east over the Andes, descended its steep slopes, and dropped into Amazon rain forest. Along the way they lost most of their men and animals. They never found El Dorado or any gold. Nor did Sir Walter Raleigh, Colonel Fawcett, or numerous others who searched. Many, like Fawcett, succumbed to illness or arrows and never returned.

JUNGLE & RIVER EXCURSIONS

Though Belém, Santarém, and other communities are great places for jungle and river excursions, they don't have nearly the selection or number of visitors that Manaus has. The most common excursion is a half- or full-day tourist-boat trip that travels 15 km (9 mi) east of Manaus to the point where the coffee-color water of the Río Negro flows beside and gradually joins the coffee-with-cream-color water of the Rio Solimões. According to Brazilians, this is where the Amazon River begins. The waters flow alongside one another for 6 km (4 mi) before merging. Many of these Meeting-of-the-Waters treks include motorboat side trips along narrow streams or through bayous. Some also stop at the Parque Ecológico do Januaury, where you can see birds and a lake filled with the world's largest water lily, the *vitória régia*.

Nighttime boat trips into the forest explore flooded woodlands and narrow waterways. Some stop for trail hikes. Some companies take you by canoe on a caiman "hunt," where caimans are caught and released. Trips to the Rio Negro's upper reaches, where wildlife is a little wilder, are also offered. Such trips usually stop at river settlements to visit with local families. They may include jungle treks, fishing (they supply the gear and boat), and a trip to Anavilhanas, the world's largest freshwater archipelago. It contains some 400

TOXIC BUG SPRAYS

10

DEET (diethyl toluamide), the active ingredient in some of the strongest insect repellents, is capable of peeling paint off a tin can, and it's equally capable of repelling blood-thirsty Amazonian mosquitoes. The less-toxic bug repellents are generally ineffective. Most health professionals agree that the benefits of avoiding malaria- and dengue-carrying mosquitoes outweigh the risks of using chemical repellents. Picaridin-based repellents are equally effective and may have a lower toxicity.

River-Village Excursions

Small Amazonian villages are wonderful places to visit. The docks and open markets are lively early in the day, and the community usually appreciates your interest. Many of these places rarely see foreigners.

Anamá, one such village, is upstream from Manaus on the Río Solimões (Rio Amazonas), about 14 hours from the city by regional boat. It has a lively, largely floating waterfront and good wildlife-watching nearby. **Alenquer,** across the Río Amazonas from Santarém, is a quintessential river town with lovely streams and waterfalls and ancient pictographs in its hinterlands. **Óbidos** is upstream from Santarém about 10 hours by regional boat in the "narrows" section of the river with a fort, complete with cannons, perching on a cliff overlooking the river. On an island, sleepy river town **Parintins** wakes up once a year for boi bumbá festivities.

Few tourists venture this deep into the culture and landscape. Only one tour company, Amazon Adventures (owned by the updater of this chapter), arranges these trips currently. But you can also just take a local boat. Someone at the boat docks can always tell you where your boat will be departing. All villages have food vendors. Your safest bet is a plate of rice and beans with beef, chicken, or fish. Smaller villages don't even have mineral water, and transportation is unreliable. Go well prepared and open-minded. In very small communities you may even be presented to the mayor or other town officials. Any attempt you make to communicate will be appreciated.

islands with amazing Amazon flora, birds, and monkeys. To arrange any of these excursions, contact an area tour operator (⇨*Tours, in The Amazon Essentials, below*).

SOCCER

Manaus's professional soccer teams, Rio Negro and Nacional, play at **Estádio Vivaldo Lima** (⊠*Av. Constantino Nery, Flores, 69010-160* ☎*092/3236–3219 or 92/8118–3474*). A taxi ride to the stadium and a ticket should each cost about R$35.

SHOPPING

Here, as in other parts of the Amazon, you can find lovely indigenous artisanal items made from animal parts. Macaws, for example, are killed in the wild for feathers to make souvenir items for tourists. As a result, there are no longer many macaws in the forests close to Manaus. Traveling home with items made from animal parts, certain types of wood, or plant fibers can result in big fines and even jail time, so beware.

SHOPPING AREAS & MALLS

The largest, most upscale mall is **Amazonas Shopping** (⊠*Av. Djalma Batista 482, Chapada, 69050-010* ☎*092/3642–3555*), with 300 stores and 38 restaurants. **Studio 5 Festival Mall** (⊠*Av. Rodrigo Octavio 2555, Distrito Industrial, 69077-000* ☎*092/3216–3517*) is a large mall.

CONTACTS & RESOURCES

BANKS & EXCHANGING SERVICES

ATMs are available at most bank branches in major cities. In smaller towns neither ATMs nor change are easy to come by: bring cash and lots of small bills.

Some banks accept only cards with Visa/Plus logos and others accept only cards with MasterCard/Cirrus logos. Banco24horas ATMs usually accept all cards, including American Express. *See "Money Matters" in Brazil Essentials for more information.*

INTERNET

Most cities, even small towns, have Internet cafés. Small pousadas and jungle lodges are about the only outposts that aren't online. In Belém, Speednet provides Internet service for R$4 an hour and is open all week 8 AM–9 PM. The Hilton charges R$8 per hour. In Santarém, Inter-net Cyber da Orla is open Monday through Saturday 9–6, at R$4 per hour. In Manaus, Cybercity is friendly and helpful, and charges R$4 per hour. Internext has 14 computers and charges R$4 per hour.

TOUR OPTIONS

Whichever tour you choose, be sure your experience includes wildlife viewing with a guide, contact with locals, and regional foods and drinks. The most popular tours run from Manaus, since it's the best organized for tourism and has the best jungle lodges. It can feel clogged with tourists at times though, which can make the less-popular starting points of Santarém and Belém more appealing.

For adventure and culture tours, see Adventure & Learning Vacations (Chapter 11).

SPECIALTY SHOPS

Ecoshop (⊠*Amazonas Shopping, Chapada, 69050-010* ☎*092/3234–8870*) sells regional art and a variety of indigenous crafts made from wood. One of the best places to buy all kinds of things, from fresh fish to hammocks and souvenirs, is **Mercado Adolfo Lisboa** (⊠*Rua Dos Barés 46, Centro, 69005-020*), down along the water. **Loja do Mamirauá,** near Teatro Amazonas, sells crafts made by inhabitants of the Mamirauá Reserve (⇨*above*). **Museu do Índio** (⊠*Rua Duque de Caxias 296, Centro, 69020-140* ☎*092/3635–1927*) has a gift shop that sells traditional crafts such as necklaces made from seeds and feathers and baskets.

10

SIDE TRIPS FROM MANAUS

Not far from Manaus you can explore black-water rivers, lakes, and beaches on the Río Negro; muddy-water rivers and lakes on the Amazon River; and waterfalls and streams north of Manaus. You can also visit caboclo villages along the rivers. Perhaps your guide or boat driver will walk through the village with you to introduce you and show you around. Wildlife watching can be done anywhere, though it gets better the farther you get from the city.

PRESIDENTE FIGUEIREDO

One of the Amazon's best-kept secrets is a two-hour drive north of Manaus. The town of Presidente Figueiredo (founded 1981) has dozens of waterfalls—up to 32 meters (140 feet) in height—and caves with prehistoric paintings and pottery fragments. The area was stumbled on during the construction of BR 174, the only highway that takes you out of the state (to Roraima and on to Venezuela), and was ultimately discovered by explorers looking for minerals, who had based themselves in Presidente Figueiredo. The area is excellent for swimming in blackwater streams and hiking through upland forest. The town has several hotels and restaurants, and there's a hydropower plant and reservoir and an archaeology museum in the area. The Centro de Proteção de Quelonias e Mamiferos Aquaticos (Center for the Protection of Turtles and Aquatic Mammals) is in Balbina, 82 km (51 mi) north of town. Get cash in Manaus because there are only two banks here, and they do not always accept international cards.

107 km (64 mi) north of Manaus.

TO & FROM
To get to Presidente Figueiredo from Manaus, take the bus labeled ARUANÃ, which runs twice a day (105 km, 1 hour and 30 minutes) from the Terminal Rodoviário Huascar Angelim and costs around R$12.50.

Adventure & Learning Vacations

WORD OF MOUTH

"I honestly saw eight wild jaguars in a three-week trip, seven of which were along the Paraguay River in or near the Taiama Ecological Station, with six spotted in one unbelievable afternoon. Jaguar sightings are not that rare on the Paraguay River because the jaguars have become habituated to the noise from boats, as this river is a major shipping route between Brazil and Argentina."

—atravelynn

Updated by
Nicholas Gill

WITH THE WORLD'S LARGEST TROPICAL ecosystem and more rivers, lakes, and ocean beaches than just about any other country, Brazil is ripe for adventure. The Amazon is one of the top places to get adventurous; here you can fish for piranha from a riverboat or hike deep into the rainforest from a lodge accessible only by canoe. The Pantanal is a great place for watching wildlife, especially crocodiles and birds, and also has jungle lodges. The canyons and mountains of central and southern Brazil are great for camping, hiking, climbing, biking, and horseback riding. Then there are the endless east-coast beaches and the ocean, popular for boating, diving, and snorkeling. Brazil's influences from Africa, Europe, and its own indigenous groups, combined with its many volunteer opportunities with estimable nonprofit organizations, also make it a great place to delve into a culturally rich learning vacation.

As in the past, today's travelers yearn to see the world's great cities, historical sites, and natural wonders. The difference is that today, far fewer travelers are content to experience all this from the air-conditioned comfort of a huge coach. Even tour operators known for their trips' five-star comfort have included soft-adventure components, such as hiking, canoeing, biking, or horseback riding, in most itineraries and added "best available" lodgings to satisfy the increased demand for visits to more traditional locales.

Choosing a tour package carefully is always important, but it becomes even more critical when the focus is adventure or sports. You can rough it or opt for comfortable, sometimes even luxurious accommodations. You can select easy hiking or canoeing adventures or trekking, rafting, or climbing expeditions that require high degrees of physical endurance and technical skill. Study multiple itineraries to find the trip that's right for you.

This chapter describes selected trips from some of today's best adventure-tour operators in the travel world. Wisely chosen, special-interest vacations lead to distinctive, memorable experiences—just pack flexibility and curiosity along with the bug spray.

For more information about planning an adventure or learning vacation, check out **South American Explorers Club** (⊠*126 Indian Creek Rd., Ithaca, NY 14850* ☏*607/277–0488 or 800/274–0568* ⊕*www. saexplorers.org*).

CHOOSING A TRIP

With hundreds of choices for special-interest trips to Brazil, there are a number of factors to keep in mind when deciding which company and package will be right for you.

■ **How strenuous a trip do you want?** Adventure vacations commonly are split into "soft" and "hard" adventures. Hard adventures, such as strenuous treks (often at high altitudes), Class IV or V rafting, or ascents of some of the world's most challenging mountains, generally require excellent physical conditioning and previous experience. Most hiking, biking, canoeing/kayaking, and similar soft adventures can be enjoyed by persons of all ages who are in good health and are accustomed to a reasonable amount of exercise. A little honesty goes a long way—recognize your own level of physical fitness and discuss it with the tour operator before signing on.

■ **How far off the beaten path do you want to go?** Depending on the tour operator and itinerary selected for a particular trip, you'll often have a choice of relatively easy travel and comfortable accommodations or more strenuous going with overnights spent camping or in basic lodgings. Ask yourself if it's the *reality* or the *image* of roughing it that appeals to you. Stick with the reality.

■ **Is sensitivity to the environment important to you?** If so, then determine if it's equally important to the tour operator. Does the company protect the fragile environments you'll be visiting? Are some of the company's profits designated for conservation efforts or put back into the communities visited? Does it encourage indigenous people to dress up (or dress down) so that your group can get great photos, or does it respect their cultures as they are? Many of the companies included in this chapter are actively involved in environmental organizations and projects with indigenous communities visited on their trips.

■ **What sort of group is best for you?** At its best, group travel offers curious, like-minded people with whom to share the day's experiences. Do you enjoy a mix of companions or would you prefer similar demographics—for example, age-specific, singles, same sex? Inquire about the group size; many companies have a maximum of 10 to 16 members, but 30 or more is not unknown. The larger the group, the more time spent (or wasted) at rest stops, meals, and hotel arrivals and departures.

If groups aren't your thing, most companies will customize a trip just for you. In fact, this has become a major part of many tour operators' business. The itinerary can be as loose or as complete as you choose. Such travel offers all the conveniences of a package tour, but the "group" is composed of only you and those you've chosen as travel companions. Responding to a renewed interest in multigenerational travel, many tour operators also offer designated family departures, with itineraries carefully crafted to appeal both to children and adults.

■ **The client consideration factor—strong or absent?** Gorgeous photos and well-written tour descriptions go a long way in selling a company's trips. But what's called the client consideration factor is important, too. Does the operator provide useful information about health (suggested or required inoculations, tips for dealing with high altitudes)? A list of frequently asked questions and their answers? Recommended readings? Equipment needed for sports trips? Packing tips when baggage is restricted? Climate info? Visa requirements? A list of client referrals? The option of using your credit card? What is the refund policy if you must cancel? If you're traveling alone, will the company match you up with a like-minded traveler so you can avoid the sometimes exorbitant single supplement?

■ **Are there hidden costs?** Make sure you know what is and is not included in basic trip costs when comparing companies. International airfare is usually extra. Sometimes domestic flights are additional. Is trip insurance required, and if so, is it included? Are airport transfers included? Visa fees? Departure taxes? Gratuities? Equipment? Meals? Bottled water? All excursions? Although some travelers prefer the option of an excursion or free time, many, especially those visiting a destination for the first time, want to see as much as possible. Paying extra for a number of excursions can significantly increase the total cost of the trip. Many factors affect the price, and the trip that looks cheapest in the brochure could well turn out to be the most expensive. Don't assume that roughing it will save you money, as prices rise when limited access and a lack of essential supplies on-site require costly special arrangements.

CRUISES

OCEAN CRUISES

Season: October–April.

Locations: Some Caribbean cruises or post-Antarctica-season cruises have ports of call in Brazil and a partial navigation of the Amazon River; more and more ships are getting inland as far as Manaus. Other ships have itineraries exclusively along the Atlantic coast of South America. You can even opt for a total circumnavigation of the continent, which usually takes 50 or more days; the norm, though, are 14- to 21-day cruises. Typical port calls in Brazil are Belém, Fortaleza, Salvador, and Rio de Janeiro.

Vessels vary in the degree of comfort or luxury they offer as well as in what is included in the price. Guided shore excursions, gratuities, dinner beverages, and port taxes are often extra. Peruse brochures carefully and ask questions to ensure that your choice of vessel is the right one for you.

Cost: Prices vary according to the ship, cabin category, and itinerary. Figure $1,550 to $4,495 for a 14-day cruise, excluding international airfare.

Cruise Companies: Celebrity Cruises; Crystal Cruises; Fred. Olsen Cruise Lines; Holland America Line; Norwegian Cruise Line; Orient Lines; Princess Cruises; Regent Seven Seas Cruises; Seabourn Cruise Line; Silversea Cruises.

RIVER CRUISES

The Amazon, home to more than 200 species of mammals and 1,800 species of birds, and providing 30% of the earth's oxygen, is the world's largest and densest rain forest. Stretching 6,300 km (3,900 mi), the Amazon is the world's longest river. From its source in the Peruvian Andes, the river and its tributaries snake through parts of Bolivia, Ecuador, Colombia, and Brazil before emptying into the Atlantic.

Whatever your style of travel, there's a boat plying the river to suit your needs. Sleep in a hammock on the deck of a thatch-roof riverboat or in the air-conditioned suite of an upscale vessel. A typical river program includes exploring tributaries in small boats; village visits, perhaps with a blowgun demonstration; piranha fishing; nocturnal wildlife searches; and rain-forest walks with a naturalist or indigenous guide to help you learn about plants, wildlife, and traditional medicines.

Season: Year-round.
Locations: Anavilhanas Archipelago; Lago Janauári Ecological Park; Manaus; Río Branco; Río Negro.
Cost: From $1,050 for seven days from Manaus.
Tour Operators: Amazon Nature Tours; Big Five Tours & Expeditions; Ecotour Expeditions; G.A.P. Adventures; Heliconia Amazônia Turismo; Latin American Escapes; Maxim Tours; Nature Expeditions International; Southwind Adventures; Swallows and Amazons; Travcoa.

River journeys along the Brazilian Amazon typically begin in Manaus and feature 3–10 days on the water, plus time in Manaus and, sometimes, Rio de Janeiro. On Big Five's 14-day trip you'll follow three days in Rio with a four-day cruise aboard the comfortable *Amazon Clipper Premium,* then continue on to Salvador and Iguaçu Falls. Travcoa's guests cruise aboard the Amazon's first luxury ship, the *Iberostar Grand Amazon*; after three days on the river you'll visit Brazil's capital, Brasília, before spending time in the Pantanal and Rio. Amazon Nature Tours, Latin American Escapes, Ecotour Expeditions, Nature Expeditions, and Southwind Adventures use the 18-passenger motorized yacht *Tucano* for their Amazon cruises that ply the mostly uninhabited Río Negro. On G.A.P.'s 42-day itinerary, explore the Amazon from Belém to Manaus and visit Bahia and Ceara states; the trip concludes with 10 days in Venezuela. Swallows and Amazons offer a variety of river programs, ranging from a traditional riverboat to a six-cabin air-conditioned houseboat with shared baths to a motorized yacht with private baths. Itineraries run from 4 to 11 days, and all include a visit with traditional *caboclo,* or river people. For Heliconia, Maxim Tours, and most of the tour operators' programs, a cruise highlight is the "Meeting of the Waters," where the dark waters of the Río Negro join the lighter waters of the Amazon.

LEARNING VACATIONS

CULTURAL TOURS

Among the many types of travel, some find the most rewarding to be an in-depth focus on one aspect of a country's culture. This could mean exploring the archaeological remains of great civilizations, learning about the lives and customs of indigenous peoples, or trying to master a foreign language or culinary skills.

Season: Year-round.
Locations: Amazon; Rio de Janeiro; Salvador.

Cost: From $943 for eight days from Salvador.
Tour Operators: Abercrombie & Kent; Amizade; Brazil Nuts; Focus Tours; G.A.P. Adventures; Maxim Tours; Nature Expeditions International; Swallows and Amazons; Wilderness Travel.

If your interest is learning about other cultures, consider Swallows and Amazons' caboclo program, which focuses on the lifestyle and culture of the Amazonian river people. You'll stay at the company's rain-forest camp in the Anavilhanas Archipelago Biological Reserve, and get to know the local family that lives on the property. Activities include canoeing, fishing, rain-forest walks, and overnight camping. Nature Expeditions' multifaceted itinerary features a three-day Amazon cruise; two days in Salvador, the spiritual and cultural center of the Bahia region; Rio; Petropolis, where you'll visit the home of a Macumba practitioner to learn about this unique religion with roots in voodoo; Paraty; and Iguaçu Falls. Maxim Tours lets you determine the number of days you'd like in the architectural and historical gems of Ouro Prêto, Olinda, and Salvador. The Afro-Brazilian and Bahian culture of Salvador and its environs are the focus of Brazil Nuts' eight-day tour. Following 10 days in Venezuela, G.A.P. Adventures moves on to the Brazilian Amazon, then works its way down the coast to Rio, exploring such points as São Luis, Fortaleza, Recife, and Salvador along the way. To add a rewarding dimension to your trip, consider an Amizade work project in Santarém, an Amazonian city of 300,000 people, where you'll help construct a center for street children.

SCIENTIFIC RESEARCH TRIPS

Joining a research expedition team gives you more than great photos. By assisting scientists, you can make significant contributions to better understanding the continent's unique ecosystems and cultural heritages. Flexibility and a sense of humor are important assets for these trips, which often require roughing it.

Season: Year-round.
Locations: Cananéia Estuary; Emas National Park; Pantanal.
Cost: From $2,946 for 13 days from Campo Grande.
Tour Operator: Earthwatch.

Earthwatch has six projects in Brazil, all focused on wildlife. Working by boat and on land on the Cananéia Estuary, volunteers will help to establish data for guiding local tourism development and protecting the region's biodiversity. Emas National Park harbors many mammal, reptile, and bird species. Scientists here are involved in assessing the distribution and numbers of carnivores in the park, and volunteers will help in this endeavor by capturing and radio-collaring jaguars, foxes, pumas, and wolves. In the Pantanal, the largest freshwater wetland on the planet, assist a multinational team of scientists in collecting data on the area's plants and animals to aid in the development of a sound conservation plan. Special projects focus on bats, giant river otters, and amphibians and reptiles.

THE OUTDOORS

11

AMAZON JUNGLE CAMPING & LODGES

Because the Amazon and its tributaries provide easy access to remote parts of the jungle, river transport often serves as the starting point for camping and lodge excursions. Many lodges and camps are within or near national parks or reserves. Accommodations range from hammocks to comfortable rooms with private hot-water baths. Nature walks, canoe trips, piranha fishing, and visits to indigenous villages are typically part of rain-forest programs led by naturalists or indigenous guides.

Season: Year-round.
Locations: Amazon Ecopark; Jau National Park; Manaus; Río Negro.
Cost: Beginning at about $1,400 for eight days from Manaus.
Tour Operators: Ecotour Expeditions; Focus Tours; Heliconia Amizônia Turismo; International Expeditions; Latin American Escapes; Maxim Tours; NatureQuest; PanAmerican Travel Services; Swallows and Amazons.

Most jungle adventures here begin with a boat trip up the Río Negro, the main tributary of the Amazon. With Swallows and Amazons, there are 19 trips throughout the Brazilian Amazon ranging 7–15 days, including stays at Araras Lodge, the company's floating jungle hotel, and canoe trips between Jau National Park and the Rio Branco. From this base, make various excursions as outlined in the introduction to this section. NatureQuest has created a rustic jungle lodge and riverboat safari combination. With International Expeditions you'll explore the rain forest and watery byways from your base at remote Uakari Lodge's cluster of floating cabañas. Focus Tours' program features the rain forest, rivers, and wildlife of the Alta Floresta region. Maxim Tours offers short stays at the comfortable Pousada dos Guanavenas or the more rustic Amazon Lodge. PanAmerican Travel's 12-day itinerary also begins with a transfer by boat from Manaus to a rain-forest lodge. In this case, it's the Amazon Ecopark, on the banks of the Río Tarumã. Here biologists and zoologists have initiated several wildlife preservation projects, including a monkey jungle, a bird sanctuary, and a botanic garden.

BIRD-WATCHING TOURS

When selecting a bird-watching tour, ask questions. What species might be seen? What are the guide's qualifications? Does the operator work to protect natural habitats? What equipment is used? (In addition to binoculars, this should include a high-powered telescope, a tape recorder to record and play back bird calls as a way of attracting birds, and a spotlight for night viewing.)

Seasons: Year-round.
Locations: Amazon; Emas National Park; Iguaçu Falls; Itatiaia National Park; Northeast; Pantanal; Southeast.

Cost: From $1,550 for seven days from Manaus.
Tour Operators: Field Guides; Focus Tours; Swallows and Amazons; Victor Emanuel Nature Tours; WINGS.

Bird habitats in Brazil range from coastal rain forests to cloud forests to open plains, and with dozens of itineraries between them, the above tour operators cover all topographies. The Pantanal, a vast area of seasonally flooded grassland, has the hyacinth macaw, bare-faced curassow, Toco toucan, and yellow-billed cardinal, while the newly described cryptic forest-falcon and bare-headed parrot are but two of many exotic species inhabiting the Amazon and coastal jungles. Brazilian avian life is so rich that Focus Tours has four tours here, Wings runs six, Victor Emanuel Nature Tours has eight, and Field Guides offers 10.

NATURAL HISTORY

Many operators have created nature-focused programs that provide insight into the importance and fragility of South America's ecological treasures. The itineraries mentioned below take in the deserts, glaciers, rain forests, mountains, and rivers of this continent, as well as the impressive variety of its wildlife.

Season: Year-round.
Locations: Bonito; Iguaçu Falls; Pantanal.
Cost: From $831 for five days from Campo Grande.
Tour Operators: Australian & Amazonian Adventures; Big Five Tours & Expeditions; Brazil Nuts; Bushtracks Expeditions; Ecotour Expeditions; ElderTreks; Explore! Worldwide; G.A.P. Adventures; Geographic Expeditions; International Expeditions; Latin American Escapes; Maxim Tours; NatureQuest; Oceanic Society Expeditions; Southwind Adventures; Travcoa; Wilderness Travel.

Covering 89,000 square mi, the Pantanal is the world's largest freshwater wetland. Most of the above companies operate Pantanal programs; many are based at Refúgio Ecológico Caiman, which offers comfortable lodgings and a staff of naturalists who lead excursions by truck, by boat, on horseback, and on foot. Jabiru storks and other wading birds, anteaters, monkeys, caimans, capybaras, and possibly jaguars are among the wildlife you might see. Oceanic Society's trip, led by two animal specialists, spends six days at a lodge on the Río Pixiam and includes an excursion to an area with the world's highest recorded number of jaguar sightings per day. ElderTreks combines the Pantanal, the Amazon, and Iguaçu on a 15-day trip. Australian & Amazonian Adventures offers two programs in lesser-known regions of the Pantanal. Before traveling to the wetlands, Bushtracks participants observe hyacinth macaws and maned wolves at Hyacinth Cliffs Lodge, then continue on to Greenwing Valley Reserve to see brown capuchin monkeys, sometimes called Einstein monkeys because of their ability to use rock tools as hammers and anvils. With G.A.P. you'll spend days in Rio, Parati, and Iguaçu, as well as the Pantanal.

OVERLAND SAFARIS

The brochure for a company that operates overland trips exclusively states in bold print: NOT YOUR EVERYDAY JOURNEY. Although definitely not for everyone, this type of travel is sure to take you far from the beaten path. It's also a great way to immerse yourself in a number of cultures and landscapes. Expect to travel by truck, bus, train, boat, or custom-built expedition vehicle—no air-conditioned coach tours here. Occasionally, you may find yourself in lodges or inns, but much of the time you'll be sleeping outdoors. Know that you're expected to help pitch tents, cook, and do other chores. The camaraderie that evolves often sparks lifelong friendships. You should be tolerant of others, willing to forego some creature comforts, and be a good sport about taking part in group activities. Companies often rank trip segments from easy to extreme. This type of trip generally attracts an international mix of physically fit adventurers between ages 18 and 50. Although the operators listed below do not have fixed upper age limits for participants, those over 60 will likely be asked to complete a health questionnaire. Note that this practice is not limited to overland journeys; many companies follow this procedure when trips involve strenuous activities or roughing it.

Season: Year-round.
Locations: Throughout South America.
Cost: From $1,320 for 32 days from La Paz, plus $390 for a "kitty," which funds such expenses as camp food, group activities, and park entrance fees.
Tour Operators: Dragoman Overland; Exodus; G.A.P. Adventures; Gecko's.

These companies offer trips that cover most of South America ranging in length from 4 to 22 weeks. Itineraries typically are composed of segments that you can take separately or combine into a longer trip. Most programs visit between three and nine countries.

PHOTO SAFARIS

An advantage of photo tours is the amount of time spent at each place visited. Whether the subject is a rarely spotted animal, a breathtaking waterfall, or villagers in traditional dress, you get a chance to focus both your camera and your mind on the scene before you. The tours listed below are led by professional photographers who offer instruction and hands-on tips. If you're not serious about improving your photographic skills, these trips might not be the best choice, as you could become impatient with the pace.

Season: August
Locations: Iguaçu Falls; Pantanal; Atlantic Rainforest; Caraça Natural Park; Chapada National Park; Caratinga Biological Station
Cost: $3,999 for 21 days
Tour Operator: Focus Tours

Focus Tours custom-designs photo tours for groups. It also has a package tour that takes you to six unique Brazilian habitats to shoot wildlife up close. Each destination has a number of endemic species and all are known as places with exceptional biodiversity. A maximum of six participants ensures that all have window seats in ground transportation. Highlights include the Pantanal, the largest freshwater wetlands on the planet, sparsely populated by humans but abundantly populated by animals. From small boats and other vehicles, you can photograph jabiru storks, caimans, capybaras, marsh deer, giant anteaters, and, with luck, the camera-shy jaguar. The price includes meals, accommodations, land transportation, and a naturalist guide.

SPORTS

A sports-focused trip offers a great way to get a feel for the part of the country you're visiting and to interact with local people. A dozen bicyclists entering a village, for instance, would arouse more interest and be more approachable than a group of 30 stepping off a tour bus. Although many itineraries do not require a high level of skill, it's expected that your interest in the sport focused on in a particular tour be more than casual. On the other hand, some programs are designed for those who are highly experienced. In either case, good physical conditioning, experience with high altitudes (on certain itineraries), and a flexible attitude are important. Weather can be changeable, dictating the choices of hiking and climbing routes. If you're not a particularly strong hiker or cyclist, determine if support vehicles accompany the group or if alternate activities or turnaround points are available on more challenging days.

CANOEING, KAYAKING & WHITE-WATER RAFTING

White-water rafting and kayaking can be exhilarating experiences. You don't have to be an expert paddler to enjoy many of these adventures, but you should be a strong swimmer. Rivers are rated from Class I to Class V according to difficulty of navigation. Generally speaking, Class I–III rapids are suitable for beginners, while Class IV–V rapids are strictly for the experienced. Canoeing is a gentler river experience.

Season: Year-round.
Location: Amazon.
Cost: $1,100 for eight days from Manaus.
Tour Operator: Swallows and Amazons.

Following a day's journey along the Río Negro, overnight in a small rain-forest lodge owned by Swallows and Amazons. The next day, set out on a six-day canoeing and camping adventure, exploring various tributaries and the lakes, channels, and flooded forest of the Anavilhanas Archipelago. Hike, fish, swim, and visit the local river people, camping at night on beaches or in the jungle.

FISHING

Season: September–May.
Location: Amazon.
Cost: From $2,495 for six days from Bélem.
Tour Operators: Augusto Albuquerque; Fishing International; FishQuest; Frontiers; G.A.P Adventures; Rod & Reel Adventures; Santana; Swallows & Amazons; Yanna Ecofishing.

Although pirapitinga, pirarucú, jancundá, and many other exotic fish inhabit the Amazon, it is the legendary peacock bass that anglers describe as the ultimate adversary. With Swallows & Amazons, you can fish the Ríos Negro and Cuieiras plus several lakes while based on a traditional riverboat with hammocks or mats for beds. Yanna Ecofishing has all the amenities of a typical upscale Amazon fishing company, including a luxury regional boat and small BassTracker fishing boats. Santana has well-run tucunaré sportfishing tours in Manaus that are popular with North Americans. Augusto Albuquerque runs a small operation setting up fishing tours for small groups to out-of-the-way places. Depending on the trip, your base will be a fishing camp, a five-star resort, or a comfortable live-aboard yacht. Fishing International will even take you by small plane to some very remote places. On Rod & Reel's Amazon trip, you'll live aboard a comfortable 30-meter (100-foot) yacht while reeling in peacock bass. Frontiers offers several choices of accommodations on the Brazilian Amazon: a fly-fishing-only lodge, floating cabins, a luxury live-aboard riverboat, or a four-person houseboat with air-conditioned rooms and private baths. FishQuest also utilizes the floating cabins, as well as lodge and yacht accommodations. The company takes you to tributaries and lagoons where it's not uncommon to catch two or three dozen peacock bass per day. One itinerary focuses on an estuary known for pirarucú, the world's largest freshwater fish, known for its fighting spirit and long runs and leaps.

HIKING, RUNNING & TREKKING

South America's magnificent scenery and varied terrain make it a terrific place for trekkers and hikers. The southern part of Argentina and Chile, known as Patagonia, and Peru's Inca Trail are especially popular. Numerous tour operators offer hiking and trekking trips to these regions, so study several offerings to determine the program that's best suited to your ability and interests. The trips outlined below are organized tours led by qualified guides. Camping is often part of the experience, although on some trips you stay at inns and small hotels. Itineraries range from relatively easy hikes to serious trekking and even running.

Season: Year-round.
Locations: Amazon basin; Bahia; Jau National Park; Rio de Janeiro.
Cost: From $466 for four days from Rio.
Tour Operators: Australian & Amazonian Adventures; G.A.P Adventures; Swallows and Amazons.

For an up-close jungle experience, join Swallows and Amazons for 11 days of trekking and camping in Jau National Park, during which you walk an average of six hours daily through thick vegetation, then relax at night in a jungle camp. This company also operates a seven-day hiking and camping adventure between the Ríos Cuieiras and Jaraqui, focusing on jungle biodiversity, animal tracking, and jungle survival skills. Australian & Amazonian Adventures' itinerary centers around scenic Chapada Diamantina, in Bahia state, and the colonial city of Lençóis. You'll hike among valleys, ravines, and mountains while exploring caves, waterfalls, natural chutes, and the region's heritage as a source of precious stones. A visit to a diamond prospecting ghost town is a highlight. G.A.P. Adventures runs longer (45 days or more) trekking tours that take you to the Pantanal, Iguaçu, and Rio.

HORSEBACK RIDING

Season: Year-round
Locations: Highlands; Pantanal
Cost: From $1,445 for seven days from Campo Grande
Tour Operators: BikeHike Adventures; Hidden Trails

Observe the flora and fauna as you ride through the vast Pantanal with Hidden Trails on a "Wildlife Safari Ride" that includes picnics, camping, and ranch stays, plus sightseeing and a show in Rio. The company also has an eight-day "Aparados da Serra," where you journey the Serra Geral between Rio Grande do Sul and Santa Catarina. Meet local ranchers and gaúchos and, perhaps, participate in a local rodeo. BikeHike Adventures incorporates horseback riding into its multisport excursions *(⇨ below)*.

MULTISPORT

Only a few years ago, multisport offerings were so sparse that the topic didn't merit inclusion in this chapter. Since then, such trips have grown in popularity every year and now form an important part of the programs of many adventure-tour operators. Innovative itineraries combine two or more sports, such as biking, fishing, canoeing, hiking, horseback riding, kayaking, rafting, and trekking.

Season: April–October.
Locations: Bonito; Rio de Janeiro; Serra do Cipó.
Cost: From $1,899 for nine days from Belo Horizonte.
Tour Operator: Australian & Amazonian Adventures; BikeHike Adventures; Mountain Travel Sobek; Swallows and Amazon.

Nearly a continent's worth of adventure on its own, Brazil has a multitude of landscapes, making it ideal for taking on a number of sports in one trip. BikeHike's nine-day adventure starts off with a three-day trek through the Cipó mountain range, including an ascent of 1,676-meter (5,500-foot) Pico do Breu, followed by river kayaking, horseback riding across wide-open plains, and an 18-meter (60-foot) rappel down a waterfall. There's even an aerial zip-line running from forest into water; gear up in a harness and take off! Australian & Amazonian Adventures has come up with a fresh way to take in Rio's most famous sites. View Tijuca, the world's largest urban forest, by peddling through it on a mountain bike; follow a hiking path for about two hours, then make a 24-meter (80-foot) climb to stand atop that Rio landmark, Sugarloaf; kayak to Cotunduba Island for snorkeling and swimming, and climb four pitches (5.8 grade) to reach the top of Corcovado. Horseback riding, rafting, hang gliding, rappelling, and surfing are other options. With Mountain Travel Sobek you'll take a three-day rafting trip down the Río Novo, spend a few days hiking in the state of Tocantins, explore the beaches of Rio, and summit Sugarloaf. Swallows and Amazon's multisport trips include mountain biking, canyoning, snorkeling, and trekking in various locations.

Tour Operators

Below you'll find contact information for all tour operators mentioned in this chapter. For international tour operators, we list both the tour operator and its North American representative. For example, Exodus is represented in North America by Adventure Center. Although those listed hardly exhaust the number of reputable companies, these tour operators were chosen because they are established firms that offer a good selection of itineraries. Such operators are usually the first to introduce great new destinations, forging ahead before luxury hotels and air-conditioned coaches tempt less hardy visitors.

Abercrombie & Kent ✉ *1520 Kensington Rd., Oak Brook, IL 60523* ☎ *630/954–2944 or 800/554–7016* ⊕ *www.abercrombiekent.com.*

Amazon Nature Tours ✉ *Box 128, Jamestown, RI 02835* ☎ *401/423–3377 or 800/688–1822* ☎ *401/423–9630* ⊕ *www.amazon-nature-tours.com.*

Amizade ✉ *Box 110107, Pittsburgh, PA 15232* ☎ *412/441–6655 or 888/973–4443* ⊕ *www.amizade.org.*

Augusto Albuquerque ✉ *Rua Rio Javarí 36, Vieralves, Manaus* ☎ *092/3635–6868* ✑ *mgasouza@ig.com.br.*

Australian & Amazonian Adventures ✉ *2711 Market Garden, Austin, TX 78745* ☎ *512/443–5393 or 800/232–5658* ⊕ *www.amazonadventures.com.*

Big Five Tours & Expeditions ✉ *1551 S.E. Palm Ct., Stuart, FL 34994* ☎ *772/287–7995 or 800/244–3483* ⊕ *www.bigfive.com.*

BikeHike Adventures ✉ *200-1807 Maritime Mews, Vancouver, British Columbia, V6H 3W7 Canada* ☎ *604/731–2442 or 888/805–0061* ⊕ *www.bikehike.com.*

Brazil Nuts ✉ *1854 Trade Center Way, Naples, FL 34109* ☎ *239/593–9959, 239/593–0267, or 800/553–9959* ⊕ *www.brazilnuts.com.*

Bushtracks Expeditions ✉ *6335 Mountain View Ranch Rd., Healdsburg, CA 95448* ☎ *800/995–8689* ⊕ *www.bushtracks.com.*

Dragoman Overland ✉ *Camp Green, Debenham, Suffolk, IP14 6LA U.K.* ⊕ *www.dragoman.com. . This company is represented in North America by Adventure Center (contact information under A, above).*

Earthwatch ✉ *3 Clocktower Pl., Suite 100, Maynard, MA 01754* ☎ *978/461–0081 or 800/776–0188* ⊕ *www.earthwatch.org.*

Ecotour Expeditions ✉ *Box 128, Jamestown, RI 02835* ☎ *401/423–3377 or 800/688–1822* ⊕ *www.naturetours.com.*

ElderTreks ✉ *597 Markham St., Toronto, Ontario, M6G 2L7 Canada* ☎ *416/588–5000 or 800/741–7956* ⊕ *www.eldertreks.com.*

Exodus This company is represented in North America by Adventure Center (contact information under A, above). ✉ *9 Weir Rd., London SW12 OLT, U.K.* ⊕ *www.exodustravel.com.*

Explore! Worldwide This company is represented in North America by Adventure Center (contact information under A, above). ✉ *Hampshire, GU14 7PA U.K.* ⊕ *www.explore.co.uk.*

Field Guides ✉ *9433 Bee Cave Rd., Bldg. 1, Suite 150, Austin, TX 78733* ☎ *512/263-7295 or 800/728-4953* ⊕ *www.fieldguides.com.*

Fishing International ✉ *5510 Skylane Blvd., Suite 200, Santa Rosa, CA 95405* ☎ *707/542-4242 or 800/950-4242* ⊕ *www.fishing international.com.*

FishQuest ✉ *152 North Main St., Hiawassee, GA 30546* ☎ *706/896-1403 or 888/891-3474* ⊕ *www. fishquest.com.*

Focus Tours ✉ *Box 22276, Santa Fe, NM 87502* ☎ *505/989-7193* ⊕ *www.focustours.com.*

Frontiers ✉ *Box 959, Wexford, PA 15090* ☎ *724/935-1577 or 800/245-1950* ⊕ *www.frontiers travel.com.*

G.A.P. Adventures ✉ *19 Charlotte St., Toronto, Ontario, M5V 2H5 Canada* ☎ *416/260-0999 or 800/708-7761* ⊕ *www.gapadventures.com.*

Gecko's This company is represented in North America by Adventure Center (contact information under A, above). ✉ *380 Lonsdale St., Melbourne, V1C 3000, Australia* ⊕ *www.geckosadven tures.com.*

Geographic Expeditions ✉ *1008 General Kennedy Ave., San Francisco, CA 94129* ☎ *415/922-0448 or 800/777-8183* ⊕ *www.geoex.com.*

Heliconia Amazônia Turismo ✉ *Rua José Clemente 500, Room 214, Manaus, AM 69010-070, Brazil* ☎ *092/3234-5915* ☎ *092/3633-7094* ⊕ *www.heliconia-amazon.com.*

Hidden Trails ✉ *659A Moberly Rd., Vancouver, British Columbia, V5Z 4B3 Canada* ☎ *604/323-1141 or* *888/987-2457* ⊕ *www.hiddentrails. com.*

International Expeditions ✉ *One Environs Park, Helena, AL 35080* ☎ *205/428-1700 or 800/633-4734* ⊕ *www.ietravel.com.*

Latin American Escapes ✉ *3209 Esplanade, Suite 130, Chico, CA 95973* ☎ *530/879-9292 or 800/510-5999* ☎ *530/879-9290* ⊕ *www.latin americanescapes.com.*

Maxim Tours ✉ *268 Rte. 206, Flanders, NJ 07836* ☎ *973/927-0760 or 800/655-0222* ☎ *973/927-1417* ⊕ *www.maximtours.com.*

Mountain Travel Sobek ✉ *1266 66th St., Suite 4, Emeryville, CA 94608* ☎ *510/594-6000 or 888/687-6235* ⊕ *www.mtsobek.com.*

Nature Expeditions International ✉ *7860 Peters Rd., Suite F-103, Plantation, FL 33324* ☎ *954/693-8852 or 800/869-0639* ⊕ *www.naturexp.com.*

NatureQuest ✉ *Box 22000, Telluride, CO 81435* ☎ *800/369-3033* ⊕ *www.NatureQuesttours.com.*

Oceanic Society Expeditions ✉ *Fort Mason Center, Bldg. E, San Francisco, CA 94123* ☎ *415/441-1106 or 800/326-7491* ⊕ *www. oceanic-society.org.*

PanAmerican Travel Services ✉ *320 E. 900 S, Salt Lake City, UT 84111* ☎ *800/364-4359* ⊕ *www.panam tours.com.*

Rod & Reel Adventures ✉ *32617 Skyhawk Way, Eugene, OR 97405* ☎ *541/349-0777 or 800/356-6982* ⊕ *www.rodreeladventures.com.*

Tour Operators

Santana ✉ *Rua dos Andrades 106, Centro, Manaus* ☎ *092/3234–9814 092/3233–7127* ⊕ *www.santanaecologica.com.br.*

Southwind Adventures ✉ *Box 621057, Littleton, CO 80162* ☎ *303/972–0701 or 800/377–9463* ⊕ *www.southwindadventures.com.*

Swallows and Amazons ✉ *Box 523, Eastham, MA 02642* ☎ *508/255–4794* ⊕ *www.swallowsandamazonstours.com.*

Travcoa ✉ *4340 Von Karman Ave., Suite 400, Newport Beach, CA 92660* ☎ *949/476–2800 or 800/992–2003* ⊕ *www.travcoa.com.*

Victor Emanuel Nature Tours ✉ *2525 Wallingwood Dr., Suite 1003, Austin, TX 78746* ☎ *512/328–5221 or 800/328–8368* ⊕ *www.ventbird.com.*

Wilderness Travel ✉ *1102 9th St., Berkeley, CA 94710* ☎ *510/558–2488 or 800/368–2794* ⊕ *www.wildernesstravel.com.*

WINGS ✉ *1643 N. Alvernon, Suite 109, Tucson, AZ 85712* ☎ *520/320–9868 or 888/293–6443* ⊕ *www.wingsbirds.com.*

Yanna Ecofishing ☎ *092/3232–2522* ☎ *092/3232–2397* ⊕ *www.yanna.com.br.*

CRUISE COMPANIES

Celebrity Cruises ☎ *800/647–2251* ⊕ *www.celebrity.com .*

Crystal Cruises ☎ *888/722–0021* ⊕ *www.crystalcruises.com .*

Fred. Olsen Cruise Lines ☎ *800/843–0602* ⊕ *www.fredolsencruises.com.*

Holland America Line ☎ *877/724–5425* ⊕ *www.hollandamerica.com.*

Norwegian Cruise Line ☎ *800/327–7030* ⊕ *www.ncl.com .*

Orient Lines ☎ *800/333–7300* ⊕ *www.orientlines.com .* **Princess Cruises** ☎ *800/774–6237* ⊕ *www.princess.com .*

Regent Seven Seas Cruises ☎ *877/505–5370* ⊕ *www.rssc.com .*

Seabourn Cruise Line ☎ *800/929–9391* ⊕ *www.seabourn.com .*

Silversea Cruises ☎ *800/722–9955* ⊕ *www.silversea.com .*

UNDERSTANDING BRAZIL

Brazilian Portuguese
Vocabulary

BRAZILIAN PORTUGUESE VOCABULARY

ENGLISH	PORTUGUESE	PRONUNCIATION

BASICS

ENGLISH	PORTUGUESE	PRONUNCIATION
Yes/no	Sim/Não	**see**ing/nown
Please	Por favor	pohr fah-**vohr**
May I?	Posso?	**poh**-sso
Thank you (very much)	(Muito) obrigado	(**moo**yn-too) o-bree-**gah**-doh
You're welcome	De nada	day **nah**-dah
Excuse me	Com licença	con lee-**ssehn**-ssah
Pardon me/ what did you say?	Desculpe/ O que disse?	des-**kool**-peh/ o.k. **dih**-say?
Could you tell me?	Poderia me dizer?	po-day-**ree**-ah mee dee-**zehrr**?
I'm sorry	Sinto muito	**seen**-too **moo**yn-too
Good morning!	Bom dia!	bohn **dee**-ah
Good afternoon!	Boa tarde!	**boh**-ah tahr-dee
Good evening!	Boa noite!	**boh**-ah nohee-tee
Goodbye!	Adeus!/Até logo!	ah-**deh**oos/ah-**teh** **loh**-go
Mr./Mrs.	Senhor/Senhora	sen-**yor**/sen-**yohr**-ah
Miss	Senhorita	sen-yo-**ri**-tah
Pleased to meet you	Muito prazer	**moo**yn-too prah-**zehr**
How are you?	Como vai?	**koh**-mo **vah**-ee
Very well, thank you	Muito bem, obrigado	**moo**yn-too **beh**-in o-bree-**gah**-doh
And you?	E o(a) Senhor(a)?	eh oh sen-**yor** (**yohr**-ah)
Hello (on the telephone)	Alô	ah-**low**

NUMBERS

1	um/uma	oom/**oom**-ah
2	dois	**doh**ees
3	três	**treh**ys
4	quatro	**kwa**-troh
5	cinco	**seen**-koh

6	seis	**seh**ys
7	sete	**seh**-tee
8	oito	**oh**ee-too
9	nove	**noh**-vee
10	dez	**deh**-ees
11	onze	**ohn**-zee
12	doze	**doh**-zee
13	treze	**treh**-zee
14	quatorze	kwa-**tohr**-zee
15	quinze	**keen**-zee
16	dezesseis	deh-zeh-**seh**ys
17	dezessete	deh-zeh-**seh**-tee
18	dezoito	deh-**zoh**ee-toh
19	dezenove	deh-zeh-**noh**-vee
20	vinte	**veen**-tee
21	vinte e um	**veen**-tee eh **oom**
30	trinta	**treen**-tah
32	trinta e dois	**treen**-ta eh **doh**ees
40	quarenta	kwa-**rehn**-ta
43	quarenta e três	kwa-**rehn**-ta e **treh**ys
50	cinquenta	seen-**kwehn**-tah
54	cinquenta e quatro	seen-**kwehn**-tah e **kwa**-troh
60	sessenta	seh-**sehn**-tah
65	sessenta e cinco	seh-**sehn**-tah e **seen**-ko
70	setenta	seh-**tehn**-tah
76	setenta e seis	seh-**tehn**-ta e **seh**ys
80	oitenta	**oh**ee-**tehn**-ta
87	oitenta e sete	**oh**ee-**tehn**-ta e **seh**-tee
90	noventa	noh-**vehn**-ta
98	noventa e oito	noh-**vehn**-ta e **oh**ee-too
100	cem	**seh**-ing
101	cento e um	**sehn**-too e **oom**
200	duzentos	doo-**zehn**-tohss

500	quinhentos	key-**nyehn**-tohss
700	setecentos	seh-teh-**sehn**-tohss
900	novecentos	noh-veh-**sehn**-tohss
1,000	mil	meel
2,000	dois mil	**doh**ees meel
1,000,000	um milhão	oom mee-lee-**ahon**

COLORS

black	preto	**preh**-toh
blue	azul	a-**zool**
brown	marrom	mah-**hohm**
green	verde	**vehr**-deh
pink	rosa	**roh**-zah
purple	roxo	**roh**-choh
orange	laranja	lah-**rahn**-jah
red	vermelho	vehr-**meh**-lyoh
white	branco	**brahn**-coh
yellow	amarelo	ah-mah-**reh**-loh

DAYS OF THE WEEK

Sunday	Domingo	doh-**meehn**-goh
Monday	Segunda-feira	seh-**goon**-dah **fey**-rah
Tuesday	Terça-feira	**tehr**-sah **fey**-rah
Wednesday	Quarta-feira	**kwahr**-tah **fey**-rah
Thursday	Quinta-feira	**keen**-tah fey-rah
Friday	Sexta-feira	**sehss**-tah fey-rah
Saturday	Sábado	**sah**-bah-doh

MONTHS

January	Janeiro	jah-**ney**-roh
February	Fevereiro	feh-veh-**rey**-roh
March	Março	**mahr**-soh
April	Abril	ah-**breel**
May	Maio	**my**-oh
June	Junho	jy**oo**-nyoh

July	Julho	jy**oo**-lyoh
August	Agosto	ah-**ghost**-toh
September	Setembro	seh-**tehm**-broh
October	Outubro	owe-**too**-broh
November	Novembro	noh-**vehm**-broh
December	Dezembro	deh-**zehm**-broh

USEFUL PHRASES

Do you speak English?	O Senhor fala inglês?	oh sen-**yor fah**-lah een-**glehs**?
I don't speak Portuguese.	Não falo português.	nown **fah**-loh pohr-too-**ghehs**
I don't understand (you)	Não lhe entendo	nown ly**eh** ehn-**tehn**-doh
I understand	Eu entendo	**eh**-oo ehn-**tehn**-doh
I don't know	Não sei	nown say
I am American/ British	Sou americano (americana) /inglês/inglêsa	sow a-meh-ree-**cah**-noh (a-meh-ree-**cah**-nah)/ een-**glehs** (een-**gleh**-sa)
What's your name?	Como se chama?	**koh**-moh seh **shah**-mah
My name is . . .	Meu nome é . . .	mehw **noh**-meh eh
What time is it?	Que horas são?	keh **oh**-rahss **sa**-ohn
It is one, two, three . . .o'clock	É uma/São duas, três . . . hora/horas	eh **oom**-ah/**sa**- ohn **doo**-ahss, **treh**ys **oh**-rah/**oh**-rahs
Yes, please/ No, thank you	Sim por favor/ Não obrigado	seing pohr fah **vohr**/- nown o-bree-**gah**-doh
How?	Como?	**koh**-moh
When?	Quando?	**kwahn**-doh
This/Next week	Esta/Próxima semana	**ehss**-tah/**proh**-see-mah seh-**mah**-nah
This/Next month	Este/Próximo mêz	**ehss**-teh/**proh**-see-moh mehz
This/Next year	Este/Próximo ano	**ehss**-teh/**proh**-see-moh **ah**-noh
Yesterday/today/ tomorrow	Ontem/hoje/ amanhã	**ohn**-tehn/**oh**-jeh/ ah-mah-**nyan**

This morning/ afternoon	Esta manhã/ tarde	ehss-tah mah-**nyan**/ **tahr**-deh
Tonight	Hoje a noite	**oh**-jeh ah **noh**ee-tee
What?	O que?	oh **keh**
What is it?	O que é isso?	oh **keh** eh **ee**-soh
Why?	Por quê?	pohr-**keh**
Who?	Quem?	**keh**-in
Where is . . . ?	Onde é . . . ?	**ohn**-deh **eh**
the train station?	a estação de trem?	ah es-tah-**sah**-on deh train
the subway station?	a estação de metrô?	ah es-tah-**sah**-on deh meh-**tro**
the bus stop?	a parada do ônibus?	ah pah-**rah**-dah doh **oh**-nee-boos
the post office?	o correio?	oh coh-**hay**-yoh
the bank?	o banco?	oh **bahn**-koh
the hotel?	o hotel . . . ?	oh oh-**tell**
the cashier?	o caixa?	oh **kahy**-shah
the museum?	o museo . . . ?	oh moo-**zeh**-oh
the hospital?	o hospital?	oh ohss-pee-**tal**
the elevator?	o elevador?	oh eh-leh-vah-**dohr**
the bathroom?	o banheiro?	oh bahn-yey-roh
the beach?	a praia de . . . ?	ah prahy-yah deh
Here/there	Aqui/ali	ah-**kee**/ah-**lee**
Open/closed	Aberto/fechado	ah-**behr**-toh/ feh-**shah**-doh
Left/right	Esquerda/direita	ehs-**kehr**-dah/ dee-**ray**-tah
Straight ahead	Em frente	ehyn **frehn**-teh
Is it near/far?	É perto/longe?	eh **pehr**-toh/**lohn**-jeh
I'd like to buy . . .	Gostaria de comprar . . .	gohs-tah-**ree**-ah deh cohm-**prahr** . . .
a bathing suit	um maiô	oom mahy-**owe**
a dictionary	um dicionário	oom dee-seeoh-**nah**-reeoh
a hat	um chapéu	oom shah-**peh**oo

a magazine	uma revista	oomah heh-**vees**-tah
a map	um mapa	oom **mah**-pah
a postcard	cartão postal	kahr-**town** pohs-**tahl**
sunglasses	óculos escuros	ah-koo-loss ehs-**koo**-rohs
suntan lotion	um óleo de bronzear	oom **oh**-lyoh deh brohn-zeh-**ahr**
a ticket	um bilhete	oom bee-lyeh-teh
cigarettes	cigarros	see-**gah**-hose
envelopes	envelopes	eyn-veh-**loh**-pehs
matches	fósforos	**fohs**-foh-rohss
paper	papel	pah-**pehl**
sandals	sandália	sahn-**dah**-leeah
soap	sabonete	sah-bow-**neh**-teh
How much is it?	Quanto custa?	**kwahn**-too **koos**-tah
It's expensive/cheap	Está caro/barato	**ehss**-tah **kah**-roh/ bah-**rah**-toh
A little/ a lot	Um pouco/ muito	oom **pohw**-koh/ **mooyn**-too
More/less	Mais/menos	**mah**-ees /**meh**-nohss
Enough/ too much/ too little	Suficiente/ demais/ muito pouco	soo-fee-see**ehn**-teh/- deh-**mah**-ees/ **mooyn**-toh/pohw-koh
Telephone	Telefone	teh-leh-**foh**-neh
Telegram	Telegrama	teh-leh-**grah**-mah
I am ill.	Estou doente.	**ehss**-tow doh-**ehn**-teh
Please call a doctor.	Por favor chame um médico.	pohr fah-**vohr** shah-meh oom **meh**-dee-koh
Help!	Socorro!	soh-**koh**-ho
Help me!	Me ajude!	mee ah-**jyew**-deh
Fire!	Incêndio!	een-**sehn**-deeoh
Caution!/Look out!/ Be careful!	Cuidado!	kooy-**dah**-doh

ON THE ROAD

Avenue	Avenida	ah-veh-**nee**-dah
Highway	Estrada	ehss-**trah**-dah
Port	Porto	**pohr**-toh
Service station	Posto de gasolina	**pohs**-toh deh gah-zoh-**lee**-nah
Street	Rua	**who**-ah
Toll	Pedagio	peh-**dah**-jyoh
Waterfront promenade	Beiramar/orla	behy-rah-**mahrr**/**ohr**-lah
Wharf	Cais	**kah**-ees

IN TOWN

Block	Quarteirão	kwahr-tehy-**rah**-on
Cathedral	Catedral	kah-teh-**drahl**
Church/temple	Igreja	ee-**greh**-jyah
City hall	Prefeitura	preh-fehy-**too**-rah
Door/gate	Porta/portão	**pohr**-tah/porh-**tah**-on
Entrance/exit	Entrada/saída	ehn-**trah**-dah/ sah-**ee**-dah
Market	Mercado/feira	mehr-**kah**-doh/**fey**-rah
Neighborhood	Bairro	**buy**-ho
Rustic bar	Lanchonete	lahn-shoh-**neh**-teh
Shop	Loja	**loh**-jyah
Square	Praça	**prah**-ssah

DINING OUT

A bottle of . . .	Uma garrafa de . . .	**oo**mah gah-**hah**-fah deh
A cup of . . .	Uma xícara de . . .	**oo**mah **shee**-kah-rah deh
A glass of . . .	Um copo de . . .	oom **koh**-poh deh
Ashtray	Um cinzeiro	oom seen-**zehy**-roh
Bill/check	A conta	ah **kohn**-tah
Bread	Pão	**pah**-on
Breakfast	Café da manhã	kah-**feh** dah mah-**nyan**

Butter	A manteiga	ah mahn-**tehy**-gah
Cheers!	Saúde!	sah-**oo**-deh
Cocktail	Um aperitivo	oom ah-peh-ree-**tee**-voh
Dinner	O jantar	oh **jyahn**-tahr
Dish	Um prato	oom **prah**-toh
Enjoy!	Bom apetite!	bohm ah-peh-**tee**-teh
Fork	Um garfo	**gahr**-foh
Fruit	Fruta	**froo**-tah
Is the tip included?	A gorjeta esta incluída?	ah gohr-**jyeh**-tah ehss-**tah** een-clue-**ee**-dah
Juice	Um suco	oom **soo**-koh
Knife	Uma faca	**oo**mah **fah**-kah
Lunch	O almoço	oh ahl-**moh**-ssoh
Menu	Menu/cardápio	me-**noo**/ kahr-dah-peeoh
Mineral water	Água mineral	**ah**-gooah mee-neh-**rahl**
Napkin	Guardanapo	gooahr-dah-**nah**-poh
No smoking	Não fumante	nown foo-**mahn**-teh
Pepper	Pimenta	pee-**mehn**-tah
Please give me	Por favor me dê	pohr fah-**vohr** mee **deh**
Salt	Sal	sahl
Smoking	Fumante	foo-**mahn**-teh
Spoon	Uma colher	**oo**mah koh-**lyehr**
Sugar	Açúcar	ah-**soo**-kahr
Waiter!	Garçon!	gahr-**sohn**
Water	Água	**ah**-gooah
Wine	Vinho	**vee**-nyoh

PRONOUNCING PLACE NAMES

NAME	PRONUNCIATION
Amazônia	ah-mah-**zoh**-knee-ah
Bahia	bah-**ee**-ah
Belém	beh-**lein**
Belo Horizonte	**beh**-loh ho-rih-**zon**-teh

Brasília	brah-**zee**-lee-ah
Fortaleza	for-tah-**leh**-zah
Manaus	mah-**nah**-oos
Minas Gerais	**mee**-nahs jyeh-**rah**-ees
Paraná	pah-rah-nah
Porto Alegre	**pohr**-toh ah-**leh**-greh
Recife	heh-**see**-fee
Rio de Janeiro	**hee**-oh day jah-**ne**-roh
Rio Grande do Sul	**hee**-oh **gran**-deh doh sool
Salvador	sahl-vah-**dohr**
Santa Catarina	sahn-**tah** kah-tah-reeh-nah
São Paulo	saohn **pow**-low

Brazil
Essentials

PLANNING TOOLS, EXPERT INSIGHT,
GREAT CONTACTS

There are planners and there are those who,
excuse the pun, fly by the seat of their pants.
We happily place ourselves among the planners.
Our writers and editors try to anticipate all the
issues you may face before and during any journey, and then they do their research. This section
is the product of their efforts. Use it to get excited
about your trip to Brazil, to inform your travel
planning, or to guide you on the road should the
seat of your pants start to feel threadbare.

GETTING STARTED

We're really proud of our Web site: Fodors.com is a great place to begin any journey. Scan Travel Wire for suggested itineraries, travel deals, restaurant and hotel openings, and other up-to-the-minute info. Check out Booking to research prices and book plane tickets, hotel rooms, rental cars, and vacation packages. Head to Talk for on-the-ground pointers from travelers who frequent our message boards. You can also link to loads of other travel-related resources.

▌RESOURCES

ONLINE TRAVEL TOOLS

For good information you may have to search by region, state, or city—and hope that at least one of them has a comprehensive official site of its own. Don't rule out foreign-language sites; some have links to sites that present information in more than one language, including English.

The search terms in Portuguese for "look," "find," and "get" are *olhar* or *achar, buscar,* and *pegar*; "next" and "last" (as in "next/last 10") are *próximo* or *seguinte* and *último* or *anterior.* Keep an eye out for such words as: *turismo* (tourism), *turístico* (tourist-related), *hotéis* (hotels), and *restaurantes* (restaurants).

The Brazil Information Center is a Washington, D.C.–based organization that promotes political and business issues rather than tourism, but its Web site has an incredible number of helpful links. The online magazine *Brazzil* has interesting English-language articles on culture and politics. *See also Visitor Information, below.*

All About Brazil Brazil Information Center (⊕ www.brazilinfocenter.org). Brazzil **Magazine** (⊕ www.brazzil.com).

Currency Conversion Google (⊕ www.google.com) does currency conversion. Just type in the amount you want to convert and

an explanation of how you want it converted (e.g., "14 Swiss francs in dollars"), and then voilà. Oanda.com (⊕ www.oanda.com) also allows you to print out a handy table with the current day's conversion rates. XE.com (⊕ www.xe.com) is a good currency conversion Web site.

Safety Transportation Security Administration (TSA; ⊕ www.tsa.gov)

Time Zones Timeanddate.com (⊕ www.timeanddate.com/worldclock) can help you figure out the correct time anywhere. Timeticker.com (⊕ www.timeticker.com) if you want to hear what time it is anywhere in the globe, visit this useful Web site.

Weather Accuweather.com (⊕ www.accuweather.com) is an independent weather-forecasting service with good coverage of hurricanes. Weather.com (⊕ www.weather.com) is the Web site for the Weather Channel.

VISITOR INFORMATION

EMBRATUR, Brazil's national tourism organization, doesn't have offices overseas, though its Web site is helpful. For information in your home country, contact the Brazilian embassy or the closest consulate (⇨ *Passports & Visas, below*), some of which have Web sites and staff dedicated to promoting tourism. The official consular Web site in New York, www.brazilny.org, has details about other consulates and the embassy as well as travel information and links to other sites. Cities and towns throughout Brazil have local tourist boards, and some state capitals also have state tourism offices. Viva Brazil provides background and travel info on Brazil's different regions as well as links that will help you arrange your trip.

Contacts Brazilian Embassy–New York (⊕ www.brazilny.org). EMBRATUR (☎ 61/3429-7774 in Brasilia, 646/378-2126 in U.S. East Coast, 310/ 341-8394 in U.S. West

Coast ⊕www.embratur.gov.br). **Viva Brazil** ⊕www.vivabrazil.com).

▌THINGS TO CONSIDER

GEAR

For sightseeing, casual clothing and good walking shoes are appropriate; most restaurants don't require formal attire. For beach vacations, bring lightweight sportswear, a bathing suit, a beach cover-up, a sun hat, and waterproof sunscreen that is at least SPF 15. A sarong or a light cotton blanket makes a handy beach towel, picnic blanket, and cushion for hard seats, among other things.

If you're going to coastal cities like Rio, Florianópolis, and Salvador in summer (December, January, and February), dress more informally and feel free to wear flip-flops (thongs) all day. Southeastern cities like São Paulo, Curitiba, and Porto Alegre, which have lower temperatures, tend to be more formal and more conservative when it comes to clothing (sometimes even Brazilians are shocked by the way people in Rio dress). In urban areas it's always a good idea to have some nice outfits for going out at night.

Travel in rain-forest areas requires long-sleeve shirts, long pants, socks, waterproof hiking boots (sneakers are less desirable, but work in a pinch), a hat, a light waterproof jacket, a bathing suit, and plenty of strong insect repellent. (Amazonian bugs tend to be oblivious to non-DEET or non-picaridin repellents.) Other useful items include a screw-top water container that you can fill with bottled water, a money pouch, a travel flashlight and extra batteries, a Swiss Army knife with a bottle opener, a medical kit, binoculars, a pocket calculator, spare camera batteries, and a high-capacity memory card or lots of extra film. *For more information, see Packing in Chapter 10.*

PASSPORTS & VISAS

PASSPORTS

When in Brazil, carry your passport or a copy with you at all times. Make two photocopies of the data page (one for someone at home and another for you, carried separately from your passport). If you lose your passport, promptly call the nearest embassy or consulate and the local police.

If your passport is lost or stolen, first call the police—having the police report can make replacement easier—and then call your embassy. You'll get a temporary Emergency Travel Document that will need to be replaced once you return home. Fees vary according to how fast you need the passport; in some cases the fee covers your permanent replacement as well. The new document will not have your entry stamps; ask if your embassy takes care of this, or whether it's your responsibility to get the necessary immigration authorization.

Go to the Web site for the Brazilian embassy or consulate nearest you for the most up-to-date visa information. At this writing, tourist visa fees are US$100 for Americans and C$72 for Canadians. Additional fees may be levied if you apply by mail. Obtaining a visa can be a slow process, and you must have every bit of paperwork in order when you visit the consulate, so read instructions carefully. (For example, in the U.S., the fee can only be paid by a U.S. Postal Service money order.)

To get the location of the Brazilian consulate to which you must apply, contact the Brazilian embassy. Note that some consulates don't allow you to apply for a visa by mail. If you don't live near a city with a consulate, consider hiring a concierge-type service to do your legwork. Many cities have these companies, which not only help with the paperwork, but also send someone to wait in line for you.

Info **Brazilian Embassy** (✉3006 Massachusetts Ave. NW, Washington, DC 20008

☎202/238-2700 ⊕www.brasilemb.org
✉450 Wilbrod St., Ottawa, ON K1N 6M8
☎613/237-1090 ⊕www.brasembottawa.org).

VISAS

Most visas limit you to a single trip—basically during the actual dates of your planned vacation. Other visas allow you to visit as many times as you wish for a specific period of time. Remember that requirements change, sometimes at the drop of a hat, and the burden is on you to make sure that you have the appropriate visas. Otherwise, you'll be turned away at the airport or, worse, deported after you arrive in the country. No company or travel insurer gives refunds if your travel plans are disrupted because you didn't have the correct visa.

U.S. Passport Information U.S. Department of State (☎877/487-2778 ⊕http://travel. state.gov/passport).

U.S. Passport & Visa Expediters A. Briggs Passport & Visa Expeditors (☎800/806-0581 or 202/338-0111 ⊕www. abriggs.com). **American Passport Express** (☎800/455-5166 or 800/841-6778 ⊕www. americanpassport.com). **Passport Express** (☎800/362-8196 ⊕www.passportex press.com). **Travel Document Systems** (☎800/874-5100 or 202/638-3800 ⊕www. traveldocs.com). **Travel the World Visas** (☎866/886-8472 or 301/495-7700 ⊕www. world-visa.com).

GENERAL REQUIREMENTS FOR BRAZIL	
Passport	Must be valid for 6 months after date of arrival.
Visa	Required for Americans (US$100) and Canadians (C$72)
Vaccinations	Yellow fever and diptheria
Driving	International driver's license required; CDW is compulsory on car rentals and will be included in the quoted price
Departure Tax	US$20, payable in cash only

SHOTS & MEDICATIONS

Vaccinations agaist hepatitis A and B, menengitis, typhoid, and yellow fever are highly recommended. Consult your doctor about whether to get a rabies vaccination. Check with the CDC's International Travelers' Hotline (⇨ *Health Warnings, below)* if you plan to visit remote regions or stay for more than six weeks.

Discuss the option of taking antimalarial drugs with your doctor. Note that in parts of northern Brazil a particularly aggressive strain of malaria has become resistant to one antimalarial drug—chloroquine). Some antimalarial drugs have rather unpleasant side effects—from headaches, nausea, and dizziness to psychosis, convulsions, and hallucinations.

For travel anywhere in Brazil, it's recommended that you have updated vaccines for diphtheria, tetanus, and polio. Children must additionally have current inoculations against measles, mumps, and rubella.

Yellow fever immunization is compulsory to enter Brazil if you're traveling directly from one of the following countries in South America (or from one of several African countries): Bolivia; Colombia; Ecuador; French Guiana; Peru; or Venezuela. You must have an International Certificate of Immunization proving that you've been vaccinated.

For more information see Health in On the Ground in Brazil, below.

Health Warnings National Centers for Disease Control & Prevention (CDC ☎877/394-8747 international travelers' health line ⊕www.cdc.gov/travel). **World Health Organization** (WHO ⊕www.who.int).

BOOKING YOUR TRIP

ACCOMMODATIONS

Unlike lodging in European countries, all hotels in Brazil have bathrooms in their rooms. The simplest type of accommodation usually consists of a bed, TV, table, bathroom, a little fridge, a telephone, and a bathroom with a shower. (Budget hotels in the Amazon or northeast don't always have hot water.) In luxury hotels you'll also generally have Internet access, cable TV, and a bathroom with a bathtub and shower. Hotels listed with EMBRATUR, Brazil's national tourism board, are rated using stars. Staff training is a big part of the rating, but it's not a perfect system, since stars are awarded based on the number of amenities rather than their quality.

If you ask for a double room, you'll get a room for two people, but you're not guaranteed a double mattress. If you'd like to avoid twin beds, ask for a *cama de casal* ("couple's bed").

Carnival, the year's principal festival, takes place during the four days preceding Ash Wednesday. ■TIP→ **For top hotels in Rio, Salvador, and Recife during Carnival you must make reservations a year in advance.** Hotel rates rise by 20% on average for Carnival. Not as well known outside Brazil but equally impressive is Rio's New Year's Eve celebration. More than a million people gather along Copacabana Beach for a massive fireworks display and to honor the sea goddess Iemanjá. To ensure a room, book at least six months in advance.

In the hinterlands it's good to look at any room before accepting it; expense is no guarantee of charm or cleanliness, and accommodations can vary dramatically within a single hotel. Also, be sure to check the shower: some hotels have electric-powered showerheads rather than central water heaters. In theory, you can adjust both the water's heat and its pressure. In practice, if you want hot water you have to turn the water pressure down; if you want pressure, expect a brisk rinse. ⚠ **Don't adjust the power when you're under the water—you can get a little shock.** Note that in the Amazon and other remote areas what's billed as "hot" water may be lukewarm at best—even in higher-end hotels.

The lodgings we list are the cream of the crop in each price category. We always list the facilities that are available, but we don't specify whether they cost extra; when pricing accommodations, always ask what's included and what costs extra. All rooms have private bathrooms, air-conditioning, telephones, and televisions unless we indicate otherwise.

Properties marked ✕🍽 are lodging establishments whose restaurants warrant a special trip.

When you book a room, you pay, in addition to the base fee, tourism fees equaling 10% of the room price plus (sometimes) R$1.50. Hotels accept credit cards for payment, but first ask if there's a discount for cash. Try to bargain hard for a cash-on-the-barrel discount, then pay in local currency.

CATEGORY	COST
$$$$	over R$500
$$$	R$375–R$500
$$	R$250–R$375
$	R$125–R$250
¢	under R$125

All prices are in reais for a standard double room in high season, based on the European Plan (EP) and excluding taxes and service charges.

Most hotels and other lodgings require you to give your credit-card details before they will confirm your reservation. If you don't feel comfortable e-mailing this information, ask if you can fax it (some places even prefer faxes). However you book, get confirmation in writing and have a copy of it handy when you check in.

Be sure you understand the hotel's cancellation policy. Some places allow you to cancel without any kind of penalty—even if you prepaid to secure a discounted rate—if you cancel at least 24 hours in advance. Others require you to cancel a week in advance or penalize you the cost of one night. Small inns and B&Bs are most likely to require you to cancel far in advance. Most hotels allow children under a certain age to stay in their parents' room at no extra charge, but others charge for them as extra adults; find out the cutoff age for discounts.

BED & BREAKFASTS

B&Bs in Brazil are comfortable, friendly, and offer a modicum of privacy. A nice option if you're looking for something a little more intimate than a hotel.

Reservation Services Bed & Breakfast.com (☎512/322-2710 or 800/462-2632 ⊕www. bedandbreakfast.com) also sends out an online newsletter. **Bed & Breakfast Inns Online** (☎615/868-1946 or 800/215-7365 ⊕www. bbonline.com). **BnB Finder.com** (☎212/432-7693 or 888/547-8226 ⊕www.bnbfinder.com). **Ipanema Bed and Breakfast** (✉contact@ipanemabedandbreakfast.com ⊕www.aithost. com.br/bed_and_breakfast/). **Pousada Koala** (✉Rua Beijupirá, Porto de Galinhas 55590-000, Pernambuco ☎81/3552-1145 ✉contato@pousadakoala.com.br ⊕www. pousadakoala.com.br). **Pousada Quintal do Mar** (✉Av. Aroeira da Praia, Bombinhas 88215-000, Santa Catarina ☎47/3393-4389 ⊕www.quintaldomar.com.br).

FAZENDAS

Another accommodation option is to stay on a *fazenda* (farm), or *hotel fazenda*, where you can experience a rural environment. They are ideal for families with kids, as most have adventure sports and programs for children. Some farms in the state of São Paulo date back to colonial times, when they were famous Brazilian coffee farms. Prices range from around $50 to $125 per day for adults, but the actual cost depends a lot on which facilities and activities you choose. The prices we give usually include all meals (but be sure to check this beforehand) and are valid for the months of January, February, July, and December (high season). You can get discounts of up to 30% during the low season.

HOSTELS

Hostels offer bare-bones lodging at low, low prices—often in shared dorm rooms with shared baths—to people of all ages, though the primary market is young travelers, especially students. Most hostels serve breakfast; dinner and/or shared cooking facilities may also be available. In some hostels you aren't allowed to be in your room during the day, and there may be a curfew at night. Nevertheless, hostels provide a sense of community, with public rooms where travelers often gather to share stories. Many hostels are affiliated with Hostelling International (HI), an umbrella group of hostel associations with some 4,000 member properties in more than 60 countries. Other hostels are completely independent and may be nothing more than a really cheap hotel.

Membership in any HI association, open to travelers of all ages, allows you to stay in HI-affiliated hostels at member rates. One-year membership is about $28 for adults. Rates in dorm-style rooms run about $15–$25 per bed per night; private rooms are more, but are still generally well under $100 a night. Members have priority if the hostel is full; they're also eligible for discounts around the world, even on rail and bus travel in some countries.

There are more than 80 hostels throughout Brazil, in Alagoas, Bahia, Ceará, Distrito Federal, Espírito Santo, Maranhão, Mato Grosso, Mato Grosso do Sul, Minas Gerais, Paraíba, Pernambuco, Piauí, Rio de Janeiro, Rio Grande do

Norte, Rio Grande do Sul, Santa Catarina, São Paulo, and Pará. You should expect to pay from $10 to $25. Brazil is among the 15 countries better served with hostels in the world, being the leader in Latin America.

Information **Federação Brasileira de Albergues da Juventude** (☎21/2286–0303 ⊕www.hostel.org.br). **Hostelling International–USA** (☎301/495–1240 ⊕www.hiusa.org).

POUSADAS

If you want the facilities of a hotel plus the family environment of an apartment, but at a lower cost, a *pousada* is a good option. Cheaper than hotels and farms, pousadas are simple inns, often in historic houses. They usually have swimming pools, parking lots, air-conditioning and/or fans, TVs, refrigerators, and common areas such as bars, laundry, and living rooms. Some have a common kitchen for guests who prefer to cook their own meals.

▌ AIRLINE TICKETS

▌**TIP→** Discount air passes that let you travel economically in a country or region must often be purchased before you leave home. In some cases you can only get them through a travel agent.

Air passes from TAM or Varig can save you hundreds of dollars if you plan to travel a lot within Brazil. These can only be purchased outside Brazil. Varig's Brazil AirPass costs $560 for five coupons, which are valid for 21 days on flights to more than 100 cities within Brazil on Varig or its affiliates, Rio-Sul or Nordeste. You can buy up to four additional coupons (a total of nine) for $100 each. TAM's 21-day Brazilian AirPass costs $399 for four coupons, with additional coupons at $100 each.

If you plan to visit more than one of the Mercosur (Southern Common Market) countries—Argentina, Brazil, Paraguay,

and Uruguay—the Mercosur Pass presents the greatest savings. It's valid on Aerolineas Argentinas, Varig, and several other carriers. You must visit at least two countries within a minimum of seven days and a maximum of 30 days. Pricing is based on mileage, ranging from $225 for flights totaling between 1,900 and 3,000 km (1,200 and 1,900 mi) to $870 for flights totaling more than 11,300 km (7,000 mi). Contact participating airlines or tour operators and travel agents who specialize in South American travel for information and purchase.

Air Pass Info **GLOBOTur** (☎800/998–5521 ⊕www.globotur.com).

▌ RENTAL CARS

Driving is chaotic in cities like São Paulo, but much easier in cities like Curitiba and Brasília. In the countryside the usually rough roads, lack of clearly marked signs, and language difference are discouraging for driving. Further, the cost of renting can be steep. All that said, certain areas are most enjoyable when explored on your own in a car: the beach areas of Búzios and the Costa Verde (near Rio) and the Belo Horizonte region; the North Shore beaches outside São Paulo; and many of the inland and coastal towns of the south, a region with many good roads.

Brazil has more than 1.65 million km (1.02 million mi) of highway, about 10% of it paved. The country's highway department estimates that 40% of the federal highways (those with either the designation *BR* or a state abbreviation such as *RJ* or *SP*), which constitute 70% of Brazil's total road system, are in a dangerous state of disrepair. Evidence of this is everywhere: potholes, lack of signage, inadequate shoulders. Landslides and flooding after heavy rains are frequent and at times shut down entire stretches of key highways. Recent construction has improved the situation, but independent land travel in Brazil definitely has its liabilities.

Some common-sense tips: before you set out, establish an itinerary and ask about gas stations. Be sure to plan your daily driving distance conservatively and don't drive after dark. Always obey speed limits and traffic regulations.

Always give the rental car a once-over to make sure the headlights, jack, and tires (including the spare) are in working condition.

Consider hiring a car and driver through your hotel concierge, or make a deal with a taxi driver for extended sightseeing at a long-term rate. Often drivers charge a set hourly rate, regardless of the distance traveled. You'll have to pay cash, but you may actually spend less than you would for a rental car.

You need an international driver's license if you plan to drive in Brazil. International driving permits (IDPs) are available from the American and Canadian automobile associations. These international permits, valid only in conjunction with your regular driver's license, are universally recognized.

CAR-RENTAL INSURANCE

Everyone who rents a car wonders whether the insurance that the rental companies offer is worth the expense. No one—including us—has a simple answer. It all depends on how much regular insurance you have, how comfortable you are with risk, and whether or not money is an issue.

If you own a car, your personal auto insurance may cover a rental to some degree, though not all policies protect you abroad; always read your policy's fine print. If you don't have auto insurance, then seriously consider buying the collision- or loss-damage waiver (CDW or LDW) from the car-rental company, which eliminates your liability for damage to the car.

Car insurance is not compulsory when renting a car, but if you have plans to drive to more than one city we strongly recommend paying for car insurance, given the bad conditions of Brazilian roads in some states and the risk of accidents. Most car-rental companies offer an optional insurance against robbery and accidents. Minimum age for renting a car is 21, but some companies require foreign clients to be at least 25 or charge an extra fee for those aged between 21 and 25.

■TIP➔ You can decline the insurance from the rental company and purchase it through a third-party provider such as Travel Guard (www.travelguard.com)—$9 per day for $35,000 of coverage. That's sometimes just under half the price of the CDW offered by some car-rental companies.

■ VACATION PACKAGES

Packages *are not* guided excursions. Packages combine airfare, accommodations, and perhaps a rental car or other extras (theater tickets, guided excursions, boat trips, reserved entry to popular museums, transit passes), but they let you do your own thing. During busy periods packages may be your only option, as flights and rooms may be sold out otherwise.

Packages will definitely save you time. They can also save you money, particularly in peak seasons, but—and this is a really big "but"—you should price each part of the package separately to be sure. And be aware that prices advertised on Web sites and in newspapers rarely include service charges or taxes, which can up your costs by hundreds of dollars.

■TIP➔ Some packages and cruises are sold only through travel agents. Don't always assume that you can get the best deal by booking everything yourself.

Each year consumers are stranded or lose their money when packagers—even large ones with excellent reputations—

go out of business. How can you protect yourself?

First, always pay with a credit card; if you have a problem, your credit-card company may help you resolve it. Second, buy trip insurance that covers default. Third, choose a company that belongs to the United States Tour Operators Association, whose members must set aside funds to cover defaults. Finally, choose a company that also participates in the Tour Operator Program of the American Society of Travel Agents (ASTA), which will act as mediator in any disputes.

You can also check on the tour operator's reputation among travelers by posting an inquiry on one of the Fodors.com forums.

Considering the sheer number of interesting places in Brazil, buying a package tour can be more convenient than researching everything yourself. Depending on how much time you can spend here, make sure your package includes the most famous and enchanting places in Brazil: Pantanal, the Amazon, Rio de Janeiro, and the Northeastern beaches.

For information on specific packages and tours, see Chapter 11, "Adventure & Learning Vacations."

Organizations **American Society of Travel Agents** (ASTA ☎703/739–2782 or 800/965–2782 ⊕www.astanet.com). **United States Tour Operators Association** (USTOA ☎212/599–6599 ⊕www.ustoa.com).

■TIP→ Local tourism boards can provide information about lesser-known and small-niche operators that sell packages to only a few destinations.

▌ GUIDED TOURS

Guided tours are a good option when you don't want to do it all yourself. You travel along with a group (sometimes large, sometimes small), stay in prebooked hotels, eat with your fellow travelers (the cost of meals sometimes included in the price of your tour, sometimes not), and follow a schedule.

But not all guided tours are an if-it's-Tuesday-this-must-be-Belgium experience. A knowledgeable guide can take you places that you might never discover on your own, and you may be pushed to see more than you would have otherwise. Tours aren't for everyone, but they can be just the thing for trips to places where making travel arrangements is difficult or time-consuming (particularly when you don't speak the language).

Whenever you book a guided tour, find out what's included and what isn't. A "land-only" tour includes all your travel (by bus, in most cases) in the destination, but not necessarily your flights to and from or even within it. Also, in most cases prices in tour brochures don't include fees and taxes. And remember that you'll be expected to tip your guide (in cash) at the end of the tour.

For special-interest tours, see Chapter 11, "Adventure & Learning Vacations."

Recommended Companies **Flytour Turismo** (⊠Av. Juruá 641, Alphaville 06455-010 ☎11/4502–2600 ⊕www.flytour.com). **Avipam** (⊠Av. Rio Branco 251, Rio de Janeiro 20040-008 ☎21/2108–0909 ⊕www.avipam.com.br).

TRANSPORTATION

Brazil is one of the biggest countries in the world, and larger than the continental U.S. This means that you'll be hard-pressed to see the Amazon, Bahia, Rio, and São Paulo during a weeklong vacation. You can, however, cover a lot of territory if your trip is well planned. If you want to start from the North/Northeast and then later on go southward, go ahead. We just do not recommend traveling around without a clear idea of the distances between destinations.

TRAVEL TIMES FROM SÃO PAULO TO	BY AIR	BY BUS
Rio de Janeiro	1 hour	6 hours
Salvador	1 hour and 30 minutes	24 hours
Manaus	2 hours	60 hours
Florianópolis	1 hour and 15 minutes	9 hours
Brasília	1 hour and 45 minutes	13 hours

▌ BY AIR

Within a country as big as Brazil, it's especially important to plan your itinerary with care. Book as far in advance as possible, particularly for weekend travel. Planes tend to fill up on Friday, especially to or from Brasília or Manaus. For more booking tips and to check prices and make online flight reservations, log on to www.infraero.gov.br

▌TIP→ Ask the local tourist board about hotel and local transportation packages that include tickets to major museum exhibits or other special events.

Reconfirm flights within Brazil, even if you have a ticket and a reservation, as flights tend to operate at full capacity.

Be prepared to pay a hefty departure tax when you leave Brazil, which runs about R$78 ($33) for international flights. A departure tax also applies to flights within Brazil; amounts vary roughly between R$11 and R$22 ($4 and $10). Although some airports accept credit cards in payment of departure taxes, it's wise to have the appropriate amount in *reais*.

Airlines & Airports Airline and Airport Links.com (⊕www.airlineandairportlinks.com) has links to many of the world's airlines and airports.

Airline Security Issues Transportation Security Administration (⊕www.tsa.gov) has answers for almost every question that might come up.

Air Travel Resources in Brazil National Civil Aviation Agency (ANAC) (☎55 61 3905–2645 ⊕www.anac.gov.br).

TRANSFERS BETWEEN AIRPORTS

Some airports offer transfers to another airport, such as Guarulhos-Congonhas, in São Paulo, or Galeão-Santos Dumond, in Rio de Janeiro. However, because the country is so big, this type of service is not common outside of Rio and São Paulo.

FLIGHTS

TO BRAZIL

Miami, Newark, New York, and Toronto are the major gateways for flights to Brazil from North America. At this writing, most flights to Brazil from North America connect through São Paulo.

Varig, a Brazilian airline and a partner with United Airlines, offers a wide range of flights within Brazil. TAM, another Brazil-based international carrier and a partner with American Airlines, flies nonstop from New York and Miami to São Paulo, with continuing service to Rio and connections to other cities. TAM also offers nonstop service between Miami and Manaus.

Continental Airlines flies nonstop from Newark to São Paulo and Delta offers nonstop service from Atlanta to São Paulo and Rio. Air Canada has nonstop service between Toronto and São Paulo. For travel within Brazil, another good option is Gol, the most reliable low-cost airline with routes that cover most major and medium-size Brazilian cities. Gol is increasing its range of international destinations, and now covers some Latin American countries. Other options are OceanAir and WebJet.

Airline Contacts Air Canada (☏888/712–7786 in North America, 11/3254–6600 in Brazil ⊕www.aircanada.com). **American Airlines** (☏800/433–7300, 11/4502–4000 in Brazil ⊕www.aa.com). **Continental Airlines** (☏800/523–3273 for U.S. and Mexico reservations, 800/231–0856 for international reservations, 0800/702–7500 in Brazil ⊕www.continental.com). **Delta Airlines** (☏800/221–1212 for U.S. reservations, 800/241–4141 for international reservations, 0800/881–2121 in Brazil ⊕www.delta.com). **TAM** (☏888/235–9826 in U.S., 0800/55–5200 in Brazil, 11/5582–8811 in São Paulo ⊕www.tamairlines.com). **United Airlines** (☏800/864–8331 for U.S. reservations, 800/538–2929 for international reservations, 800/16–2323 in Brazil ⊕www.united.com). **Varig** (☏800/468–2744 in U.S., 11/4003–7000 in Brazil ⊕www.varig.com).

WITHIN BRAZIL

There's regular jet service within the country between all major cities and most medium-size cities. Remote areas are also accessible—as long as you don't mind small planes. Flights can be long, lasting several hours for trips to the Amazon, with stops en route. The most widely used service is the Varig Ponte Aérea (Air Bridge), the Rio–São Paulo shuttle, which departs every half hour from 6 AM to 10:30 PM (service switches to every 15 minutes during morning and evening rush hours). Fares (one-way) for the Rio–São Paulo shuttle service vary from $145 (with Gol) to $170 (with TAM).

Domestic Airlines Gol (☏0300/789–2121 in Brazil ⊕www.voegol.com.br). **TAM** (☏888/235–9826 in U.S., 305/406–2826 in Miami, 800/570–5700 in Brazil ⊕www.tamairlines.com). **Varig** (☏800/468–2744 in U.S., 11/4003–7000 in Brazil ⊕www.varig.com). **Trip Linhas Aéreas** (☏084/3644–1129 in Natal, 081/3464–4610 in Recife ⊕www.airtrip.com.br). **WebJet Linhas Aéreas** (☏0800/722–1212 in Brazil ⊕www.webjet.com.br).

▌ BY BUS

The nation's *ônibus* (bus) network is affordable, comprehensive, and efficient—compensating for the lack of trains and the high cost of air travel. Every major city can be reached by bus, as can most small to medium-size communities.

The quality of buses in Brazil is good; in many cases better than in the U.S., depending on the type of bus. The number of stops at roadside cafés depends on the length of the trip. A trip from São Paulo to Curitiba, for example, which takes about 6 hours, has only one 20-minute stop. Usually buses stop at large, nice outlets with food, souvenirs, and magazines.

When buying a ticket, you'll be asked whether you want the *ônibus convencional,* the simplest option; the *ônibus executive,* with air-conditioning, coffee and water, more space between seats, and a pillow and blanket; or the *leito,* where you have all facilities of an executive bus plus a seat that reclines completely. If you're over 5 10 , buy the most expensive ticket available and try for front-row seats, where you'll have more space.

Most buses used for long trips are modern and comfortable, usually with bathrooms and air-conditioning. Note that regular buses used for shorter hauls may be labeled AR CONDICIONADO (AIR-CONDITIONED) but often are not.

▐ TIP➡ To ensure that your destination is understood, write it down on a piece of paper and present it to bus or taxi drivers, most of whom don't speak English.

Bus Information Itapemirim (☎800/723–2121 ⊕www.itapemirim.com.br/english/).
Pluma International (☎41/3212–2689 ⊕www.pluma.com.br/engli/main.htm).

▌BY CAR

Traveling by car is recommended if you meet the following criteria: you're not pressed for time, you enjoy driving even in places you do not know well, you do not want to be limited by airline/bus schedules. It's reasonably safe in most areas, a wonderful way to see the country and to visit lesser-known areas.

GASOLINE

Gasoline in Brazil costs around R$2.15 (74¢) a liter, which is about $2.75 per gallon. Unleaded gas, called *especial,* costs about the same. Brazil also has an extensive fleet of ethanol-powered cars *carro a álcool,* and you might end up with one from a rental agency. Ethanol fuel is sold at all gas stations and is a little cheaper than gasoline. However, these cars get lower mileage, so they offer little advantage over gas-powered cars. Stations are plentiful within cities and on major highways, and many are open 24 hours a day, 7 days a week. In smaller towns few stations take credit cards, and their hours are more limited. If you want a receipt, as for a *recibo.*

PARKING

Finding a space in most cities—particularly Rio, São Paulo, Brasília, Belo Horizonte, and Salvador—is a major task. It's best to head for a garage or a lot and leave your car with the attendant. The cost of parking depends on the city and the neighborhood: downtown garages, close to stores, will certainly be more expensive than those in residential areas. There are no meters; instead, there's a system involving coupons that you must post in your car's window, which allows you to park for a certain time period (one or two hours). You can buy them from uniformed street-parking attendants or

> **WARNING**
>
> It's not safe to drive at night, especially in Rio and São Paulo where drivers commonly run stop signs and traffic lights to avoid robbery. Take special note of motorcyclists at night—they're often used in robberies for a quick getaway. We strongly recommend that women do not drive alone at night.

at newsstands. Should you find a space on the street, you'll probably have to pay a fee for parking services. Or you might run into unauthorized street parking offered by the so-called *flanelinhas* (literally, "flannel wearers"), who may charge from R$2 (85¢) to R$5 ($2) in advance. This is most common in São Paulo.

No-parking zones are marked by a crossed-out capital letter *E* (which means *estacionamento,* Portuguese for "parking"). These zones, more often than not, are filled with cars that are rarely bothered by the police.

ROAD CONDITIONS

Road conditions in Brazil vary widely throughout the country. Roads in the South are often excellent, while federal, interstate roads (also known as BR) in other parts of the country are often very poor, with occasional potholes and uneven surfaces. Passenger car travel is reasonably safe in most areas, while passenger-bus hijacking, usually nonviolent, occurs at random in some areas. In major cities like São Paulo and Rio de Janeiro traffic jams are common in rush hours (8 AM, 6 PM). The same occur in other capitals, but Rio and São Paulo are undoubtedly the worst in this regard. In Brasília there are special roads for those driving faster (the so-called Eixão, where the limit is 80 km per hour/49 mi per hour). In rush hours you may find the local driving style more aggressive but, still, driving in major cities is easier than in small ones.

FROM	TO	DISTANCE
São Paulo	Rio de Janeiro	430 km
Rio de Janeiro	Búzios	180 km
Rio de Janeiro	Salvador	1,650 km
São Paulo	Belo Horizonte	590 km
São Paulo	Florianópolis	705 km
São Paulo	Foz do Iguaçu	1,050 km

Roadside Emergencies

The Automóvel Clube do Brasil (Automobile Club of Brazil) provides emergency assistance to foreign motorists, but only if they're members of an automobile club in their own nation. If you're not a member of an automobile club, you can call 193 from anywhere in the country. This is a universal number staffed by local fire departments. The service is in Portuguese only. Many motorists in major urban areas and more developed parts of the country carry cellular phones, and can be asked to assist in calling for help. In case of emergency, the fastest way to summon assistance is to call one of the following services: Fire Brigade(193); Police (190); Ambulance (192); Civil Defense (199).

RULES OF THE ROAD

Brazilians drive on the right, and in general traffic laws are the same as those in the United States. The use of seat belts is mandatory. The national speed limit ranges from 60 to 80 kph (36–48 mph). There are cameras on the streets of most cities to enforce the speed limit. Make sure you wear seat belts at all times and do not answer your cell phone. The minimum driving age is 18 and children should always sit in the back seat.

SAFETY

If you get a ticket for some sort of violation, be polite with the police officer and try to solve the issue either by accepting the ticket (if you committed the violation) or by explaining your position (if you did not commit a violation). Even though it's common to see scams in cases like this, the best option is to solve the problem as honestly as possible, especially if you're a foreigner. It's true that there are corrupt police officers, but they cannot force you to pay something you should not, and even if this does happen, you can make a complaint, though you may spend a good deal of time settling it.

ON THE GROUND

■ ADDRESSES

Finding addresses in Brazil can be frustrating, as streets often have more than one name and numbers are sometimes assigned haphazardly. In some places street numbering doesn't enjoy the wide popularity it has achieved elsewhere; hence, you may find the notation "s/n," meaning *sem número* (without number). In rural areas and small towns there may only be directions to a place rather than to a formal address (i.e., street and number). Often such areas do not have official addresses and/or don't need them.

In Portuguese *avenida* (avenue), *rua*, (street) and *travessa* (lane) are abbreviated (as *Av., R., and Trv. or Tr.*), while *estrada* (highway) often isn't abbreviated. Street numbers follow street names. Eight-digit postal codes (CEP) are widely used.

■ COMMUNICATIONS

INTERNET

If you're traveling with a laptop, carry a spare battery, a universal adapter plug, and a converter if your computer isn't dual-voltage. Ask about electrical surges before plugging in your computer. Keep your disks out of the sun and avoid excessive heat for both your computer and disks. In Brazil carrying a laptop computer signals wealth and could make you a target for thieves; conceal your laptop in a generic bag and keep it close to you at all times.

Contacts **Cybercafés** (⊕ www.cybercafes. com) lists more than 4,000 Internet cafés worldwide.

PHONES

The number of digits in Brazilian telephone numbers varies widely. The country code for Brazil is 55. When dialing a Brazilian number from abroad, drop the initial zero from the local area code.

Public phones are everywhere and are called *orelhões* (big ears) because of their shape. The phones take phone cards only.

CALLING WITHIN BRAZIL

Local calls can be made most easily from pay phones, which take phone cards only. A bar or restaurant may allow you to use its private phone for a local call if you're a customer.

If you want to call from your hotel, remember long-distance calls within Brazil are expensive, and hotels add a surcharge.

With the privatization of the Brazilian telecommunications network, there's a wide choice of long-distance companies. Hence, to make direct-dial long-distance calls, you must find out which companies serve the area from which you're calling and then get their access codes—the staff at your hotel can help. (Some hotels have already made the choice for you, so you may not need an access code when calling from the hotel itself.) For long-distance calls within Brazil, dial 0 + the access code + the area code and number. To call Rio, for example, dial 0, then 21 (for Embratel, a major long-distance and international provider), then 21 (Rio's area code), and then the number.

For local directory assistance, dial 102. For directory assistance in another Brazilian city, dial 0 + the access code + the area code of that city + 121. English-speaking operators are not available, but you can ask to talk to the supervising team, who may speak English. Another suggestion is to ask a Portuguese-speaking friend to make this call for you or even visit ⊕*www.brasiltelecom.com.br* and click "102 Online."

CALLING OUTSIDE BRAZIL

International calls from Brazil are extremely expensive. Hotels also add a surcharge, increasing this cost even more. Calls can be made from public phone booths with a prepaid phone card. You can also go to phone offices. Ask your hotel staff about the closest office, as they are less common in Brazil than pay phones.

For international calls, dial 00 + 23 (for Intelig, a long-distance company) or 21 (for Embratel, another long-distance company) + the country code + the area code and number. For operator-assisted international calls, dial 00–0111. For international information, dial 00–0333. To make a collect long-distance call (which will cost 40% more than a normal call), dial 9 + the area code and the number.

The country code for the United States is 1.

AT&T, MCI, and Sprint operators are also accessible from Brazil; get the local access codes before you leave home for your destinations.

Access Codes AT&T Direct (☎11/3885–0080 within São Paulo, 0800/703–6335 for individuals, 0800/703–6334 for companies). **MCI WorldPhone** (☎0800/890–0012). Service not accessible via mobile phones. **Sprint International Access** (☎0800/888–7800, 0800/890–8000, or 0800/888–8000).

CALLING CARDS

All pay phones in Brazil take phone cards only. Buy a phone card, a *cartão telefônico* at a *posto telefônico* (phone office), newsstand, drugstore, or post office. Cards come with a varying number of units (each unit is usually worth a couple of minutes), which will determine the price. Buy a couple of cards if you don't think you'll have the chance again soon. These phone cards can be used for international, local, and long-distance calls within Brazil. Be aware that calling internationally using these cards is extremely expensive and your units will expire pretty quickly.

If you do want to do this, buy many cards with the maximum units (50). A 20-minute card costs about $1.25; a 50-minute card costs around $2.50.

MOBILE PHONES

If you have a multiband phone (some countries use different frequencies than what's used in the United States) and your service provider uses the world-standard GSM network (as do T-Mobile, Cingular, and Verizon), you can probably use your phone abroad. Roaming fees can be steep, however: 99¢ a minute is considered reasonable. And overseas you normally pay the toll charges for incoming calls. It's almost always cheaper to send a text message than to make a call, since text messages have a very low set fee (often less than 5¢).

If you just want to make local calls, consider buying a new SIM card (note that your provider may have to unlock your phone for you to use a different SIM card) and a prepaid service plan in the destination. You'll then have a local number and can make local calls at local rates. If your trip is extensive, you could also simply buy a new cell phone in your destination, as the initial cost will be offset over time.

▌EATING OUT

Food in Brazil is delicious, inexpensive (especially compared to other countries), and bountiful. Portions are huge and presentation is tasteful. A lot of restaurants prepare plates for two people; when you order, be sure to ask if one plate will suffice—or even better, glance around to see the size of portions at other tables.

MEALS & MEALTIMES

Between the extremes of sophistication and austere simplicity, each region has its own cuisine. You find exotic fish dishes in the Amazon, African-spiced dishes in Bahia, and well-seasoned bean mashes in Minas Gerais. *For more information on regional cuisine, see About the Restaurants & Cuisine in regional chapters.*

Unless otherwise noted, the restaurants listed in this guide are open daily for lunch and dinner.

PAYING

Credit cards are widely accepted at restaurants in the major cities. In the countryside all but the smallest establishments generally accept credit cards as well. Gratuity is 10% of the total sum, and it's sometimes included in the bill; when it's not, it's optional to give the waiter a tip.

For guidelines on tipping see Tipping, below.

The restaurants we list are the cream of the crop in each price category. Properties indicated by a ✗⊡ are lodging establishments whose restaurant warrants a special trip. Price categories are as follows:

CATEGORY	COST
$$$$	over R$60
$$$	R$45–R$60
$$	R$30–R$45
$	R$15–R$30
¢	under R$15

All prices are per person in reais for a main course at dinner, excluding taxes.

RESERVATIONS & DRESS

Appropriate dress for dinner in Brazil can vary dramatically. As a general rule, dress more formally for expensive restaurants. In most restaurants dress is casual, but even moderately priced places might frown upon shorts.

WINES, BEER & SPIRITS

The national drink is the *caipirinha*, made of crushed lime, sugar, and *pinga* or *cachaça* (sugarcane liquor). When whipped with crushed ice, fruit juices, and condensed milk, the pinga/cachaça becomes a *batida*. A *caipivodka*, or *caipiroska,* is the same cocktail with vodka instead of cachaça. Some bars make both drinks using a fruit other than lime, such as kiwi and *maracujá* (passion fruit).

Brazil has many brands of bottled beer. In general, though, Brazilians prefer tap beer, called *chopp,* which is sold in bars and restaurants. Be sure to try the carbonated soft drink *guaraná,* made using the Amazonian fruit of the same name. It's extremely popular in Brazil.

▮ ELECTRICITY

The current in Brazil isn't regulated: in São Paulo and Rio it's 110 or 120 volts (the same as in the United States and Canada); in Recife and Brasília it's 220 volts (the same as in Europe); and in Manaus and Salvador it's 127 volts. Electricity is AC (alternating current) at 60 Hz, similar to that in Europe. To use electric-powered equipment purchased in the U.S. or Canada, bring a converter and adapter. Wall outlets take Continental-type plugs, with two round prongs. Consider buying a universal adapter, which has several types of plugs in one handy unit. Some hotels are equipped to handle various types of plugs and electrical devices. Check with your hotel before packing converters and adapters.

Contacts **Steve Kropla's Help for World Traveler's** (⊕www.kropla.com) has information on electrical and telephone plugs around the world. **Walkabout Travel Gear** (⊕www.walkabouttravelgear.com) has a good coverage of electricity under "adapters."

EMERGENCIES

In case of emergency, call one of the services below. Calling the fire brigade is a good otpion, since they're considered one of the most efficient and trustworthy institutions in Brazil. If you need urgent and immediate support, talk to the people around you. Brazilians are friendly and willing to help. They'll go out of their way to speak your language and find help.

If you've been robbed or assaulted, report it to the police. Unfortunately, you shouldn't expect huge results for your trouble. Call your embassy if your passport has been stolen or if you need help dealing with the police.

General Emergency Contacts **Fire Brigade (Bombeiros)** (☎193 ⊕www.bombeirosemergencia.com.br). **Police** (☎190). **Ambulance** (☎192). **Civil Defence** (☎199).

HEALTH

The most common types of illnesses are caused by contaminated food and water. Especially in developing countries, drink only bottled, boiled, or purified water and drinks; don't drink from public fountains or use ice. You should even consider using bottled water to brush your teeth. Make sure food has been thoroughly cooked and is served to you fresh and hot; avoid vegetables and fruits that you haven't washed (in bottled or purified water) or peeled yourself. If you have problems, mild cases of traveler's diarrhea may respond to Imodium (known generically as loperamide) or Pepto-Bismol. Be sure to drink plenty of fluids; if you can't keep fluids down, seek medical help immediately.

Infectious diseases can be airborne or passed via mosquitoes and ticks and through direct or indirect physical contact with animals or people. Some, including Norwalk-like viruses that affect your digestive tract, can be passed along through contaminated food. If you're traveling in an area where malaria is prevalent, use a repellent containing DEET and take malaria-prevention medication before, during, and after your trip as directed by your physician. Condoms can help prevent most sexually transmitted diseases, but they aren't absolutely reliable and their quality varies from country to country. Speak with your physician and/or check the CDC or World Health Organization Web sites for health alerts, particularly if you're pregnant, traveling with children, or have a chronic illness.

English-speaking medical assistance in Brazil is quite rare. It's best to contact your consulate or embassy if you need medical help. Seek private clinics or hospitals, since getting an appointment in the government's healthcare system is a slow process.

TIP→ If you're traveling to the Amazon, extra precautions are necessary. *For Amazon-specific health matters, see the Amazon Essentials in Chapter 10.*

DIVERS' ALERT

Do not fly within 24 hours of scuba diving. Neophyte divers should have a complete physical exam before undertaking a dive. If you have travel insurance that covers evacuations, make sure your policy applies to scuba-related injuries, as not all companies provide this coverage.

FOOD & DRINK

The major health risk in Brazil is traveler's diarrhea, caused by eating contaminated fruit or vegetables or drinking contaminated water. So watch what you eat—on and off the beaten path. Avoid ice, uncooked food, and unpasteurized milk and milk products, and drink only bottled water or water that has been boiled for at least 20 minutes, even when brushing your teeth. The use of bottled water for brushing your teeth is not necessary in large cities, where water is treated. Don't use ice unless you know it's made from purified water. (Ice in city restaurants is usually safe.) Peel or thoroughly wash fresh fruits and vegetables. Avoid eating food from street vendors.

Choose industrially packaged beverages when you can. Order tropical juices from places that appear clean and reliable. Avoid eating egg-based foods such as mayonnaise in restaurants to prevent stomach indisposition.

INFECTIOUS DISEASES & VIRUSES
The Amazon and a few other remote areas are the only places in Brazil where you really need worry about infectious diseases. Most travelers to Brazil return home unscathed, apart from a bit of traveler's diarrhea. However, you should visit a doctor at least six weeks prior to traveling to discuss recommended vaccinations, some of which require multiple shots over a period of weeks. If you get sick weeks, months, or in rare cases, years after your trip, make sure your doctor administers blood tests for tropical diseases.

Meningococcal meningitis and typhoid fever are common in certain areas of Brazil—and not only in remote areas like the Amazon. Meningitis has been a problem around São Paulo in recent years. Dengue fever and malaria—both caused by mosquito bites—are common in Brazil or in certain areas of Brazil. Both are usually only a problem in the Amazon, but dengue can affect urban areas and malaria is sometimes found in urban peripheries. Talk with your doctor about what precautions to take.

PESTS & OTHER HAZARDS
You'll likely encounter more insects than you're used to in Brazil, but they generally only present health problems in the Amazon.

Heatstroke and heat prostration are common though easily preventable maladies throughout Brazil. The symptoms for either can vary but always start with headaches, nausea, and dizziness. If ignored, these symptoms can worsen until you require medical attention. In hot weather be sure to rehydrate regularly, wear loose lightweight clothing, and avoid overexerting yourself.

OVER-THE-COUNTER REMEDIES
Mild cases of diarrhea may respond to Imodium (known generically as loperamide) or Pepto-Bismol (not as strong), both of which can be purchased over the counter at a *farmácia* (pharmacy). Drink plenty of purified water or *chá* (tea)—*camomila* (chamomile) is a good folk remedy. In severe cases rehydrate yourself with a salt–sugar solution: ½ teaspoon *sal* (salt) and 4 tablespoons *açúcar* (sugar) per quart of *agua* (water).

Pharmacies also sell antidiarrheal medicines, but an effective home remedy is the same as the rehydrating concoction: a teaspoon of sugar plus a quarter teaspoon of salt in a liter of water.

Aspirin is *aspirina*; Tylenol is pronounced *tee*-luh-nawl.

▌MONEY

Brazil's unit of currency is the *real* (R\$; plural: *reais*). One real is 100 *centavos* (cents). There are notes worth 1, 5, 10, 20, 50, and 100 reais, together with coins worth 1, 5, 10, 25, and 50 centavos and 1 real.

When in Brazil, pay for everything with credit cards or with reais.

■TIP➔**Banks never have every foreign currency on hand, and it may take as long as a week to order. If you're planning to exchange funds before leaving home, don't wait till the last minute.**

ATMS & BANKS
Your own bank will probably charge a fee for using ATMs abroad; the foreign bank you use may also charge a fee. Nevertheless, you'll usually get a better rate of exchange at an ATM than you will at a currency-exchange office or even when changing money in a bank. And extracting funds as you need them is a

safer option than carrying around a large amount of cash.

■**TIP**→ PIN numbers with more than four digits are not recognized at ATMs in many countries. If yours has five or more, remember to change it before you leave.

Nearly all the nation's major banks have ATMs, known in Brazil as *caixas eletrônicos,* for which you must use a card with a credit-card logo. MasterCard/ Cirrus holders can withdraw at Banco Itau, Banco do Brasil, HSBC, and Banco24horas ATMs; Visa holders can use Bradesco ATMs and those at Banco do Brasil. American Express cardholders can make withdrawals at most Bradesco ATMs marked 24 HORAS. To be on the safe side, carry a variety of cards. Note also that if your PIN is more than four digits long and/or uses letters instead of numbers, it might not work. If you don't have one, get a four-digit PIN before your trip. For your card to function in some ATMs, you may need to hit a screen command (perhaps, *estrangeiro*) if you are a foreign client.

Banks are, with a few exceptions, open weekdays 10–4.

CREDIT CARDS

Throughout this guide, the following abbreviations are used: **AE**, American Express; **DC**, Diners Club; **MC**, MasterCard; and **V**, Visa.

It's a good idea to inform your credit-card company before you travel, especially if you're going abroad and don't travel internationally very often. Otherwise, the credit-card company might put a hold on your card owing to unusual activity—not a good thing halfway through your trip. Record all your credit-card numbers—as well as the phone numbers to call if your cards are lost or stolen—in a safe place, so you're prepared should something go wrong. Both MasterCard and Visa have general numbers you can call (collect if you're abroad) if your card is lost, but you're better off calling the number of your issuing bank, since MasterCard and Visa usually just transfer you to your bank; your bank's number is usually printed on your card.

For costly items use your credit card whenever possible—you'll come out ahead, whether the exchange rate at which your purchase is calculated is the one in effect the day the vendor's bank abroad processes the charge or the one prevailing on the day the charge company's service center processes it at home.

Reporting Lost Cards American Express (☎800/528–4800 in U.S., 336/393–1111 collect from abroad ⊕www.americanexpress. com). **Diners Club** (☎800/234–6377 in U.S., 303/799–1504 collect from abroad ⊕www. dinersclub.com). **MasterCard** (☎800/627–8372 in U.S., 636/722–7111 collect from abroad, 0800/891–3294 in Brazil ⊕www. mastercard.com). **Visa** (☎800/847–2911 in U.S., 410/581–9994 collect from abroad, 0800/99–0001 in Brazil ⊕www.visa.com).

CURRENCY & EXCHANGE

At this writing, the real is at 1.75 to the U.S. dollar and 1.72 to the Canadian dollar.

For the most favorable rates, change money through banks. Although ATM transaction fees may be higher abroad than at home, ATM rates are excellent because they're based on wholesale rates offered only by major banks. You won't do as well at *casas de câmbio* (exchange houses), in airports or rail and bus stations, in hotels, in restaurants, or in stores.

To avoid lines at airport exchange booths, get a bit of local currency before you leave home. Don't wait until the last minute to do this, as many banks—even the international ones—don't have reais on hand and must order them for you. This can take a couple of days. Outside larger cities, changing money in Brazil becomes more of a challenge. When leaving a large city for a smaller town, bring enough cash for your trip. For an average week in a Brazilian city, a good strategy is to convert $500 into reais. This provides sufficient cash for most expenses, such as taxis and small purchases and snacks.

■TIP➡ Even if a currency-exchange booth has a sign promising no commission, rest assured that there's some kind of huge, hidden fee. (Oh...that's right. The sign didn't say no fee.). And as for rates, you're almost always better off getting foreign currency at an ATM or exchanging money at a bank.

▌ RESTROOMS

The word for "bathroom" is *banheiro,* though the term *sanitários* (toilets) is also used. *Homens* means "men" and *mulheres* means "women." Around major tourist attractions and along the main beaches in big cities, you can find public restrooms that aren't necessarily clean. In other areas you may have to rely on the kindness of local restaurant and shop owners. If a smile and polite request (*"Por favor, posso usar o banheiro?"*) doesn't work, become a customer—the purchase of a drink or a knickknack might just buy you a trip to the bathroom. Rest areas with relatively clean, well-equipped bathrooms are plentiful along major highways. Still, carry a pocket-size package of tissues in case there's no toilet paper. Tip bathroom attendants with a few spare centavos.

Find a Loo The Bathroom Diaries (⊕www. thebathroomdiaries.com) is flush with unsanitized info on restrooms the world over—each one located, reviewed, and rated.

▌ TAXES

Sales tax is included in the prices shown on goods in stores. Hotel, meal, and car rental taxes are usually tacked on in addition to the costs shown on menus and brochures. At this writing, hotel taxes are roughly 5%, meal taxes 10%, and car rental taxes 12%.

Departure taxes on international flights from Brazil aren't always included in your ticket and can run as high as R$86 ($36); domestic flights may incur a R$22 ($9.30) tax. Although U.S. dollars are accepted in some airports, be prepared to pay departure taxes in reais.

▌ TIPPING

Wages can be paltry in Brazil, so a little generosity in tipping can go a long way. Tipping in dollars is not recommended—at best it's insulting; at worst, you might be targeted for a robbery. Large hotels that receive lots of international guests are the exception. Some restaurants add a 10% service charge onto the check. If there's no service charge, you can leave as much as you want, but 15% is a good amount. In deluxe hotels tip porters R$2 per bag, chambermaids R$2 per day, and bellhops R$4–R$6 for room and valet service. Tips for doormen and concierges vary, depending on the services provided. A good tip would be at least R$22, with an average of R$11. For moderate and inexpensive hotels, tips tend to be minimal (salaries are so low that virtually anything is well received). If a taxi driver helps you with your luggage, a per-bag charge of about R$1 is levied in addition to the fare. In general, tip taxi drivers 10% of the fare.

If a service station attendant does anything beyond filling up the gas tank, leave him a small tip of some spare change. Tipping in bars and cafés follows the rules of restaurants, although at outdoor bars Brazilians rarely leave a gratuity if they have had only a soft drink or a beer. At airports and at train and bus stations, tip the last porter who puts your bags into the cab (R$1 a bag at airports, 50 centavos a bag at bus and train stations).

INDEX

PHOTO CREDITS

NOTES

NOTES

NOTES

NOTES

ABOUT OUR WRITERS

British-born **Lucy Bryson** has been based in Rio de Janeiro since 2006 and works as a freelance writer and editor. Lucy updated the Where to Eat and Where to Stay sections for Rio.

Daniel Corry is originally from Wisconsin and now resides in São Paulo with his wife, Renata. For this edition, Daniel wrote the front-of-book essays for Rio and São Paulo, and updated the Where to Eat and Where to Stay sections for São Paulo.

São Paulo resident **Ana Cristina** currently writes for *Gazeta Mercantil* and has also worked as a freelancer for *Forbes* and *Viagem e Turismo* magazine. She has traveled extensively in Western Europe and will soon be packing her things and moving to Italy. This year, Ana updated the Side Trips from São Paulo chapter.

Doug Gray moved to Rio de Janeiro in January 2007, where he spends his time writing and exploring *carioca* culture from his home in Flamengo. This year, Doug updated the Nightlife section of Rio.

Katya Hodge is a travel writer and video producer who has lived and worked in Canada, Mexico, Argentina, and Brazil. Katya updated the Shopping section of Rio.

A native of St. Petersburg, Russia, **Anna Katsnelson** developed a soft spot for Brazilian music before she fell in love with the entire country. Anna is a Fulbright Scholar and PhD candidate researching Brazilian literature in the *Cidade Maravilhosa*—Rio de Janeiro. This year, Anna took on the gargantuan task of updating Minas Gerais, Salvador and the Bahia Coast, the Northeast, and parts of the Amazon.

Husband-and-wife team **Fabio Kreusch** and **Carolina Berard Kreusch** updated the Essentials chapter of the book. Carolina is a translator, writer, and a certified guide. She currently works as a marketing manager at an international organization. Fabio specializes in finance and management. Both of them love the road.

Stephen Silva is a Brazilophile who lived in Rocinha, Rio de Janeiro, and studies at Yale University. Stephen updated the Exploring section of Rio.

A journalist from Sydney, Australia, **Simon Tarmo** is now involved in Brazil's growing wine industry and lives in São Paulo with his Brazilian wife. This year Simon updated the Exploring, Nightlife, and Shopping sections of São Paulo.

Carlos Tornquist has a PhD in soil science and is currently an environmental consultant with the Brazilian government. He and his wife Renata are avid travelers, both in Brazil and abroad. Carlos updated Brasília and the West and the South chapters of this year's guide.